The United States Army in
Operation ENDURING FREEDOM (OEF)
October 2001–September 2005

A Different Kind of War

Donald P. Wright, Ph.D.
James R. Bird
Steven E. Clay
Peter W. Connors
Lieutenant Colonel Scott C. Farquhar
Lynne Chandler Garcia
Dennis F. Van Wey

Combat Studies Institute Press
US Army Combined Arms Center
Fort Leavenworth, KS

Library of Congress Cataloging-in-Publication Data

A different kind of war : the United States Army in Operation Enduring Freedom (OEF), October 2001-September 2005 / Donald P. Wright ... [et al.].
  p. cm.
 1. Afghan War, 2001- 2. War on Terrorism, 2001- 3. United States. Combined Forces Command--Afghanistan--History. 4. United States--Armed Forces--Stability operations. 5. United States--Armed Forces--Civic action. 6. United States--Armed Forces--Civil functions. 7. Postwar reconstruction--Afghanistan. I. Wright, Donald P., 1964- II. Title.

 DS371.412.D54 2010
 958.104'7--dc22

                                                                    2009011584

First printing, May 2010.

Foreword

Since the beginning of the Global War on Terrorism, the US Army Training and Doctrine Command (TRADOC) has captured the experiences of Soldiers as they conducted difficult operations across the world in a variety of important ways. Historical accounts of the US Army's campaigns play a critical role in this process by offering insights from the past to assist Soldiers with their current—and future—operational challenges.

This volume, *A Different Kind of War,* is the first comprehensive study of the US Army's experience in Afghanistan during the first 4 years of Operation ENDURING FREEDOM (OEF). The work focuses on Army operations in the larger Joint and Coalition campaign that evolved between October 2001 and September 2005. Beginning with a description of the successful offensive against the Taliban regime, launched in late 2001 in response to the attacks of 9/11, the book then shifts to the less well-understood campaign that began in 2002 to establish a peaceful and politically stable Afghanistan.

A Different Kind of War is balanced and honest. Its publication is particularly timely as both the Army and the Department of Defense are beginning to reassess and restructure the campaign in Afghanistan. This study will shed a great deal of light on the overall course of OEF. As the title suggests, the campaign in Afghanistan was unique. While its initial phases featured the use of small teams of Special Operations Forces and air power, the campaign after 2002 evolved into a broader effort in which conventional forces were responsible for the creation of security, reconstruction, and programs to train the Afghan Army. Overall, the story in these pages is one of a relatively small number of Soldiers conducting multifaceted operations on difficult terrain and within a complex cultural environment.

A Different Kind of War was written in recognition of all the men and women who served in Afghanistan to bring stability and prosperity to that country while protecting the security of the United States. Their experiences chronicled in this book will help inform and educate all those who serve the Nation today and in the future.

Victory Starts Here!

Martin E. Dempsey
General, US Army
Commanding General
US Army Training and Doctrine Command

Acknowledgments

Constructing a study of this length and complexity was a huge task. We have benefited greatly from the large number of Soldiers and civilians who took the time to talk with us and share documents, insights, and encouragement. This study would have been impossible to complete without their contributions, and for this we are deeply indebted. Because of the contemporary nature of this history, we have relied heavily on oral interviews—approximately 140 were completed for this study alone. We would like to thank each of those who found the time to share his or her experiences with us. Additional thanks goes to those interviewees who helped us make contact with other veterans of Afghanistan and to those who shared unit records with us. Lieutenant Colonel (Retired) Ronald E. Corkran was particularly helpful in sitting for several interviews and in providing materials related to Operation ANACONDA.

Since the Contemporary Operations Study Team was established at the Combat Studies Institute (CSI) in 2005, we have enjoyed the support of General (Retired) William S. Wallace, General David H. Petraeus, and Lieutenant General William B. Caldwell IV. As commanders of the Combined Arms Center, these senior officers made the creation of ambitious historical studies like *A Different Kind of War* possible. All three have served as sponsors of this project because of their strong belief in the obligation to examine and seek insights from the Army's experiences in Iraq and Afghanistan. General George W. Casey Jr., the Chief of Staff of the Army, also reinforced the Army's interest in the contemporary history of these campaigns and served as a proponent of the team's efforts.

The authors are indebted to the other members of the Contemporary Operations Study Team in this endeavor. Specifically, we would like to thank Ms. Catherine Shadid Small for her management of the team as well as Ms. Angela McClain and Ms. Rebecca Bednarz for their roles as editors. Mr. Jerry England and Mr. Ray Barker were instrumental in organizing the voluminous amount of primary documentary material collected by the team into an accessible collection. Ms. Kim Sanborn provided the critical transcription support that transformed our interviews into usable primary sources. Ms. Robin Kern, our graphics specialist, created the maps and charts that make this study more vibrant and comprehensible. Major Jeffrey Holmes and Major J.D. Steven assisted the team by providing critical research support.

We would like to extend special thanks to the historians and archivists who worked closely with us in our research. At the US Army Center of Military History, Mr. Frank Shirer, Dr. Chris Koontz, and Ms. Dena Everett were especially helpful in providing key documents to us from their growing collection. Lieutenant Colonel Scotty Dawson (USMC), the command historian at US Central Command, welcomed our team and offered assistance in the collection of unit records. Mr. Doug Cubbison, the 10th Mountain Division command historian, provided our team with a wealth of documentation about that division's multiple deployments to Afghanistan. Ms. Donna Tabor, the US Army XVIII Airborne Corps historian, assisted by scheduling interviews and making available critical materials about the operations of the 82d Airborne Division in Operation ENDURING FREEDOM. Dr. John Lonnquest, the historian for the US Army Corps of Engineers, was instrumental in providing documents and helping us understand the Army's large-scale reconstruction effort in Afghanistan.

Closer to home, Mr. Les Grau of the Foreign Military Studies Office at Fort Leavenworth offered key insights into the Soviet experience in Afghanistan and early US operations in 2001 and 2002. The work of Mr. John McCool, Mr. Laurence Lessard, and Ms. Colette Kiszka of the Operational Leadership Experience, CSI, expanded our understanding of operations in Afghanistan.

A number of individuals reviewed early drafts of this study and we are in debt to all of them for their comments. Lieutenant General (Retired) David W. Barno and Lieutenant General (Retired) Karl W. Eikenberry made time to carefully read our work and offer important recommendations. Dr. Richard Stewart, the Chief Historian of the Army, Dr. Alexander Cochran, Historical Advisor to the Chief of Staff of the Army, and Dr. Britt McCarley, the command historian for the US Army Training and Doctrine Command, provided helpful suggestions. Dr. Kenneth Finlayson in the US Army Special Operations Command history office gave us useful comments concerning the critical role of Army Special Forces in Afghanistan.

Finally, the entire team would like to thank Colonel Timothy R. Reese and Dr. William G. Robertson, the senior leaders of CSI, for their enduring support and belief in the importance of contemporary history to today's Army. Ms. Elizabeth Weigand, an editor in CSI, also merits special acknowledgment for her transformation of a rough manuscript into a real book.

As our team gathered documents, conducted interviews, and began to write this account, we remained cognizant of the fact that many Americans, both military and civilian, made great sacrifices in their service in Afghanistan. The story in these pages belongs to them. As authors, we have tried diligently to tell their story accurately and with candor. Still, in writing this history, we have undoubtedly made mistakes of fact and interpretation. All responsibility for those errors lies on our shoulders.

Contents

Figures

Call Out Boxes

Introduction

As the sun rose on the morning of 11 September 2001, the United States (US) was at peace. American Soldiers across the country and in a number of nations across the globe woke up that day planning to conduct routine operations and training. A relatively small number of US Army units were deployed in the Balkans and the Sinai desert on peacekeeping missions. But, for most Soldiers, the day promised to be much like any other.

For the Army, as well as the entire American nation, the peaceful nature of that day was shattered when just after 0900 a United Airlines jet filled with passengers plowed into the side of the North Tower of the World Trade Center in New York City. Thirty minutes later, an American Airlines jet rammed into the South Tower. While the twin towers burned, a third airliner slammed into the Pentagon in Washington, DC, and a fourth plane, possibly headed toward the US Capitol, dove straight into a field in Pennsylvania. By noon on that day, almost 3,000 people, most of whom were Americans, were dead.

Within hours of the attack, George W. Bush, the President of the United States, identified the radical Islamic terrorist group al-Qaeda as the likely perpetrator of the attacks and began preparing the US military for retaliation actions. As the sun set on 11 September 2001, many Soldiers realized that their country was now preparing for war and that they would likely be called on to act against their country's enemies.

Many of the world's governments and international organizations immediately expressed outrage and called for solidarity with the United States. The United Nations (UN), the North Atlantic Treaty Organization (NATO), and the European Union all began deliberations on how to respond. President Bush identified the attacks as an act of war against the United States rather than using the previous practice of classifying terrorist acts as crimes. The response would thus be a military campaign rather than legal proceedings against individuals. The US Government began diplomatic negotiations and military planning to create a Coalition to support the retaliations against the terrorist network and the nations that hosted it.

In less than a month, the United States had forged a Coalition and begun attacking al-Qaeda and its supporters in a variety of ways. The most visible and dramatic means was the military campaign that began in early October 2001 against the Taliban regime in Afghanistan and its al-Qaeda allies in that country. That campaign—largely improvised and based on the innovative use of Special Operations Forces (SOF) and air power—became known as Operation ENDURING FREEDOM (OEF). Like the unconventional attack that provoked it, this campaign did not resemble past armed conflicts, a fact that led President Bush to describe it as "a different kind of war."* This study takes its title from the President's suggestion that OEF—and the broader war on terrorism—would be conducted differently from other American military campaigns.

A Different Kind of War is the third volume in the series of contemporary historical accounts by the Combat Studies Institute (CSI) of the US Army's operations since 9/11. The first two volumes, *On Point* and *On Point II*, offered preliminary histories of the US Army in Operation IRAQI FREEDOM (OIF) during initial combat operations against the Saddam regime and the

---

*George W. Bush, "Radio Address from the President to the Nation," 29 September 2001. http://www. whitehouse.gov/news/releases/2001/09/20010929.html (accessed 8 October 2008).

campaign that resulted once that regime was toppled in April 2003. *A Different Kind of War* is CSI's first study of OEF.

These preliminary studies are a result of an initiative by senior US Army commanders who hoped that historical analysis could help the Army understand its operations in Iraq and Afghanistan in a more complete way. In 2005 General Kevin Byrnes, the commander of the US Army Training and Doctrine Command (TRADOC), and Lieutenant General William Wallace, the commander of US Army Combined Arms Center (CAC), directed CSI to produce contemporary historical accounts of these campaigns. To create these studies, CSI created the Contemporary Operations Study Team (COST), composed of researchers, writers, editors, and transcribers, who would conduct interviews with participants in these campaigns, collect primary documents from Army units, and transform those materials into coherent historical accounts.

The difficulties posed by the task of writing this type of contemporary history were and remain manifold. Perhaps the greatest is that the operations that are the focus of CSI's contemporary accounts are ongoing. This not only prevents the historians from writing from the vantage point of knowing how the conflict ended, it also creates difficulties with establishing a methodological basis for research. For example, the dearth of primary sources from Taliban and other insurgent forces means that this study does not include accounts of the campaign from the adversary's perspective. Also daunting is that many if not most of the US Army documents associated with OEF in the period covered by this study remain classified and are unavailable for direct use. To be sure, a number of documents are unclassified and they were used to the maximum extent in this book. However, the problems related to the classification of military records have led the historians involved in this project to rely to a significant degree on oral interviews. While memories never allow for the perfect re-creation of events, the hundreds of interviews conducted by CSI with participants in OEF have established a solid foundation on which the authors could construct their account of the US Army in Afghanistan.

Another obstacle to the writing of contemporary histories of the Army's current campaigns is the general lack of scholarly secondary sources. The historical literature about the campaign in Afghanistan in particular is not well developed. Perhaps the best work on the first 6 months of the campaign is CSI's study of US Army Special Forces (SF) operations in Afghanistan titled *Weapon of Choice*. There are also several good secondary works on Operation ANACONDA, which took place in early 2002, and a number of good first-person accounts from military personnel involved in the early phases of OEF. Nevertheless, the scholarly literature, other than specialized articles in professional military journals, generally does not cover military operations in Afghanistan after 2002.

A Different Kind of War offers the first preliminary comprehensive historical account of OEF, tracing the development of the Afghanistan campaign from its inception in the fall of 2001 through the Afghan parliamentary elections of September 2005. To do so, the study takes a chronological approach to the story of the Army in Afghanistan in this period. The first three chapters provide the background to the campaign that began in October 2001. Chapter 1 describes the Afghan context by briefly discussing the geography, history, and culture of the country with an emphasis on the rise of the Taliban in the 1990s. Chapter 2 explains the national strategy promulgated by President Bush in response to the 9/11 attacks and the rapid formulation of US Central Command's joint and interagency campaign plan to carry out actions against the Taliban and al-Qaeda in Afghanistan. The chapter includes a discussion of the political and diplomatic complexities that the United States had to master to build a Coalition that would support operations inside Afghanistan as well as the engagement of regional powers such as Pakistan, Uzbekistan, and other central Asian republics needed to support the Coalition campaign. Chapter 3 examines the opening phase of OEF, covering the broad effort of staging and moving units and equipment to the central Asian theater as well as the preliminary air campaign.

The next three chapters examine the initial ground operations focused on the overthrow of the Taliban and the elimination of al-Qaeda. Chapter 4 discusses operations in the northern region of Afghanistan in late 2001 where SOF teams married up with anti-Taliban Afghan forces and quickly ended Taliban rule over the area. Chapter 5 examines Coalition ground operations around the capital of Kabul as well as in the southern and eastern regions of the country that were the traditional homeland of the Pashtun ethnic group and the Taliban movement. This chapter follows the ground campaign in the south and east from the airborne assault near Kandahar in October 2001 and the arrival of Hamid Karzai through the ultimately unsuccessful battle at Tora Bora in December 2001. Chapter 6 looks closely at Operation ANACONDA, the final large-scale combat action that in March 2002 essentially destroyed the remnants of Taliban and al-Qaeda organized military formations, thus achieving the Coalition's critical goals of ridding Afghanistan of Taliban rule and the presence of Osama bin Laden's terrorist organization.

The four chapters that follow focus on the evolution of the campaign in Afghanistan from mid-2002 through the parliamentary elections of 2005. Chapter 7 begins with the termination of ANACONDA and the establishment of Combined Joint Task Force-180 (CJTF-180), the command that led the transition to the next phase of the campaign designed to stabilize Afghanistan, strengthen the new government and its security forces, and support humanitarian and reconstruction operations. Chapter 8 follows the development of the CJTF-180 campaign from mid-2002 through the middle of 2003 by looking at security and reconstruction operations as well as the effort to establish the Afghan National Army. Chapter 9 examines the creation of a new Coalition headquarters called Combined Forces Command–Afghanistan (CFC-A) in late 2003, that headquarters' transformation of the Coalition effort in Afghanistan into a counterinsurgency (COIN) campaign, and the course of that new campaign through the middle of 2004. Chapter 10 concludes the narrative portion of the study by focusing on the period between May 2004 and September 2005 when the Coalition reinforced the difficult COIN campaign to set conditions for two critical elections.

The study closes with a discussion of the key implications generated by the first 4 years of OEF. Although each military campaign is unique, there are key insights offered by the Coalition's experience in Afghanistan during this period that can inform military officers and civilian officials who in the future might face the daunting task of planning similar operations in comparable conditions. What will emerge throughout the study is the overriding evolutionary nature of the campaign in Afghanistan. If that campaign at its outset appeared to be a different type of conflict with its focus on the use of air power, SOF, and indigenous forces to overthrow the Taliban government and the presence of al-Qaeda, those aspects that arguably made it unique continued to change after the toppling of the Taliban. This transformation is most starkly seen first in the transition in 2002 to a larger-scale campaign with the broader goals of nation building to prevent the return of the Taliban, and then again in 2003 when the Coalition effort transitioned to a COIN campaign.

Accompanying this evolution is the changing composition of US forces and command structure in Afghanistan. The early emphasis on maintaining a small footprint in Afghanistan meant that through the middle of 2002, the number of US troops in the country was less than

10,000 Soldiers, the majority of whom lived on large Coalition bases near the city of Kandahar and at the Bagram Airfield outside the capital of Kabul. These forces were commanded by a division headquarters that served as a CJTF. With the introduction of more conventional forces in the middle of 2002, the growing troop commitment, and expanded requirements to work with the new Afghan Government and to train Afghan security forces, the US military decided to create a larger headquarters (CJTF-180) out of the staff of the XVIII Airborne Corps and appoint the corps commander, a three-star general, as the commander.

In 2003, the Coalition added CFC-A as the theater-strategic headquarters that would oversee CJTF-180 while focusing on synchronizing political affairs and military operations. The establishment of CFC-A marked a sea change in the nature of OEF because of its introduction of a formal COIN campaign. Largely as a result of this shift, the size of the US troop commitment began growing and in 2005 would reach approximately 16,000 Soldiers as combat, aviation, logistics, and units dedicated to training security forces established their presence in Afghanistan. Further, during this period, the increasing number of US Soldiers began moving out of their large bases to live and conduct operations among the population in the southern and eastern regions of Afghanistan. However, beginning in 2003, the United States had clearly shifted its strategic focus—and the lion's share of its resources—to Iraq. Thus, the transition to COIN had to be accomplished in a theater of operations that was increasingly considered an "economy of force" effort.

Throughout this period, the American Soldier in Afghanistan displayed a remarkable amount of flexibility and toughness. In the earliest days of the campaign, the members of the SF teams showed innovation and a high degree of professionalism in their ability to translate Coalition air power in support of indigenous Afghan forces into victory over the Taliban. As the campaign transitioned after mid-2002, Soldiers and their commanders found themselves conducting a broad set of operations that included security and reconstruction operations as well as the training of Afghan forces. With the exception of the security missions, most units deployed to Afghanistan in this early period were not trained for these operations. As the Taliban gradually reasserted itself after 2002 and the Coalition transitioned toward a more comprehensive COIN campaign, US commanders found even the conduct of adequate security operations challenging given the relatively small numbers of troops available.

A Different Kind of War was written in recognition of the tens of thousands of American Soldiers, Marines, Sailors, and Airmen who served in Afghanistan during this period. These men and women, along with their Coalition and Afghan allies, endeavored to help Afghanistan achieve an amount of political stability and economic progress that would prevent the country from becoming a terrorist safe haven in the future. In the process, 122 American Service men and women lost their lives while another 640 were wounded in action.[†] Ultimately, all of the Soldiers involved in OEF, like their comrades who served in Iraq and their predecessors who fought in America's previous wars, sacrificed to protect their own nation while simultaneously assisting another people achieve peace and prosperity. The authors of *A Different Kind of War* have tried to ensure that this study accurately captures their contributions in a very difficult effort.

[†]US Department of Defense, Military Casualty Information. http://siadapp.dmdc.osd.mil/personnel/CASUALTY/castop.htm (accessed 10 April 2009).

Chapter 1

Afghanistan and the Tribulations of Nationhood

US military forces began arriving in Afghanistan in October 2001. As they entered the country, American Soldiers found they were operating in an austere, rugged, and often beautiful environment. While a small number of specialists in the US Government had maintained a close watch on Afghanistan in the years following the Soviet pullout in 1988, the US Armed Forces in general had no deep understanding of the country, its population, or its recent history, which had been marked by civil war and the rise of a radical Islamist regime called the Taliban. For many American Soldiers, Afghanistan appeared to be a place of imposing physical topography inhabited by an unknown people. Assessing the country through Western eyes, some Soldiers focused on the unfamiliar quality of the culture with which they began interacting. Major Bryan Hilferty, who deployed to Afghanistan in January 2002 as the Chief of Public Affairs for the 10th Mountain Division, expressed a commonly held first impression of the country among those Soldiers who arrived in the early months of Operation ENDURING FREEDOM (OEF). Hilferty recalled thinking, "Afghanistan was kind of a blank slate because there was no infrastructure there. There were no native newspapers, radios, television, electricity, or anything . . . there was barely water or air."[1]

These early perceptions of Afghanistan often dwelled on the alien nature of the country and tended to overlook the deeply rooted social, economic, religious, and cultural structures that together formed the environment in which American Soldiers soon began operating. This chapter examines these often-complex structures to describe the terrain—physical, political, and cultural—that influenced US military actions in Afghanistan. After a brief assessment of the country's rugged topography, the discussion will then examine Afghanistan's religious, ethnic, and social structures, focusing on the issue of Afghan identity and the evolution of national consciousness. The final section will offer an overview of Afghanistan's history with emphasis on the country's political history since the 1970s and the rise of the Taliban movement that became the chief adversary to the Coalition's political and military effort in Afghanistan.

The Lay of the Land

Afghanistan is completely landlocked, bordered by Turkmenistan, Uzbekistan, and Tajikistan to the north; China and Pakistan to the east; Pakistan on the south; and Iran to the west. A country of physical extremes, it includes flat arid deserts and towering mountain peaks. With a total land area of 252,000 square miles, Afghanistan is roughly the size of the state of Texas. This makes the country one-third larger in area than Iraq. That large territory can be divided into five regions.[2] The eastern edge contains terrain that is heavily mountainous with some peaks in the Pamir Range that are higher than 10,000 feet. The Hindu Kush Range begins in the northeast and runs southwest to form part of the high plateau that dominates the central part of the country. The capital city of Kabul is located in the Kabul River Valley on the southeastern edge of this plateau. North of the high central region is the Turkoman Plain, characterized by relatively arid terrain. To the west are the more fertile lowlands that border on Iran, and to the southwest, running from the Hindu Kush foothills to the Pakistani border south of the city of Kandahar, scrubland and desert dominate.

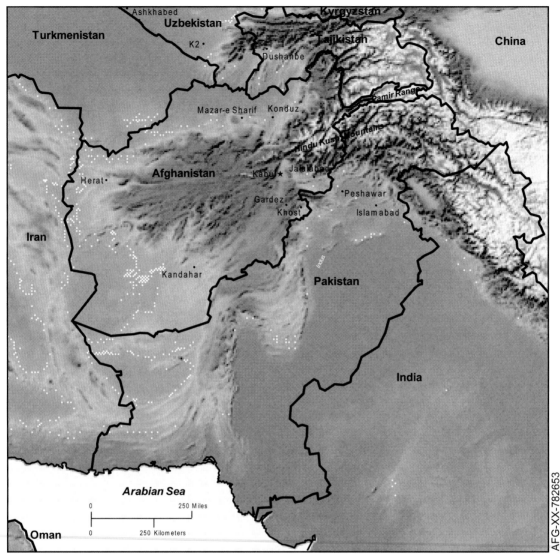

Figure 1. Afghanistan base map.

Despite its significant size, only 55,000 square miles of Afghanistan's land is arable.[3] Fertile areas are located primarily in the river valleys although irrigation has allowed for the expansion of farming into other sections, especially in the southwest. Traditional Afghan irrigation practices involve the use of buried irrigation canals, sometimes located 20 feet or more below the surface of the land, that bring water from mountain streams to fields of wheat, barley, and corn. Poppies, grown for the production of opium, became a commonly cultivated crop in the 20th century, especially in the south.

Transportation and communication in this mountainous and rural country has always been difficult. The Hindu Kush Range and the high plateau that dominate the central region make travel across the mid-section of the country slow. Slow construction of roads has exacerbated the situation. The main ground transportation artery is the Ring Road, actually a network of roads and highways of varying quality that roughly traces a circle around the circumference of

Afghanistan. The road connects the capital of Kabul to Kandahar in the southwest. From there, it runs westward to Farah and then north to Herat near the Iranian border. At Herat, the road turns east and runs toward the cities of Konduz and Mazar-e Sharif in the north-central part of Afghanistan. The rough terrain in the northern part of the country prevented the road from connecting with the capital. However, the Salang Road does link Kabul with Konduz and the northern border of Afghanistan. When American forces arrived in the fall of 2001, the Ring Road was damaged, but essentially still intact; even so, many of the country's other paved roads had been almost totally destroyed during the Soviet occupation of the 1980s.

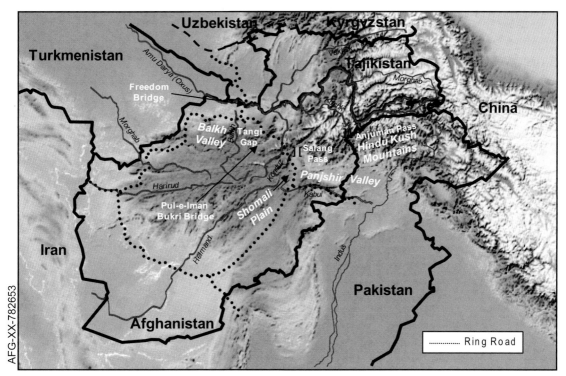

Figure 2. Afghanistan map showing Ring Road.

Afghanistan's rugged topography and minimal transportation infrastructure have prevented economic development and greater political centralization. Still, that terrain has proven beneficial at times. During the course of its history, Afghanistan has been the target of many invading forces. The mountains and the lack of roads have prevented outsiders from using military force to dominate the country. Moreover, for Afghan irregular forces, who for centuries have fought ferociously to expel outsiders, the terrain served as sanctuary from which they could attack invading armies, making their hold on the country tenuous.

Afghan Ethnic and Religious Structures

Afghanistan defies conventional Western thought about nations and nationhood. Although Afghans are united by their Islamic faith, ethnic and tribal identities divide them. These serious differences have led some to question whether the Afghan nation truly exists. This section describes the key identities and structures that dominate Afghan life as a means of describing the culture in which America Soldiers began operating in 2001.

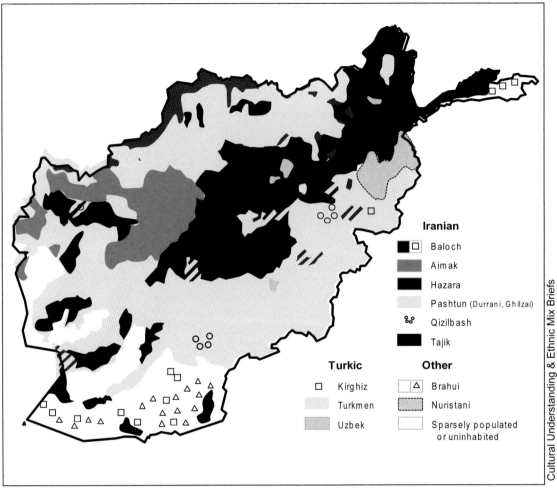

Figure 3. Ethnic map.

To be sure, scholars recognize that the process of nation building began in Afghanistan as early as 1747 and continued until the country became formally independent of Britain in 1919. The centuries of Afghanistan's existence as a state appear to have fostered at least some measure of national identity. Some have found evidence of this identity in expressions like the one made by a tribal elder from Nangarhar province, near the country's eastern border with Pakistan: "Without our land, there is no food; without our water, there is no life; without our trees and flowers, there is no soul; and without our country, there is no poetry, no music, for then we are not Afghans."[4] Shah M. Tarzi, like many Western Afghan scholars, avoids suggesting that "the Afghan people lack a sense of national consciousness."[5] Tarzi instead suggests that the Afghan sense of national identity derives from "the persistent historical pattern of foreign intervention" that predated formation of the Afghan state in 1747 (under Ahmad Shah Abdali) and continues into the modern era.[6]

Perhaps the best recent example of outside intervention serving as a uniting force is that offered by the Soviet invasion of Afghanistan in December 1979. The Soviets turned what had been a domestic political conflict between Afghan factions into a campaign that united many

Afghans against a foreign invader.[7] The intervention from outside appears to have reawakened a very real, if sometimes dormant, sense of patriotism that historically seemed to surface in Afghanistan's response to foreign threats. The Soviet experience evokes an anecdote from a previous foreign intervention in Afghan affairs. In 1809 a British envoy to the Afghan throne suggested that Afghans could enjoy a better, more peaceful quality of life if only their monarchy would accept British guidance. An elder gave this response to the envoy: "We are content with discord, we are content with alarms, we are content with blood . . . but we will never be content with a master."[8]

While this story is perhaps apocryphal, it does capture the role of division in Afghan life. These differences have become the focal point for those scholars intent on arguing that Afghanistan does not constitute a nation. One specialist in Afghan affairs, Larry P. Goodson, has asserted, "Afghanistan has never been a homogenous nation but rather a collection of disparate groups divided along ethnic, linguistic, religious, and racial lines and forced together by the vagaries of geopolitics."[9] The remainder of this section examines how the identities that compete with Afghan nationality shape social structures and practices in Afghanistan.

Ethnicity

Ethnic identity is the most striking feature of Afghan culture. Goodson has identified it as "the most important contextual factor shaping Afghanistan today, as it has been throughout Afghanistan's history."[10] The mix of ethnic groups that settled there was a product of the multiple invading forces that entered Afghanistan over the centuries and decided to stay. In this sense, Afghanistan became the ethnic crossroads of central Asia and by the 20th century featured six prominent ethnic groups and many smaller ethnic communities. The most important of these groups are the Pashtuns, the Hazara, the Tajiks, the Uzbeks, the Turkomen, and the Kirghiz.

Ethnic identities served as the foundation for more than just cultural differences, however. Louis Dupree, a historian of Afghanistan, has asserted that internal discord, caused by ethnic strife, is a key characteristic of the country's history.[11] Goodson agrees and suggests that the differences in ethnicity prevented Afghan society from uniting except in dire circumstances:

> Afghanistan's ethnic mixture has traditionally known a high propensity for violence, often between ethnic groups, subtribes, and even cousins. Only outside threats seem to unite the Afghans, and those alliances are temporary and limited. When the threat is eliminated or sufficiently reduced, people return to regular patterns of traditional warfare.[12]

What emerges from these scholarly accounts is a picture of a country that is historically more accustomed to political division than political unity. Further, those divisions along ethnic lines have led to conflict and violence between many of the groups that make up Afghan society. These patterns, rooted in centuries of history, remained a vibrant part of Afghanistan life as the 21st century began.

Any discussion of Afghanistan's ethnic groups must begin with the Pashtuns. They are the largest and historically dominant of the country's groups, comprising approximately 40 percent of the country's total estimated population of 27 million. In addition to their dominant position in present-day Afghanistan, the Pashtuns are also responsible for the founding of the first Afghan monarchy in the 18th century. This group, of Indo-European origin, moved into the area around what is today southern Afghanistan and northwestern Pakistan thousands of years ago. As an ethnic group, they are divided into several large tribal groups—the most important of which are the Ghilzai and the Durrani—and many smaller tribal and clan communities. In addition to these internal divisions, the Pashtun people are further divided by a political boundary: the border between Afghanistan and Pakistan. That frontier, arbitrarily created by the British Government in 1893, divides the Pashtuns, placing them under the jurisdiction of two countries.

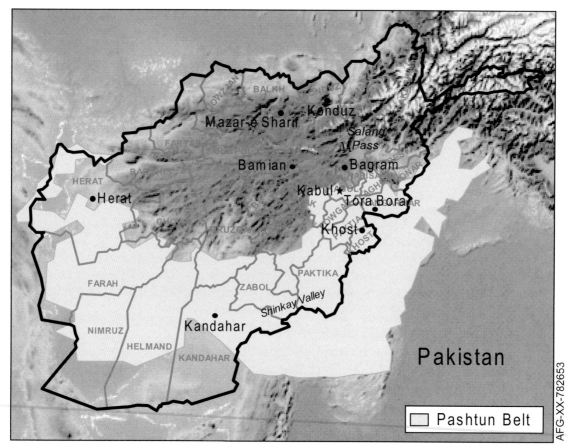

Figure 4. Pashtun Belt.

Despite the internal and artificial divisions, two things unite the many groups that make up the Pashtuns: the Pashto language and the Pashtun code of behavior called Pashtunwali. The code is actually a combination or synthesis of many tribal codes focused on several common denominators that stress the importance of kinship ties, tradition, and localism. One pair of prominent scholars of Afghanistan have noted its focus on ensuring the legacy of the people, stating that Pashtunwali is "simple but demanding. Group survival is its primary imperative. It demands vengeance against injury or insult to one's kin, chivalry, and hospitality toward the helpless and unarmed strangers, bravery in battle, and openness and integrity in individual behavior."[13] Among the Pashtuns themselves, discord, feuds, and violence often dominated intertribal and intratribal relations. Pashtunwali established the means of settling these disagreements and creating peace: "Much honor is given to Pashtuns who can successfully

---

Key Values of Pashtunwali

Hewad—Love and defense of Pashtun people (or Pashtun "nation")

Nang—Honor

Meranah—Manhood

Milmastia—Hospitality and protection for all guests

Nanawati—Requirement to provide asylum even to bitter enemies if requested

Namus—Defense of the honor of women

Badal—Action taken to avenge a death or honor of a woman

Jirga—Use of councils to settle feuds and other matters

Larry P. Goodson, *Afghanistan's Endless War:*
State Failure, Regional Politics, and the Rise of the Taliban
(Seattle, WA: University of Washington Press, 2001)

---

arbitrate the feuds that are endemic among them. Fines and blood money are devices frequently used to limit violence among rival families. Pashtunwali is a code that limits anarchy among a fractious but vital people."[14]

An aspect of the code that would come to play an important role in OEF was its establishment of the *jirga*, an all-male council or assembly of tribal elders that met to discuss and settle matters, both public and private. At the national level, the Pashtuns would sometimes convene a *loya* (grand) *jirga* to decide particularly critical problems of broad consequence. Goodson underscored the importance of this venerable form of representative assembly by chronicling a January 1987 incident that occurred near Peshawar, Pakistan: "A *jirga* of elders had settled a case in Pakistan's Khyber Agency concerning the construction of a road. When they went to deliver the verdict to the person affected, he opened fire, killing five tribal elders." Committing these murders instantly rendered the perpetrator a pariah, "because it symbolically represented the rejection of tribal will. The killer became an outlaw in the truest sense of the word, having rejected both the government and his tribe."[15] According to Goodson, the relationship between the Pashtunwali and *jirga* is that "as the Pashtunwali provided a code of behavior for the Afghan tribes, so the *jirga* . . . provided a form of government."[16]

In 2001, as US planners began to consider military and political actions in Afghanistan, the importance of the Pashtuns was not overlooked. The Taliban, the Afghan Islamist movement that had taken power in Afghanistan in the late 1990s, had originated among Pashtun tribes near the city of Kandahar. Additionally, in 2001, the Taliban regime remained heavily dominated by the Pashtuns. Perhaps more important was the decision by Coalition leaders to support Hamid

Karzai as the leader of the new government that replaced the Taliban. Karzai, a Pashtun of the Durrani tribe, was a native of Kandahar and had close relationships with other key Pashtun leaders throughout Afghanistan. For many within the Coalition leadership, Karzai represented the best chance of forming a lasting representative and stable government in Afghanistan. They certainly had taken notice of Karzai's ethnicity in championing his candidacy.

Second to the Pashtuns in size are the Tajiks, composing approximately 27 percent of the population. This ethnic group, which speaks a Persian language called Dari, is centered in the northeast of the country, but its people also inhabit the strategically important Panjshir Valley northeast of Kabul as well as the capital itself.[17] Although originally a rural people who practiced animal husbandry and farming, over the last several centuries many Tajiks have moved to urban centers, especially Kabul. As a result, some Tajiks are now less connected to their tribal groups.

Located in the central portion of Afghanistan, an area that includes the city of Bamian and known as the Hazarajat, is the next largest ethnic group—the Hazara. This group makes up about 10 percent of the population, speaks a dialect of Dari, and may be the descendants of the Mongol armies that invaded Afghanistan in the 13th century. Because they are Shia Muslims, the Hazara have periodically been the victims of religious discrimination, which has led to the movement of some in this group to western Pakistan and eastern Iran. The Taliban, for example, began targeting the Hazara in the late 1990s because of their Shia faith. Exacerbating confessional differences is the history of Pashtun attempts to subjugate the Hazara, campaigns that led to a series of Hazara uprisings in the 19th and 20th centuries.

The Uzbeks, situated primarily in Afghanistan's northern provinces, comprise the next largest ethnic population. Their traditional lands lie in the region between the northern ridges of the Hindu Kush Mountain Range and the Amu Darya (or Oxus) River, which forms the boundary between Afghanistan and the states of Uzbekistan and Tajikistan. Possessing Mongoloid features, they speak Uzbek, a Turkic language, and share their culture with fellow Uzbeks in Uzbekistan.[18]

The nomads called Aimaqs and the more sedentary farmers identified as Turkomen make up another 10 percent of the population. These two groups range across the northwestern region of Afghanistan. While the Aimaqs have a language similar to Dari, the Turkomen speak a Turkic language and maintain close ethnic and cultural ties to Turkmenistan, another former Soviet Republic that neighbors Afghanistan.

It is important to note that a feature shared by most of the large ethnic groups within Afghanistan, with the sole exception of the Hazara, is that their respective populations flow across international boundaries. Goodson contended that this has greatly influenced Afghan history: "Because all of Afghanistan's major ethnic groups either straddle the border with neighboring countries or have ethnolinguistic-religious ties to groups in [those] countries, all of those countries have built-in incentives for meddling in Afghanistan's internal affairs."[19] Interference from a number of Afghanistan's neighbors would prove to be both helpful and a hindrance once Coalition forces arrived in 2001.

Religion

Islam is the faith of Afghanistan. As noted earlier, this generally helped unite groups of the population that have distinct ethnic differences. However, there are various sects within

Islam and ways of practicing the faith that are of great importance, especially in the type of campaign the US forces began in 2001. In a study of the Taliban movement published in 2001, Pakistani journalist Ahmed Rashid characterized the type of Islam traditionally practiced in Afghanistan as "immensely tolerant—to other Muslim sects, other religions, and modern lifestyles. [Religious leaders] were never known to push Islam down people's throats and sectarianism was not a political issue until recently."[20] Other scholars agree and have emphasized the willingness of Afghan Muslims to incorporate local practice and thought.[21] Goodson, arguing that Afghans have historically rejected radical interpretations of Islam that would hold up the faith as the single guide for life, stated, "The vast majority of [Afghans] believe but are not particularly religious."[22]

Despite these conventions, religious divisions were important. Roughly 80 percent of the population of Afghanistan practiced the Sunni form of Islam. The rest were Shia. As noted above, the Shia faith of the Hazara people made them a minority that the Sunni Pashtun majority sometimes treated with harshness. Within the larger Sunni community, there sometimes appeared divisions as well. Throughout the 19th and 20th centuries, the Sufi sect—a mystical form of Islam—had made significant inroads in Afghanistan, and by the 1970s practicing Sufis held important political positions in the country.[23] More radical sects, such as the Wahabbi school of Islam, did not find Afghanistan fertile ground until the Soviet invasion, when many Wahabbists arrived in the country to fight the Soviet infidel forces. These men, often backed by Saudi funds, slowly gained influence in the 1980s and would play a major role in the rise of the Taliban in the 1990s.

Perhaps most important in this discussion of Islam and Afghanistan is the critical tenet of protecting Islamic lands from infidels. Appeals to fight the infidels had provided much of the force behind the insurgency of the mujahideen against the Soviets in the 1980s. A later section in this chapter will more closely examine this conflict. Still, those appeals were no less powerful in 2001 when military forces from Christian countries of the West began appearing in Afghanistan. Religion in general and the desire to not appear as a large non-Muslim occupation force specifically became a major factor in the Coalition's campaign in the country.

Afghanistan and the Outside World, 1800–1979

Afghanistan's location in central Asia, astride the ancient caravan routes that connected east Asia with Europe and Africa and close to the rich lands of the Indian subcontinent, gave the country a strategic importance that was obvious to many outsiders. Alexander the Great, who in the 4th century B.C. led his army to the area that would later take the name Afghanistan, was the first Western leader to seek dominance over the territory. Forces from China and other parts of central Asia also sought to add the region to their empires. They often succeeded, at least temporarily. Between the years 400 and 1700 A.D., Afghanistan came under the power of rulers such as Genghis Kahn, Tamerlane, and Babur the Tiger.

But by the end of the 18th century, an independent Afghan kingdom had managed to emerge under the leadership of a Pashtun monarchy that managed the querulous Pashtun tribes while also attempting to subjugate the other ethnic groups in the region. As a series of Pashtun rulers consolidated power into the 19th century, their territory became a focal point in the imperial rivalries of European colonial powers. Both Great Britain and Russia began to view Afghanistan as a critical buffer to their expanding empires. The British, increasingly concerned about Russian designs on their colony in India, sought control over the Afghan kingdom. Likewise, the Russians viewed Afghanistan as an obstacle to British expansion in their growing sphere of influence in central Asia. Over the course of the 19th century, both powers would partake in what historians have labeled the Great Game—the contest for control over Afghanistan that featured diplomacy, espionage, saber-rattling, and overt military force.[24] While the two Great Powers never went to war with each other directly, they did use violence and coercion in the Afghan kingdom to achieve their interests.

The British Government, for example, used its military power to fight two campaigns in Afghanistan in the 19th century and one in the early 20th century. In the first Anglo-Afghan War, a British force marched north from Indian territories to install a monarch on the throne who would be favorable to British interests. In 1840, after capturing the recalcitrant Afghan king Dost Muhammad and exiling him to India, the British Army established a garrison in the capital of Kabul to protect the newly installed Afghan ruler. In any event, by 1841 popular discontent among the Afghan population compelled the force to leave Kabul and attempt to march back to British-controlled territory. Along the way, thousands of British and Indian soldiers met their deaths at the hands of Afghan tribesmen.

This disaster did little to deter British aspirations in central Asia. In 1859 Great Britain annexed Baluchistan, a region located south and southwest of Afghanistan, making it a part of India's Northwest Frontier provinces. After becoming concerned about rising Russian influence in Kabul in the 1870s, the British pressured the Afghan monarchy into accepting the Treaty of Gandamak in 1879 in which the Afghan kingdom ceded control of its foreign policy to the British Government, and agreed to accept British military presence in Kabul. Not all Afghan factions accepted the treaty, and some tribal forces took to the field against the British. At the Battle of Kandahar in 1880, the only major engagement in what became known as the second Anglo-Afghan War, a British military victory sealed the political fate of Afghan independence.

In the three decades that passed between the Treaty of Gandamak and the Outbreak of World War I, Great Britain and Russia eventually reached an accord for central Asia that kept relations stable. Afghan domestic politics, nevertheless, were marked by an instability partly caused by conflict between traditional groups and factions advocating modernization. In 1919 the Afghan ruler Habibullah Khan was replaced by King Amanullah Kahn, who wasted little time before initiating the third Anglo-Afghan War by ordering the Afghan Army to attack south into British-held territory. British forces, weakened by 4 years of war in Europe, struggled to retain control over Afghanistan, but after several months of conflict, London agreed to end hostilities and signed the Treaty of Rawalpindi that granted Afghanistan full independence.

Independence and Invasion

In the five decades following the Treaty of Rawalpindi, a succession of Afghan leaders, working within what was ostensibly a constitutional monarchy, launched efforts to modernize some of the country's institutions. Foreign aid provided by Western powers was key in this process. As the Cold War heated up, Afghanistan attracted the attention of both the United States and the Soviet Union. Both Cold War protagonists contributed funds and advisors to Afghanistan in an effort to make the country an ally in Asia. However, by the 1960s the Soviet Union had forged a closer relationship with Afghanistan by offering military equipment and training to the Afghan Army as well as technical and financial assistance for the building of key infrastructure.

Not surprisingly, in the 1970s elements within the Afghan Army came under the influence of Marxist officers, and this group managed to erode the government's power until the Great Saur Revolution of April 1978 created a Communist regime called the Democratic Republic of Afghanistan (DRA). Leading the Communist party—the People's Democratic Party of Afghanistan (PDPA)—was Mohammed Taraki, who became head of state. Shortly after assuming power, Taraki signed a treaty with the Soviet Union, and Soviet military advisors soon began working with Afghan military units. The new Afghan Communist regime did enjoy some support in urban areas of Afghanistan, but quickly alienated the more traditional rural areas because of its introduction of sweeping social reforms.[25] The insurrection that resulted led to Taraki's dismissal from power and the installment of a new Afghan leader, Hafizullah Amin, who also failed in suppressing dissent. Concerned about a rebellious Islamic territory on its southern border, Soviet leader Leonid Brezhnev made the decision to invade Afghanistan on 27 December 1979 with a contingent of 30,000 troops that included airborne units and special forces.[26] Larger, more powerful mechanized units soon followed, and by early 1980 there were close to 90,000 Soviet troops in Afghanistan.

By 1979 maintaining control over Afghanistan had become a paramount strategic goal for Soviet leadership for two reasons. That year marked the radical Islamist revolution in Iran, a movement that threatened to spread to the rest of the Muslim world, especially to those Muslim parts of the Soviet Union that were located near Iran. In Soviet eyes, a stable Afghan Government could serve as a bulwark to the spread of the Islamic revolutionary threat. In addition, 1979 saw the rise of the Solidarity Labor Union in Poland, a far different movement but one almost as threatening to the Soviet empire. For the Soviet leadership, a strong military move in Afghanistan would send a message to the Poles and other eastern European satellite states that the Soviet Union would act against any power that appeared to be attempting to leave Soviet orbit. The Soviet intervention in Afghanistan reinforced the Brezhnev doctrine established after the Soviet invasion of Czechoslovakia in 1968 to end forcefully the "Prague Spring" and the potential loss of the country as a client state.

To a large degree, Soviet leadership hoped to model the Afghanistan intervention on the invasion of Czechoslovakia. In 1968 Brezhnev had not sought to occupy the eastern European state for any length of time. Instead, the use of military power was intended to be short termed and focused on installing a new government in Prague that would return the country securely to the Soviet fold. In this sense, the 1968 intervention was successful. Soviet and other Warsaw Pact forces did not face an armed resistance from the Czechoslovak population and were able to withdraw relatively soon after their arrival.

However, as much as the Soviet political and military leadership hoped to use the 1968 intervention in Czechoslovakia as a template for the Afghanistan invasion, the Afghan population responded far differently than did the Czechs and the Slovaks. In reaction to this invasion by an outside non-Islamic power, Afghan society broke along the fractures that had already appeared in the previous 2 years. Some Afghans, especially those associated with the Marxist party, remained Soviet partners. The Soviet leadership, for its part, viewed the Afghan partnership as crucial to achieving its goals in Afghanistan. According to Dr. Robert Baumann, a historian who has looked closely at the Soviet-Afghan conflict, Soviet military leaders in command of the intervention believed their primary mission to be the "resuscitation" of the Afghan Government and its military forces while avoiding the commitment of a large force to a lengthy campaign.[27]

Other Afghans ensured that the incursion of the non-Islamic power to the north would be neither short nor easy. Not long after the Soviets arrived, small bands of guerrillas emerged from the population to oppose the foreign invaders. Known as mujahideen or "holy warriors," these guerrillas viewed their mission as the expulsion of an infidel occupier from Muslim territory. Lightly armed and untrained in conventional tactics, mujahideen bands could hardly stand toe-to-toe when matched against Soviet formations, whose mobility and technology allowed them to quickly concentrate firepower and maneuver forces. Mujahideen leaders adapted by using time-proven tactics of the insurgent: ambush, retreat, and gradual wearing down of the enemy's will to continue the fight.

Soviet and Afghan military units fortified the capital city and conducted patrols along the highways to keep lines of communication open. This approach allowed Afghan forces to engage the guerrillas. Still, as the mujahideen resistance continued in the early 1980s and the Afghan Army proved less than capable of meeting that resistance, Soviet forces began mounting large-scale operations in the countryside with the goal of suppressing the guerrilla forces. Gradually, the Soviet approach became that of the counterinsurgent. Even so, the counterinsurgency campaign mounted by the Soviet command did not try to win support from the population, but instead focused on destroying the mujahideen by eliminating the rural population that supported the guerrillas. To do this, the Soviet and Afghan air forces relied heavily on air power, bombing villages, irrigation systems, grain storage facilities, and other elements of the rural infrastructure. As a result, by 1985 tens of thousands of Afghans had died in these attacks and nearly 5 million had fled to Iran or the Pashtun areas of Pakistan just across the Afghan border.

By the mid-1980s the Soviet leadership had also increased the number of soldiers inside Afghanistan to approximately 100,000. While often successful in temporarily removing the guerrilla presence, Soviet operations led to a relatively high number of casualties. Indeed, by 1984 Soviet forces were suffering thousands of deaths per year.[28] In any event, Soviet units usually chose not to hold the terrain, returning instead to bases near urban areas. This practice meant that control of the ground quickly reverted to the mujahideen.[29]

The decision in 1986 by the US Government to clandestinely aid the Afghan guerrillas by sending them sophisticated weaponry altered the context of the conflict. By secretly funneling American Stinger and British Blowpipe shoulder-fired, surface-to-air missiles through Pakistan into Afghanistan, the United States empowered the mujahideen to blunt Soviet aerial assaults.[30] While these weapons were not enough to forcibly eject the Soviets from Afghanistan, the introduction of these systems marked a shift in US policy and symbolized the extent to which nations bordering Afghanistan influenced Afghan affairs. Before 1986 no US-made weapons or personnel had been directly committed to the Soviet-Afghan War. By 1986 not only was the United States involved, but American officials had begun using the Pakistani Government and its intelligence arm, the Inter Services Intelligence (ISI), to channel arms and other support to the mujahideen. Forging the US-ISI military aid pipeline established the Pakistani Government as the most important regional player in the anti-Soviet resistance by giving it the power to determine which rebel groups received support and for setting priorities for distributing military supplies.

But Pakistan did more than provide weaponry to the mujahideen. The Pakistani Government allowed its tribal areas centered on the city of Peshawar in the northwest region of the country to become a headquarters for the mujahideen. Afghan guerrilla leaders not only met in Peshawar but also recruited their fighters from the refugee camps that had sprung up in the Pakistani provinces closest to the Afghan border. Moreover, the Pakistanis tacitly encouraged Muslim mujahideen from across the Islamic world to use their territory to organize and travel to Afghanistan to fight the Soviets alongside the Afghan guerrillas. According to Ahmed Rashid, tens of thousands of Muslim men from 43 Islamic countries in the Middle East, Africa, central Asia, and east Asia arrived to help the Afghan mujahideen. Although only a portion were Arab by ethnicity, these foreign volunteers came to be called "Arab Afghans" and contributed significantly to guerrilla successes in the Soviet-Afghan War.[31]

While the Soviet and Afghan forces did celebrate some victories after 1986, the situation in Afghanistan increasingly took on the character of a stalemate that the new Soviet leader, Mikhail Gorbachev, believed was not tenable. By 1987 Gorbachev had decided to withdraw his military forces over a period of 2 years. While the mujahideen on the field of battle had not defeated that army, the guerrillas had certainly made it impossible for the Soviets and their Afghan allies to exert political or military control over Afghanistan, thus preventing the Soviet Union, despite its dedication of manpower and financial resources, from achieving its goals in Afghanistan. The Soviets increased the scale of their military actions in 1987 and early 1988, including one multidivision operation called Magistral aimed at Paktia province in the southeast, in a final series of operations designed to destroy the guerrillas. However, when Soviet units began leaving in 1988, the mujahideen remained in firm control of much of the country. Historian Lester Grau summarized the Soviet experience in Afghanistan by casting the country as the site "where a modern, mechanized army tried to defeat a guerrilla force on rugged terrain in the middle of a civil war. Despite their best efforts, [the Soviet soldiers] were unable to achieve decisive military victory and their politicians finally ordered them home."[32]

Post-Soviet Afghanistan and the Rise of the Taliban

When the Soviets pulled out of Afghanistan, they left behind a puppet Communist regime that remained intact for a short time because of a continued presence of Soviet aid and advisors. At its helm stood Dr. Najibullah Ahmadzai, the former head of the KHAD, the Afghan security service that bore some similarity to the Soviet KGB.[33] Najibullah was last in a string of leaders the Soviets installed in the wake of the 1979 invasion and notwithstanding his former reputation as a hard-liner, he had little choice but to initiate a National Reconciliation Campaign that sought to broaden the base of popular support for his government. His regime suffered from lack of legitimacy, and would last only as long as Soviet benefactors were willing and able to offer support.

For their part, the mujahideen, though fragmented, continued to scorn any contact with the Najibullah government, and their conflict with the Afghan Communists continued with unremitting brutality. Still, during this period at least some guerrilla factions formed temporary alliances with the government. More than anything else, the reconciliation drive bought time to orchestrate the Soviet withdrawal and permitted the Afghan regime to reorganize itself to meet the problems it would face alone following the Soviet Army's departure.

If collapse of the Najibullah government was not a forgone conclusion when the Soviets left, it was fated to last only as long as the Soviet state, and in the end survived the demise of the Soviet

Union by little more than 2 months. What ensued after 1991 was a continuance of the struggle for mastery in Afghanistan with various factions of the mujahideen competing for power. This period, sometimes referred to as the mujahideen interregnum, left Afghanistan in chaos.

Two factions were of particular importance in this period. Gulbuddin Hekmatyar, a Pashtun, led a contingent called the Hezb-i-Islami that was itself 75-percent Pashtun and found most of its support in northeastern Afghanistan and within Pakistan's Afghan refugee population.[34] Other factions would break way from Hekmatyar's party to form half a dozen splinter parties operating out of Pakistan; but, until the rise of the Taliban, the Hezb-i-Islami remained one of the most prominent.

The second was the Jamiat-e Islami, a faction comprised primarily of Afghans from the northern minority groups, especially Tajiks and Uzbeks. Prominent within the ranks of this more northern-based faction, besides its Tajik leader, Burnahuddin Rabbani, were General Ahmed Shah Massoud, a former police chief of Herat, and Ismail Khan, also of Herat. Religious biases complicated the ethnic divide between the northern and southern (mainly Pashtun) factions.

Hekmatyar's Hezb-i-Islami was both more organizationally close-knit and ideologically strident in its Islamic zeal than was the Jamiat party. Still, Rabbani's forces were formidable. Indeed, the chaos of the mujahideen interregnum broke out partially because in 1992 Kabul fell to a non-Pashtun force composed of Tajik forces under Burnahuddin Rabbani and Ahmad Shah Massoud combined with Uzbek forces under General Abdul Rashid Dostum. Hekmatyar and the Pashtuns could not tolerate this event. Allowing Kabul to remain in those hands raised the possibility that for the first time since Afghanistan became a country, non-Pashtuns would be ruling it. Hekmatyar's response was to besiege Kabul and unleash artillery barrages on the city's residential areas, which predictably cost the lives of thousands of civilian noncombatants.[35]

Out of the factions that fought in the interregnum emerged a small group of politically unsophisticated Islamic fundamentalists that became known as the Taliban. Eventually, the Taliban evolved into a force that eclipsed others and eventually seized the reins of power in Afghanistan when it captured Kabul in late 1996.

The root of the Taliban rise to power lies not within Afghanistan but in Pakistan. Throughout the 1980s and 1990s, as the Afghan refugee population grew inside Pakistan, an entire generation of young men was exposed to a fundamentalist version of Islam taught in the many madrassas (religious schools) that thrived in the Pashtun areas around Peshawar. That interpretation of Islam, combined with the lack of employment opportunities available to refugees and the culture of violence that had developed among the mujahideen, contributed to the creation of groups that sought simple, often violent, answers to Afghanistan's problems.

This generation of youth, most of whom were Pashtuns, would play a key role in the rise of the Taliban and the shaping of their approach to political rule. In 1995, on the eve of the Taliban victory, journalist Ahmed Rashid encountered young Taliban soldiers and found them quite different from the older, more traditional Afghans:

> These boys were a world apart from the [mujahideen] whom I had got to know during the 1980s—men who could recount their tribal and clan lineages, remembered their abandoned farms and valleys with nostalgia and recounted legends and stories from Afghan history. These boys were from a generation who had never seen their country at peace. . . . They had no memories of their

tribes, their elders, their neighbors nor the complex ethnic mix of peoples that often made up their villages and their homeland. These boys were what the war had thrown up like the sea's surrender on the beach of history. . . . Many of these young warriors did not even know the history of their own country or the story of the jihad against the Soviets.[36]

Rashid then suggested that the version of Islam taught by the madrassas in the Pashtun regions was "the only prop [the young Taliban men] could hang onto which gave their lives some meaning."[37]

By 1994 these young men had begun their climb to political power. For the better part of that year, Afghanistan remained mired in the midst of the civil war. Burnahuddin Rabbani set up what amounted to a Tajik government in Kabul, and assumed the duties as its nominal president, although his own forces controlled only Kabul and the northeast, thus limiting his actual political authority. Other regional leaders and their militias held sway over the other regions of the country, and the dominant ethnic group remaining, the Pashtuns, suffered from divided leadership.

The Taliban represented one of the Pashtun groups vying for influence. Most of the initial membership of this loosely organized group formed in the region around Kandahar and were united in their disillusionment with the mujahideen leadership. Many were young graduates of the madrassas, and because of this common experience, they took the name "Taliban," an Arabic term that refers to students of the Islamic faith. The leader of the group, Mullah Mohammad Omar, came from a poor family, had been educated in a traditional madrassa, and in the 1980s opened his own madrassa in Kandahar province.

The men who formed the original core of the Taliban had learned and imparted a version of Islam that differed significantly from other fundamentalists. Some scholars of the movement have emphasized that the madrassa education instilled in Pakistan focused on returning Afghan society to an imagined premodern period in which a purer form of Islam was practiced by a more righteous Muslim society. This made the Taliban approach to governance somewhat utopian in its attempt to battle the enemies of modernity and nonorthodoxy.[38]

Originally an inchoate group of disgruntled mujahideen, the Taliban came together more formally in 1994 when Omar organized an attack against a local warlord who had kidnapped and raped several local girls.[39] The group received a boost later that year when attempts by Pakistan's Government to bolster Pakistani involvement in the Afghan economy were rebuffed by all of the major mujahideen factions. The Taliban, however, started collaborating with Pakistani interests and began a campaign in 1994 to gain control of southern Afghanistan to help establish a new trade route from the Pakistani border to Uzbekistan and Turkmenistan. The first step was a small attack by Taliban forces on Hekmatyar's men in October. By mid-November Taliban leaders had used bribes, force, and threats of force to secure a truck route through central Afghanistan.

The Taliban's backers could not have been more pleased with their performance. More importantly, as the word about the Taliban actions and their theology spread, the movement began attracting large numbers of recruits. One scholar contends that by the beginning of 1995 approximately 12,000 men from both Afghanistan and Pakistan had traveled to the Kandahar area to join Mullah Mohammad Omar.[40]

At this stage of the struggle, there existed three geopolitical centers of gravity in Afghanistan. One was Kandahar, firmly within the Taliban grip. A second was in the west in the important city of Herat where the formidable warlord Ismail Khan enjoyed Iranian support and held sway over three provinces considered by Iran to be in its strategic backyard. The third focus was Kabul, where President Rabbani's government clung to power thanks mainly to troops under the command of Ahmed Shah Massoud.

In the months that followed the attack on Hekmatyar's forces, the Taliban won control—at least temporarily—of 12 out of Afghanistan's 31 provinces. As they moved toward Kabul, opposing warlords either surrendered or fled the field.[41] As this untrained group of soldiers marched, they opened roads, disarmed local populations, and restored order by introducing a strict version of Sharia law. Their success was almost completely unexpected and continued as they captured Oruzgan and Zabol provinces without firing a shot. Helmand province was a vortex of a flourishing opium trade and proved to be more difficult for Mullah Mohammad Omar's men. The Taliban met stiff resistance, but through a combination of bribery and exploitation of local rivalries that province fell early in 1995. By February they were within striking distance of Kabul and prepared to attack.

Hekmatyar's forces, strung out between Kandahar and Kabul, became trapped between government forces to the north and the Taliban to the south. Prior to the Taliban advance, different Kabul neighborhoods had been occupied by contending mujahideen forces. With Hekmatyar trapped, Massoud decided to confront his remaining enemies in serial fashion, launching an attack first on the Hazaras—the Shia ethnic group that received support from Iran. Fearing for their position in Kabul, the Hazara leadership made a deal with the approaching Taliban. However, in the turmoil that began when the Taliban entered the capital, the Hazara leader was detained and murdered by Taliban soldiers.[42] This won the Taliban the undying enmity of the Hazaras, who evened the score 2 years later by massacring thousands of Taliban prisoners.

During the rest of 1995, Taliban fortunes waxed and waned. Massoud's forces pushed the Taliban out of Kabul in March. That same month, Mullah Mohammad Omar's advance toward the city of Herat came to a halt when it ran into Ismail Khan's ground forces backed by air power provided by Massoud. Taliban losses mounted as their poorly equipped and untrained soldiers clashed with armies that were more modern and better organized. By the fall, a steady stream of volunteers, many from madrassas in Pakistan, had replenished the movement's ranks and the Taliban leadership renewed the pressure on Herat. In September the assault on the city was renewed, forcing Ismail Khan to flee to Iran and Herat falling to the Taliban.

With Kandahar and Herat now under the control of the Mullah Omar's upstart army, much of the country had fallen under the sway of the Taliban. As long as the capital belonged to Massoud and the Tajiks, however, the Taliban could not truly assert themselves as rulers of Afghanistan. Aided by support from both Pakistan and Saudi Arabia, the Taliban leadership planned a campaign that would lead to an assault on the capital from several directions. Launched in September 1996, that attack forced Massoud to evacuate his forces from the city and deploy them to the north. Kabul was then turned over to the Taliban.

Before leaving the city, General Massoud offered former Communist President Najibullah safe passage out, but he declined, opting instead to seek asylum through United Nations (UN) channels. When that arrangement fell through, the Taliban punctuated their conquest by murdering Najibullah in a barbaric fashion—hanging his body from a light pole near the UN compound in the capital.[43] Shortly thereafter, the Taliban leadership also imposed death sentences (in absentia) on Dostum, Rabbani, and Massoud, but lacked the practical means of carrying out these executions.

The Taliban's Reign of Militant Islam

Massoud and other forces—collectively known as the Northern Alliance (NA)—continued their resistance in the northern reaches of the country from late 1996 until the attacks on the World Trade Center and Pentagon in September 2001. The Taliban ruled most of Afghanistan, creating and asserting new political, legal, and social policies based on their interpretation of Islam. As an indicator of things to come, within 24 hours after capturing Kabul, they began to proscribe the rights and privileges of women as part of an overarching plan to impose their narrow interpretation of Sharia law.

The Taliban creed claimed to be apolitical, universal, and all encompassing. According to Ahmed Rashid, the core members of the Taliban "rejected nationalism, ethnicity, tribal segmentation, and feudal class structure in favor of a new Muslim internationalism which would reunite the Muslim world."[44] The success of this approach depended on the purity and piety personified by a charismatic leader, as opposed to a solid organizational infrastructure grounded in, for example, a system of checks and balances. While claiming to be unique, the all-embracing ideology of their revolution demanded change from the top down rather than attempting to accommodate the myriad social, ethnic, and racial strands that comprised the fabric of Afghan culture.

Some actions taken by the Taliban resonated with Afghan Muslims; others did not. To the extent that they reigned in fractious warlords who recognized only their own authority, the Taliban's actions were welcomed. Still, as Rashid and other scholars have noted, that Islamic tradition "does not sanction the killing of fellow Muslims on the basis of ethnicity or sect [which certainly occurred after they came to power], and it is this, the Taliban interpretation of jihad, which appalls the non-Pashtuns."[45]

The Taliban remained something of an enigma. They emerged from obscurity in 1994, ruled for 6 years, and then were ousted by Coalition forces. One journalist suggested that, at the time of their 2001 defeat, the Taliban "were not much better understood than they were when they first emerged."[46] To some they represented less an enigma than an anomaly: "The Taliban interpretation of Islam, jihad, and social transformation was an anomaly in Afghanistan because the movement's rise echoed none of the leading Islamist trends that had emerged through the anti-Soviet war. . . . They fitted nowhere in the Islamic spectrum of ideas and movements that had emerged in Afghanistan between 1979 and 1994."[47]

Still other scholars of Afghanistan thought they could discern continuity in the Taliban: the tendency of the majority ethnic group to assert hegemony over a heterogeneous society and state to rule it effectively. The Pashtun reliance on leaders like Mullah Mohammad Omar and their treatment of minorities represent a new version of an old refrain, which a writer for the International Institute for the Study of Islam (ISIM) called person-centered politics. This view holds that, ironically, even as Mullah Mohammad Omar donned the reputed Cloak of the Prophet Mohammed in Kandahar to accept the title of Commander of the Faithful, he acted within a historical tradition "consistent with a kin-based mode of Pashtun tribal social and political organization [that] has been the defining [trait] of Afghan politics since Pashtuns first came to dominate the Afghanistan in the mid-18th century."[48] One meaningful way of interpreting the Taliban rise to power is to view it as the Pashtun choosing one of their own who was renowned for his piety and simplicity to rule Afghanistan. Although these two events occurred centuries apart, they shared a common denominator: Pashtun hegemony.

An important distinction here is the difference between state formation and state failure. It is not that a nation-state never evolved in Afghanistan; rather, most scholars view the country as a failed state whose infrastructure has been destroyed or rendered ineffective by war and other disasters. As M. Nazif Shahrani explained, "The primary reason for the failure has been the unwillingness or inability of the leadership to shift from a tribal political culture anchored in person-centered politics to a broader, more inclusive, participatory national politics based on the development of modern national institutions and ideologies."[49] Despite their universalist message, the Taliban refused to stop behaving like Pashtuns historically acted—they embodied a tribal hegemony that has scorned other tribes and traditions, and failed to reach out to broaden their base of support. This failure became very apparent when considering their treatment of women and Taliban behavior toward other Afghan ethnic and religious groups.

The mujahideen interregnum proved to be a period marked by not only widespread war and indiscriminate use of violence, but also of more targeted brutality focused on particular ethnic groups. After the Taliban gained power, the marginalized ethnicities considered the Taliban's version of Islamic justice a pretext for killing non-Pashtuns. Although a Taliban regime ruled in Kabul, much of the rest of the country remained under the control of its enemies. In May 1997 a rebellion of Shia Hazaras forestalled a Taliban takeover of Mazar-e Sharif. Replacing their losses required a transfusion of an additional 5,000 new madrassa students. In June 1997 elements opposing Taliban rule established the "United Islamic and National Front for the Salvation of Afghanistan," which would become known as the NA. But efforts to form a new "shadow government" floundered due to squabbles among Uzbek, Tajik, and Hazara factions.[50] Rashid offered a fuller explanation:

> All sides had carried out ethnic cleansing and religious persecution. The Taliban had massacred Shi'a Hazara villagers and forced out Tajik farmers from the Shomali valley. The Uzbeks and Hazaras had massacred hundreds of Taliban prisoners and killed Pashtun villagers in the north and around Kabul. The Shi'a Hazaras had also forced out Pashtuns on the basis of their Sunni beliefs. More than three-quarters of a million people had been displaced by the recent fighting—in the north around Mazar, on the Herat front and around Kabul—creating a new refugee crisis.[51]

Winter imposed its annual lull in the fighting, but by summer 1998 the Taliban had amassed sufficient combat and logistics strength, much of which came from their Pakistani and Saudi allies. This replenishment allowed for a second assault on Mazar-e Sharif. The corpses of 5,000 to 8,000 massacred civilians lay in the wake of their advance; among these were "Iranian diplomats [stationed at the Iranian Consulate in Mazar], intelligence officers, and a journalist [who had been herded] into the basement and then shot."[52] One observer described the tone of this massacre as "genocidal in its ferocity."[53] In large measure, it was retribution for Taliban losses inflicted the previous year by the NA.

The regime's attitude toward gender represented another dimension of its hatred of the Hazara. Women within this ethnic group had formerly comprised a core of opposition to the Taliban. For centuries Afghanistan's tribal culture constrained women in a vise of domesticity that limited their opportunities within society. Gender issues became muddled during the 1970s as Afghans wrestled with social issues raised by the PDPA and its Soviet mentors. If the Soviet occupation eroded traditional values, it also afforded women—especially those who numbered among the ranks of the urban middle class—greater opportunities for education and careers.[54] Predictably enough, for many this resulted in conflicting values and loyalties.

The 1992 collapse of the Najibullah government did not bode well for women who had supported the Communist government. Many suffered abuse, torture, and death at the hands of mujahideen who sought retribution for crimes committed by the former regime. In the post-Communist era, women's conduct, apparel, and fashion mirrored the return to traditional Islamic mores and values. Although Rabbani's Isamic Republic of Afghanistan neglected to codify women's rights, it did at least acknowledge the role of women in the jihad against the Soviets, as well as their right to work for a livelihood and receive an education.[55] Historically though, a woman's professional status could backfire with negative results. Some former mujahideen regarded feminine upward mobility as an indication that a woman's mind had been inoculated with atheistic, anti-Islamic values. Nonetheless, the status of Afghan women gradually improved before the Taliban rose to power. Approximately 70 percent of the teachers at Kabul University were female by the mid-1990s, along with about 8,000 members of the university's student body. The city's public school students numbered near 150,000 by that decade, and roughly 40 percent were female.[56]

Things changed dramatically and suddenly in areas conquered by the Taliban. In these regions, religious police appeared almost immediately to enforce Islamist strictures on female behavior. Typical was a public notice published by Mawlawi Rafiullah Moazin, head of Kabul's Religious Police, that warned women not to go outside their residence: "If you go outside the house you should not be like women who used to go with fashionable clothes wearing much cosmetics and appearing in front of every man before the coming of Islam. . . . If women are going outside with fashionable ornamental and charming clothes to show themselves, they will be cursed by the Islamic Shari'a and should never expect to go to heaven."[57]

A noted Afghan academic with credentials in archaeology, Sidiqa Sidiq, appealed in vain to Taliban authorities: "Based on the orders of the Holy Koran, I am requesting all the concerned brothers and individuals to release us from this detention and these chains and let us continue our education and our jobs. Under the Islamic Law that is the prime need for the development of our ruined homeland."[58] The Taliban ignored this plea, and thumbed their noses at UN requests for the universal observance of human rights. That Afghanistan had formerly been a signatory to the UN Covenant on Civil and Political Rights carried little weight with the country's new leadership.[59]

In the wake of President Najibullah's murder in 1996, media attention finally began to focus on how the Taliban treated women. Only after "Western journalists witnessed the public whipping of women with bicycle chains because they had not worn their burqas correctly" did members of the press decide that the "people's right to know" warranted moving Afghan gender issues into the spotlight of world public opinion.[60]

In their efforts to instill the values that they believed were necessary to create a pure religious society, the Taliban ushered in a brutal regime of strict behavioral standards for all Afghans. Public punishments, even for capital offenses, assumed a grim equal opportunity dimension. One episode in Kandahar entailed tying a suspected murderer between the goal posts of a soccer stadium recently renovated by the UN—where the relatives of his alleged victim executed him with an AK-47. Other examples include the stoning of a woman to death for trying to leave Afghanistan with a man who was not her blood relative.[61] The Taliban also severely curtailed many forms of social entertainment common in the West, including television, videos, music, cards, and kite flying.

Previously, the sect represented an unknown quantity to US diplomats who, if a little naïve from the vantage point of historical hindsight, had no particular reason *not* to take what the Taliban told them at face value. The latter articulated a dislike for Iran, intent to curtail poppy cultivation, and, at least initially, a disdain for the foreign Muslim presence of the Arab-Afghans. Moreover, they projected a public image of foregoing political power in favor of simply ensuring that the reins of government were in the hands of good Muslims. According to Ahmed Rashid, at least some US officials viewed the Taliban "as messianic do-gooders [not altogether unlike] born-again Christians from the American Bible Belt."[62] Despite warnings from others in the region, American diplomats could not fully grasp what the Taliban represented and promised, partially because the United States had not been integrally engaged in Afghan affairs once the Soviets withdrew at the end of the 1980s.

✦   ✦   ✦

This brief review of the physical, political, cultural, and historical structures of Afghanistan has tried to illustrate the environment in which US forces found themselves operating in 2001. These structures had developed over centuries and had proven extremely resistant to change. Perhaps the two most important elements of Afghan life that have persisted are contradictory. First, Afghan society has been and remains an amalgam of ethnic groups such as the Pashtuns who are historically mutually antagonistic. The fact that each ethnic group contains further tribal divisions only contributed to the fragmented nature of society. This social structure, not surprisingly, has historically served as a brake on political unity within Afghanistan's borders. While the country was first united as a kingdom in the 18th century, ethnic fractures continued to characterize Afghan life.

The second critical element has been the role of outside intervention in Afghan affairs. Foreign powers from the British in the 18th century to the Pakistanis and, arguably, the Americans at the beginning of this century have viewed Afghanistan as a strategic territory and have attempted to gain dominance in the country. Unified opposition composed of Afghans of all ethnic groups has met these outsiders, especially those from outside the Islamic world. Indeed, foreign armies have actually served as forces for political accord inside Afghanistan, although that accord was often short-lived.

These elements and the other deeply embedded structures examined in this discussion would come to play a major role in OEF. American Soldiers who arrived in 2001 and early 2002 would quickly discover that the country they had entered was exceedingly complex. To achieve any amount of long-term success, these Soldiers would have to deal not only with harsh physical terrain but also with a society that was quite different from their own.

Notes

1. Lieutenant Colonel Bryan Hilferty, interview by Contemporary Operations Study Team, Combat Studies Institute, Fort Leavenworth, KS, 12 December 2006, 2.

2. Dr. Robert F. Baumann, *Russian-Soviet Unconventional Wars in the Caucasus, Central Asia, and Afghanistan,* Leavenworth Paper No. 20 (Fort Leavenworth, KS: Combat Studies Institute, Command and General Staff College Press, 1993), 134.

3. Illinois Institute of Technology, Paul V. Galvin Library, "Afghanistan Country Study" (14 January 2002), 1–4. http://www.gl.iit.edu/govdocs/afghanistan (accessed 29 January 2007).

4. Major Tim Hollifield, Office of Military Cooperation–Afghanistan (OMC-A) Briefing, *Building the Afghan Army: Some Keys to Cultural Understanding.* No date/place given, slide 2.

5. Shah M. Tarzi, "Politics of the Afghan Resistance Movement: Cleavages, Disunity, and Fragmentation," *Asian Survey* 3 no.6 (June 1991), 484.

6. Tarzi, "Politics of the Afghan Resistance Movement," 484.

7. Edward Girardet et al., *Afghanistan* (Geneva, Switzerland: Crosslines Publications, 2004), 16.

8. Hollifield Briefing, *Some Keys to Cultural Understanding*, slide 1.

9. Larry P. Goodson, *Afghanistan's Endless War: State Failure, Regional Politics, and the Rise of the Taliban* (Seattle, WA: University of Washington Press, 2001), 13–14.

10. Goodson, *Afghanistan's Endless War*, 13–14.

11. Quoted in Goodson, *Afghanistan's Endless War*, 30.

12. Goodson, *Afghanistan's Endless War*, 17.

13. Nancy Peabody Newell and Richard S. Newell, *The Struggle for Afghanistan* (Ithaca, NY: Cornell University Press, 1981), 23.

14. Newell and Newell, *Struggle for Afghanistan*, 23.

15. Goodson, *Afghanistan's Endless War*, 198.

16. Goodson, *Afghanistan's Endless War*, 16.

17. Major Tim Hollifield, Office of Military Cooperation–Afghanistan (OMC-A) Briefing, *Ethnic Overview of Afghanistan*, slides 7–8; Goodson, *Afghanistan's Endless War*, 16.

18. Hollifield Briefing, *Ethnic Overview of Afghanistan*, slides 12–13; Goodson, *Afghanistan's Endless War*, 16.

19. Goodson, *Afghanistan's Endless War*, 16–17.

20. Ahmed Rashid, *Taliban: Militant Islam, Oil, and Fundamentalism in Central Asia* (New Haven, CT: Yale University Press, 2001), 82.

21. Louis Dupree, *Afghanistan* (Princeton, NJ: Princeton University Press, 1973), 104.

22. Goodson, *Afghanistan's Endless War*, 18.

23. Rashid, *Taliban*, 84–85.

24. For an excellent overview of the Great Game, see Peter Hopkirk, *The Great Game: The Struggle for Empire in Central Asia* (New York, NY: Kodansha, 1992).

25. M.J. Gohari, *The Taliban Ascent to Power* (Oxford, UK: Oxford University Press, 2000), 7.

26. Gohari, *The Taliban Ascent to Power*, 8.

27. Baumann, *Russian-Soviet Unconventional Wars*, 135.

28. Colonel V. Izgarshev, "Afganskaia bol," *Pravda*, 17 August 1989. Quoted in Baumann, *Russian-Soviet Unconventional Wars*, 148.

29. Baumann, *Russian-Soviet Unconventional Wars*, 139 and 142; for an overview of the Soviet-Afghan War, see also Anthony Arnold, *Afghanistan: The Soviet Intervention in Perspective* (Stanford, CA: Hoover Institution Press, 1986); for a more tactical perspective and small-unit vignettes on Soviet and mujahideen operations respectively, see Dr. Lester W. Grau, ed., *The Bear Went Over the Mountain: Soviet Combat Tactics in Afghanistan* (Washington, DC: National Defense University Press, 1996); and Ali Ahmad Jalali and Lester W. Grau, *The Other Side of the Mountain: Mujahideen Tactics in the Soviet-Afghan War* (Fort Leavenworth, KS: Foreign Military Studies Office, 1995).

30. Baumann, *Russian-Soviet Unconventional Wars*, 150–156.

31. Rashid, *Taliban*, 129–131.

32. Baumann, *Russian-Soviet Unconventional Wars*, 177; Grau, *The Bear Went Over the Mountain*, xxiii.

33. Library of Congress Country Studies, "Afghanistan: The Soviet Decision to Withdraw." http://lcweb2.loc.gov/cgi-bin/query/r?/frd/cstdy:@field(DOCID+af0094) (accessed 5 February 2007).

34. Goodson, *Afghanistan's Endless War*, 61–63.

35. Rashid, *Taliban*, 21.

36. Rashid, *Taliban*, 32.

37. Rashid, *Taliban*, 32.

38. Olivier Roy, as quoted in Girardet et al., *Afghanistan*, 238. This definition, taken from Roy, appears in Girardet's glossary but does not cite a specific work. However, two publications authored by Roy do appear in Girardet's bibliography on page 522: *Islam and Resistance in Afghanistan* (Cambridge, MA: Cambridge University Press, 2d Edition, 1990), and *Afghanistan: From Holy War to Civil War* (Darwin Press).

39. Rashid, *Taliban*, 25.

40. Rashid, *Taliban*, 29.

41. Rashid, *Taliban*, 29–30.

42. Rashid, *Taliban*, 34–35.

43. Rashid, *Taliban*, 48–50.

44. Rashid, *Taliban*, 86.

45. Rashid, *Taliban*, 87.

46. John Butt, "The Taliban Phenomenon," in Girardet et al., *Afghanistan*, 46.

47. Rashid, *Taliban*, 87.

48. M. Nazif Shahrani, "The Taliban Enigma: Person-Centered Politics and Extremism in Afghanistan," *International Institute for the Study of Islam (ISIM) Newsletter*, June 2000, 20–21. http://isim.leidenuniv.nl (accessed 5 February 2007).

49. Shahrani, "The Taliban Enigma," 20–21.

50. Rashid, *Taliban*, 61–63.

51. Rashid, *Taliban*, 63–64.

52. Rashid, *Taliban*, 73.

53. Rashid, *Taliban*, 74.

54. Christine Aziz and Smruti Patel, "Defiance and Oppression: The Situation of Women," in Girardet et al., *Afghanistan*, 104.

55. Aziz and Patel, "Defiance and Oppression," in Girardet et al., *Afghanistan*, 106–108.

56. Aziz and Patel, "Defiance and Oppression," in Girardet et al., *Afghanistan*, 108.

57. Aziz and Patel, "Defiance and Oppression," in Girardet et al., *Afghanistan*, 108.

58. Aziz and Patel, "Defiance and Oppression," in Girardet et al., *Afghanistan*, 108–109.

59. Aziz and Patel, "Defiance and Oppression," in Girardet et al., *Afghanistan*, 108–109.

60. Aziz and Patel, "Defiance and Oppression," in Girardet et al., *Afghanistan*, 109; see also Rashid, *Taliban*, 113.

61. Rashid, *Taliban*, 2–5.

62. Rashid, *Taliban*, 176–177.

Chapter 2

The American Response to Terror:
Planning Operation ENDURING FREEDOM

In the days that followed the attacks on 11 September 2001, it became clear that the United States (US) Government intended to take swift and decisive action. In his address to the nation, President George W. Bush announced that the United States and its friends would soon be embarking on a campaign to destroy the forces that had planned and executed those attacks. Bush stated, "America and our friends and allies join with all those who want peace and security in the world, and we stand together to win the war against terrorism."[1] Across the globe, US military forces prepared for operations. Within US Central Command (CENTCOM), the combatant command whose geographic area of responsibility (AOR) included Afghanistan, military staffs began developing a comprehensive campaign plan for widespread counterterrorist actions in a number of countries. This plan was complex and had to be built from the ground up because no previous plan for operations in Afghanistan or other nearby countries existed.

The overarching objectives of CENTCOM's plan were ambitious and required the planners to create a plan that featured both conventional units and Special Operations Forces (SOF) from a variety of nations. They also had to rely on capabilities offered by other agencies within the US Government. Despite the complexities and the demand of creating a wholly new campaign plan, by 21 September, less than 2 weeks after the assaults in New York City and Washington, DC, General Tommy Franks, the commander of CENTCOM, briefed President Bush on the concept of the plan for what was called Operation ENDURING FREEDOM (OEF).*

Figure 5. General Tommy Franks, commander of US forces in Afghanistan.

In the days following the attacks, President Bush and Secretary of Defense Donald Rumsfeld had provided the strategic vision and overall direction for OEF as well as for what became known as the Global War on Terrorism (GWOT). Working from this guidance, Franks designed OEF to eliminate Osama bin Laden and his terrorist group, al-Qaeda, and to take down the ruling Taliban regime that harbored these terrorists. The resulting campaign plan divided operations into four phases, beginning with preparing the battlefield for an air campaign and the insertion of SOF to work with and train indigenous forces and culminating in humanitarian efforts that would allow the international Coalition to help rebuild Afghanistan.

---

*Initially, Operation ENDURING FREEDOM was called Operation INFINITE JUSTICE; however, because Muslim followers believe that only God can compel infinite justice, the name was changed to ENDURING FREEDOM.

The overall approach taken by Franks and the Bush administration was multifaceted, utilizing all the elements of national power—diplomatic, informational, military, and economic—to achieve the larger goals of the new war on terrorism. From the early days of OEF, Franks and his staff worked closely with military representatives from many nations to ensure the campaign plan made the best use of international capabilities. Likewise, because gaining and retaining the support of the Afghan people became a crucial aspect of the campaign, CENTCOM mounted effective humanitarian assistance efforts. This imperative added the additional task of integrating nongovernment organizations (NGOs), like the International Conference of the Red Cross, into the plan.

This chapter provides an account of how the American Government, working with its allies, created a unique response to answer the terrorists that had perpetrated the worst attack on the United States since Pearl Harbor. The discussion will begin with a brief overview of the American experience with terrorism over the last three decades to help explain why the US Government in 2001 had no plan to attack al-Qaeda bases in Afghanistan. Following that section, the chapter will shift focus to the strategy devised by the Bush administration that would serve as the foundation for the campaign the American military and its partners were about to begin. Because international support was so critical to OEF, the discussion will then recount the efforts to work with key countries such as Pakistan and Uzbekistan and build a Coalition that would help the United States respond to the terrorist attacks of 11 September. Finally, the chapter examines the plan itself to explain how Coalition forces intended to enter a landlocked country and defeat both the Taliban regime and the al-Qaeda organization harbored by that regime.

International Terrorism and American Counterterrorism Policy, 1970–2001

In hindsight, it is perhaps difficult to understand why the US Government did not have a plan in 2001 to mount an offensive against terrorist targets in Afghanistan. After all, in the previous 3 years the al-Qaeda organization and its leader, Osama bin Laden, had used Afghanistan as a site for planning and launching two dramatic attacks on American targets. In 1998 al-Qaeda had simultaneously bombed the US Embassies in Dar es Salaam, Tanzania, and Nairobi, Kenya. These attacks killed over 200 and wounded thousands. In 2000 suicide bombers had used a huge bomb to blow a large hole in the destroyer USS *Cole* as it was moored in the harbor of Aden, Yemen, killing 17 Sailors. By early 2001 US intelligence officials were reasonably certain that al-Qaeda was responsible for both incidents.[2]

These suspicions were based on strong evidence, but did not collectively represent a trigger for a large-scale military campaign. Indeed, in 1998 the US Government chose not to initiate major military operations against the Taliban regime that was providing refuge for al-Qaeda, but instead launched missile strikes designed to kill the organization's leadership and damage its training camps. In the wake of the *Cole* bombing, the American Government gathered evidence and prepared a multifaceted response that featured diplomatic pressure on the Taliban to turn bin Laden over to the United States. At the same time, intelligence and military officials continued to plan covert efforts to kill bin Laden and other al-Qaeda leaders using SOF, cruise missiles, or non-Taliban groups inside Afghanistan.[3] In support of any future US airstrike against Osama bin Laden, CENTCOM and other US military agencies maintained a list of al-Qaeda targets at all times. This set of targets, and the preparations that had been made to strike them, were the only "plans" available to the CENTCOM commander on the morning of 11 September 2001.

This lack of a fully manifested plan for a campaign in Afghanistan should not be surprising. In the three decades that preceded the events of 9/11, a period replete with terrorist attacks against American military targets and other interests, no US administration had chosen to direct large-scale military operations against any nation that either directly conducted the attacks or harbored the groups responsible for terrorist incidents. In general, the American counterterrorism policy was a mix of diplomatic, legal, law enforcement, intelligence, and covert initiatives. In a few cases where evidence pointed to state-sponsored terrorism, the American Government did launch military actions to punish those regimes.

Perhaps the best example of a focused military response was the escalation of action against Muammar Qadhafi's Libya in the 1980s. After discovering that Libyan agents were involved in several attacks on US military personnel and installations in Europe, the Reagan administration used US air power to attack Libyan aircraft and bomb targets in the capital city of Tripoli. The US Government, however, never considered invading the country and overthrowing the Qadhafi regime, conceivably because of the relatively small scale of the attacks and their location overseas.

While the Libyan attacks were horrific and unconscionable, a military campaign aimed at regime change was not among the courses of action considered to address the Qadhafi problem. Moreover, the broad approach by the Reagan, George H.W. Bush, and Clinton administrations toward Libya that relied on economic, diplomatic, and legal policies as well as limited military actions seemed to members of these administrations to be the right response toward a terrorist state because it resulted in success. By the late 1990s the Qadhafi government had distanced itself from terrorist groups and begun working with the United States, the United Nations (UN), and the International Court of Justice to bring the Libyan officials responsible for the 1988 bombing of Pan Am Flight 103 over Lockerbie, Scotland, to trial. Until September 2001, no American political or military leader had seriously considered counterterrorism policies that departed from this general approach.

Strategy for the Global War on Terrorism

The US response to the attacks of 9/11 differed considerably from past US policy to terrorism. Unlike the Libyan-sponsored incidents or previous al-Qaeda bombings, the attacks on that September morning were directed against iconic landmarks of American power inside the country itself. These strikes by al-Qaeda hijackers also inflicted far greater casualties than previous terrorist attacks. Despite policy precedents, the Bush administration immediately considered large-scale military action once the scale of the 9/11 attacks became apparent. President Bush pledged to bring the entire spectrum of US power to the fight in Afghanistan and declared the terrorist attacks acts of war rather than crimes. As such, the military would take the lead in actions against al-Qaeda rather than playing a limited role as in the past.

Three days after the attacks, President Bush signaled his intent to use the military broadly when he signed a directive making all elements of the Ready Reserves available for up to 2 years of Active Duty.[4] One day later, on 15 September 2001, the President used very clear language at Camp David to assert the role of the Armed Forces in his response to the terrorists, stating, "The message is for everybody who wears the uniform: get ready. The United States will do what it takes to win this war."[5]

Thus, within days of the attacks, the Bush administration began using the term "war" to describe its effort against al-Qaeda and other terrorist groups and consequently began placing some governmental institutions on a war footing. In an effort to bolster homeland defense, the Department of Defense (DOD) began planning for Operation NOBLE EAGLE, the official name for homeland defense and civil support operations after 9/11. The mobilization in support of NOBLE EAGLE called up approximately 35,000 National Guard and Reserve members to provide medical and engineering support as well as general civil support.[6] The Air National Guard patrolled the skies over New York and Washington, DC, and flew random patrols over other major cities. Coast Guard Reserves patrolled the waters on both coasts. The US population overwhelming supported these steps. A *New York Times*/CBS News poll taken 2 weeks after the 9/11 attacks found that 92 percent of those surveyed believed the United States should take military action. Even if it meant the deaths of thousands of military personnel, 72 percent supported military action, and 68 percent believed the military conflict would last a year or longer.[7]

In an address to the nation on 20 September 2001, President Bush declared that Osama bin Laden and his terrorist organization were responsible for the attacks and implicated the Taliban leadership as sponsors of al-Qaeda. Although bin Laden and al-Qaeda were the primary perpetrators for the 9/11 attacks, Bush clearly stated that the goal of the United States was to look beyond bin Laden to eliminate terrorism worldwide. He declared, "Our war on terror begins with al-Qaeda, but it does not end there. It will not end until every terrorist group of global reach has been found, stopped, and defeated."[8] Bush also used this speech to announce that the US Government had given the Taliban an ultimatum demanding that they hand over all members of al-Qaeda in Afghanistan and close all terrorist camps on Afghan territory. A refusal to do so, Bush promised, would be met by military action.

Other calls for the Taliban to surrender Osama bin Laden and cease all affiliation with al-Qaeda followed. On 6 October 2001, for example, President Bush gave a final warning to the regime in Kabul, stating, "The Taliban has been given the opportunity to surrender all the terrorists in Afghanistan and to close down their camps and operations. Full warning has been given, and time is running out."[9] According to one report, on the eve of the US military offensive, the Taliban offered to try Osama bin Laden in an Islamic court.[10] However, the US Government quickly rejected this compromise.

From its incipient stage, the primary goal of US strategy in the emerging campaign against terrorism was to disrupt and destroy the al-Qaeda organization in Afghanistan and in other states that had granted al-Qaeda sanctuary. Still, President Bush explicitly attempted to distinguish the war on terrorism from a religious war against those of the Islamic faith in his 20 September address: "The enemy of America is not our many Muslim friends; it is not our many Arab friends. Our enemy is a radical network of terrorists, and every government that supports them."[11] This was an important declaration given the American desire to make the campaign a Coalition effort and limit the number of adversaries that Coalition would face. Indeed, President Bush repeatedly asked every nation in the world to join in the battle against extremism and terrorism in its many guises.

Civilian and military officials in the US Government certainly understood the impending campaign against al-Qaeda as a *war*. Furthermore, most believed that this new war would *not* resemble past armed conflicts. This imminent military effort was focused against a secretive supranational terrorist organization and because of that distinction, would likely not rely on conventional combat operations against an enemy state and its armed forces. This difference in the nature of the conflict forced American leaders to consider how they might harness all the elements of national power in the new war. Beginning in September 2001, planners for the GWOT employed a variety of means including interrupting financial networks, conducting widespread information operations, and asserting diplomatic influence in conjunction with military action.

Disrupting terrorist financial networks became a vitally important part of the overall campaign. On 23 September, just 12 days after the attacks, Bush signed Executive Order 13224 authorizing the US Government to block the assets of foreign individuals and entities that committed or posed a serious risk of committing acts of terrorism. This effort included individuals who supported or assisted terrorist organizations.[12] In addition to the Executive order, the United States and its allies worked to deny terrorist access to the international financial system and to prevent the movement of assets through alternative financial networks.

Information efforts included providing information to the Afghan population about US intentions. The United States needed to ensure that the Afghan citizens as well as Muslim allies around the world understood that a war was not being waged against Islam and Muslims, but against terrorist organizations and their illegitimate allies that ruled Afghanistan. Further, as the largest provider of humanitarian funding to Afghanistan, the United States publicly asserted its renewed commitment of aid through planned food drops and coordination with humanitarian organizations.

Intelligence gathering efforts grew exponentially after the attacks as the military and Federal Bureau of Investigation (FBI) began focusing on al-Qaeda and affiliate organizations. Lieutenant General Michael DeLong, Deputy Commander of CENTCOM, recalled that his staff immediately pulled together all available intelligence on Afghanistan and began to review counterterrorism contingency plans.[13] Although the United States had a well-developed set of intelligence services, successful intelligence operations required the sharing of information from allied countries. By 30 September 2001, over 100 nations had begun to offer intelligence support, and several dozen countries took more overt action by detaining suspected terrorists and their supporters.[14]

On the diplomatic front, President Bush and his key advisors—including Vice President Richard Cheney, Secretary of Defense Rumsfeld, and Secretary of State Colin Powell—immediately began to put together a Coalition from around the world. Making the fight against terrorism an international effort had become a cornerstone of Bush's strategy and some American military leaders quickly recognized it as equal in importance to the imminent military action in Afghanistan. DeLong, for example, contended that the construction of a Coalition was key to launching a multifaceted counterterrorist campaign that struck at terrorist groups across the globe. International organizations and leaders from nations around the world were sympathetic to the American cause, quickly denouncing the terrorist attacks and offering condolences to the victims. The victims of the attack had included citizens from over 80 countries, a fact that highlighted the international significance of the atrocity.

Some nations quickly offered military assistance while others agreed to provide intelligence and access to their airspace. Because of the complexity of worldwide negotiations and alliances, the Coalition did not fully disclose all specific pledges. Generally, offers of support involved sharing information, transportation access agreements, use of military bases, and provisions of military assets. Because Afghanistan was completely landlocked, access to airspace, ports, airfields, and roads was especially crucial to the campaign. Some nations promised border security to thwart escape attempts by al-Qaeda. Others provided substantial military assets such as aircraft, ships, equipment, and both conventional and special forces.[15] The most critical contributions came from America's traditional allies—Great Britain, Australia, Canada, and France in particular—which quickly declared that an attack on the United States was an attack on their own countries and volunteered military troops and equipment.

Support also came from international organizations such as the UN, which issued several proclamations concerning terrorism and humanitarian assistance, and the North Atlantic Treaty Organization (NATO), which offered the most dramatic initiative. In 2001 NATO was the strongest military alliance in the world and in the wake of 9/11, the organization fulfilled the promise that was at the core of its existence. Formed in 1949 to defend western Europe against a Soviet invasion, NATO had survived the Cold War as a powerful league of Western allies. NATO took military action in Bosnia, Herzegovina, and Kosovo, but 9/11 was the first time that a NATO member-nation was directly attacked. Article V of the 1949 North Atlantic Treaty, which formed the basis of the alliance, made the following assertion: "The Parties agree that an armed attack against one or more of them in Europe or North America shall be considered an attack against them all."[16] Although the organization had participated in past military actions, NATO leadership had not invoked Article V. The events of 11 September, nevertheless, called for a strong consideration of the article. Hours after the attacks, Lord Robertson, Secretary General of NATO, made a strong public statement condemning the attacks: "These barbaric acts constitute intolerable aggression against democracy and underline the need for the international community and the members of the Alliance to unite their forces in fighting the scourge of terrorism."[17]

NATO leaders felt a responsibility to uphold the alliance in the face of terrorism. At the same time, the North Atlantic Council had to consider its sometimes-tenuous relationship with Russia and the effect any action would have on central and eastern European nations who might someday join NATO. Another consideration was the sustainment of continuing missions in the Balkans and Macedonia.[18] Finally, consensus to support the United States required proof that Osama bin Laden and al-Qaeda were responsible for the attacks. Many member nations had already experienced terrorism and did not wish to incite new incidents within their borders, nor did they wish to offend their sizable Muslim populations.[19]

Within 36 hours of the attack, NATO provisionally invoked Article V, and by 4 October 2001 had gathered sufficient evidence incriminating Osama bin Laden and al-Qaeda to allow a formal invocation of Article V. As part of this declaration, the NATO allies agreed to take numerous measures to assist the United States in the fight against terrorism. The nations agreed to share intelligence and increase security for US and other allied facilities on their territories. They also gave blanket overflight clearance to US and allied military aircraft involved in the campaign and granted American forces access to ports and airfields on allied territory.[20]

In support of the military effort, NATO deployed the nine ships of the Standing Naval Forces Mediterranean (STANAVFORMED) to the eastern Mediterranean. Five NATO Airborne Warning and Control System (AWACS) aircraft and one cargo plane with 196 military and 31 civilian people deployed to Tinker Air Force Base, Oklahoma, under the command of North American Air Defense Command (NORAD), a move that freed up American AWACS aircraft to deploy to Afghanistan. While this initial NATO support enhanced American military capabilities, the United States did not initially seek substantial military forces or assets from NATO countries. Most of these nations did not have the air or Special Forces (SF) capabilities needed for the initial campaign. Instead, these allies supported other strategic objectives by providing intelligence, security, and tracking and terminating financial networks that supported al-Qaeda and their supporters. In a press conference on 20 September 2001, Deputy Secretary of State Richard Armitage discussed the importance of this level of international cooperation on all strategic aspects of the war against terrorism. Explaining that the fight against terrorism would be a sustained campaign, he stated, "And I think it is quite clear to most, if not all . . . that this is not just military in nature. It's political, it's economic, it will mean sharing of intelligence. So I think there is a role of some sort for every nation who is disgusted by terrorism and has had enough."[21]

By focusing the NATO effort toward other missions and by not asking for collective military action from the allies, the United States maintained control of the military campaign while gaining a wide degree of international support. This arrangement also benefited the allies who demonstrated their commitment to eliminate terrorism and support the United States, but were not bound by future military action.[22] French Minister of Defense Alain Richard appeared to endorse this approach and its diplomatic benefits when he remarked in early October 2001, "Our American friends have thoughtfully emphasized that defeating terrorism can only proceed from a large array of means—financial, political, diplomatic, judicial, police and intelligence-related . . . of which military force is only one among others."[23]

The endorsement of the UN also assisted the overall American approach. The UN charter stated that the organization's goals were to prevent war, affirm fundamental human rights in all nations, uphold international law, and promote social and economic progress.[24] As the largest and most important of the world's international organizations, it facilitated dialogue and cooperation for 189 countries. While only a relatively small number of member countries considered themselves military allies of the United States in 2001, the attacks of 9/11 compelled an immediate condemnation of terrorism. On 12 September 2001 UN Secretary General Kofi Annan stated, "We are struggling, above all, to find adequate words of condemnation for those who planned and carried out these abominable attacks. In truth, no such words can be found. And words, in any case, are not enough."[25] That day, the UN Security Council passed Resolution 1368 that condemned the attacks, expressed condolences to the victims, and called on all nations to combat terrorism. In addition to these strong condemnations, many nations used the General Assembly forum to publicly express their outrage at the attacks and express sympathy for the American people. James Cunningham, Acting US Ambassador to the UN, thanked these speakers for their support and urged united action to defend the founding values of the United Nations. He also reminded the General Assembly of President Bush's message that all nations had to choose between those who oppose terrorism and those who use and support terrorism, including turning a blind eye to terrorist groups active on their soil.[26]

While condemnation of the attacks and sympathy for the victims was widespread, UN members had diverse opinions concerning subsequent action and retaliation. They expressed their concerns in several debates in the General Assembly. Gaining UN consensus and support was central to the US campaign, especially because of humanitarian concerns in Afghanistan. The UN estimated at the time of 9/11 that more than 5 million Afghans required humanitarian assistance and 3.8 million relied on UN food aid for survival. Nearly 20 percent of those in need were children under the age of 5.[27] The UN called on all countries and especially neighboring countries to help prevent tragedy by contributing humanitarian aid and opening borders to those in need. In late September, with military action in Afghanistan looming on the horizon, Kofi Annan implored the international community to provide assistance:

> In accordance with international law, the borders must be open to civilians seeking refuge. At the same time, the international community must send swift and generous help, so that refugees do not become an impossible burden on the neighboring States. Innocent civilians should not be punished for the actions of their government. The world is united against terrorism. Let it be equally united in protecting and assisting the innocent victims of emergencies and disasters.[28]

The UN representative from Pakistan, Shamshad Ahmad, pledged Pakistan's full support in the fight against international terrorism and stated that over 2.5 million Afghan refugees had entered Pakistan in the last two decades with many more likely to cross the border. He also appealed to the international community to address Afghanistan's grave humanitarian situation through reconstruction and reconciliation as well as greater emphasis on economic growth in developing countries.[29]

In response to the 9/11 attacks, the UN Security Council passed Resolution 1373 to combat terrorism and monitor its implementation. Resolution 1373 made previous UN Resolution 1269 binding on all member states and furthered the strategy of the Bush administration by declaring that all nations must block any financing of terrorism, deny safe haven to any terrorist persons or entities, and prevent terrorist groups from using their territories. Further, the resolution stated that member nations should establish terrorist acts as serious criminal offenses and should bring to justice any person or any organization who participates in terrorist financing, planning, preparation, or perpetration. The UN Security Council also requested that all nations share intelligence regarding terrorist acts and assist one another in criminal investigations or criminal proceedings relating to the finance or support of terrorist acts.[30]

NATO and the UN were not the only international organizations to express solidarity with the United States. The Organization of American States, which included many Central and South American countries as well as the United States, quickly invoked the Inter-American Treaty of Reciprocal Assistance (commonly know as the Rio Treaty). Ratified in 1945, this treaty was similar to NATO's Article V in that the agreement stated that an attack against one was considered an attack against all. On 14 September 2001 Australia formally invoked the ANZUS Treaty, which pledged Australian and New Zealand support for their ally, the United States. Both Australia and New Zealand would eventually provide both SOF and naval ships for OEF.

As noted earlier in this chapter, several key nations expressed their immediate support to the United States after 9/11 and volunteered to participate in the GWOT. Great Britain, as a member of NATO, had supported the invocation of Article V. However, British Prime Minister Tony Blair went further by committing the Royal Navy, the Royal Air Force, the British Army, and British SOF to the Afghanistan campaign. The Royal Navy made available an aircraft carrier, a squadron of Harrier jets, and other capital ships while the Royal Air Force planned to use fighters, bombers, tankers, and attack helicopters.[31] President Bush recognized Prime Minister Blair's and Great Britain's contribution stating in his 20 September address to the nation, "America has no truer friend than Great Britain. Once again, we are joined together in a great cause."[32]

Canada, as a NATO member, also supported Article V and further contributed to the operation by pledging 2,000 Canadian troops including an SOF unit, six warships, six planes, and several helicopters. Canada placed the Canadian Disaster Assistance Response Team (DART) as well as three humanitarian assistance ships in readiness.[33] In addition to invoking the ANZUS Treaty, Australia committed 150 Special Air Service troops along with 1,000 other service members. Australian Prime Minister John Howard also promised to send aircraft and additional SOF if required.[34]

France allowed use of French airspace and sent a navy air defense frigate and a command and logistics vessel to support the United States. The French placed their SOF overseas in readiness and President Jacques Chirac agreed to commit French forces in the offensive.[35] Japan sent four warships from its Maritime Self-Defense Forces (MSDF) for support, intelligence, medical service, transportation, fuel, and supplies. Turkey provided blanket access to Turkish airspace as well as the use of eight air bases. Turkey Prime Minister Bulent Ecevit also authorized the deployment of SOF to train anti-Taliban fighters, and the Turkish parliament increased support for the anti-Taliban Northern Alliance (NA), which controlled territory in northeast Afghanistan. By 30 September 2001 the Department of State (DOS) had received dozens of declarations of multilateral and unilateral support. Equally important was that several Middle Eastern nations severed diplomatic ties with the Taliban, thus furthering that regime's isolation from the international community.

Securing Access to Afghanistan's Neighbors

Perhaps the most critical type of support offered to the Coalition in September and October 2001 were the overflight and landing rights made available to the Coalition by over two dozen nations.[36] Given Afghanistan's location as a landlocked country in the middle of central Asia, planners knew that securing overflight and basing assistance from Afghanistan's neighbors would be critical. Further, the United States needed access to these countries to stage Combat Search and Rescue (CSAR) units, teams that could locate and pick up pilots and crewmembers who had ejected from damaged aircraft. Without CSAR capability, both ground and air missions would be precarious.

Negotiating in this part of the world, in fact, was extremely complex because the alliances and conflicts in this region made the area a virtual political chessboard. To the north of Afghanistan were the central Asian states of Uzbekistan, Kazakhstan, Tajikistan, Kyrgyzstan, and Turkmenistan, which were independent but retained close ties to Russia. Although each claimed to be a democracy, human rights violations had damaged relations between these nations and some countries in the West. To the west was Iran, which, although a staunch opponent of the Taliban, firmly opposed joining a US-led Coalition claiming the war was a pretext for helping Israel and extending American military power in the Middle East. In late September 2001 Ayatollah Ali Khamenei, Iran's supreme leader, expressed his government's public dismissal of support for the anti-Taliban Coalition stating, "How can America, which has tampered with Iran's interests, demand help from Iran to attack the suffering, oppressed and Muslim nation of Afghanistan? . . . It is true that America's dignity has been badly damaged, but that does not mean that it can make an arrogant face and force other countries to give in to its demands. . . . It is wrong to say that those who are not with us are with the terrorists."[37]

Figure 6. Afghanistan and its neighbors.

Pakistan to the south of Afghanistan presented the most difficult challenge for the Coalition. The populous Muslim country had been involved in internal Afghan affairs for decades. In the 1980s the country's Pashtun provinces in the northwest had been the sanctuary for the mujahideen movement, and in the following decade, the Taliban drew support not only from the fundamentalist Muslims in the northwest but also from the Pakistani Government. In 2001 much of the country's population was generally sympathetic to the Taliban and not necessarily eager to support the United States. Further complicating diplomatic matters was that in the fall of 2001 Pakistan was embroiled in a disagreement with India over the Kashmir region, a conflict that threatened to escalate into nuclear war.

Within this turbulent international environment, military leaders and US diplomats worked to secure overflight, staging, and basing support. Recalling the initial planning sessions within the National Security Council following the 9/11 attacks, National Security Advisor

Condoleezza Rice remembered that the participants were struck by complexities inherent in conducting military operations in Afghanistan. She stated, "You look at the map, you look at Afghanistan and you look at where it is—I think the color kind of drained from everybody's faces. . . . I think everybody thought, 'Of all of the places to have to fight a war, Afghanistan would not be our choice.' But we didn't choose Afghanistan; Afghanistan chose us."[38]

During the course of these sessions, the central Asian nations of Uzebekistan, Turkmenistan, and Kyrgyzstan quickly rose to prominence. Luckily, when Rice and others considered these countries as allies in the GWOT, there was a foundation on which they could build. These countries had become members of the NATO Partnership for Peace Program in the 1990s, and in 1995 that program facilitated the creation of the Central Asian Battalion (CENTRASBAT) to conduct training and exercises with NATO countries and the United States. In 1998 CENTCOM Commander General Anthony Zinni used CENTRASBAT as a conduit to foster closer ties with the central Asian states by attending the opening ceremony of an exercise held in Kyrgyzstan.[39] Then on 1 October 1999 the DOD transferred these nations from European Command's AOR to that of CENTCOM. When General Franks took command of CENTCOM, he continued to promote military relationships through CENTRASBAT exercises and visited President Islam Karimov of Uzbekistan twice in the 12-month period before 9/11.[40]

Although the United States fostered military and political relationships with the independent central Asian states, the Russian Government still had multiple ties within the region and considered the area to be in their back yard.[41] On the breakup of the Soviet Union, Russia and 10 former Soviet republics, including all 5 central Asian states, formed the Commonwealth of Independent States (CIS). The CIS was not a confederation, but did facilitate coordination of security, trade, and finance among member countries and allowed Russia a great deal of influence in these matters. Russia also extended its influence through the Shanghai Five, another important regional organization formed to maintain security along the borders of the former Soviet states and China. Formed in 1996, the founding members—Russia, China, Kazakhstan, Tajikistan, and Kyrgyzstan—united to foster stability through fighting terrorism, drug trafficking, illegal immigration, and armed smuggling. In June 2001 Uzbekistan joined the alliance.[42]

Given Russia's heavy influence in the region, the United States tried to tread lightly in its dealings with the central Asian countries. Already in September 2000, General Franks was careful to ensure that support for Uzbekistan was not intended to compete with Russia's support and that CENTCOM's presence in the area was for "coordination and cooperation, not for competition."[43] Instead of fostering competition, US diplomatic strategy after 9/11 focused on gaining the support of Russian President Vladimir Putin. Putin was one of the first leaders to offer moral support after the attacks, and quickly pledged intelligence sharing and the opening of Russia's airspace for deliveries of humanitarian aid. The Russian president also urged the central Asian states to assist the United States.[44] This cooperation was vital for impending US operations in Afghanistan and was politically valuable for Putin who had an opportunity to regain international status and defuse criticism of Russia's policies toward Chechnya.[45]

While President Bush and other key US leaders worked with Moscow, US officials also traveled directly to central Asian states to seek support. On 28 September 2001, James R. Bolton, Under Secretary of State for Arms Control and International Security, visited Tashkent, Uzbekistan. General Franks arrived in the Uzbek capital 2 days later and Secretary of Defense

Rumsfeld followed the CENTCOM commander on 5 October 2001. Rumsfeld met with President Islam Karimov and secured the use of Uzbekistan's former Soviet air base Karshi-Khanabad (later known as K2) for staging, CSAR, and humanitarian missions.[46] The United States did not intend its presence in Uzbekistan to become permanent. Rather, K2 would serve as a base for ongoing operations in Afghanistan and US forces would vacate once the conflict ended. This assurance eased fears of a permanent US presence within Russia's sphere of influence.

Figure 7. Location of US Air Base at Karshi-Khanabad (K2).

Uzbekistan's border with Afghanistan was only 137 kilometers long, but was of strategic importance because of its proximity to Mazar-e Sharif and other NA strongholds. As President Bush's and the US military's emissary to Uzbekistan, Rumsfeld's ability to secure support from President Karimov was a key turning point in the planning process. Without use of the air base and airspace, the United States would have had a significantly more difficult time providing the logistics support for operations.

Karimov had not made this crucial decision without considering the benefit to his own government, however. The United States pledged military and financial support in return for the basing rights. While the terms of the agreements were not disclosed, the US Government gave Uzbekistan $118.2 million in general aid in 2002, up from a total of $24.8 million in 2001. Funding for Foreign Military Finance and International Military Education and Training grew from $3 million in 2001 to $37.7 million in 2002.[47] From Karimov's point of view, the relationship had benefits beyond the additional incoming funds. The US air base would stimulate the local economy and bring the young nation closer to the world's remaining superpower. Additionally, Uzbekistan planned to use US support to combat its own internal terrorist threat, a group called the Islamic Movement of Uzbekistan (IMU) that often fought alongside Taliban and al-Qaeda forces. Indeed, in its negotiations with Karimov, the United States pledged to target the IMU as part of the GWOT.

While US diplomats were courting Uzbekistan, other officials also visited Kyrgyzstan, Kazakhstan, and Tajikistan. All of these countries eventually issued statements of support, but Tajikistan and Kyrgyzstan went further. The former offered the use of three air bases—Kulyab, located only 96 miles from the Afghan border; Kurgan-Tyube in the south; and Khujand in the north. In addition, in December 2001 Kyrgyzstan granted the use of Manas Airport near the capital of Bishkek for use by the Coalition. This base became a major logistics hub during operations in Afghanistan.

Uzbekistan's K2 provided the platform from which operations in northern Afghanistan could be launched, but the United States also needed cooperation from Pakistan. That country shared a 2,430-kilometer border with Afghanistan and was thus critical for operations in southern and eastern areas. Until 11 September 2001 Pakistan maintained a pro-Taliban stance and offered the Afghan regime political, financial, and military support. In light of the attacks on the United States, Pakistan had to give serious consideration to President Bush's ultimatum that "any nation that continues to harbor or support terrorism will be regarded by the United States as a hostile regime."[48] When faced with this statement, Pakistan quickly chose to side with the United States against Osama bin Laden and on 13 September, Pakistan President General Pervez Musharraf announced that Pakistan would give "unstinted cooperation" to the United States.[49]

Unlike the former Soviet states where US relationships were relatively new, Pakistan was over 50 years old and had maintained an uneasy relationship with the United States for several decades. This relationship had begun in the early years of the Cold War when the United States and Pakistan aligned out of US concerns about Soviet expansion into South Asia and Pakistani anxiety about India. Conflicts between India and Pakistan in 1965 and 1971 strained these links, although the relationship grew much tighter in the 1980s when Pakistan served as the conduit for US military aid to the mujahideen. In the 1990s, as Pakistan experienced political turmoil, ties between the two countries became strained again and finally broke in 1998 after Pakistan tested a nuclear weapon and the US applied economic sanctions.

The attacks of 9/11 provided Pakistan the opportunity to go from pariah to partner in the eyes of the United States. While a US partnership would be economically and diplomatically advantageous for Pakistan in many respects, President Musharraf faced a difficult decision. Within Pakistan, public opinion did not generally support the United States. Many Pakistanis regarded the United States with skepticism fostered by the belief that once Pakistan's usefulness had expired, the country would be cast off and forgotten, much like what had happened after the Soviet withdrawal from Afghanistan.[50] This skepticism was seen in a number of polls conducted in 2002. According to a Pew Global Attitudes Survey of that year, only 22 percent of Pakistanis had a favorable image of the United States in 1999–2000, and by 2002 this percentage dropped to only 10 percent. Additionally, only 20 percent of those surveyed favored the United States' declaration of a GWOT, while 45 percent opposed it.[51]

As one of the few nations who recognized the Taliban as a legitimate government, Pakistan had many deep-seated connections to the regime in Kabul. The Taliban's origin in the Pashtun ethnic group, a people who lived straddling the border between Pakistan and Afghanistan, was only the most obvious tie. While border control was a known problem, managing the flow of terrorist groups and refugees seemed to be an insoluble problem for the Pakistani Government. Any Pakistani policy in support of US actions in Afghanistan had to take the interests of Pakistan's Pashtun citizens under consideration.[52] This was especially true of Pakistan's many Islamic fundamentalists who cooperated with al-Qaeda and Osama bin Laden and offered no great support to the Musharraf regime. Any abrupt change of policy had the potential to ignite violent reaction.

President Musharraf assessed his options and quickly came to a decision. Weighing the pros and cons of cooperating with the United States, he concluded that, militarily and economically, Pakistan did not have the strength or social cohesion to sustain an attack by the United States.[53] For this reason, Pakistan decided to join the GWOT and offer immediate tangible support to the United States. President Musharraf's strategy firmly and vocally placed the needs of his country and people first.

On 13 September 2001 Musharraf's government agreed to take several important steps mandated by the Bush administration. Following the American demarche, Pakistan had to stop al-Qaeda operatives at its border and end logistical support for bin Laden. And, in its relations with the Taliban, the Musharraf government had to cut off all shipments of fuel to the regime and prevent Taliban recruits from entering Afghanistan from Pakistan. If the evidence implicated bin Laden and al-Qaeda and the Taliban continued to harbor them, Pakistan had to break all relations with the Taliban government.[54] Ultimately, Pakistan agreed to 74 basing requests including CSAR, communication relay stations, and medical evacuation sites.[55] These negotiations included the right to use Pakistani bases near the cities of Pasni, Dalbandin, and Jacobabad as forward operating bases (FOBs).[56]

These measures were not easy for Musharraf to accept because of the significant dissent within his own government and military. More ominously, these events occurred as fears of nuclear conflict between Pakistan and India escalated over differences that had been festering for decades. Throughout 2000 and into 2001, troops and militants had assembled in the border region of Kashmir and increasingly came into armed conflict. This tension between the south Asian countries was at the forefront of President Musharraf's mind as he worked with US diplomats and was a catalyst in his decision to side with the United States.[57]

In return for Pakistan's extensive military cooperation, the country was compensated with over $1 billion in US assistance and several billion dollars from international organizations. The Bush administration also allowed Pakistan to reschedule $379 million of its $2.38 billion debt owed to the United States. The American Government offered other forms of assistance including funds for health, education, food, counternarcotics programs, border security, and law enforcement. As members of the international Coalition against terrorism, both Japan and the European Union suspended sanctions against Pakistan and promised debt relief, aid, and trade concessions.[58]

Prelude to Planning

The diplomatic efforts to build a Coalition and convince key regional powers such as Pakistan and Uzbekistan to collaborate must be considered an integral aspect of the overall campaign, especially given the curtailed timeframe allowed to both diplomats and planners. What loomed in front of all officials in the US Government—civilian and military—was the enormous challenge of quickly projecting forces into Afghanistan to destroy al-Qaeda before the organization's leaders slipped away.

While American diplomats continued to negotiate basing rights and other key details, military planners, primarily at CENTCOM, forged ahead with the daunting task of drawing up a campaign plan on a blank slate. This plan included operations in Afghanistan but had a truly global scope.[59] Estimates suggested that al-Qaeda had cells in approximately 60 nations including the United States, and the goal of the US strategy was to eradicate each one of these. Since most terrorists were operating from countries within CENTCOM's AOR, that combatant command became a primary focus for the GWOT.[60]

As one of five geographically defined unified commands, CENTCOM was responsible for military activity in southwest and central Asia and northeast Africa, an area that encompassed 27 nations. In the past, CENTCOM had conducted successful missions to liberate Kuwait from Iraq and led humanitarian operations in Somalia and Kenya. On 9/11, even as the second plane was crashing into the World Trade Center, CENTCOM immediately activated its Crisis Action Team (CAT) to begin planning a response.[61] These organizations were specialized teams drawn from all joint command staff sections that immediately assembled to begin assessing the situation and devising possible resolutions in response to a crisis. On 11 September, while the President and his advisors met to discuss the circumstances and devise a national strategy, the CAT at CENTCOM had already begun its work.

On 9/11 General Franks, the CENTCOM commander, was making an official visit to the island of Crete. Without a secure telephone line in his hotel room, Franks quickly moved to the roof of the building where he could use an encrypted satellite link to communicate with his CENTCOM staff.[62] Back in Tampa, Florida, where CENTCOM's headquarters is located, the command's deputy commander, Lieutenant General DeLong ordered the CAT to stand up and told regional commanders to lock down their bases. Rumsfeld ordered the Armed Forces to Defense Condition (DEFCON) 3, and military bases around the world went to Threat Condition (THREATCON) Delta. Franks recalled that as soon as he turned on the television in his Crete hotel room, he knew war was imminent. As he flew back to the United States, Franks was already in planning discussions with his onboard staff and the senior leadership at CENTCOM.

On the morning of 11 September, President Bush was visiting an elementary school in Florida. Once he was notified of the attacks in New York and Washington, DC, he boarded Air Force One and flew to Barksdale Air Force Base (AFB) in Louisiana and then to Offutt AFB in Nebraska before returning to the White House later that afternoon. President Bush communicated with the National Security Council from Offutt AFB, and then assembled his entire team once he completed an address to the nation. The following morning Bush made contact with British Prime Minister Blair and discussed the veracity of the evidence against al-Qaeda and the possible ultimatums for the Taliban. That weekend Bush and the National Security Council met at Camp David to develop both an immediate response and the beginnings of an overall strategy. The group discussed the need to form an international Coalition, the scope of the war that they would declare, how to think about Afghanistan, and the methods to use in pursuit of al-Qaeda.[63]

CENTCOM was quickly pulled into the planning at the national level. Franks recalled that on 12 September Secretary Rumsfeld directed him to "prepare credible military options and bring them to me."[64] By that date Franks understood that the imminent campaign would have two objectives: destroy al-Qaeda in Afghanistan and remove the Taliban from power.[65] The next 10 days flew by as planners in Tampa considered a full range of courses of action to attain these goals. By doctrine, the US military creates campaign plans that coordinate military operations of all kinds so that they attain national strategic goals. Put another way, the campaign plan is the means of transforming military action into successful accomplishment of strategic objectives. Often, CENTCOM and the other regional combatant commands developed campaign plans for future contingencies based on threat assessments and current US policy. For example, after the 1991 DESERT STORM operation that drove the Iraqi Army out of Kuwait, CENTCOM created a campaign plan for future military operations against Saddam Hussein and continued to develop that plan throughout the 1990s. While critical to military success, campaign plans are normally complex, requiring dozens of planners who need detailed information and analysis as well as a great deal of time. The planning effort takes into consideration terrain, weather, enemy strengths and weaknesses, as well as friendly forces and capabilities available. Further, planning staffs need to know in detail how friendly forces will travel into an area and often spend years developing deployment schedules.

As noted earlier, CENTCOM did not have a developed plan on the shelf for conventional ground operations in Afghanistan, nor did its planners have the type of detailed information required to immediately construct a detailed plan. Moreover, the command did not have much time to collect this information. What CENTCOM did have was a list of al-Qaeda locations that could become targets for air and cruise missile strikes. However, General Franks determined that the Bush administration was going to demand a far more sweeping campaign that would involve American Soldiers on the ground in Afghanistan. The leadership of CENTCOM and the planning teams thus began scrambling to learn as much as they could about Afghanistan's history, culture, and terrain.

To facilitate this learning process, CENTCOM invited experts from around the world to brief the military members working in Florida. This group of specialists included diplomats such as Dr. Zalmay Khalilzad, an Afghan-American who at that time held a position on the National Security Council, as well as academics from various think tanks and universities.[66] These lecturers discussed the cultural and ethnic history of Afghanistan, including the traditional role of tribes and approaches to principles such as loyalty and honor. An extremely valuable source of expertise came from former Russian generals who served in Afghanistan and historians of the Soviet-Afghan War of the 1980s who offered critical insights about that conflict. Lester Grau, a historian and author of two books on the tactics used by both sides in the Soviet-Afghan War, briefed CENTCOM planners about what the Taliban might do to defend their regime.

Armed with this expertise, military planners began work on an initial operation order that would guide Coalition forces in the deployment and early combat phases of the campaign. They would then transform that order and the overall vision for the campaign into a more complete plan that established objectives and phases, and defined key concepts such as center of gravity (COG) and lines of operation (LOOs), all of which are necessary for the complete expression of how a military force intends to achieve the overall end state of a campaign. The concept of the COG was particularly important to planners and was drawn from the thinking of military theorist Carl von Clausewitz who suggested that these centers represented the source of power for both sides in an armed conflict. Campaign planners might identify the adversary's military units as the enemy's COG or they might decide that the COG was actually the political leadership of the enemy nation.

During CENTCOM's planning process, the command's staff came to see the strategic-level COG as the continued support for the upcoming campaign from both the American population and the international community. Additionally, CENTCOM viewed its ability to project power into Afghanistan as the operational-level COG. When these planners shifted focus to the al-Qaeda and Taliban enemy, they calculated that the COG for the former would be its well-developed financial network that undergirded its operations in Afghanistan and elsewhere. The Taliban's COG could be found, they believed, in their military forces, and that power was a result of the Taliban commanders' ability to retain cohesion among units that were made up of disparate tribes and ethnic groups. If that cohesion could be attacked, this strength might be diminished.

The LOOs were critical as well and were best understood as conceptual devices used to describe the directions of effort made by a military force. Traditionally, military planners used *geographic* LOOs to describe the sequential path taken by a military force to travel to the ultimate enemy objective. However, nonconventional campaign plans that were not based on seizing terrain en route to a specific geographic objective might have *logical* LOOs that described the various types of efforts to be mounted by a military force to attain its objectives. Examples of logical LOOs included security, reconstruction, governance, and training of indigenous forces. Developing the logical LOOs for the campaign in Afghanistan was an important task and it would take weeks of analysis and development before they were approved and published.

Assessing Campaign Options

CENTCOM's immediate objectives for the campaign were to overthrow Taliban rule in Afghanistan and eliminate the al-Qaeda organization in that country.[67] In early planning sessions, Secretary Rumsfeld emphasized that the opening stages of the campaign had to change the balance of power in Afghanistan by denying Taliban military power while enabling anti-Taliban forces.[68] This emphasis on Afghan proxies suggested that impending operations in Afghanistan would be different in comparison to other recent American military campaigns.

Instruction from Soviet experts provided vital texture to information gained from imagery intelligence and other means. Insights gained from the Soviet experience included the need to understand the role of Islam and the strength of Afghan religious beliefs. Many Afghans had viewed Soviet forces as infidel invaders and felt they had a duty to fight the foreign force for reasons of faith. The Soviets had made little allowance for the effect their intervention would have on the deeply religious Afghan population. Alexander Lyakhovsky, a Soviet general who commanded troops in Afghanistan, wrote, "[We] completely disregarded the most important national and historical factors, above all the fact that the appearance of armed foreigners in Afghanistan was always met with arms in the hands [of the population]. This is how it was in the past, and this is how it happened when our troops entered (Afghanistan)."[69]

Historical lessons were at the forefront of thinking as the CENTCOM commander and his staff developed the plan. They focused on the British experience in Afghanistan in the 19th century as well as the Soviet intervention, viewing them both as examples of the wrong type of approach to take in Afghanistan. US Air Force Lieutenant General Victor Eugene Renuart, who served as the CENTCOM Director of Operations (J3) in 2001, asserted that in the planning process, the historical experiences of these other armies were extremely powerful and suggested strongly that the United States had to avoid sending sizable numbers of troops to Afghanistan: "It was very, very important that we not relearn the lessons of the Russians, that we not get mired in large forces, that we not allow ourselves to be pinned down to big installations that could become easy targets, and that we not be seen as occupiers in the early stages because that would draw the same reactions that the Brits and the Russians drew."[70] According to Renuart, CENTCOM's historical analysis suggested that any large foreign element would inevitably face an armed and violent Afghan opposition unified across ethnic and political divisions.[71]

These insights led planners at CENTCOM to two key conclusions. First, they determined that the plan had to avoid the presence of a large Coalition ground force that might inflame the Afghan population. Second, they concluded that the Coalition effort had to achieve its goals quickly and turn political power over to the Afghans themselves as soon as possible. Both of these key realizations led CENTCOM planners to view the NA as the linchpin of the campaign. Renuart recalled that during the planning process in September 2001, the importance of this group ballooned. Renuart stated, "The ability to take forces from the NA, empower them, and have them take on a large portion of this ground operation was critically important to us."[72] Not only did the NA promise to provide the bulk of the ground forces, they would also put an Afghan face on the campaign and might provide the future political leadership of a post-Taliban Afghanistan. For Renuart, one of the most striking aspects of the CENTCOM plan was this reliance on the NA as the "ground component" of the Coalition effort.[73] This decision, however, tacitly transformed key alliance commanders such as Rashid Dostum and Fahim Khan into subordinates of General Franks. The CENTCOM commander and his staff would then have to figure out ways to ensure the Coalition's intent would be met by these distant Afghan leaders.

Supporting the use of the proxy force was the hard realities of Afghanistan's location. While US leaders were working to secure basing and staging assistance from neighboring countries, this assistance was by no means assured during this first week after the attack. A large number of ground troops could not be sustained without substantial staging facilities, and the NA did not have the facilities to host a large force. Because of the high mountains and distance from US staging areas, heavy artillery could not easily be airlifted into place.[74] Further, although President Bush assured military leaders they would have the time necessary to build up their forces, deploying a large contingent of ground troops would take longer than desired. These factors all strengthened the imperative of a small presence or footprint of Coalition forces.

As the CENTCOM staff began considering these factors, Franks received a directive from the President and Secretary Rumsfeld telling CENTCOM to develop a broad set of options ranging from a limited air campaign that used air and missile strikes to a large-scale inter-vention by ground forces.[75] The airstrike option would be similar to attacks against al-Qaeda facilities in 1998 after the African Embassy bombings. On the other extreme, the conventional force option would involve up to three light infantry battalions in direct combat against enemy forces.[76] After much consideration, the planning team arrived at three specific courses of action. The first would be a major Tomahawk land attack missile (TLAM) strike. The TLAM was an all-weather missile that had a range of about 870 miles and could be launched by US Navy ships in the Persian Gulf. With their sophisticated guidance mechanisms, the TLAM could hit targets in the rough terrain of Afghanistan making the missile an ideal weapon for certain types of targets.[77] This choice provided instant retaliation with little risk to US Armed Forces.

The second course of action was a TLAM strike followed by or concurrent with Global Power sorties.[78] The Global Power Program was the unclassified name for the US Air Force's long-range conventional strike aircraft such as B-1, B-2, and B-52 bombers that could strike al-Qaeda camps and Taliban bases with precision Joint Direct Attack Munitions (JDAMs). This option would require 3 to 10 days and also provided little risk to US forces.[79]

The third course of action combined cruise missiles, bombing missions, and small SOF teams composed of US Army SF Soldiers and Air Force combat air controller elements. These SOF units would provide intelligence support and air support to NA forces. US Army SF possessed the requisite training and experience in a myriad of tasks, including advising foreign armies, and SF teams were prepared to act quickly and covertly while operating in the austere environment of Afghanistan. The Air Force combat air controllers could identify enemy targets and guide ordnance onto these targets using laser target designators and other devices, making these teams a lethal joint combination.

CENTCOM leadership favored the third course of action, because it combined the advantages of an air campaign with a presence on the ground that could enable the NA and signal the Coalition's determination without provoking Afghan concerns about foreign intervention. Although the NA was much smaller than the ruling Taliban, they had maintained their fighting forces for years and been quite effective in defending their territory from the Taliban. The goal for SOF was to convince the various warlords and tribal factions within the alliance to work together to defeat the Taliban. To win them over, these small American teams would promise the NA that they could deliver a huge amount of firepower in the form of missiles and bombs. Acting as forward observers, the American troops could use their technology to guide ordnance onto specific Taliban targets, regardless of how well hidden they might be.

In the eyes of the CENTCOM planners, this type of combined campaign would have a secondary benefit. Lieutenant General DeLong maintained that CENTCOM leaders realized that Taliban forces were dug in and the location of key targets such as political leaders were difficult to confirm. However, according to DeLong, aerial attacks on suspected Taliban and al-Qaeda positions had the potential to reveal those targets. DeLong explained, "You start hitting the enemy and they have to move. If they move, they can't attack, and if they move you can see them. So what we wanted was to see them move so we could get after them because they were dug into different places where we couldn't find them."[80] As the enemy began to change locations, sensors in the air and teams on the ground could then detect them and engage them with NA forces or with Coalition air power.

CENTCOM did give serious consideration to a broader intervention with larger conventional units. In his memoirs, General Franks stated that in the early planning sessions in mid-September 2001 he gave his staff a fourth course of action that did involve a larger contingent of conventional ground forces. Franks recalled that he told his planners, "We've discussed three options. Here's a fourth. Run the first three simultaneously, as the lead-in for the deployment of conventional American ground combat forces."[81] For the CENTCOM commander, this course of action would actually be what is called a *sequel* in US joint military doctrine. Sequels are major operations that follow initial phases of a campaign and are contingent on conditions. In the case of Franks' fourth course of action, the success of the NA and SOF teams in their offensive against al-Qaeda and the Taliban would determine whether the sequel involving conventional US forces was necessary. In actuality, Franks and his key staff officers assumed that this sequel would likely occur. Indeed, in the final plan for OEF, CENTCOM made provisions to insert a force of approximately 10,000 to 12,000 US Soldiers and Marines that would exploit the gains made by the NA and ensure remaining enemy concentrations were defeated.[82]

After reviewing the three courses of action, Secretary Rumsfeld and Chairman of the Joint Chiefs of Staff General Hugh Shelton supported the third choice. In addition, they also required that CENTCOM include in their plan measures that would minimize damage to the country so the reconstruction could commence immediately and Afghans could quickly take charge of a new government.[83] President Bush's promise that the campaign in Afghanistan was not against

Islam or the Afghan people remained a key principle for this campaign. To put substance behind this statement, the CENTCOM staff began planning for humanitarian assistance operations that would be conducted concurrently with combat actions. President Bush approved the overall campaign concept on 21 September, enabling CENTCOM leaders and planners to focus on the fine points of the plan. General Franks expected to begin the initial air and SOF portions of the campaign plan in the first week of October 2001.[84] With 2 weeks remaining, the CENTCOM commander and his staff had a great deal to do.

Planning the Campaign

As the CENTCOM planners developed the critical details of the campaign in Afghanistan, they decided that it should consist of four phases. The first phase was called "Set Conditions and Build Forces to Provide the National Command Authority Credible Military Options," an unwieldy title but a set of vital operations and actions that included the finalization of basing, staging, and overflight agreements with countries surrounding Afghanistan.[85] Phase I involved communicating with NA leaders to lay the groundwork for the arrival of Coalition forces. This phase would also include the delivery of thousands of humanitarian daily rations (HDRs), consisting of a nutritious, culturally sensitive diet of barley and lentil stew, prepared for airdrops to assist the Afghan population. By the fall of 2001, NGOs had largely pulled out of Afghanistan because of the imminent military operations, and delivering these rations to hungry populations in the country was a central Coalition concern. According to the plan, US Air Force C-17s would travel from Ramstein Air Base, across Turkmenistan and Uzbekistan, and into Afghanistan to drop hundreds of thousands of HDRs.[86]

Phase II, "Conduct Initial Combat Operations and Continue to Set Conditions for Follow-On Operations," marked the beginning of airstrikes to hit al-Qaeda and Taliban targets and the completion of the deployment of SOF teams to work with the NA.[87] Tomahawk missiles, B-2 Stealth bombers, and B-52s were scheduled to take out training bases, early warning radars, tactical aircraft, and major air defense systems.[88] Once the initial strikes reduced the enemy's minimal antiaircraft capability, fixed-wing aircraft would attack targets across Afghanistan. Taking off from the British island of Diego Garcia and Navy carriers in the Arabian Sea, these sorties would be among the longest combat flights ever attempted. Each plane had the capacity to drop 25 tons of precision guided munitions.[89] As air operations progressed, SOF teams would infiltrate Afghanistan and begin to contact and work with the NA.

Once the NA and their SOF counterparts gained the initiative against the Taliban, a force of up to 12,000 US combat troops would enter the country to begin Phase III, "Conduct Decisive Combat Operations." CENTCOM's end state for this phase was the toppling of the Taliban regime and elimination of al-Qaeda in Afghanistan.[90] While the size of this force would dwarf the small SOF element that had entered the country earlier, the relatively small footprint would grant Coalition commander's flexibility and give them a rapid reaction capability without appearing as an army of occupation.[91] To mitigate this appearance, CENTCOM planners would direct these units to seize and hold only that ground that was required for support bases.

The final phase was called "Establish Capability of Coalition Partners to Prevent the Re-Emergence of Terrorism and Provide Support for Humanitarian Assistance Efforts." Franks and his staff had designed this phase as a 3- to 5-year effort to work with Coalition partners to help create conditions in Afghanistan that would prevent the reemergence of terrorist groups.[92] They had not, however, conceived this as a nation-building endeavor for the US military. There was no articulation of specific goals such as the fosering of a new Afghan Government or Afghan security forces that would help prevent a return of al-Qaeda or other terrorist organizations. Instead, the OEF plan directed the US and its Coalition partners to provide basic humanitarian aid and civil affairs assistance to a general restoration of stability inside Afghanistan. Clearly, CENTCOM planners were concentrating most heavily on deploying the right forces into central Asia and defeating the Taliban and al-Qaeda. What would come after that victory never really came into clear focus in this initial vision for OEF.

This four-phase plan set mission, objectives, phasing, and tasks for the Coalition military strategy in Afghanistan. General Franks later supplemented the plan with nine logical LOOs: political-military coordination, support to the opposition, direct attack of al-Qaeda and Taliban leadership, attack cave and tunnel complexes, reconnaissance and direct action, operational fires, operational maneuver, information operations, and humanitarian assistance.[93] These LOOs were types of efforts that Coalition units conducted simultaneously. The LOOs not only allowed the staff and the commander to focus overall actions, but also permitted them a means of assessing progress in achieving milestones.

While not explicitly laid out in the campaign plan, the LOOs were seen by CENTCOM leaders as the chief pathways to success in Afghanistan. Political-military actions involved the efforts to secure basing and staging support from allied nations as well as efforts to isolate the Taliban regime by denying the Taliban outside support. Support to the opposition was the focus of initial SOF coordination with the NA and subsequent efforts to recruit other Afghan groups to an anti-Taliban Coalition.[94]

Coalition SOF also had the mission to attack al-Qaeda and Taliban leadership directly. This leadership included the al-Qaeda figures Osama bin Laden and Ayman al-Zawahiri as well as critical Taliban leaders Mullar Mohammad Omar and Dadullah Lang among others. Direct action focused on the enemy's strategic COG, and because economic and political sanctions were not an effective strategy against the Taliban regime, elimination was the key.[95] The operational fires LOO directed firepower at enemy concentrations from both the air and on the ground, breaking up Taliban concentrations and depriving the enemy of the means of communication and maneuver. Friendly operational maneuver, on the other hand, attempted to use the Coalition's advantages in strategic and operational lift to grant Coalition ground forces the ability to move quickly in a country that lacked developed infrastructure. Information operations also became an essential LOO because of the need to reach the Afghan population. The Coalition needed to convince the Afghan citizenry of the positive benefits of the Coalition's presence to gain and retain its support.

The SOF who would advise the NA and direct the precision guided munitions in the early operations against the Taliban were critical throughout the campaign. As small and elite units, SOF were uniquely suited for this mission because of their specialization in strategic reconnaissance, direct action, and unconventional warfare (UW), a term that described a broad spectrum of operations that are usually conducted by a surrogate or indigenous force that is assisted by an outside element. By 2001 US joint doctrine defined UW as including guerrilla warfare, sabotage, clandestine, and other indirect operations. SOF's specialized and rigorous training, specialized equipment, and unique tactics allowed them to undertake operations not suited for conventional forces. These elite units fell under US Special Operations Command (USSOCOM) whose mission was to lead, plan, synchronize, and, as directed, execute global operations against terrorist networks. The Army service component command within USSOCOM was US Army Special Operations Command (USASOC) located at Fort Bragg, North Carolina. Within USASOC, Soldiers from the Active Army, National Guard, and Army Reserve served in the Special Forces, Rangers, Aviation, Support Units, Civil Affairs, and Psychological Operations. Collectively, they were known as Army Special Operations Forces (ARSOF).

Planning the SOF and Air Campaigns

As CENTCOM developed its plan in mid-September 2001, SOF planners in Special Operations Command Central (SOCCENT), a component command that controlled joint SOF within the CENTCOM AOR, began their own planning process. The ARSOF on the staff of that command received the intent from General Franks, understood that they would be preparing for UW, and began building a seven-phase plan for a US-based insurgency. According to ARSOF doctrine, a US-based insurgency occurred when SF trained or developed an organized resistance movement to help advance US interests. SF in Afghanistan would train the NA as a sponsored insurgency against the Taliban and al-Qaeda. SOCCENT planners, however, had to ensure that their concept was nested with Franks' overall approach. One SF staff officer within CENTCOM described how the SOF officers carefully synchronized their UW plan with Franks' plan. Less than a week after the attacks of 9/11, SOCCENT had briefed its plan to the CENTCOM commander and gained his approval.

Formulating a campaign plan was an arduous process that involved drawing on doctrine and lessons learned from Afghanistan's history as well as devising innovative ways to target al-Qaeda and the Taliban. Combining SOF and conventional forces along with the allied NA was groundbreaking. Further, successfully transmitting commander's intent from General Franks to Afghan tribal leaders demonstrated the communication abilities of those on the ground as well as the statesmanship of General Franks who was able to forge political-military relationships. Renuart summarized the campaign plan saying, "It was taking the sophistication, the technology, and the capabilities that we had and placing them on a battlefield, which was not unlike the face of the moon, with relatively unsophisticated warriors, taking on a reasonably well equipped and reasonably sophisticated enemy."[96] Campaign planners worked tirelessly to complete the campaign plan in a very short period. Even so, Phase I of OEF would begin in mid-September and Phase II would start in early October while planners were still developing the details of the campaign plan. Only in late November 2001 did General Franks publish the final version of his plan for OEF.

Essential to the plan was the ability to locate and destroy key Taliban and al-Qaeda strongholds, both those that were preplanned and those that presented themselves as targets of opportunity. SOF forces working with the NA would track the enemy's movements and locations and send intelligence back so targets could be developed. This intelligence was essential because the Coalition did not have a large number of preplanned targets before the bombing campaign began on 7 October. In most air campaigns, high-value targets (HVTs) include key government and military buildings, utilities, and transportation systems. However, the Taliban-run government was heavily decentralized and did not rely on traditional physical strongholds in the capital of Kabul. Commercial and transportation infrastructure was nearly nonexistent, so there were very few bridges, railroads, or energy plants to target. Instead, the only preplanned targets were a few buildings used by al-Qaeda and Taliban leadership, some al-Qaeda training bases, and a few tactical aircraft and antiaircraft batteries.[97]

To assist in identifying targets, Coalition forces on the ground benefited from the presence of US Air Force Tactical Air Control Parties (TACPs). These teams made excellent use of laser designators and other tools to locate enemy targets for engagement. Although cutting edge technology allowed targeting in real time, Soldiers still needed to employ caution to ensure they did not inflict excessive collateral damage. The improved picture of the engagement zone allowed more care to be taken to ensure the campaign did not cause a great deal of damage to noncombatants and nonmilitary targets, a demand specifically requested by the Bush administration. Secretary Rumsfeld personally approved every medium- or high-collateral damage target. To convert high- and medium-collateral targets to low collateral, the CENTCOM staff considered hitting the target at a time of day when fewer people were present, using a different type of weapon or a more precise weapon, or changing the direction of the blast.[98] After the campaign began, this caution would sometimes slow down the pace of the war and there would be instances in which CENTCOM overrode the Combined Air Operations Center's (CAOC's) tactical execution authority for strategic considerations of collateral damage.[99] Some would later express what they felt was bureaucratic rigidity in CENTCOM and the DOD when the campaign opened and there was great care in identifying and acting on targets.[100]

A Joint, Combined, and Interagency Effort

When General Franks and his planners began designing the campaign for OEF, they started from the assumption that the plan would include the involvement of all four military Services as well as participation from other agencies within the US Government. SOF from each Service, for example, would work together with joint conventional forces. Air support from the Air Force, Navy, and Marines would assist the Army and Marine forces on the ground. Additionally, representatives from other Federal agencies such as the DOS would be critical to the campaign from its inception. Commenting on the success of General Franks' efforts to create a joint plan, Chairman of the Joint Chiefs of Staff General Richard B. Myers praised Franks in November 2001, saying, "In my view, General Franks . . . has effectively called on the strengths and unique capabilities that the different services bring to this fight."[101]

CENTCOM planners also believed that success in the Afghanistan campaign rested on the coalescing international Coalition. While the US military was exceptionally strong, the planners understood that the military forces of allies could contribute unique capabilities and would bolster the effect of the Coalition on the world stage. Thus, Franks and his staff made a concentrated effort to integrate Coalition forces while maintaining unity of purpose and unity of command.

Within 3 days of the 9/11 attacks, Coalition military commanders started to arrange to provide assistance with CENTCOM's planning. Space within the CENTCOM headquarters was at a premium, however, and there was literally no place to create offices for these Coalition allies. In response, CENTCOM Chief of Staff Colonel Michael Hayes created the "Coalition Village" for foreign officers near the combatant command's headquarters at MacDill Air Force Base in Tampa. Hayes contracted with a local company to rent 20 trailers that were fully equipped with data lines, computers, phones, and other equipment. As autumn progressed, the number of trailers increased first to 40 and then 80, reflecting the enormous increase in Coalition integration. These Coalition members proved vital in the campaign planning process, not only for operations in Afghanistan, but also in the larger GWOT effort in areas such as the Horn of Africa.

The Plan for Humanitarian Assistance

Because the Coalition campaign was focused on al-Qaeda and the Taliban rather than against the Afghan people, the United States wanted to ensure the war did not deprive the innocent people of Afghanistan of food and other necessities. President Bush stipulated that humanitarian assistance be a vital component of the campaign. As noted earlier, Phase I of the campaign plan included humanitarian drops. Actions of this type carried through the next two phases and culminated with Phase IV during which the Coalition would turn to immediate humanitarian needs and to larger reconstruction projects that would rebuild Afghanistan, hopefully preventing the Taliban and al-Qaeda from regaining a foothold in the country. General Franks considered this phase to be the longest within the plan, assuming that it would require 3 to 5 years for the Coalition to reach its goals.[102]

Humanitarian assistance was especially critical because Afghanistan had long been one of the poorest nations in the world. An April 2001 UN report found that living conditions in Afghanistan were among the worst in the world. The UN estimated that only 25 percent of the population had access to potable water and only 10 percent had adequate sanitation.[103] Access to education and the quality of education were poor, and literacy rates hovered around 25 percent. Medical services were almost nonexistent. The UN also estimated that since 2000, up to 700,000 Afghans left their homes because of drought or armed violence. While most were displaced within Afghanistan, some 170,000 crossed the border into Pakistan and over 100,000 left for Iran.[104]

On 6 September 2001, just 5 days before the 9/11 attacks, the UN humanitarian coordinator for Afghanistan warned,

> Human suffering in Afghanistan has largely outstripped the capacity and resources of the aid community due to both the magnitude and the depth of the crisis. The catastrophe is a gradually cumulative humanitarian disaster of enormous proportions. Conflict, drought, displacement, grinding poverty, and human rights abuses add up to a deadly combination.[105]

The United States, historically the largest provider of humanitarian aid to the Afghan people, had sent hundreds of millions of dollars in 1999 and 2000 to help provide housing, medical care, and education.[106] In May 2001, after a visit by US officials to the impoverished country, Secretary of State Powell had announced a $43 million aid package for distribution through the UN and various NGOs. The United States was determined to maintain its support for the Afghan people even as Taliban rule became more oppressive.

How to continue funneling aid to the Afghan population and thereby maintain broad support from that population became one of CENTCOM's most difficult planning challenges in the fall of 2001. Staff from almost all international organizations (IOs) and NGOs who were working throughout Afghanistan quickly relocated to Pakistan and neighboring countries, expecting the imminent Coalition offensive to make conditions very dangerous for aid workers. With almost all the aid organizations leaving the country and winter quickly approaching, the humanitarian situation was perilous.[107]

The humanitarian aid element of the campaign plan was designed to help assuage this crisis situation and to support President Bush's promise that this was not a war against the Afghan people. At the CENTCOM level, the planning staff viewed the humanitarian actions as supporting combat operations through their ability to win "hearts and minds" and mitigate immediate humanitarian crises so that the military could focus on defeating the Taliban and al-Qaeda. For the United States, the humanitarian aspects of the plan would set conditions by providing initial relief and creating a secure environment into which the IOs and NGOs could them move and begin their operations.

The CENTCOM plan assumed that Coalition military forces would support NGOs and IOs throughout the country while retaining focus on combat operations. Thus, planners did not expect to provide security support for all relief convoys moving inside Afghanistan. Even if that had been a desirable objective, the small ground force made it impossible. Instead, CENTCOM planned to rely on the existing infrastructure as much as possible and to allow Afghans, NGOs, and Coalition partners to take the lead, especially on reconstruction operations.

✦ ✦ ✦

The campaign plan formulated in the aftermath of the attacks of 9/11 gave life to President Bush's strategy for taking the fight to Osama bin Laden and al-Qaeda. Bin Laden had struck at the nation's homeland, and the United States resolved to strike back using the nation's military, political, and diplomatic resources. However, believing that the campaign required widespread international support, the US Government built a Coalition against al-Qaeda and other terrorist groups. The Taliban's former ally, Pakistan, joined this effort and became an important ally against terrorism.

As the headquarters charged with the military portion of President Bush's strategy to destroy the terrorist enemy, CENTCOM quickly composed a plan that projected military power into a distant and foreboding part of the world. That plan was equally remarkable in the way it integrated air power, SOF, and conventional units. But whether the audacious concept would prove successful was not clear to anyone when the campaign began in early October, just 26 days after the 9/11 attacks.

Notes

1.   President George W. Bush, "Statement by the President in His Address to the Nation," 11 September 2001. http://www.whitehouse.gov/news/releases/2001/09/20010911-16.html (accessed 11 March 2009).

2.   *The 9/11 Commission Report: Final Report of the National Commission on Terrorist Attacks Upon the United States* (Washington, DC, 2004), 115–119, 194.

3.   *The 9/11 Commission Report: Final Report of the National Commission on Terrorist Attacks,* 126–143.

4.   President George W. Bush, "President Orders Ready Reserves of Armed Forces to Active Duty," *Executive Order Ordering the Ready Reserve of the Armed Forces to Active Duty and Delegating Certain Authorities to the Secretary of Defense and the Secretary of Transportation*, 14 September 2001. http://www.whitehouse.gov/news/releases/2001/09/20010914-5.html (accessed 11 March 2009).

5.   President George W. Bush, "President Urges Readiness and Patience," Remarks by the President, Secretary of State Colin Powell and Attorney General John Ashcroft, Camp David, Thurmont, MD, 15 September 2001. http://www.whitehouse.gov/news/releases/2001/09/20010915-4.html (accessed 18 September 2008).

6.   Gerry J. Gilmore, "Bush Authorizes Guard and Reserve Call-Ups," *American Forces Press Services*, 14 September 2001. http://www.defenselink.mil/news/Sep2001/n09142001_200109148.html (accessed 29 January 2007).

7.   Richard L. Berke and Janet Elder, "NY Times/CBS Poll," *New York Times,* 25 September 2001, A1.

8.   George W. Bush, President Addresses Joint Session of Congress, 20 September 2001. http://www.whitehouse.gov/news/releases/2001/09/20010920-8.html (accessed 19 September 2008).

9.   "Radio Address of the President of the Nation," 6 October 2001. http://www.whitehouse.gov/news/releases/2001/10/20011006.html (accessed 12 March 2009).

10.   "US Rejects Taliban Offer to Try Bin Laden," 7 October 2001. *CNN.com*. http://archives.cnn.com/2001/US/10/07/ret.us.taliban/ (accessed 19 September 2008).

11.   Bush, President Addresses Joint Session of Congress, 20 September 2001.

12.   George W. Bush, "Blocking Property and Prohibiting Transactions With Persons Who Commit, Threaten to Commit, or Support Terrorism," Executive Order 13224, 23 September 2001.

13.   Lieutenant General Michael DeLong and Noah Lukeman, *Inside CentCom: The Unvarnished Truth about the War in Afghanistan and Iraq* (Washington, DC: Regnery Publishing, 2004). 20.

14.   "Operation Enduring Freedom Overview," White House Fact Sheet, 1 October 2001. http://www.state.gov/s/ct/index.cfm?docid=5194 (accessed 1 January 2007).

15.   David J. Gerelman, Jennifer E. Stevens, Steven A. Hildreth, "Operation Enduring Freedom: Foreign Pledges of Military & Intelligence Support," *CRS Report for Congress* (17 October 2001), 1.

16.   The North Atlantic Treaty, 4 April 1949, Article V.

17.   Lord Robertson, Secretary General of NATO, "Statement by the Secretary General of NATO," PR/CP(2001)121, 11 September 2001. http://www.nato.int/docu/pr/2001/p01-121e.htm (accessed 6 December 2001).

18.   Tom Lansford, *All for One: Terrorism: NATO and the United States* (Aldershot, UK: Ashgate Publishing Limited, 2002), 74.

19.   Lansford, *All for One*, 70.

20.   Lord Robertson, NATO Secretary General, "Statement to the Press on the North Atlantic Council Decision on Implementation of Article 5 of the Washington Treaty following the 11 September Attacks against the United States," 4 October 2001. http://www.nato.int/docu/speech/2001/s011004b.htm (accessed 6 December 2006).

21.   Richard Armitage, US Deputy Secretary of State and Lord Robertson, Secretary General of NATO, "Press Availability: U.S. Deputy Secretary of State Armitage and NATO Secretary General Lord Robertson," 20 September 2001. http://www.nato.int/docu/speech/2001/s010920a.htm (accessed 6 December 2006).

22.   Lansford, *All for One*, 88, 92.

23.   Mr. Alain Richard, "The European Union, A Rising Feature on the International Stage," Remarks by the Minister of Defence of France, 12 Forum, *Bundeswehr & GesellschaftWelt am Sonntag,* Berlin, 2 October 2001. http://www.defense.gouv.fr/sites/defense/english_contents/the_ministry_of_defence/ archive/the_minister_of_defence_1998-2002/discours/051001.htm (accessed 6 December 2006).

24.   Charter of the United Nations, Preamble, 26 June 1945.

25.   United Nations, "Words Alone Inadequate as Response to Terrorist Attacks, Secretary General Tells Opening of Fifty-sixth General Assembly," Press Release SG/SM7851, GA 9906, 12 September 2001.

26.   United Nations, "Opening of the Fifty-sixth Session, General Assembly Condemns Heinous Acts of Terrorism Perpetrated in Host City and Washington," Fifty-sixth General Assembly Plenary, 1st Meeting, 12 October 2001.

27.   United Nations, "In Afghanistan, A Population in Crisis," Press Release AFG/145, ORG1336, 24 September 2001.

28.   United Nations, "Plight of Civilian Afghan Population Desperate, Says Secretary-General: Those Deliberately Withholding Food and Attacking Relief Workers will be Held Responsible," Press Release SG/SM/7968, AFG/146, 25 September 2001.

29.   United Nations, "United Nation's Role Essential in 'Moral Imperative' of Preventing Conflict General Assembly Told, As Debate Continues on Secretary-General's Report," Press Release/9916, Fifty-sixth General Meeting, 9th Meeting (AM), 25 September 2001.

30.   United Nations, "Security Council Unanimously Adopts Wide-Ranging Anti-terrorism Resolution," Press Release SC/7158, Security Council, 4385th Meeting (Night), 28 September 2001.

31.   Gerelman, Stevens, and Hildreth, "Foreign Pledges of Military & Intelligence Support," 13–14.

32.   Bush, President Addresses Joint Session of Congress, 20 September 2001.

33.   Gerelman, Stevens, and Hildreth, "Foreign Pledges of Military & Intelligence Support," 7.

34.   Gerelman, Stevens, and Hildreth, "Foreign Pledges of Military & Intelligence Support," 6.

35.   Gerelman, Stevens, and Hildreth, "Foreign Pledges of Military & Intelligence Support," 9–12.

36.   "Operation Enduring Freedom Overview," White House Fact Sheet, 1 October 2001.

37.   Nazila Fathi, "Iran Won't Joint US Campaign, Leader Says," *New York Times* (27 September 2001), B2.

38.   "Frontline with Condoleezza Rice," *PBS Online,* 12 July 2002. http://www.pbs.org/wgbh/ pages/frontline/shows/campaign/interviews/rice.html (accessed 6 December 2006).

39.   William C. Lambert, "US-Central Asian Security Cooperation: Misunderstandings, Miscommunications & Missed Opportunities," in *Security Assistance, U.S. and International Historical Perspectives, Proceedings from the Combat Studies Institute 2006 Military History Symposium*, edited by Kendall Gott and Michael Brooks (Fort Leavenworth, KS: Combat Studies Institute Press, 2006), 128.

40.   General Tommy Franks, *American Soldier* (New York, NY: HarperCollins, 2004), 256.

41.   A. Elizabeth Jones, Assistant Secretary for European and Eurasian Affairs, "Testimony before the Senate Foreign Relations Committee, Subcommittee on Central Asia and the Caucasus," Washington, DC, 13 December 2001.

42.   "Russia and Central Asia," Berlin Information Center for Transatlantic Security (BITS). http:// www.bits.de/NRANEU/CentralAsia.html#II (accessed 10 January 2007).

43. "CENTCOM Commander Franks Press Conference in Uzbekistan," 27 September 2000, transcript archived at the Department of State, Press Relations.

44. Gerelman, Stevens, and Hildreth, "Foreign Pledges of Military & Intelligence Support," 7.

45. Elizabeth Wishnick, *Growing US Security Interests in Central Asia* (Carlisle, PA: Strategic Studies Institute, 2002), 23.

46. *The 9/11 Commission Report* (New York, NY: W.W. Norton & Company, 2004), 61.

47. Jim Nichol, "Central Asia's Security Issues and Implication for US Interests," *CRS Report for Congress* (updated 7 February 2006), footnote 21.

48. Bush, President Addresses Joint Session of Congress, 20 September 2001.

49. "Pakistan Vows to Help US 'Punish' Attackers," *Cable News Network,* 13 September 2001. http://archives.cnn.com/2001/WORLD/asiapcf/central/09/13/pakistan.support/index.html (accessed 28 March 2007).

50. Robert Wirsing, "Precarious Partnership: Pakistan's Response to U.S. Security Policies," *Asia-Pacific Center for Security Studies, Special Assessment* (2003), 2. http://www.apcss.org/Publications/SAS/SASAPResponse030320/PrecariousPartnershipPakistansResponsetoUSSecurityPolicies.pdf (accessed 14 May 2007).

51. "What the World Thinks in 2002," *The Pew Global Attitudes Project* (Washington, DC: Pew Center for People and the Press, 4 December 2002), 4, 69.

52. Ahmed Rashid, "Pakistan, the Taliban and the US," *The Nation,* 8 October 2001, 1. http://www.thenation.com/doc/20011008/rashid (accessed 21 January 2007).

53. Pervez Musharraf, *In the Line of Fire* (New York, NY: Free Press, 2006), 202.

54. *The 9/11 Commission Report,* 331.

55. Franks, *American Soldier,* 273.

56. Nadeem Malik, "US Military Seeks Deeper Roots in Pakistan," *Asia Times Online,* 30 January 2002. http://www.atimes.com/c-asia/DA30Ag01.html (accessed 14 February 2007).

57. "Address by President General Pervez Musharraf to the Pakistani Nation," 19 September 2001. http://www.un.int/pakistan/14010919.html (accessed 17 January 2007).

58. Peter R. Blood, Foreign Affairs, Defense and Trade Division, "Pakistan–U.S. Relations," *CRS Issue Brief for Congress,* 10 March 2002, 7, 11.

59. Congress, Senate, Senate Armed Services Committee, "Prepared Testimony of U.S. Secretary of Defense Donald H. Rumsfeld before the Senate Armed Services Committee on Progress in Afghanistan," 31 July 2002. http://www.defenselink.mil/speeches/2002/s20020731-secdef.html (accessed 20 January 2007).

60. Lieutenant General Michael DeLong, interview by Contemporary Operations Study Team, Combat Studies Institute, Fort Leavenworth, KS, 8 January 2007, 2.

61. DeLong and Lukeman, *Inside CentCom*, 18.

62. Franks, *American Soldier,* 243.

63. "Frontline with Condoleezza Rice."

64. "Frontline Interview with General Tommy Franks," *PBS Online* Archive, 12 June 2002. http://www.pbs.org/wgbh/pages/frontline/shows/campaign/interviews/franks.html (accessed 6 December 2006).

65. Franks, *American Soldier,* 252.

66. DeLong, interview, 8 January 2007, 5; "Frontline Interview with General Tommy Franks."

67. Franks, *American Soldier,* 255.

68. Donald Rumsfeld, "Statement of the Secretary of Defense," United States Department of Defense, No. 560-01, 1 November 2001. http://www.defenselink.mil/releases/2001/b11012001_bt560-01.html (accessed 6 December 2006).

69. Svetlana Savranskaya, "The Soviet Experience in Afghanistan: Russian Documents and Memoirs," *Volume II: Afghanistan: Lessons from the Last War*, 9 October 2001, Document 21. CC CPSU Letter on Afghanistan, 10 May 1088 [Source: Alexander Lyakhovsky, *Tragedy and Valor of Afghan*, Iskon, Moscow, 1995, Appendix 8, Translated by Svetlana Savranskaya. http://www.gwu.edu/~nsarchiv/NSAEBB/NSAEBB57/soviet.html (accessed 20 January 2007).

70. General Victor Eugene Renuart, interview by Contemporary Operations Study Team, Combat Studies Institute, Fort Leavenworth, KS, 31 May 2007, 3.

71. Renuart, interview, 31 May 2007, 3.

72. Renuart, interview, 31 May 2007, 3.

73. Renuart, interview, 31 May 2007, 5.

74. DeLong, interview, 8 January 2007, 4.

75. DeLong, interview, 8 January 2007, 4.

76. Lieutenant Colonel Tom Reilley, interview by 47th Military History Detachment, 18 May 2002, 6.

77. Saul Ingle, "First Strike: Launching of Tomahawk Missiles from USS John Paul Jones As Part of War on Terrorism," *All Hands* (December 2001): 34–35.

78. Franks, *American Soldier,* 259.

79. DeLong and Lukeman, *Inside CentCom*, 23.

80. DeLong, interview, 8 January 2007, 4.

81. Franks, *American Soldier*, 261.

82. Franks, *American Soldier*, 271.

83. DeLong and Lukeman, *Inside CentCom,* 23.

84. Franks, *American Soldier*, 281.

85. Franks, *American Soldier,* 269.

86. Franks, *American Soldier*, 269–273.

87. *The 9/11 Commission Report*, 337.

88. Franks, *American Soldier*, 270; DeLong and Lukeman, *Inside CentCom*, 34.

89. Franks, *American Soldier*, 271.

90. *The 9/11 Commission Report*, 337.

91. Franks, *American Soldier*, 271.

92. Franks, *American Soldier*, 271.

93. General Tommy Franks, Presentation to the Army War College, April 2002, slide 9.

94. Renuart, interview, 31 May 2007, 3.

95. Renuart, interview, 31 May 2007, 3.

96. Renuart, interview, 31 May 2007, 5.

97. DeLong and Lukeman, *Inside CentCom*, 34.

98. DeLong and Lukeman, *Inside CentCom*, 34.

99. Grant, "The War Nobody Expected."

100. Henry A. Crumpton, "Intelligence and War: Afghanistan, 2001–2002," in *Transforming U.S. Intelligence,* edited by Jennifer E. Sims and Burton Gerber (Washington, DC: Georgetown University Press, 2005), 173.

101. Jim Garamone, "Joint Force Concept Comes of Age in Afghanistan," *DefenseLink*, 15 November 2001. http://www.defenselink.mil/news/Nov2001/n11152001_200111151.html (accessed 9 February 2007).

102. Franks, *American Soldier*, 272.

103. United Nations, "Senior Inter-Agency Network on Internal Displacement Mission to Afghanistan," *Findings and Recommendations from the UN Special Coordinator on Internal Displacement from Mission*, 25 April 2001, 1.

104. UN, "Senior Inter-Agency Network on Internal Displacement," 1.

105. United Nations, "Daily Press Briefing by the Office of the Spokesman for the Secretary-General," *United Nations Press Briefing*, 6 September 2001. http://www.un.org/News/briefings/docs/2001/db090601.doc.htm (accessed 25 January 2007).

106. "U.S. Largest Single Donor of Aid to Afghans," US State Department Archives, 2 October 2000. http://usinfo.state.gov/is/Archive_Index/U.S._Largest_Single_Donor_of_Aid_to_Afghans.html (accessed 25 January 2007).

107. Olga Oliker et al., *Aid During Conflict: Interaction Between Military and Civilian Assistance Providers in Afghanistan, September 2001– June 2002* (Santa Monica, CA: RAND Corporation, 2004), 42.

Chapter 3

Opening Moves:
The Preliminary Phases of the Campaign

Between 12 September and 7 October 2001—the 26 days during which US Central Command (CENTCOM) developed its campaign plan for Operation ENDURING FREEDOM (OEF)—the US Armed Forces expended much effort in preparation for America's response to 9/11. As the four phases of the CENTCOM plan clearly established, this campaign would not consist solely of airstrikes and cruise-missile attacks. Instead, the plan called for regime change in Afghanistan and the destruction of al-Qaeda and its support facilities in that country. Historically, objectives such as these are difficult to achieve with air power alone. They are best realized by the development of complex plans that place forces on the ground and provide for the support and sustainment of those forces while they move toward the objectives. However, before the United States and its Allies even gained proximity to those goals, they had to accomplish a series of exceedingly difficult tasks including the mobilization of forces; the gaining of indigenous support in Afghanistan and surrounding nations; the deployment of troops, equipment, and supplies; and the preparation of the battle area for the commencement of ground operations. This chapter will briefly examine the key actions taken by the US Government to prepare for major ground operations in Afghanistan, including the initial logistics and Combat Search and Rescue (CSAR) effort and the air campaign launched by CENTCOM.

Mobilization

OEF began with the US Government's efforts to place the US Armed Forces and key federal agencies on a war footing. On Friday, 14 September 2001, the US Congress passed a joint resolution titled "Authorization for Use of Military Force" that allowed the President to use the Armed Forces against the terrorist groups responsible for the 9/11 attacks.[1] That same day, President George W. Bush authorized the mobilization of America's Reserve Components. That directive allowed Secretary of Defense Donald Rumsfeld, on the recommendation of the Joint Chiefs of Staff (JCS), to order the activation of 35,500 military reservists.[2]

In the past, large-scale mobilizations of military reservists were reliable indicators of a nation preparing for war. Yet, the mobilization by the United States in September and October 2001 was somewhat different. Primarily it was small in contrast to the mobilization for past conflicts. In his initial orders, Rumsfeld called for only 10,000 Soldiers, 13,000 Airmen, 7,500 Marines, and 3,000 Sailors.[3] To seasoned military observers, the numbers hardly seemed to indicate that the United States was preparing any kind of serious counterattack. Indeed, most of these troops were mobilized to support what became known as Operation NOBLE EAGLE (ONE)—the security operations in American cities and airports that immediately followed the terrorist attacks. What was not apparent to many at this point was that the campaign about to take shape would portend a different style of warfare that did not require a large number of troops. Indeed, few Reserve and National Guard Soldiers would participate in the initial operations in Afghanistan.

The first priority of the US Government's response was the security of the homeland. ONE, as noted above, was the Department of Defense's (DOD's) effort to provide security within the borders of the continental United States (CONUS). The Army's portion of that effort included both Active Duty and Reserve Component units. Beginning on 11 September, Regular forces were immediately deployed to secure military installations and sensitive sites around the country. In most cases, those duties were turned over to National Guard and Army Reserve units and personnel as they mobilized and deployed to their assigned missions in the next few weeks.

For ONE, the Army National Guard and US Army Reserve mobilized 16,298 Soldiers between 12 September and 5 December 2001.[4] The types of National Guard units mobilized generally consisted of military police and infantry organizations. The Army Reserve, likewise, mobilized many military police and military intelligence units as well. These units were typically assigned missions to provide security for myriad locations—on both military installations and key civilian sites, to include civilian airports. Few were tasked to support OEF.

Though the Army Reserve contribution to the initial callup for OEF was small, that of the US Air Force was both enormous and critical to the initial phases of the campaign. For the Army to successfully support CENTCOM's plan, its troops had to enter the theater of operations. Only the Air Force could accomplish that task. To support both ONE and OEF, the Air Force mobilized 227 units of various types. No less than 54 of these units were airlift and refueling outfits that would soon play critical roles in the deployment of Army units into Uzbekistan and Pakistan.

Securing Regional Bases

The salient characteristic of the opening phases of OEF was that it required air power. The staging of forces and the logistics support for those forces once they began operations in Afghanistan could not be done in ways used in recent campaigns. In Operation DESERT STORM, for example, the US Army secured seaport facilities through which massive amounts of supplies could be trucked or railed to a depot close to the area of operations (AO). From there the supplies were distributed to units in large quantities. That conventional approach was impossible for OEF. Afghanistan's landlocked position in central Asia precluded the use of seaports near the country. Those neighboring countries, such as Pakistan, that did possess seaports would not allow US military convoys to rumble along their already inadequate highways to reach Afghanistan. Further, Afghanistan's transportation infrastructure was severely outdated. Rail transportation into Afghanistan was not available and roads were in such disrepair that they were almost unusable. Thus, movement into Afghanistan had to be conducted through the air.

This realization presented another challenge. On 11 September 2001 there were few countries in the region that were interested in making airfields available for Coalition air operations. As the previous chapter of this study demonstrated, one of the key efforts in the US planning process was to secure the rights to landing and overflight in the region. One of the first nations to offer the use of an airfield was Pakistan. Despite the unpopularity of such a decision among Islamic fundamentalists in his own country, President Pervez Musharraf offered the use of several fields to the United States, most importantly the Shahbaz Air Base in the city of Jacobabad in the center of Pakistan. Shahbaz was close enough to key AOs in Afghanistan that United States Air Force (USAF) Special Operations Forces (SOF) and CSAR units could use the base for their missions.[5] However, Shahbaz was too far from bases in Europe from which Air Force cargo planes would fly to support operations in Afghanistan. CENTCOM planners needed an airfield that was closer to the European airfields yet still within central Asia.

Figure 8. Major regional air bases in support of OEF.

Fortunately, the former Soviet Republic of Uzbekistan on Afghanistan's northern border signaled its potential willingness to cooperate with the Coalition. Uzbekistan possessed several former Soviet air force bases that met the basic needs of the CENTCOM commander. American negotiators originally pushed the Uzbek Government for the use of a base at Samarkand, but were rebuffed.[6] The Uzbeks instead offered the use of a base at Karshi-Khanabad, a name quickly shortened to K2 by military planners. On closer look, the negotiators found that K2 could provide the United States an aerial port of debarkation (APOD) for troops operating in Afghanistan, and a location to establish a small, though critical, supply depot to support those operations. The airfield was sufficient, but not ideal. The old Soviet-built runways had extensively deteriorated and required repair and expansion.[7] Despite their serviceable quality, the K2 runways were too short to handle the large C-5 Galaxy cargo planes used by the US

Air Force to transport large numbers of troops, large pieces of equipment, or big shipments of materiel. Planners had to send C-5s from the United States or elsewhere to Ramstein Air Base in Germany, or other US bases in Spain, Italy, or Turkey, where they were unloaded and their cargo transferred to smaller C-17 or C-130 aircraft for haul into K2.[8] The time needed for these long flights and to load and unload the cargo at each stop would be a significant factor for logistics and therefore operational planning efforts.

The K2 airfield support facilities were also in complete disrepair in 2001 and required a huge renovation effort. Few buildings were actually intact; those that were livable were occupied by Uzbek military personnel. Tents would initially serve as the living and working quarters for US military personnel. Environmental conditions in the area presented other problems. The subsoil on the base was severely contaminated with old jet fuel and the vapors that resulted caused potential health problems. Asbestos was another concern.[9]

Despite its dilapidated character, the United States did not immediately obtain permission from Uzbekistan to use the K2 Air Base. However, negotiations went on through early October as US and Uzbek officials came closer to an agreement. The agreement was critical to the start of the air campaign because K2 would be needed for staging potential CSAR operations once Coalition aircraft began operations over Afghanistan.

Establishment of Lines of Communications (LOCs) and the Deployment of Forces

While the US and the Uzbek diplomats finalized arrangements for the use of K2, US Transportation Command (TRANSCOM) and the Air Force pressed forward with their work to support the CENTCOM campaign plan and concurrently prepare other pending operations. Transport planes from the United States loaded with troops and equipment slated for K2 arrived in Spain, Sicily, and Turkey in late September and early October.[10] To the great concern of military planners at TRANSCOM and other commands, the number of airplanes parked on the tarmacs at these locations continued to increase and were idle at a time when they were needed to support other operations around the globe.

One of those operations was called BRIGHT STAR, a multinational exercise co-organized by the United States and Egypt to foster cooperation and stability among allies in the eastern Mediterranean and Middle East areas. BRIGHT STAR was an annual event held in Egypt and consisted of up to 60,000 troops from as many as 24 countries. Scheduled for 8 October to 2 November 2001, many on the CENTCOM staff believed it should be canceled after the events of 9/11 and because of the impending campaign in Afghanistan. US Marine Lieutenant General Michael DeLong, the Deputy Commander of CENTCOM, recalled that he and General Tommy Franks both agreed that the exercise should take place because it would allow CENTCOM to funnel people and equipment into the area of responsibility (AOR). After the very successful exercise, over 9,000 troops remained in the Middle East and south-central Asia to provide security and build or improve port facilities; billeting; airfields; and command, control, and communications nodes.[11] The decision to execute BRIGHT STAR also reinforced to the world that the United States was committed to its allies and had the capacity to both participate in the exercise and still fight a war. Arguably, the most important outcome was the ability that the American exercise participants provided CENTCOM to rapidly establish the LOC to support the opening stages of OEF.[12] Colonel Mark Wentlent, who served on the staff of US Third Army, maintained that his involvement in BRIGHT STAR significantly helped him and his colleagues become the Combined Forces Land Component Command (CFLCC) headquarters a few months later.[13]

As BRIGHT STAR progressed, advance parties from CONUS-based SOF units began arriving at the K2 Air Base even before an agreement was made between the US and Uzbek Governments. The initial Army elements into K2 were a 3-man team from Fort Campbell, Kentucky, and an 11-man team from Special Operations Command Central (SOCCENT), a Special Operations headquarters subordinate to CENTCOM, which arrived during the negotiations. The teams landed with the mission to prepare the way for the impending arrival of US forces at the airfield. They conducted surveys of the base; decided locations for the parking, loading, and unloading of Coalition aircraft; and coordinated with the Uzbek airfield commander to determine the facilities available for Coalition use. Eventually, the Uzbek official granted one building, which became the tactical operations center (TOC). But the Americans were able to begin the purchasing of fuel, building materiels, and other supplies to repair and operate the airfield for the coming air campaign.[14]

Because of the pressure in DOD and CENTCOM to keep the US footprint in the region small, campaign planners sought to conduct a ground war that differed from earlier US conflicts. As the previous chapter established, CENTCOM desired to use Special Forces (SF) teams working in conjunction with anti-Taliban Afghan militias and Coalition aircraft to defeat the enemy, rather than rely on large conventional forces. Although reliance on SF allowed for a very light footprint, those teams still required a great deal of support in the form of airlift. Colonel Phillip McGhee, Deputy Chief of Staff for Resource Management for United States Army Special Operations Command (USASOC), expressed his surprise at the amount of airlift that was needed to transport one SF group, a formation consisting of three SF battalions and support elements. McGehee recalled, "The amount of airlift it took to get one [SF] group in theater just amazed me. It took almost fifty C-17s to get 3,000 guys and their equipment into theater."[15]

Once Uzbekistan granted formal permission to use K2 on 5 October 2001, the American transport planes waiting in Europe and elsewhere quickly launched to clear the ramp space at the backed up air bases. Nevertheless, the onslaught of planes almost immediately congested the limited ramp and taxi space at K2 creating a huge traffic jam. Air traffic controllers were overwhelmed, and offload teams struggled to keep up using the limited offloading equipment they had. Aircraft began arriving at K2 every 2 hours, and the base population swelled from 100 to 2,000 in just 1 week.[16]

Company A, 528th Special Operations Support Battalion (A/528th SOSB), the first US Army unit to arrive at K2 on 4 October, attempted to handle the arriving cargo planes. The company normally performed the mission of receiving, sorting, and issuing supplies; the US Air Force Theater Airlift Control Element (TALCE) assigned the mission to unload aircraft at K2 arrived the day before but without its cargo handling equipment. The 528th Soldiers then pitched in to help the TALCE unload the incoming planes through muscle power.[17] In a unique twist, the SOF provided the initial logistical support to the Army. Doctrinally, the geographic combatant commander and his subordinate component commanders support SOF once in theater. However, because OEF commenced so rapidly, the SOF were the first to arrive in Uzbekistan and had to begin building the base. Thus, conventional Army units were supported by the SOF support unit for about 30 days until the Army could build its capability for logistical support.[18]

Among the arrivals on 5 October was the 16th Special Operations Wing of the Air Force Special Operations Command (AFSOC), the advance party of the 5th Special Forces Group (SFG), elements of the 160th Special Operations Aviation Regiment (SOAR), elements of the 112th Signal Battalion, and the lead elements of the 1st Battalion, 87th Infantry (1-87 IN), a unit that belonged to the US Army 10th Mountain Division and soon responsible for securing the entire airfield.[19] These early arrivals were quickly followed by other logistics, signal, civil affairs, and psychological operations (PSYOP) units.

Among the first logistics units to arrive at the Uzbek base was Logistics Task Force (LTF) 530, which arrived from Fort Bragg in mid-November. LTF 530 was a composite organization pasted together to meet the logistics needs of the units at K2. It was composed of the battalion headquarters and service company (HSC) of the 530th Service and Supply Battalion, and the 58th Maintenance Company of the 7th Transportation Battalion. Consisting of only 174 personnel, this unit took over A/528th SOSB's mission and provided virtually every class of supply required by the other organizations at K2. In addition, the HSC also provided billeting, food, laundry and bath, and sanitation services to the compound, while the 58th Maintenance Company provided all vehicle and equipment maintenance support less that required by the helicopter units.[20] This composite unit would continue operations well into the following year as the footprint continued to grow at K2.

CENTCOM planners originally intended to use the K2 airfield as the base for CSAR operations that would retrieve downed aviators during the initial air campaign. To this end, when Colonel Frank Kisner, commander of the 16th Special Operations Wing arrived, he quickly established a Joint Special Operations Task Force (JSOTF) headquarters knowing that the CSAR operation would soon involve other Services' SOF elements.[21] One of those elements, the 2d Battalion, 160th SOAR from Fort Campbell, began arriving on 5 October 2001. To conduct CSAR operations as well as other missions that might emerge, 2-160 SOAR was equipped with MH-47E and MH-60L helicopters. In an amazing feat of teamwork, the battalion mechanics unloaded the aircraft from the cargo planes, assembled them, conducted tests, and had them ready for operations within 48 hours of arrival.[22] That achievement was critical because the air campaign was set to begin on 7 October.

The Air Campaign

As early as 12 September, an air campaign against Taliban forces in Afghanistan had been on the table as a viable response, at least in part, to the attacks of 9/11. As the Bush administration's strategy for the war against terror evolved and the planning for the initial campaign took shape during mid- to late-September, the Air Force and Navy positioned assets in and around the Middle East and Asia to support an air campaign in Afghanistan. On 14 September the Navy ordered two ships carrying 235,000 barrels of marine diesel fuel to Diego Garcia Island in the Indian Ocean. Concurrently, 28,000 gallons of aviation fuel was ordered to be delivered to Moron Air Base in Spain, which had been used as a staging base for Air Force tanker aircraft. Other actions included the recall of tankers from test programs and the limiting of the Air Force bomber fleet to only essential flying so that repairs and scheduled maintenance could be completed before assigning them to missions in Afghanistan.[23] All these actions, and more, were sure indicators of the impending air campaign.

By the end of September, USAF long-range precision strike aircraft were ready for combat missions and many had been repositioned to forward operating bases such as Diego Garcia and other locations throughout southern Europe and the Middle East. A large number of the B-52 Stratofortresses that deployed to Diego Garcia had been modified to carry AGM-86C Conventional Air Launched Cruise Missiles (CALCMs), along with Joint Direct Attack Munitions (JDAMs) and cluster bombs. The B-1B Lancer supersonic bombers, which were based at Diego Garcia as well as in the Persian Gulf country of Oman, were also capable of carrying JDAM precision guided munitions, cluster bombs, and Mark 82 500-pound iron bombs. The B-2A Spirit stealth bombers, however, remained based at Whiteman Air Force Base in Missouri. With several in-flight refuelings, the B-2A was capable of flying round trip, nonstop, from Whiteman to Afghanistan and back, and could deliver thousand-pound JDAMs, as well as deep penetrating precision-guided bombs on each mission. In addition to these strike aircraft, a large number of additional USAF attack and tanker aircraft had been flown to the Middle East, Turkey, and Pakistan in preparation for OEF.

The US Navy had been preparing to support operations over Afghanistan as well. When the 9/11 attacks occurred, the carriers USS *Carl Vinson* and *Enterprise* and their corresponding battle groups were conducting operations in the Indian Ocean. By 18 September two other carriers, the *Theodore Roosevelt* and the *Kitty Hawk,* had been ordered to the area as well. The latter ship, sailing from her homeport at Yokosuka, Japan, had left almost her entire air wing there so that she could function as a platform for launching helicopters from the 160th SOAR that would transport SOF into Afghanistan from the south.[24]

US Air Force Lieutenant General Charles Wald, commander of the Joint Forces Air Component Command (JFACC) for CENTCOM, was responsible for planning and executing the air campaign. Wald's mission statement was clear: "On order, Combined Forces Air Component Command provides air support for friendly forces working with the Northern Alliance and other opposition forces in order to defeat hostile Taliban and al-Qaeda forces and to set the conditions for regime removal and long-term regional stability." Wald's command would operate from the newly established Combined Air Operations Center (CAOC) at Prince Sultan Air Base, Saudi Arabia.[25]

The planning and preparation for the air campaign was not without problems. Delays resulted from a number of issues involving the problems with negotiations over K2, proper target designation, a shortage of approved targets, and a heavy emphasis on collateral damage avoidance. For example, all potential targets were scrutinized in painstaking detail not only at the CAOC, CENTCOM, and onboard Navy aircraft carriers, but also by military attorneys in the Pentagon. Each routinely assessed potential target lists before approving targets for planned raids and airstrikes.[26] Frustrated with the situation, General Franks, the CENTCOM commander, stepped in and put a stop to at least some of the micromanagement from the Pentagon. Franks wrote in his memoirs that he told the Chairman of the JCS, General Myers, "I am not going along with Washington giving tactics and targets to our kids in the cockpits and on the ground in Afghanistan."[27]

The planning and other preparations continued up to the night of 7 October when the attacks began. In a televised address to the nation on 8 October, President Bush announced, "On my orders, the United States military has begun strikes against al-Qaeda terrorist training camps and military installations of the Taliban regime in Afghanistan."[28] The first night of bombing was far from overwhelming in either scope or effect. Only 31 preplanned strategic targets in the vicinities of Kabul, Kandahar, Shindand, Herat, Mazar-e Sharif, and Sheberghan were hit. These targets did not include frontline Taliban positions. The opening-round attacks were conducted by Air Force B-2 stealth bombers from Whiteman, the B-1B and B-52 bombers from Diego Garcia, and by Navy F-14 and F/A-18 fighters from aircraft carriers in the Arabian Sea. Joining the ordnance dropped by the aircraft were Tomahawk missiles fired by US Navy cruisers and destroyers as well as submarines belonging to both the United States and the United Kingdom.[29]

The goal of the initial wave of air attacks was to gain uncontested control of Afghan airspace by destroying Taliban air defense capabilities. To this end, US planners focused attacks in the first several days on surface-to-air missile sites; early warning radars; command, control, and communications facilities; airfields; and aircraft. While the Taliban air defense system was not well developed, the threat to Coalition aircraft was real. On the first night of the air offensive, for example, Coalition pilots reported a small number of incidents in which Afghan soldiers directed antiaircraft artillery and surface-to-air missiles at their aircraft.[30] Still, within days, the air campaign had achieved air supremacy in the skies over Afghanistan.

The Coalition also sought to erode the Taliban's ground forces and general capability to oppose the upcoming Coalition ground campaign. After the first day, strikes targeted Taliban tanks and artillery as well as training facilities in Kabul and Kandahar. On the fifth day, Air Force aircraft dropped the first 5,000-pound laser-guided bombs on al-Qaeda mountain cave sanctuaries.

By the end of the first week of the air campaign, Coalition aircraft had dropped over 1,500 bombs and munitions of various types. As the second week began, AC-130 gunships and F-15E Strike Eagles from Jaber Air Base in Kuwait, the first land-based fighters to enter the campaign, joined the fray and began attacking Taliban troop concentrations and vehicles. With the bulk of the primary targets destroyed or damaged, the Coalition target list expanded to focus on emerging targets or "targets of opportunity."[31]

In addition to the bombing, on the first night of the air campaign C-17 Globemasters, flying from Ramstein Air Base in Germany, began dropping food and medical supplies to the Afghan population that, as the previous chapter noted, was suffering from decades of war and social dislocation. That turmoil had by late 2001 left a majority of Afghanistan's 27 million citizens impoverished.[32] During the first 4 nights of the air campaign, C-17s airdropped nearly 150,000 humanitarian daily rations (HDRs) to the needy Afghans.[33]

While the humanitarian air drops were an integral part of the campaign plan, these drops were actually controversial in the civilian humanitarian assistance community. Detractors claimed that they were ineffective, expensive, and motivated by political concerns. Some nongovernment organizations (NGOs) and international organizations (IOs) in Afghanistan felt that the airdrops were a PSYOP mission and the use of the term "humanitarian" for these missions was incorrect.[34] A further point of contention was that both cluster bombs and aid packages had yellow packaging. Civilian workers on the ground contended that the two could easily be confused. Although there were no reported instances of Afghans confusing the two, the Coalition changed the color of the HDR packages.[35] Despite these concerns, during the early October timeframe, the Coalition dropped more humanitarian rations than bombs.

Coalition PSYOP in the Opening Phases

While CENTCOM directed the initial phase of the air campaign, Coalition leaders began efforts to engage and win over the Afghan population to their cause. To explain to the Afghan people why the Coalition was attacking their country, CENTCOM directed several efforts to focus on distributing critical messages to the population. At Fort Bragg, North Carolina, the Special Operations (SO) 4th Psychological Operations Group (POG) began its air war effort 2 days before the initial OEF airstrikes. On 5 October, the EC-130 "Commando Solo" aircraft, from the 193d Special Operations Wing of the Pennsylvania Air National Guard, began broadcasting radio transmissions across Afghanistan. The Joint Psychological Operations Task Force (JPOTF), which became active on 4 October at Fort Bragg, North Carolina, scrambled to develop messages that would capture the minds of the Afghans. However, the development of radio transmissions, leaflets, and other PSYOP products and their distribution would not be an easy task in a time-constrained environment.

Fortunately for the Coalition forces, Dr. Ehsan Entezar, a native Afghan who spoke the Dari and Pashto languages; Dr. David Champagne, who had worked with the Peace Corps in Afghanistan; and Dr. Joseph Arlinghaus, an intelligence analyst at Fort Bragg who had served since 1982, were already working as civilians in CENTCOM's Strategic Studies Detachment (SSD) within the 4th POG. As Dr. Champagne explained, the SSD had people "with over 100 years of cumulative experience working on [OEF] which was unheard of in the government. That didn't exist in any other agency."[36] Despite this, the 4th POG found itself challenged by scrutiny from officials at the Pentagon. Captain Troy O'Donnell, a JPOTF planner who worked at CENTCOM headquarters in Tampa, Florida, from September 2001 to January 2002, experienced Pentagon micromanagement first hand. During the first 2 months of the campaign, final products had to go through a lengthy approval process with the Office of the Under Secretary of Defense for Policy (OUSD[P]) at the top of the chain.[37] As O'Donnell remembered, the OUSD(P) was "really telling us what to produce and in some instances the medium they wanted. But they didn't understand the target audience and they didn't understand really, I think, the intent of what General Franks wanted us to be able to accomplish when we went out."[38] By the December timeframe, however, OUSD(P) began to realize the 4th POG's expertise and allowed the approval process to centralize at CENTCOM, with Franks as the final approving authority.[39]

One of 4th POG's initial operations was to coordinate the messages that would be broadcast from Commando Solo. The group's experts quickly developed a variety of radio scripts—all with different themes, objectives, and target audiences—that were recorded in both the Dari and Pashto languages. One message focused on the innocent victims of 9/11, stating, "On September 11, 2001, thousands of people were killed en masse in the United States . . . policemen, firefighters, teachers, doctors, mothers, fathers, sisters, brothers all killed. Why?"[40] The staff of the 4th POG also used music to focus the attention of the Afghan populace on the messages the Coalition hoped to disseminate. Colonel James Treadwell, who commanded the group in 2001, stated that the use of traditional jovial Afghan music was a calculated decision.

> The Taliban had banned music on the radio. We used the power of music. We would have music interspersed with a short spot after every song. Then, if we were passing out information, there might be two or three minutes where we would speak, but we would always go back to music because nobody is going to turn to a radio station if it is just somebody preaching to them.[41]

Because of the quick development of the PSYOP campaign, individuals from the 4th POG had to supply the Afghan music from their personal collections.[42] Though most Afghans did have access to radios, the Coalition eventually airdropped small portable radios with the preset frequency throughout the country.[43]

The overall messages of these broadcasts were designed to encourage the Taliban to cease support of al-Qaeda, to undermine Taliban and al-Qaeda morale, to promote the legitimacy of US operations, and to convince Afghan citizens that they were not the target of US attacks.[44] The Soldiers in the 4th POG also employed strong direct themes such as the inevitable defeat of both the Taliban and al-Qaeda, and rallying support for the NA.[45] Once the Coalition took out the main Taliban radio station, Commando Solo began broadcasting updates and messages on the same frequency that very day.

Due to Afghanistan's low literacy rates, leaflets had to be simple and many messages were transmitted orally via radio broadcasts. Leaflets were designed to appeal to the general public and were targeted toward specific geographic regions in Afghanistan to reflect tribal differences and ethnic diversity.[46] One leaflet featured bin Laden moving pawns with Taliban faces on a chessboard. This image was chosen because chess was once a popular Afghan pastime before the Taliban banned the game.[47] Other leaflets explained the humanitarian drops, stressed that the American forces were a friendly rather than an occupying force, and warned about landmines remaining from previous conflicts.[48] A large majority of the leaflets simply instructed the Afghans to tune their radios to the Coalition's broadcasting station.

Thousands of leaflets accompanied the numerous HDRs that were dropped to the Afghan people. Leaflets printed at Fort Bragg either were flown directly from Bragg or were transported by rented U-Haul trucks to McGuire Air Force Base, New Jersey, where they were packed into MK-129 leaflet bombs. To keep up with demand, forward teams deployed to Diego Garcia also printed leaflets. If intelligence, surveillance, and reconnaissance (ISR) assets spotted activity in the mountains, leaflets pre-positioned at Diego Garcia could be dropped within 6 hours.[49]

The JPOTF also developed and printed hundreds of thousands of leaflets that were shipped to Diego Garcia and initially disseminated by B-52 bombers over Afghanistan beginning 15 October. Up to 80,000 leaflets could be packaged in a single MK-129 or modified Rockeye leaflet bomb.[50] In due course, F-16, F-18, A-6, and MC-130 aircraft would also perform high altitude leaflet drops in the AOR. One such leaflet, written in both Pashto and Dari, described US intentions in Afghanistan as honorable, and pictured an Afghan man and an American Soldier shaking hands. Another portrayed radio towers and gave the frequencies for receiving Commando Solo broadcasts. Other leaflets explained how to properly use the daily rations and warned Afghans to stay clear of unexploded ordnance.[51]

The air campaign that began in early October was a multifaceted effort designed to destroy, degrade, or demoralize Taliban and al-Qaeda forces. Concurrently, the air effort sought to prevent large-scale suffering of the Afghan people while seeking to convince the populace that the Coalition efforts were designed to ultimately help the Afghan people. Ultimately, the campaign met its primary objective of gaining air superiority over Afghanistan so that land forces could enter the country and begin to work against the Taliban with the full support of the Coalition's air power. Indeed, air power would prove to be far more decisive once the initial air campaign was over and Coalition Soldiers were on the ground.

Boots on the Ground: Joint Special Operations Task Force–North (JSOTF-N) Enters the Theater

In September CENTCOM and SOCOM designated 5th SFG, based at Fort Campbell, Kentucky, as the core of the special operations unit designated by the unwieldy title Joint Special Operations Task Force–North (JSOTF-N). It was a good fit in the sense that the 5th SFG had trained for missions in the CENTCOM AOR. This meant that many of its Soldiers were fluent in the main languages and understood the cultural norms of the region.[52]

The commander of the 5th SFG, Colonel John Mulholland, and the group headquarters arrived at K2 Air Base on 10 October. Two days later, JSOTF-N was officially established with Mulholland as the commander. Since no Joint Forces Special Operations Component Command (JFSOCC) was yet established in theater, Mulholland served as the commander of joint SOF as well, despite the fact that his small SF group headquarters was not staffed or equipped to function in such a role. This command arrangement would continue to pose significant challenges to Mulholland and his staff until a formal JFSOCC was established in November.[53] One advantage, however, was that Mulholland had direct access to General Franks, the CENTCOM commander.

Initially, the primary mission of JSOTF-N was to coordinate and provide CSAR for Coalition aircrews that might have to bail out or crash land during the air campaign. Fortunately, this mission was never required and the task force's focus would quickly transition to the insertion of ODAs into Afghanistan to link up with NA units for the ground campaign. Because Mulholland was the senior US Army officer at K2, he also took tactical control (TACON) of the other Army units at the air base. The largest of these was the 1st Battalion, 87th Infantry (1-87 IN) from the 10th Mountain Division stationed at Fort Drum, New York, a force of about 700 Soldiers. The 1-87 IN had been deployed to K2 to perform the base security mission and provide quick reaction force (QRF) teams for CSAR operations. The battalion's mission would evolve into much more as the ground campaign developed.

Over the next week, other units continued to arrive at K2, further taxing the abilities of the JSOTF staff. Not only did this relatively small staff have to plan for and prepare for the coming ground operations, it also had to wrestle with mundane matters like billeting for incoming units on the already cramped air base, unloading and spotting cargo from incoming aircraft, feeding the troops, sanitation, and general housekeeping requirements. Nevertheless, the staff continued to prepare for the infiltration of its ODAs into Afghanistan.[54]

✦   ✦   ✦

On 12 October planning began in earnest for the insertion of the ODAs. Two MH-60L helicopters from the 2d Battalion, 160th SOAR, paved the way for the initial insertions on the night of 16 October by flying over the mountains and unloading equipment at a helicopter landing zone (HLZ) near General Abdul Rashid Dostum's headquarters in Afghanistan. Three nights later, ODA 595 assembled at the back of an MH-47E helicopter at K2 Air Base for the long flight into Afghanistan.[55] Remarkably, just over 5 weeks had passed since the World Trade Center buildings had fallen. Within those 5 weeks, the Coalition had planned a complex response to the 9/11 attacks and then launched the initial deployment of forces into theater as well as the air attack that had begun destroying enemy forces in Afghanistan. In mid-October US Army SOF were ready to begin the initial phase of the ground war. Unlike preceding American wars, SOF would be the main effort for this fight. Instead of selecting the US military's powerful conventional units as the American vanguard on the ground, leaders at the Pentagon and at CENTCOM had chosen these small teams to deal the fatal blows to the Taliban and al-Qaeda. It would indeed be a different kind of war.

Notes

1. Congress, Joint Resolution, *Authorization for Use of Military Force*, 107 Cong., S.J. Res. 23, *Congressional Record*, Vol. 147 (18 September 2001). http://www.usconstitution.net/newsarch_01.html (accessed 20 February 2007).

2. Gerry J. Gilmore, "Bush Authorizes Guard and Reserve Call-Ups," *DefenseLink,* 14 September 2001. http://www.defenselink.mil/news/newsarticle.aspx?id=44884 (accessed 17 December 2008).

3. Gilmore, "Bush Authorizes Guard and Reserve Call-Ups."

4. "National Guard and Reserve Mobilized as of Dec. 5," 5 December 2001. *DefenseLink.* http://www.defenselink.mil/releases/release.aspx?releaseid=3176 (accessed 17 December 2008).

5. Forrest L. Marion, "Building USAF 'Expeditionary Bases' for Operation ENDURING FREEDOM-AFGHANISTAN, 2001–2002," *Air & Space Power Journal*, 3. http://www.airpower.maxwell.af.mil/airchronicles/cc/marion.html (accessed 31 July 2007).

6. Major General (Retired) Dennis Jackson, interview by Contemporary Operations Study Team, Combat Studies Institute, Fort Leavenworth, KS, 16 January 2007, 9.

7. Jackson, interview, 10 January 2007, 17.

8. Harold Kennedy, "More Life Needed, Avers US Transportation Chief," *National Defense Magazine*, July 2002. http://www.nationaldefensemagazine.org/issues/2002/Jul/More_Lift.htm (accessed 1 February 2007).

9. Colonel Robert Landry, interview by 130th Military History Detachment, 1 June 2002, 4.

10. Charles H. Briscoe et al., *Weapon of Choice: US Army Special Operations Forces in Afghanistan* (Fort Leavenworth, KS: Combat Studies Institute Press, 2003), 67.

11. Lieutenant General Michael DeLong and Noah Lukeman, *Inside Centcom: The Unvarnished Truth about the Wars in Afghanistan and Iraq* (Washington, DC: Regnery Publishing, 2004), 43; Lieutenant General Michael DeLong, interview by Contemporary Operations Study Team, Combat Studies Institute, Fort Leavenworth, KS, 8 January 2007, 7.

12. DeLong and Lukeman, *Inside CentCom*, 43; DeLong, interview, 8 January 2007, 7.

13. Colonel Mark Wentlent, interview by 47th Military History Detachment, 1 May 2002, 6.

14. Briscoe et al., *Weapon of Choice,* 64–66.

15. Colonel Phillip McGhee, interview by Contemporary Operations Study Team, Combat Studies Institute, Fort Leavenworth, KS, 18 December 2007, 7.

16. Briscoe et al., *Weapon of Choice,* 67.

17. Briscoe et al., *Weapon of Choice,* 66, 72.

18. McGhee, interview, 18 December 2007, 5.

19. Briscoe et al., *Weapon of Choice,* 45.

20. Kenneth Finlayson, "Not Just Doing Logistics: LTF 530 in Support of TF Dagger," *Veritas*, vol. 3, no. 2, 2007 (Fort Bragg, NC: United States Special Operations Command), 45–46.

21. Briscoe et al., *Weapon of Choice,* 66, 72.

22. Briscoe et al., *Weapon of Choice,* 71–72.

23. Benjamin S. Lambeth, *Air Power Against Terror: America's Conduct of Operation Enduring Freedom* (Santa Monica, CA: RAND Corporation, 2005), 83.

24. Lambeth, *Air Power Against Terror,* 65.

25. Lambeth, *Air Power Against Terror,* 83.

26. Esther Schrader, "Response to Terror; War, on Advice of Counsel," *Los Angeles Times,* 15 February 2002, sec. A, p. 1.

27. Tommy Franks, *American Soldier* (New York, NY: HarperCollins, 2004), 295.

28. George W. Bush, "Presidential Address to the Nation," 8 October 2001. http://www.whitehouse.gov/news/releases/2001/10/20011007-8.html (accessed 10 July 2007).

29. Lambeth, *Air Power Against Terror,* 79–80.

30. Lambeth, *Air Power Against Terror,* 84.

31. Lambeth, *Air Power Against Terror,* 93.

32. US Agency for International Development, "USAID Fact Sheet on Humanitarian Aid for Afghanistan," 26 April 2002, 1–12. http://geneva.usmission.gov/press2002 (accessed 23 January 2007).

33. Gerry J. Gilmore, "Air Force Fliers Continue Afghan Food Drop Operations," *American Forces Press Service,* 12 October 2001, 1–2. http://www.defenselink.mil (accessed 17 January 2007).

34. Olga Oliker et al., *Aid During Conflict: Interaction Between Military and Civilian Assistance Providers in Afghanistan,* September 2001–June 2002 (Santa Monica, CA: RAND Corporation, 2004), 44–45.

35. Oliker et al., *Aid During Conflict,* 46.

36. Dr. David Champagne, interview by Contemporary Operations Study Team, Combat Studies Institute, Fort Leavenworth, KS, 20 March 2007, 5.

37. Major Troy O'Donnell, interview by Contemporary Operations Study Team, Combat Studies Institute, Fort Leavenworth, KS, 20 March 2007, 11.

38. O'Donnell, interview, 20 March 2007, 11.

39. O'Donnell, interview, 20 March 2007, 11.

40. Douglas W. Jaquish, "Uninhabited Air Vehicles for Psychological Operations—Leveraging Technology for PSYOP Beyond 2010," *Air & Space Power Journal—Chronicles Online* (6 April 2004), 2. http://www.airpower.maxwell.af.mil/airchronicles (accessed 14 March 2007).

41. Colonel (Retired) James Treadwell, interview by Contemporary Operations Study Team, Combat Studies Institute, Fort Leavenworth, KS, 8 January 2007, 5.

42. Treadwell, interview, 8 January 2007.

43. Champagne, interview, 20 March 2007, 8–9.

44. Christopher J. Lamb and Paris Genalis, *Review of Psychological Operations Lessons Learned from Recent Operational Experience* (Washington, DC: National Defense University Press, 2005), 45–46, 172.

45. Richard L. Kiper, "Of Vital Importance: The 4th PSYOP Group," *Special Warfare* (September 2002), 19–20.

46. Robert K. Ackerman, "Infowarriors Ensure Local Citizenry Gets the Message," *Signal Magazine* (March 2002), 21.

47. Douglas Waller, "Using Psywar Against the Taliban," *Time Online,* 10 December 2001. http://www.time.com/time/columnist/waller/article/0,9565,187810,00.html (accessed 31 January 2007).

48. James A. Schroder, "Observations: ARSOF in Afghanistan," *Special Warfare* (September 2002): 51.

49. Treadwell, interview, 8 January 2007, 9.

50. Treadwell, interview, 8 January 2007, 5.

51. Herbert A. Friedman, "Psychological Operations in Afghanistan," *Perspectives: The Journal of the Psychological Operations Association* 14, no. 4 (2002), 1–4.

52. General Bryan "Doug" Brown, interview by Contemporary Operations Study Team, Combat Studies Institute, Fort Leavenworth, KS, 11 January 2007, 3.

53. Major Mark G. Davis, "Operation ANACONDA: Command and Confusion in Joint Warfare," Masters Thesis, School of Advanced Air and Space Studies, Air University, Maxwell AFB, AL, June 2004, 619–620.

54. Briscoe et al., *Weapon of Choice,* 79.

55. Briscoe et al., *Weapon of Choice,* 96.

Chapter 4

Collapse of the Taliban in Northern Afghanistan

In October 2001 most observers of the Coalition's air campaign in Afghanistan believed that Operation ENDURING FREEDOM (OEF) was progressing slowly and that the Taliban retained a tight grip on power over much of the country. Almost no one—either inside or outside the Coalition—considered the collapse of the Taliban regime imminent. Master Sergeant Armand J. (John) Bolduc, who in early October was preparing to lead one of the first US Army Special Forces (SF) teams into Afghanistan, expected the worst. As the leader of Operational Detachment–Alpha (ODA) 585, Bolduc informed his men that they might not survive and advised them to fight to the death rather than surrender or be taken prisoner.[1] Yet, in just over 6 weeks, Bolduc and approximately 100 SF Soldiers and airmen empowered the Northern Alliance (NA) to decisively defeat the Taliban in northern Afghanistan.

This striking victory was the result of a unique set of circumstances. The provinces to the northeast of Kabul were populated by non-Pashtun ethnic groups and served as the base of operations for the NA, which was dominated by Uzbeks and Tajiks. In his original vision for OEF, General Tommy Franks had proposed the use of a small number of US Soldiers to seize the initiative and begin assisting the NA in operations against the Taliban, thus avoiding the appearance of an outright invasion.[2] Initially, Joint Special Operations Task Force–North (JSOTF-N), established at Karshi-Khanabad (K2), would plan and direct the infiltration of these teams. The first two teams to enter Afghanistan arrived on 19 October and began making contact with the NA commanders in the northern areas. Soon, those Special Operations Forces (SOF) teams would be directly involved in combat against both Taliban and al-Qaeda forces and would greatly assist in the critical battles for the cities of Mazar-e Sharif, Taloqan, and Konduz that would lead to the NA victory in the north.

The Taliban Enemy

As the first chapter of this study established, the Taliban movement had formed in the chaotic aftermath of the Soviet withdrawal. Led since the mid-1990s by Mullah Mohammad Omar, the militant group was intent on establishing an Islamist government in Afghanistan and on driving foreign influence from the country. Affiliation with al-Qaeda in 1996 signaled the Taliban's tacit support for spreading global Islamist extremism beyond Afghanistan. By 2001 the Taliban controlled an estimated 80 percent of Afghanistan.[3]

But the ruling regime did not command a single military force. Instead, in the fall of 2001 the 40,000 to 50,000 combatants organized to fight for the Taliban regime in Afghanistan were essentially organized in three distinct components: indigenous Taliban, non-Afghan Taliban, and al-Qaeda forces trained by and associated with Osama bin Laden.[4] The three groups were then organized nominally into five divisions. Funding and logistical support for Taliban activities in Afghanistan came primarily from Pakistan; however, sympathetic Muslim organizations from various parts of the globe also contributed. This led to the influx of Arabs, Pakistanis, Uzbeks, Chechens, and central Asians who eventually were organized into the non-Afghan elements in the Taliban force. Taliban units were generally armed with Kalashnikov (AK-47) assault rifles, 7.62-mm PK general-purpose machineguns, antiaircraft guns and missiles, rocket and grenade launchers, mortars, makeshift-armed vehicles, and a limited number of Soviet-era tanks and artillery pieces.[5]

The quality of both the Taliban's military leadership and its soldiers varied widely. While Mullah Omar was the commander in chief, the army was overseen by a military council and a general staff. Senior officers tended to change position frequently, however, and no single body was invested with either operational control or setting overall strategy. Both the Afghan and non-Afghan Taliban soldiers served on a less than permanent basis. Although some were conscripted, many were volunteers either from Pashtun tribes or Pakistani madrassas. As such, both commanders and troops on the front lines changed often during the course of a typical campaign as some returned home and others arrived to take their places. Thus, these forces did not make up a professional standing army but a military organization that had more traditional characteristics. Pakistani journalist Ahmed Rashid described many indigenous Taliban units as having more in common with a *lashkar* or tribal militia than with a regular military force.[6] Historically, Afghan *lashkars* were formed by Pashtun commanders from unpaid volunteers when tribal leaders felt threatened or wanted to exert power. This practice affected the structure of the Taliban's indigenous units, making their formations dependent on individual leaders, politics, and financial conditions. Coalition and NA units made use of these vulnerabilities in late 2001 as they induced defections from many indigenous Taliban units.

The foreign Taliban, who comprised approximately 25 percent of the regime's military force, were far better trained and enjoyed a higher level of morale derived from their desire to wage jihad. Of the foreign groups, those associated with al-Qaeda had received the best training and displayed the most zeal in combat against Coalition and NA forces. Stephen Biddle, an analyst at the US Army Strategic Studies Institute, has pointed out that the Taliban recognized the superiority of the foreign elements and relied greatly on them in the fall of 2001 as the NA and their American allies began the ground campaign.[7]

The Northern Alliance

The anti-Taliban Northern United Front, known more commonly as the NA, was led during the summer of 2001 by ousted Afghan President Burnahuddin Rabbani and his military commander General Ahmad Shah Massoud, the charismatic Tajik mujahideen leader who was known as the "Lion of the Panjshir." As the fall of 2001 began, the NA controlled only the Panjshir Valley in the northeast region of the country, the Shomali Plains north of Kabul, and several other small enclaves in the northern, central, and western regions of Afghanistan.[8]

The leadership of the NA suffered a devastating blow on 9 September 2001 when General Massoud was assassinated in Takhar province by two al-Qaeda suicide bombers posing as journalists. Shortly after his death, dire predictions arose regarding the possible disintegration of the NA. Massoud had been considered an exceptional military strategist and had successfully engineered key coalitions among disparate anti-Taliban guerrilla groups that hardened the NA.

Massoud's death did not lead to the disintegration of the NA; however, four distinct components within the Alliance rose to the surface. The largest contingent was made up of ethnic Tajik forces commanded by General Mohammed Fahim Khan. Fahim, former head of intelligence for the NA, rose to take the position of overall military commander immediately following Massoud's demise. In Ghowr and Herat provinces, in west Afghanistan, General Mohammed Ismail Khan took charge of additional ethnic Tajik NA forces. Known as the "Lion of Herat," Ismail had been a mujahideen commander during the Soviet invasion and had previously served as governor of Herat province. Ethnic Uzbeks, under General Abdul Rashid Dostum, formed a third element of the Alliance. In the 1980s, General Dostum's militia had controlled six provinces in northern Afghanistan. His stronghold had been the city of Mazar-e Sharif, the country's fourth largest city, which Dostum lost to the Taliban in 1999. The final faction of the NA was the Hizb-i-Wahdat (Unity Party), comprised of ethnic Hazara fighters led by Karim Khalili. The Taliban had driven this group out of central Afghanistan in 1998, but Khalili and his fighters had managed to survive.[9]

During the summer of 2001, prior to the US intervention in Afghanistan, the NA was short on manpower, inadequately trained, and poorly equipped. Its forces were capable only of maintaining a military stalemate with the Taliban. Although troop strength estimates varied at the time, it was likely that the NA could muster only about 20,000 combat forces to support upcoming US operations.[10] Most NA forces were armed with AK-47 rifles; PK machineguns; ZGU-1 heavy machineguns; single- and multi-barrel rocket launchers; and a limited number of artillery pieces, tanks, and other armored vehicles. The NA had also retrofitted light trucks and BMP-1 infantry fighting vehicles with 32-shot 57-mm rocket pods recovered from Russian Mi-24 and Mi-25 combat helicopters. The Alliance also maintained a small air wing that included approximately a dozen Soviet-built helicopters. Logistics support for the NA was difficult at best and came primarily from the central Asian countries to the north. Supply routes from Tajikistan, for example, were long, arduous, and susceptible to Taliban interdiction. Thus, NA commanders relied on local markets to purchase food and other perishable supplies.[11]

The Insertion of the ODAs

Extensive inclement weather in early October 2001 combined with the treacherous mountain terrain and Taliban antiaircraft fire to significantly delay US Central Command's (CENTCOM's) schedule for the insertion of US Army SF ODAs (also known as A Teams). Since the beginning of the air campaign, Secretary of Defense Donald Rumsfeld had pushed hard for SOF presence in Afghanistan. According to a number of sources, in early October Rumsfeld continuously directed pointed queries about the ODAs to the planners at CENTCOM, asking, "When are the Special Forces people going to get in?"[12] Since becoming the head of the Department of Defense (DOD), Rumsfeld had championed the use of SOF. Once OEF began, Rumsfeld placed great stock in the capacity of SOF to play a decisive role in the campaign. At a news conference on 18 October 2001, Rumsfeld asserted that SOF brought specific capabilities that air power could never offer, stating, "there are certain things they [aircraft] can't do—they can't crawl around on the ground and find people."[13]

On the evening of 19 October 2001, the first of several SF elements infiltrated Afghanistan. Eleven members of ODA 555, onboard MH-47 Chinook helicopters, arrived late in the evening at the Astaneh camp in Panjshir Valley and received their initial briefing.[14] Within a few days, ODA 555 would link up with NA's General Bismullah near Bagram. That same night, the 12 men of ODA 595 infiltrated the Darya Suf Valley on MH-47s to join General Dostum's forces in Dehi, some 60 miles south of Mazar-e Sharif.[15] Not long after, the team split into two sections—one accompanying Dostum to his headquarters, the other remaining at Dehi. On 25 October ODA 585 landed near Dasht-e Qaleh then moved south to join General Bariullah Khan's NA forces near Konduz. On 31 October ODA 553 was inserted into Bamian province, northwest of Kabul, to support Hazara Commander Karim Khalili. Next, an eight-man command-and-control element, known as an Operational Detachment–Charlie (ODC), was inserted to assist General Dostum and his staff on 3 November. On 4 November ODA 534 landed at Darya-e Balkh to support NA General Atta Mohammed. This detachment soon split into two six-man teams, one remaining with Atta Mohammed's command group

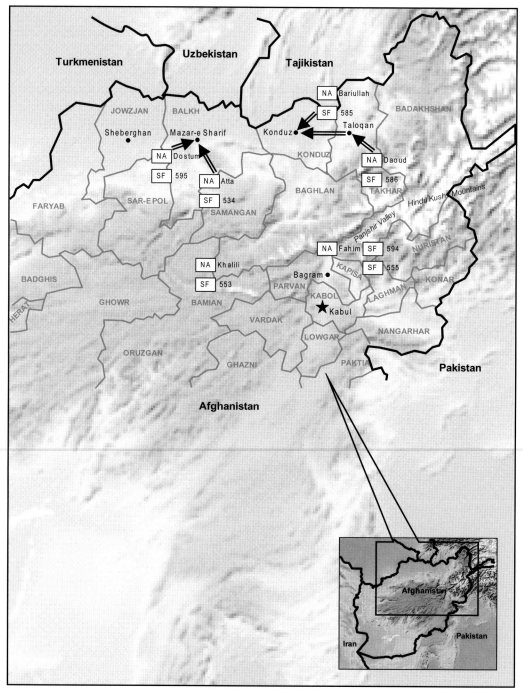

Figure 9. ODA and NA operations, northern Afghanistan, October–December 2001.

while the other moved ahead to join forward NA elements. Finally, ODAs 586 and 594 were flown to a remote landing zone near the Tajik border on 8 November. From there, ODA 586 flew south to link up with General Daoud Khan near Farkhar. ODA 594 moved farther south to the Panjshir Valley.[16]

Beginning in early October, 5th Special Forces Group (SFG) A Teams had been kept in isolation facilities (ISOFAC) at Fort Campbell, Kentucky, where they prepared for operations in Afghanistan without contact from any outsiders. Their mission was complex and difficult, but once they reached K2 Colonel John Mulholland, the 5th SFG commander who had transformed his command into the JSOTF-N, described the SOF mission in a single straightforward statement: "Advise and assist the Northern Alliance in conducting combat operations against the Taliban and al-Qaeda, kill, capture, and destroy al-Qaeda, and deny them sanctuary."[17] The overly broad statement provided the JSOTF-N commander and his teams the freedom to make decisions with limited operational constraints and the appropriate amount of flexibility necessary to complete the mission. Since there had been no off-the-shelf plan for operations in Afghanistan, the 5th SFG began with a clean slate. "Basically, we wrote our own plan," Mulholland explained, adding, "it was heavily guided by Special Forces Unconventional Warfare doctrine which proved to be very relevant to the situation."[18] Unconventional warfare (UW) was a doctrinal term used by the US Army to describe operations in which SF Soldiers deploy to a foreign country and partner with that country's indigenous forces to conduct a variety of operations including intelligence collection, sabotage, guerrilla warfare, and conventional combat actions. Mulholland pushed this emphasis on UW down to his subordinates, allowing them great latitude in how to conduct this type of campaign. Captain Dean Newman, ODA 534 team leader, recalled that his "entire mandate consisted of a handful of PowerPoint slides that told him to conduct unconventional warfare, render Afghanistan no longer a safe haven for terrorists, defeat al-Qaeda, and coup the Taliban."[19] Newman stated that he was afforded remarkable discretion in carrying out the team's mission, asserting, "We were given an extraordinarily wonderful amount of authority to make decisions."[20]

Mazar-e Sharif: The Starting Point

Roughly 2 weeks after the arrival of the first ODAs in northern Afghanistan, Mazar-e Sharif became the first Taliban-controlled city to fall to NA forces. Strategically situated in the Balkh River Valley approximately 35 miles south of Uzbekistan, the city is the capital of Balkh province and has been a major regional trading center since the days of Alexander the Great. As the fourth largest city in Afghanistan and with an estimated population of 200,000 Uzbeks, Tajiks, and Turkomen, Mazar-e Sharif was named in honor of the son-in-law of the Prophet Mohammed, Hazarate Ali, who was enshrined there in a blue-tiled mosque built during the 12th century.

In the late 1990s, control of the city shifted several times between forces led by General Dostum and the Taliban. In 2001 Mazar-e Sharif had been under the control of the Taliban for several years. Once hostilities began in October, the Taliban government moved 3,000 to 5,000 soldiers to the region, and as the month progressed, additional reinforcements were arriving daily from Pakistan by way of Konduz.[21]

For Coalition leaders, Mazar-e Sharif had to be the first objective of the new campaign. In late October 2001, General Franks, the CENTCOM commander, had met with NA commander

Fahim Khan in Tajikistan and both had eventually agreed to focus operations in the north, specifically against the cities of Mazar-e Sharif, Taloqan, and Konduz. Franks and his staff viewed Mazar-e Sharif as critical because its strategic location and airport allowed for the creation of a logistics node inside Afghanistan and a staging area for future operations against Taloqan.[22] Gaining a supply base with an airport before the onset of winter was especially important for Franks who anticipated major humanitarian crises as a result of the military operations. During the meeting, General Fahim brought up the importance of the capital of Kabul. Franks promised that the Coalition would help the NA take Kabul, but was adamant about starting with Mazar-e Sharif and securing the north before moving south. Franks then sealed the deal by granting Fahim both financial and logistical assistance.

By the time Franks and Fahim met, JSOTF-N had inserted two ODAs and an ODC in the Mazar-e Sharif vicinity to help the NA capture the city. ODA 595, which had joined up with General Dostum south of the city, wasted little time calling in its first series of airstrikes on 21 October against Taliban positions in the Beshcam area, about 8 miles from Dostum's headquarters.[23] Pleased with the potential power promised by the airstrikes, Dostum radioed the opposing Taliban commander and announced, "This is General Dostum speaking. I am here, and I have brought the Americans with me."[24] Captain Mark Nutsch, the ODA 595 team leader, then moved his men forward to Cobaki and directed additional airstrikes on Taliban tanks,

---

The Horses They Rode in On

On 19 October 2001, Operational Detachment-Alpha (ODA) 595 infiltrated into Afghanistan and linked up with General Rashid Dostum and his Northern Alliance (NA) forces in the Darya Suf Valley some 70 miles south of Mazar-e Sharif. General Dostum's only modes of transportation were horses and mules; thus, for the next several weeks, ODA 595 rode into battle on horseback, side-by-side with NA fighters.

The commander of ODA 595, Captain Mark D. Nutsch, was well prepared for this task. A full-fledged, highly skilled, cowboy from Alma, Kansas, Nutsch had been a rodeo rider and calf-roping champion at his college alma mater, Kansas State University, prior to joining the Army and becoming a Special Forces officer. Although their Afghan saddles were too small and the stirrups too short, ODA 595 team members were able to successfully keep up with General Dostum during a series of battles leading to the eventual Taliban defeat at Mazar-e Sharif on 10 November.

Along the way, Nutsch, his men, and the NA forces that they supported liberated more than 50 towns and cities, killed or captured thousands of Taliban and al-Qaeda soldiers, and destroyed hundreds of enemy vehicles, bunkers, and weapons systems. In his first field report (25 October), Captain Nutsch declared "We are doing amazingly well with what we have . . . . Frankly, I am surprised that we have not been slaughtered." After Mazar-e Sharif fell to NA forces, General Dostum expressed his gratitude to Nutsch and ODA 595, stating, "I asked for a few Americans. They brought with them the courage of a whole Army."

Special Forces Soldier on horseback.

Courtesy of US Army SFGOARMY.COM/i

Kalev Sepp, "Meeting the 'g-chief': ODA 595," *Special Warfare*, September 2002.

artillery, and a command post near Chapchal.[25] In quick succession, NA forces took control of several villages in the district south of Mazar-e Sharif, assisted in great measure by additional airstrikes directed by ODA 595.

On 26 October Nutsch sent a three-man element to Omitak Mountain to intercept enemy troops moving south toward Dostum's forces and to conduct further airstrikes. Then, during the evening of 28 October a US Air Force Tactical Air Control Party (TACP) arrived, allowing Captain Nutsch to split ODA 595 into four three-man elements along with a two-man command and control cell comprised of himself and a radio operator. The next day saw the arrival of the ODC 53, commanded by Lieutenant Colonel Max Bowers, to provide command and control support for ODA 595, ODA 534, and General Dostum's NA forces in preparation for the impending battle.

With these early actions putting the Taliban on the defensive, General Dostum was ready to move north and retake Mazar-e Sharif with a full complement of US support personnel: SF teams, an SF command and control element, and an Air Force TACP that carried satellite radios for contacting strike aircraft and Special Operations Forces Laser Acquisition Markers (SOFLAM) for pinpointing enemy targets. US cargo aircraft had also managed to drop much-needed food, ammunition, and supplies to NA forces in preparation for this next phase of operations.[26] Additionally, since no vehicles were available and paths in the region consisted primarily of winding mountain trails at elevations in excess of 6,000 feet, NA forces and their American counterparts were forced to travel on horseback and by mule.

The Role of the US Air Force on the Ground

Typically, two Air Force Special Operations Command (AFSOC) Terminal Attack Controllers accompanied each Army Special Forces ODA on combat operations during Operation ENDURING FREEDOM. Everyone wanted a terminal attack controller on his team and these airmen had a dramatic effect on the battles of Mazar-e Sharif, Taloqan, and Konduz in northern Afghanistan. Their primary function was to coordinate and control all joint close air support missions conducted by US Air Force, Navy, and Marine Corps attack, fighter, and bomber aircraft in support of Special Operations Forces and Northern Alliance operations on the ground. They used laser designators and special GPS equipment to direct hundreds of air strikes on Taliban and al-Qaeda troops, tanks, personnel carriers, and assorted vehicles. The Air Force controllers also proved proficient at controlling a variety of aircraft from fighters to B-52s and AC-130s. These aircraft often carried a mix of munitions (precision-guided and/or iron "dumb" bombs of varying sizes) that necessitated split-second decision-making by the controllers regarding which ordnance was best suited for which targets.

One controller, whose team had been nearly overrun in the Balkh Valley south of Mazar-e Sharif, noted that "there is no doubt in my mind that air power allowed the Northern Alliance to move through that valley virtually unimpeded. Close air support helped cut down the amount of time it would have taken for the alliance to advance, and it reduced the loss of life that would surely have resulted from direct action." These men, whose roles are often overlooked, were critical in the early Coalition victories against the Taliban.

Technical Sergeant Ginger Schreitmueller,
"Profile: Staff Sgt. Matt," *DefendAmerica,* February 2002

During the week of 29 October, ODA 595 teams spread out across the region south of Mazar-e Sharif to prepare for the final assault.[27] On 4 November ODA 534, commanded by Captain Newman, linked up with General Atta Mohammed's forces in the Balkh River Valley.[28] The intent at this point was for Dostum to keep moving through the Darya Suf Valley, while Atta Mohammed pushed north in the Balkh. Once they met, the combined force, which also included an NA group led by General Mohammed Mohaqqeq, would continue up the Balkh Valley and attack the Taliban stronghold at Tangi Gap.

On 5 November General Dostum's men were ready to move. The operation began at dawn when MC-130 aircraft dropped two 15,000-pound BLU-82 "Daisy Cutter" bombs on Taliban locations at Aq Kuprok. However, one of ODA 595 teams had crept close to Taliban positions and the Taliban commander counterattacked, attempting to trap the team. Close air support (CAS), Joint Direct Attack Munitions (JDAMs), and strafing runs by F-14s disrupted the Taliban attack and assisted the SOF in escaping safely. Other 595 teams had similar success directing airstrikes from B-52s, a Predator unmanned aerial vehicle (UAV), and other aircraft against key Taliban command and control sites. In one case, an SOF-controlled bomb killed high-ranking Taliban commander Mullah Razzak. In another, an attack on Taliban forces by F-18 Hornet aircraft was followed by NA forces launching a cavalry charge against the remaining enemy, many of whom had begun to retreat northward.[29]

At this point, NA forces were closing in on Mazar-e Sharif from the south and southwest. Taliban commanders in the city continued to funnel reinforcements to the south and continued to put up some resistance. As a result, SOF teams directed Coalition air power against these

---

Early Look at Hell

On 5 November 2001, two officers with General Rashid Dostum's Northern Alliance forces south of Mazar - e Sharif were monitoring Taliban defensive positions located about 3,000 meters away. Soon, an MC-130 Combat Talon aircraft approached and released a huge wooden pallet containing a 15,000 pound high explosive BLU-82 bomb over the enemy position. The pallet separated and fell away; then, a drag parachute deployed from the back of the bomb as it slowly floated toward the Taliban target.

Suddenly, there was a tremendous explosion and a crushing shock wave that knocked both men to the ground, leaving one unconscious. A giant mushroom-shaped cloud (that resembled a nuclear blast) rose from the impact site. One of the officers finally commented, "We were nearly a mile away from the blast and it beat the crap out of us. What was it like out there on the Taliban lines?" He would soon answer his own question, noting "they're getting an early look at what hell is like." Moments later a second BLU-82 was dropped on the same Taliban position. Mazar-e Sharif fell to Dostum's troops that night.

The BLU-82 epitomized the US military's ability to make a huge impact on the battlefield with a small force. Few of these weapons would be used in OEF and not all would have the equivalent effect as the two outside of Mazar-e Sharif. But the overall use of air-delivered munitions proved decisive in enabling the Northern Alliance to defeat the Taliban in northern Afghanistan in 2001.

Gary C. Schroen, *First In* (New York, NY: Ballentine Books, 2005).

moving Taliban units, which often fled back to the north.[30] As the NA forces and their American partners displayed the amount of firepower they had at their command, local Afghan Taliban began defecting.

On 9 November General Dostum began his final push. In preparation for the assault, ODA 595 Soldiers called B-52 strikes on Taliban defenders who were dug in on the reverse slope of a ridge outside the city. As the NA force moved, a Taliban rocket barrage and minefields slowed Dostum's forward progress. But by late afternoon, NA forces fought off last-ditch Taliban counterattacks and, led by Captain Nutsch on horseback, seized the ridge.[31] The next day, NA troops seized the city airport allowing General Dostum and his SF advisors to ride into Mazar-e Sharif where they were greeted warmly by the population.[32]

Fighting in the city would resume, nevertheless, when several hundred Taliban, who had taken refuge in the former Sultan Razia girl's school, refused to surrender. An estimated 300 Taliban fighters, mostly Pakistanis and other non-Afghans, were subsequently killed when US airstrikes destroyed the school.[33] In the aftermath of the assault, the NA took nearly 3,000 Taliban prisoners in the city and the surrounding area.[34] This quick victory would have been highly unlikely without the marriage of NA forces and Coalition air power that the ODAs made possible. Even the Taliban regime tacitly acknowledged the role that air power had played in the taking of Mazar-e Sharif. On 10 November the Bakhtar News Agency quoted a Taliban official as stating, "For seven days continuously they have been bombing Taliban positions. They used very large bombs."[35]

Securing the North: Konduz and Taloqan

ODA 585 arrived at a village close to the Tajik border on 25 October. After linking up with NA forces, Master Sergeant Bolduc and his team met with local NA commander General Bariullah Khan at a safe house to plan the joint operation that would ultimately capture the city of Konduz. Bariullah, though, was skeptical of the team's capabilities. "I have been here for three years with hundreds of men and could do nothing—what are you going to do with 10 men?" he asked.[36] Despite his concern, Bariullah arranged a meeting for ODA 585 with Fahim Khan, the Supreme NA Commander. Fahim agreed to give Bolduc a few days to prove his team's worth. Bariullah, Bolduc, and five members of ODA 585 then moved to the NA front line, which consisted of four observation posts extended over 6 miles of rugged terrain located about 40 miles northeast of Konduz, an important city in northern Afghanistan located to the east of Mazar-e Sharif. From the observation point, Bolduc could see several Taliban fortifications running north to south along the opposite ridgeline. Bolduc immediately called for airstrikes against these enemy targets. Unfortunately, the first bombing runs missed the Taliban fortifications, leaving General Bariullah unimpressed. Moments later, two Marine Corps F-18 Hornets made four passes over the target area, destroying two enemy command bunkers and several sections of Taliban trench lines. Bariullah now saw the light. "We proved to him that we could be an asset and this was only our third day in country," recalled Bolduc.[37]

By early November ODA 585 was manning an observation post which overlooked the village of Chickha and calling in airstrikes. For the remainder of the month, the SOF Soldiers continued bombing the Taliban day and night, wearing them down mentally and physically. Eventually, this allowed NA fighters to overrun Taliban positions, capture the town of Chickha, and push south toward Konduz.[38]

General Bariullah's offensive bogged down briefly, and, to better assess the enemy defensive situation up ahead, Bolduc sent a three-man observation team to find a more suitable vantage point. The observation team sent back invaluable intelligence reports describing Taliban defensive positions in detail. With this critical information, Bariullah now felt ready to resume NA offensive operations. An attack was planned for dawn the next day, but Bariullah called it off at the last minute for no apparent reason. Bolduc was forced to cancel the CAS missions he had arranged and to recall his observation team. Then, in another surprise move, General Bariullah launched his attack without notifying ODA 585. The frontal assault was a dismal failure that led to the deaths of several hundred NA soldiers and three reporters who were covering the offensive. In explaining the NA defeat, Bolduc emphasized the lack of air support which left them exposed to enemy fire, contending, "they were like ducks in a barrel with no air cover."[39] After the failed assault, Bariullah apologized to Bolduc, explaining that he wanted to achieve victory on his own, without assistance from the SOF team.

The following day, nevertheless, offered another chance to dislodge the Taliban defenders. With the assistance of the Coalition air support, the NA forces overran the enemy fighters who had just defeated them. Bariullah and Bolduc then moved farther west and established a new command center about 40 miles north of Konduz. From this location, the SOF team and the NA sent out a reconnaissance team to gather information about Taliban forces in the city and came close to being overrun 10 miles north of Konduz. However, the timely arrival of two F-18s allowed the team to withdraw unharmed.[40] Two days later, General Bariullah's NA forces moved unchallenged to the outskirts of the city.

While General Bariullah and ODA 585 were approaching Konduz from the north, ODA 586 and NA forces commanded by General Daoud Khan were moving toward Konduz from the

Figure 10. ODA 586.

southeast. ODA 586, commanded by Captain Patrick O'Hara, had flown into Afghanistan to link up with General Daoud. By 10 November ODA 586 team members were discussing the mission to capture both Konduz and Taloqan over dinner with Daoud at his safe house in the town of Farkhar. Daoud claimed to have several thousand men as well as some artillery and armored vehicles. The next day these forces, acting on their own initiative, easily seized Taloqan.

This was a significant victory for the NA, because until the Taliban capture of Taloqan in September 2000, the city served as the headquarters of General Ahmad Shah Massoud. On 11 November ODA 586 moved into Taloqan where O'Hara reorganized the team into a three-element rotation with one section along the NA front lines directing CAS operations, another recovering and overseeing supply matters, and the third preparing for the next day's series of CAS missions.

On 13 November the Taliban counterattacked Daoud's forces west of Taloqan along the road to Konduz. The ODA 586 forward element was forced to reposition to a new observation post, but was quickly able to call in a series of airstrikes that destroyed the attacking Taliban forces. General Daoud had expected that the move west to Konduz would be as easy as the capture of Taloqan. Instead, Daoud and ODA 586 would have to fight all the way to the outskirts of Konduz. Tactically, the NA now began moving slowly and deliberately, allowing air power to suppress and destroy Taliban positions ahead of them before moving forward to occupy the positions. Captain O'Hara described the advance up the road to Konduz in the following way: "Bomb the mountain, then hit it with artillery, then take the mountain. The next day we are going to go to the next mountain. . . . [Daoud] did that for 2 weeks and we did that with him, trying to advance as quickly as possible."[41] This combination of tactics proved to be extremely lethal against the Taliban forces that had no weapons to defeat the aircraft and little protection against the bombings.

In the NA attack on 15 November, for example, Coalition CAS accounted for an estimated 386 Taliban killed or wounded. Three hundred additional Taliban casualties were reported on 17 November. The men of ODA 586 had taken great risks to launch these attacks on the Taliban. They came under enemy fire almost daily on the march to Konduz, and in several instances had to call for emergency CAS to protect their own lives.[42] Their bravery, though, was pivotal to setting conditions for the final assault on Konduz.

By 23 November Daoud had captured the city of Khanabad and was moving toward Konduz, 15 miles to the west. During the move from Taloqan to Khanabad, ODA 586 controllers directed hundreds of airstrikes against Taliban and al-Qaeda troops, trucks, tanks, and mortar positions along the way. O'Hara had kept accurate records for the daily bomb damage assessments and later confirmed the destruction of 51 Taliban trucks, 44 bunkers, 12 tanks, and 4 ammunition dumps. In addition, O'Hare reported that more that 2,000 enemy soldiers had been killed or wounded in the 10 days of fighting.[43]

At the same time that General Daoud was closing on Konduz from the east and General Bariullah was approaching from the north, General Dostum was moving in from the west. All three NA commanders were attracting support from the local populations and by the time they surrounded the city, NA ranks included approximately 30,000 fighters.[44] Each NA general then began his own surrender negotiations. After holding out for several days, a few thousand Taliban forces, which included numerous Uzbeks, Chechens, Pakistanis, and Arabs, finally acknowledged the bleakness of their desperate situation and surrendered Konduz to the NA over a 4-day period beginning 23 November. Captain O'Hara and ODA 586 were the first Americans to enter the city. Dostum set many of the Afghan Taliban free, while his forces held foreign and al-Qaeda fighters as prisoners. With the fall of Mazar-e Sharif, Taloqan, and Konduz, the strategically important cities of northern Afghanistan were now in the hands of NA forces.

Concurrent Civil-Military Operations

As noted earlier in this study, CENTCOM planners had sought to create a campaign plan for OEF in which combat operations and humanitarian assistance would occur simultaneously. Northern Afghanistan became the first stage on which the Coalition attempted to do these types of operations concurrently. To support humanitarian relief assistance for the Afghan people, CENTCOM had requested that Combined Forces Land Component Command (CFLCC) establish an appropriate organization to coordinate these relief activities. Lieutenant General Paul Mikolashek, CFLCC commander, then created the Combined Joint Civil Military Operations Task Force (CJCMOTF), composed of elements from the 377th Theater Support Command, the 122d Rear Operations Center, and the 352d Civil Affairs (CA) Command to conduct the humanitarian assistance operations. The CJCMOTF formed in Atlanta and Tampa, moved to Kuwait, and eventually deployed to Kabul in early December 2001.

The planning for humanitarian assistance operations in theater had begun just 4 days after the air campaign began. On 11 October an officer from the 96th CA Battalion deployed to Islamabad, Pakistan, to establish a Civil-Military Operations Center (CMOC) and to organize

---

Humanitarian Rations from the Sky

Developed in the early 1990s by the Department of Defense Humanitarian Assistance Team, humanitarian daily rations (HDRs) were similar to the military meal, ready-to-eat (MRE) that offered a variety of single-portion foods in sealed pouches. HDRs were designed to feed large populations of refugees in emergency situations. Each HDR provides sustenance for one day (2,200 calories), and did not include animal products in order to comply with worldwide religious restrictions. The HDR packages were colored yellow to make each packet highly visible. In Afghanistan, Coalition aircraft dropped HDRs without parachutes. This "flutter-down" method created wide dispersion and hopefully precluded hoarding and altercations over large pallet-load airdrops.

Unfortunately, at the same time that the Coalition was dropping HDRs, its aircraft were also dropping cluster bombs in Taliban concentrations. Each cluster bomb contained over 200 cylindrically-shaped bomblets that were colored yellow like the HDRs. About 5 percent of these bomblets failed to explode, thereby creating the potential for being mistaken for HDR packets. Realizing the potential danger of mistaking bomblets for rations, the Coalition used the Commando Solo aircraft to warn the Afghan population in Dari and Pashto about the differences between the HDRs and the deadly munitions.

The final OEF humanitarian daily ration airdrop occurred on 13 December 2001. By that time, US military aircraft had dropped nearly one million packets in support of the Afghan people. In 2002, the Pentagon changed the HDR packet color from yellow to red.

Deborah Zabarenko, "US Offers Lesson on
How to Tell Cluster Bombs from Food Packs,"
The Washington Post, 30 October 2001.

Coalition Humanitarian Liaison Cells (CHLCs) to deconflict humanitarian and combat operations, conduct assessments, and identify potential relief projects. Later that month a liaison officer and several CA teams from the 96th CA Battalion deployed to the K2 Air Base in support of the 5th SFG. One of these teams relocated to Mazar-e Sharif in late November and a second would move onto the Bagram Air Base near Kabul after it was occupied in October.[45]

During this same period, Humanitarian Assistance Survey Teams (HASTs) from the 96th CA Battalion joined the ODAs in place in the north. Their mission was to assist NA leaders and to initiate collaborative efforts with local Afghan civilians. Some HAST members began wearing civilian clothes in an effort to blend in with Afghans. Nongovernment organizations (NGOs) complained about this practice, however, thinking that locals would be unable to distinguish between Soldiers (in civilian attire) and NGO personnel. Shortly thereafter, CENTCOM ordered CA Soldiers in Afghanistan back in uniform.[46] After the NA victory in Mazar-e Sharif, Soldiers from the 96th CA Battalion, the 5th SFG, and the 10th Mountain Division began working on a number of humanitarian projects including the opening of a new hospital.[47] The hospital, completed in part by specialists from the country of Jordan, quickly put a staff of 20 surgeons to work and by mid-January 2002 had treated approximately 8,000 patients.[48]

Qala-i Jangi Prison Uprising

Figure 11. Fortress of Qala-i Jangi.

The Taliban collapse in northern Afghanistan had led to the surrender of thousands of Taliban and al-Qaeda fighters to victorious NA forces. True to the Afghan fighting tradition, NA leaders accepted at face value the word of the captured Taliban that they would not engage in any further hostilities. Because of this promise, NA Soldiers rarely searched their captives for weapons in a thorough manner. What local NA commanders seemed to have overlooked was that many of those surrendering were non-Afghan Taliban—Pakistanis, Chechens, and others—as well as members of al-Qaeda who would not follow Afghan customs. Approximately 1,000 of these prisoners were taken to the 19th-century Qala-i Jangi fortress, 6 miles west of Mazar-e Sharif, that had served as a Taliban military base and most recently as General Dostum's headquarters.[49]

On 24 November, the day of their arrival at the makeshift detention facility, Taliban captives killed two NA commanders in separate handgrenade suicide attacks.[50] Despite these unexpected attacks, the NA failed to expand the force guarding the prison, which consisted of only about 100 soldiers.[51] The next morning two officers, unaccompanied by security, arrived to interrogate the Taliban and search for al-Qaeda members. Several Taliban wandered freely within the compound, having been untied by the guards to wash and pray.[52] The American presence provoked the Taliban and one attacked a guard with a rock and grabbed an AK-47 assault rifle.[53] Within minutes, the remaining guards fled and enemy forces seized control of the fortress. One of the officers escaped in the turmoil. The other officer, was killed, after having shot three Taliban, thus becoming the first American casualty of hostile fire in Afghanistan.[54]

Later that afternoon, American SF and British Special Air Service (SAS) Soldiers led by Major Mark Mitchell of 3d Battalion, 5th SFG, arrived at Qala-i Jangi and took control of the situation. For the remainder of the day, they called in airstrikes on the south end of the compound where the Taliban had concentrated. On 26 November additional SF troops and Soldiers from the 10th Mountain Division flown in from K2 joined the US and British forces at the prison. Mitchell established a new command post and positioned an NA tank in the northeast corner of the facility. Unfortunately, a misdirected 2,000-pound bomb dropped from a Coalition aircraft struck the north wall of the command post later that morning, killing several NA soldiers and wounding five US and two SAS Soldiers.[55] That evening, Coalition leaders on the ground directed two AC-130 Spectre gunships in strafing runs against the Taliban end of the prison. By the next day, the surviving Taliban were nearly out of food, water, and ammunition. NA tanks shelled a building where the remaining prisoners held out. By late that afternoon, the fighting ended and an SF team was able to recover the fallen Soldier's body. For his leadership in action, Major Mitchell was later given the Distinguished Service Cross, the first award of this decoration since the Vietnam War.

A group of Taliban survived, however, by hiding in the basement of the prison complex. For several days they refused to come out despite being doused with burning oil.[56] Finally, on 1 December, 86 Taliban prisoners emerged and surrendered after the basement had been flooded with frigid well water. Among the survivors was the so-called "American Taliban," John Walker

---

The Death Ray

Air Force AC-130H "Spectre" and AC-130U "Spooky" gunships heavily supported US Special Operations Forces in northern Afghanistan during the fall of 2001. In November, an AC-130 was providing suppressive fires to ODA 595 and General Rashid Dostum's Northern Alliance forces near the city of Konduz when Dostum overheard the gunship's female fire support officer's voice over the radio. He immediately summoned Mohammed Fazal, a recently-captured former Taliban chief of staff, to listen to the radio conversation. Dostum convinced Fazal that the voice was the "Angel of Death," waiting overhead to use the "Death Ray" on Taliban holdouts in Konduz. Fazal immediately grabbed a radio and ordered the remaining Taliban forces to surrender.

AC-130 gunships flew out of Oman during the initial months of OEF and were instrumental in every Northern Alliance attack in northern Afghanistan, especially those in Konduz and in the Qala-i Jangi prison uprising. The side-firing gunship's primary missions include close air support, air interdiction, and force protection. Integrated sensor, navigation, and fire control systems allow the aircraft to operate at night, in adverse weather, and over extended liter times, while providing both surgical strike or saturation firepower.

AC-130H Spectre gunships are configured with a 40-mm Bofors cannon (rate of fire up to 120 rounds per minute) and one 105-mm Howitzer cannon (rate of fire 10 rounds per minute). The AC-130U Spooky (also know as the U-Boat) gunship has a 25-mm GAU-12 Gatling gun (rate of fire 1,800 rounds per minute), advanced sensors, and a new fire control radar system, and is capable of engaging two targets simultaneously.

CAPT. Mark, no last name available,
PBS Frontline, "Campaign Against Terror Interview:
U.S. Special Forces ODA 595," 8 September 2002.

Lindh, who was treated at the Afghan hospital in the city of Sheberghan, interrogated at Camp Rhino in southern Afghanistan, and transported to the USS *Peleliu* in the Arabian Sea.[57] Many of the Taliban and al-Qaeda members involved in the Qala-i Jangi insurrection were among the first arrivals at the newly established detainee facility called Camp X-Ray, which the US Government had established at the Guantanamo Bay Naval Base in Cuba.[58]

For his part, General Dostum felt betrayed by the Taliban uprising at the prison. He had hoped that his humane treatment of the prisoners would be regarded as a gesture of reconciliation. As a result, he had not directed his subordinates to search the prisoners as thoroughly as they should have in the circumstances. "We treated them humanely . . . we did not search them well enough because we trusted them," he would later remark. "That was a mistake."[59]

Logistics Operations in the Early Campaign

Prior to OEF, Army Special Operations Forces (ARSOF) were accustomed to deploying and operating independently in small teams. Thus, their logistics needs were limited. In 2001 the existing, nondeployable, Special Operations Support Command (SOSCOM) with one support battalion, two forward support companies, and one headquarters company was sufficient to meet ARSOF team-oriented logistics requirements.

However, when the 5th SFG deployed to K2 and became the JSOTF-N, the assigned forward support element—Alpha Company, 528th Special Operations Support Battalion—was nearly overwhelmed with the enormity of logistics requests. There were approximately 400 Soldiers in the entire 528th Support Battalion to provide combat service support for 15,000 Soldiers in the ARSOF. This ratio appears inadequate in contrast to conventional force ratios that normally allow for 3,300 support personnel for a combat division that normally has 15,000 Soldiers.[60] Nevertheless, the Soldiers of the 528th shouldered the huge burden at K2 by quickly establishing a warehouse, a clothing distribution center, a dining facility, and ration and refueling points. The 507th Corps Support Command replaced the 528th in December 2001 after SF combat operations in northern Afghanistan had subsided.[61]

Soldiers and Army civilians from the 200th Materiel Management Center (MMC), 21st Theater Support Command (TSC) in Kaiserslautern, Germany, also provided logistics support to SOF personnel during the early days of OEF. A special OEF cell was established at 200th MMC headquarters to provide, as they claimed, "corner-cutting, on-the-fly, I-want-it-now, customer-driven" support services as "unconventional as the war being fought."[62] The cell operated 24 hours a day and was in direct contact with US troops on the ground in Afghanistan via satellite phones and e-mail. When certain items were not readily available in the system, MMC members used their Government credit cards to make the necessary purchases on the local German economy. When cargo parachutes were in short supply, the cell had hundreds more sent to Germany by Federal Express. During the first 60 days of OEF, the 21st TSC air-dropped dozens of Western saddles, 12,000 pounds of horse feed, 2 million humanitarian meals, 2 million pounds of wheat, 93,000 blankets, specialized batteries, nonmilitary tactical gear, camping equipment, mountaineering clothing, plus tons of extra equipment and supplies.[63]

Without doubt, the workhorse airlift aircraft in the early months of OEF was the C-17 Globemaster III. The Air Force had recently purchased 80 of these aircraft to replace the aging C-141 fleet for intertheater long-range transport missions. C-17s carried a larger payload and could operate from smaller, unimproved, airfields. Typically, C-5 Galaxy or commercial aircraft airlifted personnel and equipment from US aerial ports of embarkation to staging bases. To accommodate this movement, the Air Force established two air bridges—one flowed eastward from Moron Air Base in Spain, Rhein-Main and Ramstein Air Bases in Germany, and Incirlik Air Base in Turkey; the other moved westward from Andersen Air Base on Guam to Diego Garcia in the Indian Ocean. At these intermediate staging bases, aircrews transferred cargo from the larger C-5s to C-17s for delivery to the theater. Unfortunately, a single C-17 could not accommodate all the cargo from a C-5 transport. This discrepancy caused considerable backlog and congestion at the various staging bases and resulted in split theater shipments.

From the beginning of the air war until mid-December 2001, C-17s air-dropped more than 2 million humanitarian daily rations for the Afghan population.[64] Since there were no in-theater bases initially, these food drop missions often lasted up to 30 hours and required a third pilot joining the C-17 crews to rotate rest periods. Despite the fact that there had been no CENTCOM or Air Mobility Command off-the-shelf plan for airlift to Afghanistan, the Coalition air forces used innovation and flexibility to deal with the significant challenges posed by the operations in central Asia.[65]

Explaining the Taliban Collapse in the North

US civilian and military officials had expected defeating the Taliban would take much longer than it actually did. However, the speed with which the NA routed the Taliban in northern Afghanistan resulted from an unprecedented combination of military efforts: SOF directing precision-guided airstrikes in support of an indigenous ally against enemy forces. In many battles in the north, the Taliban enemy, which often outnumbered NA forces, were not in contact with the NA and were only visible through sensors used by the ODAs. In these situations, SOF-directed US air power was the combat multiplier that enabled an outnumbered NA to destroy Taliban infantry and armor and to liberate northern Afghanistan in just over 6 weeks. SOF executed their UW campaign precisely in accordance with their doctrine. ODAs not only directed deadly airstrikes, but also influenced the decisionmaking of NA commanders on the ground, thereby shaping NA tactics. According to Colonel Mulholland, commander of JSOTF-N, the Taliban faced a classic dilemma. If they massed, they would be annihilated by devastating airstrikes. If they dispersed, they would be, in Mulholland's words, "overwhelmed and defeated piecemeal by NA ground forces."[66] For Mulholland, the ODAs were the key, serving as "the ultimate 'bridging force,' joining methods and techniques of warfare that had not changed in hundreds of years to 21st century capabilities"[67]

These tactics presented US forces maximum effectiveness with minimal risk. Al-Qaeda units did attempt two counterattacks, yet US SOF suffered no casualties in any of the battles in the north. The principal reason for this was that CAS controllers attached to ODAs used laser illuminators and Global Positioning System (GPS) equipment to engage Taliban fighters at significant stand-off distances. For example, on the march toward Mazar-e Sharif in October, SOF controllers were able to acquire Taliban targets at ranges of up to 10 kilometers.[68] The resulting technique took on a new name, ground-directed interdiction (GDI), and differed from typical CAS in which supported forces are normally in direct contact with the enemy. GDI facilitated attacks on moving targets, ensured compliance with CENTCOM rules of engagement, and enabled the concentration of devastating effects without concentrating physical forces.[69] US Army Colonel Mike Findley, the former Commander, Special Operations Command, Joint Forces Command, argued that although the mix of players in the GDI equation was unprecedented, the NA (along with its SOF advisors) was essentially no different than any other conventional ground maneuver force requiring periodic joint fire support.[70] Matching concentrated firepower with nimble ground maneuver elements to vanquish an enemy force has always been a principal factor for success in warfare. As such, JSOTF-N became by default the functional ground force (supported) commander directing ODA/NA maneuver units against the Taliban and employing complementary US air support whenever needed.

Some observers have suggested that the quick victories over the Taliban in the north and elsewhere resulted from the pitting of a modern force against a poorly-trained, incompetent, and unmotivated enemy.[71] This may have been true during the first few days of SOF-directed US bombing, when the enemy was exposed and easily acquired. The Taliban learned quickly and by November 2001 had adopted a variety of cover-and-concealment techniques and began taking cover and dispersing their troops. These efforts proved at least partially successful in minimizing the devastating effects of American airstrikes, and would serve the Taliban well in future actions such as the assault on Tora Bora and Operation ANACONDA. Additionally, although Afghan Taliban were often hesitant to stand and fight, the foreign forces that had received sophisticated military training were significantly more likely to hold their positions and even mount counterattacks.

The power of the SOF/NA combination was magnified by important innovations in the use of aerial platforms during the initial months of OEF. The expanded use of UAVs, such as Predator and Global Hawk, provided both faster reaction times and longer dwell times than did conventional piloted aircraft. This enabled significantly improved data fusion, near constant surveillance of Taliban activity, and major reductions in sensor-to-shooter link times. Unfortunately, teams on the ground could not communicate directly with UAV operators. On the other hand, improved capability to transmit and receive data permitted aircrews to retarget during flight and to strike targets repeatedly if necessary.

Despite some initial growing pains, the Combined Air Operations Center (CAOC) at Prince Sultan Air Base provided an unprecedented level of timely air support for SF ODAs and the NA. Air Force and Navy cooperation and integration was generally harmonious from the start as all CAOC members focused on sharing information and on the common objective of defeating the Taliban. Improved technology provided CAOC operators with proximate real-time theater connectivity, situational awareness, and the ability to deliver devastating firepower on demand.[72]

A few controversies did arise. Military and civilian personnel at CENTCOM and in Washington exercised high levels of centralized control over mission planning and execution, thereby interfering with timely target approval decision cycles.[73] This practice, coupled with restrictive rules of engagement that sometimes required Judge Advocate General (JAG) officers influencing target choices, rear-area scrutinizing of live Predator data, lengthy mission distances (up to 15 hours flight time from Diego Garcia), limited loiter capability, and the fact that CENTCOM and CAOC were separated by eight time zones detracted from air power reaction times as new targets emerged. Additionally, other US Government agencies flew armed Predators within the area of responsibility (AOR) in support of covert operations without advising the CAOC. To address this issue, liaison officers at CENTCOM, CAOC, and JSOTF-N developed a broad-based coordination plan that integrated all friendly OEF participants—SOF, covert SOF, and NA.[74] Eventually, JSOTF-N established a limited Air Support

Operations Center (ASOC) to coordinate joint fires and began using other procedures to help eliminate friendly fire incidents.[75]

Fortunately, commanders quickly resolved the few difficulties that arose early on in OEF. For example, JSOTF-N's assumption of the role of "supported" command clarified command relationships among the participants. Also, CENTCOM requested the first-time use of commercial satellites to address the demand for data transmission bandwidth.[76] This, though, did not completely alleviate occasional range and reliability problems with targeting systems, data links, and frequency modulation (FM) tactical radios encountered by infiltrated SOF. In addition, extensive aviation operations in mountainous terrain revealed the high-altitude lift limitations of MH-60 Black Hawk helicopters. Although Black Hawk crews flew hundreds of dangerous OEF support missions, several such missions involving flights into mountainous terrain were, of necessity, shifted to the larger and more powerful MH-47 Chinooks. Taking time to assess variations in aircraft capabilities complicated mission planning for commanders, but never seriously endangered the support Coalition SOF was able to give to their indigenous partners in the NA.[77]

✦　　✦　　✦

In fewer than 2 months, the NA, supported by US SOF and air power, decisively defeated the Taliban and al-Qaeda forces in northern Afghanistan and liberated 6 provinces, 3 key cities, and nearly 50 additional smaller towns and villages in the region. NA forces killed nearly 10,000 enemy soldiers and took several thousand more prisoners. The unique combination of small SOF teams (trained eyes on the ground), strike aircraft/bombers, and precision-guided munitions brought about the remarkable accomplishments realized during combat operations in the north. SOF also provided tactical advice to the NA and dealt adroitly with various Afghan factions, rivalries, and tensions. The seven ODAs and one ODC that entered the northern region certainly maintained the imperative of keeping the Coalition footprint small and proved that devastating firepower and other technological advantages could be brought to bear by small, highly-trained units.

In the early battles for Mazar-e Sharif and for the other population centers in the north, American forces gained valuable insight into how the Taliban and al-Qaeda would fight. Moreover, CENTCOM had demonstrated to doubters that the United States could rapidly project destructive land, sea, and air power over exceptionally long distances. US combat participants proved the concept of "jointness" to be both viable and workable, as all—SOF, conventional Army, Navy, Air Force, and Marines—cooperated in support of the OEF mission. Defeating the Taliban and establishing a strategic foothold in northern Afghanistan would be critical to the rest of the OEF campaign by creating an anchor point for NA power and a platform from which to project that power.

The NA commanders now turned their focus to the capital of Kabul and the promise of taking control of the entire country. At the same time, CENTCOM and JSOTF-N had begun conducting UW in the south of Afghanistan where the Taliban had deep roots amongst the Pashtun population. The victorious battles in the north were critical to the campaign and set the stage for even greater victories. However, both the capital and the south of the country would have to be secured for the Coalition to achieve its overall goal of ridding Afghanistan of the Taliban and al-Qaeda.

Notes

1. Phillip O'Connor, "Two Men Who Fought Terror," *St. Louis Post-Dispatch,* 22 February 2004, sec. A, p. 1.

2. House Armed Services Committee, *Statement of General Tommy R. Franks,* 107 Cong., 27 February 2002, 7–8.

3. Ali A. Jalali, "Afghanistan: The Anatomy of an Ongoing Conflict," *Parameters* (Spring 2001): 92–93.

4. Stephen Biddle, *Afghanistan and the Future of Warfare: Implications for Army and Defense Policy* (Carlisle, PA: US Army War College Strategic Studies Institute, 2002), 13.

5. Jalali, "Anatomy of an Ongoing Conflict," 92–94.

6. Ahmed Rashid, *Taliban: Militant Islam, Oil, and Fundamentalism in Central Asia* (New Haven, CT: Yale University Press, 2001), 99–100.

7. Biddle, *Afghanistan and the Future of Warfare,* 14.

8. Fiona Symon, "Afghanistan's Northern Alliance," *BBC News Online* (19 September 2001), 3. http://news.bbc.co.uk/2/hi/south_asia/1552994.stm (accessed 31 January 2007).

9. Symon, "Afghanistan's Northern Alliance," 2.

10. Rory McCarthy, "Warlords Bury their Differences in Readiness for Long and Bloody Battles," *The Guardian* (7 November 2001), 1. http://www.guardian.co.uk/waronterror/archive/0,,554661,00.html (accessed 9 February 2007).

11. Jalali, "Anatomy of an Ongoing Conflict," 92–95.

12. Both General Tommy Franks and Deputy Secretary of Defense Paul Wolfowitz attest to this pressure from Secretary of Defense Rumsfeld. See General Tommy Franks, *American Soldier* (New York, NY: HarperCollins, 2004), 299–300. See also, "Interview: Paul Wolfowitz," *PBS FRONTLINE.* http://www.pbs.org/wgbh/pages/frontline/shows/campaign/interviews/wolfowitz.html (accessed 23 January 2007).

13. US Department of Defense, "DOD News Briefing—Secretary Rumsfeld and Gen Myers," *DefenseLink News Transcript,* 18 October 2001, 8. http://www.defenselink.mil/transcripts/transcript.aspx?transcriptid=2130 (accessed 21 February 2007).

14. Brigadier General John Mulholland, interview by Contemporary Operations Study Team, Combat Studies Institute, Fort Leavenworth, KS, 7 May 2007, 6.

15. William Knarr and John Frost, *Operation Enduring Freedom Battle Reconstruction* (Alexandria, VA: Institute for Defense Analyses, 2004), I-1, V-6.

16. Andrew Birtle, *Afghan War Chronology* (Washington, DC: US Army Center of Military History Information Paper, 2002), 3.

17. "The Liberation of Mazar-e Sharif: 5th SF Group Conducts UW in Afghanistan," *Special Warfare* 15, no. 2 (June 2002): 39; Mulholland, interview, 7 May 2007, 4.

18. Mulholland, interview, 7 May 2007, 3.

19. Max Boot, "Special Forces and Horses," *Armed Forces Journal* (November 2006): 18–25. http://www.armedforcesjournal.com/2006/11/2146103 (accessed 1 April 2007).

20. Boot, "Special Forces and Horses," 18–25.

21. Knarr and Frost, *Battle Reconstruction,* V-5.

22. Franks, *American Soldier,* 310–312.

23. Dale Andrade, *The Battle of Mazar-e Sharif, October–November 2001* (Washington, DC: US Army Center of Military History Information Paper, 2002), 2; Knarr and Frost, *Battle Reconstruction,* V-7.

24. Boot, "Special Forces and Horses," 18–25.

25. Knarr and Frost, *Battle Reconstruction,* V-8.

26. Thom Shanker and Steven Lee Myers, "U.S. Special Forces Step up Campaign in Afghan Areas," *New York Times,* 19 October 2001, 1. http://query.nytimes.com/gst/fullpage.html?res= 9E00E2 DB133EF93AA25753C1A9679C8B63 (accessed 2 January 2008).

27. Knarr and Frost, *Battle Reconstruction,* V-11.

28. "Liberation of Mazar-e Sharif," 37.

29. Andrade, *Battle of Mazar-e Sharif,* 2.

30. Biddle, *Afghanistan and the Future of Warfare,* 10.

31. Knarr and Frost, *Battle Reconstruction,* V-27, 28.

32. Andrade, *Battle of Mazar-e Sharif,* 2.

33. Carlotta Gall, "A Deadly Siege At Last Won Mazar-e Sharif," *New York Times,* 19 November 2001, sec. B, p. 1. http://query.nytimes.com/gst/fullpage.html?res=9C0DE0D7103BF93AA25752C1A9 679C8B63&n=Top/Reference/Times%20Topics/Organizations/T/Taliban (accessed 2 January 2009).

34. Birtle, *Chronology,* 4.

35. Dexter Filkins and Thom Shanker, "Afghan Rebels Report Capture of Major City from the Taliban," *New York Times,* 10 November 2001, sec. A, p. 1. http://query.nytimes.com/gst/fullpage.html? res=9A03EEDF1538F933A25752C1A9679C8B63 (accessed 2 January 2009).

36. Master Sergeant Armand J. Bolduc, e-mail interview by Contemporary Operations Study Team, Combat Studies Institute, Fort Leavenworth, KS, 21 August 2007.

37. Bolduc, e-mail interview, 21 August 2007.

38. Birtle, *Chronology,* 5.

39. Bolduc, e-mail interview, 21 August 2007.

40. Master Sergeant Armand J. Bolduc, interview by Contemporary Operations Study Team, Combat Studies Institute, Fort Leavenworth, KS, 4 September 2007, 2.

41. Captain Patrick O'Hara, interview by Contemporary Operations Study Team, Combat Studies Institute, Fort Leavenworth, KS, 27 July 2007, 9.

42. O'Hara, interview, 27 July 2007, 10.

43. Patrick O'Hara, "ODA 586 (Texas 11) Historical Vignette of Afghanistan," unpublished document, undated.

44. Johanna McGeary, Massimo Calabresi, and Mark Thompson. "Shell Game," *Time* 158, no. 24 (3 December 2001), 26. See also, O'Hara, interview, 27 July 2007, 8–9, for a description of General Daoud's informal recruiting of local fighters on the road to Konduz.

45. William Flavin, *Civil Military Operations: Afghanistan* (Carlisle, PA: US Army Peacekeeping and Stability Operations Institute, 2004), 91.

46. Flavin, *CMO,* 91.

47. Jim Garamone, "Humanitarian Success Story in Afghanistan," *Armed Forces Press Service,* 18 January 2002, 1–2. http://www.defenselink.mil/news/newsarticle.aspx?id=43839 (accessed 2 January 2009).

48. Garamone, "Humanitarian Success Story in Afghanistan," 1–2.

49. Jennifer Whittle and Steve Alvarez, "Special Forces Officer Honored for Heroism in Mazar-e Sharif Prison Battle," *DefendAmerica News,* 14 November 2003, 1–2. http://www.defendamerica. mil/articles/nov2003/a111403a.html (accessed 23 January 2007); Carlotta Gall, "In Tunnels Full of Bodies, One of Them Kept Firing," *New York Times,* 30 November 2001, sec. B, p. 3. http:// query.nytimes.com/gst/fullpage.html?res= 9904E6D8153DF933A05752C1A9679C8B63 (accessed 2 January 2009).

50. Alex Perry, "Inside the Battle at Qala-i Jangi," *Time* 158, no. 25 (10 December 2001): 52.

51. Bay Fang, "They Were All Fighting to Die," *U.S. News & World Report* 131, no. 24 (10 December 2001): 18–21.

52. Fang, "Fighting to Die," 18–21.

53. Carlotta Gall, "U.S. Bomb Wounds G.I.'s as Battle Rages at Fort," *New York Times,* 27 November 2001, sec. A, p. 1. http://query.nytimes.com/gst/fullpage.html?res=9900EED71E3AF934A15752C1A96 79C8B63 (accessed 2 January 2009).

54. George J. Tenet, Director of CIA, "Statement on the Death of a CIA Officer in Afghanistan," Central Intelligence Agency (CIA) Press Release, 28 November 2001.

55. Kalev Sepp, "Uprising at Qala-i Jangi: The Staff of the 3/5th SF Group," *Special Warfare* 15, no. 3 (September 2002): 17.

56. Gall, "In Tunnels Full of Bodies," sec. B, p. 3.

57. "CNN Presents House of War: "The Uprising at Mazar-e Sharif," 3 August 2002. http://www. cnn.com/CNN/Programs/presents/shows/house.of.war/interactive/interactive/house.of.swf (accessed 3 March 2007); Daniel Klaidman and Michael Isikoff, "Walker's Brush with bin Laden," *Newsweek* 139, no. 1 (7 January 2002): 20–21.

58. US Department of Defense, "Rumsfeld Visits, Thanks U.S. Troops at Camp X-Ray in Cuba," *DefenseLink News Transcripts,* 27 January 2002, 1. http://www.defenselink.mil/news/Jan2002/ n01272002_200201271.html (accessed 3 March 2007).

59. Fang, "Fighting to Die," 18–21; Perry, "Battle at Qala-i Jangi," 51; Dostum confirmed through his personal secretary, Issan Eari in an unrecorded telephone interview with Dr. Peter Connors of the Contemporary Operations Study Team on 1 September 2007, that he did indeed regret not having searched Taliban/al-Qaeda prisoners more thoroughly after capturing Konduz in November 2001. Issan explained that the situation in Konduz was extremely confusing at the time. Issan also suggested that Dostum ordered his men to carefully search the prisoners, but this order was not properly carried out. Dostum, hoping to create reconciliation, did not confirm that his order had been enacted.

60. Jorge E. Rodriguez, "What's Missing in ARSOF Logistics?" *Army Logistician* 36, no. 1 (January/February 2004): 7–9.

61. Richard L. Kiper, "We Support to the Utmost: The 528th Special Operations Support Battalion," *Special Warfare* 15, no. 3 (September 2002): 13–15.

62. Dennis Steele, "Unconventional Logistics," *Army* 52, no. 11 (November 2002): 58.

63. Steele, "Unconventional Logistics," 58–59.

64. Olga Oliker et al., *Aid During Conflict: Interaction Between Military and Civilian Assistance Providers in Afghanistan*, September 2001–June 2002 (Santa Monica, CA: RAND Corporation, 2004), 47.

65. Daniel L. Haulman, *Intertheater Airlift Challenges of Operation Enduring Freedom* (Maxwell AFB, AL: Air Force Historical Research Agency, 2002), 1–12.

66. Mulholland, interview, 7 May 2007, 10.

67. Mulholland, interview, 7 May 2007, 10.

68. Biddle, *Afghanistan and the Future of Warfare,* 26.

69. Michael Noonan and Mark Lewis, "Conquering the Elements: Thoughts on Joint Force (Re)Organization," *Parameters* (Autumn 2003): 38.

70. Mike Findley, Robert Green, and Eric Braganca, "SOF on the Contemporary Battlefield," *Military Review* (May/June 2003): 11.

71. See, for example, Anthony H. Cordesman, *The Ongoing Lessons of Afghanistan: Warfighting, Intelligence, Force Transformation, and Nation Building* (Washington, DC: Center for Strategic and International Studies, 2004), 16–23.

72. Benjamin S. Lambeth, *Air Power Against Terror: America's Conduct of Operation Enduring Freedom* (Santa Monica, CA: RAND Corporation, 2005), 83.

73. See, for example, Lieutenant General (Retired) Paul T. Mikolashek, interview by Contemporary Operations Study Team, Combat Studies Institute, Fort Leavenworth, KS, 13 December 2006, 9.

74. Lambeth, *Air Power Against Terror,* 353.

75. Findley, Green, and Braganca, "SOF on the Contemporary Battlefield," 12–13.

76. Cordesman, *Ongoing Lessons of Afghanistan,* 43.

77. Conrad Crane, *Final Report: The U.S. Army's Initial Impressions of Operation Enduring Freedom and Noble Eagle* (Carlisle, PA: US Army War College, 2002), 4.

Chapter 5

Success in the South and East

The situation in southern and eastern Afghanistan differed markedly from the circumstances in the north. Unlike operations in the northern part of Afghanistan, where Operational Detachment–Alpha (ODA) teams worked with the multiethnic Northern Alliance (NA) to bring down the Taliban, ODAs in the south and southeast did not have the opportunity to work with a well-established anti-Taliban organization and needed to either manufacture resistance to the Taliban or nurse extant opposition within the local population to maturity. Making this problem more difficult was that the Taliban movement emerged from the areas around the southern city of Kandahar, and the movement's most ardent supporters remained located in that region and the southeastern provinces along the Pakistani border. In the eastern region, seizing control of Kabul presented both a military and a political challenge. If that seizure occurred at the hands of the Tajik- and Uzbek-dominated NA, the Pashtun majority within the country might be irrevocably alienated from the Coalition. Clearly, for the ODAs that would begin working in the south and the east, significant obstacles lined the path that led to the overthrow of the Taliban regime.

Still within 2 months of arriving in Afghanistan, the ODAs worked with indigenous forces of several different types to capture Kabul in November, seize Kandahar in early December, and destroy much of Osama bin Laden's al-Qaeda forces at Tora Bora in mid-December. Throughout these operations in southern and eastern Afghanistan, Coalition military leaders continued to rely on the partnership between indigenous anti-Taliban forces, small teams of Special Operations Forces (SOF), and highly-focused close air support (CAS). This formula worked well through the middle of December as key anti-Taliban Pashtun leaders such as Hamid Karzai and Gul Agha Sherzai emerged to work with Coalition forces and rapidly build their own military forces. The collaboration of these elements culminated in early December with the remarkably quick capture of Kandahar, the key objective in the south.

However, the collaboration between Special Forces (SF) advisors and anti-Taliban militia developed differently during the fighting in the Tora Bora Mountains in early to mid-December. There, on the border with Pakistan, a potent mix of cultural differences, inter-Afghan political agendas, and international frictions prevented Coalition forces from annihilating al-Qaeda forces in Afghanistan and capturing Osama bin Laden. While the actions at Tora Bora were generally successful in removing al-Qaeda as a fighting force, that battle revealed that the Coalition's ability to rely on Afghan militia forces in the south had significant limits.

Initial Moves: Identifying Pashtun Allies in the South

For the ODAs designated for operations in eastern and southern Afghanistan, it was vital to find, link-up, and work with legitimate anti-Taliban Pashtun leaders who would help the Coalition seize Kandahar—the center of Pashtun life in Afghanistan. By the late 20th century, there were roughly 17 million Pashtuns living along both sides of the Afghan–Pakistani border, and any outside power that wanted to significantly influence Afghan affairs needed a champion from within the Pashtun ethnic group.[1] Coalition military and political leaders recognized early that operations could not solely rely on the NA; ultimate victory would required support from the Pashtun population. Fortunately, the US Government quickly found a Pashtun leader who was willing to serve at the head of an anti-Taliban Pashtun movement. His name was Hamid Karzai and he would quickly emerge as an ally not only in the effort to dislodge the Taliban, but also in the nation-building process that would immediately ensue after the Taliban's defeat.

Little known by Americans before the dramatic events of September 2001, Karzai was born in 1957, the son of Abdul Ahad Karzai, just outside Kandahar. Abdul Karzai had served as deputy speaker of the Afghanistan Parliament in the 1960s and was a tribal elder of the Popalzai, one of the key Pashtun tribes. Hamid Karzai's maternal grandfather, Khair Mohammad Khan, had fought in Afghanistan's War of Independence in 1919 and had served as the deputy speaker of Afghanistan's Senate. Karzai thus enjoyed an impeccable pedigree that in 2001 positioned him as a potential player in the post-Taliban Afghan government.

Figure 12. Hamid Karzai.

In any event, it was not just Karzai's lineage that thrust him into the forefront of the anti-Taliban forces' efforts.[2] Karzai had played a significant role in just about every major event in Afghanistan since the 1979 Soviet invasion. After receiving his Master of Arts degree in International Relations in 1983 from Shimla University in India, Karzai returned to his home country and joined the mujahideen, serving the anti-Soviet resistance in a variety of capacities. He was the Director of Information for the National Liberation Front (NLF) and eventually moved into the post of deputy director of the NLF's Political Office. After the Soviet withdrawal, Karzai received an appointment as the director of the foreign affairs unit within the transitional post-Soviet government led by Mohammad Najibullah. After the mujahideen ousted Najibullah's communist Democratic Republic of Afghanistan regime in 1992, Karzai was tabbed as the interim government's Deputy Foreign Minister. When civil war broke out, Karzai attempted to bring the disparate sides together at a *loya jirga* (grand council), but failed.

With the rise of the Taliban, Karzai and his family became fierce opponents of Mullah Mohammad Omar's movement and of his al-Qaeda allies, a stance that forced them to leave Afghanistan. In August 1999 assassins killed Abdul Ahad Karzai in Quetta, Pakistan, while he was attempting to organize resistance to the Taliban regime. This event consolidated Hamid Karzai's position as an anti-Taliban figure able to garner support from fellow Pashtuns as well as other Afghan ethnic groups.

Karzai's potential looked very promising, but Coalition leaders believed they would have to recruit other Pashtun leaders if they were to conduct a successful campaign in the south and east. Gul Agha Sherzai was the next obvious candidate. Prior to the Taliban taking power in the 1990s, Sherzai had exerted political control over the area around Kandahar. He had fought with the mujahideen against the Soviets and maintained close ties with the Pakistani Inter Services Intelligence (ISI) agency. While Sherzai would ultimately prove to be a valuable resource to the United States in driving the Taliban from Kandahar, his power was based on his political standing in the Kandahar region. Because of this, Sherzai had sometimes been identified as a warlord. By turning to men like Karzai and Sherzai, Coalition leaders hoped to cultivate favor among the Pashtuns and enable not just a military decision against the Taliban, but a political coup de main that would bring a new government supported by all ethnic groups.[3]

Ground Operations Begin: Objectives RHINO and GECKO

In mid-October, 2 weeks after the beginning of the air campaign, US ground forces would make their first appearance in southern Afghanistan. The US Army Ranger and SOF units that hit the ground first hoped to set the right conditions for the ODA efforts in the region. On the night of 20 October 2001, about 200 Rangers from the 3d Battalion, 75th Ranger Regiment, conducted a parachute assault on a small desert airfield about 50 miles southwest of Kandahar dubbed Objective RHINO. The purpose of the operation was to secure the airfield and use it as a forward arming and refueling point (FARP) for helicopters ferrying troops of an elite SOF task force, which would be conducting a follow-on mission from the airfield.[4]

The objective area was divided into smaller objectives: TIN, IRON, and COBALT. The last of these was a walled compound that appeared to be a billeting area for Taliban troops. The 3d Battalion's A Company was to clear Objectives TIN and IRON, then set up blocking positions to oppose any Taliban counterattacks that might develop. Company C's mission was to assault and clear Objective COBALT, the walled compound.[5]

Before the Rangers parachuted onto the objective, strikes by a variety of aircraft hit the targets to suppress and perhaps kill many of the enemy forces near the objectives. The US Air Force directed B-2 Stealth Bombers to hit the various target areas around RHINO, especially TIN, with 2,000-pound bombs, and were followed up by AC-130 gunship strafing runs.[6] The airstrikes proved remarkably successful, eliminating 11 Taliban fighters on Objective TIN and forcing 9 more to withdraw.[7] The AC-130 attacked several structures within COBALT and effectively quelled resistance there that might have contested the parachute drop and the follow-on assault into the walled compound.[8]

The 3d Battalion's attack went off relatively smoothly. Once on the ground, the Rangers of A Company immediately attacked and secured their objectives without incident. Company C then attacked the walled compound at COBALT. With the exception of one enemy fighter who was quickly killed, there was no resistance. During the attack, members of the 9th Psychological Operations (PSYOP) Battalion began broadcasting messages via loudspeaker urging any surviving enemy soldiers to give up to the Americans.[9] The US elements at RHINO quickly cleared all buildings, destroyed weapons caches, and secured the field. In less than 20 minutes, several MC-130 aircraft landed and prepared to refuel the SOF helicopters and extract the Rangers. Within a few more minutes a flight of choppers landed at the FARP and began refueling.[10] Phase I was complete. The next phase, the operation to seize Objective GECKO, was about to begin.

Objective GECKO was a residential compound southwest of Kandahar that, according to Coalition intelligence, potentially housed a target of significant value—Mullah Mohammed Omar, the leader of the Taliban. According to a US Special Operations Command (USSOCOM) history of the operation, the SOF mission going into GECKO was to "disrupt Taliban leader-ship and [al-Qaeda] communications, gather intelligence and detain select personnel."[11] A short time after refueling at the FARP, the helicopters were en route to the compound carrying about 90 highly trained SOF soldiers who were intent on killing or capturing Mullah Mohammed Omar. Shortly before the choppers landed near the compound, AC-130 Spectre gunships and MH-60 Blackhawk helicopters pounded the residence with a variety of weapons. Once on the ground, the elite force took less than an hour to seize and clear Omar's compound. Failing to find the Taliban leader at the site, the troops gathered valuable intelligence, after which they evacuated the objective and returned to RHINO.[12] Once the SOF choppers departed RHINO, the Rangers boarded the MC-130s and departed. The entire operation lasted just over 5 hours after the parachute assault.[13]

The operations to capture Objectives RHINO and GECKO were designed to have as much of a psychological impact as a military one. The Taliban simply did not have a well-developed air force and so the loss of the airfield did not have any meaningful military effect on their war effort. However, the operation was meant to have a significant influence on the thinking of the political and military leadership of the Taliban and its al-Qaeda allies. The day after the assault, Chairman of the Joint Chiefs of Staff, US Air Force General Richard B. Myers, asserted that the operations near Kandahar displayed the Coalition's military dominance, stating, "U.S. forces were able to deploy, maneuver and operate inside Afghanistan without significant interference from Taliban forces. They are now refitting and repositioning for potential future operations against terrorist targets in other areas known to harbor terrorists."[14] General Tommy Franks, the CENTCOM commander and overall commander of Operation ENDURING FREEDOM (OEF), reinforced this point, stating that these operations were conducted to show the Taliban, and perhaps the Afghan people at large, "that we will go anywhere we choose to go."[15]

Despite Omar's absence at Objective GECKO, the operations did achieve some success. The raids on Objectives RHINO and GECKO demonstrated that the Taliban was powerless to prevent the Coalition military command from focusing land forces on any target within the borders of Afghanistan at the time of its choosing. The Taliban's attention on any impending battles was doubtless fixed to the north where the bulk of its fighting force faced the NA. The south was supposed to be secure, but these raids proved to the Taliban and the country's popula-tion that it was not.

The ODAs Enter: The Fall of Kabul

On the same day that the Rangers landed at RHINO, US Central Command (CENTCOM) and Joint Special Operations Task Force–North (JSOTF-N) inserted another SF team much closer to the historic political capital of Afghanistan—the city of Kabul. As noted in the previous chapter, ODA 555 was the first team inserted into the Panjshir Valley in northeast Afghanistan on 19 October 2001. This team, nicknamed the "Triple Nickel," arrived with the mission of working with the NA forces of Generals Bismullah Khan and Mohammed Fahim Khan to seize the Shomali Plains located between the city of Bagram and the capital of Kabul. The team met with the NA commanders at the old Soviet Air Base near Bagram and discovered that the dilapidated control tower at the field made a superb observation post. From that site, the team could observe the Taliban front lines and call in airstrikes against their positions.[16] Sergeant First Class "Frank," a member of ODA 555, recalled the first day that he was taken up into the tower:

[An NA commander] takes us up into the tower. We didn't go down there to call any of our aircraft in, we were just going to survey the front lines, and he starts pointing out all the enemy positions. [We were] like, "You mean that's al-Qaeda right there, and that's Taliban?" He knew. "Yes, General so-and-so lives in that house. This is where his lines are."[17]

Frank and the others quickly gathered their laser designating equipment and called for CAS:

[The NA commander] just started pointing out the targets where all the gun positions were, where all the commanders were, the radios. We just started taking them out with the laser, one by one. [The commander and his men] were giggling. They were all laughing and joking about it and slapping each other on the back. They were happy as hell. The food got a lot better that day.[18]

For the next 3 weeks, the ODA directed multiple airstrikes against the Taliban, softening their positions.[19]

Such tactics, as well as discussions between NA leaders and local Taliban commanders, were repeated several times up and down the lines before the final assault. Still, the negotiations and planning for the attack took time and the impression that the offensive was stalled worried some senior American political and military officials. Lieutenant General Dan K. McNeill, the commander of the XVIII Airborne Corps in 2001, recalled that in early November the general anxiety within the DOD and Bush administration generated pressure on CENTCOM to get the NA moving again. Eventually, General Franks directed McNeill to prepare plans for an airborne operation that would drop American paratroopers near Kabul or elsewhere to draw Taliban troops away from the front lines north of the capital, thus allowing the NA to approach the city.[20]

Despite the concerns inside the Coalition command, the much-anticipated NA attack began on 13 November, with the forces under Fahim and Bismullah moving forward, ahead of schedule, to attack the Taliban defenses. The enemy resistance rapidly fell apart, clearing the way through the Shomali Plains all the way to the capital. This sudden success caught Coalition leaders by surprise, and they became concerned that the sudden conquest of the capital by the NA would threaten Pashtun leaders and scuttle any chances to create a new, stable, multiethnic government in Afghanistan. Indeed, around the time of the NA offensive, Pakistani President Pervez Musharraf communicated his interest in the proper treatment of Pashtun interests in any post-Taliban state, and Coalition leaders hoped to allay the concerns of this critical ally.[21] Regardless of political desires in Washington, DC, and Islamabad, Pakistan, the NA found no reason to wait for negotiations once Taliban forces disintegrated and widespread disorder erupted in the capital. On 14 November 2001 the troops of General Fahim Khan rolled into Kabul and liberated the city from 5 years of despotic rule by the Taliban.[22]

The ODAs Go to Work in the South

To win over the Pashtuns in the south and begin operations against the Taliban, the Coalition planned to insert two ODAs near the city of Kandahar. Major Donald Bolduc was a member of Special Operations Command and Control Element (SOCCE) 52, which had tactical control of the two ODAs. Bolduc explained the mission:

Basically from November 2001 until complete, we were to provide C2 [command and control] and conduct unconventional warfare in order to advise and assist Hamid Karzai and Gul Sherzai in organizing anti-Taliban forces, which was what they were called at that time, and to conduct combat operations against the Taliban and al-Qaeda forces.[23]

Bolduc further described the key tasks that the ODAs had to accomplish with their Afghan partners:

> We were to secure Kandahar City, develop a plan to stabilize Kandahar City, and operate from a secure base, and then concentrically improve that security from Kandahar City, which was considered the cultural and religious center of gravity, out to other provinces in the south, and then, on order, exfiltrate the operational area.[24]

Coalition leaders also understood that they could not simply leave the area once Kandahar was out of the Taliban grip, but had to set conditions for the next phase of the campaign. Major Bolduc asserted that the end state for the ODAs was the creation of "a stable, safe, and secure Kandahar City ready to transition to more formalized humanitarian assistance and nation-building operations."[25] This objective was ambitious, especially considering the small Coalition presence, which in November 2001 consisted of the 27 Soldiers of the two ODAs and SOCCE 52.[26]

Hamid Karzai would have to play a key role if the effort in the south was to have any serious chance. In early October 2001 Karzai decided that the time was right for his return to Afghanistan. On either 8 or 9 October, he and three colleagues riding on two motorcycles crossed the Pakistan border to enter Afghanistan. Before Karzai departed, several of his friends warned him that Taliban forces heavily patrolled the border areas and that an attempt to get through in such a manner was very risky. Undeterred, Karzai and his friends made it through and proceeded to Shorandam, a small village close to Kandahar. There he began recruiting fighters to help him overthrow the Taliban.[27]

Karzai was not entering an Afghanistan that was entirely hostile to his cause. During the previous 5 years, Karzai and his allies had been busy making contacts among other Pashtuns in and outside of Afghanistan who wanted to overthrow the Taliban. Many of these contacts were former mujahideen who had known Karzai in the 1980s. He thus had an extensive network of friends, acquaintances, and anti-Taliban sympathizers with whom he could begin work on his return. Still, there was a great deal to do to transform these contacts into an armed resistance.[28]

In early November 2001, after spending several weeks talking to the people in the areas around Kandahar, Karzai believed that the population was prepared for political change. He also came to the realization that he would need Coalition support to force the Taliban out of power. Karzai recalled that he used a satellite phone and "called Rome and I called Islamabad and I told the [US] Embassy there and the consulate that I needed help. They said, 'Where are you?' I said, 'I'm in this area.'... Then they came and helped, dropped parachutes." To his followers' amazement, the American planes dropped bundles containing not only weapons and ammunition, but also food and other supplies. The aid could not have been more timely. On the following day, Karzai and his followers, now numbering about 150 men, were attacked by about 500 Taliban troops. That attack was successfully repulsed with the aid of the US-supplied weapons.[29]

While the food, weapons, and other supplies were a huge boost to Karzai's band, some in his following realized that it was not enough. After a number of days of wandering in the

Hamid Karzai and His Satellite Phone

The members of ODA 574 who worked closely with Afghan opposition group leader Hamid Karzai learned that he was not a typical military leader. Karzai's charisma and knowledge of Afghanistan made him a natural choice to lead the anti-Taliban resistance. While Karzai had no formal military training, he did use one unconventional weapon with devastating effectiveness—the satellite phone.

Upon his return to Afghanistan in early October 2001, Karzai quickly realized that he did not have the required resources to take on the Taliban. So, to use Karzai's own words, he "called the United States." Karzai's phone calls to the US (actually, the US Embassy in Rome and the US consulate in Islamabad) started a flood of aid, supplies, and weaponry to this most prominent Pashtun anti-Taliban leader. Eventually, ODA 574 was inserted to provide Karzai military advice and to train his growing band of men. But Karzai also used his "sat phone" for intelligence, diplomacy, and interviews.

ODA 574 team member Captain Jason Amerine, the ODA leader, stated, "The biggest tool in his intelligence network was the [satellite] telephone. He had them spread all over the province with key trusted leaders. So he was able to get word right away of anything going on. . . . He worked the phones constantly. . . . It was something. He'd get phone calls like that all the time. Whenever the phone rang, all of us were kind of wondering who's calling next. Maybe it was the BBC or maybe it was another senior Taliban leader trying to surrender. The satellite telephone was his greatest weapon. Arguably, it was our greatest weapon in the war, especially in the Pashtun tribal belt."

Karzai also addressed the Bonn Conference via his trusty cell phone, and did numerous TV and print interviews—all the while trying to raise an anti-Taliban force and gather intelligence. The emerging Afghan leader had to do a lot of different tasks that would normally be farmed out to subordinate staff officers which Karzai did not have. Lieutenant Colonel David Fox asserted that Karzai handled the majority of the personnel, intelligence, operations, and logistics tasks that kept his small anti-Taliban group going in the fall of 2001. Fox recalled that Karzai was "doing everything, and I don't know [how] he did it. He was giving interviews, speeches, working with his commanders, working with the Americans. He was working on about three or four hours sleep a night. He would get up fresh in the mornings and begin, ready to start the day again."

Hamid Karzai, "Interview with President Hamid Karzai,"
PBS Frontline (7 May 2002).

Captain Jason Amerine, "The Battle of Tarin Kowt,"
PBS Frontline (12 July 2002).

Lieutenant Colonel David Fox, "Interview: Lt. Col. David Fox,"
PBS Frontline (no date given).

mountains trying to avoid contact with the Taliban, some of his men came to him and, as Karzai remembered, told him, "Hamid, life is difficult. The Taliban will come and get us one day. . . . Look, we must ask for American help." Karzai relented, picked up the phone, and made another call to the Americans to ask for SF support. He remembered that he was told by someone at the embassy, "Fine, we can do that." The effort to get help from America was "Easy. Quite easy," he recalled.[30]

Karzai was instructed to mark a helicopter landing zone (HLZ) with small fires and wait for an ODA that would arrive at the site at a specific time. Karzai remembered, "We lit the fires and they just came—very easy, exactly on the minute that they told . . . they would be there, on the very minute. Our people couldn't believe it."[31]

Arrival of ODA 574

ODA 574 arrived in southern Afganistan to link up with Hamid Karzai and his band of Pashtun fighters. According to Captain Jason Amerine, the ODA leader, the team's mission was to "infiltrate the Oruzgan province, link up with Hamid Karzai and his Pashtun fighters, and advise and assist his forces in order to destabilize and eliminate the Taliban regime there."[32] Amerine and his team immediately evaluated the situation in terms of men, intelligence, supplies, and the enemy.

On his arrival, Amerine quickly sat down with Karzai to establish a relationship with him and understand the situation as Karzai comprehended it. During the course of the initial meeting, Karzai told the American officer that the key to winning Kandahar as well as Oruzgan province was to capture the town of Tarin Kowt, located to the north of Kandahar. Amerine explained:

> Hamid Karzai described Tarin Kowt as the heart of the Taliban movement. He said that all the major leaders of the Taliban movement had families in and around Tarin Kowt. Mullah Omar was from Deh Rawod, which was just to

Figure 13. Karzai with ODA 574.

DOD Photo

the west of Tarin Kowt. So the seizure of Tarin Kowt would represent such a psychological victory for us. He believed that, by taking Tarin Kowt, all of the Pashtun villagers would essentially surrender at that point, or turn completely to our cause.[33]

Amerine then gathered his team, pulled out some maps, and developed a strategy to take Tarin Kowt. That plan amounted to a siege. Karzai's forces along with their SF advisors would close off the mountain passes leading into the town. Karzai had reasoned that once that was accomplished, the town would simply surrender. Additionally, he informed Amerine that there were already friendly fighters in Tarin Kowt who would foment an uprising if necessary. Given the small numbers of troops that were available—the 12-man ODA and the 150 Afghan fighters in Karzai's band—Amerine told Karzai that they would have to create a larger force.[34]

Bringing in more weapons and ammunition, Karzai and the ODA began building a volunteer militia. Hundreds of people arrived to try and get weapons, but most were only interested in protecting their own homes and villages. With the recruiting effort just starting, news arrived on 16 November that stunned both Karzai and his newly arrived American comrades: the people in Tarin Kowt had already seized the town and wanted help.[35] If Karzai was correct, the Taliban would have to quickly and forcefully restore their control of the town.[36]

The Taking of Tarin Kowt

The news of the uprising presented Amerine and Karzai with a dilemma. If they moved into Tarin Kowt and the Taliban launched a counterattack, Karzai's forces were too small to defend the town. It was doubtful that enough reliable and capable volunteers could be recruited to make much difference before the Taliban would likely begin such an assault. Still, Amerine knew he had the trump card of American air power on his side. It was a difficult choice, but Amerine and ODA 574 decided to support Karzai's insistence that they go immediately to Tarin Kowt and take advantage of the military—and political—opportunity.[37]

Piling into a motley collection of beat-up trucks and other vehicles sent by village elders, the ODA and their Afghan partners bounced along the mountain roads to the village. En route, Karzai worried that the population of Tarin Kowt might be angry that American Soldiers had accompanied his force to the town. His fears were quickly allayed though when the people warmly welcomed the Soldiers.[38]

Once in the village, Karzai left military matters to ODA 574. He stayed busy getting in touch with other Pashtun leaders in the area, constantly recruiting fighters, supporters, and, conversely, undermining the Taliban's rule. Many of the area's most important people came to speak with him. From them he learned where al-Qaeda elements were located. He also discovered that many of the Islamic clerics in the region were supportive of his actions. Early that evening, other informants brought him the news that he had been expecting: a large force of Taliban were en route to Tarin Kowt.[39]

Karzai quickly requested that Amerine meet him and his local supporters to explain the situation. The Afghan leaders proceeded to matter-of-factly mention that hundreds of Taliban troops were approaching the town and that the enemy force, mounted on a large number of trucks, would probably arrive "in the next day or two." Amerine remembered, "It took me a second to digest it. At that point, I said, 'Well, it was nice meeting all of you. I think we need to organize a force now and do what we can to defend this town.'"[40]

The captain attempted to excuse himself so that he could start getting things ready to oppose the threat. His Afghan hosts, however, would not hear of it. Since it was the first day of Ramadan, they insisted that he stay, drink tea, eat, and talk. Sensing that he could not embarrass his hosts, Amerine stayed just long enough to satisfy their request, then quickly made his exit, but not before asking Karzai to send every fighter he could find to the ODA's headquarters as soon as possible.[41]

Returning to his men, Amerine pulled them together and told them about the impending arrival of the Taliban forces, stating, "Well they're coming from Kandahar. We know it's a large

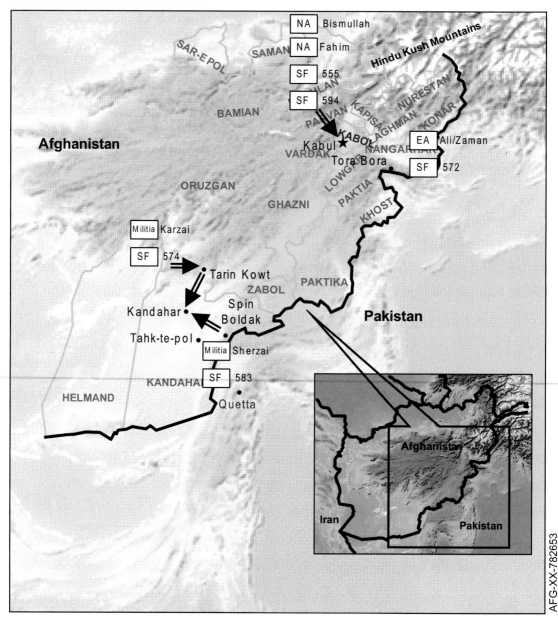

Figure 14. ODA and anti-Taliban operations, south and east, October–December 2001.

convoy." The captain then ordered a number of actions. His communications sergeant began contacting the team's SOCCE to inform their headquarters about the imminent assault. The team's Air Force enlisted terminal attack controller (ETAC) passed warning orders through those channels to let the Air Force and Navy know that their CAS services would soon be required at Tarin Kowt. Amerine's team worked into the night to arm all the new Afghan fighters that showed up and develop a plan to hold the town.[42]

Amerine had a limited force at his disposal: the 12 men of ODA 574 and only several dozen of Karzai's Afghan fighters.[43] Sometime around midnight, Amerine moved with this group to the outskirts of the village. There he spotted a plateau from which the team could direct airstrikes onto the vehicular approaches to Tarin Kowt. In addition, from the plateau the team could observe the main road as it came through a pass at the south end of the valley. That road led to Kandahar and was one of two axes of advance that the approaching Taliban forces could use to attack Tarin Kowt. Amerine surmised that the Taliban would arrive on this road. He guessed correctly.[44]

Early on the morning of 17 November, Amerine received an intelligence report from F-18 Navy jet fighters that "a convoy of 8 to 10 vehicles" was heading north on the Kandahar–Tarin Kowt road.[45] Amerine explained what happened next:

> So my combat controller looked at me and said, "OK, well, this is what we see." At that point, we hadn't fired a shot in the war, really; that was sort of the commencement of actual fighting for us. The whole team was in a small room. There really was kind of a moment of silence. A lot of the men had been to war. It wasn't that the experience was that new to a lot of the people on the team. But at the same time, it was the first shot of the war for us. . . . I'd hoped to say something a little bit more eloquently, but I just said, "Well, smoke 'em."[46]

After the tense buildup, the first bomb missed the target. The second one did not.[47] Using a laser designator, the team's ETAC directed a storm of bombs onto the Taliban convoy causing significant destruction and confusion. As the pilots continued their work and the Taliban struggled to avoid the bombardment, the situation began to look like Karzai and ODA 574 had won a tremendous victory.

Then something inexplicable happened that Amerine described as feeling like "we were seizing defeat from the jaws of victory."[48] Karzai's men panicked. The lack of training among these militiamen demonstrated itself with graphic clarity when the Afghan fighters decided for some reason that the battle was not going well and their best option at that point was to withdraw to Tarin Kowt. To make matters worse, Karzai was not present at the battle area, and the men of ODA 574 could not communicate with the panic-stricken Afghan tribesmen.[49] The Afghans hopped into the vehicles and were only prevented from driving off immediately by the members of ODA 574 who literally stepped in front of the vehicles to get them to stop. If the trucks left, the Americans had no way to get back to Tarin Kowt. Amerine later dryly observed that in a future situation like this, the ODA team needed to make sure they kept the truck and car keys before deploying for a fight.[50] Reluctantly, the troops of ODA 574 jumped aboard the trucks and went with their charges back to the village.

With the Taliban still continuing its advance, ODA 574 and Karzai had to turn the situation around. Back at Tarin Kowt the team met with Karzai and after a quick consultation, ODA 574 sped south of town again to find another spot to establish a final defensive position. After urging Karzai to speed as many Afghan fighters as he could to them, ODA 574 found a new site from which to observe Taliban vehicles, and the air attack on the enemy convoy began anew.[51]

With the renewal of the attacks on the Taliban, ODA 574 ran into a new and wholly unexpected problem: many civilians from Tarin Kowt had begun arriving on the outskirts of the town to watch the battle. The ODA team had not expected to have to deal with this type of situation. Captain Amerine called it a "circus atmosphere" where Afghan children attempted to rummage through their equipment and older civilians meandered around the defensive position. One member of ODA 574 pleaded with an English-speaking Afghan to at least send the children back to Tarin Kowt because of the danger of the situation.[52] Thankfully none of the townspeople was injured as the pace of the attacks on the Taliban convoy increased.

Initially, the leading trucks were targeted to slow the convoy down. When those vehicles were destroyed, the Coalition aircraft simply began working their way back through the convoy which was now very spread out. Sometime after 0800, another unexpected surprise struck the ODA. Two of the Taliban trucks had found an alternate route into Tarin Kowt and dismounted 10 to 20 fighters at the edge of town. The American troops began to hear small arms fire to their flank, which indicated the enemy was close by. The mounting gunfire caused Amerine to think perhaps the battle was lost. Unbeknownst to him, a number of villagers had moved to the threatened area and fought off the Taliban intruders. That action actually signaled the end of the battle. For the next 2 hours, the remnants of the convoy took hit after hit from CAS sorties as the Taliban tried to make their way back to Kandahar.[53]

One final obstacle emerged the evening after the battle and caused Karzai great concern. One of the local mullahs called on Karzai to speak with him. He was deeply concerned that the mullah, who would speak for the others, was going to tell him that the Taliban attacked because there were Americans in Tarin Kowt and that Karzai and the others must leave. If this belief was communicated, Karzai believed that the people in the region would also turn against his liberation efforts. His fears were thankfully dashed when the mullah instead told him, "If the Americans hadn't been here, we would have all been killed."[54] That statement was an indication that the military victory had also become a political success.

ODA 574 and Hamid Karzai's small force, assisted greatly by Coalition air support, had clearly triumphed over the Taliban at Tarin Kowt. Colonel John Mulholland, commander of JSOTF-N, later viewed the engagement at Tarin Kowt as "pivotal for the [entire operation in the] south."[55] Furthermore, Mulholland argued that the Taliban recognized the potential threat posed by Karzai to their legitimacy in the region and made a strong effort to force Karzai's group out of Tarin Kowt. According to Mulholland, when that attack failed, the Taliban grew greatly concerned about their hold on the southern area of Afghanistan.[56]

This belief seemed borne out by the success Hamid Karzai enjoyed in rallying other Pashtuns to his cause. Captain Amerine not only witnessed firsthand the destruction of the Taliban forces, he also saw the reaction of other Pashtun Afghans to Karzai. He realized the tremendous psychological and political importance the victory had, and its resultant impact on the enemy.[57] Karzai's tireless work in securing political support from the various groups in the Tarin Kowt area—and elsewhere as it would turn out—made ODA 574's future tasks less difficult. Amerine explained:

With the religious mullahs on our side, we were really in psychologically with the Pashtun tribes. Rapport had been established, trust had been gained, and now we could get on with fighting. Now we can become task-focused on "Let's get to Kandahar, and let's end this war." So in that regard, it was just psychologically a crushing victory for us. Hamid would later tell me that, in his eyes, that fight broke the back of the Taliban.[58]

Karzai later remarked that the battle was "a turning point. . . . I recognized there [was] a much wider legitimacy thing than I perceived we had. We actually underestimated the whole thing all along, the impact that this movement of ours had, the legitimacy that there was. This was our miscalculation—which is good."[59]

Karzai deserves more credit than he is given as a military leader. This is not to suggest that Karzai understood the intricacies of military tactics or operational art. However, Karzai's influence in winning the support of the population around Tarin Kowt, and later, much of the Pashtun population in and around Kandahar, clearly magnified the power of his small force. Karzai's clear and correct assessment of Tarin Kowt as the enemy center of gravity was borne out by succeeding events. Understanding his limitations, Karzai did not interfere with ODA 574's ability to conduct the battle against the Taliban convoy at Tarin Kowt. Conversely, his clear appreciation for the political situation—something the ODA team lacked—helped make Tarin Kowt a key victory in the fight to evict the Taliban from Afghanistan.

The battle of Tarin Kowt was clearly an instance where the plan to use an ODA team in conjunction with US air power to collaborate with an indigenous element worked almost flawlessly. The elements fit together seamlessly: SF working with indigenous troops, CAS, and a politically savvy tribal leader moving together toward a common goal. This was a textbook example of how a small, well-trained force could employ unconventional warfare for a superlative result.

Although the victory at Tarin Kowt had the Taliban reeling, they were by no means defeated. ODA 574 and Karzai's force were strategically positioned to move on Kandahar from the north, but the group still had too little combat power to take the city by itself. More indigenous support was needed and the effort to mobilize just such support was already underway.

ODA 583 and Gul Agha Sherzai

Following the victory at Tarin Kowt, planners at JSOTF-N wanted to maintain the positive momentum against the Taliban. To do this, they focused on identifying another Pashtun leader in the area south of Kandahar that might enable the next phase in the campaign in the south. Gul Agha Sherzai appeared to be the most promising candidate. Shortly after the Battle of Tarin Kowt, ODA 583 was sent to the Shahbaz Air Base near the Pakistani town of Jacobabad to prepare for its mission inside Afghanistan. The ODA leader, Captain Smith, had been informed that Sherzai was a fairly insignificant Pashtun figure, but because the United States needed more Pashtuns to take up arms against the Taliban in the south, no one at JSOTF-N or CENTCOM wanted to ignore any political figures that could become rallying points.[60] It later became clear to Smith that the information on Sherzai he received was largely incorrect and incomplete. Smith described his intelligence briefing in the following way:

> The initial report on Sherzai was horrible. I received a PowerPoint slide with an old picture of him that stated something to the effect that he was the son of a famous [mujahideen] who fought the Soviets and was the former Governor of Kandahar. At the top of the slide, the name Karzai had been scratched out in pen and Sherzai written in. It was quite a classy piece of intel that I wished I had kept to demonstrate how little we knew.[61]

Fortunately, prior to ODA 583's infiltration, Smith was able to acquire more accurate intelligence on Sherzai from an American intelligence official who would accompany the team on the mission.[62]

The benefits of enlisting Sherzai seemed obvious. Another anti-Taliban Pashtun group operating south of Kandahar could force the Taliban to spread their already rapidly dwindling resources more widely.[63] But the United States understood that Sherzai did not have the same national level influence in Afghanistan as Karzai. Nevertheless, the United States needed leaders at various levels of influence and from different ethnic groups to fight the Taliban. To US leaders, Karzai was a well-educated man who spoke English fluently and exhibited a great deal of political sophistication. He thus presented himself as a potential leader at the national level. Sherzai, on the other hand, did not speak English and had at best, a regional power base. Still, Sherzai offered a way of mobilizing more popular Pashtun support. As Smith later explained, Sherzai looked like a typical Afghan warlord, but "he was our warlord and seemed to fit our purposes as to getting after the Taliban and [al-Qaeda]."[64]

On 18 November, the day after the battle of Tarin Kowt, Smith, along with two other members of ODA 583 slipped into Afghanistan onboard an MH 53 "Pave Low" helicopter and landed in the Shin Naray Valley south of Kandahar just before midnight. There to greet him was Sherzai himself and 10 or so of his men. Led to a "small mud-walled hut," Smith and Sherzai began talking about future cooperation. Not surprisingly, Sherzai asked Smith for supplies, weapons, and ammunition, among other things. Smith delayed answering until he could better assess the potential of Sherzai and his forces.[65]

The following morning, Smith and his colleagues set out to review Sherzai's troops. The team judged Sherzai's Afghans to be between 650 and 800 men, clearly a much larger force than Karzai's group. However, to Smith, these soldiers looked more like an armed mob than a military organization:

> Sherzai's forces were lightly armed with a mix of small arms. Ammo was generally scarce. There were some light mortars and heavy machineguns that were inoperable. Uniforms were nonexistent and were a mix of local Pashtun garb. Vehicles were four-door Toyota pick-up trucks, tractors, a few sedans and motorcycles, and several large trucks. The force was organized (or unorganized) with numerous commanders of varying loyalty and men under their command.[66]

Sherzai, however, asserted that he could recruit 500 more fighters if needed. That was enough to convince Smith to request the insertion of the rest of his team, and the remainder of ODA 583 joined Sherzai's band on the evening of 21 November to start the offensive northward to capture Kandahar.[67] The United States had now become partners with two anti-Taliban Pashtun leaders, and both fixed their sights on capturing Kandahar, arguably the most important political center of gravity in the south.

Smith's plan to advance north centered on the main avenue of approach from the Afghan–Pakistan border, Highway 4. ODA 583 recommended an operation that advocated a westward movement through the Shin Naray Valley to the town of Tahk-te-pol with the eventual goal of blocking Highway 4 to cut the Taliban supply line into Pakistan. After capturing Tahk-te-pol, Smith then proposed a bold movement north to seize the Kandahar Airport, the key to the city. Sherzai generally approved of the plan, but he suggested that the combined force mask its approach to the Taliban garrison stationed in Tahk-te-pol by using a neighboring mountain range as a shield, then surprising the garrison by coming in behind it—from the north. Smith agreed to the change and on 22 November the combined Afghan and US force, 800 strong, piled into a collection of about 100 vehicles and began the trek to Tahk-te-pol.[68]

Arriving at a point about 5 miles from the town late on 23 November, the force stopped to ponder the next move. Sherzai and Smith agreed to initially try to negotiate for the surrender of Tahk-te-pol, thus capturing it without bloodshed. However, to make sure his force was protected and ready to fight if necessary, Sherzai deployed about half of it on a low ridge east of the town. The rest of his troops remained at the initial position while Sherzai sent a delegation to parlay for the surrender.[69]

On receiving Sherzai's negotiators, the Taliban leaders in the area agreed to talks, but in the meantime attempted to send troops to surround and destroy Sherzai's force. This ploy resulted in a 2-hour firefight between the two forces. ODA 583 ordered Sherzai's men to fall back to a stronger position and directed airstrikes against the Taliban. A Spectre AC-130 gunship arrived overhead and destroyed six Taliban trucks. The consensus among the Afghans and Americans was that the Taliban would attempt to wipe out Sherzai's force in the morning. Much to everyone's surprise and relief, the Taliban had abandoned Tahk-te-pol overnight and on the following day, 24 November, Sherzai's Afghans and ODA 583 entered the town. The capture of Tahk-te-pol meant that Taliban supplies from Pakistan traveling north on Highway 4 were effectively cut off, but it did not mean that Kandahar would immediately fall into the hands of anti-Taliban forces. Before Kandahar could be subdued, Sherzai's forces and ODA 583 needed to capture the bridge spanning the Arghastan Wadi, the dried-up river bed that was a major obstacle between their position and the city. Once the bridge was secure, the combined force could move on to the Kandahar Airport.[70]

At this point, Sherzai seemed reluctant to continue his move north. His American advisors encouraged him to go on with the advance, although they also recommended that Sherzai send out robust detachments north and south of Tahk-te-pol to warn of any advancing Taliban force.[71] On 25 November, as Sherzai's main element moved northward toward Kandahar, the Afghan commander of the southern reconnaissance detachment reported the capture of a truckload of Arab al-Qaeda fighters.[72] This commander then told Smith that enemy forces were moving up from Spin Boldak north toward Kandahar and that the ODA needed to take action against them.[73]

While concerns grew about Taliban reinforcements moving into the area, Sherzai's main force approached the bridge at Arghastan Wadi on 25 November and seized it. The force then continued to move north and approached the entrance to the Kandahar Airport. There they met fierce resistance and guessed that they were facing well-trained al-Qaeda terrorists. The heavy fighting forced Smith and Sherzai's forces back to the bridge. Sherzai decided to move his force back to Tahk-te-pol that evening, while Smith opted to place his ODA on a ridge to the south, which commanded the bridge.[74]

For the next week, the ODA's Tactical Air Control Party (TACP) working around the clock called in airstrikes against the al-Qaeda and Taliban forces in and around the Wadi and the Kandahar Airport. Enemy casualties were undoubtedly high, while the United States did not lose a single aircraft to hostile fire.[75] Despite the casualties, the enemy held Sherzai in check and the advance stopped.

Karzai's Offensive Renewed

While Sherzai's advance ground to a halt, Hamid Karzai's force to the north of Kandahar continued to find success. Karzai and the men of ODA 574 had little time to bask in their victory over the Taliban at Tarin Kowt. Shortly after the battle, Karzai and ODA 574 were joined by a more senior and experienced American officer, Lieutenant Colonel David Fox, and four other SF Soldiers. Fox, the commander of 2d Battalion, 5th Special Forces Group (SFG), linked up with Karzai early in the morning of 28 November.[76] While the US element with Karzai grew by four with Fox's arrival, Afghans were coming more frequently and in larger numbers to pledge their loyalty to Karzai. So many young Pashtuns arrived that Karzai urged the ODA to move south toward Kandahar because the newcomers were young men who, according to Amerine, were starting to get "rowdy."[77] Karzai and his advisors decided to keep the force fairly small, and resumed the advance toward Kandahar without the bulk of the newcomers.[78]

The drive south from Tarin Kowt was memorable for Fox and the rest of ODA 574. As the motley group moved south over the bumpy roads, individual trucks and cars continually raced up on the berm to see Karzai in person.[79] The whole process seemed surreal, but no one was hurt by these enthusiastic maneuvers, nor was the convoy attacked by the Taliban during the trek south toward Kandahar. For Major Donald Bolduc, the leader of SOCCE 52 who was now with ODA 574, the experience proved exasperating:

> It was crazy because [the Afghans] didn't understand convoy operations. They were turning around and driving back and forth passing each other. So, on our first stop, I said, "Hey, sir. We have to get control of this. Here is my recom-mendation." So we got the ODA . . . and Karzai together and we told Karzai to tell everybody that they could not pass a certain vehicle. So we organized it so we had organization and control of the recon element and the main body and then behind that was everything else.[80]

Eventually the group arrived at the village of Shawali Kowt where Karzai's force finally encountered a sizable Taliban element.[81]

The Arghendab Bridge near the village of Sayd Alim Kalay had to be captured to eradi-cate the last significant Taliban presence north of Kandahar. Rooting the Taliban out proved tougher than expected. At one point, Karzai informed Lieutenant Colonel Fox that the Taliban was on the way to attack the combined US-Afghan anti-Taliban force. Then Karzai and his men suddenly left, leaving the ODA to defend the north side of the Arghendab Bridge and a ridgeline just beyond the bridge.[82] Fox did not want to abandon the position as he did not like the idea of having "to fight over the same ground again" and thus refused to yield, calling in repeated airstrikes against the Taliban forces on the south bank of the riverbed and the high ground beyond.[83] By directing airstrikes, ODA 574 kept the enemy at bay.[84] The following day, 4 December, Karzai and the bulk of the troops returned to ODA 574.[85] After a sharp firefight, Taliban forces abandoned their positions across the river.[86] The military campaign to liberate

Kandahar continued, but Hamid Karzai was soon forced to focus on larger concerns that would play a major role in the overall US strategy to topple the Taliban.

The New Afghan Leader

While the campaign to evict the Taliban from Kandahar continued from both north and south of the city, political events outside of Afghanistan were moving quickly. On 14 November 2001 the United Nations (UN) had passed a resolution that endorsed a conference of Afghan groups to move the country in a new political direction. As described in a later chapter, that conference convened in Bonn, Germany, in late November and by early December had approved a new Afghan Interim Authority (AIA). However, as December began, the conference still needed to find a leader who could guide Afghanistan on its new political path.

Although ODA 574 did not have an intimate knowledge of what was happening in Germany, many senior Coalition officers knew about the conference and its implications for the Coalition campaign. Colonel Mulholland, JSOTF-N commander, recalled that he and his staff "were very aware of the Bonn Conference and [what was] going on there. I was requesting and receiving updates on what was happening politically when they were available. . . . It was really a political battle every bit as much as a military one."[87] This reality was underlined by the fact that in the midst of the Kandahar campaign, Karzai was unexpectedly asked to speak to the conference via satellite phone. By this point, it was clear that he was under consideration for a senior position in the new Afghan Government.

According to Karzai, his address to the conference was anything but an auspicious moment. He had a cold and sat in an unheated room among a number of fellow Afghans.[88] Karzai had no prepared remarks so he made a few spontaneous comments about the challenge and necessity of putting aside differences and working for the benefit of the nation as a whole.[89] Despite the lack of a written speech and inspiring surroundings, the conference nominated him to be the chairman of a governing committee that would take the reins of power if and when the Taliban regime was toppled. On 22 December 2001 Karzai would formally accept that position.

Karzai's tremendous potential as a leader of the anti-Taliban opposition made him a natural target for Taliban assassins. Considering what had happened to Ahmad Shah Massoud and other anti-Taliban leaders, Karzai's assassination was not a farfetched possibility. Indeed, Captain Amerine, the commander of ODA 574, possessed intelligence that Karzai was the target of Taliban assassination squads. Considering his new status as the nominated leader of the AIA, the men of ODA 574 now had an additional burden: the personal security of Hamid Karzai. Karzai had Afghan bodyguards, but they were not professionally trained, which forced ODA 574 to ensure they protected the Afghan leader properly. Amerine remembered that on many mornings when he arrived to meet with Karzai, he found a number of bodyguards asleep.[90] Karzai had by mid-November become a very well-known figure that many Afghans wanted to see or talk to in person. The new AIA president was also deluged with media requests for interviews. This kind of exposure, so necessary for Karzai to increase his political influence, also made him a highly visible and thus vulnerable target.

Ironically, it was not Taliban assassins that gave Hamid Karzai his closest brush with death. On the morning of 5 December—the same day that Karzai learned of his selection by the Bonn Conference—at least six of Karzai's group and two members of ODA 574 were killed by a Joint Direct Attack Munition (JDAM) bomb dropped from a B-52 bomber.[91] After advancing over the Arghendab Bridge, Lieutenant Colonel Fox and Captain Amerine received intelligence regarding a small Taliban force in a nearby cave. To remove any threat posed by this force, the ODA's TACP called in an airstrike.[92] A hand-held Viper laser target designator system carried by one of the TACP's members transmitted the target's Global Positioning System (GPS) coordinates to a B-52 overhead, which then dropped the JDAM. Instead of hitting the target, however, the JDAM landed on the Viper laser designator, very close to Karzai and ODA 574's position.[93] Karzai initially thought that the building he occupied had been hit by al-Qaeda with some type of high-powered explosive.[94] Sadly, that was not the case.

Inexperience and technical issues led to the tragedy. There were two new TACP members on duty and, according to Fox, the most experienced operator was sleeping after a long shift.[95] The less experienced airman had been responsible for directing the Viper designator at the Taliban in the cave, but in the process the batteries in the device died. The airman quickly replaced the batteries. However, apparently unknown to the TACP airmen, when new batteries were inserted into the Viper, the system automatically zeroed out all data and transmitted its own GPS coordinates as a self-test operation.[96] Fox explained what happened next:

> So the navigator asks the TACP to confirm the grid coordinates and he reads the grid coordinates, but when you are only talking 1,000 meters from the target and you are using geo[graphic] coordinates you are talking one second off. So the navigator asks him to confirm and he confirms, which are the coordinates to the Viper, which is 30 feet from my position, and he launches the JDAM. The aircraft was at 25,000 feet. I'm not sure how long it takes for that JDAM to impact, but it lands right on top of the Viper.[97]

The resulting explosion killed or mortally wounded three ODA members and wounded every other member of the team. It also wounded 65 Afghan militiamen and even Karzai was struck in the face by a shard of glass.[98]

The strike was devastating. Still, the surviving ODA members, although wounded, sprang into action to get medical treatment for those hurt by the blast.[99] Major Bolduc suffered a dislocated hip in the blast, but he immediately popped it back in place and focused on assisting the casualties.[100] Coalition aircraft evacuated all the wounded, including the Afghans.

Hamid Karzai, incidentally, refused evacuation because he anticipated a breakthrough in the talks concerning Kandahar. His intuition was correct and the situation developed very quickly soon after the JDAM hit. By noon, Karzai was talking by telephone to Taliban authorities in Kandahar, and they were signaling interest in negotiating the surrender of Kandahar. Developments south of Kandahar had forced the Taliban's hand.

Culmination South of Kandahar

In the south, ODA 583 and Sherzai's opposition group had progressed to the Arghastan Bridge near the Kandahar Airport when the offensive stalled on 25 November in the face of significant al-Qaeda and Taliban resistance.[101] Having been driven back to the high ground south of the wadi, ODA 583 and part of Sherzai's force spent the next week calling in airstrikes against enemy positions at the airport and around the bridge.

The position at the bridge was a natural strongpoint and was easily defended. Captain Smith, the commander of the ODA, remembered,

There wasn't a fixed line per se, just guys in and around the bridge and dry canal structures. . . . The problem was, there were so many natural fighting positions around there that developing a formal defensive line was unnecessary. The canals and [wadis] in the area were really maze-like and lended to a natural web or elastic defense.[102]

Sherzai's forces repelled a Taliban attack on their position south of the Arghastan Bridge and on 2 December, they moved across the bridge and took up positions in front of both Taliban and al-Qaeda units who mounted a tenacious defense using the rugged terrain to conceal themselves from ODA 583 and Sherzai's men as they regrouped. This might have worked had US aerial reconnaissance not detected the concentration of troops on Sherzai's left flank. Sherzai ordered an assault on the Taliban forces in this area early on 4 December. His men overwhelmed the defenders and Sherzai aggressively urged his men to continue the pursuit and capture the Kandahar Airport. This proved to be premature as Sherzai's forces were repulsed by heavy Taliban and al-Qaeda gunfire and artillery support. US airstrikes called in by the attached TACP blunted a follow-on Taliban counterattack and retained the Arghastan Bridge for Sherzai, but not before his forces had taken significant casualties.[103]

While Sherzai's northern advance stalled, his southern outposts were hit by the Taliban near the town of Spin Boldak. The half-hearted Taliban assault consisted mainly of mortar and rocket attacks on one of the main positions in the vicinity of that town. Sherzai's commander in the south had continued to report the build-up of enemy forces toward Spin Boldak and forced Captain Smith to split ODA 583 into three four-man elements. Smith now sent one of the teams to assess the reported enemy movements to the south. There, the element encountered a "real target-rich environment" along Highway 4 just as the Afghan commander had described.[104] The SF element went to work bringing Coalition CAS down on the enemy concentration. Eventually, Captain Smith went down to the area to assess the situation and recalled seeing "a lot of burning vehicles."[105]

The strikes blunted the southern attacks, but Sherzai's troops found Taliban personnel huddling under a bridge to escape the air assault. The TACP directed another attack on the troops there, eliminating a significant majority of the enemy force. After the battle, Smith inspected the remains of the enemy force and concluded that they were al-Qaeda rather than Taliban, recalling, "a lot of bodies in nice camo[uflage] uniforms lying around and other AQ indicators."[106]

The Fall of Kandahar

With the south seemingly secure and the Arghastan Bridge under his control, Sherzai could turn his full attention toward the Taliban forces defending Kandahar.[107] Instead of a dramatic battle to wrest Kandahar from the Taliban, however, the city was to ultimately fall without a fight. Earlier, the ODA 583 commander, Captain Smith, had been ordered by Colonel Mulholland to prevent Sherzai and his command from entering Kandahar. Historically, Karzai and Sherzai had not always gotten along and there was a great risk of fighting between the forces of those two men should they bump into each other in the city. In addition, Smith's and Sherzai's troops had been struggling for over a week to try and seize the airport. Smith badly wanted that prize and so attempted to convince Sherzai that the airport was the real objective.[108]

On 6 December Smith talked Sherzai into sending a reconnaissance detachment to the west to determine if there was a threat from that direction. The following day, Smith and his ODA were in the vicinity of the airport entrance when Sherzai came roaring up in a convoy to let the captain know that the city had fallen and invited ODA 583 to join him at his former palace in Kandahar.[109] Smith soon learned that the reconnaissance force sent to the west had instead made its way into the city without encountering resistance and had proceeded all the way to the provincial governor's palace. Sherzai now could not be stopped and he too made his way to the palace. Though told not to enter the city, Smith recalled his rationale for ultimately deciding to disregard Mulholland's order:

> I determined that first, I had to maintain rapport with Sherzai and accept his invitation; second, that he had made it to the palace . . . so maybe things were somewhat safe; third, that if there was an implied intent to prevent forces of Sherzai and Karzai from conflicting I could do it better in the city than out-side the city; fourth, making ballsy unexpected moves had served me well so far; fifth, Colonel Mulholland couldn't blame me if I made an on the ground assessment that going in would do more good than not going in if a positive advantage presented itself; and sixth, the whole team was itching to get into the city and the fighting was quickly dying down around the airport.[110]

Thus Smith concluded that Mulholland had no clear understanding of the extremely fluid situation facing the team and decided that they would enter the city with Sherzai's men. When later contacted, Mulholland had no objections to the decision by ODA 583 to enter Kandahar with Sherzai.[111] With the entry of Sherzai's forces into Kandahar, the initial combat actions aimed at overthrowing Taliban political control of Afghanistan concluded.

Consolidating Control

On the same day that Sherzai and his soldiers were making their final approach to Kandahar and the JDAM strike nearly killed Hamid Karzai, Taliban leaders agreed to surrender the city to Karzai's opposition group. The US air medical evacuation (MEDEVAC) of the wounded Americans and Afghans from the JDAM accident may have had an unintended but fortu-itous impact on the Taliban negotiators.[112] Fox noted that the Taliban delegation may have mistakenly assumed that this was a massive demonstration of US combat power instead of a MEDEVAC operation.[113] Whatever the reason for the Taliban surrender, the end seemed some-what anticlimactic.

Unfortunately, the fall of the city led to problems between the two anti-Taliban forces. Kandahar surrendered to Karzai on 5 December, but his forces did not enter the city until 2 days later. Sherzai's forces were able to take actual possession of the city on 7 December by arriving first and managing to take control of the main buildings in Kandahar, including the governor's palace. Sherzai's action initially infuriated Karzai.[114] In exchange for surrendering Kandahar, the Taliban commander in Kandahar, Mullah Naqeebullah, had been promised the governor-ship of Kandahar, but Sherzai's occupation of the palace seemed to nullify that deal. Karzai seriously considered a military operation to evict Sherzai.[115] Fox elaborated:

> It was everything I could do to calm Karzai down because Karzai was pre-pared to conduct a military action to force Sherzai out of the mansion and out of Kandahar. So I looked at him and I sat down with him and I said, Listen, because the fall of Kandahar and the surrender was really the final stage. The

country, at that point, was pretty much secure. The Taliban had fallen apart and had either gone back into the mountains or had dispersed into Pakistan or wherever. So I asked him, "Do you want to start a civil war? You are on the verge of starting a war."[116]

Cooler heads prevailed and Karzai insisted that the mullah yield all military and political power, and only then could he keep his religious title and his home in Kandahar.[117] A few days later, Karzai, Sherzai, and Naqueebullah concluded negotiations that solved the outstanding issues and averted a potentially serious crisis.[118]

Not everyone was happy with the turn of events, however. Less than a day after the governor's palace fell and Kandahar was secured, an improvised explosive device (IED) consisting of 24 antitank mines and 15 155-mm artillery shells was found on the roof of the palace and neutralized.[119] Had the improvised device detonated when Karzai and Sherzai were in the palace together, the blast likely would have killed both of them. The bomb demonstrated that the Taliban and their al-Qaeda confederates remained active even if the Taliban had lost political control of the country.

While Karzai had been negotiating the surrender of Kandahar, some Taliban and al-Qaeda leaders had escaped from the city. Coalition leaders and their Afghan allies could not identify with any certainty the identities of those who fled, and it remains unclear whether Osama bin Laden or Mullah Mohammad Omar were among that group. Fox was present during almost all of the negotiation process and was confident that the enemy had always intended to evacuate the city, but that Karzai did not acquiesce to their escape. Fox contended:

> I am sure that key Taliban leaders escaped during negotiations for the surrender in the south. I am absolutely certain that Karzai knew nothing about it. What I believe is that the Taliban believed if they kept Karzai at bay in the north and Sherzai at bay in the south, [with these] negotiations and a set date to surrender, this gave them the time to pick up, get in their vehicles and drive off.[120]

Fox noted that Karzai had dictated unconditional terms to the Taliban and al-Qaeda forces, compelling them to give up their weapons and vehicles before becoming prisoners of the US Army.[121] The promise of captivity forced the enemy to look for ways out of the city that was imperfectly sealed off by Karzai's and Sherzai's forces.

Tora Bora: An Opportunity Lost

With the fall of the major centers of Taliban power—Mazar-e Sharif, Konduz, Kabul, Tarin Kowt, and Kandahar—the sweep of the war was pushing the fleeing Taliban soldiers and their al-Qaeda allies who had not been killed or captured toward sanctuaries near the Pakistan border, or even into the uncontrolled Pakistani tribal areas of the Northwest Frontier province. The two primary sanctuaries within Afghanistan were located well northeast of Kandahar. One sanctuary was in Paktia province in the Shahi Kowt Valley, but that location would not be identified by Coalition intelligence sources as a major concentration point until late January 2002. The other sanctuary was located in the Spin Ghar (White Mountain) region of Nangarhar province about 45 miles southwest of the city of Jalalabad.[122] That refuge was in a valley called Tora Bora.

As the Kandahar campaign ended, intelligence indicated that Taliban and al-Qaeda leaders and fighters seemed to be moving toward Tora Bora.[123] Tora Bora had previously sheltered the mujahideen against the Soviets and since the late 1990s, had been improved by al-Qaeda as a training area and refuge. The complex consisted of a series of defensive positions and caves dug into the steep sides of the mountains and along the valley floor. The caves held large stocks of food, weapons, ammunition, and other supplies stockpiled to enable al-Qaeda to make a stand against a larger force.[124]

The valley was 9.5 kilometers wide, 10 kilometers long, and surrounded by 12,000- to 15,000-foot mountains that formed a concave bowl facing northeast. The primary avenue of approach into the area was from the town of Pachir Agam south through the Milawa Valley that joined the Tora Bora Valley at its eastern end. Most of the al-Qaeda positions were spread along the northern wall of the valley. Because the high mountains and steep terrain made CAS much less effective, any successful assault against the enemy would have to include ground troops.[125] The valley was also only 15 kilometers from the Pakistan border. Any al-Qaeda terrorists that wished to escape the valley could walk along one of several possible escape routes to reach the border, a journey that would take approximately 17 hours. Although the Coalition could block these escape routes by placing forces in blocking positions, the nearness of Tora Bora to the Pakistani border made that risky. The Coalition did not want those elements to mistakenly cross the border or otherwise come into conflict with Pakistani troops.

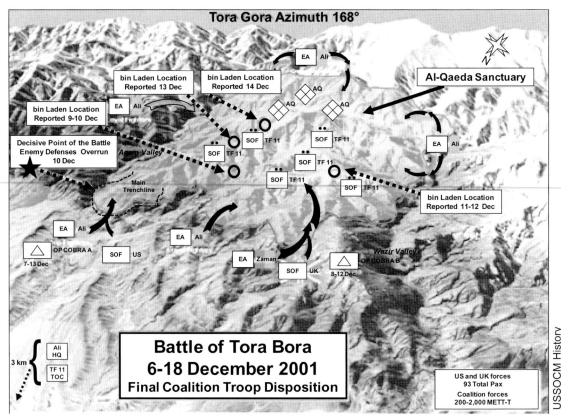

Figure 15. Battle of Tora Bora.

Intelligence from various sources indicated that the population in the Spin Ghar region of Nangarhar province was sympathetic to al-Qaeda. With that organization's presence in the area for many years, a large proportion of the local tribesmen had become beneficiaries of employment and trade with Osama bin Laden's group. Additionally, the sources indicated that al-Qaeda and Taliban strength was significant, but reports were not definitive and only offered estimates of between 300 and 3,000 enemy troops in the region.

More important to the Coalition leadership were the intelligence reports that suggested bin Laden and other senior al-Qaeda leaders were taking refuge in the Tora Bora Valley.[126] With the evidence now available, it is almost certain that at least Osama bin Laden was at Tora Bora and made good his escape as the Coalition attack culminated in mid-December. Several official government and former government sources affirm this view.[127] Additionally, in early 2005, the Department of Defense (DOD) released a document from a purported eyewitness, a detainee at Guantanamo Bay, who had fought under bin Laden during the Afghan-Soviet War and claimed that he helped the al-Qaeda leader escape from Tora Bora in December 2001.[128]

Given the importance of Tora Bora as a refuge for both al-Qaeda leadership and the remnants of their forces in Afghanistan, Coalition leaders began deliberating about the means of assaulting the enemy redoubt. In keeping with the efforts to maintain a small footprint in the country, General Franks and his staff at CENTCOM sought Afghan allies for the fight. Moreover, the fact that the Coalition did not have the right type of conventional combat forces in the region made Afghan proxies more important. The opposition group forces that would ultimately team with the United States at Tora Bora were a collection of small local militias numbering approximately 2,500 fighters that were grouped under the label "Eastern Alliance (EA)." The alliance was comprised of four anti-Taliban groups led by Commanders Hajji Qadir, Hajji Zahi, Mohammed Zaman Ghun Shareef, and Hazrat Ali. Only the last two leaders commanded a significant force to put into the field, and the last, Ali, would emerge as the primary commander at Tora Bora due to his connections with the NA. Ali had previously fought alongside Ahmad Shah Massoud and was considered to be the most loyal to the overall anti-Taliban effort.

Ali became the "security chief" of the EA, while Zaman was named the Jalalabad commander, but the two were rivals rather than friends.[129] The majority of Ali's men were ethnic Pashay, while Zaman's men were Pashtun, thus the two groups disliked and distrusted each other. During the assault on Tora Bora, there were times when the two factions shot at each other rather than at their Taliban and al-Qaeda foes and the fighters. The antipathy the leaders and their respective militias held for each other did not bode well for a successful outcome against a determined enemy.

On the Coalition side, CENTCOM had little to offer in the way of ground forces to help Ali and the others in their assault on Tora Bora. The 1st Battalion, 87th Infantry (1-87 IN), a part of the 10th Mountain Division's force in the theater, was tied up with security missions at K2, Mazar-e Sharif, and Bagram Airfield. The US conventional forces in the theater—the 1st Battalion, 187th Infantry (1-187 IN), a unit that belonged to the 2d Brigade of the 101st Airborne Division, at Shahbaz Air Base in Pakistan and US Marine Task Force 58 that had arrived at Kandahar Airfield in late November—were also busy with security tasks. Even had these forces been available, there were few aviation lift assets in Afghanistan making the primary problem of transport into the Spin Ghar region essentially impossible to solve. Franks simply appeared not to have any ground forces inside CENTCOM's area of responsibility to assist the EA.

However, once Coalition military leaders began receiving credible intelligence reports offering positive identification of enemy forces in the region, they began committing forces to the fight. In late November, Coalition airstrikes began hitting targets in the Spin Ghar, killing and wounding many of the enemy and wreaking destruction on their vehicles and facilities. Meanwhile, Mulholland, now armed with the evidence of a large al-Qaeda presence near Tora Bora, decided to send an ODA to develop the situation further. Coalition leaders had decided to rely on the SF/Afghan partnership that had worked so well elsewhere.

Arrival of ODA 572

As promised, Mulholland directed ODA 572, under the command of Master Sergeant Jefferson Davis, to Jalalabad on 2 December 2001 to link up with Hazrat Ali. The team soon found that forging a close relationship with Ali and other EA leaders at Tora Bora would be difficult. First, Ali refused to wait for ODA 572's arrival and the team discovered that he had already commenced operations without coordinating with US representatives. When Master Sergeant Davis finally linked up with Ali on 4 December at his headquarters near Pachir Agam, he and his team immediately ran into problems. Misunderstanding the role the ODA was to play, Ali demanded that the special operators directly participate in combat, a mission that ran contrary to their main roles of advising and coordinating air support. Because of the problems between ODA 572 and Ali, Mulholland ordered the team back to Jalalabad until the issues could be sorted out. After some additional negotiations and explanations with Ali, the ODA returned to Pachir Agam on 6 December.

The reappearance of ODA 572 also returned the CAS capability that would soon tip the scales in favor of the EA. With Ali's concurrence, the ODA's plan was to divide into two teams and each would establish an observation point (OP) from which to direct the CAS for Ali's force. The air attacks would destroy, damage, or otherwise suppress the al-Qaeda positions thereby allowing Ali's men to advance through the Milawa Valley into the mouth of the Tora Bora Valley. There they would move against remaining pockets of resistance. On 7 December one-half of ODA 572 set up an OP on the eastern ridgeline and commenced the airstrikes. The following day, the other half set up on the northwestern side of the valley and began operations.[130]

Until 8 December ODA 572 operated under the loose control of JSOTF-N. The following day, Task Force (TF) 11—a Coalition SOF organization focused on capturing or killing enemy leaders—arrived and took control of all Coalition operations in the area. Committed to the region by General Franks, TF 11 consisted of 50 elite American troopers as well as contingents from British SOF.[131] While the new task force was not equivalent to an American infantry battalion, these troops could be used in close combat alongside Ali's troops. The task force mission, like that of the ODA, was to support Ali's offensive and kill or capture as many al-Qaeda leaders and troops as it could find.

Soon after his arrival, the TF 11 commander conducted a reconnaissance of the al-Qaeda defenses and realized he was up against a strong opposition. On 10 December he decided to both reinforce the two ODA OPs with some of his troops and establish additional OPs farther forward. That afternoon Ali sent him word to send some SOF troops forward to support an impending attack. Two special operators were sent and the attack went forward. Around 1600 that day, some of Ali's men reported that they had cornered Osama bin Laden. The TF commander immediately ordered all of his available force forward to locate, capture, or kill the al-Qaeda leader. However, the early dusk of Afghan winters in the mountains meant that TF 11 would not arrive at the reported area until after dark. Nonetheless, the men piled into trucks and sped forward.

Unfortunately, the TF commander then encountered a problem that had plagued the operations from the beginning. En route to the specified location, TF 11's convoy met Ali's convoy on the road coming out of the valley. The EA commander had ceased operations for the night and had left the two TF 11 men who had accompanied him on the attack stranded and alone near the al-Qaeda positions. It was the holy month of Ramadan in the Muslim world and Ali's men were going home to break their fast. Upon encountering the TF 11 convoy, Ali promised the American commander that he would turn around and reinforce the pursuit, but he did not follow through on this pledge.[132] While the two stranded Soldiers were able to make their way back to safety, bin Laden made his escape.

One member of ODA 572 explained how the Ramadan holiday played a key role in the fight at Tora Bora:

> One of the biggest problems you have when you work with forces like this—indigenous-type forces—is their logistic system. They don't have a well-developed logistic system like we have. . . . Pretty much all their meals either had to be prepared straight from either raw materials or animals and what-not—cooked freshly right there for them. So a lot of the problems during the battle is, they'll go battle all day. Then when they pull back, it's not like a retreat they're going from the enemy; it's dinnertime. . . . Then the enemy moves back forward and reoccupies position. Then they got to go up there and try to retake it again.[133]

Another team member emphasized this problem, noting that the religious holiday exacerbated the situation, "Yes, it was a big, big problem because it was Ramadan at the time. They're not eating or drinking, really, all day. When it's their time to eat and drink, they want to eat and drink."[134]

Early in the battle the ODA OPs would bring in CAS to destroy the Taliban and al-Qaeda positions. The bombardment would force the survivors to retreat; then Ali's men would occupy the recently vacated ground. However, at night, the EA troops would pull back to eat and drink and the al-Qaeda forces would return to their original positions. The next day the process was repeated.[135] Because of this pattern, the TF 11 commander decided to keep his force close to the front. He hoped that with his own men occupying terrain at night it would convince the Afghan commander to keep his troops forward after dark to hold the ground they had taken during the day.[136] The effort did not immediately bear fruit.

Despite the slow pace that the EA approach required, enemy forces in the valley were increasingly under pressure and their positions were becoming less tenable each day. Much of this pressure was provided by the highly-accurate air support that was directed by the TF 11 Soldiers and the ODAs. On 10 and 11 December alone, the air controllers on these SOF teams called in airstrikes on al-Qaeda positions for 17 continuous hours.[137]

In reaction, some Taliban and al-Qaeda leaders attempted to use negotiations to extricate themselves. On the night of 11–12 December, al-Qaeda elements contacted Zaman and tried to negotiate a cease-fire so they could surrender to the Afghan forces. The negotiations came as a surprise to the men of ODA 572. One staff sergeant on the team recalled:

> One of the interpreters that we did work with—who we had with us all the time—came in and said, "Stop. No more bombs." When he would do that, usually it meant that General Ali's troops were about to move forward again. But it turned out that we were like, "Why are we stopping for so long?" He's like, "No, no. Don't drop any more." It turned out that one of the other commanders had rigged up a bargain, I guess, to receive a large surrender.[138]

When members of ODA 572 realized what was happening, they immediately attempted to end the cease-fire. According to one ODA member, the Taliban and al-Qaeda forces wanted to "lay down their weapons and then walk away," which Afghan custom would have allowed.[139] Because the members of ODA 572 were certain that the forces at Tora Bora were al-Qaeda and that Osama bin Laden might be there as well, they considered conditional surrender unacceptable. One noncommissioned officer (NCO) on the ODA recalled that there was only one type of negotiation that would have been acceptable: "it's a complete unconditional surrender, and [the Taliban and al-Qaeda forces] are processed as prisoners" by the United States.[140]

Once the American opposition became known, the cease-fire ended and Coalition forces renewed their effort to reduce the enemy positions at Tora Bora. In the minds of the American Soldiers in the region, however, this process was excruciatingly slow. Most alarming was that all the terrain taken by the combination of EA forces and CAS during the day was ceded back to al-Qaeda at night when the Afghan militia retreated to their bases lower in the valley. The constant retreat had one unintended advantage. Soldiers in TF 11, armed with night observation and target acquisition equipment and powerful and accurate sniper weapons, became the masters of the night. With no friendly forces in the area after dark, the Tora Bora Valley and its accompanying slopes were a virtual free-fire zone and the dead bodies of al-Qaeda fighters carted off the field the next day in EA trucks were proof of the special operators' lethality. Only on 14 December did the process change when American commanders convinced Ali to keep his men forward and occupy ground already seized.[141] By this date, al-Qaeda forces had been severely mauled and were not able to defend this terrain.

The fighting continued at Tora Bora until 17 December. As the fighting concluded, the combat took on a brutal quality as al-Qaeda's most dedicated fighters remained in the caves to cover the retreat of their leadership. This resistance allowed large numbers of al-Qaeda and Taliban fighters, along with their leaders to slip over the high, snowy, passes of the Spin Ghar into Pakistan.

When hostilities ended in the valley, CENTCOM directed ODA 561 to travel to the valley on 20 December and begin searching the cave complexes that studded the mountains in and around Tora Bora to determine whether wounded or killed al-Qaeda leaders had been left behind. In the process, they found no evidence that any of the key al-Qaeda or Taliban leaders had been killed or wounded in the combat.[142]

With that team's departure several days later, operations by US forces in the Tora Bora region essentially ended. Nevertheless, many questions remained and the most important of these focused on how the combined American and Afghan force had allowed such a large contingent of enemy escape. The mission at Tora Bora had been to cut off and capture or kill large numbers of al-Qaeda and Taliban fighters, and the Coalition forces in the valley had achieved some success in this. Estimates had placed the number of enemy in the hundreds or perhaps thousands and Coalition operations had taken a large toll on these enemy formations. One SOF commander later estimated enemy killed in action (KIA) at 250, but he arrived on the field well into the fight.[143] The JAWBREAKER team that was calling in airstrikes in the Milawa Valley was successfully engaging enemy troops with CAS almost 2 weeks earlier. EA forces had sharp engagements with the enemy even before ODA 572 arrived and that team began calling in airstrikes early on as well.

On the other hand, it is unlikely that as many as 1,000 enemy troops were killed, as some observers have estimated.[144] Still, using the lower estimates of enemy KIA and given historic ratios of wounded in action (WIA) to killed, another 750 fighters would have sustained some level of injury during the fight. Because of the harsh weather and sanitary conditions of the environment at that time, a number of these wounded men would have eventually succumbed to their wounds. In addition, Coalition forces accepted the surrender of a number of al-Qaeda and Taliban forces, but the exact figures remain unclear. These numbers offer an approximate total of 1,100 enemy KIA, WIA, and enemy prisoners of war (EPWs) as a conservative estimate of total enemy casualties. Even if the enemy forces in the Tora Bora region numbered as high as 3,000, the above casualty estimate is a significantly large percentage given historic averages for losses in battle. It is even more impressive when one considers that few of the EA fighters and none of the US or British participants were lost in the fighting at Tora Bora. However, this estimate also suggests that as many as 1,500 fighters may have escaped to fight another day. Some of them likely made their way to the Shahi Kowt Valley in Paktia province and would fight Coalition forces again 3 months later.[145]

The actions at Tora Bora undoubtedly dealt a severe blow to those Taliban and al-Qaeda elements that remained active in Afghanistan after the fall of Kabul and other major Coalition successes that fall. As a result, operations in the valley were clearly not perceived as a victory because of the flight of so many enemy fighters and the likely escape of Osama bin Laden and other key leaders. The reasons for this incomplete success were myriad. Some observers have emphasized the lack of Coalition conventional forces that might have closed down the exit routes to Pakistan. Clearly, in December 2001, CENTCOM did not have combat forces in the theater equipped and trained to conduct sustained operations in the wintry elevations of the Spin Ghar Mountains. Even if these forces had been available, their use in blocking positions to seal the passes into Pakistan was probably unrealistic. The problems associated with inserting and supplying multiple battalion-sized units, spread out across mountainous terrain, were almost insurmountable. As noted earlier, there were not yet enough Army airlift assets in theater, for example, to put a force of this size into position and resupply them on a regular basis. Negotiating with the Pakistani Government over the role of these forces, operating so close to the border, would have added more complications.

An additional explanation of the incomplete success at Tora Bora was the nature of the EA and its relations with US forces. The rivalry between the various militia groups created rifts in the alliance and made command and control difficult. In fact, diplomacy became the primary means of persuading the Afghan chieftains to work together and move toward a common purpose. Furthermore, at some points in the battle, diplomatic skills were not enough to keep the alliance together and the individual leaders began acting unilaterally. Given the poor relations between the two primary commanders, Ali and Zaman, it is somewhat surprising that operations went as well as they did.

✦　　✦　　✦

Although the Tora Bora operation was tarnished by the lost opportunity to capture or kill Osama bin Laden, the overall Coalition campaign in southern and eastern Afghanistan to oust the Taliban and evict al-Qaeda from the country must be considered a success. The plan to work with indigenous anti-Taliban Afghan groups to drive the Taliban from Kabul and Kandahar worked brilliantly. Indigenous leaders like Hamid Karzai proved to be critical not only for the achievement of American political goals in Afghanistan, but also for the ODA team that worked with Karzai at the tactical level. Although Karzai did not have much military acumen, his political savvy and intimate knowledge of the country and culture was a critical enabler that made the campaign much more feasible. Karzai readily admitted that he could not handle the military aspects of the campaign and wisely turned that element over to members of ODA 574 who essentially took command of Karzai's opposition group. The ODA leader, in turn, accepted Karzai's assessment of the political landscape and the two achieved a resounding victory at Tarin Kowt, which led to the fall of the Kandahar and, arguably, sowed the seeds of the Taliban's demise. ODA 583's experience with Gul Agha Sherzai proved to be equally successful. Only at Tora Bora did this form of unconventional warfare (UW) not prove to be as fruitful.

Coalition practices and technology were not the only explanation for the success in the south, east, and north of Afghanistan in the fall and early winter of 2001. The leadership, organization, and tactics of the Taliban and its al-Qaeda allies were equally important. Because the Afghan-Soviet War and the resultant civil war devastated Afghanistan, the country possessed almost no production infrastructure or modern and financial institutions. Thus, the Taliban could not adequately outfit and equip their forces with modern tanks, artillery, or ground-to-air missiles that might have beaten back Coalition ground and air forces.

Despite this, the Taliban government in October and November 2001 initially attempted to defend fixed positions using its antiquated weaponry. Because the Taliban and al-Qaeda troops largely manned these static sites, they were highly vulnerable to extremely accurate CAS sorties. Thus, they suffered huge casualties in terms of men killed or captured and equipment destroyed.

The Taliban and al-Qaeda were actually better suited to unconventional tactics rather than the conventional operations they tried to conduct. Once driven out of or otherwise freed from fixed positions, they would become a more potent fighting force. No longer would they have to wait for attacks against them; they could seize the initiative, at least locally, deciding where and when to attack. This transformation of the Taliban and al-Qaeda from conventional fighters to the unconventional began at Tora Bora. Bin Laden, Mullah Omar, and their military commanders realized that they could not stand up to US military might and melted into the mountains of southern and eastern Afghanistan and the tribal regions of Pakistan to escape. In these sanctuaries they would begin to reconstitute and eventually sally forth to strike US and Coalition forces then disappear back into the mountains to blend in with the local population.

Before that reconstitution was complete, however, there remained one more sanctuary in Afghanistan that held a large number of al-Qaeda and Taliban fighters. That refuge was in the Shahi Kowt Valley in Paktia province to the southwest of Tora Bora. Many of the enemy's toughest fighters, including some that had survived the Coalition's assault on Tora Bora, began assembling there in January and February 2002. The Coalition's effort to eliminate these forces would lead to the biggest engagement of the campaign in Afghanistan.

Notes

1.   Larry P. Goodsen, *Afghanistan's Endless War: State Failure, Regional Politics, and the Rise of the Taliban* (Seattle, WA: University of Washington Press, 2001), 14–15.

2.   Islamic Republic of Afghanistan, "A Brief Biography of President Hamid Karzai. http://www.president.gov.af/english/president_biography.mspx (accessed 14 March 2007).

3.   Shahzada Zulfiqar, "Altered States," *Newsline* (January 2002). http://www.newsline.com.pk/NewsJan2002/newsreport1.htm (accessed 15 March 2007).

4.   Charles H. Briscoe et al., *Weapon of Choice: US Army Special Operations Forces in Afghanistan* (Fort Leavenworth, KS: Combat Studies Institute Press, 2003), 109.

5.   United States Special Operations Command History Office, *United States Special Operations Command HISTORY, 1987–2007, 20th Anniversary Edition* (MacDill AFB, FL: USSOCOM, 2007), 90.

6.   Gaea Levy, "Objectives Rhino and Gecko: SOF's Opening Salvo in Operation Enduring Freedom," *Tip of the Spear,* November 2006, 41.

7.   Briscoe et al., *Weapon of Choice*, 111.

8.   Levy, "Objectives Rhino and Gecko," 41.

9.   Briscoe et al., *Weapon of Choice*, 111.

10.   *USSOCOM History*, 90.

11.   *USSOCOM History*, 90.

12.   *USSOCOM History*, 90.

13.   Briscoe et al., *Weapon of Choice*, 113.

14.   US Department of Defense. "DOD News Briefing—Gen Myers." *DefenseLink News Transcript,* 20 October 2001. http://www.defenselink.mil/transcripts/transcript.aspx?transcriptid=2145 (accessed 1 April 2007).

15.   General Tommy Franks, "After Action: Evaluating the Military Campaign," *PBS Frontline*, 8 September 2002. http://www.pbs.org/wgbh/pages/frontline/shows/campaign/interviews/franks.html (accessed 27 August 2007).

16.   *USSOCOM History*, 90.

17.   "Interview: U.S. Special Forces ODA 555 (SFC "Frank" [no last name available]," *PBS Frontline* (undated). http://www.pbs.org/wgbh/pages/frontline/shows/campaign/interviews/555.html (accessed 4 September 2007).

18.   "Interview: ODA 555 (SFC "Frank")."

19.   *USSOCOM History*, 90.

20.   Lieutenant General Dan K. McNeill, interview by Contemporary Operations Study Team, Combat Studies Institute, Fort Leavenworth, KS, 16 June 2008, 3.

21.   Douglas J. Feith, *War and Decision: Inside the Pentagon at the Dawn of the War On Terrorism* (New York, NY: HarperCollins, 2008), 132.

22.   *USSOCOM History*, 90.

23.   Lieutenant Colonel Donald Bolduc, interview by Contemporary Operations Study Team, Combat Studies Institute, Fort Leavenworth, KS, 23 April 2007, 4.

24.   Bolduc, interview, 23 April 2007, 4.

25.   Bolduc, interview, 23 April 2007, 4.

26.   Lieutenant Colonel Donald Bolduc, *Operations in Southern Afghanistan* Briefing, udated, slide 9.

27.   "Campaign Against Terror, Interview: President Hamid Karzai," *PBS Frontline* (7 May 2002). http://www.pbs.org/wgbh/pages/frontline/shows/campaign/interviews/karzai.html (accessed 29 March 2007).

28.   "Interview: Karzai."

29.   "Interview: Karzai."

30. "Interview: Karzai."

31. "Interview: Karzai."

32. "Campaign Against Terror, Interview: U.S. Army Captain Jason Amerine," *PBS Frontline* (12 July 2002). http://www.pbs.org/wgbh/pages/frontline/shows/campaign/interviews/amerine.html (accessed 29 March 2007).

33. "Interview: Amerine."

34. "Interview: Amerine."

35. "Interview: Amerine."

36. "Interview: Karzai."

37. "Interview: Amerine."

38. "Interview: Karzai."

39. "Interview: Karzai."

40. "Interview: Amerine."

41. "Interview: Amerine."

42. "Interview: Amerine."

43. Briscoe et al., *Weapon of Choice*, 156; Bolduc, *Ops in Southern Afghanistan* Briefing, slide 9.

44. "Interview: Amerine."

45. "Interview: Amerine."

46. "Interview: Amerine."

47. "Interview: Amerine."

48. "Interview: Amerine."

49. "Interview: Karzai."

50. "Interview: Amerine."

51. "Interview: Amerine."

52. "Interview: Amerine."

53. "Interview: Amerine."

54. "Interview: Amerine."

55. "Campaign Against Terror, Interview: Colonel John Mulholland," *PBS Frontline* (no date given). http://www.pbs.org/wgbh/pages/frontline/shows/campaign/interviews/mulholland.html (accessed 1 April 2007).

56. "Interview: Mulholland."

57. "Interview: Amerine."

58. "Interview: Amerine."

59. "Interview: Karzai."

60. Briscoe et al., *Weapon of Choice*, 165.

61. Captain Smith, interview by Contemporary Operations Study Team, Combat Studies Institute, Fort Leavenworth, KS, 18 April 2007, 4.

62. Smith, interview, 18 April 2007, 4.

63. Max Boot, "Special Forces and Horses," *Armed Forces Journal* (November 2006). http://www.armedforcesjournal.com/2006/11/2146103 (accessed 1 April 2007).

64. Smith, interview, 18 April 2007, 4.

65. Briscoe et al., *Weapon of Choice*, 166.

66. Smith, interview, 18 April 2007, 4.

67. Briscoe et al., *Weapon of Choice*, 166–167.

68. Briscoe et al., *Weapon of Choice*, 167.

69. Briscoe et al., *Weapon of Choice*, 167–168.

70. Briscoe et al., *Weapon of Choice*, 169.

71. Briscoe et al., *Weapon of Choice*, 169.

72. Briscoe et al., *Weapon of Choice*, 169

73. Smith, interview, 18 April 2007, 10.

74. Smith, interview, 18 April 2007, 10.

75. Briscoe et al., *Weapon of Choice*, 170.

76. "Campaign Against Terror, Interview: Lt. Col. David Fox," *PBS Frontline* (no date given). http://www.pbs.org/wgbh/pages/frontline/shows/campaign/interviews/fox.html (accessed 1 April 2007).

77. "Interview: Amerine."

78. "Interview: Amerine."

79. "Interview: Fox."

80. Bolduc, interview, 23 April 2007, 10–11.

81. "Interview: Amerine."

82. Colonel David G. Fox, interview by Contemporary Operations Study Team, Combat Studies Institute, Fort Leavenworth, KS, 30 November 2006, 10.

83. Fox, interview, 30 November 2006, 12.

84. Fox, interview, 30 November 2006, 10.

85. Fox, interview, 30 November 2006, 10.

86. Briscoe et al., *Weapon of Choice*, 176–177.

87. "Interview: Mulholland."

88. "Interview: Karzai."

89. "Interview: Karzai."

90. "Interview: Amerine."

91. Briscoe et al., *Weapon of Choice*, 179–180.

92. Fox, interview, 30 November 2006, 12.

93. Fox, interview, 30 November 2006, 12.

94. "Interview: Karzai."

95. Fox, interview, 30 November 2006, 13.

96. Fox, interview, 30 November 2006, 13; Briscoe et al., *Weapon of Choice*, 181.

97. Fox, interview, 30 November 2006, 13.

98. Fox, interview, 30 November 2006, 13.

99. Fox, interview, 30 November 2006, 13.

100. Bolduc, interview, 23 April 2007, 13.

101. Briscoe et al., *Weapon of Choice*, 174–175.

102. Smith, interview, 18 April 2007, 9.

103. Briscoe et al., *Weapon of Choice*, 175.

104. Smith, interview, 18 April 2007, 9.

105. Smith, interview, 18 April 2007, 9.

106. Smith, interview, 18 April 2007, 11.

107. Briscoe et al., *Weapon of Choice*, 175.

108. Smith, interview, 18 April 2007, 11.

109. Briscoe et al., *Weapon of Choice*, 178.

110. Smith, interview, 18 April 2007, 12.

111. Briscoe et al., *Weapon of Choice*, 179.

112. Fox, interview, 30 November 2006, 13.

113. Fox, interview, 30 November 2006, 13.

114. Briscoe et al., *Weapon of Choice*, 182.

115. Fox, interview, 30 November 2006, 14.

116. Fox, interview, 30 November 2006, 14.

117. Briscoe et al., *Weapon of Choice*, 182.

118. Briscoe et al., *Weapon of Choice*, 183.

119. Fox, interview, 30 November 2006, 19.

120. "Interview: Fox."

121. "Interview: Fox."

122. Briscoe et al., *Weapon of Choice*, 213.

123. Briscoe et al., *Weapon of Choice*, 213.

124. *USSOCOM History*, 93.

125. Briscoe et al., *Weapon of Choice*, 213.

126. *USSOCOM History*, 94; Briscoe et al., *Weapon of Choice*, 213.

127. *USSOCOM History*, 98.

128. "Detainee Helped Bin Laden Flee, Document Says," *Washington Post* (23 March 2005), A2.

129. Philip Smucker, "How bin Laden got away: A day-by-day account of how Osama bin Laden eluded the world's most powerful military machine," *Christian Science Monitor,* 4 March 2002. http://www.csmonitor.com/2002/0304/p01s03-wosc.html (accessed 4 May 2007).

130. *USSOCOM History*, 95.

131. *USSOCOM History*, 95.

132. *USSOCOM History*, 95.

133. "Campaign Against Terror, Interview: U.S. Special Forces ODA 572 (Master Sergeant Shane)," *PBS Frontline* (no date given). http://www.pbs.org/wgbh/pages/frontline/shows/campaign/interviews/572.html (accessed 8 April 2007).

134. "Campaign Against Terror, Interview: U.S. Special Forces ODA 572 (Staff Sergeant Bill)," *PBS Frontline* (no date given). http://www.pbs.org/wgbh/pages/frontline/shows/campaign/interviews/572.html (accessed 8 April 2007).

135. "Campaign Against Terror, Interview: U.S. Special Forces ODA 572 (Staff Sergeant Jeff)," *PBS Frontline* (no date given). http://www.pbs.org/wgbh/pages/frontline/shows/campaign/interviews/572.html (accessed 8 April 2007).

136. *USSOCOM History*, 96.

137. *USSOCOM History*, 96.

138. "Interview: U.S. Special Forces ODA 572 (SSG Jeff)."

139. "Interview: U.S. Special Forces ODA 572 (MSG Shane)."

140. "Interview: U.S. Special Forces ODA 572 (MSG Shane)."

141. *USSOCOM History*, 97.

142. Briscoe et al., *Weapon of Choice*, 215.

143. *USSOCOM History*, 97.

144. Briscoe et al., *Weapon of Choice*, 215.

145. Tommy Franks, *American Soldier* (New York, NY: Regan Books, 2004), 377.

Chapter 6

Operation ANACONDA

Following the fighting at Tora Bora, the military situation in Afghanistan in late December 2001 and January 2002 settled down. With all of the known Taliban and al-Qaeda forces destroyed, captured, or scattered, US and Coalition military forces in the region were poised to more fully transition into Phase IV of US Central Command's (CENTCOM's) campaign plan that would feature stability operations. In political terms as well, the conditions appeared auspicious to begin this shift. The Taliban regime had been removed and Hamid Karzai had been installed as the head of an interim government of Afghanistan that would become a partner to the United Nations (UN) and the Coalition in supervising the country's path to a more stable political future. If done with the proper energy and resources, this campaign transition would help cement the notion that Coalition forces were there to help, not occupy. Thus, deliberations among Coalition leaders began to focus on reconstruction projects and humanitarian aid. As those discussions evolved, Coalition planners, as this chapter will show, began considering a significant redeployment of combat forces.

At the Karshi-Khanabad (K2) Airfield in Uzbekistan, Major General Franklin Hagenbeck, commanding general of the 10th Mountain Division, became heavily involved in planning for this transition. Hagenbeck's division headquarters had arrived at K2 on 12 December 2001 to function as the Combined Forces Land Component Command (CFLCC) (Forward). This command served as the representative for Lieutenant General Paul T. Mikolashek, the Third US Army/CFLCC commanding general (CG) in the theater of operations. As such, Hagenbeck's headquarters was responsible for commanding and controlling virtually all Coalition ground forces and ground force operations in the theater, to include security of Coalition airfields in Afghanistan, Uzbekistan, and Pakistan, as well as the logistics operations set up to support those forces.

As combat operations wound down, Hagenbeck's staff officers began discussions with their counterparts at CFLCC about returning forces to their home stations. In fact, on 25 January Hagenbeck, Lieutenant Colonel David Gray, the 10th Mountain Chief of Operations (G3), and Major Paul Wille, the assistant G3, traveled to Camp Doha, Kuwait, to brief the CFLCC staff regarding the plan for redeploying the division headquarters.[1] Hagenbeck recalled that at this meeting "it was the general consensus from everyone that the war, the fight, in Afghanistan was done."[2] This conclusion would prove premature. At roughly the same time that Hagenbeck was in Kuwait, various intelligence assets in theater, primarily signals intelligence (SIGINT) and human intelligence (HUMINT), were developing a picture of increased enemy activity in Paktia province in the southeast of Afghanistan centered on the towns of Gardez, Khost, and Ghazni. There were indications that some of the al-Qaeda and Taliban fighters who had escaped from Tora Bora had gravitated to that area as well as into Pakistan. Estimates of al-Qaeda members in the Paktia region ran as high as 1,000 fighters.[3]

The intelligence about possible enemy formations in Paktia province would eventually lead to the planning and execution of the single largest combat action of Operation ENDURING FREEDOM (OEF)—Operation ANACONDA. In this action, which would take place over 18 days in late February and early March 2002, more than 2,000 Coalition ground troops would enter the Shahi Kowt Valley to conduct search and destroy operations against a large concentration of al-Qaeda and Taliban fighters. The end result—several hundred enemy troops killed, wounded, or captured and the rest driven underground or into Pakistan—would be a critical strike against the remnants of the enemy in Afghanistan. While Operation ANACONDA was an unequivocal victory, Coalition forces encountered significant difficulties in the Shahi Kowt Valley. The discussion that follows highlights many of the problems faced by the Coalition

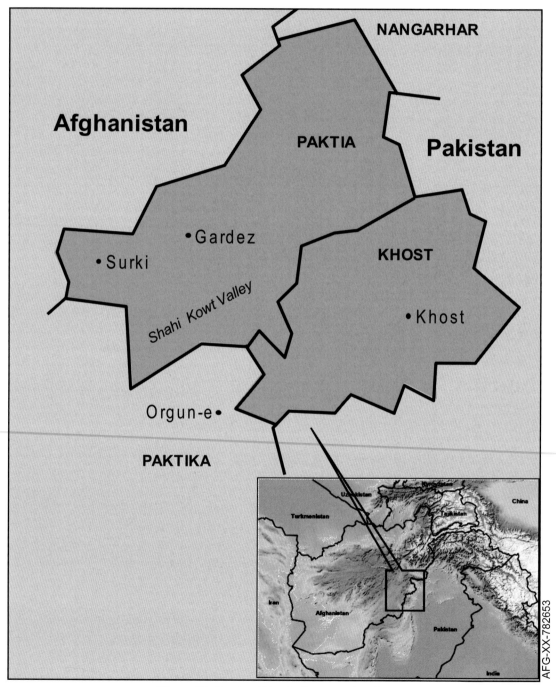

Figure 16. Gardez–Khost–Orgun-e triangle.

forces during the battle against entrenched al-Qaeda and Taliban elements that stood and fought in the valley.

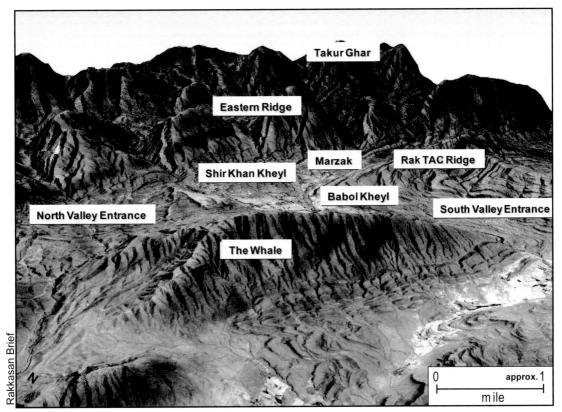

Figure 17. View of Shahi Kowt Valley from the north.

Paktia Province and the Soviet-Afghan War

The US-led Coalition was not the first military force to mount combat operations in the Shahi Kowt Valley. Indeed, in the 1980s the Soviet Army launched numerous campaigns into the region in attempts to destroy mujahideen control over the valley. The Soviet experience, therefore, provides important historical context for Operation ANACONDA.

Paktia province is located in southeastern Afghanistan adjacent to the Northwest Frontier province of Pakistan. The provincial capital, Gardez, sits in the middle of a large valley running northeast to southwest, which forms the northwestern third of the province. Splitting Paktia down the middle third is a huge range of rugged mountains with numerous peaks that rise well over 10,000 feet above sea level. The southeastern third of the province consists of the eastern foothills and, relative to the center third, low rolling hills that extend to the border of Pakistan.

Few paved roads cross the province. The main highway runs west from the city of Khost, located in the eastern hills, over the mountains to Gardez. The road heads north from the provincial capital, exits the province by crossing over another small mountain range, and continues north to Kabul, about 80 miles away. The other major route runs down the valley southwest out of Gardez toward Kandahar, about 250 miles away. Largely inaccessible to vehicular traffic, the province is an ideal location for a nonmechanized armed force to regroup and refit. Afghans have also recognized it as an ideal place for such a force to do battle against a modern foe that seems to hold technological advantages.

Such was the case during the Soviet-Afghan War in the 1980s. The mujahideen forces opposing the Red Army in southeast Afghanistan centered their defenses in Paktia province on the central mountain range. Their defenses were particularly well placed and strong along the highway between Gardez and Khost. The latter city was garrisoned by a sizable Soviet force that relied on supplies coming in from Kabul through Gardez. Determined to deny use of that road as a supply route, in 1981 Afghan fighters successfully sealed it off and laid siege to Khost. As a result, the Soviets were forced to resupply the garrison through airlift.

During the 7 years that followed, the Soviet Army conducted numerous operations in the Gardez–Khost area seeking to bring the mujahideen to battle and to relieve Khost. On 20 March 1982 the mujahideen ambushed a reconnaissance platoon of a Soviet mechanized battalion at the village of Shir Khan Kheyl located in the Shahi Kowt Valley.[4] In August 1983 the Soviets conducted their first major offensive in Paktia province followed by another in November the following year. In August and September 1985 the Russians conducted one of the largest offensives of the war to break the blockade of the Gardez–Khost road and resupply the garrison. They succeeded in breaking through to Khost, but the mujahideen reestablished the siege and again blocked the road once the Soviet relief column pulled back to Gardez.[5]

In November 1987 the Soviet Army launched Operation MAGISTRAL, the largest campaign of the war. The 40th Army, consisting of about five divisions and air support, again battled its way through the mountains from Gardez to Khost. After a significant fight at Satukandav Pass, a key chokepoint on the road, the 40th Army successfully pushed through the mountains and relieved Khost. But as they had done repeatedly in the past, the mujahideen flowed back into the mountain defenses and cut off Khost as the Soviet relief column withdrew to Gardez. The difference this time was that Operation MAGISTRAL was used by the Soviets to set conditions for their departure from Afghanistan.[6] The mujahideen had lost the battle, but won the war when Soviet troops began officially pulling out in 1988.

In Paktia province, the mujahideen had achieved success largely by holding the high ground and making the enemy fight their way up to them. These guerrilla bands were exceptionally good at conducting hit-and-run ambushes with small arms against small detachments, especially convoys, and were generally successful in denying the use of roads to a largely roadbound mechanized army. Though the Soviets had the combat power to bull their way through whenever and wherever they chose, that combat power was not strong enough to conduct such operations anytime or anywhere in Afghanistan. Thus, when they conducted a large operation to clear an area of the enemy, the mujahideen would simply melt away in small elements and return after the Soviets had departed.

Conversely, the Soviets, despite their generally overwhelming superiority in firepower, were loath to fight the mujahideen at close quarters. Instead, Soviet commanders preferred to engage the enemy with heavy weapons at distances of 300 meters or greater—out of rocket-propelled grenade (RPG) and AK-47 range—if the enemy could be detected early enough.[7] These timid tactics almost guaranteed the guerrillas an opportunity to escape and fight another day if the battle went against them.

As the war progressed, the Soviets began making extensive use of helicopters for airmobile and air assault operations. Operations that included air assault and airborne units were generally more successful than those conducted by mechanized forces alone. Typically, the air assault elements would function as an anvil to block the enemy escape routes and lines of communications, while the mechanized ground force would function as a hammer to drive the guerrillas into the kill zones. However, the Soviet's general lack of adequate helicopter lift capacity—critical to inserting the right number of troops in the right place—limited the overall effectiveness of these operations. Adding to this problem was that the trained air assault and airborne regiments in country required for such missions were generally understrength and often missing many of their subordinate battalions.[8] Despite the potential that air assault operations promised in the war against the mujahideen, the Soviets were never able to exploit them fully in the mountains of Paktia province or elsewhere that the Afghan guerrillas chose to stand and fight.

A New Mission for a Renewed Threat

The nature of the combat between Coalition and Taliban forces in late 2001 differed significantly from the operations during the Soviet occupation. Nevertheless, by February 2002 Coalition operations had established a pattern. The pressure to keep the numbers of military personnel in Afghanistan small led to a ground warfare that was unusual. The general pattern of the ground fighting since October followed what seemed to have become a standard set of tactics and procedures. Afghan Militia Forces, those groups that had fought as partners of the US Special Operations Forces (SOF), had engaged and routed the Taliban and its al-Qaeda allies. Once a combined Afghan—Operational Detachment–Alpha (ODA) team detected the enemy, the Special Forces (SF) advisors routinely proceeded by calling in close air support (CAS) to break up or destroy the enemy force. After the airstrikes had pounded the enemy into stunned inaction or retreat, the team would move forward to pursue, capture, or complete the destruction of the enemy force.

These tactics were ideal for three related reasons. First, it required a very light footprint of Coalition forces, which meant operations could be easily supported logistically. Second, the small number of troops demonstrated to the Afghans, and the world, that the Coalition was not an invading army but was there as a force for liberation. This appearance was important to the US Government in general and Secretary of Defense Donald Rumsfeld in particular. Though there was no official force cap placed on CENTCOM forces flowing into Afghanistan, the pressure to keep numbers low was keenly felt by all deploying commanders as they tailored their units for operations in country. Finally, the Coalition approach on the ground played to the strengths of the SF teams trained to advise and assist indigenous forces in what was called unconventional warfare (UW).[9] Not unimportant was that the practice of UW nested perfectly with Rumsfeld's and CENTCOM's emphasis on retaining an Afghan face on the campaign to free Afghanistan from Taliban rule.

Even after most of the Taliban and al-Qaeda military concentrations had disappeared from the battlefield after December 2001, the partnerships between the ODAs and Afghan militia forces endured. Operations relying on these partnerships were overseen by the Joint Special Operations Task Force–North (JSOTF-N), located at K2, and the Combined Joint Special Operations Task Force–South (CJSOTF-S), which had been established in December 2001 at Kandahar Airport. When on 6 January 2002 JSOTF-N received a mission to begin planning for what was originally to be a sensitive site exploitation (SSE) mission in the Gardez–Khost region, they immediately conceived the mission within the UW context.[10] The SOF planners designed an operation in which Afghan militia, assisted by ODAs from the 5th Special Forces Group (SFG), would move into the area to engage and destroy the Taliban and al-Qaeda remnants that intelligence sources had identified there.[11]

Colonel John Mulholland and his staff set to work gathering intelligence on the area of operations (AO) while some of his ODAs began training and preparing several militia bands for the upcoming operation. Over the next 3 weeks, several ODA teams joined Afghan militiamen and reconnaissance teams from Australian Special Air Service's (SAS) Task Force (TF) 64 to look closely into the area around Gardez and Khost. The information these teams garnered indicated that there were indeed enemy fighters in the area, but none of the teams were able to actually observe activities in the Shahi Kowt Valley. In addition, several indigenous Afghan scouts that CJSOTF-S had sent into the valley were never heard from.[12] Toward the end of the month, ODA 594 was conducting a mission near the Shahi Kowt Valley when its Afghan security personnel urgently warned the team leader not to go there. The Afghans reported that local villagers claimed the enemy had indeed concentrated in the valley. Based on the report from ODA 594, Mulholland refocused his intelligence efforts on the Shahi Kowt Valley.[13] The more information Mulholland gained about the enemy in the valley, the more he became convinced he did not possess the combat power to accomplish the mission with which he had been charged. "It was beyond my ability with my small force to do something about it because we were confident there was a sizable concentration of bad guys in there," Mulholland recalled.[14]

In early February, Mulholland met with Major General Hagenbeck and Commodore Robert Harward, the US Navy Special Operations officer who commanded CJSOTF-S, to discuss future operations in the Shahi Kowt Valley. In this meeting, Mulholland explained the situation to Hagenbeck and Harward, informally suggesting that since this operation was going to need additional assets to ensure success—and employing such assets would be beyond the capabilities of JSOTF-N to control—that CFLCC (Forward) should take over the planning, command, and control of any offensive in the valley. Hagenbeck agreed and over the next several days the two commanders, along with their staffs, put together a briefing for Lieutenant General Mikolashek recommending that course of action. In early February they presented the brief to Mikolashek who agreed with the recommendation.[15] A few days later, in a video teleconference (VTC) Mikolashek advised Hagenbeck to "learn how to spell Bagram," thereby hinting that CFLCC (Forward) would soon be moving into Afghanistan to become more directly involved in the upcoming operation.[16] Indeed, on 13 February 2002 Mikolashek ordered Hagenbeck to move CFLCC (Forward) to the airfield located at Bagram and 2 days later the headquarters was officially redesignated as Combined Joint Task Force (CJTF) *Mountain* and assumed responsibility for the planning and execution of what had then become known as Operation ANACONDA.[17]

CJTF *Mountain*

Though designated as a CJTF, the headquarters of the 10th Mountain Division, consisting of only 167 officers and Soldiers, was hardly the proper size to serve as the staff of a CJTF. Before it had deployed to K2, the headquarters had deployed part of its staff to missions in Bosnia, Kosovo, the Sinai Desert, and the Joint Readiness Training Center (JRTC) at Fort Polk, Louisiana. The division's primary intelligence officer (G2) was one of those deployed

10th MT Afghanistan and OP ANACONDA Brief

Figure 18. 10th Mountain Soldiers in the Shahi Kowt Valley.

and would be sorely missed in the planning for ANACONDA. Additionally, some of the division staff had been left at Fort Drum to perform post security missions in the wake of 9/11. Additional assets missing for the planning and the execution of ANACONDA were the 20th Air Support Operations Squadron (ASOS) and the headquarters' Tactical Air Control Party (TACP), both of which were normally associated with the division and were critical to coordinating CAS with US Air Force units. The 20th ASOS had already deployed in October to support JSOTF-N and the TACP was left behind due to Department of Defense (DOD) pressure to keep the deployment numbers low. The 10th Mountain Division had been tasked to perform logistics and force protection functions at K2. Thus, division planners had not made arrangements to deploy the TACP.[18]

By doctrine, a CJTF headquarters is a much larger organization whose staff possesses all the assets and sections needed to plan, conduct, and support the full range of Coalition operations. Joint task forces are also responsible for conducting direct coordination with the various theater-level headquarters that command and support it. Such was not the case with CJTF *Mountain*. As Major General Hagenbeck explained, "Were we in fact a CJTF? I will tell you we were in name primarily, but names are powerful. It did bring all these disparate organizations together from across the Services and we had a small contingent embedded in that 167 now from some of the other Services, so I won't say it was a CJTF in name only."[19] But Hagenbeck did encounter problems, especially in creating a plan for ANACONDA that required close coordination with the air support staff at CENTCOM:

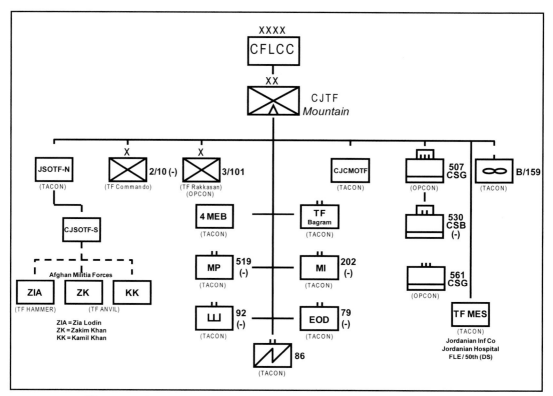

Figure 19. CJTF *Mountain* task organization for Operation ANACONDA.

There was confusion because as we began to develop our battle plans and to work in air power for fire support because we had no artillery, and we saw this retrospectively, there were many that believed that we still were an append-age of the CFLCC and therefore [CFLCC] should be dealing directly with CENTCOM and with the Combined Forces Air Component Commander (CFACC) in Saudi Arabia and Prince Sultan Air Base (PSAB). If we truly were a CJTF, we would have had direct lines working with them to develop the plans. So confusion did reign.[20]

Despite the problems inherent in the headquarters organization, Hagenbeck, Mulholland, Harward, and their teams moved forward on developing the plan for ANACONDA.

Planning Begins

The experience of Tora Bora was still fresh as the planning for ANACONDA proceeded, specifically the problems encountered when the Coalition relied on the Afghan militia forces of the Eastern Alliance to ensure the destruction of al-Qaeda forces in the Tora Bora Valley. The willingness of Afghan militia commanders to negotiate with the enemy allowed large numbers of Taliban and al-Qaeda leaders and fighters to escape. The lack of conventional troops that might have served to block that escape and the dearth of airlift capabilities that would have prevented the deployment of those conventional forces had they existed had pushed the Coalition toward its reliance on the militia groups.[21] Although al-Qaeda forces endured hundreds of casualties at Tora Bora, the operation had become a political and public relations defeat as well as an overall military failure for CENTCOM because of the escape of senior al-Qaeda leaders including Osama bin Laden. Nobody in the Coalition wanted a repeat of that outcome. Whatever enemy forces existed in the Shahi Kowt Valley had to be captured or killed.

Planning an operation that intends to destroy an enemy located in rugged terrain is a very complicated task. The Shahi Kowt is a 60-square mile bowl-shaped area about 15 miles due south of Gardez. The valley is bound on the east by a range of tall, steep mountains known as the Eastern Ridge, and a smaller, lower hill mass named Tergul Ghar on the west. US Soldiers rechristened Tergul Ghar as "The Whale" because its appearance was similar to a hill at the National Training Center (NTC) at Fort Irwin, California, which for decades had been known by the same nickname.[22] The valley runs northeast to southwest and has two primary entrances/exits. The first is on the north end of the valley and enters from northwest. The other, larger entrance enters the valley from the southwest past the village of Surki. The Eastern Ridge was dominated by one particularly tall mountain known as Takur Ghar, located across the valley adjacent to the southern entrance.

The steepness of the whole ridgeline made finding suitable helicopter landing zones (HLZ) for inserting airmobile troops difficult. The terrain was such that troops could be landed on tops of peaks or low in the foothills, but landing options in between were few. Additionally, to surmount the mountains the helicopters had to carry fewer Soldiers and/or less equipment per load. The Eastern Ridge and the Whale were pockmarked with caves and folds that were ideal hiding places and defensive positions. If the enemy were to get to the high ground and defend from those positions, they would indeed be difficult to dislodge or kill. Positions on the ridges would also give enemy gunners clear shots at any slow-moving aircraft that entered the valley.

The difficulties presented by the harsh terrain were exacerbated because Coalition intelligence officers had only the vaguest idea of the enemy situation in the Shahi Kowt Valley. Early estimates of the enemy strength spanned the range from as few as 50 to as high as 1,000 Taliban and al-Qaeda fighters. The final intelligence estimate issued just prior to the operation settled on a number of 150 to 200 fighters and approximately 1,400 villagers, fighters' family members, and other noncombatants in the valley. The enemy appeared to be concentrated primarily in three small villages—Shir Khan Kheyl, Babol Kheyl, and Marzak—located in the south-central part of the valley.[23]

CJTF *Mountain* planners assumed that the enemy in the Shahi Kowt Valley, like Taliban and al-Qaeda forces encountered previously, would be armed primarily with AK-47s, RPG-7s, 82-mm mortars, and a few old Soviet DShK 12.7-mm machineguns nicknamed "Dishkas." The task force's intelligence officers believed that the most likely course of action the enemy would pursue would be for the frontline fighters to resist only long enough to allow their leaders to escape, then they too would attempt to escape using the trails (known as ratlines) that wound through various draws leading south and east out of the valley toward Pakistan. The fighters would attempt to escape by mixing in with the local villagers in the refugee flow. The estimate of the most dangerous course of action held that the enemy would disperse, reconsolidate, and then conduct guerrilla attacks against the Coalition forces in the near future. Experience with the enemy since October 2001 as well as the intelligence gleaned up to that point in time strongly suggested that the least likely course of action was that the enemy would defend and fight to the bitter end.[24]

Organizing the Fighting Force

The perceived most likely enemy course of action, the terrain of the Shahi Kowt Valley, and the mix of forces available to CJTF *Mountain* dictated the development of the plan for ANACONDA. Since the expected Taliban and al-Qaeda reaction was escape, the planners at CJTF *Mountain* knew they needed more ground forces and resources other than the ODA teams and Afghan militia units under JSOTF-N's control. Hagenbeck asked for and received operational control (OPCON) of a number of conventional units that had been flowing into the theater since October.

The first of these units was TF *Rakkasan*, commanded by Colonel Francis "Frank" Wiercinski. The TF consisted, at that point, of the Headquarters, 3d Brigade, 101st Airborne Division; two infantry battalions; an aviation battalion; and assorted support units all located at the Kandahar Airfield. The first battalion was the 2d Battalion, 187th Infantry (2-187 IN) commanded by Lieutenant Colonel Charles A. "Chip" Preysler. The 2-187 IN was one of Wiercinski's organic infantry battalions from Fort Campbell, Kentucky, and had arrived in mid-January. The other battalion was the 3d Battalion, Princess Patricia's Canadian Light Infantry (3-PPCLI), which had just arrived from Edmonton, Canada, during the first week of February. Both battalions were employed in conducting security and force protection operations at the Kandahar Airfield.[25]

Another of Wiercinski's battalions, the 1st Battalion, 187th Infantry (1-187 IN), was also conducting security and force protection operations, but at the Shahbaz Air Base in Jacobabad. Commanded by Lieutenant Colonel Ronald Corkran, the 1-187 IN reported directly to CFLCC (Forward), not to Wiercinski. The battalion had been conducting its mission at Jacobabad since mid-November 2001, but its subordinate units had also conducted a few quick reaction force (QRF) and SSE missions.[26]

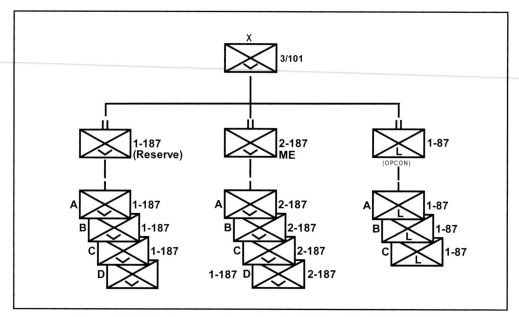

Figure 20. TF *Rakkasan* task organization for Operation ANACONDA.

The final conventional force committed by Major General Hagenbeck to the initial operations in the valley was a battalion that he already owned—the 1st Battalion, 87th Infantry (1-87 IN), commanded by Lieutenant Colonel Paul LaCamera. Like the other battalions, the 1-87 IN had been involved in airfield security and force protection operations at K2 since early October 2001. Unlike the other battalions, however, the 1-87 IN had been running a split operation between K2 and Bagram Airfield near Kabul. Since November the battalion had maintained a company at Bagram to provide security to the forward tactical operations center (TOC) set up there by JSOTF-N. LaCamera's battalion had also run various QRF missions and had become involved in both the efforts to quell the Qala-i Jangi Prison uprising and in detainee operations at Sheberghan Prison.[27] Eventually, these three US Army battalions would be brigaded together under TF *Rakkasan* for the operation. Control of 3-PPCLI would revert to CJTF *Mountain*.

Hagenbeck also had tactical control (TACON) of a wide array of SOF. The first and foremost of the SOF organizations was Mulholland's JSOTF-N, which would exercise OPCON of participating ground SOF organizations not actually part of the special operations TF. For ANACONDA, JSOTF-N committed at least five ODAs from the 5th SFG—542, 563, 571, 574, and 594—to the operation. Three of the five were assigned the task to prepare participating Afghan militia units for the mission.

OPCON to JSOTF-N was CJSOTF-S, a combined and joint organization consisting of the 3d Battalion, 3d SFG (3-3 SFG); US Navy Sea, Air, Land (SEAL) teams, and SOF teams from various Coalition nations to include Denmark, France, Germany, and Norway.[28] The 3-3 SFG also allocated five ODAs (372, 381, 392, 394, 395) to the operation of which three were assigned to help prepare the participating Afghan militia units. Also OPCON to JSOTF-N was TF 64, the Australian SAS unit.

The Afghan militia forces that would become involved in ANACONDA consisted of three Pashtun units. The first force, led by Commander Zia Lodin, consisted of approximately 600 men. ODAs 594 and 372 advised and trained Zia's force, which would be chosen to be the main effort and designated TF *Hammer* for the upcoming operation. The other two Afghan units were led by Zakim Khan and Kamel Khan and each consisted of about 400 to 500 fighters. ODAs 542 and 381 partnered with Zakim's force and ODAs 571 and 392 worked with Kamel's unit. These two forces would be designated as TF *Anvil* for ANACONDA.[29]

In short, the collection of units Hagenbeck had available for the operation was diverse in origin and capabilities. The force consisted of everything from essentially untrained irregular militia fighters to highly skilled SOF soldiers considered the world's elite. The troops came from at least nine different countries, which reflected the Coalition nature of the operation. ANACONDA would also be a joint operation, involving units from the US Army, Navy, and Air Force. The leadership and operational challenges facing Hagenbeck and his subordinate commanders would be manifold.

The Final Scheme of Operation ANACONDA

In thinking about the scheme of maneuver for ANACONDA, the CJTF *Mountain* staff looked for historical insights. They noted that when conducting operations in the Shahi Kowt Valley, Soviet ground units typically entered the valley through either the northern or southern entrances. At least twice in the 1980s, the Soviets used these avenues of approach and suffered heavy casualties both times. CJTF *Mountain* planners anticipated that the enemy expected the

Coalition to use the same routes.[30] In fact, Coalition planners did intend to advance into the valley from those directions with two forces that would collectively act as a "hammer." But because they believed that the al-Qaeda enemy would be trying to escape, they hoped to put in place an "anvil" consisting of a number of forces—American and Afghan—in blocking positions (BPs) along the high ground on the eastern and southern sides of the valley.

Using that concept as their foundation, between 15 and 22 February planners and staff personnel from CJTF *Mountain*, JSOTF-N, and other agencies put together the operations plan for ANACONDA. As the days progressed and the operation became more complex, CJTF *Mountain* and Major General Hagenbeck asserted command authority over the planning. Ultimately, Hagenbeck assigned the following mission to Coalition forces involved in the operation:

> On order, CJTF *Mountain* attacks to destroy (capture or kill) AQ [al-Qaeda] vicinity OBJ Remington (Shir Khan Kheyl), and to identify or disrupt AQ insurgency support mechanisms and exfiltration routes into Pakistan. BPT [Be prepared to] conduct follow-on operations to clear selected objectives and interdict AQ movements in AO Lincoln.[31]

Further, the CJTF *Mountain* commander defined success by articulating his proposed end state for the operation. Hagenbeck viewed the operation as a victory only when all al-Qaeda forces in the Gardez-Khost region were killed or captured.[32]

Figure 21. The village of Shir Khan Kheyl.

10th MT Afghanistan and OP ANACONDA Brief

To accomplish the mission, CJTF *Mountain* assigned each subordinate element tasks that supported the goal. About 3 days prior to D-day, which was set for 28 February, SOF reconnaissance teams from CJSOTF-S would move into the ANACONDA area where they could observe the objective and other key locations and report enemy activity, strengths, and locations. On 27 February TF *Anvil* would move out from Khost (Kamel Khan) and from Orgun-e (Zakim Khan) and set up the outer ring for what would eventually become concentric rings of BPs. Their mission was to kill or capture any enemy personnel who successfully evaded the inner ring of BPs that were to be established at the south end and east side of the valley.

Zia's appropriately named TF *Hammer* was designated as the main effort for the operation. The TF *Hammer* mission was to move in trucks the night before the attack began on the road south from Gardez. The force would split into two assault elements on approaching the Whale. One element would move on Axis COPPER in the north and approach the northern entrance to the Shahi Kowt Valley until it reached Phase Line (PL) EMERALD. The other element would move on Axis BRASS in the south and approach the valley's southern entrance until it too reached PL EMERALD. At EMERALD, both elements would hold in place until the US Air Force had attacked several preselected targets located in the valley and on the Whale. Once the Air Force had completed its work, the northern element would set up a BP in the northern entrance. Zia's men in the south would then proceed to attack into the valley and clear the three villages on Objective REMINGTON. If the enemy retreated, Zia's force would pursue and destroy the enemy by running them east and south into the guns of troops manning the inner ring of BPs.[33]

Establishing the inner ring was the mission assigned to Wiercinski's TF *Rakkasan*. The inner ring consisted of seven BPs designed to close off the primary ratlines that ran through the draws in the Eastern Ridge leading east and south out of the valley toward Pakistan. The BPs were named for the wives and girlfriends of several *Rakkasan* Soldiers and were designated alphabetically from north to south.[34] Preysler's 2-187 IN, the brigade's main effort, was assigned the four BPs in the north: AMY, BETTY, CINDY, and DIANE. Given that Preysler was provided only three Chinooks for the initial lift, he selected Captain Franklin Baltazar's C Company to make the first insertion and to establish BETTY, CINDY, and DIANE, the three BPs closest to the objective. AMY would remain unmanned until Captain Kevin Butler's A Company was inserted using three CH-47s 11 hours after the operation began (H+11). Preysler and his tactical command post (TAC) would go in on the first lift with Baltazar's troops.[35]

The three southern BPs—EVE, GINGER, and HEATHER—were assigned to LaCamera's 1-87 IN. Also provided with only three CH-47s, LaCamera opted to bring in portions of two rifle companies on the initial insertion. He assigned BP EVE to Captain Roger Crombie's A Company. Crombie, with only one CH-47, could bring in one platoon on the initial insertion. Crombie also had to squeeze his headquarters and a 12-man scout element onto his chopper, thereby precluding the ability to bring any of his company's 60-mm mortars along, at least initially.[36]

LaCamera assigned BPs GINGER and HEATHER to Captain Nelson Kraft's C Company. Provided with two CH-47s, Kraft could load two of his platoons, but also had to make room for LaCamera's TAC. Additionally, LaCamera wanted to bring along a battalion mortar section, thereby reducing the number of troops Kraft could bring, but adding a critical capability that no other *Rakkasan* force would have available on D-day.[37] This was particularly important

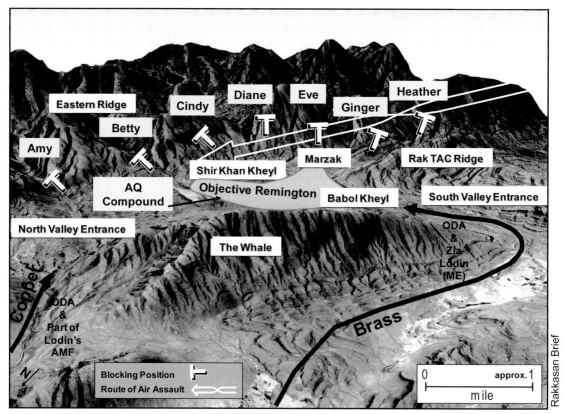

Figure 22. Concept of the Operation (Shahi Kowt Valley).

because TF *Rakkasan* had not deployed with its organic field artillery battalion. Thus, there would be none of the indirect fire support normally available to a battalion commander from brigade level.

Back at Fort Drum, 1-87 IN's mortar platoon had recently gone through testing with the new 120-mm mortar before acquiring the system as part of a change to the battalion's table of organization and equipment (TOE). LaCamera decided to bring the weapons when his battalion was deployed overseas to K2. He further decided to bring one of the 120-mm tubes along with his 81-mm mortars for the initial insertion of Operation ANACONDA with the idea that he could provide both his battalion and 2-187 IN (which was not bringing any mortars in on the first lift) with indirect fire.[38] The 120-mm mortar had a range of over 7 kilometers and could easily reach up to and past BP BETTY to provide Preysler's troops fire support if needed. For the second lift at H+11, Crombie would receive another Chinook and would be able to bring in one other platoon (his third platoon was the battalion reserve) and his mortars. Kraft would also get one chopper to bring in his last rifle platoon.

The TF *Rakkasan* reserve and QRF was Corkran's 1-187 IN. Although his battalion would remain at Bagram during the initial insertion, Corkran and four of his key leaders were to accompany Wiercinski and the brigade TAC to be inserted on a ridgeline just west of BP HEATHER. Corkran and his men were tasked to provide security to the TAC, while at the same time getting familiar with the terrain and battlefield in the event his battalion was committed to the fight. The plan was for the TAC to remain on the ridge for about 90 minutes or until Preysler and LaCamera had the operation well in hand. Wiercinski then planned to move the TAC back to Bagram and control things from there or return to the AO when 1-187 IN was committed, actions all dependent on how the situation developed.[39]

As the CJTF *Mountain* planners developed and finalized the plan, the units that were to execute it prepared for the operation. Between 16 and 25 February TF *Rakkasan* units flowed into the increasingly cramped Bagram Airfield. On arrival, the units conducted drills and rehearsals, including a "fly away" rehearsal designed to see how fully loaded CH-47s would perform at high altitude HLZs. In their small base near the town of Gardez, the ODAs feverishly worked to train their Afghan charges, while at the same time keeping them in the dark about the upcoming operation. Fearing that one or more of the Afghan troops would let the word get out about the plan, the SF advisors planned not to tell the Afghan militia units anything until they had crossed the line of departure.[40]

Once the plan was completed, Hagenbeck and Mulholland briefed it to General Tommy Franks via VTC on 26 February. Franks gave his approval and D-day was set for 28 February. Unfortunately, the winter weather in Afghanistan did not cooperate. A snowstorm lashed the Gardez–Khost area beginning the day of the VTC with Franks. The blizzard lasted for 2 days and delayed the departure of the Afghan militia units and their ODAs as well as preventing the insertion of TF 64 and other surveillance teams. As a result, surveillance of the Shahi Kowt Valley did not begin 72 hours prior to the operation as planned. Indeed, the most fortunate teams managed to begin their reconnaissance 36 hours before ANACONDA. While these delays would have a negative impact on the operation—especially the lack of accurate information about the enemy situation—they did not stop the mission from going forward. On 1 March the two halves of TF *Anvil* moved out from their respective locations to establish their BPs. Operation ANACONDA was underway.

The Opening Phase

After midnight on 2 March Commander Zia and the troops of TF *Hammer*, accompanied by ODAs 594 and 372, departed Gardez in a column of 39 trucks, busses, and other vehicles. From the beginning, the column experienced difficulties that threatened to disrupt the operation. The recent snows and rain had turned the dirt roads into mushy, slippery quagmires that significantly slowed movement through terrain that was difficult to negotiate in daylight. En route, several trucks became stuck and at one point a large bus turned over injuring several fighters. Once the injured troops were evacuated, the column continued to move until it arrived at a small village west of the Shahi Kowt Valley. There, the force split and the southern element headed down Axis BRASS toward the village of Surki. The northern element, under the direction of Chief Warrant Officer 2 Stanley L. Harriman of ODA 372, headed for PL EMERALD and a small hill near the northern entrance that had been dubbed the "Little Whale."[41]

Not long after the northern element split off, it came under what was initially believed to be enemy mortar fire. The lead high-mobility multipurpose wheeled vehicle (HMMWV) was struck by a round that killed Harriman and two Afghans. By the time the attack abated, 2 other SF Soldiers and 13 Afghans were wounded. It soon became apparent that the attack came not from enemy mortars but an AC-130 Spectre gunship that had accidentally identified the column as enemy and opened fire. This event forced the northern element to stop and focus its attention on evacuating the wounded, and caused the leaders of the southern column to also halt and ponder how to proceed with the mission.[42]

After getting word that the casualties were on their way to Gardez, the commander of ODA 594, moving with Zia and the southern element, ordered his column to continue forward. Zia had been convinced to cooperate with his SF advisors on this operation partly because of the promise of air power to support his attack. The Afghan leader knew how effective the airstrikes had been in the operations of the Northern Alliance and he saw the chance for his units to receive the same support. As the column deployed and advanced toward the southern end of the Whale, Zia and his men expected the hill mass to erupt in a hail of bombs. The ODA members had told him that the Coalition's air forces had prepared to launch a massive hour-long bombardment on the hill. Instead, Coalition aircraft delivered only seven Joint Direct Attack Munitions (JDAMs) against targets on the Whale.[43]

Alerted by the attacks, enemy mortar crews and riflemen on the Whale soon began directing fire against Zia's troops as they advanced. "Where are the planes?" Zia kept asking his advisors.[44] The ODA commander could only shrug his shoulders. The young SF captain had no way of knowing what had happened with the air support. After suffering several casualties, Zia angrily withdrew his men and rallied them at a position near the southern tip of the Whale.[45] For the time being, Zia's troops were not going anywhere, and TF *Hammer* had ceased to be the main effort.

TF *Rakkasan* Enters the Valley

As TF *Hammer* struggled through the mud and darkness en route to their attack positions, the assault troops of TF *Rakkasan* gathered at Bagram Airfield and prepared to board their helicopters. Morale was high and the troops were excited about finally getting to fight the enemy directly instead of pulling security at the ramshackle Kandahar Airport.[46] The night was extremely dark, so Soldiers were busily moving around the flight line using night vision goggles (NVG) to see their way to their respective assembly areas and conduct last minute inspections of weapons and equipment.[47] The weather was also humid, cold, and cloudy—perfect conditions for hypothermia—and many of the Soldiers were bundled up with cold weather gear in an attempt to keep warm. At about 0500 the CH-47 Chinook transport helicopters took off and headed almost due south for the hour-long flight to the Shahi Kowt Valley.

The CH-47s carrying TF *Rakkasan* belonged to TF *Talon*, commanded by Lieutenant Colonel James Marye. As the aircraft departed Bagram, they immediately ran into a thick fog, making an already difficult flight almost impossible. However, Marye and his pilots found a literal hole in the clouds. Corkran recalled the flight and the auspicious moment when a clear path was located:

> It was foggy and there were a lot of clouds and there were serious mountains. I don't know if you have been to Bagram or not, but it is fairly impressive of how ugly it is mountain-wise . . . instead of getting antsy, [the pilots] found a split between the two layers of clouds, like some thermal inversion thing going there . . . they found this layer of about 40 feet of split that you could see 7 miles.[48]

The pilots, Corkran stated, "flew that cloud layer through the mountains right up to the objective."[49]

As they left Bagram, the six Chinooks had been joined by two UH-60 Blackhawk command and control (C2) helicopters, and several AH-64 Apache helicopters. As these aircraft sped through the skies, Wiercinski and other *Rakkasan* leaders listened to the chatter on the radio. They soon became aware that the northern element of TF *Hammer* had taken casualties and things were not going according to plan. In the cold dawn, the line of helicopters soon flew over the large valley to the west of the Shahi Kowt, passed the south entrance, and made a 180-degree turn back to the northeast. As they approached the valley, the six Chinooks spread out to head for their respective HLZs and were soon on the ground.

Up in one of the C2 aircraft, Lieutenant Colonel Corkran and his security team felt as if they were freezing to death. The helicopter door gunners had to keep the Blackhawk's doors open all the way to the objective area so they could return fire if necessary. When the helicopter touched down on the high ridge west of BP HEATHER, Corkran and the others quickly exited. Corkran recalled, "I was so cold I couldn't move my fingers which had only been clad in a pair of raggedy nomex gloves so that I could write and track the air assault execution matrix in our alternate C2 aircraft." He added that as he left the helicopter, he was thinking, "Oh, God. I can't even move my fingers. I'm going to die here fumbling around with my frozen hands if we make contact."[50]

As the security team scrambled to secure the HLZ for Colonel Wiercinski's Blackhawk, the TF *Rakkasan* commander was studiously observing the valley below with some foreboding. He remembered,

> Very early on I could tell there were no civilians in those three towns. There were no colors, no smoke, no animals, no hanging clothes, nothing to identify it as a populated area, with people living there. I looked down and asked, "What's wrong with this picture?" There were no civilians in there. They had moved them out.[51]

When Wiercinski's Blackhawk approached the HLZ, it was struck by small arms fire and a glancing blow by what was probably an RPG. The chopper was not seriously damaged and was able to land the brigade TAC and still take off.[52]

Once the pounding beat of rotor blades had vanished into the distance, the nine men of the brigade TAC and the security team were quickly joined by a two-man SOF Special Reconnaissance (SR) Team called Mako-31. The 11 were now positioned on a high, very steep knife-like ridge that would soon become known as Rak TAC Ridge. As Wiercinski looked off to the north, he continued to study the villages. It now dawned on him that "there was nothing but bad guys there. The place did not have the look of anything else in Afghanistan. It had the look of a battlefield." He then thought, "This is going to be a fight."[53]

Suddenly, off to the southeast, from the direction of BP HEATHER, they heard small arms fire. What initially sounded like a few random shots rapidly built into a crescendo of noise. Corkran remembered thinking, "Come on guys. You're all picking on one guy down there and now we are turning this into what is beginning to sound like a company live fire."[54] What he did not realize at the time was that what he was hearing was predominantly enemy fire. Lieutenant Colonel LaCamera and his C Company were about to experience a battle for their lives.

HLZ 13A

The three CH-47s allotted to LaCamera's 1-87 IN approached their assigned HLZs at about 0615 on 2 March. Crombie's A Company (-) and the scouts headed for HLZ 5 located on a high ridge just south of BP EVE. The other two choppers headed for HLZs 13A and 13 located between BPs GINGER and HEATHER. The lead Chinook, carrying LaCamera, C Company commander Captain Kraft, and Kraft's 1st Platoon landed at 13A while the other carried the 2d Platoon, the battalion mortar section, and the battalion S3, Major James Hall, who was leading the alternate TAC at HLZ 13.[55]

Sprinting off the aircraft, the troops spread out and laid flat on the ground while they waited for the choppers to depart. At HLZ 13A, when the Chinook was no more than 30 feet off the ground, the small group that included LaCamera and Kraft began receiving small arms fire from the slopes of Takur Ghar, the huge mountain to their east. Kraft recalled that the fire "didn't appear to be very well aimed. There were bullets flying overhead, but nothing too extreme, in my opinion, and nothing, in my opinion, to change an operation."[56] The company commander grabbed his 1st Platoon leader and ordered him to move off to the west and establish BP HEATHER.[57]

Within seconds of giving that order, a heavy machinegun opened up, pinning down the 1st Platoon. An RPG soon followed the gun. Technical Sergeant John McCabe, the battalion's enlisted terminal attack controller (ETAC), saw the round coming. "Out of the corner of my eye, in slow motion, I see this object land right in front of us," McCabe recalled. "It was either a mortar round or an RPG. Now after thinking about it, I think it was actually an RPG. It dudded out—it did not go off."[58]

Down at HLZ 13, Kraft's 2d Platoon had also come under fire. The platoon leader contacted Kraft via radio to inform him about the contact and ask for orders. The company commander realized the platoon could actually direct fire on the enemy positions that were pinning down the units at HLZ 13A. He told his lieutenant to take up positions and begin suppressing the enemy. As he was talking with 2d Platoon, another RPG round sailed into Kraft's position and landed about 2 feet from where he was kneeling. Fortunately, it too failed to explode. Kraft remembered that his radio-telephone operator (RTO) "looked up at me with eyes bigger than you can imagine and said, 'Sir, we need to get out of here.'"[59]

Spying the bowl-shaped depression where he had planned to put his command post (CP), Kraft ordered the 1st Platoon to move into it by using bounds and suppressive fire. Within a short time, the platoon, Kraft's CP, and LaCamera's TAC were all located in the "Bowl." This low ground provided ample cover from the enemy's fire, most of it now passing harmlessly overhead. From the Bowl, Kraft could see HEATHER and reasoned that he could still establish that BP with little interference from the enemy on Takur Ghar. He issued orders and soon the 1st Platoon departed down the ridge to set up the BP.[60]

In discussing the situation with his 2d Platoon leader, and knowing their position on the map, Kraft knew that the platoon could still cover the location where BP GINGER was to be established, even if the enemy prevented him from actually putting troops there. He could still block the exfiltration of enemy fighters along Route JEEP, which was what his mission called for. It was not ideal, but Kraft decided it would have to do.[61]

At about 0730 the 1st Platoon leader called to tell Kraft that BP HEATHER was established. No sooner did Kraft get that message than he learned that the platoon was also receiving fire from a mountain to the west. Kraft quickly moved over to that side of the Bowl and peered across the draw. Up on the ridge he could see somewhere between 50 to 100 enemy troops, who were probably al-Qaeda given their black battle dress uniforms. As they moved along the ridge, some of them were firing at his 1st Platoon. The 1st Platoon was returning fire and hitting many of the enemy fighters. Kraft recalled it was like watching a carnival game "when you have the ducks going around in a circle and you shoot and they go down and they just continue going around. It was just like that."[62]

BP EVE

At this point the operation in the southern end of the valley seemed to be well in hand, even if the sudden and intense enemy contact had surprised the Soldiers of C Company. Kraft's unit was not the only element of 1-87 IN to make contact with the enemy, however; its brother company to the north had experienced enemy contact as well. Crombie's Company A was supposed to land on HLZ 5. Instead, as the Chinook carrying Crombie, his 1st Platoon, and the scouts approached the landing zone, the pilot determined he could not land there due to the rough terrain. The chopper drifted farther and farther down the slope to the northwest until it touched down on Route CHEVY, the trail leading directly into the draw where BP EVE was to be established. Crombie and his troops scrambled off the aircraft and went to ground. Once the Chinook departed, the troops got up and prepared to move, only to discover about 100 yards away a number of enemy troops holding AK-47s and an RPG. "They were young, probably 14 years old," Crombie remembered. "If they were older guys we probably would have had some big problems on the LZ, but they were probably scared out of their wits."[63] The M203 gunners fired a few grenade rounds and, according to Crombie, "that was it."[64]

As the scouts took off to the south to establish observation posts between EVE and GINGER, Crombie ordered his troops, now consisting of only 22 men from the 1st Platoon, to move off to the east up the draw to EVE. Within a short time, the BP was established. Looking toward the southwest, Crombie could see right down into the village of Marzak. Just as Wiercinski and Corkran had noted, Crombie immediately recognized that the village was empty, especially of women and children. "They'd probably been gone for a week. You just got that feeling," he recalled.[65] But Crombie could see 10 to 12 men moving out of the village. To him, too, the situation was now obvious: "If they've got weapons, they're the enemy."[66]

Crombie grabbed his ETAC and told him to get a CAS aircraft up on the net to attack the men leaving the village. Instead, they both discovered that attempting to gain access to CAS on this day would lead to a great deal of frustration. Crombie remembered, "On the first day when the opportunity presented itself more frequently, we couldn't get a bomb—we couldn't pay for one—because the focus was on Charlie Company, 1-87 and the battalion TAC in the south. . . . At that point, one bomb would have saved us from tracking down 10 or 12 al-Qaeda guys later, but we couldn't get it."[67] Instead, A Company would spend most of 2 March watching and hearing the battle rather than participating in it.

Insertion of 2-187 Infantry

Farther to the north at about 0615 Lieutenant Colonel Preysler was landing with the 2-187 TAC and Baltazar's C Company at three different HLZs. Baltazar's 3d Platoon, tasked to establish BP DIANE, landed at HLZ 4. His 1st Platoon, with responsibility for BP CINDY, landed at HLZ 3. Preysler's TAC, Baltazar, and the 2d Platoon landed at HLZ 1. The scene at HLZ 1 was similar to what the other companies had experienced on their landings. Baltazar

Figure 23. The al-Qaeda compound near HLZ 1.

recalled, "Initially, when I landed, there was no contact. Everybody rushed off the helicopter and kind of waited until the Chinooks flew off. Then, I would say, within a minute, we heard small arms fire."[68] This time, by contrast, the fire was not directed at the troops at his LZ. Baltazar soon received a call from his 1st Platoon at HLZ 3 saying they were already in contact.[69]

Once on the ground, Preysler eyed a walled compound just northeast of the HLZ that had caught his attention during the planning for the operation. The compound was situated at the southeastern foot of a large east-west ridge that cut the Shahi Kowt in two. The building had struck him as a likely enemy strongpoint and he originally did not want to use that LZ. His anxiety was calmed somewhat by reports from reconnaissance teams before the operation that suggested the compound was unoccupied, so he decided to go ahead with HLZ 1 for the air assault. Preysler now watched as a squad from the 2d Platoon bounded across a dry creek bed between the HLZ and the compound and entered the structure to search it.[70]

At about that time, the remaining troops still deployed on HLZ 1 began to receive fire from three enemy fighters high on the ridge behind the compound. In addition to the small arms fire, an RPG round sailed over Preysler's head and landed in the perimeter. Preysler told Baltazar, "We have to move. We are too exposed here."[71] Soon, part of the 2d Platoon was laying down suppressive fire while the remaining troops bounded into the compound. They were then followed by the rest of 2d Platoon. Fortunately, Preysler was able to bring Apache helicopters to his location and those aircraft quickly killed the three enemy fighters on the ridge.[72]

Inside the compound, Preysler discovered two things. First, the compound had indeed been occupied, probably by the three men killed by the Apaches, if not others as well. Baltazar's men found two mortar tubes, a cache of RPG rounds, an American night vision device, a few handheld radios, and a great deal of foreign currency. There were also six beds indicating

Figure 24. AH-64 Apache conducting close air support on D-day.

that perhaps more than the three dead men had been living there. Apparently, the enemy had departed in a rush because they had left their shoes and a pot of hot tea brewing on the fire.[73] The second thing that Preysler realized was that the compound was not really a tenable position. The high ridge to the north looked right down into it. Not surprisingly, enemy fighters on the ridge began placing effective small arms fire into the compound's open courtyard at about that time. To counter the fire, Preysler's forward observer attempted to contact the 1-87 IN's 120-mm mortar squad in the south to put indirect fire on the enemy on the ridge, but discovered that the crew was busily engaged in supporting its own battalion. The 2-187 IN would not see any fire support from 1-87 on 2 March.[74]

Meanwhile, Baltazar had decided not to move his CP into the compound. He opted instead to set up on the outside under the cover of the eastern wall. There he noticed that the compound was now receiving fire from the vicinity of where BP CINDY was to be established. A call was again sent out to the Apaches and within minutes the aircraft had taken out those troops as well.[75] Close to an hour into the operation, Preysler decided to move a squad onto the ridge to clear off the enemy located in that area and thereby provide the vulnerable compound with some protection. Just as he was about to tell Baltazar what he wanted, the compound was shaken by concussions from large explosions. Several missiles had struck enemy positions on the ridgeline, the nearest only 300 meters from the compound. Apparently the pilot of a Predator unmanned aerial vehicle (UAV) had been watching the enemy fighters on the ridge who had been engaging the compound and the attack helicopters, and decided to launch the guided missiles onto their positions.[76]

With the enemy now disrupted, the elements in the compound began moving, but instead of clearing the ridge, Preysler decided it was time for the 2d Platoon to head for BP BETTY. Sometime after 0700 Preysler and Baltazar, along with their troops, left the compound and headed northeast over the ridge for their preplanned positions. After a 5-hour movement, Baltazar arrived near the BP, while the 2d Platoon escorted Preysler and the TAC farther north to a position between BETTY and AMY. The platoon then turned south to link up with Baltazar and establish the BP. By this time, 1st Platoon had already established BP CINDY. The 3d Platoon, making a difficult climb up the Eastern Ridge to their position, would establish DIANE a little later in the day.[77] By mid-afternoon, the 2-187 IN had completed its initial task and all three BPs were in place.

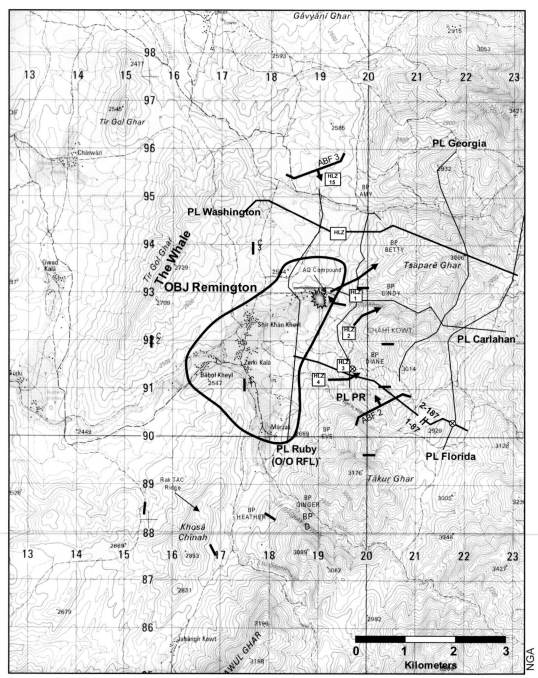

Figure 25. Operation ANACONDA, TF 2-187, 2 March 2002.

Rak TAC Ridge

At about the same time Kraft's 1st Platoon was conducting its shooting gallery firefight at BP HEATHER, the Soldiers on Rak TAC Ridge noticed three men to the north moving south on a parallel ridge toward their position. The men could very well have been part of the group that had been trying to slip by the 1st Platoon at BP HEATHER. The troops on Rak TAC Ridge were not sure if these men were enemy combatants, because they were still too distant to be recognized. One of the men appeared to be carrying something large slung over his shoulder by a dangling strap. As Wiercinski and Corkran were discussing whether they should engage these strangers, several Apaches flew up the valley on a gun run to support the embattled 1-87 IN down near GINGER. Wiercinski and Corkran watched as the unidentified men turned and opened fire on the choppers. That decided the issue.[78]

Though Wiercinski was committed to engaging the confirmed enemy fighters, he still had to decide how he was going to do it. The three enemy fighters had suddenly increased to nine, almost equal in number to their own group on the ridge. The *Rakkasan* commander decided to direct an airstrike at them, but the JDAM hit too low on the ridge to kill any of them. The next attempt involved an Apache that flew directly over the TAC position west to east, dipped its nose just beyond the crest, and launched several rockets while hovering only 6 feet over Wiercinski and his small element. The rockets also failed to kill any of the fighters. The enemy squad simply took cover and proceeded toward the TAC's position again once the Apache departed.[79]

Figure 26. Members of TF *Rakkasan* TAC on Rak TAC Ridge.

Apparently, the enemy fighters were still oblivious that there were American Soldiers on top of the ridge. Left with no choice, the men of the TAC chose to ambush the enemy fighters as they came closer. The SOF team located with Wiercinski initiated the action with their noise-suppressed M4 assault rifles. After killing one of the fighters when the ambush began, Corkran and others spent the next several hours picking off the remainder in a sort of cat and mouse game. Eventually all nine Taliban fighters were killed with no losses to the TF *Rakkasan* TAC.[80]

By this time, it was late morning and the plan for the TAC to remain on the ground for only 90 minutes had long been forgotten. The plan had changed not so much because of the enemy activities on Rak TAC Ridge, but because the battle near the Bowl had turned very ugly.

The Battle at the Bowl

Not long after Kraft had observed his 1st Platoon engaging the Taliban fighters, 82-mm mortar rounds began falling on BP HEATHER. The strange aspect about the mortar fire was that the rounds were coming from tubes located on the slopes of Takur Ghar as well as the mountain just to its south. Since the mortars in the east were supporting the enemy fighters to the west, Kraft suspected that the two elements possessed communications capabilities and were coordinating their efforts. Within about 15 or 20 minutes, several volleys had fallen precisely on the 1st Platoon's position and had wounded at least 10 Soldiers, including the platoon leader and platoon sergeant.[81]

Earlier, LaCamera had asked Kraft if he had thought about establishing a company strongpoint between the two BPs. In his planning, the C Company commander had considered this, but he wanted his platoon leaders to have the chance to operate in a more decentralized manner. At any rate, after the rapid succession of casualties in the 1st Platoon, Kraft changed his

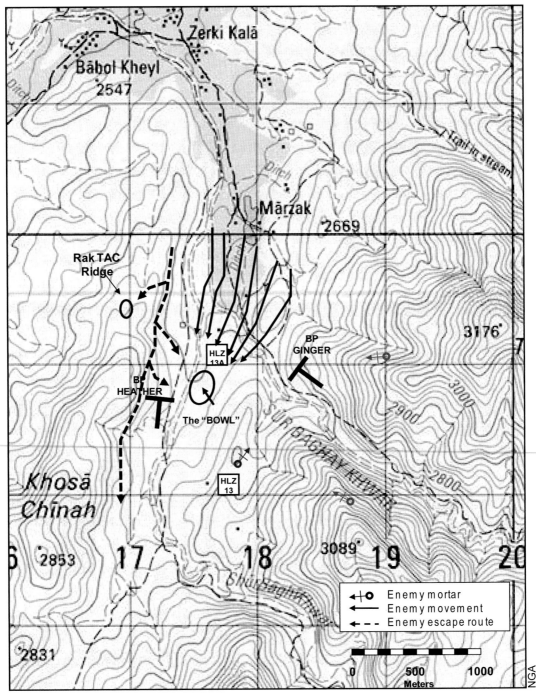

Figure 27. Operation ANACONDA, 1-87 in the Bowl, 2 March 2002.

mind and ordered most of his 2d Platoon to move up from HLZ 13 and consolidate with him at the Bowl. One squad would stay near HLZ 13 with the mortars to maintain indirect fire on the enemy to the east. When the 2d Platoon arrived, Kraft sent them to BP HEATHER to help 1st Platoon move its casualties and the rest of the platoon into the Bowl. By about 0830 the consolidation was complete.[82]

For the next hour, C Company hunkered down in its position and traded fire with the enemy while LaCamera and the ETACs attempted to acquire and coordinate CAS sorties to hit the enemy positions. At about 0930, the troops in the Bowl started receiving heavy machinegun and small arms fire from the north. The company was then fighting in three directions. According to Kraft, "We were fighting off, in my best estimate, 50 to 100 [enemy fighters] in the west, 50 to 100 in the east, and 50 to 100 to our north."[83] It soon became apparent that the troops in the north, which were wearing black al-Qaeda battle dress, were attempting to maneuver against the American infantrymen in the Bowl. "They were popping in and out of the [ravines] and heading toward our position," Kraft recalled.[84]

At about 1000, after a number of the enemy fighters from this new threat were killed, the first Coalition fixed-wing aircraft showed up on station. The aircrafts' first target was the al-Qaeda element in the north, which they quickly destroyed. Technical Sergeant McCabe, the battalion ETAC, had meanwhile been trying to coordinate for CAS to strike the positions on Takur Ghar. He was finally able to raise the aircraft that went by the call sign "Blade," a B-52 bomber whose pilot informed McCabe that he had on board 24 Mark 82 500-pound bombs. McCabe was able to plan for a strike that would bring the bomber on a route south to north and lay the bombs in a path parallel to C Company's position and about 700 meters to its east. The sergeant estimated that the enemy positions were only about 500 meters away, but he was leery of bringing such a devastating load in that close to friendly troops. He estimated that with the 700-meter standoff distance, the enemy would still be within the 200-meter blast radius of the 500-pound bombs.[85]

One minute before the B-52 strike, McCabe yelled over to LaCamera and Kraft that the plane would soon be dropping its bombs and the troops needed to stay down. "So everybody basically drew down off the ridge a little bit," McCabe recalled. "They stopped doing their suppressive fires and basically everybody got on their bellies, hands over their heads, getting ready for the airstrike. At the moment that it came in, it was loud and furious."[86] Unfortunately, the strike failed to do much damage, although as McCabe remembered, "it definitely boosted the morale. Having a B-52 drop 24 Mark-82's that close to 'friendlies,' yes, that's a hell of a booster."[87]

The real heroes to the troops of C Company that day, however, were the Apache pilots of the 3d Battalion, 101st Aviation Regiment, nicknamed the "Killer Spades." This unit had trained to operate by taking up hide positions behind hills and other terrain features, pop up to fire at the enemy, and then return to the safety of the masking feature. This tactic minimized exposure to enemy fire. Because of the terrain and the way the enemy and friendly troops were positioned, the Apaches could not operate in that manner at the south end of the Shahi Kowt. Instead, they were forced to make moving gun runs along a canyon-like route, firing into the side of the mountain as they went. If they chose to use their rockets, they would have to stop, hover, and take aim to have any hope of hitting the enemy. The pilots knew these methods would expose the Apaches to close-range direct fire, but they gamely accepted the risk.

The Apaches made their runs from the south of C Company and flew north through the BP HEATHER draw. As they flew through, they were met by a hail of fire from the enemy troops concentrated there. McCabe stated, "I do recall seeing 2.75 [inch] rockets coming off of the Killer Spades. They shot their 30-mm at them. . . . Again, they would fire their weapon systems, continue flying, and they received heavy ground fire from the guys. I believe they made probably four attacks, at best."[88] At the end of those runs that morning, five of the six Apaches available had to return to Bagram. They had become too damaged to continue flying combat missions in the Shahi Kowt Valley.

The 120-mm mortar crew near the Bowl had also been busy trying to contribute to the overall effort. Still positioned about 300 meters south of the Bowl, it was conducting counterfire missions against the enemy mortars on the high ground to the east. McCabe happened to be looking at the 120-mm mortar position when an enemy mortar round struck right in the middle of it, but miraculously none of the men were injured. McCabe later remarked, "How they survived that, it still just boggles me."[89] The mortar crewmen dusted themselves off and rapidly moved to a second position to begin firing again. Then, the crew was soon struck by a second enemy mortar round. This time they suffered several casualties and the 120-mm mortar was knocked out of action.[90]

LaCamera decided it was time to consolidate everybody at his location. While C Company provided heavy suppressive fire, the mortar crew and the squad from 2d Platoon dragged the wounded men to the west and then north behind a small ridge to stay out of the open kill zone that lay between C Company and the second mortar position. Eventually all the troops were assembled in the Bowl.[91]

While the Bowl provided a level of safety from the enemy's small arms fire, it was a good target for the enemy mortars. With the American troops concentrated in a relatively small area, it was easier to drop mortar rounds into the depression and expect to cause casualties. Indeed, it was the 82-mm mortars, manned by well-trained Taliban and al-Qaeda crews that ultimately produced the greatest number of casualties in C Company. Hall recalled that the enemy troops "weren't very good shots with their weapons, but their mortar fire was accurate in that they adjusted fire. . . . These guys took awhile to adjust the rounds, but once they did adjust the rounds they served a purpose, they executed."[92] The enemy not only knew how to fire their weapons, they understood prudent tactics as well. They would fire their mortars as long as they were confident that no Coalition aircraft were in the area. Once a plane or helicopter was spotted, the mortar crew would move into a cave or a hide position until the aircraft departed. Then the crew would resume firing.[93]

Although the 82-mm mortars were the most lethal enemy weapon that day, small arms fire remained a problem. The C Company Soldiers had to maintain positions on the lip of the Bowl to provide return fire on the enemy. The problem was that if a Soldier lay on the east side of the Bowl, the enemy in the west had a shot at his back. Conversely, those on the west side were being shot at by the enemy up on the high ground to the east. Of course the Soldiers down in the Bowl were the most likely to be hit by mortar fragments. As Major Hall remembered it, "NCOs had worked hard to convince the Soldiers that they could get up there [on the lip] and still be safe, which was quite a challenge, but they did it. The Soldiers performed—they were true warriors, getting up on those ridgelines . . . when they mortared you, you'd want to get up there [on the lip] and [when] they'd snipe you, you'd want to go back. It [was] kind of a Catch 22 situation."[94]

Before noon, an 82-mm mortar round landed in the Bowl about 25 feet from the battalion TAC. That one shell wounded Hall, the battalion command sergeant major, the fire support officer, the operations NCO, and one of the RTOs. Though LaCamera was with the group of men at the TAC, he suffered no wounds. By noon, the number of wounded men in the Bowl had reached 20; the vast majority had been hurt by mortar rounds.[95]

The battalion surgeon and his medics performed heroically that day. As the casualties piled up, LaCamera faced the decision of whether to bring in medical evacuation (MEDEVAC) choppers in broad daylight and risk getting them shot down or wait until dark when the al-Qaeda and Taliban fighters were expected to break off the engagement. The surgeon, who had been wounded, told LaCamera that he and his medics could stabilize even the most seriously wounded at that point and keep them alive until dark. LaCamera called Wiercinski and told him that his wounded men could wait until nightfall to be evacuated.[96]

As the wounded increased, the force in the Bowl faced another emerging problem: a shortage of ammunition. When C Company began to receive fire on the LZs, many of the troops had dumped their rucksacks to return fire and maneuver on the enemy if necessary. As the elements moved off to their planned locations and later as the company consolidated in the Bowl, many Soldiers had left their rucks where they had dumped them. Unfortunately, much of the spare ammunition from their basic load was still in the packs. This was particularly true of the ammunition for the M240 machineguns. To compensate for the ammunition shortage, Kraft ordered the troops to direct fire at targets they could clearly identify and not use suppressive fire techniques, which expended a great deal more ammunition. Additionally, the company commander sent Soldiers to retrieve some of the rucksacks that were accessible, which further eased the ammunition shortage.[97]

The battle continued throughout the day. With one out of every four men stranded near GINGER now wounded, Colonel Wiercinski, still up on Rak TAC Ridge, began to reevaluate the original plan. There were no civilians to worry about and the enemy was aggressively fighting, not attempting to flee. Additionally, LaCamera and the elements of 1-87 IN in the Bowl were at a distinct disadvantage. Faced with a larger enemy force that held the high ground around him, LaCamera could not effectively seize the initiative even had his force been entirely healthy. He and his command were pinned down.

Later that afternoon, Wiercinski decided on a new plan. He contacted Preysler and told him that the 2-187 IN was now the main effort. Wiercinski also directed Preysler to move 2-187 IN TAC and C Company platoons to the base of the valley (below their respective BPs) and get into pickup zone (PZ) posture. The TF *Rakkasan* commander wanted to consolidate the units at another HLZ and have it sweep through the valley in lieu of Zia's Afghan units.

However, after he passed on the plan to Baltazar and as Preysler's TAC began movement to the PZ, Wiercinski reconsidered again.[98] Wiercinski now decided to extract the elements of LaCamera's 1-87 IN out of the south and return it to Bagram where the wounded could be treated, and to send Crombie's A Company, 1-87 IN, north to link up with Preysler's battalion. Preysler would pull Crombie's company and all the platoons of his C Company up to the vicinity of HLZ 15 to secure that location to bring in fresh troops (which would include Preysler's own A Company).[99] In any event, the plan would have to wait until dark when US forces' fighting capabilities were overwhelming and the enemy could be suppressed to the point where helicopters could land near LaCamera's position.

The sun set around 1800 that evening and soon after an AC-130 gunship arrived on station over the Bowl. With superb night-capable optics and an impressive array of miniguns and 40-mm and 105-mm cannon, the Spectre gunship was soon detecting and hitting the enemy with accurate and concentrated fire. Kraft later described the Spectre support as "awesome."[100] Within an hour, enemy fire had diminished to the point that LaCamera felt it was safe to bring in two Blackhawk MEDEVAC choppers to get his most critically wounded Soldiers out.[101] The helicopters landed just to the west of the Bowl. As Soldiers struggled to get the wounded men loaded, the LZ began to take fire once again. Immediately, the troops on the perimeter returned fire to suppress the enemy. Though the two Blackhawks had to remain in this vulnerable location as the wounded were loaded, they eventually departed safely for Bagram with the first 14 Soldiers wounded in action (WIA).[102]

Wiercinski contacted LaCamera to discuss his situation and relay the new plan. LaCamera told the TF *Rakkasan* commander that he wanted to bring in C Company's reserve, the 3d Platoon, that night. Thus reinforced, LaCamera believed he could hold the Bowl. Wiercinski overruled his battalion commander and told him that the 1-87 IN was going to be pulled out and sent to Bagram to refit for future operations.[103]

Meanwhile, the AC-130 had departed to refuel, but once it was back on station, LaCamera was given an hour for his men to locate their rucksacks, and any other previously discarded equipment, while under the protection of the Spectre's guns.[104] At about midnight, additional helicopters landed near the Bowl and the 1-87 IN departed for Bagram. During 18 hours of almost continuous combat, the battalion sustained 26 casualties, but miraculously none became fatalities.[105] The Taliban and al-Qaeda fighters that opposed them were not so lucky.

Reinforcing the Operation: The Valley on Day 2

During the night, Wiercinski decided to bring in his reserve battalion, the 1-187 IN. But before he had a chance to direct this phase of the operation, the *Rakkasan* commander decided to pull his own command post out of the valley. At about 0300 on 3 March, aircraft landed near Rak TAC Ridge, extracted Wiercinski and his small element, and then headed for Bagram.[106]

Once back at Bagram, Lieutenant Colonel Corkran received his new mission—land his 1-187 IN at HLZ 15 at the northern end of the valley near BP AMY and send it south along the Eastern Ridge to clear it of enemy all the way to BP DIANE. As he prepared his battalion for the mission, Corkran also received an additional mission—clear the BP AMY draw prior to the sweep along the Eastern Ridge. The enemy had been directing mortar fire at Preysler's position from somewhere in that vicinity and the positions were believed to be in the draw. A senior SOF officer who had a sniper team observing the draw had requested that the ravine be searched and cleared. At Bagram, that officer told Corkran, "If you try to go over the mountain, it will become something horrendous for you. I have a sniper team, Juliet 01 [J01], that can see up the valley. So if you will trust me on moving up the valley with my guys and putting your snipers up where they can look down, you can make a pretty quick move of this to get up there."[107] With the assurances of the SOF officer that 1-187 would have plenty of early warning of any enemy movement in or near the draw, Corkran agreed to the plan.[108] The 1-187 IN was to land at HLZ 15 at noon on 3 March.

By about 1800 on 2 March the enemy fire at HLZ 15 had died down enough to bring in the next contingent of fresh troops, Preysler's own A Company, 2d Battalion, 187th Infantry (A/2-187 IN) commanded by Captain Kevin Butler, along with Baltazar's 60-mm mortar platoon. On A/2-187 IN's arrival at approximately 2000, Butler established the initial HLZ 15 perimeter defense.

Figure 28. Troops of 1-187 Infantry in AMY draw.

Meanwhile, Crombie, with Company A, 1-87 IN and the 1-87 IN Scout Platoon had been ordered to move north to link up with Baltazar's 3d Platoon at BP DIANE. From there, the two units would move to BP CINDY to pick up 1st Platoon, and then would consolidate with Preysler, Baltazar, and the 2d Platoon at or near BP BETTY. From there, the group would move to HLZ 15. Crombie knew that the movement was going to be easier to plan than execute because of the rugged terrain between BPs EVE and DIANE. After walking all night, Company A, 1-87 IN had moved only 500 meters. As dawn approached on 3 March, the ground began to level out and the movement sped up.[109]

Lieutenant Colonel Preysler had expected to receive a call well before dawn reporting that Crombie had linked up with the 3d Platoon at DIANE. The linkup did not occur, however, until well after first light. Preysler was concerned that his platoons might get engaged piecemeal during the daylight, so he ordered them all to start moving to HLZ 15 for consolidation. The battalion commander arrived at the LZ with Baltazar and the 2d Platoon before noon and set up a perimeter. Meanwhile, Crombie, with the 3d Platoon attached, ran into enemy resistance near the same compound that had held up Preysler the day before. After a significant firefight but sustaining no casualties, Crombie's men dumped their rucksacks and continued to march north.[110]

As Crombie's force moved, another part of Corkran's 1-187 IN was loading into choppers at Bagram. For this mission, Corkran had only his own C Company commanded by Captain Patrick Aspland, the 3d Platoon of D Company, the battalion Scout Platoon, and a sniper team from a Canadian Army unit. His A Company and the rest of his D Company had remained at Shahbaz Airfield at Jacobabad, and his B Company and mortars were held in reserve. To provide Corkran additional combat power, Wiercinski attached B Company, 1st Battalion, 87th Infantry (B/1-87 IN), commanded by Captain Christopher Cornell, to the 1-187 IN, which then made Corkran's command a TF. The TF took off for HLZ 15 at noon.[111]

At HLZ 15, Preysler and Baltazar began to receive mortar fire from a lone 82-mm mortar located on the Whale. The enemy mortar crew was crafty and well trained. The very first round landed only 30 meters from Preysler's CP. Several CAS sorties attempted to take out the position, but it was no easy target. "You could see the aircraft way above us, up high, kind of circling, and sometimes you could hear it," Preysler recalled, "so as soon as they saw that, [the mortar crew] went to ground. So the aircraft, after it checked in and got its coordinates, would conduct its attack, and then 5 minutes after it flew away, the mortar gunner would come back up and drop a couple of rounds just to let us know he was still there."[112]

During the flight to HLZ 15, Corkran could hear from the radio chatter that there was enemy fire on the LZ. The air mission commander was instructed to take the aircraft on a long orbit around the AO to see if the fire would die down and thus allow the aircraft to land. But, the fire did not slacken and the choppers were running low on fuel. Corkran recalled, "We were going to go out and land at one of the refuel sites. There was a refuel site they had near Khost, but they ended up waving us off and

Figure 29. Airstrikes hitting enemy troops in GINGER pass

saying, 'Return to base.' . . . so I was like, 'Got it. No big deal. We will retry again.'"[113] In any event, the aircraft carrying Cornell's B Company, 1-87 IN, did not get the abort message, and proceeded into HLZ 15 while the rest of TF 1-187 flew back to Bagram. Fortunately, neither the choppers nor B Company suffered any losses or damage on the hot LZ.[114]

The rest of Corkran's TF 1-187 IN finally arrived at the LZ at about 2000 on 3 March. Once on the ground, and after a bit of frustration with terrain orientation due to the location where the choppers landed, Corkran soon began movement toward the AMY draw, picking up Cornell's B Company, 1-87, on the way.

The movement up AMY draw was slow going due to the darkness and the rough, rocky terrain. In addition to the SOF team called J01 providing eyes on the draw, TF 1-187 had an AC-130 providing additional observation and firepower. Corkran felt secure that any enemy in the draw would be picked up and dealt with effectively, but sometime after midnight he was notified through his ETAC that his AC-130 coverage had been suddenly pulled away. This move appeared to reflect priorities elsewhere in the valley.

Back down at HLZ 15, Colonel Wiercinski, who had brought his TAC back into the AO earlier that night, was with Lieutenant Colonel Preysler in the 2-187 IN TAC discussing the situation in the valley. Suddenly two CH-47s flew over the men. "We were both surprised like, 'Who else is coming in?'" Preysler recalled.

> We saw the [refueling] probe, so we knew they weren't ours and they were
> SOF helicopters. But they flew over our position headed up toward . . . [Takur

Ghar], and landed up there. Then the next thing we knew this helicopter flew over us again from the south to the north and landed about 700 meters from our position. That was when we got word of what had happened, that they had some casualties up there.[115]

There was trouble on the top of the largest mountain in the Shahi Kowt.

Disaster on Takur Ghar

The MH-47 (call sign Razor 03) that had landed near Preysler was an aircraft from the 160th Special Operations Aviation Regiment (SOAR) on a mission to insert a US Navy SEAL team called Mako-30 on the top of Takur Ghar for a special reconnaissance mission. The purpose of the move was to put observers above GINGER pass after the decision to withdraw 1-87 IN had been made. Once it was on the mountain, the SEAL team could easily survey the draw and call in airstrikes on any enemy activity.

Along with another 160th SOAR MH-47 (call sign Razor 04), Razor 03 had stopped at a forward arming and refueling point (FARP) after arriving from Bagram earlier that night. At 0230 on 4 March, the two aircraft lifted off from the FARP and about 15 minutes later Razor 03 approached the top of Takur Ghar. As the helicopter pulled up to land, crewmembers spotted evidence that the enemy occupied the summit. Once on the ground, there was a slight delay in Mako-30's exit from the helicopter. The delay was just long enough for a concealed al-Qaeda fighter to launch an RPG at the Chinook. The resulting explosion knocked out the aircraft's electrical power and hydraulics, rendering the 7.62-mm miniguns and the pilot's multifunctional displays, radios, and other flight control equipment useless.[116]

The Chinook's rear ramp had been in the down position to allow the exit of the SEAL team, but with the hydraulics leaking all over the floor it was now impossible to get it back up. As the pilot attempted to take off and get the chopper out of danger, one of the SEALs, Petty Officer First Class Neil Roberts, slipped on the oily floor and fell. Roberts slipped farther toward the ramp as the chopper nosed up in the air while lifting off. Razor 03's rear M-60 gunner attempted to keep Roberts from sliding out, but instead, both slipped off the ramp and out of the Chinook. Fortunately for him, the gunner was tethered to the inside of the chopper, but Roberts fell to the ground 6 feet below.[117] With the intercom system down, the pilot was oblivious to the fact that Roberts had fallen out and continued flying north trying to assess the seriousness of the damage. Soon notified that a SEAL was still at the LZ and that a man was dangling out the back of his aircraft, the pilot decided to go back for the SEAL as soon as the gunner was back inside. However, just as the ramp gunner was recovered, the Chinook began to shudder and the pilot knew he had to find a safe place to land or he would crash into the mountains below.[118] When the pilot safely put the Chinook down, he was only 700 meters from Preysler's TAC.[119]

Razor 04, unable to contact Razor 03 by radio, called the AC-130 then on station in the valley. The Spectre pilot told Razor 03's pilot that Razor 04 had been forced down and provided the coordinates to where the Chinook then sat. Armed with Razor 03's location, Razor 04 flew back into the valley, rescued the crew and the remaining members of the SEAL team, and flew them to Gardez.[120]

Back at Bagram, the QRF from A Company, 1st Battalion, 75th Ranger Regiment (A/1-75) was notified of the situation. At about 0400 the QRF commander, Captain Nathan Self, began to plan the rescue mission. At the same time, the Mako-30 team leader and the pilot of Razor 04 made a quick assessment of the situation and decided that the Chinook crew would reinsert the SEAL team on Takur Ghar to try and rescue Roberts. At about 0420 the Chinook left Gardez en route for the mountain, and just before 0500 Mako-30 was successfully inserted at the same LZ where Roberts had fallen.[121]

Immediately on insertion, Mako-30 came under enemy fire. In the fight, Technical Sergeant John Chapman, the team's Air Force combat controller, was mortally wounded. The team broke contact and, sliding in the snow, moved about 800 meters down the south slope to safety. During the descent, two of the SEALs were hit by enemy fire.[122] With one man dead and two wounded, Mako-30's mission had rapidly changed from rescue to survival.

At about the time that Mako-30 was inserted on the mountain, Captain Self, who was not aware that the SEALs had been reinserted on top of Takur Ghar, led his 22-man Ranger QRF onto two Chinooks—Razor 01 and Razor 02—at Bagram. Accompanied by an ETAC and a three-man Air Force Combat Search and Rescue (CSAR) team, they began flying toward the Shahi Kowt Valley. By the time these aircraft arrived near Takur Ghar, the sun was up and the mission pilot, flying Razor 01, became concerned that the two choppers would be landing in daylight and on a very small LZ. The pilot was also concerned that if the aircraft were to receive fire on landing, as had two others already, the two Chinooks might collide in their hurry to get away. He decided to send Razor 02 to Gardez and bring its load of Rangers in later. Razor 01 was going in alone.[123]

A little after 0600 as Razor 01 approached the LZ it too received heavy and accurate fire. Struck by bullets and an RPG round, the big Chinook made a hard landing on Takur Ghar, but not before the copilot was struck in the leg with a bullet. Both door gunners were also hit during the approach, and Sergeant Phil Svitak, the right door gunner, died as a result.[124]

Unable to take off, the Chinook became an easy target as bullets ripped through the aircraft and the men inside. As Self and the Rangers attempted to exit the aircraft, they ran into a withering blast of small arms fire. In rapid succession, three more men were killed or wounded. The enemy was all around the chopper and firing into it from multiple directions. Desperately the Rangers attempted to set up a defensive position at the back of the downed chopper and return fire. Gradually, they were able to suppress their adversaries enough to allow the ETAC to start coordinating CAS strikes against the enemy positions.[125]

Around 0700, 45 minutes after Razor 01 had landed, the ETAC succeeded in bringing two F-15 aircraft on station. After several dry runs, the two fighters made several strafing runs, firing their 20-mm cannons into the enemy positions on the mountaintop. Though the strafing runs did not have an immediate effect on the enemy, the presence of the US Air Force certainly heightened the morale of the stranded QRF.[126]

Back at Gardez, Razor 02, carrying the other 13 Rangers from the QRF, took off for the mountain at about the time the F-15s arrived. En route, Mako-30 contacted Razor 02 and told him that the LZ was hot and that the F-15s were about to make their strafing runs. The SEAL team leader also informed Razor 02 that his team was not on top of the mountain but down slope on the south side. After the F-15s departed, the chopper pilot landed his load of Rangers only 300 meters from the SEAL team at around 0730. Once on the ground, Staff Sergeant Arin K. Canon, the leader for the second QRF element, contacted Self and informed him where the other half of the QRF landed. A quick look at the map told them that Canon's team would have a 2,000-foot climb at altitudes of over 8,000 feet to reach the stranded half of the QRF. Nevertheless, Self ordered the sergeant to move out—the force on top was in dire need of help.[127]

As Canon and his section struggled its way up Takur Ghar, Self and his group continued to receive fire. The enemy had now begun using 82-mm mortars and was attempting to bracket the downed MH-47 where the CSAR team was treating the wounded. As the rounds came closer to the aircraft, Self and one of the Chinook pilots decided the wounded needed to be moved to a safer location. They chose a depression about 20 meters from the chopper.[128]

Once the injured were moved to the new position, Self realized that if his force was to be extracted, he needed to take out a key enemy position on the very top of the mountain, only about 100 meters away. Otherwise, no friendly helicopters would be able to safely land. Self and five other men began to assault the enemy strongpoint, but were quickly driven back. The enemy troops were entrenched in a well-fortified bunker. CAS seemed to be the only solution.[129]

Self's ETAC went to work getting two F-16s lined up for a strike on the bunker. After one of the "Vipers" dropped two 500-pound bombs and failed to knock out the bunker, the ETAC acquired the services of a Predator armed with Hellfire missiles. The Predator pilot failed to hit the position with the first Hellfire, but the second successfully struck the bunker and killed the enemy inside. Though resistance from the bunker was eliminated, enemy mortar fire remained a problem. However, shortly after the Predator did its work, Self noticed that the mortar fire had shifted down hill. He knew now that Canon and the rest of the QRF were getting close, and by 1100 the two elements conducted a successful link-up.[130]

The combined QRF cleared the top of the mountain and by 1130 notified CJTF *Mountain* at Bagram that the PZ they had selected was free of the enemy and available for extraction. That message had hardly been sent when the entire American force once again came under RPG and machinegun fire. The enemy had returned in force.[131]

This development forced CJTF *Mountain* to cancel the mission of the 70-man QRF that had assembled at Bagram. Instead, the extraction time was pushed back to 2015 when darkness hindered the enemy and AC-130 Spectre support would be available. For the remainder of the day, the Rangers traded long-range fire with the enemy and watched as a parade of aircraft from various services and nations came to their aid.[132] A little after 2000, two MH-47s landed and began extracting the wounded and the Air Force CSAR team. Once on their way to Gardez, those Chinooks were followed into the PZ by two other aircraft that picked up the remaining force and the bodies of the men who had been killed during the action, including Petty Officer First Class Neil Roberts. The entire operation on Takur Ghar had lasted about 17 hours.

What had started out as a special reconnaissance mission had turned into a series of daring rescue attempts, each degenerating into close combat against a determined enemy. Obviously, the fact that SOF planners did not know the enemy was on Takur Ghar, in such strength and in such well prepared positions, was a serious intelligence failure. In retrospect, it is clear that the SEAL team should not have been sent there. The initial contact with the enemy caused the failure of the mission and, more importantly, the loss of Neil Roberts. The follow-up rescue attempts resulted in the deaths of six more men and numerous others wounded.

Still, the battle was a testimony to the increasing effectiveness of Army–Air Force joint operations and the fighting tenacity of the American Soldier. Captain Self and the rest of the men on the mountain would have been hard pressed even to survive the day without the efforts of the ETAC, the CSAR personnel, and, of course, the pilots overhead who brought so much to the fight. Moreover, the battle drove home the point that the American Soldier is committed to never abandoning a fellow Soldier on the battlefield. It was a tragedy that six men died trying to rescue one. But, it is safe to say that, as long as they thought Roberts was alive and knew his approximate location, those men believed they had an important and honorable mission.

Clearing the Eastern Ridge

The fight on Takur Ghar also drove home the point that al-Qaeda and Taliban forces in the Shahi Kowt Valley were not going to flee. Instead, they planned to fight to the death and take as many American Soldiers with them as possible. The enemy fighters who had reinforced Takur Ghar was only one indicator of this fact. Further confirmation came when Coalition military intelligence picked up a signal from a commander in the Islamic Movement of Uzbekistan (IMU) located somewhere outside the valley who was urging subordinates and local Afghans to conduct jihad and fight the infidels inside the valley. The exhortations were effective as several hundred fighters attempted to enter the valley during the operation.[133]

These were the enemy troops that Corkran's, and later LaCamera's, Soldiers were to fight over the next several days, but not in BP AMY draw. After walking all night, TF 1-187 IN arrived around dawn at the point in the draw right below where the J01 SOF team was positioned. Dropping off supplies there for the team, the battalion continued toward its objective, which consisted of several caves in the draw where military intelligence personnel believed the enemy mortar crews might be hiding. They discovered several mud huts and two Soviet-made 57-mm towed antiaircraft guns, neither of which showed any recent use. Corkran then received a call from Colonel Wiercinski ordering him to move back out of the draw, turn south, and clear the Eastern Ridge of enemy troops all the way down to BP GINGER.[134]

Immediately turning back, the TF made good time in the daylight. It soon arrived back in the valley and Corkran halted the column to issue instructions. He put Cornell's B Company, 1-87 IN, in the lead and the TF began its movement south. Cornell's company, moving in a maneuver called bounding overwatch where one element provides covering fire while another moves forward, had traveled about 1,700 meters when it ran into the same al-Qaeda compound that Presysler and Crombie had encountered. Cornell contacted Corkran about the structure and soon the two men were scanning the position with binoculars. After determining that the compound was likely clear of enemy, Corkran turned to Cornell and told him to go clear the area.[135]

Company B cautiously moved to the compound, but encountered no resistance. Once inside, Cornell and his troops noticed that the food Preysler's troops had discovered sitting on the table 2 days before was still there undisturbed. Also inside were the mortar tubes, weapons, and ammunition.[136] While Cornell's men cleared the compound, Corkran received additional orders from TF *Rakkasan* to go only as far south as BP DIANE. Corkran then ordered Cornell to turn west and occupy BP CINDY while the rest of the TF continued to head south. Aspland's C Company, 1-187 IN, now took up the lead.[137]

TF 1-187 IN's movement toward BP DIANE was resolute but cautious. Not only was the potential for enemy contact a concern, but there were old Soviet antipersonnel mines strewn across the area as well. Complicating the problem was the snow that still covered the ground in patches. "We had some old Soviet maps with where we thought mine concentrations were, but stuff had shifted over the years with the ice and snow and all that kind of stuff, so we were pretty nervous about that," Corkran recalled.[138]

By the afternoon of 4 March, TF 1-187 IN had arrived near BP DIANE. Aspland deployed C Company to establish that BP while Corkran moved his TAC and the platoon of D Company to a

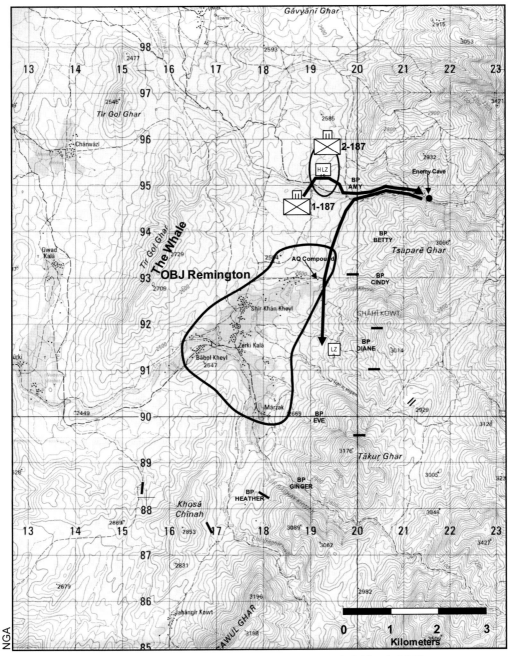

Figure 30. Operation ANACONDA, TF 1-187, 4–6 March 2002.

point about midway between the two line companies, establishing mutually supporting BPs integrated to cover the central part of the Shahi Kowt Valley. In their new positions, the men of TF 1-187 IN had a commanding view of the valley. Corkran recalled,

> What we had was almost amphitheater like. We had a commanding view of Shir Khan Kheyl all the way across to Babol Kheyl, but we couldn't really see (it was sort of down and below our line of sight) into Marzak. But we had a great view of the valley and we didn't have to go down there to stand on it to see it.[139]

By the evening of 4 March, all BPs from AMY to DIANE had been reestablished by the units of TF *Rakkasan*, but the enemy's primary route seemed to be the pass through the mountains leading southeast from where BP GINGER was supposed to have been established. GINGER had to be closed and Colonel Wiercinski selected LaCamera's 1-87 IN to do it.

Insertion of TF *Summit*

Back at Bagram, LaCamera was preparing to take his battalion back into the valley. Since part of Crombie's A Company was still in the Shahi Kowt Valley, LaCamera gave that company's two remaining platoons, which had stayed at Bagram on 2 March, to Captain Kraft to reinforce his badly depleted C Company.[140] Wiercinski further reinforced 1-87 IN with C Company, 4th Battalion, 31st Infantry (C/4-31 IN)—a unit that belonged to the 10th Mountain Division and had just arrived from Kuwait—and B Company, 1-187 IN, which was the brigade reserve. Additionally, LaCamera received Corkran's 81-mm mortar platoon. Now with three full companies and other attachments, TF 1-87 IN was ready to reenter the fight, this time named after the battalion's historic call sign—TF *Summit*.

At about 1630 on the afternoon of 4 March, TF *Summit* was inserted into HLZ 3 just to the west of BP DIANE under the overwatching guns of Aspland's C Company. Once on the ground, LaCamera received a mission change via radio. CJTF *Mountain* wanted him to seize the top of Takur Ghar Mountain and clear it of the enemy. Preysler, back near HLZ 15, was listening to the conversation. He recalled,

> Somebody told [LaCamera] that he was going to have to attack the hill and move all the way up to the top of GINGER and I will never forget his response. It was, "Yeah, I'll do that, but somebody back there is not seeing the same map I am." In other words, if you saw the terrain, it was just a tall snow covered mountain that just dominated.[141]

TF *Summit* began its move before dark. Stumbling up the steep and rocky grade, the troops made it about one quarter the way up the side of the mountain, over terrain described by Kraft as "ungodly,"[142] before settling into a patrol base to endure a cold, snowy night. During the night, the TF received two groups of visitors. The first was Roger Crombie and his now undermanned A Company. They had retraced their steps from HLZ 15 during the day and rejoined the TF at the patrol base for the remainder of the mission. The second group was several Taliban fighters who came down from the mountain in a snowstorm to surrender, some of the very few enemy fighters who did so during Operation ANACONDA.[143]

The next day LaCamera received a new mission, much to his and his Soldiers' relief. Instead of climbing to the top of Takur Ghar, TF *Summit* was directed to secure a downed helicopter somewhere to the northwest of Takur Ghar. LaCamera's plan was to send C Company, 4-31

IN, to an overwatch position to the west; Kraft's C Company, 1-87 IN, was sent to another overwatch position on high ground to the north, and Crombie's A Company, 1-87 IN, was sent to secure the helicopter.[144] After dark Crombie moved his company uneventfully into position. Kraft, however, ran into a 7- to 10-man Taliban squad that opened fire with small arms. For the movement, though, Kraft had received the assistance of an AC-130 that made short work of the enemy fighters. Once C Company, 1-87 IN, was in position, Crombie's A Company made the search of the target area but found no helicopter. The reports of the downed helicopter had been inaccurate.[145]

The following morning dawned cold, crisp, and clear. TF *Summit* was now situated on various pieces of high ground south of Corkran's TF 1-187 IN and on the western slopes of Takur Ghar. From their positions to the southeast of the villages, the troops of TF *Summit* could clearly look down into the towns of Objective REMINGTON. What they could see were enemy troops hurriedly loading what appeared to be civilian sport utility vehicles (SUVs) as well as other enemy activity in all three villages. Kraft, who had brought his own mortars with him this time, opened fire on the enemy vehicles. LaCamera had also brought along the battalion's 81-mm mortars and the remaining 120-mm mortars that had not been brought in on 2 March. Soon, all TF *Summit* mortars were busy dropping rounds on the Taliban and al-Qaeda fighters. Kraft recalled that the mortars "were pretty successful in destroying a lot of enemy personnel in two villages that day."[146]

By 6 March TF *Summit* had pushed almost all the way to the original BP GINGER. The enemy was effectively cut off from escape to the east. Still, the Taliban and al-Qaeda fighters did not seem to be running. As TF *Summit* had seen, many were still concentrated in the villages in the valley. It was apparent that there were no civilians in the valley, and as a result, CJTF *Mountain* had declared Shahi Kowt Valley a free-fire zone. Numerous CAS sorties soon arrived to soften up the area for follow-on assaults into the villages.

By this time, Zia Lodin was ready to send his troops back into the fight. His confidence had been renewed, especially by the news that JSOTF-N had requested the assistance of Afghan mechanized forces to participate in a joint operation with his units. The two Afghan commands were to conduct a simultaneous sweep of the Whale and the valley villages. The preparatory bombardment for this new operation began on 6 March.

Operation GLOCK, 6–12 March 2001

From 6 to 9 March Coalition aircraft pounded the Whale and the villages. The violence of the airstrikes caused several al-Qaeda troops to surrender, some while still carrying their weapons. While the airstrikes took place, ODAs 394, 594, and 372 prepared their Pashtun militiamen for their role in what became known as Operation GLOCK.

The plan called for Zia's men to move past the western side of the Whale and assemble at an assault position at the south end of the mountain. An Afghan mechanized force would concurrently move to the northern entrance to the valley. The signal to begin the attack was the dropping of a 15,000-pound BLU-82 "Daisy Cutter" bomb by the US Air Force on the top of the Whale at 0500 the day of the operation. At that signal, the two forces would conduct a converging attack toward the villages with Coalition aircraft in support.[147]

The Afghan mechanized force consisted of about 600 men, 4 T-54 tanks, 6 BMP armored personnel carriers, and several truck-mounted rocket launchers. The unit was commanded by General Gul Haidar, an ethnic Tajik, and was composed primarily of Tajiks, traditional adversaries of the Pashtun. Thus, it was no easy task to get Zia and Haidar to collaborate and plan the mission. The SF personnel involved in the negotiations between the two Afghan militia commands accomplished an extraordinary feat in getting these two commanders to work together.[148]

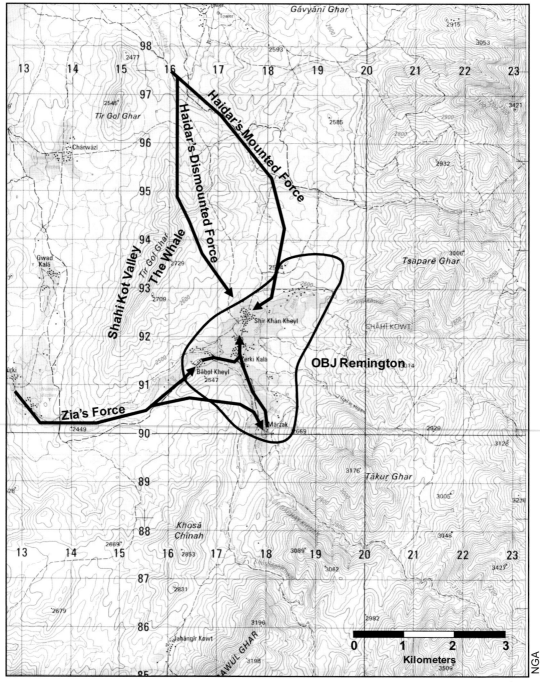

Figure 31. Operation ANACONDA Glock, 11–12 March 2002.

The Tajiks arrived on 8 March and after 2 days of negotiations and planning, moved to their assault positions on the afternoon of 10 March. While Zia's force positioned in the south, Haidar's troops moved directly to the planned jump off point. However, instead of holding in place at the base of the Whale as planned, the dismounted elements began climbing the north end of the mountain even as the Coalition aircraft were dropping bombs on the summit. Once on top, the Tajiks constructed a huge bonfire despite the existence of enemy troops on the mountain and the potential for attracting mortar fire. The presence of Haidar's men on the top of the Whale thus forced the cancellation of the Daisy Cutter mission set for dawn the next day.[149]

On the morning of 11 March, Haidar's men on the Whale began a sweep of the summit, but Haidar was nowhere to be seen. The ODA 394 team leader working with Haidar's command soon discovered that the Tajik commander had opted to remain with the mounted force as it drove through the valley toward the villages and left leadership of the dismounted force to his second in command. Almost as soon as the dismounted troops saw the three villages in the valley below, the SF advisors found they could not hold Haidar's men to their task. The Tajiks took off headlong down the eastern slope of the Whale, headed for the villages to search for whatever spoils might be available. The "attack" was fast becoming chaos.[150]

As Haidar's mounted force entered the valley on the north, they soon encountered what they believed to be enemy forces to their east along the high ground. The tanks halted and opened fire. The "enemy" they were shooting at, however, was Frank Baltazar's C Company, 2-187 IN, at BP BETTY. After scrambling to locate a VS-17 reflective panel, the *Rakkasans* were able to signal to the Tajik tankers that they were friendly forces and the firing ceased.[151]

Meanwhile Zia's force, a more disciplined group, swept their end of the Whale and entered the villages of Babol Kheyl and Marzak. The Pashtuns cleared both and continued north until they met Haidar's troops, who had just cleared—and looted—Shir Khan Kheyl. The valley villages were devoid of enemy by that afternoon and Operation GLOCK concluded.

While GLOCK was in progress, the units of TF *Rakkasan* held in place and conducted localized patrols, fire missions, and engaged targets of opportunity. Few direct fire engagements occurred after 5 March, indicating that many of the enemy had already been killed or wounded, and some, no doubt, had decided to make their escape. Beginning on 9 March, TF *Rakkasan* began exfiltrating its battalions and sending them back to Bagram. On 12 March the rest of the TF was successfully extracted. Nevertheless, Operation ANACONDA was not yet complete.

TF *Commando* and Operation HARPOON

By 12 March contact with the enemy had become sporadic and any direct contact was either at long range or with CAS. Most enemy fighters remaining in the valley by this time were dead, in hiding, or attempting to make their way out. Most of the latter were probably Taliban; those who remained were probably al-Qaeda. If any fighters stayed, they most likely intended to fight to the death. But, the total number of these forces remained unclear to Coalition intelligence. For most CJTF *Mountain* leaders, there was an assumption that an enemy presence remained and that the Whale was the most likely location of that threat. The sweep of that feature by the Tajik militia force during Operation GLOCK had been insufficient, and CJTF *Mountain* now had additional conventional forces available to complete that task.

The headquarters of the 10th Mountain Division's 2d Brigade, commanded by Colonel Kevin Wilkerson, had been at K2 and in Afghanistan almost as long as the 10th Mountain Division's headquarters. Arriving on 21 December 2001, the 2d Brigade had already provided the C2 for several missions, including operations involving 10th Mountain units at Mazar-e Sharif and detainee operations at Sheberghan Prison. The 2d Brigade, designated TF *Commando*, would execute operations for the second half of Operation ANACONDA.

For the various missions for which TF *Commando* would be responsible, Major General Hagenbeck provided Wilkerson with several nondivisional units and one organic battalion under its operational control. On 10 March Hagenbeck ordered 3-PPCLI to Bagram from Kandahar and put it under TF *Commando*.[152] He also provided Wilkerson with HMM-165, a Marine helicopter battalion possessing three CH-53 "Sea Stallion" heavy lift helicopters, six CH-47s (attached from the Army's 159th Aviation Regiment), and five AH-1 Cobra attack helicopters organic to HMM-165.[153]

The CJTF *Mountain* CG had also ordered Lieutenant Colonel Stephen Townsend, commander of 4th Battalion, 31st Infantry (4-31 IN), to deploy his battalion headquarters from Fort Drum to Bagram to assume C2 of his two infantry companies that were in Afghanistan. The 4-31 IN, nicknamed the "Polar Bears" for their service in Siberia in World War I, was one of the 2d Brigade's three organic battalions. The battalion's C Company had already deployed into the ANACONDA AO earlier with LaCamera's 1-87 IN. The battalion's A Company, which had arrived at Bagram about 8 March, would be attached to the 3-PPCLI for the first TF *Commando* mission, dubbed Operation HARPOON.[154] Townsend's TAC, however, would not arrive in Afghanistan in time to take part.

The main effort of Operation HARPOON would be the 3-PPCLI, commanded by Lieutenant Colonel Patrick Stogran. The "Princess Pats" had arrived at Kandahar over several days beginning 7 February 2002. There, the battalion was attached to Wiercinski's 3d Brigade and assigned to the airfield security mission. Because the battalion also had an attached "Coyote" light armored vehicle (LAV) squadron, Stogran had directed that element to conduct presence patrols and interact with the local Afghan residents around the airfield perimeter.[155] The Coyote had a surveillance system that allowed its operators to see 15 to 20 kilometers in the desert, a capability that was lacking with the US battalions conducting airfield security missions. The LAV unit would play no role in ANACONDA, but would in follow-on missions along the Pakistani border.[156]

Early on 10 March Wiercinski contacted Stogran and told him that the 3-PPCLI would soon be conducting an air assault mission into the Naka Valley southeast of Takur Ghar to intercept and destroy enemy forces there. Right after Stogran finished his conversation with Wiercinski, he notified the senior Canadian officer in the theater, a rear admiral who worked in the CENTCOM headquarters, of the impending mission. The admiral told the 3-PPCLI commander, "No, your objective is actually the Whale. . . . I just came out of a meeting with [CENTCOM commander] General Franks and General Franks said you were attacking the Whale, which is sort of the hard nut on the western flank."[157] Confused, Stogran called Wiercinski back and informed him of his conversation with the admiral. The TF *Rakkasan* commander initially assured Stogran that the 3-PPCLI's target was indeed the Naka Valley, but a short time later changed the story—"You are going for the Whale."[158]

The 3-PPCLI deployed to Bagram via C-130 transport planes that afternoon. On arrival, Stogran learned that his battalion was attached to TF *Commando* and he would be working for Wilkerson instead of Wiercinski. Additionally, Stogran discovered that Company A, 4-31

IN, commanded by Captain John Stevens, would be attached to him for the operation. This caused Stogran some concern, as he had no understanding of the capabilities and readiness of the American unit or its commander. Nevertheless, Stogran and his staff went to work planning the operation.

Rakkasan Brief

Figure 32. Troops of 3d Battalion, PPCLI climb the Whale.

The plan for HARPOON was to insert the battalion at an HLZ at the north end of the Whale. The company from 4-31 IN, now code named "Strike" Company to differentiate it from the Canadian's own A Company, would sweep the spine of the Whale. The 3-PPCLI's Company A would sweep the Whale's sloping eastern foothills. Between Strike and A Companies, C Company would fill the void, while B Company followed in reserve. In front of the formation, Stogran planned to send his reconnaissance platoon to detect the enemy and report locations. The battalion would sweep the mountain moving from the northeast to southwest until reaching the southern entrance to the valley. The Whale's western slope was extremely rugged and steep, so the plan to clear that area was for the scouts and Strike Company to scan that side to detect any enemy presence there.[159]

As the planning developed, Stogran was notified that friendly Afghans were on the Whale and conducting clearing operations, so HARPOON was postponed. These operations were the aborted efforts of Gul Haidar on 11 March during Operation GLOCK. It soon became evident that the Afghan forces had not adequately performed their mission and it was still necessary to clear the Whale in a more careful fashion. Thus, Stogran was told that HARPOON was back on.[160] D-day was set for 13 March.

Just after daybreak on the 13th, the first lift, consisting of A and B Companies and part of Strike Company, arrived at the HLZ, a bowl-shaped area just to the east of the spine. Just as with the initial insertions on 2 March, there was not enough lift capability to bring in the entire battalion so the remainder would follow the next morning. Stogran directed his A Company to secure the HLZ for the follow-on elements while he sent B Company to the northeast to search out enemy. The following morning the rest of 3-PPCLI arrived, and shortly thereafter Stogran put the battalion on line and began the movement south.[161]

The movement over the Whale was initially uneventful. There appeared to be no enemy around and only a few caches of ammunition and small arms were found. Movement was slow due to the incredibly heavy loads the men were carrying. Stogran knew he had to adjust to a new technique if he was not going to exhaust his men to the point that they were combat ineffective. Major Mark Campbell, commanding the 3-PPCLI Combat Support Company, recalled:

About halfway through the first day of the actual advance, the CO [Stogran] said, "Okay. We have to be smart about this," and what he did was he had the companies essentially establish company patrol bases, drop their rucksacks with a security force, sort of fan out and scour that area, if you know what I mean, within about an hour or 2-hour walk, and then go back, pick up their

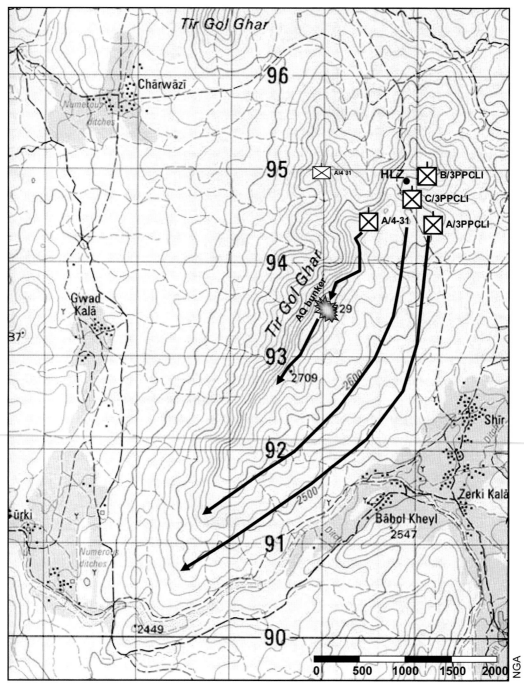

Figure 33. Operation ANACONDA, HARPOON, 13–17 March 2002.

rucksacks, move, establish a new sort of firm base, and then fan out again and check out all the reentrance points in caves and do their demolitions and sensitive site exploitation stuff.[162]

At night, the companies set up patrol bases and waited to resume movement the following day at first light.

During the first 2 nights on top of the Whale, Stogran noticed that there were sharp firefights off to the east in the valley. Since there appeared to be no threat on the high ground, he surmised that these enemy elements were exfiltrating down into the valley and running into the Afghans and their SF advisors who had been down there since they had entered the villages a few days before. "That was very frustrating because we could not move fast enough to actually engage [the enemy]," Stogran recalled.[163]

Late in the day on 15 March, the Canadian scouts reported an enemy bunker on the spine close to what was the topographical high point of the Whale. The Strike Company commander was notified of the location and given the task to take out the position. Stevens' men conducted the attack quickly and with no friendly casualties. By dusk, the American company had taken out the three defenders with AT-4s and seized the position. This incident was to be the only contact that the 3-PPCLI would make with a live enemy during the operation.[164]

Over the next 2 days, the battalion discovered many more caches of weapons and ammunition. The Canadians retained anything of intelligence value they found while their engineers efficiently blew the caches in place. The battalion reached the south end of the Whale on 16 March, having also cleared portions of the steep western slopes. The mission complete, the 3-PPCLI was ordered to exfiltrate over the next 2 days. After what was termed a "pretty treacherous descent" down the western slope to get to the PZ, the last Canadian soldier was lifted out of the AO on 18 March.[165]

Operation POLAR HARPOON

The operation the 3-PPCLI was originally tasked to perform—the sweep of Takur Ghar and the valley to its east—was still a necessary mission. So, while the Canadians were clearing the Whale of enemy troops, weapons, and munitions, Townsend's battalion TAC was en route to Bagram to assume control of its companies. Company C, under Captain Gregory Kozelka, had returned to Bagram when TF *Rakkasan* was pulled out of the valley and had been resting and refitting for its next mission. Stevens' A Company, 4-31 IN, had returned to Bagram from the Whale on 16 March, the day before the rest of the 3-PPCLI began pulling out. The 4-31 IN TAC had arrived that same day and was immediately tasked by Wilkerson to conduct the mission that had been pulled from the 3-PPCLI almost a week before.[166]

Townsend and his staff developed the plan over the next 36 hours and then briefed it to Wilkerson. Developing the plan was not an easy task due to the chronic lack of hard intelligence on the enemy. Townsend remembered:

> Information was pretty sketchy, which was a little bit of a surprise to me because Special Operations Forces had been up there and we had all these national [Intelligence, Surveillance, and Reconnaisance] platforms working the area. But information as to what I would find up there was pretty darn sketchy. We had discovered trenches, we had discovered bunkers with overhead cover, but

we didn't really have a lot of knowledge about that other than what I was able to garner from a couple of the Special Operators who had fought up there briefly and had withdrawn off the ridgeline.[167]

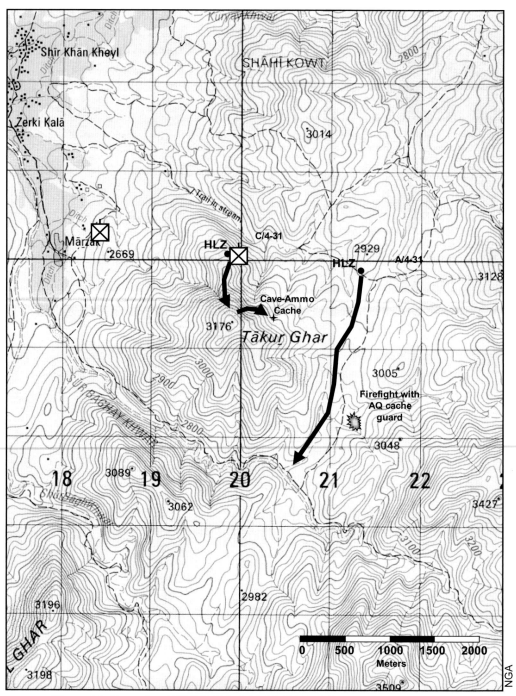

Figure 34. Operation ANACONDA, POLAR HARPOON, 18–19 March 2002.

Nevertheless, armed with what information he could glean, Townsend developed a two-company air assault that was designed to satisfy both tasks—clear the top of Takur Ghar and clear the valley to the east.

The plan for Operation POLAR HARPOON called for inserting C Company, 4-31 IN, onto a ridgeline 800 meters to the north of the peak. That company would climb to the top and both clear the summit and provide A Company, 4-31 IN overwatching fires as it cleared the valley below. A Company would be inserted into an HLZ on the valley floor to the northeast of Takur Ghar and clear the valley from north to south to a point where the valley met with the GINGER draw that skirted Takur Ghar on the south. Townsend's TAC and the battalion mortars were to insert with C Company on the side of the mountain.[168]

The operation began at dawn on 18 March with the battalion lifting off at Bagram. The flight encountered no problems en route, but Townsend suddenly became concerned as his CH-47 pilot touched down on the ridgeline. He remembered:

> We landed on top of the ridgeline and as I looked out the windows as my troops were disembarking I thought, "Where in the heck has he landed? I can't tell that we have landed." Well, as I came off the ramp myself, I realized that he had not landed. The ridge was so narrow that his rear two wheels only and his ramp were on the mountain. His ramp was on the ridgeline and his front two wheels were hovering out in the air and he was at max power. In fact, my Soldiers were clinging to small shrubs and bushes on the ridge to keep from tumbling down the ridge and a medical aid bag and an assault pack did in fact go tumbling down the ridge.[169]

The second Chinook followed the first and unloaded the rest of the TAC, mortars, and C Company, 4-31 IN, then flew northward toward Bagram. It was quickly apparent to the battalion's leaders that to climb the remaining 1,500 feet to the top was going to be difficult at that altitude. Opting to leave the mortars on the HLZ, Townsend and Kozelka led their troops on the slow, arduous ascent up the mountain.[170]

Meanwhile, down below, Stevens' A Company was inserted in the valley and began its sweep without the overwatch element yet in place. The company had little difficulty finding abandoned bunkers and caches. The troops busied themselves with gathering any documents or other items of intelligence value, then wired any discovered weapons and ammunition for destruction with explosives. At one point, they located a huge ammunition bunker and blew it in place, only to realize that the cave in which the ammunition was stored was then blowing shrapnel and chunks of other debris from west to east across the company's line of march. Stevens was forced to move his troops to the far side of the valley and make rushes over the "kill zone" to get them safely across. The ammunition in that bunker continued to explode for about 6 hours.[171]

Once on top of Takur Ghar, Kozelka's troops spread out and began their search. Not knowing what they would find, Townsend was glad that his troops did not have to fight for the top. "It was basically abandoned," he recalled. "There was nothing up there but dead al-Qaeda. But, when we got up there, I realized there were trenches, prepared defensive positions, hidden bunkers, hidden command and control facilities, and some crew-served weapons that were still operational up there."[172] In addition to the enemy equipment, C Company Soldiers were able to recover much of the US equipment that had been abandoned in the attempts to recover Neil Roberts.[173] One of the items was the helmet of Sergeant Bradley S. Crose, one of the QRF Rangers who had been killed in the fighting on 3 March.[174]

As it turned out, C Company did not find all of the discarded US equipment. Later in the day, as A Company approached its limit of advance, Soldiers spied several bunkers. Not sure if the positions were occupied, Stevens called for mortar fire and sent some men to engage the positions with AT-4s. Some troops even got close enough to lob a few handgrenades into one bunker. It turned out that none of the positions were manned, but it was not long before the Soldiers did make contact. As one of Stevens' platoons was clearing a small draw, the platoon sergeant, posted with the squad in the overwatch position, noticed an enemy position higher up in the draw. One squad had already passed the suspected location and the next, along with the platoon headquarters, was approaching it. The sergeant radioed the platoon leader who then led a squad toward the suspected enemy. Suddenly, an al-Qaeda fighter armed with a US-made M249 Squad Automatic Weapon (SAW) popped up out of a hole a mere 15 yards away. The American troops fired and quickly killed him. Searching the draw, the platoon not only recovered the SAW but other US equipment that had been deposited there for safekeeping. Townsend felt that the action revealed the enemy's intent in the aftermath of ANACONDA, asserting, "It was my assessment that al-Qaeda, when they withdrew from the battlefield there to head toward Pakistan, left this guard behind to guard their stuff because they knew if they were caught with it while they were moving it would look bad for them."[175]

That action effectively ended POLAR HARPOON, and as it turned out, ANACONDA as well. The companies remained in patrol bases that night, and the following morning, 4-31 IN prepared to be airlifted back to Bagram. "I remember that on 19 March 2002, which was my birthday, I was sitting on top of Takur Ghar Mountain," Townsend recalled. "We were listening to the radio, and it came across the satellite communications (SATCOM) radio, which was the only way we had to talk all the way back to Bagram, that the commander-in-chief, then General Tommy Franks, the CENTCOM Commander, . . . had come to Bagram and announced that Operation ANACONDA was officially over."[176] Later that morning, the battalion's Soldiers made their way to their respective PZs and were flown back to Bagram.

At Bagram, Townsend assembled his troops to talk to them about what they had just experienced. What he had to say was applicable to all of the American Soldiers who had just entered combat for the first time and killed other human beings. His words that day were poignant:

> First of all, I support you in what you did. If you feel as I do, 3,000 dead Americans on September 11 is all the justification you need. Now, some of you might consider yourselves lucky to have the chance to get one of them, and that's okay. If you feel good about it, keep it to yourself. Don't make other people listen to it. But most of you probably say to yourselves "I didn't want to kill anybody. I was just doing my job." To those people I want to say don't feel bad about what you have to do.[177]

Townsend then added a note of warning: "Don't let this cloud your vision. There may be more of it to be done in the days ahead."[178]

ANACONDA was not a perfect military operation. There had been significant challenges in establishing a clear picture of the enemy's locations, strength, and intent. Additional problems with the tailoring of forces and equipment, CAS, indirect fire support, and sufficient lift capabilities also affected combat operations in the Shahi Kowt Valley. Indeed, just months after the battle, Major General Hagenbeck openly addressed some of the problems encountered by US ground forces in the valley, especially those that prevented infantry units from coordinating quick response attacks with Coalition fixed-wing aircraft.[179] As noted earlier in this chapter, not all ground forces who needed CAS, especially in the initial hours of the operation, received it in a timely fashion or at all.

At any rate, given the many shortcomings and issues facing the staffs and commanders who planned and conducted the operation, ANACONDA must be considered an overall success. First and foremost, the operation supported CENTCOM's military objectives in Afghanistan. Coalition actions in the valley successfully destroyed al-Qaeda forces and the organization's training bases, both of which were objectives in Franks' original plan for OEF.[180] According to CJTF *Mountain's* estimates, over 800 al-Qaeda and Taliban fighters were killed during the operation. Coalition forces also destroyed or captured 26 mortars, 11 artillery pieces, and 15 DShK heavy machineguns. Additionally, those forces captured and searched 5 compounds, 62 other buildings, and cleared 41 cave complexes.[181] American estimates of the number of enemy killed are not universally accepted and some accounts suggest that the number of al-Qaeda and Taliban fighters killed in the Shahi Kowt Valley was as low as 200. Still, this smaller total would indicate an approximate number of 800 wounded enemy fighters, given historical killed in action (KIA)/WIA rates for combat actions similar to ANACONDA. When even these lower estimates of the effects on the enemy are considered against the Coalition's casualty count that totaled less than 70 killed and wounded, the operation should be considered a success.

Perhaps more important than the operation's casualty count was ANACONDA's qualitative effect on the enemy. Many of the al-Qaeda members who were killed were the seasoned fighters who formed the backbone of that organization's training base in Afghanistan. In summarizing the result of the operation, General Hagenbeck, the CJTF *Mountain* commander, described the enemy's losses in the following terms:

> They were . . . the hard core cadre that had been doing the training for a number of years in Afghanistan of these tens of thousands of terrorists that were trained there. If you think of them in terms of the captains and majors and drill sergeants that might run our schools at Fort Benning or Fort Sill, that was who these characters were. They were war veterans.[182]

Ultimately, Hagenbeck believed that the operation in the valley would have a lasting effect on al-Qaeda's capabilities, asserting, "we took out something that they could not replace overnight, the people, and then also this locality, this sanctuary, where they could actually do the training."[183]

✦   ✦   ✦

ANACONDA was the largest, and arguably the most successful, combat operation of the Coalition campaign in Afghanistan. By the end of March 2002, the ability of the Taliban and it al-Qaeda allies to conduct significant military operations in Afghanistan had been shattered. Within 5 months every battalion that had participated in the battle had left Afghanistan to return to their home stations in the United States and elsewhere. The units and commanders that followed them in Afghanistan intended to build on the success of ANACONDA. However, they were less focused on large-scale combat operations than on moving the campaign into its final phase by refocusing Coalition efforts on humanitarian assistance and strengthening the viability and capacity of the new Afghan nation. Coalition leaders hoped that if these efforts were successful, they would not have to mount another ANACONDA in the future.

Notes

1. Lieutenant General Franklin L. Hagenbeck, interview by Contemporary Operations Study Team, Combat Studies Institute, Fort Leavenworth, KS, 30 March 2007, 6; Lieutenant Colonel Paul Wille, interview by Contemporary Operations Study Team, Combat Studies Institute, Fort Leavenworth, KS, 14 December 2006, 4.

2. Hagenbeck, interview, 30 March 2007, 6.

3. Colonel Michael Hawrylak, interview by 47th Military History Detachment, Camp Doha, Kuwait, 21 May 2003, 29; Brigadier General John Mulholland, interview by Contemporary Operations Study Team, Combat Studies Institute, Fort Bragg, NC, 7 May 2007, 6.

4. Lester W. Grau, ed., *The Bear Went Over the Mountain: Soviet Combat Tactics in Afghanistan* (Washington, DC: National Defense University Press, 1996), 2.

5. Lester W. Grau and Michael A. Gress, eds., *The Soviet-Afghan War: How a Superpower Fought and Lost* (Lawrence, KS: University of Kansas Press, 2002), 32–33; Grau, *The Bear Went Over the Mountain*, 65.

6. Grau, *The Bear Went Over the Mountain*, 60–64.

7. Grau and Gress, *The Soviet-Afghan War*, 312.

8. Grau and Gress, *The Soviet-Afghan War*, 311.

9. Major Mark G. Davis, "Operation ANACONDA: Command and Confusion in Joint Warfare," Masters Thesis, School of Advanced Air and Space Studies, Air University, Maxwell AFB, AL, June 2004, 61.

10. Davis, "Operation ANACONDA," 70.

11. Hawrylak, interview, 21 May 2003, 29.

12. Mulholland, interview, 7 May 2007, 6–7.

13. Charles H. Briscoe et al., *Weapon of Choice: US Army Special Operations Forces in Afghanistan* (Fort Leavenworth, KS: Combat Studies Institute Press, 2003), 279.

14. Mulholland, interview, 7 May 2007, 7.

15. Mulholland, interview, 7 May 2007, 7.

16. Mulholland, interview, 7 May 2007, 8.

17. Richard W. Stewart, *The United States Army in Afghanistan, Operation Enduring Freedom, October 2001–March 2002*, CMH Publication 70-83-1 (Washington, DC: Center of Military History, 2006), 32.

18. Davis, "Operation ANACONDA," 30–33.

19. Hagenbeck, interview, 30 March 2007, 7.

20. Hagenbeck, interview, 30 March 2007, 7.

21. Davis, "Operation ANACONDA," 68.

22. Briscoe et al., *Weapon of Choice*, 280.

23. Stewart, *OEF, October 2001–March 2002*, 32; Davis, "Operation ANACONDA," 96.

24. 3d Brigade, 101st Airborne Division, *After Action Report* Brief, undated, slides 54–58.

25. Colonel Charles A. Preysler, interview by Contemporary Operations Study Team, Combat Studies Institute, Fort Leavenworth, KS, 8 May 2007, 3; Major Peter Dawe, interview by Contemporary Operations Study Team, Combat Studies Institute, Fort Leavenworth, KS, 16 May 2007, 2, 5.

26. Lieutenant Colonel (Retired) Ronald Corkran, telephone interview by Contemporary Operations Study Team, Combat Studies Institute, Fort Leavenworth, KS, 9 May 2007, 4–5.

27. Major Nelson Kraft, telephone interview by Contemporary Operations Study Team, Combat Studies Institute, Fort Leavenworth, KS, 9 May 2007, 5–6.

28. Briscoe et al., *Weapon of Choice*, 281.

29. Briscoe et al., *Weapon of Choice*, 281.

30. Davis, "Operation ANACONDA," 103.

31. CJTF *Mountain, Operation Anaconda, Combat Operations* Brief, 26 February 2002, slide 2.

32. CJTF *Mountain, Operation Anaconda, Combat Operations* Brief, 26 February 2002, slide 6.

33. Stewart, *OEF, October 2001–March 2002*, 32–33; Briscoe et al., *Weapon of Choice*, 283.

34. Corkran, telephone interview, 9 May 2007, 23.

35. Preysler, interview, 8 May 2007, 4. Preysler had only two companies with which to conduct his mission. B Company, 2-187 IN was sent to secure a safe house in Khost, and D Company remained at Kandahar to perform the airfield security mission.

36. Major Roger Crombie, interview by Operational Leadership Experiences Project Team, Combat Studies Institute, Fort Leavenworth, KS, 30 March 2006, 7; Major James Hall, interview by 130th Military History Detachment, Bagram, Afghanistan, 15 March 2002, 3.

37. Kraft, telephone interview, 9 May 2007, 8.

38. Lieutenant Colonel (Retired) Bruce Stanley, discussion with Contemporary Operations Study Team, Combat Studies Institute, Fort Leavenworth, KS, 14 May 2007.

39. Lieutenant Colonel (Retired) Ronald Corkran, e-mail interview by Contemporary Operations Study Team, Combat Studies Institute, Fort Leavenworth, KS, 8 May 2007, 5.

40. Davis*,* "Operation ANACONDA," 111, see chapter 4, footnote 39.

41. Briscoe et al., *Weapon of Choice*, 285.

42. Briscoe et al., *Weapon of Choice*, 285–286.

43. Briscoe et al., *Weapon of Choice*, 286. According to Major Mark Davis, a combination of late sorties by the Air Force, messages by the SOF reconnaissance team to stop the strikes that hit near their position, and a weapons malfunction in a B-1B bomber were responsible for the smaller number of airstrikes that morning. See Davis, "Operation ANACONDA," 109.

44. Briscoe et al., *Weapon of Choice*, 46.

45. Briscoe et al., *Weapon of Choice*, 286.

46. Hall, interview, 15 March 2002, 3.

47. Corkran, telephone interview, 9 May 2007, 12.

48. Corkran, telephone interview, 9 May 2007, 12.

49. Corkran, telephone interview, 9 May 2007, 12.

50. Corkran, telephone interview, 9 May 2007, 12.

51. Austin Bay, "A Full Report on Operation ANACONDA—America's First Battle of the 21st Century, A Complete After Action Interview with COL Wiercinski." http://www.strategypage.com/on_point/20020627.aspx (accessed 30 May 2007).

52. Bay, "A Full Report on Operation ANACONDA"; Corkran, e-mail interview, 8 May 2007, 4.

53. Bay, "A Full Report on Operation ANACONDA."

54. Corkran, telephone interview, 9 May 2007, 14.

55. Kraft, telephone interview, 9 May 2007, 8; Hall, interview, 15 March 2002, 4.

56. Kraft, telephone interview, 9 May 2007, 8

57. Kraft, telephone interview, 9 May 2007, 8.

58. Technical Sergeant John McCabe, interview by 130th Military History Detachment, Bagram, Afghanistan, 8 March 2002, 3.

59. Kraft, telephone interview, 9 May 2007, 9.

60. Kraft, telephone interview, 9 May 2007, 9.

61. Kraft, telephone interview, 9 May 2007, 10.

62. Kraft, telephone interview, 9 May 2007, 10, 18.

63. Crombie, interview, 30 March 2006, 8.

64. Crombie, interview, 30 March 2006, 8.

65. Crombie, interview, 30 March 2006, 8.

66. Crombie, interview, 30 March 2006, 8.

67. Crombie, interview, 30 March 2006, 10.

68. Major Franklin Baltazar, telephone interview by Contemporary Operations Study Team, Combat Studies Institute, Fort Leavenworth, KS, 10 May 2007, 8.

69. Baltazar, telephone interview, 10 May 2007, 8.

70. Preysler, interview, 8 May 2007, 7; Baltazar, interview, 10 May 2007, 8.

71. Preysler, interview, 8 May 2007, 7.

72. Baltazar, interview, 10 May 2007, 9.

73. Baltazar, interview, 10 May 2007, 9–10.

74. Preysler, interview, 8 May 2007, 8.

75. Baltazar, interview, 10 May 2007, 9.

76. Preysler, interview, 8 May 2007, 8.

77. Baltazar, interview, 10 May 2007, 12.

78. Corkran, telephone interview, 9 May 2007, 14.

79. Corkran, telephone interview, 9 May 2007, 14–15.

80. Corkran, telephone interview, 9 May 2007, 15.

81. Kraft, telephone interview, 9 May 2007, 10.

82. Kraft, telephone interview, 9 May 2007, 10.

83. Kraft, telephone interview, 9 May 2007, 11.

84. Kraft, telephone interview, 9 May 2007, 11.

85. McCabe, interview, 9 May 2007, 5.

86. McCabe, interview, 9 May 2007, 6.

87. McCabe, interview, 9 May 2007, 6.

88. McCabe, interview, 9 May 2007, 7.

89. McCabe, interview, 9 May 2007, 8.

90. McCabe, interview, 9 May 2007, 8.

91. Hall, interview, 15 March 2002, 5.

92. Hall, interview, 15 March 2002, 5.

93. Hall, interview, 15 March 2002, 5.

94. Hall, interview, 15 March 2002, 6.

95. Hall, interview, 15 March 2002, 6; Kraft, telephone interview, 9 May 2007, 13.

96. Hall, interview, 15 March 2002, 7.

97. Hall, interview, 15 March 2002, 7; Kraft, telephone interview, 9 May 2007, 13.

98. Preysler, interview, 8 May 2007, 11.

99. Preysler, interview, 8 May 2007, 11.

100. Kraft, telephone interview, 9 May 2007, 13.

101. Kraft, telephone interview, 9 May 2007, 13.

102. Kraft, telephone interview, 9 May 2007, 13; Hall, interview, 15 March 2002, 7.

103. Kraft, telephone interview, 9 May 2007, 14.

104. Major Nelson Kraft, *Lessons Learned from a Light Infantry Company during Operation ANACONDA* Brief, undated, slide 3.

105. Corkran, telephone interview, 9 May 2007, 17.

106. Corkran, telephone interview, 9 May 2007, 17–18.

107. Corkran, telephone interview, 9 May 2007, 18.

108. Corkran, telephone interview, 9 May 2007, 18.

109. Crombie, interview, 30 March 2006, 13.

110. Preysler, interview, 8 May 2007, 12–13.

111. Corkran, e-mail interview, 8 May 2007, 6.

112. Preysler, interview, 8 May 2007, 13.

113. Corkran, interview, 9 May 2007, 20.

114. Corkran, interview, 9 May 2007, 20.

115. Preysler, interview, 8 May 2007, 14–15.

116. Briscoe et al., *Weapon of Choice*, 297–298.

117. Briscoe et al., *Weapon of Choice*, 298.

118. Briscoe et al., *Weapon of Choice*, 299.

119. Preysler, interview, 8 May 2007, 14.

120. Briscoe et al., *Weapon of Choice*, 300.

121. Briscoe et al., *Weapon of Choice*, 302.

122. Department of Defense, "Executive Summary of the Battle of Takur Ghar," 24 May 2002, 6.

123. Briscoe et al., *Weapon of Choice*, 304–305.

124. Briscoe et al., *Weapon of Choice*, 306.

125. Briscoe et al., *Weapon of Choice*, 308

126. Briscoe et al., *Weapon of Choice*, 309.

127. Briscoe et al., *Weapon of Choice*, 309–310.

128. Briscoe et al., *Weapon of Choice*, 311.

129. Briscoe et al., *Weapon of Choice*, 311.

130. Briscoe et al., *Weapon of Choice*, 312–313.

131. Briscoe et al., *Weapon of Choice*, 313.

132. Briscoe et al., *Weapon of Choice*, 315–316.

133. Hagenbeck, interview, 30 March 2007, 11.

134. Corkran, telephone interview, 9 May 2007, 19; Headquarters, 1st Battalion, 187th Infantry, Memorandum: Subject: Task Force 1-187 IN After Action Report: Operation ANACONDA, 21 March 2001, 1.

135. Corkran, telephone interview, 9 May 2007, 21–22.

136. Corkran, telephone interview, 9 May 2007, 22; Corkran, e-mail interview, 8 May 2007, 8.

137. TF 1-187 IN After Action Report, 1.

138. Corkran, telephone interview, 9 May 2007, 22.

139. Corkran, telephone interview, 9 May 2007, 23.

140. Kraft, telephone interview, 9 May 2007, 15.

141. Preysler, interview, 8 May 2007, 15.

142. Kraft, telephone interview, 9 May 2007, 15.

143. Kraft, telephone interview, 9 May 2007, 15.

144. Kraft, telephone interview, 9 May 2007, 17.

145. Kraft, telephone interview, 9 May 2007, 16–17.

146. Kraft, telephone interview, 9 May 2007, 17.

147. Briscoe et al., *Weapon of Choice*, 322.

148. Briscoe et al., *Weapon of Choice*, 322.

149. Briscoe et al., *Weapon of Choice*, 322–323.

150. Briscoe et al., *Weapon of Choice*, 324.

151. Baltazar, interview, 10 May 2007, 21–22.

152. Major Fred Wolanski, interview by Contemporary Operations Study Team, Combat Studies Institute, Fort Leavenworth, KS, 14 May 2007.

153. 2d Brigade, 10th Mountain Division, *"Commandoes," Afghanistan: December 2001–April 2002 After Action Review* Briefing, slide 27.

154. Colonel Stephen J. Townsend, interview by Contemporary Operations Study Team, Combat Studies Institute, Fort Leavenworth, KS, 11 May 2007, 3.

155. Lieutenant Colonel Patrick Stogran, interview by Contemporary Operations Study Team, Combat Studies Institute, Fort Leavenworth, KS, 18 May 2007, 7–8.

156. Stogran, interview, 18 May 2007, 5.

157. Stogran, interview, 18 May 2007, 7–8.

158. Stogran, interview, 18 May 2007, 7–8.

159. Stogran, interview, 18 May 2007, 10.

160. Stogran, interview, 18 May 2007, 9.

161. Stogran, interview, 18 May 2007, 10–11.

162. Major Mark Campbell, interview by Contemporary Operations Study Team, Combat Studies Institute, Fort Leavenworth, KS, 21 May 2007, 6–7.

163. Stogran, interview, 18 May 2007, 15.

164. Dawe, interview, 16 May 2007, 9.

165. Campbell, interview, 21 May 2007, 9.

166. Townsend, interview, 11 May 2007, 6.

167. Townsend, interview, 11 May 2007, 6.

168. Townsend, interview, 11 May 2007, 7.

169. Townsend, interview, 11 May 2007, 7.

170. Townsend, interview, 11 May 2007, 7–8.

171. Townsend, interview, 11 May 2007, 8.

172. Townsend, interview, 11 May 2007, 8.

173. Townsend, interview, 11 May 2007, 8.

174. Dennis Steele, "U.S. Army Line Battalion in the War on Terrorism: The Mountains," *Army Magazine*, June 2002. http://findarticles.com/p/articles/mi_qa3723/is_200206/ai_n9124771 (accessed 9 May 2007).

175. Townsend, interview, 11 May 2007, 8–9.

176. Townsend, interview, 11 May 2007, 11.

177. Steele, "The Mountains."

178. Steele, "The Mountains."

179. See Robert H. McElroy, "Interview with Franklin L. Hagenbeck—Afghanistan Fire Support for Operation Anaconda," *Field Artillery*, September–October 2002, 8.

180. General Tommy Franks, *American Soldier* (New York, NY: HarperCollins, 2004), 338.

181. CJTF *Mountain,* Headquarters, 10th Mountain Division, *Afghanistan and Operation ANACONDA* Brief, undated, slide 19.

182. Hagenbeck, interview, 30 March 2007, 13.

183. Hagenbeck, interview, 30 March 2007, 13.

Chapter 7

Success Out of Victory: Changing Course in Mid-2002

In March 2002 Afghanistan appeared to be a nation ready to rise from the ashes of Taliban rule. While Mullah Mohammad Omar and Osama bin Laden had escaped the grasp of Coalition forces and their Afghan allies, the Taliban's armed forces—and their al-Qaeda confederates—had been captured or killed almost in entirety. The vestiges of these forces had scattered and sought refuge in remote corners of Afghanistan or across the border in Pakistan. With these military threats defeated, leaders in both the Coalition and Hamid Karzai's interim government faced the difficult task of transforming military victory into an enduring political and economic settlement that would constitute success for the Afghan population and for the Coalition. On the Coalition side, this challenge entailed the creation of new plans to ensure post-Taliban Afghanistan continued to move toward stability.

This chapter focuses on the 3 months that followed the conclusion of Operation ANACONDA during which CENTCOM and the Coalition made critical decisions about their future operations in a dramatically altered Afghanistan. Unquestionably, the most important decision came in the spring of 2002 when Coalition leaders reached the conclusion that the great majority of their forces would not be departing Afghanistan anytime soon. Despite the victory in the Shahi Kowt Valley, the new Afghan state was still in its infancy and required nurturing if it was to endure. With Coalition strategic success contingent on the survival of this nascent state, officials in the United States and Europe began planning a new campaign that demanded security missions to prevent the military and political resurgence of the Taliban as well as reconstruction operations and programs to train Afghan security forces. With the decision to extend the Coalition presence in Afghanistan came a change in command structure and force levels. These transitions essentially ended the campaign that centered on Special Operations Forces (SOF), which had defined the first 6 months of operations and initially made Operation ENDURING FREEDOM (OEF) appear as a unique conflict. After spring 2002, conventional units would become the core of the Coalition's presence, even as the nature of the conflict in Afghanistan retained characteristics that many would describe as unconventional.

Spring 2002: Optimism and Anxiety

ANACONDA had inflicted a major defeat on Taliban and al-Qaeda forces. Afterwards, many of the Taliban that had survived ANACONDA, Tora Bora, and other Coalition actions and remained loyal to Mullah Omar hid within the population. In April 2002 General Tommy Franks, CENTCOM commander, admitted that the Coalition was aware of the presence of Taliban remnants in Afghanistan, stating, "I will say right now we do not see [large groupings of enemy forces.] What we see are smaller groups, we see groups of enemy soldiers trying to blend in with communities if you will."[1] That summer, the new Afghan Interior Minister Ali Jalali confirmed the existence of semidormant Taliban forces inside Afghanistan. To help discern likely Taliban actions in the near future, Jalali recalled the words of a 17th-century Pashtun guerrilla leader: "When you encounter a stronger enemy force, avoid decisive engagement and swiftly withdraw only to hit back where the enemy is vulnerable. By this you gain sustainability and the ability to fight a long war of attrition."[2] Thus, anxiety concerning the security of the new Afghan state persisted even after the significant victory in the Shahi Kowt Valley.

Still, both the Coalition and the Afghan Interim Authority (AIA) intended to pursue the political road map established at the Bonn Conference in December 2001. The agreement signed at the conference codified a basic consensus shared among members of the Coalition, the United Nations (UN), the larger international community, and Afghan representatives about the political future of Afghanistan. The cornerstone of the Bonn Agreement was its call for an emergency loya jirga, or grand council, scheduled to convene no later than June 2002 and charged "to lead Afghanistan until such time as a fully representative government can be elected through free and fair elections."[3] Those elections, according to the agreement, were to be held no more than 2 years after the emergency loya jirga. To help foster a stable environment in which this political process could work, the UN Security Council on 20 December 2001 passed Resolution 1386 that, in addition to sanctioning the Bonn Agreement, called for creating a military security force to "assist the Afghan Interim Authority in the maintenance of security in Kabul and its surrounding areas, so that the Afghan Interim Authority as well as the personnel of the United Nations can operate in a secure environment."[4] This new security element would stand separately from OEF and concentrate its efforts on securing the capital of the new Afghan Government.

The new UN-sponsored security force became known as the International Security Assistance Force (ISAF). The United Kingdom (UK) assumed the lead for providing command and control (C2) for ISAF and appointed Major General John McColl to command the organization. By early 2002, 18 other nations had pledged military forces to this command, which began operations that winter. A detailed seven-page Military Technical Agreement completed on 4 January 2002 outlined the rules of engagement (ROE) and established a clear separation between ISAF and Coalition forces, stating, "'Coalition Forces' are those national military elements of the US-led international coalition prosecuting the 'War on Terrorism' within Afghanistan. The ISAF is not part of the 'Coalition Forces.'"[5] The Military Technical Agreement was essentially a bilateral contract between ISAF and the AIA. It formalized the partnership between a new sovereign Afghanistan and a military force sanctioned by the United Nations.[6]

During the weeks of Operation ANACONDA, concerns about Afghanistan's future grew. In the first quarter of 2002, UN officials had painted a cautiously optimistic picture of prospects for consolidating the new interim government. On 27 February, for example, Kieran Prendergast, the UN's Under-Secretary-General for Political Affairs, reported to the Security Council that although security threats remained in Afghanistan, on balance the country's political progress had exceeded expectations.[7] Prendergast noted that by that date, ISAF strength levels were approaching their full complement of 4,500 soldiers, that the World Food Program had successfully delivered more than 325,000 metric tons of food, and that the return of UN and nongovernment organizations (NGO) to Afghanistan promised a significant improvement in the conduct of humanitarian assistance missions.

Despite the generally upbeat quality of February 2002 assessments, a report made by UN Secretary General Kofi Annan cast recent developments in a more pessimistic light. Annan recognized the instability in Afghanistan, stating, "Insecurity remains the prime cause of concern for Afghans across the country."[8] He then listed the continued presence of Taliban and al-Qaeda militants as one cause of the general sense of insecurity, but added that conflicts between political and military groups vying for power and criminal organizations seeking to take advantage of the instability were contributors as well.[9] This apparent change in tone by UN officials was symptomatic of a new reality. By late March 2002, Operation ANACONDA had forced international observers—both civilian and military—to adjust the lens through which they viewed conditions in Afghanistan. The loya jirga, set for June 2002, remained on schedule as the AIA's top priority. To ensure this milestone was reached, the Coalition began increasing its forces while ISAF consolidated its presence in Kabul.

On the day that ANACONDA ended, the United Kingdom announced it would commit a brigade-size infantry task force consisting of approximately 1,700 Royal Marines from the 45th Commando Regiment to augment US efforts in Afghanistan. Dubbed Task Force (TF) *Jacana*, the UK deployment would constitute the largest projection of British military force since the end of the Gulf War in 1991.[10] British officials publicly emphasized the distinction between their ISAF contingent, discharging international peacekeeping responsibilities in and around Kabul, and TF *Jacana,* sent specifically to engage the enemy. As Secretary of State for Defence Geoffrey Hoon noted during his address to the House of Commons, "These troops are being deployed to Afghanistan to take part in warfighting operations. We will be asking them to risk their lives. Their missions will be conducted in unforgiving and hostile terrain against a dangerous enemy. They may suffer casualties."[11] Next to the American troop commitment, the British contribution to OEF would be the largest of the 37-nation Coalition by the end of July 2002.[12] It also signaled that neither the United States nor the United Kingdom—the senior partners in OEF—were taking the relative peace of the late spring as a sign of a pacified Afghanistan.

As TF *Jacana* prepared for its OEF deployment, US leadership reassessed the American stance on reconstruction and nation building. In mid-April 2002, approximately 1 month after the end of ANACONDA, President George W. Bush, addressing an audience at the Virginia Military Institute (VMI), praised the "good progress" visible in Afghanistan. He remarked, "It's important for Americans to know this war will not be quick and this war will not be easy. . . . The battles in Afghanistan are not over."[13] The President vowed that OEF would not replicate earlier military episodes in Afghanistan's troubled history. Typically, he said, these involved "initial success, followed by long years of floundering and ultimate failure. We're not going to repeat that mistake."[14] In addition to announcing the intention of America and its Coalition allies to "stay until the mission is done," President Bush empowered advocates of a greater American commitment to Afghanistan's economic reconstruction. He invoked the memory of George C. Marshall, a 1901 graduate of VMI and Army Chief of Staff during World War II who was also the architect of the Marshall Plan, to stress the need for the United States and other donor countries "to help Afghanistan . . . develop an economy that can feed its people" without falling back into destructive practices like opium cultivation.[15]

In Afghanistan, Major General Franklin Hagenbeck, the commander of Combined Joint Task Force (CJTF) *Mountain*, was attempting to gain a better understanding of the situation and make some rudimentary plans for action. Across Afghanistan, Coalition military leaders began reaching out to the population to build rapport with local leaders and gain information. In the weeks after Operation ANACONDA, Hagenbeck personally met with tribal elders and other leaders to "get a grasp of the culture and live with the Afghans day in and day out."[16] According to Hagenbeck, the process entailed a calculated personal risk that the Afghans "would cut your throat when you fell asleep at night; and we were not unaware of all that."[17]

The information he gained from local villagers, according to Hagenbeck, confirmed "what we thought had happened . . . that al-Qaeda had taken a beating. I mean these local people were telling me that al-Qaeda had lived among them for 10 years [sic] now."[18] However, the vestiges of bin Laden's group remained in the country and were highly visible to the population. Local leaders told Hagenbeck that the non-Afghans that made up the al-Qaeda rank and file "stuck out like a sore thumb."[19] The CJTF *Mountain* commander believed this made the remnants of the enemy "separate and distinct and I think there was an opportunity, a fleeting opportunity, where we could have killed them all."[20]

Annihilating the enemy, though, might have required pursuing fleeing al-Qaeda and Taliban elements across the border into Pakistan, a move that international law and the ROE would not allow. Hagenbeck later came to appreciate the reasons behind this proscription:

> We didn't pull the trigger for political reasons, which I understand now. I was out of my mind at the time. In retrospect, again, [deciding against cross-border operations] was in many ways a smart thing to do. It potentially could have collapsed the [friendly] Musharraf government [in Pakistan] at a time when we didn't need that.[21]

Indeed, the spring of 2002 was not a propitious time to put significant pressure on the Musharraf government. By May 2002 India and Pakistan were on the brink of nuclear war over terrorist attacks in India that the Indian Government believed had been sponsored by the Pakistani Government.

Some of Hagenbeck's visits took him to the frontier area on the Pakistani border and he used meetings with local leaders to explain the rationale behind the Coalition presence. In these discussions, he emphasized "that we were [in Afghanistan] for blood retribution because of 9/11 and we were going after the guys who did it."[22] The message resonated fairly well with the Afghans. "Their response to-a-person," said General Hagenbeck, "basically was, 'Okay. You can do that. You can stay here. We will be neutral until you dishonor us, our families, or our tribes. Then we will be your enemy.'"[23] The challenge for American commanders would be to take a broad approach to the new environment in Afghanistan that allowed them to pursue the enemy while retaining the support—or at least the neutrality—of the Afghan population.

Hagenbeck and his staff began framing this new approach, which represented the first attempt by a senior Coalition command to articulate the overall direction for the military campaign in Afghanistan since US Central Command (CENTCOM) published the original OEF campaign plan in November 2001. For the CJTF *Mountain* commander, future Coalition efforts had to revolve around full spectrum operations. Hagenbeck drew this term from US Army doctrine that described full spectrum operations as the simultaneous execution of offensive, defensive, and stability operations such as reconstruction projects. By conducting full spectrum operations, US Army units could tailor their approach to the varying conditions across a country in which one region might harbor an entrenched enemy force and a neighboring region might be peaceful and welcoming of Coalition reconstruction efforts. Hagenbeck recognized that CJTF *Mountain*'s planned approach would set conditions for the new headquarters that would be deploying to Afghanistan in mid-2002 to take over Coalition operations.

Pressure on the Enemy: Security Operations in Mid-2002

In his April speech at VMI, President Bush described how Coalition combat units were conducting Operation MOUNTAIN LION to take the fight to a dangerous enemy who remained active in Afghanistan. MOUNTAIN LION was the first large-scale security operation mounted by CJTF *Mountain* in the immediate post-ANACONDA period. Hagenbeck and his staff had launched this offensive in an attempt to do two things. First, the operation would take advantage of that short window of opportunity in which, they believed, the Coalition could easily identify the remnants of the Taliban and al-Qaeda and deal them a fatal blow. CJTF *Mountain* intelligence had located key areas in southeast Afghanistan in Paktia, Paktika, and Oruzgan provinces along the Pakistani border that had served and possibly were still providing sanctuaries to enemy groups. Planning for Operation MOUNTAIN LION focused specifically on what the CJTF *Mountain* staff identified as the decisive points for operation: the towns of Gardez, Khost, and Orgun-e.[24] By eliminating these forces, the operation would help achieve the second objective—a secure environment in which the June 2002 loya jirga could take place.

Hagenbeck envisioned Operation MOUNTAIN LION as a 90-day campaign that saw a succession of week-long missions launched by battalion-size or smaller elements. These forces would move from Bagram and Kandahar on helicopters into the targeted areas where they would conduct full spectrum operations—intelligence, cordon and search, raids, and humanitarian assistance—focused on capturing or killing Taliban and al-Qaeda groups.[25] The first of these smaller operations began in early April when the 1st Battalion, 187th Infantry (1-187 IN), an element of TF *Rakkasan*, flew from Kandahar and landed in an area southwest of the town of

---

The CH-47 Chinook: The Army's Workhorse in Afghanistan

During the first 4 years of Operation ENDURING FREEDOM, the US Army relied heavily on helicopters to move forces and materiel around Afghanistan. These aircraft were particularly important in magnifying the effect of the relatively small number of Coalition forces that until 2004 spent most of their time on a small number of bases. Of all the aircraft employed by the US Army in OEF, it was the CH-47 Chinook that bore the brunt of the heaviest work.

The Chinook had been designed in the 1950s as a heavy lift helicopter. Its tandem rotors gave the aircraft capabilities to lift and transport as well as fly at speeds of up to 170 knots and reach altitudes higher than smaller helicopters. The CH-47 saw service with US forces in Vietnam, the Persian Gulf, and other major and minor operations.

The CH-47's capabilities made it ideal for a variety of missions in OEF. Special Operations versions of the aircraft were heavily involved in the first 3 months of the campaign in Afghanistan. The Chinook's ability to transport 35 to 55 Soldiers made it ideal for the air assault portion of Operation ANACONDA.

Beginning in the middle of 2002, as the campaign slowly shifted focus from offensive to stability operations, the CH-47 arguably remained the most important piece of equipment in the Coalition's arsenal. The aviation units that flew the Chinook continued to support air assault missions in security operations such as MOUNTAIN LION, which put pressure on enemy formations in the south and southeast areas of the country. But these units also delivered food, water, ammunition, and other supplies needed to sustain the Coalition combat power.

Mountain-side PZ. Note the terrain and the fact that the CH-47's front wheels are in the air.

Khost in Paktia province. The unit's target was a large training and supply base near the village of Zhawar Kili. That location was only several miles from the Pakistani border and had served as a logistics base for anti-Soviet mujahideen in the 1980s. By late 2001 Coalition intelligence had confirmed that al-Qaeda had recently used the sprawling cave and tunnel complex as both a headquarters and a training base. The mission of 1-187 IN, and a small Afghan security force that joined the American battalion, was to move into the area and carefully search the complex. Although they did not find any enemy forces in the sanctuary, the Soldiers of 1-187 IN methodically cleared the facility, gathered information from the site and from the local population, and delivered humanitarian aid to the village that had provided the Afghan unit. By 7 April 2002 the *Rakkasan* Soldiers had completed the mission and flown back to Kandahar.[26]

Hagenbeck then turned to British and Canadian forces to continue the momentum begun by 1-187 IN. TF *Jacana* launched Operation PTARMIGAN on 16 April 2002 and directed the British marines, with some American units in support, back to Paktia province for several days to sweep through the rough terrain in search of enemy forces that might have returned after ANACONDA. In May the British followed PTARMIGAN with Operation SNIPE, which sent UK troops into areas of southeastern Afghanistan that previously had not been visited by the Coalition. According to the British Ministry of Defence, the mission in SNIPE was to "clear and destroy any terrorist infrastructure located there, and render it safe for humanitarian assistance."[27] British forces did not encounter the enemy during Operation SNIPE, but did uncover a significant cave network that contained huge arms caches. The successful destruction of the arms caches marked one of the largest controlled explosions detonated by UK Soldiers since the end of World War II.

Once the British concluded SNIPE, Canadian forces became the main effort. The 3d Battalion, Princess Patricia's Canadian Light Infantry Regiment (3-PPCLI), which had participated in Operation ANACONDA, mounted Operations HARPOON and TORII in May. Lieutenant Colonel Patrick Stogran, the 3-PPCLI commander, described Operation TORII as "essentially a sensitive site exploitation into Tora Bora," and planned primarily on the basis of satellite intelligence.[28] The Canadians swept through the area and, as in Paktia province, failed to find any organized remnants of the enemy. Instead, Stogran recalled that they uncovered "quite an extensive bunker structure built along the ridgeline, and we found that there were about 20 [non-Afghan] foreigners who had been killed [during the December 2001 Tora Bora operation] who had been buried in quite a monument down in the village."[29] CJTF *Mountain* had given the Canadians a broad mandate to examine the Tora Bora area and show the resolve of the Coalition to use military force if necessary. Major Peter Dawe, the operations officer for 3-PPCLI, described how the battalion commander interpreted that intent by moving the unit from Kandahar into a fortified position near Tora Bora from which dismounted patrols moved into smaller villages.[30] Dawe emphasized that during the patrols, the Canadians not only demonstrated the Coalition's military strength but distributed food and other humanitarian assistance to win over the support of the population.[31]

In general, by the spring of 2002, Coalition planning and C2 had become reasonably efficient processes. Unfortunately, one incident in April revealed what could happen when close coordination between Coalition partners did not occur. On 17 April 2002, 3-PPCLI was conducting a live-fire training exercise when an American F-16 fighter/bomber apparently mistook the Canadians as enemy forces and, according to a US Army officer involved in the resulting investigation, dropped a 500-pound bomb, killing four and seriously wounding eight PPCLI soldiers.[32] The incident demonstrated the level of complexity and danger faced by units conducting routine operations in Afghanistan, even after most enemy forces had been eliminated.

Not long after the end of Operation TORII, an Australian Special Forces (SF) team met with resistance from small Taliban groups near the town of Khost. A 6-hour firefight ensued, during which the Australians called in close air support (CAS) from US AC-130 and helicopter gunships. This unexpected engagement spawned Operation CONDOR, an action conducted primarily by British forces in late May. Four companies from TF *Jacana* moved by helicopter into the region and swept through finding only weapons caches, which they destroyed.[33]

The enemy resistance outside of Khost worried Coalition and AIA leaders. With the loya jirga set for the first week of June, CJTF *Mountain* believed it had to prevent all Taliban and al-Qaeda attacks to ensure the political process moved forward. To do this, TF *Jacana* launched Operation BUZZARD in late May that targeted suspected enemy concentrations in Paktia province, especially the area between Khost and the Pakistani border. British leaders directed the Royal Marines to make close contact with the local populace during the operation.[34] Major Richard King, a spokesman for TF *Jacana*, emphasized the shadowy nature of the enemy and the Marines' need to draw information from the population. King contended that at the time Operation BUZZARD was ongoing, "the terrorist organizations have really filtered back into the population, and are not easily identifiable. So as we do in Northern Ireland, we patrol to bring the locals on [our] side, but also gain intelligence against the terrorist organizations."[35] To assist this effort, Brigadier General Roger Lane, TF *Jacana* commander, used a radio program to reassure the local people of Paktia province that the Coalition had no quarrel with Islam, and no long-term intention of maintaining a permanent presence in Afghanistan.[36]

During the 4 weeks of Operation BUZZARD, the Royal Marines had strong indications that enemy fighters were in the region. Nevertheless, these forces did not mount attacks on the task force. One Marine told a journalist, "[the enemy] are there, but they are not coming out to fight."[37] On 20 June 2002, while Operation BUZZARD was still underway, Mr. Hoon, the British Secretary of State for Defence, told the Parliament that 45 Commando's deployment would end when the operation concluded. "The phased drawdown of the force," said Mr. Hoon, "will begin on 4 July and, subject as always to operational demands, should be complete by late next month."[38]

The course charted by the Canadians in the late spring of 2002 paralleled that of TF *Jacana*. On 21 May, about 2 weeks after completing Operation TORII, Canada's Minister of National Defence announced that the 3-PPCLI would soon redeploy to Canada.[39] However, in late June, the Canadian soldiers launched Operation CHEROKEE SKY, a mission designed to build on the success of the completed loya jirga. The operation took the battalion northeast from their base at the Kandahar Airport into Zabol province to suppress suspected Taliban and al-Qaeda forces in that region.[40] The warning order issued to TF *Rakkasan* tasked 3-PPCLI to conduct operations to deny al-Qaeda and Taliban the use of key facilities to forestall enemy action against the Afghan Transitional Authority (ATA) and its recently reconstituted Afghan National Army (ANA).[41] During the weeklong operation, the soldiers of 3-PPCLI conducted sweeps through suspected enemy locations; recovered cached weapon systems; and distributed food, blankets, and school supplies.[42]

In the midst of Operation MOUNTAIN LION, the AIA convened the loya jirga. On 11 June 2002 approximately 2,000 Afghans, chosen from slates of provincial party candidates

---

Task Force *Bowie*—An Early Interagency Success

In the weeks after the 9/11 attacks, CENTCOM commander General Tommy Franks directed Brigadier General Gary L. Harrell to create a joint interagency task force (JIATF) to support Coalition operations in Afghanistan. Harrell, a veteran of several elite Special Operations units, immediately began recruiting individuals from the FBI, NSA, and other agencies in the US Government to serve on the JIATF that eventually became known as Task Force *Bowie*. Joining these men was a Marine Reserve officer who in civilian life was a detective from the New York City Police department.

This group of approximately 50 people organized in Florida and then deployed to Bagram Air Base in November 2001. Housed in a small building on the base, the task force began operations as an intelligence "fusion cell" in which information from a variety of sources including Army Special Forces ODAs could be collected and synthesized into a larger and more precise picture of the enemy. Task Force *Bowie* also tasked units and organizations with the collection of specific information, much of which concerned high-value targets in al-Qaeda and the Taliban.

The JIATF operated at Bagram into the spring of 2002 and departed once CJTF-180 arrived in May. Brigadier General Harrell was proud of the task force's accomplishments and expressed great faith in the interagency approach to solving difficult problems, especially those that involve collecting and understanding a difficult enemy in an unfamiliar setting. For that reason, Harrell viewed Task Force *Bowie* as an excellent model for future JIATFs. In fact, the task force was so successful that it continued to work in support of CENTCOM even after Harrell was transferred to a new position. In the summer and fall of 2002, the organization made important contributions to CENTCOM's planning for operations in Iraq and elsewhere in the Middle East.

Major General Gary L. Harrell, interview by
Contemporary Operations Study Team, Combat Studies Institute, 11 October 2007.

Matthew Bogdanos, with William Patrick,
Thieves of Baghdad (New York, NY: 2005).

---

or appointed based on membership in specific religious or political organizations, arrived in Kabul and began deliberations about the future of Afghanistan. Although traditionally participants in loya jirgas were exclusively male, the Loya Jirga Commission, established by the Bonn Agreement to oversee the 2002 meeting, ensured that 160 women were among the thousands that convened in Kabul. The delegates deliberated for several days before agreeing to the establishment of an ATA with Hamid Karzai as interim president. A week later, Karzai had completed forming his cabinet. While observers noted that the new government featured too many military leaders, especially those from the Northern Alliance, the loya jirga had served the purpose set at Bonn to put Afghanistan on the path toward a democratic future.

The conclusion of Operation CHEROKEE SKY in early July 2002 signaled the end of Operation MOUNTAIN LION. On 13 July the Coalition claimed that the lengthy series of smaller operations had attained its primary objectives of engaging identified enemy remnant forces and creating a secure environment in which the loya jirga could convene.[43] For General Hagenbeck, Operation MOUNTAIN LION represented "the first real effort, if you will, to go out and show a presence across the country . . . to let people know that we could go anywhere in the country with the blink of an eye."[44] Certainly, the success of the loya jirga, the establishment of the ISAF, and CJTF *Mountain's* ability to seize the military initiative suggested strongly that the Coalition's vision for a new Afghanistan was becoming a reality. To reinforce the efforts made in the first 6 months of 2002, at the end of May the US military made a significant change in its command structure. That change, the arrival of a new CJTF, would change the complexion of the campaign yet again.

The Creation of Combined Joint Task Force-180 (CJTF-180)

When the 10th Mountain Division headquarters deployed to Afghanistan in late 2001, its role was to serve as the forward headquarters for Combined Forces Land Component Command (CFLCC), the headquarters belonging to CENTCOM that oversaw all Coalition ground force operations throughout the combatant command's area of responsibility (AOR). The 10th Mountain Division's headquarters, in turn, would command all land forces inside Afghanistan. Major General Hagenbeck, the 10th Mountain Division's commanding general, recalled that the entire process of choosing his headquarters for CFLCC (Forward) had been improvised and thus provided little time for his staff to prepare.

Worse was that in the fall of 2001, most of the division's troop units and staff were preparing for deployment to the Balkans and other peacekeeping missions. As a result, Hagenbeck had fewer than 200 Soldiers serving on his staff when the order for deployment to the Karshi-Khanabad (K2) Air Base arrived, far less than the normal headquarters staff of a US Army division.[45] When Hagenbeck's headquarters became CJTF *Mountain* in early 2002, taking on the additional burdens of C2 for all US forces and for units belonging to Coalition partners, the challenge became even greater. Lieutenant General Paul T. Mikolashek, who commanded CFLCC after 9/11, expressed regret that a way had not been found "to get our headquarters in [earlier] rather than [have] the 10th Mountain Division do it. Although . . . they did fine."[46] Mikolashek felt that in retrospect it would have been better to have a more robust CFLCC headquarters element in the theater, especially for the immense logistical and transportation tasks entailed in operating in central Asia.[47]

Other difficulties surrounding the OEF command structure emerged in early 2002. In February, as the situation in the Shahi Kowt Valley pushed CFLCC (Forward) to consider a large-scale operation, Hagenbeck briefed the CENTCOM commander on his tentative plan for ANACONDA and suggested that CFLCC (Forward) be designated a combined and joint headquarters to oversee the operation. General Franks agreed, but ordered Hagenbeck to avoid adopting the title of CJTF *Afghanistan* as the designation of this new command. As General Hagenbeck recalled the conversation, Franks believed the word "Afghanistan" suggested that the new CJTF would be responsible for Coalition strategy and political affairs inside Afghanistan. Instead, according to Hagenbeck, Franks wanted the new CJTF to be focused on "the tactical level of the fight and the operational level."[48] The CENTCOM commander expressly directed that all matters related to strategy and politics be reserved for his own headquarters.

Although Hagenbeck, his staff, and the subordinate commanders of CJTF *Mountain* complied fully with General Franks' guidance, realities after ANACONDA engendered some doubts about the proper Coalition command structure in Afghanistan. By April 2002 the changing circumstances suggested that political and strategic imperatives were precisely those that needed the most attention. While no senior military leaders were suggesting that tactical-level operations had become irrelevant, many had come to believe that the campaign needed to move into the next phase, a transition that entailed civil-military operations (CMO) at many levels as well as careful political and diplomatic assistance to the new Afghan Government.

The rapidly changing situation sparked animated discussion throughout the chain of command. The most important aspects of the discourse, Hagenbeck recalled, consisted essentially of two parts. Franks first emphasized that the Coalition "needed somebody on the ground that could handle the political aspects and it took somebody with more than a two-star rank . . . somebody who had at least the equivalent [three-star] rank of the component commanders who reported to General Franks."[49] The CENTCOM commander essentially wanted a senior general officer in Afghanistan whose talents allowed him to focus on strategic and diplomatic matters alongside Afghan officials, Coalition counterparts, and diplomats representing their respective governments. Presumably, an officer with the rank of lieutenant general equivalent or higher would have greater experience with Coalition partners, the UN, other international organizations (IOs), and NGOs. The second important dimension of this discussion concerned the proper size of the headquarters. Because it was possible to do only so much with 167 people—the size of the 10th Mountain Division staff when it deployed to K2—General Hagenbeck assumed that a corps headquarters, commanded by a lieutenant general, would serve as a "much more robust headquarters to do things larger than tactical operations."[50]

Long before Franks began discussing these matters with Hagenbeck, the CENTCOM commander had been laying the foundation for the creation of a more robust headquarters in Afghanistan. In fact, as early as February 2002 Franks asked the commander of the US Army's XVIII Airborne Corps, Lieutenant General Dan K. McNeill, to travel to Afghanistan and meet with Hagenbeck, Ryan Crocker—the ambassador to the Karzai government and the future ambassador to Iraq, and other Coalition leaders to gain an understanding of the situation on the ground.[51] McNeill recalled that on his arrival, Crocker and others asked when his corps headquarters was deploying to Afghanistan, a question that surprised him because no formal decision had been made by Franks or anyone else in the chain of command. However, when McNeill left Kabul, just as Operation ANACONDA began, he did so with the understanding that he would be returning soon.

McNeill also traveled to Washington, DC, that spring to get guidance from Department of Defense (DOD) officials and senior Army leaders. The XVIII Airborne Corps commander recalled that Secretary of Defense Donald Rumsfeld, Chief of Staff of the Army General Eric Shinseki, and Chairman of the Joint Chiefs of Staff General Richard B. Myers emphasized the Coalition's need to avoid looking and acting like an occupying army.[52] According to McNeill, General John Keane, the Army Vice Chief of Staff, told him, "Don't you do anything that looks like permanence. We are in and out of there in a hurry."[53] In this way, the military leadership in the Pentagon reinforced the importance of the force cap and the imperative of preventing the Coalition from becoming enmeshed in a long campaign. The problem that lay in front of McNeill was how to attain Coalition military objectives in Afghanistan with a limited force and a limited amount of time.

McNeill recalled that while senior military and civilian officials never gave him a carefully crafted mission statement, it was clear they wanted the Coalition forces to do two things: continue operations to kill or capture the Taliban and al-Qaeda forces that might still reside in Afghanistan and supervise the creation of Afghan security forces.[54] The second requirement was unexpected and had been developed in early 2002 as DOD and CENTCOM became involved in discussions with the Karzai government about the fielding of a new Afghan Army that would defend the country from al-Qaeda and Taliban once the Coalition departed.[55] Ultimately, Rumsfeld approved a CENTCOM proposal to spend approximately $4 million to train and equip a new army.

At the same time that Lieutenant General McNeill received this guidance, senior leaders in the Pentagon had been warning against Coalition forces becoming involved in "nation building," a term that suggested reconstruction and governance projects that would prevent a quick exit from Afghanistan. Despite the concerns about "mission creep," it was clear that with the adoption of the mission to train Afghan military forces, the Coalition's role in the country was beginning to expand. Again, the conundrum facing McNeill, and the commanders who followed, would be how to attain their objectives while maintaining the relatively small Coalition presence in Afghanistan.

The DOD made the final decision to deploy the XVIII Airborne Corps headquarters in mid-March 2002. However, for the corps headquarters to oversee the next step in the campaign, it would have to transform into a CJTF that could synchronize the operations of US Navy, Marine Corps, and Air Force units and the actions of Coalition forces.[56] During March and April, staff officers in the corps headquarters considered the various options for transitioning to a CJTF. Much of the discussion revolved around the proper sizing of the staff that would form the core of the CJTF headquarters.[57] The starting point was the creation of a Joint Manning Document (JMD). Brigadier General Stanley McChrystal, the XVIII Airborne Corps Chief of Staff, recalled that the corps headquarters standing operating procedure (SOP) directed the staff to expand to approximately 800 people when it transitioned to a joint task force (JTF).[58] The addition of representatives from the military forces of Coalition nations, required to transform the JTF into a CJTF, would add still more people to the staff.

At this point in the planning process, geopolitical realities began to have a critical effect on the size of the CJTF headquarters. First, there was the Coalition's force cap to ensure that its military organizations created only a light footprint in Afghanistan. No senior official in the US Government appears to have mandated a specific force level to Coalition leaders. However, in the late winter and spring of 2002, primary staff officers in XVIII Airborne Corps understood that the informal cap was 7,000 US servicemen and women.[59] Colonel Richard D. MeGahan, who served as the Personnel Officer (G1) for the XVIII Airborne Corps and then held the same position when the corps' staff deployed in 2002 as part of the new CJTF, asserted that this number drove his planning for OEF. MeGahan recalled that CENTCOM acted as if this was an official cap, yet he never found any explicit guidance from the Pentagon or any other authority concerning a nonnegotiable limit on US forces in Afghanistan.[60]

Formal or informal, this cap directly affected the capacity of the new CJTF. Brigadier General McChrystal noted concerns about the overall size of the staff heavily influenced the shaping of the CJTF structure. He recalled, "As we started to build, we culled [the 800 number] back down significantly; but there came great pressure with instructions to cull that down even more. So . . . we culled back down as much as we could, ending up with the number of 368 on the Joint Manning Document."[61] Thus, the Corps headquarters faced its impending deployment staffed to a level that amounted to less than half the authorizations mandated by its SOP for transitioning to a CJTF.

The mandated level of 368 staff personnel applied to the CJTF headquarters, but as McChrystal noted, was not inclusive: "There were requirements for some communications, intelligence, and a few other support [personnel] that were absolutely required for the head-quarters but not reflected on the JMD . . . a tremendous amount of time and effort was spent on trying to get that down to size."[62] The fact that few if any people inside XVIII Airborne Corps headquarters possessed any firsthand knowledge of Afghanistan did not make matters any easier. Key leaders in the headquarters were trying to identify minimal acceptable staffing levels within the theater of operations while concurrently trying to conceptualize what that the-ater looked like. General McChrystal asserted that it was "not an easy task to cut [the staff size to] less than half when we haven't been in theater yet; you don't know what you need and what you don't need. So, you are trying to extrapolate what you think the situation will be."[63]

Another major concern shaping the structure of the new CJTF was the possibility that the XVIII Airborne Corps and its subordinate units would become involved in operations else-where in the Global War on Terrorism (GWOT). Lieutenant General McNeill recalled that dur-ing the planning process, General Shinseki and General Keane directed him to leave half of his corps headquarters at Fort Bragg, North Carolina, in case the Army had to use corps' units like the 82d Airborne Division to react to terrorist strikes or mount other campaigns that loomed on the horizon.[64] McNeill believed that both senior officers at that time suspected the United States was moving closer to war in Iraq and wanted to retain the capabilities of the XVIII Airborne Corps headquarters for that contingency.

As deployment of the newly-christened CJTF-180 headquarters began in May 2002, CENTCOM described the new command as creating "additional focus and efficiency to the Afghanistan mission" by providing "a single senior officer who will be responsible for the majority of forces and activity" in the country.[65] By that date, the staff of the CJTF had final-ized their equivalent of a campaign plan. CJTF-180's plan and guidance from CENTCOM emphasized that Coalition forces were still in Phase III—Decisive Combat Operations—of the overall OEF plan initiated in October 2001 by General Franks. The CJTF-180 leadership recognized that fact in its mission statement that described the nature of the campaign as full spectrum operations that prioritized security operations focused on destroying remaining al-Qaeda and Taliban forces and other elements hostile to the ATA.[66] However, the CJTF-180 plan also directed operations that fit more comfortably within Phase IV of the original OEF plan, which aimed at supporting the new Afghan Government after the toppling of the Taliban. In McNeill's campaign, Coalition forces would conduct operations in support of the Afghan Army, the Karzai government, and the Afghan population.

To give further guidance to its subordinate units, the CJTF-180 plan used five lines of effort to define how Coalition forces would achieve its mission. A line of effort, like a line of opera-tion, is a doctrinal term used by campaign planners to describe a general category of opera-tions that collectively result in a specific objective and end state. CJTF-180's lines of effort were tactical combat operations, establishment and training of the ANA, support to the ISAF, CMO, and information operations. The last line of effort, information operations, described the Coalition's use of information to build support for the Coalition and the ATA while undermin-ing the Taliban and al-Qaeda. Ultimately, McNeill and his staff hoped that operations along these lines of effort would result in the attainment of a well-defined end state—the emergence of an Afghanistan that was stable politically and militarily and would no longer serve as a potential haven for terrorist groups that had the ability to strike globally. The challenge once McNeill and his headquarters arrived in Afghanistan was to quickly gain an understanding of the terrain, the enemy, and the overall political situation so they could translate their campaign plan into actual operations.

Civil-Military Operations: Fall 2001–Spring 2002

During the first 8 months of the Coalition's presence in Afghanistan, combat missions—often referred to as offensive operations—had remained the focus of the overall effort. As CJTF-180 began arriving in Afghanistan in May 2002, the situation was changing and by mid-summer, CMO had taken on an increasing significance. US joint military doctrine in 2001 defined CMO as those activities "that establish, maintain, influence, or exploit relations between military forces, governmental and nongovernmental civilian organizations and authorities, and the civilian populace in a friendly, neutral, or hostile operational area in order to facilitate military operations, to consolidate and achieve operational US objectives."[67] This broad definition appeared to allow Coalition commanders an open approach to CMO without committing their limited assets to a true "nation building" effort that American senior officials wanted to avoid.

To conduct CMO in previous campaigns and contingency operations, the US Army has relied on its engineer, medical, logistical, and civil affairs (CA) units. These units were the assets that are trained, equipped, and staffed to execute reconstruction, humanitarian and medical assistance, and governance operations. Not surprisingly, these types of units would become critical to the effort in Afghanistan. However, Coalition commanders sought a novel approach to controlling CMO by establishing a somewhat unusual command structure. This command, which served as the initial headquarters for US CMO in Afghanistan, was known as the Combined Joint Civil-Military Operations Task Force (CJCMOTF).

CFLCC Commander Lieutenant General Mikolashek created the CJCMOTF in late 2001 around elements of the 377th Theater Support Command, the 122d Rear Operations Center (ROC), and the 352d CA Command. In October of that year, once CENTCOM realized that the campaign in Afghanistan would involve humanitarian assistance operations, Mikolashek had contacted Brigadier General David E. Kratzer, deputy commander of the 377th Theater Support Command.[68] Kratzer recalled that Mikolashek informed him that he was to be brought back on Active Duty as commander of the CJCMOTF. His response was, "Great, what is that?"[69] Mikolashek explained what the acronym represented and that the command was designed to be a joint-level headquarters. Although a logistician with no formal experience in CA, Kratzer felt that Mikolashek had provided him with the latitude and all the tools necessary for success. In fact, Kratzer thought that his lack of connections to the CA branch allowed him to approach the new command with a fresh perspective and was ultimately a benefit.[70]

Mikolashek's personal selection of Kratzer to command CJCMOTF reflected a strongly-held view within CENTCOM that the organization's importance warranted a general officer as commander. CFLCC formed the core of the CJCMOTF from 50 Soldiers assigned to the 122d Rear Area Operations Center (RAOC), a Georgia Army National Guard unit that had already been activated, and by early November 2001 occupied trailers co-located with CFLCC headquarters in Atlanta. After a 4-day planning session, the command's advance party that included Kratzer and his deputy departed for Afghanistan.

CENTCOM and CFLCC planners had designed the CJCMOTF to operate with a staff of 50 based on assumptions of how CMO would be conducted in OEF. Simply put, Kratzer's command would coordinate the key agents in the distribution process—the NGOs. A 2002 study conducted by the US Army Peacekeeping and Stability Operations Institute (PKSOI) labeled this approach as "wholesale aid distribution" and described it more fully by emphasizing the military's role as one player in a system that made use of civilian networks whenever possible and enabled those networks by providing key assistance, especially transportation assistance. In this method, military headquarters ceased coordination once security was established in the area and the civilian networks were fully capable of delivering aid across the country.[71]

While there were benefits to this approach, there were serious questions in late 2001 about its feasibility in war-torn Afghanistan. The key advantages were obvious: it required relatively few soldiers and equipment and thus would help prevent Coalition forces from becoming enmeshed too deeply in broad reconstruction efforts. Still, the deployment of the CJCMOTF worried senior Coalition leaders about the campaign veering off course. Kratzer recalled that in 2001 General Franks "told me directly, with his finger in my face, that I would not get involved in nation building."[72] The disappearance of NGOs during the Taliban era and the violence and instability that accompanied the arrival of Coalition forces in October 2001 suggested "wholesale aid distribution" was not viable in Afghanistan. After the fall of Kabul in November 2001, however, some NGOs involved in aid distribution returned to the country and still more returned in early 2002 as ISAF and Coalition forces secured larger portions of the Afghan countryside.

The operations of the 96th CA Battalion (BN) offer an excellent window into the ways that early Coalition CMO worked and how it fit into the broader "wholesale aid" approach. Soldiers from this unit arrived in Afghanistan in October 2001 and were the first civil-military affairs specialists to reach the theater.[73] The original mission of the 96th CA BN was to serve as a coordination agency for projects planned by NGOs and to ensure that humanitarian assistance operations were focused on secure regions of the country. In earlier deployments, such as the peacekeeping missions in the Balkans, the Army had established similar agencies called Civil-Military Operations Centers (CMOCs) to coordinate aid efforts while gaining credibility with NGOs and UN agencies. These organizations, though, sometimes spurned contact with any entity related to military organizations because they regarded CMOCs and other agencies as part of a larger attempt to use humanitarian aid for specific national interests. In deference to NGO and UN sensitivities over this issue, in late 2001 the 96th CA BN created the expediently-named Coalition Humanitarian Liaison Cells (CHLCs) that, like the CMOCs, were supposed to focus on coordination and assistance rather than making decisions about the nature of the aid and its recipients.[74] By the fall of 2002, 10 of these 6-person teams would be established near large cities like Kandahar and Herat as well as smaller towns like Khost.

Because of the nature of the campaign in Afghanistan, the CHLCs could not always function simply as CMOCs. In some cases, rather than *coordinating* aid delivery, the CHLCs became agencies that *directly provided* assistance on the ground, especially in emergencies and in regions that were not secure. Major Luther Webster, who supervised CHLC operations in early 2002, explained that the CHLCs were sent to key areas where Coalition leaders believed CMO could make a difference in winning local support. They were combined with Army SF Operational Detachment–Alpha (ODA) teams and divided the mission into two parts. According to Webster, the CHLCs "would do the Civil Affairs part. The ODA would do the more combat-type operations. It was determined that it was a win/win situation for both. We'd be dealing with the local leaders, the local ministers, the local warlords, while they were focused more on combat operations."[75] For the Coalition command that in 2001 and 2002 was faced with a dearth of troops and other resources, the CHLCs provided a means of extending the reach of the military campaign into regions far from Kabul and Kandahar.

That reach often took the shape of "quick impact projects" that the small cells could plan and deliver to alleviate the negative affects of combat operations on a local area, build credibility with local populations, and broaden support among those people for the new Afghan Government.[76] The CHLC concept proved so successful that it inspired the creation of experimental Joint Regional Teams, which would later evolve into Provincial Reconstruction Teams that would be subsequently deployed throughout Afghanistan. The Coalition's decision to provide direct delivery of humanitarian assistance and quick action projects also signaled a move away from the partnership with NGOs and IOs.

Civil-Military Operations: Obstacles and Achievements

As early as November 2001, the availability of resources became a significant obstacle to conducting CMO. Even before CJCMOTF deployed into theater, Brigadier General Kratzer had established contact with leaders in the 96th CA BN who told him that adequate funds had become a critical problem. Kratzer recalled, "I had talked to them before we deployed—said we are coming. What do you need? They said we need vehicles and we need money. If you're not bringing cash, we'll love to see you, but you're not going to help us."[77] The CA BN was so short of funds that their quarters in Kabul was a house rented by the British Government's Department for International Development (DFID), an agency much like the US Agency for International Development (USAID).[78]

For the new CJCMOTF commander, the next 4 months were dominated by efforts to obtain funds and other resources required for accomplishing his mission. When the CJCMOTF advance party arrived at Bagram Air Base on Christmas Eve 2001, they brought with them a suitcase containing a million dollars in US currency to rent houses, lease vehicles, and conduct other business. The CJCMOTF commander soon used the suitcase full of American currency to good effect by doing everything necessary to properly equip and house his headquarters and outlying civil-military nodes, including the CHLCs. This currency, nevertheless, could not be used to fund the many projects the CHLCs were in the midst of planning.

The core of the funding challenge was more than just a matter of having enough dollars to meet CJCMOTF's expenses. It was mainly a question of flexibility in using established funds for projects in Afghanistan, and determining who could authorize these expenditures. The 2002 PKSOI study judged the funding process used in support of CMO in this early stage of OEF "restrictive and bureaucratic."[79] Because the necessity for the OEF deployment came as a surprise after 9/11, the Coalition had not yet created flexible funding procedures. Most of the money available to CJCMOTF fell under the category of Overseas Humanitarian, Disaster, and Civic Aid (OHDACA) funds. Theoretically, this money was a tool that could be used in support of quick impact humanitarian aid projects generated by CHLCs. Prior to Kratzer's arrival in the theater of operations, approval authority for dispensing these funds remained at DOD level. "The approval process," the PKSOI study asserted, "became bureaucratic, and the availability of contracting officers and transportation to get contracting officers to key areas was a restraint."[80] The situation cried out for a decentralized approval authority that could distribute OHDACA funds to cover the quick impact projects identified by the CHLCs.

Obtaining that authority was uppermost on Kratzer's priority list. "So here I am," he recalled, "with a million dollars to sustain myself and not a penny to do the mission . . . I was on the border of . . . being insubordinate and at one point sent a message saying either give me the money or send me home. . . .We raised a lot of interest."[81] Forcible arguments and appeals with commanders and financial managers throughout the chain of command eventually bore fruit. Before his departure from Afghanistan in April 2002, Kratzer arranged for his command to have approval authority to sign off on CJCMOTF projects. In retrospect, he argued that this decentralization of authority for disbursing of funding was the linchpin in the success attained by the CHLCs and should become the standard practice for future US Army operations.[82]

By May 2002, on the eve of the arrival of CJTF-180, CJCMOTF had used $2.56 million to support a diverse set of projects that included the refurbishment of roads, bridges, schools, and medical facilities.[83] The early months of the campaign also focused on wells and irrigation, two types of projects that were critical in the dry climate of Afghanistan. One large-scale irrigation effort in this period that attempted to help the Afghans recover from decades of war and instability was the Herat Desilting project. Begun in March 2002, the project sought to dredge and fix the major irrigation canals around Herat that had fallen into disuse because of neglect during the Taliban period. Major Webster, who was involved in planning the project, described the effect of the problem on agricultural conditions in the area: "Over the Taliban years . . . they just [silted] up and the water wasn't flowing. Farms weren't being irrigated. Basically nothing was growing because you couldn't get water to it."[84] Once the CJCMOTF obtained funding, the project took off, ultimately employing 40,000 people who, using mostly hand tools, constructed approximately 300 miles of trenches and canals to reclaim 400 hectares of arable land.[85]

In the spring of 2002, the CHLC's successful practices began to generate friction between the CJCMOTF and nonmilitary humanitarian assistance providers. In part, these challenges surfaced because of rapid diplomatic progress made during the period in which Operation ANACONDA occurred. On 28 March 2002 the UN Security Council passed Resolution 1401 that established a United Nations Assistance Mission in Afghanistan (UNAMA). The new mission was to create an administrative framework that would bring order to the humanitarian assistance and reconstruction efforts.

The UNAMA charter altered the improvised system that had been put in place after OEF began in October 2001. The Security Council resolution enjoined prospective donor agencies to provide humanitarian assistance directly wherever the need surfaced, but also encouraged them to work "through the Afghan Interim Administration and its successors" in providing recovery and reconstruction assistance.[86] A study conducted by the Afghanistan Research and Evaluation Unit (AREU) declared this proposed system of working through the AIA a "radical departure from standard international aid practice in complex emergencies" in its involvement of a particular regime, one whose sovereignty was, in some opinions, dependent on a foreign military force.[87]

Despite the concerns, UNAMA developed a regional model for coordinating foreign aid delivery throughout Afghanistan. The AIA, for its part, by April 2002 had drafted a codified "National Development Framework," which held that Afghanistan's "developmental agenda must be owned domestically, and the recipient country must be in the driver's seat."[88] The AIA also established its own Afghan Assistance Coordination Authority (AACA) whose charter was to work with UN agencies and NGOs to create programs that would address the new Afghan Government's needs and would be directed toward shoring up that government as well as fostering Afghan civil society.[89]

Some in the aid community chafed at the new environment emerging that spring simply because the new organizations and guidelines seemed confusing and redundant.[90] When AREU conducted its study in the April–May timeframe, several organizations existed side-by-side in the Afghan theater of operations, all perceiving aid coordination as fundamental to their respective charters. In addition to UNAMA and the AIA's AACA, a British Civil Military Cooperation (CMIC) element was on the ground in Kabul supervising aid connected with the ISAF deployment. CJCMOTF's arrival in theater, according to the AREU study, only "added to the crush of . . . nongovernment organizations (NGOs), donors, and private sector organizations."[91] Much of this seemed heavy-handed to a largely civilian aid community long accustomed to operating independently.

Some aid providers focused on the CJCMOTF, viewing it as less humanitarian assistance than "aid-induced pacification." The notion that the Coalition and ISAF had invaded humanitarian space became commonplace in the NGO community. The spread of CHLCs' across the Afghan countryside created the appearance, in some minds, of a competition in which poorly-resourced NGOs that lacked the security capacity to venture into unsecured remote areas were destined to lose. Once Brigadier General Kratzer's efforts overcame the funding obstacles, the CHLCs arguably became the most effective purveyors of humanitarian assistance and quick impact aid projects in Afghanistan. The built-in force protection gained by co-locating CHLCs with SF operational detachments addressed personal safety issues in ways no NGOs could match. Some of the Soldiers serving on the CHLCs believed that the Afghans recognized the Coalition's capacity to deliver humanitarian and reconstruction assistance. According to Major Webster, "The CHLCs were immediately respected; [they] immediately established rapport with the local leaders, and immediately saw projects getting done."[92] Webster attributed the CHLC success specifically to the availability of funds and the ability to operate in the provinces where the need was greatest but the security tenuous.[93]

The command structure that allowed for this deployment of the CHLCs hardly allayed NGO misgivings about CMO. As noted earlier in this chapter, previous US peacekeeping operations in places such as the Balkans had conditioned NGOs to expect access to CMOCs that included workspace, communications nodes, and a staff that could provide critical information. The CMOC served the purpose of coordinating NGO efforts and ensuring that security operations did not come into conflict with the NGO projects. CJCMOTF had followed precedent and created two CMOCs in Afghanistan, CMOC North and CMOC South, but they had little control in coordinating the actions of the CHLCs other than to provide logistical support. The PKSOI study explained the situation, contending, "When civil affairs [cells] deployed to Afghanistan, this function [CMOC] lapsed. . . . CHLCs in their areas coordinated with the NGOs in support of their high-impact projects, but did not perform traditional CMOC functions" associated with previous peacekeeping campaigns.[94] This state of affairs left the NGOs dissatisfied.

Friction between CJCMOTF and NGOs reached a peak during the first week of April 2002 over a CJCMOTF policy that allowed CHLC Soldiers in remote areas to wear civilian clothes as a force protection measure. Lieutenant General Mikolashek, the CFLCC commander, had concurred with this decision and in Brigadier General Kratzer's opinion, the policy had made a major impact, contending, "[It] absolutely contributed to our early success that we were allowed to operate in civilian clothes. It allowed our teams to live in communities, and come and go in a very quiet way, and not [to] either raise interest or to cause any kind of belligerence."[95] For the CJCMOTF commander, the policy was aimed equally at safeguarding his troops and creating rapport with local Afghans.

Many aid workers viewed the policy differently. NGO officials believed that enemy forces who opposed the Coalition would discover that US Soldiers were dressing in civilian clothes and consider all aid workers, civilian and military, as targets.[96] According to one report, NGO representatives sent a letter to US National Security Advisor Condoleezza Rice complaining that Soldiers conducting CMO were often wearing civilian clothes when they worked on their projects in the provinces.[97] But Brigadier General Kratzer was not convinced that the NGO concerns had a great deal of merit. In his view, the allegations that CHLCs were attempting to mimic the appearance of NGOs was unfounded.[98] Although the controversy garnered command attention at the highest levels, Coalition leaders defused the conflict through compromise. In late April 2002 the Center for Defense Information reported that new American policy dictated that US troops providing humanitarian and reconstruction assistance in Afghanistan while wearing civilian clothes were to wear items of apparel that would differentiate them from civilian aid workers.[99]

Despite this agreement, friction between aid organizations and the Coalition persisted. Higher-level leaders in NGOs and UNAMA continued to distance themselves from OEF commanders well into the spring of 2002. The inability of UNAMA officials to find time to meet personally with the CJCMOTF commander was perhaps the most apparent sign of this friction. The relationship changed when CJTF-180 arrived in May 2002. That month, Lieutenant General McNeill and Brigadier General Kratzer succeeded in gaining an audience with a senior UNAMA official. The meeting signaled the willingness of UN officials to begin building a more constructive relationship and, for the remainder of 2002, the connections between UNAMA, the NGOs, and Coalition forces improved.

A New Government and a New Army

After arriving in Afghanistan in late 2001, Brigadier General Kratzer's duties quickly expanded. Not only did he command the CJCMOTF, but by February 2002 also took the title of Chief of the Office of Military Cooperation–Afghanistan (OMC-A). In early 2002 this office represented the main thrust of the Coalition's effort to assist the new Karzai government. For Kratzer, the dual responsibilities meant that he would have to rely on the talents of other officers to lead the daily operations of the OMC-A. Assisting him with these governance operations was Colonel Mike Weimer, who arrived at the American Embassy in Kabul in February 2002 to serve as Kratzer's deputy in OMC-A.[100]

In the broadest sense, anything related to fostering the legitimacy and authority of the AIA or its successors was part of the Coalition's governance effort. To the extent that CJCMOTF was a conduit for delivering humanitarian assistance to the Afghan people, for example, or facilitating the completion of short-term reconstruction projects, it became part of this effort by making the Karzai regime appear more effective to its constituents. However, OMC-A, as part of the American Ambassador's country team, was the most active proponent of governance operations in 2002. The office's goal was to establish working relationships with key individuals within Afghanistan's nascent Ministry of Defense to accomplish overall objectives established by the Bonn Agreement. Colonel Weimer stated that the mission of OMC-A "predominately, is to be the military liaison for the [American] Ambassador, and that liaison officer goes over to the host country to liaise with, in this case, the Minister of Defense, General Delawar, and the Afghan National Army, or at least the beginnings of what I would call the Afghan Ministry of Defense."[101]

All of this activity occurred within the greater context of the international effort to reestablish Afghanistan's military, police, and judicial organizations. In early 2002 the United States joined Germany, Italy, Japan, and the United Kingdom in an agreement on what was called Security Sector Reform (SSR). Germany took the lead in reform of Afghan police forces and created a comprehensive 5-year training program focused on tactics, criminal and narcotics investigations, traffic control, and Islamic law.[102] The Germans designed their program to produce competent, well-trained Afghan police officers. However, the Afghan police sector desperately needed immediate reforms and the German-led police academy could not produce results quickly enough nor could Germany commit the necessary funds required to accelerate the training program.[103] The US supplemented the police training program with $26 million to produce a sufficient number of patrolmen for the Afghan presidential elections scheduled for fall 2004.[104]

Italy, with assistance from the United Nations and the United States, undertook reforms of the justice system. After decades of conflict, Afghanistan did not have a tradition of rule of law. Thus, Italy focused on rewriting the legal code and training judges and Ministry of Justice officers to enforce the rule of law. The Italians also made plans to improve prison and detention facilities.[105] The United Kingdom focused on counternarcotics. In 2002 poppy production was under 1,300 metric tons but would soon increase.[106] Poppy production financed insurgent groups and warlords and the heroin that resulted from poppies fed European markets. Therefore, the United Kingdom had a vested interest in tackling this problem. The UK strategy included law enforcement as well as helping foster alternative livelihoods for the agricultural sector.[107]

Japan led the Disarmament, Demobilization, and Reintegration (DDR) project, officially called the Afghan New Beginnings Program. The DDR program intended to convince regional militias to disband and either join the ANA or find other jobs. This was a difficult program to implement for several reasons. First, to convince militia members to disarm and leave militias, they needed sustainable employment. Japan, with UN assistance, spent a considerable amount of time establishing training centers to teach job-related skills. To succeed, the Japanese DDR program in 2002 needed funding to staff these training centers and provide housing for the former militiamen. Difficulties in attaining funds for these components of the program unfortunately delayed large-scale demobilizations of the country's militias.

The United States' role in security sector reform was to rebuild the ANA into a professional fighting force loyal to the democratically elected government of Afghanistan. OMC-A was the vanguard of the American effort to construct this new force. Under normal circumstances, the State Department would set the administrative wheels in motion to create an OMC. However, because General Franks anticipated the need for that kind of military element to support the embassy and to provide military-to-military contact with the AIA Ministry of Defense (MOD), CENTCOM placed the initiative on a fast track.

The CENTCOM commander's interest in the quick establishment of OMC-A is understandable, given Franks' concerns about the nature of the Coalition campaign. By quickly establishing indigenous security forces, CENTCOM could hand off responsibilities for security to the Afghans and withdraw much of the Coalition's land forces. But in early 2002, Afghanistan's police and army were essentially nonexistent. In March 2002 UN Secretary General Kofi Annan recognized this and stated that the entire Bonn Agreement agenda largely depended on the establishment of effective Afghan security forces. "Proper management of the security sector," Annan asserted, "is the necessary first step toward [Afghan national] reconciliation and reconstruction; indeed, managing this sector may be considered the first reconstruction project."[108] For Annan, the path to creating a legitimate and representative government in Afghanistan that would be capable of creating a stable environment started with the creation of new security forces loyal to that government.

The obstacles on this path were significant. In addition to the remnants of the Taliban, Afghanistan faced threats posed by warlords that in early 2002 controlled whole regions of the country. Ali A. Jalali, Karzai's interior minister that year, regarded the growing problem with warlords as inseparable from the fundamental issue of Afghan sovereignty. The AIA's leaders could ill afford to have the new Afghan political process come to resemble the historical patterns of the previous decades. Nevertheless, by the spring of 2002, the emerging military situation troubled the Interior Minister because it replicated conditions that resembled the warlord interregnum of the 1990s. As Jalali reviewed the Afghan military units that would come to exist by mid-2002, he found that much of the Afghans under arms owed allegiance to specific leaders rather than to the new Karzai government.[109] In the summer of 2002, for example, he described the Afghan Army as a mix of units that were loyal to a variety of regional leaders. Holding this structure loosely together was a patchwork of alliances that sought to achieve a balance of provincial military power inside Afghanistan. If the alliances broke down, the country might be pulled apart by civil war yet again.

Building and Training an Afghan National Army (ANA)

In February, shortly after their arrival in the theater of operations, a portion of the British-led ISAF under Major General McColl began training the first battalion of what was called an Afghan National Guard (1st BANG). The demographic makeup of this group, comprised of roughly 600 prospective soldiers, purportedly reflected Afghanistan's ethnic diversity.[110] As Kofi Annan drafted his 18 March report to the UN, members of the 1st BANG were still about 2 weeks away from their graduation. Even as these soldiers went through their training, a lively discourse erupted over the model best suited for use in building the new ANA.

Arriving at a consensus of what the Afghans could support presented a definite challenge to the Coalition. As the Secretary-General explained in his report, debate centered on "two papers produced respectively by the International Security Assistance Force, which proposed a force of about 50,000, and the [Afghan] Ministry of Defense, which suggested a force of 200,000."[111] Little doubt existed about the high levels of expertise in technology, warfighting doctrine, or training among the British soldiers or their ability to train Afghans. However, at this delicate juncture, their colonial tradition, justly or unjustly, fueled Afghan national sensitivities. While acknowledging that 21st century mentalities differed markedly from those in play during the 19th century, the disparity between the Afghan and British plans for building an ANA potentially threatened the larger SSR effort.

Both OMC-A and the British regarded the 200,000 figure as far too high. Afghan officials explained that a force of this size would be capable of controlling the country's borders and preventing unwanted incursions from terrorists, warlords, or drug-runners sheltering in regions contiguous with Pakistan's Northwest Frontier province. Some in the Coalition believed that the figure had more to do with a lingering Soviet military influence than any real calculation of the country's military needs. According to Colonel Jeffery Marshall, who soon assumed responsibility for training the ANA, the Afghan Ministry of Defense (MOD) was "structured initially like an old Soviet Ministry of Defense, very unwieldy and very bureaucratic and not functional."[112] It came as no surprise, then, that key players within the MOD, including Deputy Defense Minister Lieutenant General Atiquallah Baryalai, believed that the AIA's continued existence depended on the size and centralized control of its military establishment.[113]

Negotiations over the best way to shape and field the new ANA continued through the spring and summer. The unwieldy nature of the Afghan proposal was emphasized by an assessment team sent by CENTCOM in the spring to analyze the options. That team immediately recognized the Afghan MOD template as outmoded, unaffordable, and almost impossible to resource. Rather than taking an adversarial stance, however, the team members worked alongside OMC-A to arrive at a consensus amenable to the AIA. During the time of transition in mid-2002, the most notable accomplishment of Brigadier General Kratzer, Colonel Weimer, and others who served and worked with OMC-A was the forward momentum of the ANA project they helped generate. Much of this progress was based on the relationship they built gradually with the Afghan people. Looking back on the experience, Kratzer asserted that "building the Afghan Army took a thousand cups of tea."[114]

To observers, the most visible sign of progress would have been the growing energy devoted to training Afghan Army units. As noted earlier, British forces within ISAF had launched the program in February 2002. On 1 May 2002, OMC-A greatly reinforced this effort by committing US Soldiers in Afghanistan to the training of Afghan recruits and the formation of ANA units. Colonel Weimer credited General Franks in pushing aside or ignoring a number of bureaucratic obstacles to ensure that American troops became involved in the training effort early. Rather than securing funds and other resources first and then slowly establishing a training site and a program of instruction, Weimer remembered, "The process was absolutely reversed. The [trainees] arrived first, and the OMC mission in that regard was to help set the conditions and stage for [the training] mission to begin."[115] Even as they were still getting organized, Weimer's OMC-A team negotiated with the Afghan MOD to identify a demographically acceptable cross-section of recruits and obtain possession of the Kabul Military Training Center (KMTC), a compound that had lain dormant for 4 years after being closed by the Taliban. OMC-A immediately started spending $4 million to restore the infrastructure to acceptable levels for the training of soldiers and worked briskly to prepare to get ready to train the first three (ANA) battalions and the first two border guard battalions.[116]

The key to the OMC-A plan at this stage was securing the US Army's 1st Battalion, 3d Special Forces Group (SFG) as the unit responsible for training the ANA and border guard battalions. SF Soldiers were trained to conduct the Foreign Internal Defense (FID) mission, which included the training of indigenous security forces. The men of the 1st Battalion, 3d SFG were experienced trainers and had worked with soldiers from a variety of foreign armies. The pressures of the situation in Afghanistan that spring, however, made the ANA mission difficult. Coalition and Afghan leaders sought to have trained Afghan forces available around the middle of June, the date of the loya jirga. Lieutenant Colonel Kevin McDonnell, the commander of the 1st Battalion, 3d SFG, emphasized that the training schedule and graduation goals posed a significant challenge to his Soldiers. McDonnell told a journalist that his training mission was daunting, expressing a preference for having "six months to one year" to train each battalion rather than the 10-week training cycle timetable driven by national political imperatives.[117]

The training effort began haltingly. In April 2002 the British ISAF completed the training of 550 Afghan soldiers, but only 400 remained on duty as of the beginning of June. Attrition affected the American effort as well. When the SF battalion opened its course at KMTC, its leaders expected 605 prospective recruits to report for duty. Only 400 arrived on schedule. Lieutenant Colonel McDonnell recognized that retaining trained soldiers was often difficult in a country like Afghanistan, which was still unstable and whose future was still uncertain. He suggested that the ANA training program in early summer 2002 was just beginning to show progress: "If you've got the three stages of crawl, walk, and run, right now we're doing the crawl."[118] However rudimentary this beginning might have been, the Coalition had made yet another transition aimed at preparing the new Afghan state to stand on its own.

✦　✦　✦

This chapter has focused on the 3-month period in mid-2002 when the nature of OEF began to change in a fundamental manner. Very few senior political officials or their military commanders had expected the campaign to transition in the ways that it changed in the spring and summer of 2002. The original campaign plan for OEF, for example, made no provision for Coalition forces participating in the construction of a new Afghan Army or in supervising irrigation projects in the western provinces of Afghanistan. Yet, in May 2002, just weeks after ANACONDA concluded, American SF Soldiers found themselves training Afghan soldiers and CA specialists had become involved in a myriad of projects large and small in the far-flung regions of the country. At the same time, US Army officers with more seniority had become directly involved in assisting the Afghan Government design its new Army.

In recognition of this transition point, the Coalition itself made a significant change in command structure. Rather than move forward in an ad hoc arrangement in which a small vestigial division headquarters—CJTF *Mountain*—continued to serve as the senior headquarters of Coalition forces, the CENTCOM commander created a CJTF and deployed it to Afghanistan. CJTF-180, based on roughly half of the XVIII Airborne Corps' headquarters staff, arrived in May 2002 and immediately began to assert control over tactical military operations while it augmented the Coalition's capacity to deal with strategic and operational level issues, especially those that pertained to fostering the stability of the new Afghan Government. Both militarily and diplomatically then, the Coalition moved in mid-2002 from deposing a rogue, terror-sponsoring regime to underwriting the legitimacy of a new Afghanistan ushered in by the Bonn Agreement.

This period of transition marked several critical successes, the most important of which was the conduct of the emergency loya jirga, which began on 11 June 2002. The jirga's peaceful selection of an ATA served as the next sign of political progress along the path established by the Bonn Agreement. Yet less than a month later, on 6 July, Abdul Qadir, an official chosen by the loya jirga to serve as one of Afghanistan's new vice presidents, died alongside his driver when two unknown assailants ambushed their car. This incident drove home the fact that while it had overthrown the Taliban regime, the Coalition had only begun the campaign to transform Afghanistan into a stable and successful state.

Notes

1. "CinC CENTCOM and the Chief of the Defence Staff: Press Conference—26 April 2002, *Operation Veritas*, UK Ministry of Defence, 26 April 2002. http://www.operations.mod.uk/veritas/press_brief_26apr.htm (accessed 6 July 2007).

2. Quoted in Ali A. Jalali, "Rebuilding Afghanistan's National Army," *Parameters*, Autumn 2002, 73.

3. United Nations, *Agreement on Provisional Arrangements in Afghanistan Pending the Re-Establishment of Permanent Government Institutions*. http://www.un.org/News/dh/latest/afghan/afghan-agree.htm (accessed 19 January 2009).

4. "Security Council Resolution 1386 (2001) on the Situation in Afghanistan," *Security Council Resolutions-2001*, 20 December 2001. http://www.un.org/Docs/scres/2001/sc2001.htm (accessed 2 May 2007).

5. "Military Technical Agreement Between the International Security Assistance Force (ISAF) and the Interim Administration of Afghanistan ('Interim Administration')," 4 January 2002.

6. "NATO in Afghanistan Factsheet," North Atlantic Treaty Organization, 21 February 2005. http://www.nato.int./issues/afghanistan/040628-factsheet.htm (accessed 22 May 2002).

7. United Nations Press Release, SC/7311, "Afghanistan Political Progress Faster than Expected; Security Threats Remain, Under-Secretary-General for Political Affairs Tells Security Council." http://www.un.org/News/Press/docs/2002/sc7311.doc.htm (accessed 4 December 2008).

8. Kofi Annan, "The Situation in Afghanistan and its Implications for International Peace and Security," *Report of the Secretary-General*, General Assembly Fifty-sixth session, United Nations, NY, 18 March 2002.

9. Annan, "Situation in Afghanistan and its Implications."

10. Emily Clark and Mark Burgess, "Action Update (Complete Archive)," *Center for Defense Information Terrorism Project*, 8 October 2001–1 September 2002. http://www.cdi.org/terrorism/actionupdate-archive-pr.cfm (accessed 28 February 2007), see entry under 18–24 March 2002.

11. "The Secretary of State for Defence's Statement in the Commons—18 March 2002," *Operation Veritas*, UK Ministry of Defense, Statement, 18 March 2002. http://www.operations.mod.uk/veritas/statements (accessed 30 May 2007).

12. Senate Armed Services Committee, *Statement of General Tommy R. Franks, Commander, US Central Command*, 31 July 2002.

13. "President Outlines War Effort: Remarks by the President to the George C. Marshall ROTC Award Seminar on National Security," Office of the Press Secretary, The White House, 17 April 2002. http://www.whitehouse.gov/news/releases/2002/04 (accessed 3 July 2007).

14. "President Outlines War Effort."

15. "President Outlines War Effort."

16. Lieutenant General Franklin L. Hagenbeck, interview by Contemporary Operations Study Team, Combat Studies Institute, Fort Leavenworth, KS, 30 March 2007, 13.

17. Hagenbeck, interview, 30 March 2007, 13.

18. Hagenbeck, interview, 30 March 2007, 13.

19. Hagenbeck, interview, 30 March 2007, 13.

20. Hagenbeck, interview, 30 March 2007, 13.

21. Hagenbeck, interview, 30 March 2007, 17.

22. Hagenbeck, interview, 30 March 2007, 13.

23. Hagenbeck, interview, 30 March 2007, 13.

24. CJTF *Mountain*, Headquarters, 10th Mountain Division, *Afghanistan and Operation ANACONDA* Brief, undated, slide 42.

25. *Afghanistan and Operation ANACONDA* Brief, slide 41.

26.   "US Troops Finish 'Operation Mountain Lion,'" *CNN.com./TRANSCRIPTS,* 7 April 2002. http://transcripts.cnn.com/TRANSCRIPTS/0204/07/sm.04.html (accessed 25 January 2009).

27.   "Operation Snipe," *Operation Veritas*, UK Ministry of Defence, 13 May 2002. http://www.operations.mod.uk/veritas/snipe.htm (accessed 6 July 2007).

28.   Lieutenant Colonel Patrick Stogran, interview by Contemporary Operations Study Team, Combat Studies Institute, Fort Leavenworth, KS, 18 May 2007.

29.   Stogran, interview, 18 May 2007.

30.   Major Peter Dawe, interview by Contemporary Operations Study Team, Combat Studies Institute, Fort Leavenworth, KS, 16 May 2007.

31.   Dawe, interview, 16 May 2007.

32.   Major David Baker, interview by Center for Military History, Interview # 48 EF I 0008, 18 May 2002, Kandahar Airfield, Afghanistan, 6.

33.   "Operation Condor," *Operation Veritas*, UK Ministry of Defence, 22 May 2002. http://www.operations.mod.uk/veritas/condor.htm (accessed 4 December 2008); Linda Kozaryn, "British-led Coalition Battle al-Qaeda, Taliban Fighters," *American Forces Press Service News Articles*, 17 May 2007. http://www.defenselink.mil/news/newsarticle.aspx?id-44048 (accessed 4 December 2008); Clark and Burgess, "Action Update (Complete Archive)," see "Coalition Operations" under 13–19 May 2002.

34.   "UK Marines in New Afghan Mission," *BBC News*, 29 May 2002. http://news.bbc.co.uk/1/hi/world/south_asia/2014774.stm (accessed 16 August 2007).

35.   "UK Marines in New Afghan Mission"; "Marines Launch Operation Buzzard in Afghanistan," *ABC News Online*, 30 May 2002. http://www.abc.net.au/news/newsitems/200205 (accessed 16 August 2007).

36.   "UK Marines in New Afghan Mission."

37.   "UK Marines in New Afghan Mission."

38.   Mr. Geoffrey Hoon, "Operations in Afghanistan," *House of Commons Hansard Debates, Part 5,* 20 June 2002. http://www.publications.parliament.uk/pa/cm200102/cmhansrd/vo020620 (accessed 16 August 2007).

39.   "Operation Apollo," *Backgrounder: Land Force Western Area*, n.d., Department of National Defence/Canadian Forces. www.army.forces.ca/lfwa (accessed 17 August 2007).

40.   Major Mark Campbell, interview by Contemporary Operations Study Team, Combat Studies Institute, Fort Leavenworth, KS, 21 May 2007, 12.

41.   "Task Force *Rakkasan* Warning Order #2," 21 June 2002.

42.   "Canadian Forces' Contribution to the International Campaign Against Terrorism," *Canadian Forces Backgrounder*, Canadian Department of National Defence, BG-02.001p, 7 January 2004. http://www.forces.gc.ca/site/Newsroom/view_news_e.asp?id+490 (accessed 17 August 2007).

43.   Major Robert Forte, Combined Task Force *Mountain* Briefing, *Operation Mountain Lion Assessment Briefing*, 13 July 2002, slide 5.

44.   Hagenbeck, interview, 30 March 2007, 15–16.

45.   Hagenbeck, interview, 30 March 2007, 4.

46.   Lieutenant General (Retired) Paul T. Mikolashek, interview by Contemporary Operations Study Team, Combat Studies Institute, Arlington, VA, 13 December 2006, 15.

47.   Mikolashek, interview, 13 December 2006, 15.

48.   Hagenbeck, interview, 30 March 2007, 6.

49.   Hagenbeck, interview, 30 March 2007, 12.

50.   Hagenbeck, interview, 30 March 2007, 12.

51.   General Dan K. McNeill, interview by Contemporary Operations Study Team, Combat Studies Institute, Fort Leavenworth, KS, 16 June 2008, 4.

52.   McNeill, interview, 16 June 2008, 4.

53.   McNeill, interview, 16 June 2008, 4.

54. McNeill, interview, 16 June 2008, 4.

55. Douglas J. Feith, *War and Decision: Inside the Pentagon at the Dawn of the War on Terrorism* (New York, NY: HarperCollins, 2008), 150.

56. Brigadier General Stanley A. McChrystal, interview by 49th Military History Detachment, Bagram Airfield, Afghanistan, 7 July 2002, 2.

57. McChrystal, interview, 7 July 2002, 3.

58. McChrystal, interview, 7 July 2002, 3.

59. Colonel Richard D. MeGahan, interview by 49th Military History Detachment, Bagram Airfield, Afghanistan, 8 July 2002, 16.

60. MeGahan, interview, 8 July 2002, 16.

61. McChrystal, interview, 7 July 2002, 3.

62. McChrystal, interview, 7 July 2002, 3.

63. McChrystal, interview, 7 July 2002, 3–4.

64. McNeill, interview, 16 June 2008, 7.

65. Press Release, Combined Joint Task Force Headquarters, MacDill AFB, FL, Release Number 02-05-01, 14 May 2002. www.centcom.mil/sites/uscentcom1 (accessed 28 February 2007).

66. McNeill, interview, 16 June 2008, 7–8.

67. Joint Publication 1-02, *DOD Dictionary of Military and Associated Terms* (Washington, DC, 2001), as quoted in William Flavin, *Civil Military Operations: Afghanistan* (Carlisle, PA: US Army Peacekeeping and Stability Operations Institute, 23 March 2004), v.

68. Major General David E. Kratzer, interview by 47th Military History Detachment, Camp Doha, Kuwait, 16 July 2002, 1.

69. Kratzer, interview, 16 July 2002, 1.

70. Kratzer, interview, 16 July 2002, 1.

71. Flavin, *Civil Military Operations: Afghanistan*, 17–18.

72. Kratzer, interview, 16 July 2002, 7.

73. Flavin, *Civil Military Operations: Afghanistan*, 19.

74. Flavin, *Civil Military Operations: Afghanistan*, 19; Major Luther Webster, interview by US Army Center for Military History, Kabul, Afghanistan, 18 October 2002, 1.

75. Webster, interview, 18 October 2002, 1.

76. Coalition Joint Civil Military Operations Task Force, *Coalition Joint Civil-Military Operations (CJCMOTF)* Brief, January 2002, MacDill AFB, FL, as quoted in Flavin, *Civil Military Operations: Afghanistan*, 19.

77. Kratzer, interview, 16 July 2002, 6.

78. Kratzer, interview, 16 July 2002, 5.

79. Flavin, *Civil Military Operations: Afghanistan*, xvi.

80. Flavin, *Civil Military Operations: Afghanistan*, xvi.

81. Kratzer, interview, 16 July 2002, 5.

82. Kratzer, interview, 16 July 2002, 5.

83. Flavin, *Civil Military Operations: Afghanistan*, 21.

84. Webster, interview, 18 October 2002, 5.

85. Flavin, *Civil Military Operations: Afghanistan*, 21.

86. UN Security Council Resolution 1401, 4501st Meeting, 28 March 2002, Report of the Secretary General, "The Situation in Afghanistan and its Implications for International Peace and Security," 18 March 2002.

87. Nicholas Stockton, *Strategic Coordination in Afghanistan*, Afghanistan Research and Evaluation Unit, August 2002, 21.

88. "National Development Framework Draft for Consultation (without annexes)," Kabul, April 2002, attached as Appendix E to Stockton, *Strategic Coordination in Afghanistan*, 62.

89. UN General Assembly Security Council, "The Situation in Afghanistan and its Implications for International Peace and Security," 18 March 2002, 3.

90. Stockton, *Strategic Coordination in Afghanistan*, 6.

91. Stockton, *Strategic Coordination in Afghanistan*, 1.

92. Webster, interview, 18 October 2002, 1.

93. Webster, interview, 18 October 2002, 1.

94. Flavin, *Civil Military Operations: Afghanistan*, 22.

95. Kratzer, interview, 16 July 2002, 9.

96. Clark and Burgess, "Action Update (Complete Archive)," see entry under 1–7 April 2002.

97. Clark and Burgess, "Action Update (Complete Archive)," see entry under 15–21 April 2002.

98. Kratzer, interview, 16 July 2002, 9.

99. Clark and Burgess, "Action Update (Complete Archive)," see entry under 15–21 April 2002.

100. Colonel Mike Weimer, interview by 47th Military History Detachment, Camp Doha, Kuwait, 1 May 2002, 2.

101. Colonel (Retired) Michael Weimer, interview by Contemporary Operations Study Team, Combat Studies Institute, San Antonio, TX, 6 September 2007, 3.

102. Seth G. Jones et al., *Establishing Law and Order After Conflict* (Santa Monica, CA: RAND Corporation, 2005), 118.

103. Major General Craig Weston, interview by Contemporary Operations Study Team, Combat Studies Institute, Fort Leavenworth, KS, 14 December 2006; Brigadier General William Garrett, written interview by Contemporary Operations Study Team, Combat Studies Institute, Fort Leavenworth, KS, 18 July 2007.

104. United States Government Accountability Office, "Afghanistan Security: Efforts to Establish Army and Police Have Made Progress, but Future Plans Need to be Better Defined," GAO-05-575, June 2005, 9.

105. Jones et al., *Establishing Law and Order,* 118.

106. Office of National Drug Control Policy, "Estimated Poppy Cultivation in Afghanistan," Press Release, 28 November 2003. http://www.whitehousedrugpolicy.gov/NEWS/press03/112803.html (accessed 29 August 2007).

107. "Afghanistan Fact Sheet Jan 2003," United Kingdom Department for International Development, 29 January 2003. http://wwww.reliefweb.int/rw/rwb.nsf/AllDocsByUNID/9d624e84e3da4d40c1256cbd004ceafc (accessed 28 August 2007).

108. Annan, "Situation in Afghanistan and its Implications," 11.

109. Jalali, "Rebuilding Afghanistan's National Army," 78–79.

110. "Secretary of State for Defence's Statement in the Commons—18 March 2002."

111. Annan, "Situation in Afghanistan and its Implications," 10.

112. Brigadier General Jeffery Marshall, interview by Contemporary Operations Study Team, Combat Studies Institute, Washington, DC, 31 May 2007, 5.

113. Marshall, interview, 31 May 2007, 5.

114. Kratzer, interview, 16 July 2002, 11.

115. Weimer, interview, 1 May 2002, 20.

116. Weimer, interview, 1 May 2002, 20.

117. Anthony Davis, "Basic Training," *Time*, 3 June 2002. http://www.time.com/time/printout/0,8816,257159,00.html (accessed 5 July 2007).

118. Davis, "Basic Training."

Chapter 8

CJTF-180 Takes the Lead:
Maintaining Momentum, July 2002 to July 2003

In mid-July 2002 US Deputy Secretary of Defense Paul Wolfowitz visited Afghanistan to meet with Hamid Karzai and other Afghan political leaders to gain a sense of the conditions in the country. In Kabul, Wolfowitz spoke publicly about the changes in Afghanistan and emphasized that the United States did not plan to pull its troops out of the country until the institutions introduced in the previous 6 months had settled. In his comments, Wolfowitz emphasized that the US campaign would be a broad effort that included economic reconstruction and the training of Afghan security forces as well as security operations. He asserted that the United States was committed to "strengthening those national institutions that can move Afghanistan forward, enable Afghanistan to overcome the wounds of 20 years of civil war—and if I can put it also, from an American point of view—that would keep Afghanistan from going back to being a sanctuary for terrorism."[1] This statement essentially endorsed the tentative efforts the Coalition had begun earlier in 2002 to rebuild Afghanistan's security forces and its physical and economic infrastructure.

The initial Coalition reconstruction program was not the only topic of discussion at this event. Reporters asked Mr. Wolfowitz about the recent Coalition aerial assault that resulted in scores of casualties and over 20 fatalities. This attack had come in support of an operation launched by US Special Forces (SF) near the town of Tarin Kowt in Oruzgan province at the beginning of July.[2] While searching for weapons caches and Taliban fighters in the region, SF units reported they had called in close air support (CAS) when unknown enemy forces fired on them. The Coalition bombers and AC-130 gunships had then attacked a number of sites near the location of the SF teams. Women and children were among the casualties, and Afghan authorities soon announced that the Coalition aircraft had actually targeted a wedding party where traditional Pashtun celebratory gunfire had been mistaken for an enemy threat. While the facts continued to be disputed and Coalition authorities promised a full investigation, Afghans launched organized protests and President Karzai and his foreign minister publicly reproved Coalition forces for the mistake and cautioned them about future operations. The tragic incident served as a reminder of the difficulties facing the Coalition in creating an approach in Afghanistan that balanced rebuilding and humanitarian assistance programs with the judicious application of force.

In June 2002 Combined Joint Task Force-180 (CJTF-180), commanded by Lieutenant General Dan K. McNeill, became the headquarters responsible for the Coalition's campaign in Afghanistan. As noted in the previous chapter, CJTF-180 arrived at Bagram Airfield with a campaign plan that defined Coalition operations as full spectrum operations focused on creating a stable Afghanistan that would no longer serve as a haven for terrorist. In the plan, the Coalition commander and staff further described their intended operations by defining four lines of effort along which these operations would be directed: security, civil-military, information, and the training of Afghan security forces. For McNeill, the CJTF-180's campaign began in the midst of Phase III, Decisive Combat Operations, of US Central Command's (CENTCOM's) original plan for Operation ENDURING FREEDOM (OEF). This meant that McNeill and his staff expected security operations to be his headquarters' focus during the final 6 months of 2002.

As Afghanistan became more stable, the campaign would gradually transition to Phase IV, Humanitarian Assistance and Support to the New Afghan Government, in which CJTF-180's effort would become more focused on reconstruction and training the Afghan security forces.[3]

In the process of launching and sustaining the Coalition campaign, CJTF-180 and its subordinate commands encountered unforeseen obstacles and opportunities. To conduct successful security operations, for example, CJTF-180 had to gather intelligence from Afghans and other individuals in detention about the location and status of the enemy. Coalition detainee and interrogation operations, however, suffered from both a lack of guidance and resources, weaknesses that, in the short-term, created problems for the overall intelligence collection effort and, in the long-term, bred legal and public relations difficulties for the United States and its allies in Afghanistan. In its approach to reconstruction and training the Afghan National Army (ANA), CJTF-180 was energetic in the creation of new organizations to make the transition to Phase IV smooth and effective. The introduction of the Provincial Reconstruction Teams (PRTs) to improve Afghan infrastructure and the formation of Combined Joint Task Force (CJTF) *Phoenix* to assist with the training of the ANA are the best examples of Coalition innovation during this period. The greatest overall challenge facing the Soldiers of CJTF-180 was how to retain the momentum generated during the first 6 months of 2002 as the nature of the campaign broadened but resources remained essentially the same.

CJTF-180 Begins its Mission

At the beginning of July 2002, Lieutenant General McNeill had been leading CJTF-180 for 1 month. The creation of CJTF-180 clearly signaled the Coalition's sustained commitment to Afghanistan despite the Bush administration's unease in becoming involved in nation building. Still, concerns lingered among senior American civilian and military officials about appearing as an army of occupation. The central problem for CJTF-180 was how to create a stable security environment in Afghanistan without relying too heavily on Coalition military forces—a practice Coalition leaders believed might alienate the Afghan population.

In the summer of 2002, security operations had primacy over other aspects of the Coalition campaign, yet McNeill planned to take a broad approach. He first separated the tactical-level responsibilities for security operations from his own duties, giving the former to the commander of Combined Task Force (CTF) 82, which would arrive that summer to replace CTF *Mountain* (formerly CJTF *Mountain*). As the senior Coalition military official, McNeill assumed responsibility for what he called the "political-military piece."[4] No less crucial than the security operations, this aspect of the campaign required more diplomatic acumen than military

Figure 35. Ismail Khan.

Personal collection of Professor Thomas H. Johnson

skill. For McNeill, working the political-military component of the Coalition effort entailed building relationships with the Afghan Transitional Authority (ATA), helping President Karzai develop his government's capacity, and assisting in negotiations with powerful regional leaders like Ismail Khan and Abdul Rashid Dostum concerning the integration of their militia forces into the new Afghan security structure.

McNeill characterized the Coalition's broad program in Afghanistan as full spectrum operations at all levels. To better synchronize a campaign of this nature, McNeill took control of all civil-military operations (CMO) by asserting command over the Combined Joint Civil Military Operations Task Force (CJCMOTF). CJTF-180 also gained operational control (OPCON) over Combined Joint Special Operations Task Force–Afghanistan (CJSOTF-A), the SOF headquarters established earlier in 2002 when Joint Special Operations Task Force–North (JSOTF-N) and Combined Joint Special Operations Task Force–South (CJSOTF-S) had combined. Since the spring, the Soldiers of the CJSOTF had played a critical role in the training of the ANA and this effort continued after CJTF-180 arrived. But McNeill gave greater emphasis to the overall ANA program by taking formal control of the Office of Military Cooperation–Afghanistan (OMC-A) from the US Embassy.

Other transitions placed McNeill's command in flux. By July the tactical-level units from the 10th Mountain Division and the 101st Airborne Division, including TF *Rakkasan*, had all departed Afghanistan; the CTF *Mountain* headquarters staff followed in early September. They were replaced by CTF 82, formed from the headquarters of the 82d Airborne Division and led by the division's commander, Major General John R. Vines. CTF 82's headquarters was at Bagram Airfield, and Vines based TF *Panther*, his primary maneuver element, at the Kandahar Airfield. TF *Panther* was under the command of Colonel James L. Huggins and featured two infantry battalions from the 3d Brigade of the 82d Airborne Division and one attached infantry battalion from the division's 1st Brigade. Huggins also enjoyed support from artillery, aviation, military intelligence, and other enabling units. TF *Panther* deployed to Afghanistan in late June 2002 and would serve under CTF 82 until 5 December 2002.[5] At that point TF *Devil*, a unit formed around the 1st Brigade, 82d Airborne Division arrived to take the lead in tactical-level security operations.

Fostering Security

Once CTF 82 established its headquarters in Afghanistan, Major General Vines' forces were CJTF-180's primary means of engaging the Taliban and al-Qaeda. CTF 82 launched security operations initially from Coalition bases at the Bagram Airfield, Kandahar, and eventually from a handful of smaller forward operating bases (FOBs), such as Salerno, Shkin, or Orgun-e in southeastern Afghanistan, in reaction to the enemy.[6] None of the tactical-level units in CTF 82 had responsibility for specific areas of operation (AOs), but focused their raids and cordon and search operations on enemy elements that attacked Coalition forces or otherwise made their presence known. Lieutenant General McNeill, the CJTF-180 commander, recognized the nature of the fight, but did not believe the Coalition had the quality or quantity of intelligence to launch preemptive pinpoint strikes against this elusive foe. Consequently, he directed Major General Vines to focus his security operations on locations where the enemy was suspected to be hiding. McNeill envisioned CTF 82's tactical-level campaign as "a rolling series of operations going on all the time" that would generally prevent the Taliban and al-Qaeda from reforming into a serious threat.[7]

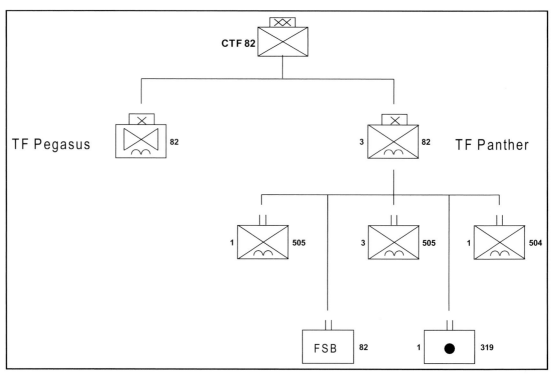

Figure 36. CTF 82 task organization, fall 2002.

For Vines and his command, this approach also meant that the Coalition's conventional combat power, the equivalent of a large brigade of approximately 5,000 Soldiers, had much of the responsibility for conducting security operations across Afghanistan. This effort was aided by the International Security Assistance Force (ISAF), which secured the capital of Kabul, and the Combined Joint Special Operations Task Force (CJSOTF), which focused part of its assets on the border region. Still, the reinforced US Army brigades that deployed to the country as part of CJTF-180 held the lion's share of the security burden. The Coalition's approach that mandated conventional forces return to their bases at Bagram, Kandahar, or the smaller FOBs once security operations concluded heightened the difficult nature of this task. While this imperative certainly met the original Coalition intent to avoid appearing as an occupying army in a land that punished outside invaders, it also meant that Coalition forces in 2002 did not intend to assert complete control over the Afghan countryside.

Beginning in August 2002, CTF 82 began a series of operations aimed at locating and destroying the enemy that many believed was in hiding and waiting for the proper opportunity to disrupt the political and military progress made up to that date. To keep pressure on the suspected threat, TF *Panther*'s actions took American Soldiers back into areas where previous fights had occurred to find both insurgents and their weapons.

Operation MOUNTAIN SWEEP

On 19 August 2002 the Soldiers of the 1st Battalion, 505th Parachute Infantry Regiment (1-505 PIR) and the 3d Battalion, 505th Parachute Infantry Regiment (3-505 PIR) boarded helicopters at the Kandahar and Bagram Airfields and flew south toward Paktia province. These units formed the main maneuver force for TF *Panther*'s Operation MOUNTAIN SWEEP, the largest security mission in Afghanistan since Operation ANACONDA in March. MOUNTAIN SWEEP represented a continuation of the type of missions launched by CJTF *Mountain* in the spring and early summer, but was far more focused than MOUNTAIN LION. By August CTF 82 and TF *Panther* had decided to target suspected Taliban forces southwest of the town of Gardez near the Shahi Kowt Valley. Coalition intelligence suggested that this area harbored a key Taliban official and large arms caches.

During the week that followed the initial insertion of the two battalions, the paratroopers conducted seven cordon and search operations focused on specific villages and compounds. The 3-505 PIR landed in the Zormat district, an area southwest of Gardez that had towns and villages located in open farmland in the central area and in mountainous terrain on the southern and northern edges. Lieutenant Colonel Martin Schweitzer, the battalion commander, used his four rifle companies and a scout platoon as the main elements in the series of cordon and search missions. In these operations, Schweitzer also made use of an attached composite multipurpose unit called Team CMO that included a civil affairs (CA) section, engineers, military interrogators, linguists, medics, and public affairs specialists to arrange for humanitarian assistance, plan reconstruction projects, and gather information.[8] Also joining the paratroopers were two Special Forces Operational Detachments–Alpha (ODAs) that had been working in the province since the spring of 2002.[9] The ODAs were accompanied by allied Afghan militia forces.

Over the course of the 6-day operation, elements of 3-505 PIR moved from village to village across the district. In most cases, the paratroopers conducted air assaults, landing near their objectives and then quickly moving into position near the village. In one instance, however, Soldiers from the battalion conducted a 13-kilometer foot march to approach one site. The ODAs and Afghan militia played an important role in the cordon and search operations, according to Lieutenant Colonel Schweitzer.[10] Once the Soldiers of the 3-505 PIR set the cordon in place around the village, the SF Soldiers and Afghans would gain entry using their language and knowledge of cultural norms. Schweitzer's troops would then conduct a thorough search of the dwellings and other buildings. These techniques led to the capture and detention of three Afghans suspected of being involved with the Taliban and the seizing of a significant amount of weapons and ammunition. Unfortunately, because of gaps in the intelligence and the possibility that news of MOUNTAIN SWEEP had reached the population in the Zormat area before US Soldiers arrived, the 3-505 PIR did not find the Taliban official thought to be in the district.[11] Colonel Huggins, the TF *Panther* commander, suspected that intelligence leaks had led to the loss of the element of surprise. On 25 August, the last day of MOUNTAIN SWEEP, Huggins stated, "I have no doubt that [the enemy] had advance warning that we were coming."[12]

Despite the sense that the operation had been compromised, Huggins and CJTF-180 leaders believed that Operation MOUNTAIN SWEEP had been a success. As in MOUNTAIN LION, the Coalition demonstrated its ability to move considerable combat force into distant regions of Afghanistan and conduct large-scale security operations where Taliban and al-Qaeda groups were operating. Still, within CJTF-180, the integration of SF and Afghan militia into conventional operations did raise questions about the Coalition's overall approach in areas like Zormat. Colonel Huggins and Lieutenant Colonel Schweitzer believed strongly that the conventional forces had worked well with the ODAs and had conducted the cordon and search operations appropriately.[13] Moreover, both leaders saw Operation MOUNTAIN SWEEP as a good model for future security operations. In contrast, several members of the ODAs involved in the operation differed, suggesting that in a few of their searches of Afghan dwellings, the Soldiers of TF *Panther* used techniques that were more suited to conventional combat operations.[14] The SF officers did believe that ODAs, with their depth of experience in the region and close relationship with the Afghan militia forces, could serve as key enablers for conventional infantry forces like 3-505 PIR as they sought to operate effectively within the Afghan culture. Huggins noted that in the wake of MOUNTAIN SWEEP his command closely reviewed all techniques and procedures to ensure that they were following the best practices, especially those that guided close interactions with Afghans during cordon and search operations.[15]

TF *Panther*'s security missions continued into the fall of 2002. But in September, CTF 82 made a significant change in how it deployed units in Afghanistan. Instead of maintaining almost all of its forces at Bagram and Kandahar Airfields, Major General Vines, the commander of CTF 82, chose to build FOBs in a handful of locations closer to the southern and southeastern provinces where Taliban and al-Qaeda groups were finding refuge. CTF 82 established the largest base called FOB Salerno just north of the city of Khost. Other FOBs near the towns of Asadabad, Shkin and Orgun-e—all sites close to the Pakistani frontier—followed by the end of the year. Salerno quickly grew as the entire 3-505 PIR, part of an aviation battalion, an SF ODA, and other units moved into the base. Schweitzer recalled that by the end of 2002, Salerno had become still larger as a runway capable of accommodating C-130 transport aircraft became functional. From the base, the 3-505 PIR launched a number of security and stability operations into the surrounding provinces. The decision to create the FOBs did generate some

DOD Photo by SPF Eric E. Hughes

Figure 37. US Soldiers from CTF 82 during MOUNTAIN SWEEP.

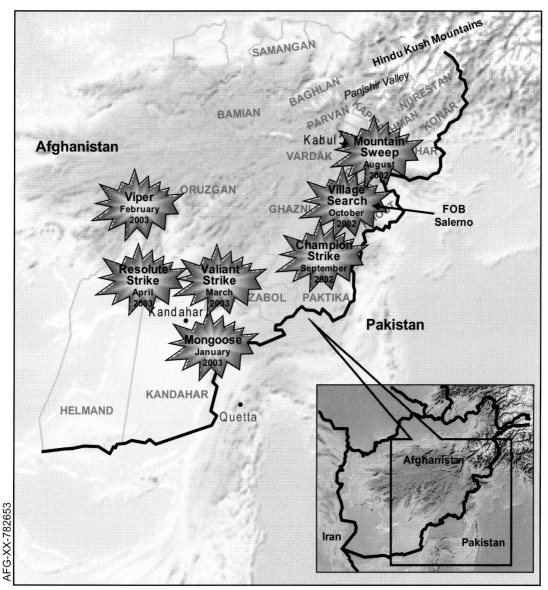

Figure 38. Major CJTF-180 security operations, August 2002–April 2003.

risk by placing Western forces closer to the Afghan population who might view the move as an encroachment on their cultural and territorial sovereignty. On the other hand, in 2002 the bases enabled the Coalition to contest more effectively those regions of the country that the enemy had chosen as sanctuaries.

In early October 2002, for example, the 3-505 PIR used FOB Salerno to launch Operation VILLAGE SEARCH.[16] This operation focused on four villages near the Pakistani border suspected of harboring both Taliban fighters and weapons caches. But to engage the villages, the paratroopers used techniques that were less aggressive than those used during MOUNTAIN SWEEP, indicating that they had paid attention to the comments made by the ODAs after that operation. During VILLAGE SEARCH, unit leaders explained their intentions to village elders, asked permission to search homes, and had female Soldiers search the women. In addition, while searches were in progress, CA teams politely inquired about medical conditions and the general needs of the villages to identify potential reconstruction projects.[17]

The searches did uncover significant stockpiles of weapons and ammunition, including one cache of 250 rocket propelled grenades (RPGs) and thousands of rounds of heavy machinegun ammunition that belonged to a young Afghan man who had fled to Pakistan.[18] A second large cache was discovered in a village less than a mile from the Pakistan border. During this part of the operation, the Soldiers of 3-505 PIR became involved in a tense standoff with Pakistani militiamen who believed the American Soldiers had crossed into Pakistan.[19] Lieutenant Colonel Schweitzer, the battalion commander, requested CAS and prepared his mortar platoon to fire a warning shot before the Pakistanis disengaged.[20] This incident illustrated the unique characteristics of the Coalition's security operations in Afghanistan. For leaders like Schweitzer and his superiors in Kandahar and Bagram, the task was clear—prevent enemy forces from affecting the progress in Afghanistan by denying them sanctuaries in the southern and southeastern regions, most importantly Paktia and Paktika provinces. The presence of the Pakistani frontier, as well as uncooperative Pakistani security forces along it, made that relatively straightforward task almost impossible to achieve in any permanent sense.

The Transition to TF *Devil*

In 2002 Coalition planners chose to deploy tactical formations such as TF *Panther* in Afghanistan for 6 months. This practice followed the pattern set during previous deployments like the peacekeeping efforts in the Balkans in the 1990s. For this reason, on 10 January 2003

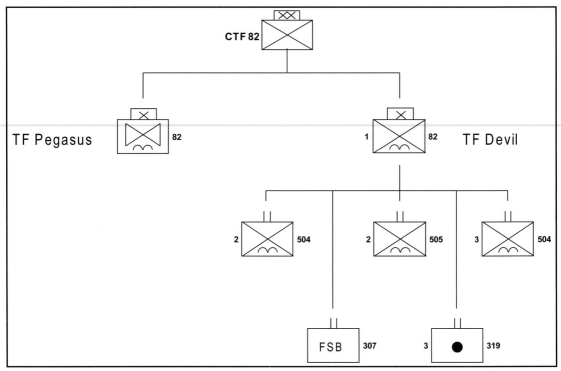

Figure 39. CTF 82 task organization, spring 2003.

TF *Panther* turned over authority for tactical security operations to TF *Devil*, comprised primarily from the units of the 1st Brigade, 82d Airborne Division. The new brigade-size TF would serve in Afghanistan until the late spring of 2003 and, like TF *Panther*, located most of its forces at the Kandahar Airfield while deploying smaller elements at the FOBs located in provinces where Taliban and al-Qaeda were seeking refuge. From these bases, the Soldiers of TF *Devil* conducted security patrols around their facilities, dispatched CA and psychological operations teams into cities and towns, and reacted to the common incidents of enemy small arms and indirect fire.[21]

The TF punctuated these routine activities with a series of larger operations. In January the command launched Operation MONGOOSE to search for enemy groups and weapons caches in the Adi Ghar Mountains southeast of Kandahar.[22] The mission, conducted by the 2d Battalion, 504th (2-504 PIR) came in reaction to contact between US aircraft and Taliban forces. After Coalition helicopters took fire in the area, CAS converged on the Adi Ghar region. Intelligence gathered near the attacks suggested there were hundreds of Taliban soldiers hiding throughout the cave complexes in the area. TF *Devil* units carefully searched through the region to identify and destroy the caves that had originally been constructed in the 1980s by the anti-Soviet mujahideen.

Operation VIPER, the next major security operation mounted by TF *Devil*, began on 19 February 2003 with the 2-504 PIR conducting air assaults into the Baghran Valley in Helmand province, a Taliban stronghold. The mission during VIPER was to use cordon and search operations to clear villages in the valley of unauthorized weapons and hostile forces.[23] The series of search operations took the Soldiers of the 2-504 PIR across the Baghran Valley and they ultimately detained eight Afghans suspected of affiliation with the Taliban.[24] Captain Andrew Zieseniss, one of the battalion's company commanders, emphasized the deliberate and painstaking character of the Coalition's mission in early 2003. Zieseniss asserted, "It's not a war where we're fighting a conventional army like World War II. There are bad guys in civilian clothes. It's old-fashioned detective work, digging through hay stacks, literally."[25]

Less than a month after Operation VIPER, TF *Devil* mounted a two-battalion air assault that inserted the 2-504 PIR, the 3-504 PIR, and Romanian and Afghan Army units into eastern Kandahar province. In this operation, called VALIANT STRIKE, company-size elements landed near targeted villages and towns and moved into positions to begin cordon and search actions. The dismounted movement through the mountainous terrain was grueling but often resulted in the discovery of small arms, crew-served weapons, land mines, mortar rounds, and rockets. These captures were not always easy. The village compounds were often labyrinthine, and enemy insurgents and their sympathizers had in some cases concealed weapons and equipment in haystacks, wells, and even under piles of manure. The American paratroopers also detained a number of Afghans who they suspected were involved in anti-Coalition activity.[26]

VIPER and VALIANT STRIKE demonstrate how TF *Devil* sought to keep the enemy off guard by hitting targets with large forces in two provinces in relatively quick succession—an innovation that appeared to pay dividends. The operations also demonstrate the continuing evolution of the US Army's tactical procedures in OEF. Accounts of the techniques used during these actions reveal that the Soldiers of TF *Devil* were cautious in their operations, attempting to avoid unnecessary alienation of the Afghan population. Most critical was the paratroopers' use of negotiation rather than force in conducting these search operations. Rather than breach compound or house walls and enter villages aggressively, unit leaders often partnered with CA specialists and linguists to engage village and town elders.[27] The American commanders requested Afghan assistance in identifying and inventorying weapons, ammunition, and other military equipment and explained to the Afghan leaders how they would proceed with searching including pledges to segregate village women and have them searched by female American Soldiers.

Both of these large-scale operations were examples of the overall maturation of tactical operations during OEF. UNIFIED VENTURE, DELIBERATE STRIKE, and other missions later in the spring of 2003 would take the TF *Devil* paratroopers back into the unstable provinces along the Pakistani frontier and would build on the experiences of previous security operations. Although these actions enjoyed success, the Coalition had made only limited gains in understanding the organization and the intent of the enemy its Soldiers faced in places like Kandahar and Helmand provinces. The struggle to develop a clear picture of a shadowy adversary led to less than decisive operations during CJTF-180's first year of operations.

Understanding the Elusive Enemy: Coalition Intelligence and Detainee Operations in 2002 and 2003

When US forces arrived in Afghanistan in October 2001, they brought with them an intelligence system that was a relic of the Cold War. During the decades that followed World War II, the Army collected information about its enemies and potential adversaries primarily using signals intelligence (SIGINT) and imagery intelligence (IMINT). These two forms of intelligence relied on the American advantage in technology to listen to enemy communications and monitor enemy locations and facilities with spy aircraft and satellites. The other important form of gathering information, human intelligence (HUMINT), had become more prominent during the Vietnam War when the interrogation of prisoners and other detainees offered precise intelligence about a shadowy insurgent enemy who often eluded detection by SIGINT and IMINT systems. But by the time the Berlin Wall fell in 1989, the Army was devoting relatively few resources to the gathering of intelligence through interrogations and other forms of HUMINT collection. Nevertheless, HUMINT proved to be very important to the peacekeeping and peace-enforcement operations that the Army mounted in the Balkans and elsewhere in the 1990s. Still, only 30 percent of the assets in the US Army's intelligence force in 2001 were HUMINT units.

The military's general lack of attention to developing the capacity to collect and analyze HUMINT meant that US forces in Afghanistan initially struggled to use this intelligence discipline to understand the Taliban and al-Qaeda enemy. Most important was the lack of preparation among US intelligence organizations for large-scale interrogation operations and the detainee operations with which interrogations are often intertwined. The US Army in the 1990s had conducted regular training for these operations that simulated complex interrogations within enemy prisoner of war (EPW) facilities. These exercises were based on Army doctrine that gave responsibility for interrogation operations to the Military Intelligence (MI) Corps. Those MI units that specialized in HUMINT normally contained teams of trained interrogators, many of whom spoke and conducted interrogations in foreign languages. In almost all cases, formal interrogations occur in or near detention facilities where prisoners of war or other detainees are held. However, according to the doctrine at the time, US Army interrogators did not run detention centers. They worked within or next to facilities that were staffed and commanded by Military Police (MP) units. MP Soldiers served as the "prison guards" who oversee the housing, feeding, medical support, and other aspects of a detainee's care. When a detainee was interrogated, the MPs were responsible for escorting the detainee to the interrogation site where the MI interrogators took control. Once the interrogation ended, the MPs returned the detainee to his or her cell. This was the doctrinal foundation that the US military used for detainee and interrogation operations in both Iraq and Afghanistan through 2004.

In the first 6 weeks of OEF, Coalition SOF and their Afghan allies had been responsible for the relatively small number of detentions and interrogations that took place after the surrender of Taliban and al-Qaeda forces. That all changed when Taliban forces in the city of Mazar-e Sharif capitulated and became the prisoners of General Dostum's Northern Alliance troops. As chapter 4 documented, thousands of these prisoners were confined at the ancient Qala-i Jangi Prison in late November 2001. When Coalition officers arrived to interrogate suspected al-Qaeda detainees, the prisoners began to riot, killing one American and eventually taking over the fortress. After several days of sustained Coalition bombing, the prison was once again under the control of the Northern Alliance. Inside, Dostum's troops found less than 100 detainees still alive. These men were immediately transferred to a prison in the city of Sheberghan. At the same time, Coalition and friendly Afghan forces were capturing other Taliban and al-Qaeda fighters near Kabul and Kandahar. By early December 2001, there were over 4,000 detainees in custody and the task of holding and interrogating this growing number of detainees was simply too large for the Coalition intelligence assets in Afghanistan.[28]

CENTCOM reacted in December by directing TF 202 and elements of the 10th Mountain Division to move to Kandahar Airfield from their location at Karshi-Khanabad (K2). TF 202, formed from elements of the 202d MI Battalion (BN) augmented by Reserve and National Guard Soldiers, specialized in HUMINT operations. By late December the TF headquarters had been established at Kandahar and its Soldiers had begun detainee operations at the airfield. The TF 202 commander had also formed mobile interrogation teams (MITs) and sent them to Sheberghan Prison, to the Bagram Airfield near Kabul, and to other locations where the number of detainees was growing. The team located at Bagram quickly became part of TF *Bowie* (see chapter 7), a joint interagency group that combined intelligence specialists from the Coalition SOF community with other agencies within the US Government. The TF 202 team at Bagram assisted TF *Bowie* with the interrogation of high-level Taliban and al-Qaeda officials detained by Coalition SOF. By the end of December, TF 202's Soldiers were not only involved in interrogations but also conducting counterintelligence operations and translating the thousands of Taliban and al-Qaeda documents found during searches of enemy facilities.

Most of the TF's resources were devoted to running the Joint Interrogation Facility (JIF) at Kandahar Airfield. When the MI Soldiers arrived in Kandahar, they had worked with US Marines from CTF 58 who had deployed to the airfield in late November 2001 to build a detention camp and an adjacent interrogations facility. The Marines served as the guards and were responsible for the care of the detainees. The involvement of the MI Soldiers with the detainees was limited to interrogations. When TF *Rakkasan*, the 3d Brigade of the US Army's 101st Airborne Division, arrived in Kandahar in early 2002, its attached MP Company took over responsibility for the detention site.

For the next 6 months, the interrogators in the JIF and the MITs conducted hundreds of interrogations with detainees of various nationalities and loyalties. A small number of these interrogations uncovered links between detainees and al-Qaeda. In those cases where the detainee appeared to be a member of the terrorist group or to hold a large amount of intelligence about al-Qaeda, TF 202 transferred the individual to the new detention site at Guantanamo Bay, Cuba (GTMO).

In the early months of their operations, the MI Soldiers at the JIF had to deal with the austere living conditions of the undeveloped Kandahar Airfield and a detainee population that was growing in complexity. Perhaps the most pressing problem was the lack of linguist support. The detainees in the facility spoke a large variety of languages including Pashto, Dari, Urdu, Arabic, and Russian. By contrast, the US Army had very few speakers of Pashto, Dari, and Urdu, and TF 202 waited for 45 days while the Department of Defense (DOD) hired and deployed contract linguists who could work as translators. In the meantime, the TF leadership tried to find local Afghans who could work as linguists at the JIF.

Equally difficult was the scope of the mission in the JIF. In the fall of 2002, Coalition leaders were focused on finding the al-Qaeda leaders and disrupting attacks that many in the West suspected were planned for the months following 9/11. These objectives led CENTCOM to issue a broad directive to TF 202 to hold for interrogation all those detainees who were interviewed and found to be members of al-Qaeda, Taliban leaders, non-Afghan members of the Taliban, and anyone else the interrogator believed "may pose a threat to US interests, held intelligence value, or may be of interest for US prosecution."[29] According to Major David Carstens, who served as the operations officer for TF 202 in Kandahar, these categories were far too vague and expansive. Carstens asserted that the CENTCOM guidance led to the detention of many individuals who after thorough interrogation proved to offer no information of value about al-Qaeda or the Taliban. Faced with problems of a ballooning detainee population, the leaders of TF 202, on their own initiative, fine tuned the screening criteria based on experience and began aggressively looking for procedural ways to release the detainees they believed should no longer be held by the Coalition.[30]

When CJTF-180 became the Coalition's senior military headquarters in May 2002, the 519th MI BN, an element that was organic to the XVIII Airborne Corps, deployed to Afghanistan to take control of HUMINT operations. Although most of TF 202 returned to the United States, the unit did leave one reinforced company in Afghanistan to assist the 519th. By that date, the Coalition had established its primary detention facility and JIF at Bagram Airfield, although Kandahar and other sites remained active as temporary detainee holding activities. Under CJTF-180, HUMINT operations were essentially planned and commanded from Bagram where the TF had created an intelligence fusion cell within its CJ2 staff section. Using larger counterintelligence and interrogation teams, the HUMINT effort became more efficient during 2002 and early 2003.[31]

The Evolution of Interrogation Policy and Incidents of Abuse in OEF, 2002–2003

Issues concerning interrogation and detention policies and practices affected the overall development of HUMINT procedures. Because most of the HUMINT collected in Afghanistan came from members of the Taliban and al-Qaeda detained on or near the battlefield, the issue of detainee legal status and treatment became an important aspect of Coalition operations. According to the official review of the DOD's detainee operations conducted by Vice Admiral A.T. Church in 2005, a document known as *The Church Report*, DOD's understanding of the legal status of those individuals detained in Afghanistan changed several times between 2001 and 2005. In October 2001, when US forces entered Afghanistan, this issue had yet to be resolved. Several months later in January 2002, Secretary of Defense Donald Rumsfeld directed in a memorandum that al-Qaeda and Taliban detainees were not to be afforded the legal status of EPWs that, under the Geneva Protocols, would have given these detainees specific protections. However, that memorandum also asserted that, despite this conclusion, US forces were to treat all detainees "humanely and to the extent appropriate and consistent with military necessity, in accordance with the principles of the Geneva Conventions of 1949."[32] This legal stance and requirement for humane treatment was further reinforced in President George W. Bush's memorandum of 7 February 2002 sent to the Vice President, the Secretary of Defense, the Chairman of the Joint Chiefs of Staff, and the Secretary of State.[33] These rulings influenced how Soldiers involved in detainee and interrogation operations in Afghanistan perceived detainees because it established that the individuals they were holding and questioning were not EPWs to whom all the protections of the Geneva Conventions were legally extended at all times. Detainees in Coalition hands in Afghanistan were referred to as persons under control (PUCs) instead of EPWs or detainees.

Likewise, interrogation policies developed slowly and haltingly in the first year of OEF. When TF 202 Soldiers arrived in late 2001, they received no special guidance on which techniques or "approaches" were allowed for use in inducing a detainee to speak openly during an interrogation. Between October 2001 and January 2003, interrogators relied on the approaches allowed in US Army Field Manual (FM) 34-52, *Intelligence Interrogation,* published in 1992. That manual allowed Army interrogators to use 14 techniques or "approaches" designed to break down the resistance of prisoners of war or detainees to questioning. This set of approaches included direct questioning, elevation or de-escalation of a detainee's fear (fear up/down), and provision of incentives. None of the techniques allowed for the use of physical contact; deprivation of sleep; or withholding of food, water, or shelter.

In the early months of TF 202's operations, American interrogators found that most of the detainees who arrived at the JIF were terrified by their detention and apprehensive about their future. Few of them attempted to mislead or challenge the MI Soldiers during interrogations. The willingness of the detainees to talk diminished over time and forced the Soldiers to consider which approaches were authorized to degrade the detainees' resistance to questioning. According to *The Church Report*, at some point in late 2002 interrogators in the 519th MI BN began going beyond the approaches explicitly described in FM 34-52. They introduced both stress positions and sleep adjustment as techniques designed to wear down the resistance of some detainees.[34] The former technique entailed directing the detainee to hold a strenuous physical position such as kneeling on a hard cement floor. Sleep adjustment involved changing the detainee's sleep pattern, but was not exactly the same as sleep deprivation. *The Church Report* documented that these techniques were introduced in Afghanistan because they had been initiated in the detention facility at GTMO earlier in 2002 and "migrated" from that facility to Bagram Airfield.

In early 2003 CJTF-180 began an attempt to give more definition to this rather loosely defined interrogation policy. The deaths of two detainees at the Bagram detention facility in December 2002 spurred this process. Lieutenant General McNeill, commander of CJTF-180, initiated a formal investigation of the incidents and investigators found that the deaths involved

---

Medical Assistance to the Afghans

Medical assistance to indigenous populations has been a part of US military campaigns throughout the 20th century. By 2002 these programs, often known as Medical Civic Action Programs or MEDCAPs, had become an integral element in OEF. Certainly, bringing medical aid to impoverished Afghan communities was part of the overall efforts mounted by the Coalition Humanitarian Liaison Cells (CHLCs) and the Provincial Reconstruction Teams (PRTs). But other US units provided MEDCAP support as well. This type of humanitarian assistance was especially critical in 2002 and 2003 as the new Afghan Government was just beginning to exert its authority and did not yet have the ability to establish even rudimentary healthcare in the provinces.

In all 2002 the 339th Combat Support Hospital (CSH), a Reserve unit from the Pittsburgh, Pennsylvania, area, supported a number of MEDCAPs. In September its doctors and medical specialists traveled to a village north of Kabul and treated 800 Afghans, half of whom were children. They followed this operation up by teaming with the 82d Forward Support Battalion to hold a clinic in a town near the city of Kandahar where they examined and treated approximately 1,400 Afghans. Lieutenant Colonel James Post, the commander of the 339th (CSH), noted that many of the patients the American doctors saw were suffering from malnutrition and conditions caused by a lack of clean water for drinking and bathing. Not surprisingly, the American doctors dispensed a large amount of deworming medicine to treat perhaps the most common ailment caused by the lack of safe water.

In 2002 and after, the CHLCs and PRTs focused a great deal of effort on drilling water wells in many communities to provide sources of potable water. And the US-led Coalition would continue to send MEDCAPs into the Afghan countryside to improve the health of the population and demonstrate the Coalition's commitment to fostering progress in Afghanistan.

Matthew Acosta, "KAF MEDCAP Treats Against Worms," *Freedom Watch*, 13 November 2002.

Jim Garamone, "US Medics Treat Afflicted Afghans," *DefenseLink*, 23 September 2002.

---

detainees who had been handcuffed to overhead objects to keep them awake. According to the investigation, MP and MI Soldiers also beat and kicked these two detainees. In both cases, investigators found that blunt force trauma to the legs was the cause of death.[35] None of the actions that led to the abuse and deaths of the detainees were officially sanctioned by senior leaders in Afghanistan.[36] Nor were they found to be among the sanctioned approaches in FM 34-52 or in any policy in effect at GTMO. These deaths were the tragic result of abusive and undisciplined Soldiers who chose to treat the individuals under their control inhumanely.

On 21 January 2003 the Director of the Joint Staff at the Pentagon requested information from CJTF-180 about interrogation techniques in use in Afghanistan.[37] Lieutenant General McNeill responded by asking his Staff Judge Advocate to write a memorandum describing the approaches used at the time and 3 days later CJTF-180 sent a list of the techniques to DOD, noting that FM 34-52 was the only reference in use although interrogators also relied on experience gained in the previous year of OEF.[38] CJTF-180's memorandum recommended that the enclosed list of techniques be approved. *The Church Report* documented that in the absence of any response from DOD, CJTF-180 assumed that the recommended techniques were approved for use in Afghanistan. In early 2003 McNeill prohibited several techniques that were believed to have contributed to the deaths at Bagram in December 2002.[39] However, the large majority of approaches in use in late 2002 remained in effect for another 2 years.

CJTF-180 and the Reconstruction Effort

While CJTF-180 endeavored to collect intelligence that would enable the effort to create greater security, McNeill also sought to use the CJCMOTF to foster greater stability in Afghanistan. For its part, the CJCMOTF struggled to meet its objectives under the new CJTF-180 headquarters. As the command's Soldiers performed their assessments, met with local leaders, and measured the pulse of the local populations, CJCMOTF leaders wrestled with how best to execute their mission. While the structure of the task force remained the same, its leadership changed twice in the 6 months after CJTF-180 arrived in Afghanistan.

In the summer and fall of 2002, reconstruction efforts continued to gain momentum. The CJCMOTF completed an increasing number of projects and shepherded previously nominated projects through the laborious approval and funding process. The command continued to emphasize the digging of wells and school construction and refurbishment, but also began sponsoring periodic medical clinics known as Medical Civic Action Programs (MEDCAPs). Reconstruction efforts were intended to gain support from the Afghans for the better way of life offered to them by the Karzai government and to demonstrate the Coalition resolve to help them. At a minimum, Coalition officials believed that reconstruction projects could sway a villager's residual support away from the Taliban or al-Qaeda members still operating inside Afghanistan.

The CJCMOTF campaign in the latter half of 2002 benefited from the arrival of the 489th CA BN, which replaced the Soldiers of the 96th CA BN. The 489th, commanded by Lieutenant Colonel Roland de Marcellus, used its 117 Soldiers to man the existing Coalition Humanitarian Liaison Cells (CHLCs) located in Herat, Kandahar, Bamian, Mazar-e Sharif, Konduz, and Kabul.[40] From these relatively stable and secure cities, the CHLC members traveled into the provinces to perform assessments, nominate projects, and meet with local leaders to measure the pulse of the populations.

Sometime between June and August 2002, CJTF-180's Lieutenant General McNeill directed Lieutenant Colonel de Marcellus to establish three additional CHLCs in areas that were less permissive but of critical importance because of cultural and historic ties to the Taliban. Shortly thereafter, CA Soldiers established additional CHLCs near Khost, at FOB Salerno, and near Gardez and Jalalabad.[41] The Afghan governors of these areas had personally requested that CHLCs be established in their provinces.[42] They knew that the CHLCs in other provinces had brought jobs and opportunities for the local Afghan people.

However significant the reconstruction effort had been up to this point, it became clear to the Coalition's leadership that more needed to be done and faster. Nevertheless, obstacles in funding projects remained as did friction between the CJCMOTF and civilian aid agencies. Reconstruction operations began with a project nomination from a Soldier in the field—usually a CA Soldier supporting a particular unit. This nomination was a formal assessment of a particular need. The information required included a description of the project, the planned review process or management of the contracted project, who the project would benefit and how the project would benefit the local population, a risk assessment with mitigating factors that could

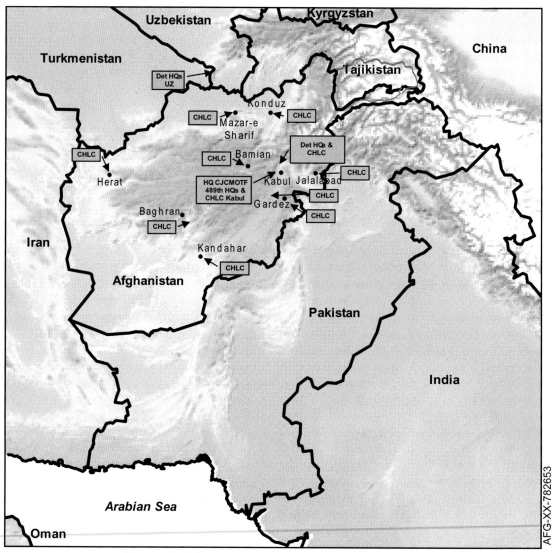

Figure 40. Disposition of CJCMOTF and CHLCs, 2002.

anticipate any negative outcomes, an itemized list of funding needs, and a priority value based on the national needs.[43] The CJCMOTF staff set the priorities without regular consultation with the CHLC that had nominated the project.[44]

The next step would require approval from CJTF-180 and CENTCOM. Certain projects could be authorized at each level—dependent on the estimated cost for completing the project. Still, there was a hesitancy to nominate any projects that would cost $300,000 or more due to the assumption within the CJCMOTF that such projects would not be approved.[45] The Office of the Secretary of Defense would have to personally review and approve anything at this level.[46] Beginning in October 2002, this policy began to change. According to Colonel George Maughan, projects were "capped at $300,000," but the CJCMOTF could get an exception on a case-by-case basis.[47]

Although digging a well for a village should have been less expensive than building a school, costs were not set and would change based on the complexity of the project. Unfortunately, the gruelingly slow process of justifying the project need, gaining approval, and receiving funds was not conducive to many projects that were easy to identify. Projects added to the CJCMOTF list often encountered a 3 or 4 month lag time before funding arrived.[48] The only funding process organic to the CJCMOTF and its supporting CHLCs was through the Department of State (DOS) Overseas Humanitarian, Disaster, and Civic Aid (OHDACA) used primarily to fund DOD humanitarian assistance activities.[49] According to the RAND National Defense Research Institute, OHDACA was a very effective tool for the CJCMOTF in providing direct and active assistance even if these activities developed slowly.[50]

The CJCMOTF had other concerns as well. Increasingly, the TF leaders had become frustrated with the refusal by various international organizations (IOs) and nongovernment organizations (NGOs) to coordinate or to overtly support the military's efforts to conduct reconstruction and humanitarian aid operations. Although these organizations ran internal coordination meetings, they tended to avoid inviting Soldiers. Nor did their representatives attend CJCMOTF coordination meetings. Instead, CHLC personnel took to meeting independently with IOs and NGOs. A related source of frustration originated in the CJCMOTF command's perception of competition between the military and civilian aid efforts, based at least in part on misunderstanding of what the CJCMOTF was intended to do. Captain Benjamin Houston, a member of the Kandahar CHLC in 2002, recognized that the CJCMOTF became closely wedded to the idea of using OHDACA funds rather than serving as a coordination agency that would enable the entire reconstruction and humanitarian assistance effort. Houston recalled, "CJCMOTF got immediately blinded [by] OHDACA, OHDACA, OHDACA . . . they forgot they were actually a Civil Affairs Task Force."[51] Houston believed that CJCMOTF's ability to direct projects led to the environment of mistrust, "The problem with that was that it created a competition to where instead of working with NGOs, we were competing with NGOs."[52]

Some of the commanders and senior staff within the CJCMOTF fostered this sense of competition in which the military authority aggressively protected its projects from NGO interference.[53] For some within the TF, transitioning projects to IOs and NGOs was viewed as a failure—not as an achievement—partly because success in the military reconstruction effort was defined by the number of OHDACA projects and the amount of money spent. This pitting of the military against the civilian sector was not conducive to gaining IO or NGO participation and would only be reversed after significant effort in late 2002.[54]

On 28 August 2002 Colonel Maughan of the 360th CA Brigade took the reins of the CJCMOTF. By mid-November the command included approximately 300 CA Soldiers who made up the CHLCs and worked in direct support of CTF 82.[55] Maughan identified his unit's mission as twofold as CJTF-180 moved closer to a full transition to Phase IV of its campaign plan. First, the direct support (DS) and general support (GS) companies within the CJCMOTF would provide the personnel to man the CHLCs. They would coordinate with the provincial government leaders to determine where they preferred reconstruction take place and in what manner. Second, the CJCMOTF staff received the nomination and prioritized the funding for reconstruction. Maughan also created and implemented a national government-level ministerial team originally envisioned in late 2001 but not established. The original plan called for 40 personnel, but was reduced to only 15 CA Soldiers who worked within key areas of Karzai's early government, such as Minister of Finance and Minister of Education.[56] At the same time, the CJCMOTF began referring to the CHLCs as Civil Affairs Team–Alpha (CAT-As), which was a doctrinal term that describes a CA element that offers general support to local populations. The CHLC concept had emerged as an ad hoc idea in October–December 2001.[57] Now, almost a year had passed and the CJCMOTF was under the command of experienced CA officers.

The Evolution of Joint Regional Teams/Provincial Reconstruction Teams

In the spring of 2002, before CJTF-180 had arrived, leaders in the CJCMOTF had begun thinking about ways in which the reconstruction effort in Afghanistan could be rationalized and improved. Their thoughts turned to a new type of organization that might be able to link key personnel from the DOD, DOS, United States Agency for International Development (USAID), or other stakeholders that could review a project nomination together and thereby rapidly reduce the nomination-to-implementation cycle.[58] Some used the term "joint regional teams" (JRTs) to describe the notional organization. As the summer of 2002 progressed, this idea gained strength, leading some CA specialists to envision the JRT concept as a "super CMOC on steroids."[59]

The idea was introduced to Hamid Karzai but, according to Interior Minister Ali Jalali, Karzai preferred the term "Provincial Reconstruction Teams" because the president did not like the connotation of the term "regional." For Karzai, that term suggested that the teams would work for regional leaders and he did not want to empower the men who had been warlords in the past and sought to retain their military strength and independence from the control of the Kabul-based government.[60] After a short period of negotiation, the JRTs became known as Provisional Reconstruction Teams (PRTs). Lieutenant Colonel Michael Stout, an experienced CA officer, took the basic concept and breathed life into it.

In September 2002 Stout had arrived from the United States Institute of Peace (USIP) to do a study about the effectiveness of the CJCMOTF as it approached its 1-year anniversary. Stout had helped write the doctrine for the command and briefed the director of the CJTF-180 staff, Brigadier General Benjamin Mixon, about the purpose and intent of the study he was hoping to do. During the course of his briefing, he discussed the lack of an authorized Political–Military (POL-MIL) Plan for Afghanistan, a concept that would guide the Coalition in their strategic engagement with the new government of Afghanistan. Coincidentally, Stout had an unsigned draft of this plan with him and it would soon become the authorizing document for the PRTs. The POL-MIL Plan had been created earlier in 2002 by the US DOS Director for the Political-Military Bureau for Contingency Planning and Peacekeeping (PM-CPP) under the management of Mr. Dennis Skocz. Stout explained the significance of the POL-MIL Plan as follows: "The United States Agency for International Development (USAID) was identified in that POL-MIL Plan to be the lead Federal agency, most importantly, and, number two, they would have all the funding to be able to do the development, reconstruction, and that kind of (CMO) in Afghanistan."[61] At a 19 September 2001 conference, Dennis Skocz had contrasted conventional military planning with the political component in POL-MIL planning. He explained that military planning occurred at operational level with heavy emphasis on logistics and command and control, while POL-MIL planning directed a coordinated multiagency effort at strategic level where decisions are negotiated with a host nation government.[62]

The commissioning and eventual creation of a POL-MIL Plan may not have been well communicated to DOD. In December 2001 Ambassador James F. Dobbins, who was serving as the US Representative to the Afghan Opposition in 2001, directed Skocz's department to produce this document—similar to what he had commissioned them to do for him when he served in Kosovo.[63] Skocz's staff was relatively small for such a critical task. They were comprised of one-third Foreign Service Officers (FSOs), one-third military personnel, and one-third civilians with occasional interns augmenting their meager team of 12.[64] The avalanche of required tasks associated with collaborating with the United Nations (UN), multiple agencies, and international countries resulted in a final product that was created through revised iterations.[65] The drafts were then sent to the various stakeholders who would submit a response. Skocz's team was able to produce this POL-MIL Plan in a mere 6 weeks and sent it to Ambassador Dobbins prior to his departure for Afghanistan.[66] The State Department plan featured a Kabul-centered approach that emphasized political and economic long-term viability for Afghanistan following the collapse of the Taliban.[67]

POL-MIL Plans are central to campaigns like OEF that require not just joint and Coalition operations but an interagency effort from the governments involved. These plans clearly identify national level strategies and should define the end state or goal of the conflict with adequate detail. A well-constructed plan clearly assigns elements of national power—military, economic, diplomatic—to specific objectives and should serve as the cornerstone of the combatant command's or joint task force's campaign plan. Most importantly, in the long term, it is the key transition document for strategic, operational, and tactical operations. Simply put, the POL-MIL Plan is a roadmap for assisting countries like Afghanistan to achieve political and social stability.[68]

Lieutenant Colonel Stout's knowledge of the POL-MIL Plan and his experience turned his temporary duty in Afghanistan into a much larger mission. Lieutenant General McNeill and his staff identified Stout as the expert they needed to establish the PRTs while providing a logical transition strategy that would take the burden of the reconstruction from DOD to DOS. Stout's initial task was to establish the first four PRTs with the first three as pilots in the towns of Gardez, Bamian, and Konduz. According to Stout, the pilot PRTs were intended "to flesh out the concept for the CJTF Commander and figure out what it should look like . . . we had a USAID representative that was going to be embedded with the PRT, we had a Department of State representative that was going to be on the ground assigned to the team, and then, most importantly, there was a representative from President Karzai's government."[69] Thus, the PRT concept was the linchpin in that transition because the new organization would team up the military reconstruction agencies with DOS, USAID, and Afghan Government representatives.[70] This inclusion of transition partners was essentially unprecedented and allowed McNeill and other Coalition military leaders a means of envisioning a path toward the end of foreign military presence in Afghanistan.

The first three pilot PRTs were established in early 2003 and had the US as the lead country. President Karzai requested the first team be established in an unstable area to help extend the reach of his government, and he chose Gardez where the inaugural PRT opened in January 2003. The Bamian PRT, located in that north-central city, opened on 2 March 2003. Finally, the Konduz PRT began operations on 10 April 2003. On 10 July 2003 the first non-US sponsored PRT located in the northern city of Mazar-e Sharif opened with the United Kingdom (UK) serving as the lead country. The 360th CA Brigade would provide the expertise and manning but could not provide security forces or logistical support for the PRTs because there were no additional resources available in the CENTCOM area. Lieutenant Colonel Carl E. Fischer, who served as a planner in CJTF-180 in late 2002 and 2003, was involved in establishing the structure and manning for the initial PRTs. Fischer recalled that in late 2002 when CJTF-180 requested 500 to 600 additional combat arms Soldiers to serve on the security elements for the PRTs, those requests came back unfilled by the Army.[71] He contended that the demand for combat arms units—specifically US Army infantry battalions—to support Operation IRAQI FREEDOM (OIF) meant that no forces were available to help secure the PRTs.

Consequently, CTF 82 had to provide combat forces as well as logistical, communications, and aviation support for the new teams to ensure they were defended, supplied, and mobile. The PRT concept was an important step forward in the Coalition campaign in the view of senior military commanders. Despite the fact that the logistical, transportation, and security needs of the PRTs took resources away from CTF 82 and that command's security operations, Major General Vines, CTF 82 commander, recognized the utility of the teams. Vines stated that his command "paid the biggest part of the bill in terms of numbers though because of the security and some of the support, and it certainly was painful to support."[72] But Vines concluded that the PRTs made a positive overall contribution to CJTF-180's campaign even in the first months of their operations.

In addition to representatives from the CJCMOTF, each of these PRTs were to include at least one representative from USAID, DOS, and, if possible, the US Department of Agriculture. A representative from the Afghan Ministry of the Interior also served on the team to help mediate and guide interactions with the local population. This pairing of DOD and DOS entities was revolutionary, but also become a recruitment challenge considering that civilians in agencies such as the DOS could not be easily deployed into combat zones in countries like Afghanistan.

The establishment and manning of the first PRT at Gardez serves as a good example of how the overall concept developed in late 2002 and early 2003. Lieutenant Colonel Stephen C. Walker, the commander of the 450th CA BN (Airborne), was heavily involved in the establishment of the first team and recalled that in late December 2002 his unit sent the first 30 Soldiers to the new mud-walled PRT compound near Gardez.[73] The nonmilitary members of the team at that point included six representatives from international organizations, but with the exception of the representative from the United Nations Assistance Mission in Afghanistan (UNAMA), these civilians would travel 3 hours back to Kabul each night because of the constant rocket attacks on the compound in early 2003.

The security situation gradually improved as CJTF-180 assigned more resources to the team. By April 2003 the PRT consisted of a US SF ODA that brought with it medical, engineering, and other specialized skills; an infantry platoon from CTF 82; and 12 CA Soldiers.[74] Additionally, the PRT gained six members from the IOs who remained in Gardez throughout their tour. Still, conducting CMO in the insecure region around Gardez was a challenge and forced the PRT to travel in large groups, thus diminishing the number of projects it could begin and monitor at any given time. At sites like Bamian, where the threat was less, the CA Soldiers were more mobile and the PRT needed a smaller security force.

Despite the IOs that joined the Gardez team, all involved in the Afghan reconstruction effort did not readily accept the PRT concept. IOs, NGOs, and even some representatives of the US DOS had serious objections to the structure and intent of the teams. The final recommendations, in a January 2003 brief by Barbara Stapleton of the British Agencies Afghanistan Group, captured the general stance of many aid workers toward the PRTs. Stapleton contended that among the civilian aid agencies there was a preference for extending the presence of the ISAF beyond Kabul. However, this consensus held that the PRTs were not the best method because of the likelihood that Coalition military forces would be involved in projects that were beyond their level of collaborative experience.[75] Deborah Alexander, USAID Field Program Manager for Afghanistan in 2002, also voiced concerns about the PRTs:

> I like the regional team concept . . . I think the work they've done has been terrific. I'm happy that the Civil Affairs teams are expanded, but I'm not happy that there is an expansion of other military forces. I'm real concerned about how this is going to be perceived because I think if I have my finger on the pulse, I think it's going to be seen as an occupation, that these military regional teams are going to be seen as taking over their country.[76]

These assessments represent a perspective that CJCMOTF and CJTF-180 leadership worked to counter through better communication, interaction, and coordination. Selling the PRT concept would take time.

As the PRT concept evolved, the CJCMOTF continued to fund and enable a variety of reconstruction projects. As of 1 January 2003, CJCMOTF had received 492 project nominations and had approved 305 OHDACA-funded projects valued at $14,020,986. CJTF-180 at that time was in the process of transferring 26 approved projects with an estimated value of $1.722 million to NGOs or other agencies for execution.[77] By early 2003 the types of projects assumed by Coalition forces and the civilian aid community spanned a wide spectrum, ranging from MEDCAP projects such as a clinic in Kandahar that treated 1,400 civilians to the large-scale renovation of the Avecina Pharmaceutical Plant, which not only made medicine available but also laid the groundwork for employment of hundreds of Afghans.[78] CJTF-180 was still in Phase III of its campaign, but the further growth of the overall reconstruction effort, especially the introduction of the PRTs, suggested that the Coalition leadership believed OEF was moving closer to a fuller transition to the next phase.

Building a Better Afghan Army

One of the objectives of the CJCMOTF and the PRTs was to enhance the legitimacy and capacity of the new ATA. Given the lingering security threats from the Taliban and al-Qaeda as well as the continued presence of regional leaders who had retained their own military forces after the fall of the Taliban regime, the creation of a new ANA was not just about the legitimacy of the ATA but concerned its very survival. To tackle the daunting task of establishing a new army, essentially from the ground up, CJTF-180 took charge of the OMC-A, revised the blueprints and roadmap for the ANA's development, and attempted to further the Disarmament, Demobilization and Reintegration (DDR) program to defuse the serious threats posed by the many militias that still existed outside the control of the ATA.

Perhaps the most immediate problem facing OMC-A in the summer of 2002 was the continuing debate about the overall size and structure of the ANA. As explained in the previous chapter, Afghan military officials had favored a very large force that resembled Soviet models from previous decades. The Coalition had argued for a smaller, more streamlined military establishment. When CJTF-180 arrived in late May 2002, the Afghans had essentially conceded but no real blueprint existed for the future ANA. US Army Colonel Jeffery Marshall, who initially worked for CJTF-180 and then became a member of OMC-A, succinctly summarized the predicament facing the team in late summer 2002: "We inherited a high level design with no implementing details and no real underlying details of how to do that."[79] He became the head of a team that included Soldiers from Canada, Romania, United Kingdom, and France, that was charged with creating a new ANA design. It would become the long-range planning document that would guide the initial fielding of the ANA.

That plan, and the modifications that resulted from it, was based on building an army of about 70,000 soldiers. In December 2002 Hamid Karzai endorsed that number in a presidential decree, which established the basic framework for the ANA. Most of those soldiers would serve in light infantry divisions although OMC-A planned for the eventual creation of mechanized forces and combat service units. The Coalition also intended to form the ANA in three phases, each of which would take approximately 2 years.[80] In Phase I, which would be completed by June 2004, three milestones would be reached: the first battalions of the ANA would be formed into what OMC-A called the Central Corps that would be based in Kabul; the Ministry of Defense would be established; and Afghanistan would have a functioning Border Command that safeguarded its frontiers. The mission of the Central Corps was to serve as a counterbalance to regional leaders and conduct security operations independent of Coalition forces.[81] Phase II, which would end in June 2006, would see the completion of the construction of the Central Corps so that it could secure the capital and the early steps in creating a small air force. The final phase was intended to end in June 2008 with the completion of a fully functioning Ministry of Defense and some regionally-based corps. Between 2002 and 2004, OMC-A planned to train and equip 24 army battalions.

OMC-A's plans met Afghan realities and by late summer 2002 some of the inertia in the ANA effort began to erode the optimism initially held by many in both the Coalition and the ATA. On 29 August 2002, for example, Afghan Finance Minister Ashraf Ghani stated that the lack of the presence of the central government's military force made the population uneasy. Ghani asserted, "We are in danger of losing the confidence of the Afghan people. Historically, this means that they take security into their own hands, and the country [descends into anarchy] and the leaders are hanged. I do not know how far along we are in this cycle, but I will be honest that I am not getting a full night's sleep lately."[82] The Finance Minister and others were essentially reacting to the slow growth of the Afghan Army's units. The first battalion of the ANA (1st BANA) graduated with 308 new soldiers on 23 July 2002. The second ANA Battalion followed on 14 August 2002 with 300 additional soldiers from the Kabul Military Academy. However, problems in housing and specialized training led to difficulties in making those first units capable of mounting operations. Worse was the attrition inside these initial units. The original OMC-A plan was to train 602 Soldiers per battalion.[83] But desertions quickly made that goal unattainable. Eventually, the ATA and the Coalition agreed to combine the Afghan National Guard forces, trained separately by UK units, with the 1st BANA in an effort to mitigate the attrition rates.

Meanwhile the funding for salaries of the new soldiers and officers was still finding its way through the US Government's bureaucracy. To keep the ANA project moving forward, the French Government agreed to provide the first two battalions' pay. To some degree, this put the program on a better foundation and sent a signal to potential recruits. On 3 October 2002 the 3d BANA graduated with 358 soldiers after experiencing a loss of 8 men during its training, an attrition rate of only 2 percent. While the 1st and 2d BANAs had received no advanced training after their initial basic course and were not yet conducting operations, the Coalition made great efforts to give the 3d BANA specialized classes that would prepare them for combat and other operations as soon as possible. Indeed, the 3d BANA would be the first recognized operational unit of the ANA when it began conducting security operations in Paktika province on 4 February 2003.[84]

Building the first three battalions of the ANA was frustrating, because the recruiting base for the ANA was primarily the hundreds of thousands of militia members in Afghanistan. Inducting these men—many of whom were former mujahideen or Taliban supporters—into a new army did not automatically make them loyal to the central government. Indeed, these individuals had formerly sworn allegiance to an individual commander or warlord, not a distant political leader who they had never seen in person. Still there were ways of improving the process of transforming these men into reliable supporters of the new government. According to Dr. Eshan Entezar, an Afghan Specialist who worked for the US Army at Fort Bragg, North Carolina, these recruits had to be carefully transitioned into the new military institution to erode loyalties to warlords and other militant groups that might prevent the flourishing of the ANA. Entezar contended, "Just giving [the recruit] showers and good food and good salary does not make him loyal. . . . It's important how they're treated, the rules and regulations. No favoritism, all of those things."[85] Even then, the ANA would have to overcome many cultural obstacles that militated against building a truly national army.

The "Valley Forge of the Afghan National Army": Growth of OMC-A and the Creation of CJTF *Phoenix*

In October 2002 US Army Major General Karl Eikenberry became the chief of OMC-A. By that point planning and designing the ANA was well underway. As noted earlier, three light infantry battalions had already been trained and two more—the 4th and 5th BANAs—had begun the training process.[86] Moreover, OMC-A was planning to initiate the training for seven more BANAs between late October 2002 and June 2003.[87] One of these units would be a light infantry battalion like the first five BANAs, but the other six would include a quick reaction battalion, two mechanized battalions, and combat service support units. The scope of the OMC-A project was growing bigger and broader.

As Eikenberry began to comprehend the scale of the task facing OMC-A, he realized that his organization did not have what was required to create the ANA. Eikenberry described what he found after he deployed to Kabul: "When I arrived in early October 2002, my own headquarters on the ground as a two-star general consisted of about 15 people working out of a couple of offices in the US Embassy, as an adjunct to that there was a small planning staff, and then the actual training mission was being conducted by a Special Forces battalion that was on the ground."[88] He concluded, "The mandate [to build the ANA] was clear and it was a central task, but it is also fair to say that up until that time there had been few resources committed."[89] This point was driven home in December 2002 when Eikenberry visited the Kabul Military Training Center (KMTC) on the eastern side of the city and found the conditions deplorable for both the new Afghan soldiers and their American advisors. He recalled that the food and the sanitary conditions were terrible and there was no heat inside the barracks. Eikenberry remembered thinking, "This is the Valley Forge of the Afghan National Army."[90]

This reaction came with the realization that creating a new military institution that could protect the nation of Afghanistan from foreign and internal threats was going to be a long and arduous process. Indeed, Eikenberry recalled being struck by the immensity of the task given to the Soldiers of OMC-A and their Afghan partners. He stated, "It was just an extraordinary set of challenges. I have been in the service for 33 plus years and I have never seen a set of infrastructure challenges, leadership challenges, and organizational challenges as we were facing in Afghanistan in October 2002."[91] Success for OMC-A would require more than just the training and equipping of light infantry battalions. Instead, Eikenberry and his command were really in the business of constructing an entire military edifice to include the Ministry of Defense, a General Staff, and all the other institutions and facilities that fall under that type of structure.

Consequently, Eikenberry and his staff restated the OMC-A mission by articulating the four primary goals they hoped to achieve. The first was to "Design, coordinate, and oversee the organizing, training and equipping of the Afghan National Army." Second, the OMC-A needed to "Assist the ANA in developing the military institutions, organizations, regulations, doctrine and systems needed to support a professional military force." Further, the OMC-A would "Assist in the reform of the Ministry of Defense and General Staff so they can provide effective management and operational oversight of the Afghan Armed Forces." Finally, the OMC-A would "Assist the transitional government, a Ministry of Defense, General Staff, and ANA that was representative of the nation, not dominated by any one ethnic group.[92]

To accomplish all of these tasks, Eikenberry realized that he needed a much more robust headquarters staff and asked Lieutenant General McNeill to transfer some officers from CJTF-180 and request more personnel support from CENTCOM to build the headquarters' capability.[93] Within several months, the OMC-A headquarters team grew to 50 staff members.[94] Nevertheless, the larger staff did not meet all the challenges facing OMC-A. As the project became far broader than just training small tactical units, the Coalition's reliance on US SF and other allied units as trainers was no longer feasible.[95]

Eikenberry and OMC-A first turned to Coalition allies for assistance with training in the fall of 2002. He asked for the British to conduct the training for noncommissioned officers (NCOs), and they began building a program for that purpose. The French Army likewise began conducting the officer training for the ANA. Small contingents from the Romanian, Bulgarian, and Mongolian Armies assisted by forming mobile training teams (MTTs) that provided instruction on how to operate and maintain Soviet-designed weapons and equipment.[96]

Far more important was OMC-A's decision in the spring of 2003 to create a new TF that would serve as the central core of trainers for the ANA. That organization took the name CJTF *Phoenix* to signify the rebirth of Afghanistan's professional army. For the new CJTF, Eikenberry turned to the US Army's conventional forces, and Forces Command (FORSCOM) assigned an augmented US Army infantry brigade, the 2d Brigade, 10th Mountain Division, to provide a headquarters and training teams.

The 2d Brigade, 10th Mountain Division began moving to Afghanistan in May 2003 and started training the ANA that summer. However, it did not deploy with all of its units. One of its battalions, 2d Battalion, 22d Infantry Regiment (2-22 IN) was assigned to TF *Warrior*, which would serve under CJTF-180 beginning in mid-2003. A second unit, 2d Battalion, 14th Infantry Regiment (2-14 IN) deployed in support of OIF that spring. CJTF *Phoenix* then began with an augmented brigade headquarters, one infantry battalion, and the brigade's forward support battalion—a force of approximately 1,000 Soldiers.

OMC-A further revised the approach the Coalition would take in training the ANA by directing CJTF *Phoenix* to organize it Soldiers into MTTs and embedded training teams (ETTs). The general concept dictated that the MTTs conduct initial training for all ANA soldiers at KMTC. Specialized training for non-infantry units would occur thereafter. Then the MTTs would leave and the ETT, consisting of 10 to 15 Soldiers who would live with the ANA battalions and mentor them during actual operations, would arrive and take responsibility for the next phase of the ANA unit's development. This program, which will be described in more detail in the next two chapters, was a critical innovation in the Coalition's effort to build the ANA.

✦   ✦   ✦

During the year that followed the establishment of a large combined and joint headquarters in Afghanistan in June 2002, the nature and scope of the Coalition's campaign in the country essentially changed. Although Lieutenant General McNeill's CJTF-180 created a broad campaign plan that attempted to use security operations to help rid Afghanistan of Taliban, al-Qaeda, and other threats, the Coalition's objectives and targeted end state demanded non-combat oriented operations as well. Thus, the CJTF-180 commander directed his efforts toward reconstruction operations and building the new Afghan Army, both of which supported the larger objective of legitimizing the central Afghan Government and enabling its reach into the provinces.

These changes took the campaign in directions not imagined by General Tommy Franks in 2001 or the SOF commanders who led the initial phases of OEF that overthrew the Taliban and destroyed the al-Qaeda presence in Afghanistan. Yet those new directions by 2002 had become critical to achieving US interests in the country and the region. The problems created by this shift were evident in the year that immediately followed the establishment of CJTF-180. US conventional forces mounted a rolling series of security operations that temporarily suppressed the enemy, but had effects that were less than permanent. US Army intelligence units that sought to understand the irregular enemy forces operating within these areas also struggled to devise ways of gaining a coherent picture of the Coalition's adversaries. The leaders and Soldiers of the CJCMOTF struggled to create a means of pushing the right type of aid to the provinces and in doing so created the PRT, an innovation that would have a lasting impact on CMO in Afghanistan and elsewhere. Finally, Coalition leaders faced the difficult problems inherent in creating a modern professional army in a developing country that had been disrupted for decades by insurgency and civil war. The challenges for the Coalition would only become greater in late 2003 as the disorganized Taliban forces began regrouping and focused organized attacks that promised to undo much of what US Soldiers and their partners had accomplished during the previous 18 months.

Notes

1.   "Deputy Secretary Wolfowitz Press Briefing with Afghan Foreign Minister," *US Department of Defense News Transcript*, 15 July 2002. http://www.defenselink.mil/transcripts/transcript. aspx?transcriptid=3601 (accessed 26 January 2009).

2.   Linda D. Kozaryn, "New Weapons Cache Found: Oruzgan Deaths Investigated," *Defend America*, 8 July 2002. http://www.defendamerica.mil/archive/2002-07/20020708.html (accessed 5 February 2009).

3.   10th Mountain Division, *10th Mountain Afghanistan and Opn Anaconda Brief*, undated, slide 33.

4.   General Dan K. McNeill, interview by Contemporary Operations Study Team, Combat Studies Institute, Fort Leavenworth, KS, 16 June 2008, 10.

5.   "TF 3-505th PIR Operation Enduring Freedom (OEF) After Action Review," 5 December 2002.

6.   Major General Benjamin Mixon, interview by Center for Military History, 22 October 2002.

7.   McNeill, interview, 16 June 2008, 10.

8.   TF 3-505th PIR, *AAR Comments for OPERATION MOUNTAIN SWEEP*, 26 August 2002, 1.

9.   *Operation MOUNTAIN SWEEP AAR* from ODAs 986 and 314, 25 August 2002, 1.

10.   Lieutenant Colonel Martin Schweitzer, paraphrased in Major Scott A. Jackson, *Tactical Integration of Special Operations and Conventional Forces Command and Control Functions*, School of Advanced Military Studies Monograph, US Army Command and General Staff College, Fort Leavenworth, KS, 2003, 34.

11.   "TF *Panther*, 3d Brigade, Battle Captain After Action Review," 27 August 2002.

12.   "Largest Afghan Campaign since Anaconda Ends," *CNN*, 25 August 2002. http://archives.cnn. com/2002/WORLD/asiapcf/central/08/25/afghan.operation/index.html (accessed 10 February 2009).

13.   Schweitzer, paraphrased in Jackson, *Tactical Integration of Special Operations,* 34; Colin Soloway, "I Yelled at Them to Stop," *Newsweek,* 7 October 2002. http://www.newsweek.com/id/65868/ page/1 (accessed 10 February 2009), 2–3.

14.   *Operation MOUNTAIN SWEEP AAR* from ODAs 986 and 314, 25 August 2002, 1.

15.   Soloway, "I Yelled at Them to Stop," 2–3.

16.   David Zucchino, "The Changing Face of Battle," 14 October 2002. http://www.dailytimes.com. pk/default.asp?page=story_14-10-2002_pg7_11 (accessed 16 August 2007).

17.   Zucchino, "The Changing Face of Battle."

18.   Zucchino, "The Changing Face of Battle."

19.   Zucchino, "The Changing Face of Battle."

20.   Zucchino, "The Changing Face of Battle."

21.   See TF *Devil, Significant Actions Daily Staff Journal*, March 2003.

22.   "TF Devil Operation Mongoose After Action Review," 18 March 2003, 16.

23.   Desert Devil Dispatch, *TF Devil Newsletter* I, Issue 7, 28 February 2003, 3.

24.   "America and the War on Terror," *Soldier Magazine* 58, Number 9, September 2003, 27.

25.   Desert Devil Dispatch, *TF Devil Newsletter* I, Issue 7, 28 February 2003, 3.

26.   "Operation Valiant Strike," *Army*, 1 May 2003, 1.

27.   "Operation Valiant Strike," 1.

28.   Lieutenant Colonel David Carstens, interview by Contemporary Operations Study Team, Combat Studies Institute, Fort Leavenworth, KS, 9 April 2008, 6.

29.   Carstens, interview, 9 April 2008, 19.

30.   Carstens, interview, 9 April 2008, 41.

31.   Major Ron Stallings and Sergeant First Class Michael Foley, "CI and HUMINT Operations in Support of Operation Enduring Freedom," *Military Intelligence Professional Bulletin,* October–December 2003, 44–45.

32. Vice Admiral A.T. Church III, *Review of Department of Defense Detention Operations and Detainee Interrogation Techniques (The Church Report)*, 7 March 2005, 186–187.

33. Church, *Review of Department of Defense Detention Operations,* 187.

34. Church, *Review of Department of Defense Detention Operations,* 196, 201.

35. Church, *Review of Department of Defense Detention Operations,* 235.

36. Church, *Review of Department of Defense Detention Operations,* 232–233.

37. Church, *Review of Department of Defense Detention Operations,* 196.

38. The list of techniques remains classified and is redacted in the publicly released version of *The Church Report*. See Church, *Review of Department of Defense Detention Operations,* 197–198.

39. Church, *Review of Department of Defense Detention Operations,* 196.

40. Lieutenant Colonel Roland de Marcellus, Commander, 489th CA Battalion, interview by Center for Military History, 9 October 2002.

41. de Marcellus, interview, 9 October 2002.

42. de Marcellus, interview, 9 October 2002.

43. Karen Gadbois, *Improving the Financial Resourcing Process for Civil/Military Operations*, Strategy Research Project, 19 March 2004, Carlisle Barracks, PA: US Army War College. http://www.strategicstudiesinstitute.army.mil/ksil/files/000110.doc (accessed 22 August 2007).

44. Captain Benjamin Houston, 401st CA Battalion, interview by Center for Military History, 28 October 2002.

45. Olga Oliker et al., *Aid During Conflict, Interaction Between Military and Civilian Assistance Providers in Afghanistan, September 2001–June 2002* (Santa Monica, CA: RAND Corporation, 2004). http://www.rand.org/pubs/monographs/2004/RAND_MG212.pdf (accessed 22 August 2007).

46. Oliker et al., *Aid During Conflict.*

47. de Marcellus, interview, 9 October 2002.

48. Houston, interview, 28 October 2002.

49. Tome H. Walters Jr. "The Office of Humanitarian Assistance and Demining: Supporting Humanitarian Needs Around the Globe—Brief Article," *DISAM Journal*, Winter 2000. http://findarticles.com/p/articles/mi_m0IAJ/is_2_23/ai_71837319 (accessed 22 August 2007).

50. Oliker et al., *Aid During Conflict.*

51. Houston, interview, 28 October 2002.

52. Houston, interview, 28 October 2002.

53. Houston, interview, 28 October 2002.

54. Houston, interview, 28 October 2002.

55. Colonel George P. Maughan, interview by Contemporary Operations Study Team, Combat Studies Institute, Fort Leavenworth, KS, 24 August 2007.

56. Maughan, interview, 24 August 2007.

57. Major Mike DeJarnette, 96th CA Battalion Liaison to Islamabad, Pakistan, interview by Center for Military History, 5 November 2002.

58. Major General David E. Kratzer, telephone interview by Contemporary Operations Study Team, Combat Studies Institute, Fort Leavenworth, KS, 5 July 2007.

59. Colonel Michael Stout, 352d CA Command, interview by Contemporary Operations Study Team, Combat Studies Institute, Fort Meade, Maryland, 22 May 2007.

60. Ali Jalali, interview by Contemporary Operations Study Team, Combat Studies Institute, Fort Leavenworth, KS, 1 June 2007, 7–8.

61. Stout, interview, 22 May 2007.

62. Woodrow Wilson International Center for Scholars, *Proceedings of the Conference, The U.S. Role in the World: Enhancing the Capacity to Respond to Complex Contingency Operations*, Washington, DC, 19 September 2001, 13–14.

63. Mr. Dennis Skocz, notes from telephone interview by Contemporary Operations Study Team, Combat Studies Institute, Fort Leavenworth, KS, 17 September 2007, 1.

64. Skocz, notes from telephone interview, 17 September 2007, 2.

65. Skocz, notes from telephone interview, 17 September 2007, 2.

66. Skocz, notes from telephone interview, 17 September 2007, 2.

67. Skocz, notes from telephone interview, 17 September 2007, 1.

68. Colonel Michael Stout, *Afghanistan: Effects Based Operations as a "Roadmap to Transition,"* US Army War College Briefing.

69. Stout, interview, 22 May 2007.

70. Stout, interview, 22 May 2007.

71. Lieutenant Colonel Carl E. Fischer, interview by Contemporary Operations Study Team, Combat Studies Institute, Fort Leavenworth, KS, 18 January 2007, 4.

72. Major General John R. Vines, interview by Contemporary Operations Study Team, Combat Studies Institute, Fort Leavenworth, KS, 27 June 2007, 6.

73. Lieutenant Colonel Stephen C. Walker, interview by 326th Military History Detachment, 18 April 2003, 4.

74. Walker, interview, 18 April 2003, 4–5.

75. Barbara J. Stapleton, *A British Agencies Afghanistan Group Briefing Paper on the Development of Joint Regional Teams in Afghanistan,* January 2003. http://www.baag.org.uk/downloads/reports/barbara_JRT_report.pdf (accessed 22 July 2007).

76. Deborah Alexander, USAID Field Program Manager for Afghanistan, interview by Center for Military History, 15 November 2002.

77. CJTF-180, Memorandum for the Commander (ATTN: CJCMOTF LNO to CJTF180), OHDACA Status Report as of 1 January 2003, 5 January 2003.

78. Matt Mientka, *US Medics Reach Out In Afghanistan*, December 2002. http://www.usmedicine.com/article.cfm?articleID=550&issueID=45 (accessed 23 August 2007).

79. Brigadier General Jeffery Marshall, interview by Contemporary Operations Study Team, Combat Studies Institute, Washington DC, 24 May 2007.

80. OMC-A, CSA Brief, *Afghan National Army,* 28 November 2002, slide 3.

81. OMC-A, CSA Brief, *Afghan National Army,* 28 November 2002, slide 3.

82. Major Christopher M. Chambers, Deputy Director, OEMA (ANA Reconstruction Team, CJTF-180), *Recruiting for the Afghan National Army* Brief, 3 October 2002.

83. Staff Sergeant Tyler Ekwell, 401 CA BN, CHLC 11, interview by Center for Military History, 28 October 2002.

84. "America and the War on Terror," *Soldier,* 25.

85. Dr. Ehsan Entezar, interview by Center for Military History, 18 October 2002.

86. Colonel Timothy Reese, *Successful Fielding of the Afghan National Army, Central Corps* Brief, 3 April 2003, slide 6.

87. OMC-A, *Building the Afghan National Army* Brief, January 2003, slide 54.

88. Lieutenant General Karl Eikenberry, interview by Contemporary Operations Study Team, Combat Studies Institute, Fort Leavenworth, KS, 27 November 2006, 3.

89. Eikenberry, interview, 27 November 2006, 3.

90. Eikenberry, interview, 27 November 2006, 10.

91. Eikenberry, interview, 27 November 2006, 10.

92. Colonel Timothy Reese, *Office of Military Cooperation—Afghanistan Command Information* Brief, slide 7.

93. Eikenberry, interview, 27 November 2006, 8.

94. Colonel Timothy Reese, interview by Contemporary Operations Study Team, Combat Studies Institute, Fort Leavenworth, KS, 26 June 2007.

95. Reese, interview, 26 June 2007.

96. Eikenberry, interview, 27 November 2006, 5–6.

Chapter 9

The Shift to a New Approach: OEF May 2003 to April 2004

In the summer of 2003, the Coalition began making a series of critical changes in the way it approached the campaign in Afghanistan. Over the previous 12 months, Combined Joint Task Force-180 (CJTF-180), the senior Coalition military headquarters, had viewed its campaign as still focused on decisive combat operations (Phase III) aimed at destroying Taliban and al-Qaeda remnants. But Lieutenant General Dan K. McNeill, the commander of CJTF-180, had envisioned that campaign gradually transitioning to the next phase—humanitarian assistance and support to the new Afghan Government—by the middle of that summer. By May 2003, that transition had occurred. The major expansion of the Afghan Army training program in 2002 and the introduction of the Provincial Reconstruction Teams (PRTs) in early 2003 were signs of this gradual transition. On 1 May 2003 Secretary of Defense Donald Rumsfeld reinforced this idea by traveling to Kabul and declaring that security levels in Afghanistan were such that a more formal transition to the next phase of the campaign could occur: "We have concluded we're at a point where we clearly have moved from major combat activity to a period of stability and stabilization and reconstruction activities. The bulk of this country today is permissive, it's secure."[1] This widely-held belief about the nature of the campaign had a number of critical and immediate affects on the shape of Operation ENDURING FREEDOM (OEF).

Just weeks after Rumsfeld's statement, McNeill and the bulk of his staff from the US Army's XVIII Airborne Corps that had formed the core of CJTF-180 departed Afghanistan. The Coalition passed command of the combined task force and its 11,000 members to Major General John R. Vines who had recently commanded Combined Task Force (CTF) 82. The Soldiers of CTF 82, most of whom had come from the US Army 82d Airborne Division, had begun redeploying to the United States in April. Beginning in May 2003, the US Army's 10th Mountain Division headquarters and other combat and support elements of the division arrived to replace the departing forces, but this transition would take most of the summer. The 10th Mountain headquarters then became the staff for CJTF-180 under Major General Vines, significantly reducing the size and capacity of the senior military command in Afghanistan.

However, by the fall of 2003, Coalition officials had decided that the campaign in Afghanistan required a headquarters that could focus primarily on operations at the theater strategic level where political affairs were integrated with military matters. Additionally, the campaign had become a more complex effort that involved a combined joint task force that included a number of nations as well as various agencies of the US Government. As a combined joint task force based on a division headquarters, CJTF-180 did not have the proper manning or expertise to direct the campaign at this level. Moreover, CJTF-180 was not well suited to direct theater-strategic affairs while also overseeing the military campaign at the tactical and operational levels.

For these reasons, in the fall of 2003 the Coalition created a new senior military headquarters called Combined Forces Command–Afghanistan (CFC-A). US Army Lieutenant General David W. Barno became the first commander of CFC-A. Barno not only began directing political-military affairs for the Coalition but also formally shifted the Coalition approach in Afghanistan to counterinsurgency (COIN). This type of effort would require close coordination between military and political agencies as well as between the Coalition and the Afghan Government.

This chapter covers these dramatic shifts in command structure and campaign direction through the spring of 2004 by first examining the implications of CJTF-180's evolution in the spring of 2003. Then the discussion will focus on the insurgent enemy that began to coalesce in early 2003 and how it evolved over the next 18 months. Finally, the chapter will look at the establishment of CFC-A in the fall of 2003 and the COIN campaign it launched, which significantly changed the way Coalition combat forces were deployed and operated in Afghanistan. CFC-A's COIN campaign also featured a continuing emphasis on reconstruction, the training of Afghan security forces, the engagement of regional leaders and their militias, and the fostering of a close partnership between CFC-A, Coalition political leaders, and the Afghan Government. Making this shift in approach more difficult were the larger transitions scheduled for 2003. In August 2003 a NATO command was set to take leadership of the International Security Assistance Force (ISAF) partly in preparation for Afghanistan's constitutional loya jirga that was supposed to meet in December 2003 to approve a new constitution for the country. Ushering Afghanistan peacefully through these key transitions was a paramount goal for the Coalition.

Restructuring CJTF-180

On 27 May 2003 Lieutenant General McNeill turned over command of CJTF-180 to Major General Vines. Because McNeill left with much of his headquarters staff, the CJTF-180 that Vines directed would look quite different. In fact, after the change of command, Vines found himself in charge of a much smaller headquarters than the one McNeill had led, which numbered close to 400. As noted earlier, the core of the new CJTF-180 staff came from the 10th Mountain Division headquarters. Vines recalled that he and other senior leaders had decided to "flatten out" the command organizations in OEF by integrating the operational-level responsibilities, normally handled by corps-level headquarters, into a tactical-level division headquarters.[2] The 10th Mountain Division staff received some augmentation to its staff as well as training from the US Joint Forces Command before it deployed in 2003 to operate in this way.[3]

There were a number of reasons behind the decision to make this change. Vines suggested that by placing operational-level and tactical-level responsibilities in one headquarters, the new CJTF-180 avoided redundancies and thus operated with greater efficiency. Some senior officers, including Vines, have also noted that as the United States moved toward war with Iraq in early 2003, US Central Command (CENTCOM) became very careful about the number of troops and other resources it directed toward Afghanistan. Vines noted that in late 2002 and early 2003 CENTCOM was "under enormous pressure not to over commit resources to Afghanistan to make sure everything possible was available for Iraq."[4]

While Vines did not state that this was the specific rationale behind the downsizing of CJTF-180, Lieutenant General Barno, who would take command in OEF later in 2003, offered a more direct assessment. Barno suggested that the decision to staff the CJTF with the 10th Mountain Division headquarters originated in the desire to conserve manpower and other resources for the campaign in Iraq.[5] Certainly by late 2003, it had become clear to a number of officers on Barno's staff that Operation IRAQI FREEDOM (OIF) had become the main effort in the Global War on Terror (GWOT).[6] Thus, the campaign in Afghanistan had, in their minds, clearly evolved into an economy of force campaign in the larger war. The doctrinal term "economy of force" denotes a military action conducted apart from and in support of the main effort. In this sense, OEF certainly remained critical to the larger global effort, but had become less important than the campaign in Iraq, which began in March 2003. After 2005, several high-level US military officials clearly identified OEF as an economy of force campaign. In December 2007, for example, Admiral Michael Mullen, Chairman of the Joint Chiefs of Staff, stated publicly that the effort in Afghanistan was "by design and necessity, an economy of force operation. There is no getting around that. Our main focus, militarily, in the region and in the world right now is rightly and firmly in Iraq."[7] In practical terms, however, the designation of OEF as something other than the main effort had emerged as early as 2003 and it meant that after OIF began, the campaign in Iraq would receive the bulk of the resources available leaving those in Afghanistan to make do with what remained.

Regardless of the motives behind the decision to alter CJTF-180, the senior Coalition military headquarters in Afghanistan was now based on a division staff. This change had an affect on the capacity of both commander and staff. After he became the new CJTF commander, Vines admitted that he could no longer focus on the tactical aspects of the campaign. Instead, Vines found that he had to take on the higher-level duties previously handled by McNeill such as directing the Combined Joint Civil Military Operations Task Force (CJCMOTF) and the Afghan National Army (ANA) training program under CJTF *Phoenix*. The new CJTF-180 commander also began working closely with Zalmay Khalilzad, the American Special Envoy to Afghanistan, and meeting with Afghan political officials such as Hamid Karzai with whom he talked on a regular basis.[8] By mid-summer, Major General Lloyd Austin, the new commander of the 10th Mountain Division, joined CJTF-180 as the Deputy Commanding General for Operations and paid close attention to tactical-level operations as Vines became increasingly enmeshed in his operational-level duties. However, as the staff of the XVIII Airborne Corps departed Afghanistan, the CJTF-180 headquarters lost a significant number of senior officers who could not be replaced by the incoming headquarters of the 10th Mountain Division.

The new CJTF-180 did not alter the direction in which the campaign had begun moving under Lieutenant General McNeill. Vines pursued the reconstruction program by overseeing the CJCMOTF and an increasing number of PRTs while also monitoring CJTF *Phoenix*'s efforts. To continue putting pressure on the enemy forces located primarily in the southern and southeastern provinces, CJTF-180 employed TF *Warrior,* a brigade-size combat organization built around the 1st Brigade, 10th Mountain Division. Like McNeill, Vines maintained tactical control (TACON) of the Combined Joint Special Operations Task Force–Afghanistan (CJSOTF-A), which generally had three battalions in the theater involved in a mix of security and foreign internal defense (FID) operations.

The Evolving Enemy and the Coalition Counterinsurgency Response

Despite Secretary Rumsfeld's belief that the campaign in Afghanistan had entered a new phase of stability, Coalition forces still faced a lethal enemy threat in 2003. The reality was that the enemy had not been completely vanquished in early 2002, but had focused on regrouping in the year following Operation ANACONDA. While these groups reconstituted, Coalition soldiers in the latter half of 2002 and first 6 months of 2003 had become the targets of sporadic Taliban direct and indirect fire, with the forward operating bases (FOBs) in the southern and southeastern provinces perhaps the most common targets of enemy mortar crews and rocket teams.

As spring 2003 became summer and then fall, enemy attacks increased in frequency and violence and began to focus on Afghan civilians, Afghan security forces, and representatives of international organizations (IOs) and nongovernment organizations (NGOs).[9] On 7 June 2003, for example, a suicide bomber in a taxicab collided with an ISAF bus killing 4 German personnel and 1 Afghan bystander, and injuring 29 others. This attack on ISAF workers was the most deadly assault on civilians to date. Two months later, on 17 August, an estimated 400 Taliban crossed the Pakistani border and attacked 2 police stations killing 7 Afghan police officers and signaling a strategic shift to targeting Afghan officials as well as Coalition members. On 1 September Taliban forces followed the attack on the police station by assaulting Afghan security officers who were guarding a reconstruction project along the Kabul–Kandahar road.[10] All told, in 2003, 12 NGO staff members died in attacks and the number would double in 2004.[11]

Other Coalition officials and agencies documented this uptick in violence. Scholars at the RAND Corporation traced a seasonal increase from 10 attacks of all kinds in Afghanistan in the first quarter of 2002 to 30 in the fourth quarter of 2002, and then rising further to nearly 40 attacks by the fourth quarter of 2003.[12] On the ground in Afghanistan, the staff of the CJSOTF-A tracked an increase in monthly insurgent incidents through 2003 and into 2004.[13] Captain Tim Wolfe, an officer in the 3d Special Forces Group (SFG) operating in Kandahar, noted in 2003, "The Taliban are targeting UN workers, NGOs, and friendly Afghans to show that nothing has changed to better their lives."[14] August 2003 proved to be one of the most deadly months since OEF began with more than 220 Afghan soldiers and civilians killed by Taliban forces.[15]

Despite Coalition efforts, the enemy had found ways to regroup and retaliate. Combat operations in 2001 and early 2002 had devastated organized resistance from the Taliban and al-Qaeda. The leaders of CJTF-180 had followed that success by launching security operations in 2002 and the first half of 2003 that attacked identified enemy concentrations. Still, pockets of enemy forces found safe havens in the mountains of Afghanistan along the border of Pakistan and inside Pakistan itself.[16] Ahmed Rashid, a specialist on the Taliban and its relations with Pakistan, has asserted that in the Pakistani province of Baluchistan—especially in and around the city of Quetta—the Taliban leadership found refuge and began to reorganize, plan future operations, and recruit new members to fill their depleted ranks.[17]

A number of agencies and organizations fostered these activities. The Jamiat Ulema-e Islam (JUI) party, which had won enough votes in Pakistan's 2002 legislative elections to give them control of the provincial government in Baluchistan, had a natural affinity for the Taliban. JUI was a political organization that espoused a traditional form of Islam and ran a network of conservative madrassas or religious schools in the region. The party had been involved in the initial formation of the Taliban in the 1990s and once again offered support. Other agencies, possibly those connected to the Pakistani Government, also lent assistance to Taliban resistance forces by helping them procure arms, equipment, and vehicles.[18] By August 2003 Taliban groups had become so powerful in Pakistan that they controlled a large suburb of Quetta.[19] Ahmed Rashid has further stated that at times Pakistani military forces provided direct assistance, including medical care for those wounded in operations to the north, to Taliban crossing into Afghanistan.[20]

Of course not all Taliban soldiers had to infiltrate into Afghanistan from Pakistan; many had simply remained in the country after the fall of the Taliban government in late 2001. By the middle of 2003, these forces had begun reorganizing and were targeting Western interests. Mullah Omar, the Taliban leader, created a council of 10 prominent Taliban leaders and 4 committees focused on military, political, cultural, and economic affairs.[21] According to Rashid, within Afghanistan, this leadership body directed Taliban fighters to form into small militia groups of 25 to 100 members. Khalid Pushtun, a spokesperson for the Afghan Government in Kandahar, stated in the fall of 2003: "The Taliban were always in Afghanistan. . . . They were just waiting for some kind of green light to start fighting the American and Afghan authorities."[22] Certain factors in 2003 may have contributed to this perceived green light, such as US attention being diverted to the invasion of Iraq, which had created concern around the country about the resiliency of US interest in Afghanistan. Ali Jalali, who served as Afghanistan's Interior Minister beginning in January 2003, believed "the intervention of Iraq shifted attention from Afghanistan at a time [when] everything was favorable to rebuild that country," and that the US-led Coalition missed "golden opportunities" to capitalize on the hope and goodwill of the Afghan people after ousting the Taliban.[23]

Another factor at play in the Taliban's regrouping was the Bush administration's continued and very public backing of Pakistan's President, Pervez Musharraf. Despite the growing power of the Taliban forces inside Pakistan, which was evident to many observers, the administration asserted its belief in the partnership with Pakistan. In June 2003, during a visit to Camp David, President George W. Bush described the common threat of global terror on the United States and Pakistan and lauded President Pervez Musharraf's commitment to reform: "Pakistan's support was essential in our campaign against the Taliban. . . . Today, both our countries are working with the Afghan Government to build a stable, democratic Afghanistan with secure border regions that are free from terror and free from extremism."[24] Earlier in the year, Afghan President Hamid Karzai had communicated a different message, clearly identifying the Taliban threat that found sanctuary in Pakistan. His efforts were dismissed and, at home, his credibility faltered. Nevertheless, the United States appeared unwilling to threaten the general cooperation of the Pakistani Government by directly confronting them about the growth of Taliban power on Pakistani soil.

This diplomatic decision left Coalition forces in Afghanistan to face the growing threat. By directly targeting Afghan security forces, Afghan civilians, and unarmed aid workers, Taliban forces were highlighting the weakness of the transitional government and thus showing its lack of legitimacy. At times, Taliban leaders emphasized this political objective. In mid-2003, for example, a Taliban mullah asserted, "We have the American forces and the puppet regime of Karzai on the run. They will collapse soon."[25] These political aspirations led many in the Coalition to classify the reemerging enemy an insurgency.

Joint military doctrine in 2003 defined an insurgency as "an organized movement aimed at the overthrow of a constituted government through use of subversion and armed conflict."[26] This definition stresses the overt political objectives that separate insurgent movements from terrorist groups who tend to focus on the use of violence for coercion and destruction rather than the introduction of new political orders. In contrast, insurgent groups tend to be "overtly" politically focused.[27] Terrorism and insurgency expert Bard O'Neill emphasized the political nature of an insurgency when he defined it "as a struggle between a nonruling group and the ruling authorities in which the nonruling group consciously uses political resources (e.g., organizational expertise, propaganda, and demonstrations) and violence to destroy, reformulate or sustain the basis of legitimacy of one or more aspects of politics."[28] Given the enemy goal to overthrow the Afghan Transitional Authority (ATA), the resurfacing Taliban fit the definition of an insurgent force, albeit one that used terrorist attacks.

Another feature that differentiated terrorist groups from insurgencies was their respective organizational structures. Generally, terrorist groups have been loosely structured with autonomous factions and cells serving as the chief organizing units. In contrast, insurgent organizations tended to be more overt in their posture and were structured in a more hierarchical fashion, often resembling military organizations.[29] While the cellular structure of al-Qaeda indicates a terrorist group, its overt posture and the considerable "scope and scale" of its operations in Afghanistan indicated an insurgency.[30] In describing the classical insurgent movement characteristic of the Communist revolutions of the 20th century, Chinese leader Mao Zedong described an organization that was centrally controlled and focused on central political objectives. Mao's paradigm, however, was not universal. By the late 20th century, decentralized insurgencies characterized by regional and ethnic ties also came to exist in many countries and appeared to be emerging in Afghanistan in the early 21st century.[31] The realization among Coalition leaders that the Afghan enemy was strengthening and sought to topple the ATA heavily influenced the new headquarters that took command in the fall of 2003.

A New Command and a New Approach

In October 2003 Lieutenant General Barno began forming the staff of CFC-A, the new theater strategic headquarters for OEF. This small staff—beginning essentially as a "pocket" staff built around a core of six officers—faced a major challenge. Before taking command, General John Abizaid, the commanding general of CENTCOM, told Barno that he was to establish a new headquarters that would focus on political-military affairs and to build necessary relationships with Karzai's government, the US–Afghanistan Embassy, and the ISAF.[32] These had become tasks critical to the overall effort; yet, after the XVIII Airborne Corps returned to the United States in May 2003, CJTF-180's staff had arguably become too small to adequately handle affairs at the high operational and theater strategic level. The CENTCOM commander believed that a headquarters dedicated to working at these levels would give the Afghan Government the attention and support it required.

Figure 41. Lieutenant General David Barno.

Because the important Coalition and Afghan political figures were all located in Kabul while most of the military operations were located in Bagram, there was a physical and psychological separation between military and diplomatic efforts. Barno sought to correct the separation by establishing the new headquarters for CFC-A in Kabul and locating his office just two doors down from Zalmay Khalilzad, the newly appointed ambassador to Afghanistan.[33] The relocation of the new headquarters from Bagram to Kabul was a strategic decision that paid significant dividends. Lieutenant Colonel Tucker B. Mansager, the CFC-A political-military chief in 2003, contended that this single decision had a major impact:

The benefit of physical collocation of senior military and diplomatic leaders and their staffs cannot be overemphasized; nearly all other lessons learned were influenced by physical proximity and its beneficial effect on personal interaction and coordination. Being in the same place allowed more agility and speed in dealing with rapidly developing crises.[34]

Mansager added that in his estimation, Barno's move to Kabul signaled to the Afghans, Coalition allies, and international observers that the United States "was entering a phase of Enduring Freedom focused on reconstruction and stability."[35]

Perhaps most importantly, relocating with the Embassy demonstrated Barno's emphasis on the nonmilitary instruments of the campaign. In fact, the CFC-A commander felt so strongly about the role to be played by the Embassy that he loaned five officers from his small headquarters to the Embassy to augment Khalilzad's equally undersized staff.[36] This group of officers became the Embassy Interagency Planning Group, which served as the major liaison between the new Coalition military headquarters and the American political representatives in the Embassy.[37]

Through close cooperation with the US Embassy, Barno was attempting to harmonize military action and political plans, thus creating unity of effort, a doctrinal term that describes the synchronization of the key instruments of national power—diplomatic, information, military, and economic—within a larger campaign. The interagency planning group, led by Barno and Khalilzad, matured into an integrated team that endured for several years and coordinated the civilian and military effort in Afghanistan. Barno began meeting daily with the US Ambassador and key Embassy staff, a practice that led to streamlined staff work and decisionmaking. By 2005, this close relationship led to the creation of an integrated Country Team that was successful in building close relationships with UN representative Jean Arnault, ISAF commanders General Jean Louis Py and Lieutenant General Richard Hillier, and Canadian Ambassador Christopher Alexander. Ultimately, the interagency coordination led to a political-military campaign plan—replete with lines of operation (called lines of effort)—that had taken into account the interests and opinions of Coalition partners. That success allowed the Coalition to present a unified effort and collective front to the Afghan Government and the broader international community.

While Barno sought to use his small staff to forge relationships and establish a coordinated campaign, the overall dearth of manpower in the headquarters made this task difficult. In CENTCOM's original plan, the CFC-A headquarters was to be a small "pocket" staff of roughly a dozen officers that would be able to rely on lower-level Coalition staffs in Afghanistan if necessary.[38] But once Barno began analyzing the mission of CFC-A, he realized that CENTCOM's idea of a pocket staff was seriously flawed. The final Joint Manning Document (JMD) for CFC-A called for approximately 400 officers and relied heavily on contributions by Coalition nations. Despite its new design, the CFC-A staff grew slowly. By mid-2005, Barno had gradually built a staff of roughly 270 personnel, giving CFC-A a more robust capacity over time even if the headquarters was not quite as large as its commander desired.

Barno found that the Coalition nations as well as the American military services were hard pressed to provide officers to fill his staff.[39] There were multiple reasons why this was the case. But a predominant cause was that in the summer of 2003, as the structure and mission of CFC-A was under development, the US Department of Defense (DOD) was in the midst of establishing CJTF-7, the new senior Coalition military headquarters in Iraq. Thus, Barno found his new command competing for resources. Coalition partners were also slow in contributing officers to the staff of the new headquarters. The CFC-A commander continued to search for ways to augment their staff structure for the next 18 months. Barno contended that it was only through "an immense amount of time, energy, and effort" that the CFC-A staff approach 400 officers, many of whom came from the US military's individual ready reserve (IRR).[40]

While CFC-A attempted to improve its staff structure, Lieutenant General Barno and his command forged ahead with their mission. General Abizaid, CENTCOM commander, had told Barno that his job was "big POL and little MIL," meaning that CFC-A was to focus on political matters at the theater strategic level, especially those aspects of the campaign closely tied to the Afghan Government and other regional powers such as Pakistan. Despite this guidance, the mission, in Barno's estimate, quickly became "big POL and big MIL" as he became intimately involved in both political matters and military operations.[41] By being at this level and having the ability to look broadly at the emerging threat, the capabilities of the Coalition, and the needs of the young Afghan state, Barno tried to integrate both political and military aspects of the campaign into a new approach.

Within weeks after arriving in Kabul, Barno and his staff began to assess the threats to the Coalition project in Afghanistan. They took into account the broad range of problems facing the new Afghan Government and the nuances that distinguished those groups that opposed both the Coalition and the ATA. CFC-A concluded from the analysis that there were really three conflicts occurring simultaneously in Afghanistan.[42] The first conflict pitted the Coalition and Afghan Government forces against al-Qaeda and closely related terrorist organizations composed primarily of non-Afghans that espoused a radical version of Islam and operated in the southern and southeastern provinces along the Afghan–Pakistan border. The second conflict featured the insurgent networks of the Taliban and the Hizb-i Islami Gulbuddin (HIG) faction. The native Afghans involved with the Taliban movement were driven by their Pashtun identity as much as they were by the militant form of Islam that formed the ideology of the Taliban. The pockets of remaining Taliban tended to be near Kandahar in the south and the adjoining provinces of Zabol, Oruzgan, and Ghazni, and along the mountainous Pakistani frontier where they had training bases and other facilities. In the northeastern provinces of Nuristan, Konar, Laghman, and Nangarhar, the former mujahideen and militia leader Gulbuddin Hekmatyar and his insurgent group, HIG, mounted operations against Coalition forces and Afghan security units. Although the HIG, Taliban, and al-Qaeda organizations were distinctive, there were indications by the fall of 2003 that leaders of all three were increasingly interested in collaboration.

Finally, the third conflict was the struggle to prevent remaining "centrifugal" forces from disrupting a peaceful transition to democracy led by the ATA. The CFC-A staff viewed this threat as primarily composed of regional leaders who maintained militias. Despite the Disarmament, Demobilization, and Reintegration (DDR) program launched by the UN as part of the Bonn agreements and conducted with significant success by Japanese forces in Afghanistan, these men had held on to military forces that granted them great authority in specific parts of the country.[43] Former mujahideen and Northern Alliance leaders like Abdul Rashid Dostum and Atta Mohammed had formally given their support to the ATA, but in the fall of 2003 they and their forces had become embroiled in a violent feud that threatened to start a new civil war. Other organizations such as poppy producers and criminal groups also undermined the authority of the Afghan Government either directly or indirectly.

Taking this analysis into account and considering the slow but steady rise in violence, the CFC-A staff began to formulate an approach that would address all of these conflicts. One of the first steps in the formulation of that plan was to identify the center of gravity (COG) for the campaign. Barno recalled that he viewed CJTF-180's campaign between the summer of 2002 and the fall of 2003 as "a very limited effort focused on the enemy."[44] His assessment was that during this period, the campaign had actually "morphed into an effort that needed to focus on the population if it was going to be sustainable over time."[45] That meant that the primary thrust of the CFC-A's approach had to be more focused on the rebuilding of the physical and social infrastructure of Afghanistan. Ultimately, the command would view their effort as a classic COIN campaign that focused 80 percent of its resources on civil affairs and political initiatives and the remaining 20 percent on military actions.

For these reasons, Barno turned away from classifying the Taliban and other enemy forces as the COG, and instead looked to the people of the country:

> We specifically identified the population of Afghanistan as the center of gravity of our effort, and so anything we did that jeopardized the population's support for that effort, population's support for their government or for the degree of hope which they all had for their future, that put the entire mission in Afghanistan at risk.[46]

In other words, the CFC-A commander believed that the Coalition would achieve success in the campaign not by focusing on destroying the enemy but by strengthening the people's support for the Afghan Government and the Coalition's plans for Afghanistan. Success with this type of approach implied that the population would reject the Taliban, al-Qaeda, HIG, and other disruptive forces. Instead of actively aiding these groups or even remaining neutral, the population would assist the efforts of the Coalition and Afghan security forces to eliminate the threats they posed.

For Barno, success in this approach was contingent on the ability of the population to tolerate Coalition operations. Much of this attitude was based on Barno's belief that Coalition security operations before mid-2003 had focused too heavily on destroying the enemy and less on winning and retaining the support of the population. Barno asserted, "In our emerging strategy, I viewed the tolerance of the Afghan people for this new international military effort as a 'bag of capital,' one that was finite and had to be spent slowly and frugally."[47] That realization led him to conclude that Coalition operations had to help preserve capital rather than expend it.

From this early assessment, the CFC-A built a COIN campaign strategy based on five interagency "operational" concepts that Barno called pillars. The first pillar was called *Defeat Terrorism and Deny Sanctuary* and categorized operations and actions that placed continual pressure on the enemy. While Special Operations Forces (SOF) teams would continue their search for al-Qaeda's senior leaders, other Coalition forces would conduct full spectrum operations, which Barno described as a mix of combat operations aimed at insurgents, negotiations among rival groups, and reconstruction missions. The second pillar was called *Enable Afghan Security Structure* and referred to the growing efforts to rebuild the ANA and the Ministry of Defense (MOD) as well as the Afghan National Police and the Ministry of Interior.

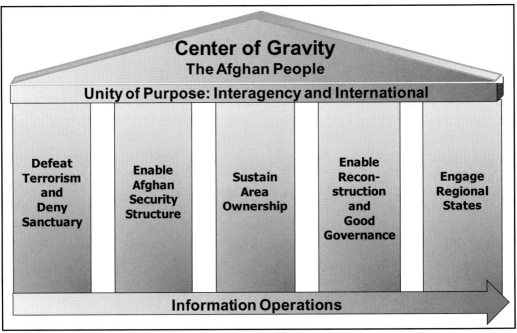

Figure 42. Pillars of CFC-A campaign.

CFC-A would rely heavily on Afghan security forces to win the support of the population and extend the legitimacy of the ATA.

With the third pillar, *Sustain Area Ownership*, the CFC-A instituted a dramatic change in the way US military units operated within the country. Prior to fall 2003, the small number of Coalition maneuver forces operated primarily out of Bagram, Kandahar, or the small number of FOBs from which they would launch operations that often took them deep into the Afghan countryside. Once on the ground, they attacked the small number of Taliban and al-Qaeda units that were flushed into the open or chose to stand and fight. But because of the limited number of maneuver units and the brevity of the security operations, the Coalition could neither gain a detailed understanding of conditions in that region nor create a durable security environment. Enemy groups either reemerged or moved back into these areas once Coalition forces returned to their bases. To correct this deficiency, the third pillar mandated the creation of areas of operation (AOs) for TF *Warrior*, the reinforced brigade that served as CJTF-180's maneuver force. CFC-A would assign brigades that arrived later in 2004 similar AOs. Through ownership of AOs, Soldiers could familiarize themselves with the local population and key leaders. The move into unit areas was also intended to send a message to the Afghan population that the Coalition was committed to making their lives better. Barno hoped that building better relations with Afghan communities would allow his Soldiers to collect better information. In turn, better intelligence would lead to more focused combat operations and more timely reconstruction projects.

Pillar three dovetailed with the fourth pillar called *Enable Reconstruction and Good Governance.* At the core of this pillar was the PRT concept that had been designed and fielded to facilitate and coordinate the Coalition's efforts to rebuild Afghan infrastructure and government institutions. Governance projects would focus on democratic elections and development of the ATA, both of which would also undermine the strength of regional leaders and poppy growers. Finally, the fifth pillar, *Engage Regional States,* required CFC-A to continue diplomacy with bordering nations such as Pakistan, Tajikistan, and Uzbekistan.*

To breathe life into this approach, Barno delegated responsibility for specific pillars to his subordinate commands. CJTF-180 would bear the burden for the security operations and reconstruction efforts that supported pillars 1, 3, and 4. The Office of Military Cooperation– Afghanistan (OMC-A) would focus on pillar 2. Finally, Barno, working closely with his staff and US Embassy officials, pursued the initiatives at the center of pillar 5.[48]

Given the nature of OEF as an economy of force campaign, the CFC-A commander understood that his resources were limited. The number of troops available to Barno in late 2003, for example, was approximately 14,000. Once these forces took ownership of their AOs, they would be spread very thin across the southern and southeastern provinces where the enemy had a strong grip. In some AOs, battalions composed of 800 Soldiers took responsibility for entire provinces that were the size of small New England states. This stark reality meant that Barno could not expect the tactical-level forces available in OEF in late 2003 to secure the population in any complete sense. The small number of Coalition units in Afghanistan simply could not occupy and patrol every Afghan village and town in the contested provinces. Troop levels would grow during his tenure as commander of CFC-A, as Barno requested and in 2004 received an additional brigade of US Soldiers. More units arrived in 2004 and 2005 when CFC-A received reinforcements for major events, such as elections which called for increased security. But these units were relatively small in size and remained in Afghanistan for short periods of time. When asked to look back and assess troop levels during 2004 and 2005, Barno unequivocally asserted that given the limitations driven by operating in a theater that was an economy of force mission, "I was very comfortable with the troops I got. . . . I felt very comfortable having that many forces in country and being able to accomplish the mission in the environment we had there."[49]

The underlying reason for this attitude about force levels was that Barno did not base his approach on the principal of using Coalition maneuver units to secure Afghan communities. He simply did not have enough troops to accomplish that difficult task. Instead, Barno rested his campaign on the idea that the maneuver units could develop an acute understanding of their areas and then conduct a mix of offensive, stability, and information operations that would clear the enemy out of the AO and win the support of the population for the Coalition and the ATA. In this effort, the maneuver unit would be assisted by an increasing roster of competent and dependable Afghan security forces as well as a growing number of PRTs. This multifaceted and synchronized approach would, in Barno's thinking, ensure that the population remained on the side of the Coalition and the Afghan Government. That support would prevent the enemy from returning and regaining a foothold.

Providing Security: Combat Operations

The nucleus of the CJTF-180's effort was TF *Warrior*, the largest component of which was the 1st Brigade, 10th Mountain Division. The augmented brigade's 5,000 Soldiers were divided

---

*By early 2005, CFC-A expanded the number of lines of operation in its campaign plan to 12. These included counterinsurgency and counterterrorism, but also economic development, social development, and counternarcotics efforts.

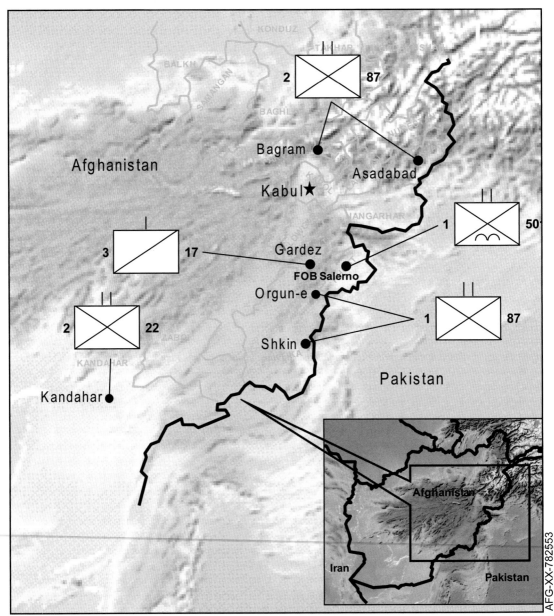

Figure 43. TF *Warrior* disposition—2003.

into four light infantry battalions; one field artillery battalion; a forward support battalion; a cavalry troop; and a large number of intelligence, signal, engineer, and military police elements. Eventually, once CFC-A established its "area ownership" initiative in late 2003, these units would begin taking control of their own AOs, primarily in the south and east of the country. Moreover, by the spring of 2004, CFC-A and CJTF-180 would create two regional headquarters in the south and east that provided greater command and control for TF *Warrior*'s tactical units.

When the Soldiers of TF *Warrior* began arriving in the summer of 2003, however, that transition was in the future. Units like the 1st Battalion, 87th Infantry (1-87 IN) began deploying across Afghanistan according to the template established by CJTF-180 in 2002. The Soldiers of 1-87 IN conducted operations from FOBs at Orgun-e, Shkin, and several other locations along the Pakistani border. Further to the east, a troop from the 3d Squadron, 17th Cavalry Regiment operated out of the Gardez FOB. 2d Battalion, 22d Infantry (2-22 IN) moved into Kandahar Airfield and provided the quick reaction force (QRF) for southern Afghanistan. 2d Battalion, 87th Infantry (2-87 IN) secured Bagram Airfield as well as a small base near Asadabad and provided the QRF for northern Afghanistan. 1st Battalion, 501st Parachute Infantry Regiment (1-501 PIR), a unit based in Alaska, joined the TF in fall 2003 and deployed to FOB Salerno near Khost. The batteries of the 3d Battalion, 6th Field Artillery (3-6 FA) were deployed at various FOBs to provide indirect fire support to these units as they conducted missions near the bases.

TF *Warrior* also contained a significant number of Coalition forces. Four hundred Soldiers from Romania's 151st Infantry Battalion "Black Wolves" were based at the Kandahar Airfield. They provided airfield security as well as convoy security for civil affairs (CA) operations. The 250 Soldiers of French Task Group *Arès* operated in the border region southeast of Kandahar with a primary mission to interdict Taliban and al-Qaeda infiltrators. Using a technique called "nomadisation," Task Group *Arès* soldiers ran frequent and random reconnaissance patrols that yielded valuable intelligence concerning the terrain, population, and enemy locations. The new intelligence allowed the French to focus their cordon and search raids and humanitarian aid efforts. The Italian TF *Nibbio II* was based at FOB Salerno, north of Khost, until September 2003. This 800-soldier airborne battalion conducted patrols that led to the seizure of several weapons caches and facilitated relationships with local Afghans near Khost.

The CJSOTF-A, under the operational control (OPCON) of CJTF-180, had approximately 4,000 special operators from the US Army, Navy, Marines, Air Force, and Coalition components from 7 countries. With a staff built around the headquarters of the US Army's 3d SFG, the CJSOTF-A's primary mission was to conduct unconventional warfare that included combat operations and humanitarian operations in support of its primary mission. Because of the nature of their work, the CJSOTF-A was not given a specific AO, but had one battalion of US Army Special Forces (SF) based out of Bagram that operated in the eastern part of Afghanistan and a second battalion in Kandahar that focused on the south.[50]

For many of the Soldiers in TF *Warrior*, this was the second deployment to Afghanistan. Some noticed huge changes when they arrived in 2003: bigger structures, larger forces, and a better-developed logistics system.[51] The veterans in the TF also realized that the enemy had matured. Alpha Company Sergeant Christopher Below noted, "They've adapted to our body armor—they know where to shoot us. These guys may be the hard-core survivors. They seem more trained than the guys in [Operation] ANACONDA."[52]

Despite some improvements, conditions at the FOBs, where CJTF-180 had concentrated much of its combat power, remained difficult. Conditions were austere. For example, FOB Shkin, located just 7 kilometers from the Pakistani border along a key infiltration route, consisted of a small number of wood or mud buildings and guard towers inside mud walls that were about 15 feet high and surrounded by triple strand concertina wire.[53] For this reason and because of their isolation, the Soldiers of 1-87 IN sometimes referred to the base as "The Alamo."[54] A landing strip and Afghan militia positions lay outside the wire. In the summer of 2003, the compound accommodated about 300 Soldiers from 1-87 IN and Coalition SOF.

**Sustaining Full Spectrum Operations:
The 10th Forward Support Battalion (FSB) in OEF**

Supporting the thousands of Soldiers of CJTF-180 required extensive combat service support (CSS) operations. In 2003 the 10th Forward Support Battalion (FSB) of the l0th Mountain Division arrived in Afghanistan to support Task Force (TF) *Warrior*. Like the 30th FSB of the 82d Airborne Division that had provided CSS to Combined Task Force 82, the Soldiers of the 10th FSB found themselves supporting not just US Army units but Marine, Air Force, Special Operations, Coalition, and Afghan units as well.

Operating primarily from Kandahar Airfield, approximately 450 members of the 10th FSB moved all types of supplies to the units of TF *Warrior* deployed to smaller bases in the provinces of eastern and southern Afghanistan. To do this, the battalion had been augmented with Soldiers from the US Army Reserve and Army National Guard that brought expertise in specific logistics skills such as fuel storage and handling. Although a large amount of supplies traveled by helicopter, the 10th FSB also contracted with Afghan "Jingle" trucks to transport a variety of items and reduce the burden on Coalition aircraft. The 10th FSB also provided much needed medical care through its medical company and attachments from the 44th Medical Brigade and the 911th Forward Surgical Team.

From July 2003 to May 2004, the 10th FSB provided over 3,000 cases of MREs and over 100,000 gallons of potable water to customers each week. The unit also maintained close to a million gallons of fuel in support of both aircraft and wheeled vehicles. Despite the great demands placed on the 10th FSB by the Coalition's conduct of a complex campaign in difficult conditions, the efforts of the CSS Soldiers ensured that the units of TF *Warrior* always had the supplies they needed.

Lieutenant Colonel Rodney D. Edge, "10th Forward Support Battalion
'On Steroids' Supporting Full-Spectrum Combat Operations,"
Quartermaster Professional Bulletin, Spring 2004.

The state of the latrines, showers, and dining facility were less than ideal—a problem that unit leaders found difficult to solve when Coalition forces were so widely deployed and logistical support, stationed at the larger bases, were equally distant.

The placement of FOB Shkin and the other FOBs along or near the infiltration routes from Pakistan made contact between Coalition units and enemy forces a regular, almost daily, occurrence. Most attacks came from rocket or mortar fire that caused few casualties. Units like 1-87 IN would conduct routine combat and stability operations normally within a radius of 15 or 20 kilometers of the FOB.[55] The exceptions were the large-scale security operations, discussed later in this section, that focused tactical-level units on a particular region in search of the Taliban and al-Qaeda facilities and force concentrations. The routine operations within the sphere of the FOBs included mounted combat patrols, dismounted combat patrols, cordon and searches, and small security missions in support of PRT or other humanitarian activities. Mounted patrols, one of the most common operations launched from the FOBs, normally consisted of a rifle platoon distributed across four high-mobility multipurpose wheeled vehicles (HMMWV), each of which was equipped with a crew-served direct fire weapon such as a .50-caliber M2 machinegun or an MK-19 40-mm grenade launcher. The platoon normally enjoyed attachments such as a 60-mm mortar section, a sniper team, medics, and a forward observer.[56]

As noted earlier, combat operations and contact with the enemy were routine events, and a brief summary of these cases cannot do justice to their scope and complexity. However, several examples of small unit actions can serve to provide insights into the type of operations conducted at the tactical level. One of the most dramatic and deadly came on 29 September 2003. The 2d Platoon from A Company, 1-87 IN, operating out of FOB Shkin, was conducting a routine mounted patrol of the main infiltration route through the Pakistani frontier when enemy mortar fire and rocket-propelled grenades (RPGs) began impacting around the unit's HMMWVs. One Soldier was immediately wounded, and the enemy fire continued unabated. Captain Ryan L. Worthan, the company commander, then moved out of the FOB with another platoon and together moved toward the sites where they suspected the enemy mortars were located. Elements of A Company quickly moved onto open ground that provided a clear field of fire and a large enough area to accommodate a medical evacuation (MEDEVAC) helicopter, which was on its way to pick up the wounded Soldier. The enemy fire intensified and another Soldier was hit by sniper fire. As the helicopter flared to land and pick up the wounded, dozens of enemy fighters began firing from positions on the ridgelines surrounding the site. Major Paul Wille, the executive officer (XO) of the 1-87 IN stationed at FOB Shkin during the fight, contended that Company A had moved into "a horseshoe-shaped engagement area" in which a determined and well-armed enemy force was directing both direct and indirect fire.[57]

The strength of that fire forced the MEDEVAC helicopter to pull out. As it did, some of the Soldiers near the landing zone found a wire that they traced to an insurgent position prepared to detonate a mine near where the helicopter was going to land. Fortunately, they had killed the insurgent in the position earlier in the battle before he was able to detonate the device. While the company continued to take fire, unit leaders on the ground and at the FOB coordinated for close air support (CAS) to suppress the enemy on the high ground. Soon, several Apache helicopters and two A-10 ground support aircraft arrived, placed lethal fire on the enemy fighters on the ridgelines, and brought the fight to an end.[58] By that time, unfortunately, Private First Class Evan O'Neill, the Soldier who had been hit three times by a sniper, had died of his wounds. Leaders of 1-87 IN estimated that 20 al-Qaeda and Taliban fighters had been killed before the firefight was over.[59]

Cordon and search operations were also critical in TF *Warrior*'s effort to disrupt the enemy's attacks. Some searches focused on finding weapons caches. For example, in late December 2002 Soldiers from 2-87 IN conducted a 4-day operation along the main road from Kabul to Jalalabad, an area in which HIG insurgents were active and in which RPG attacks on Coalition supply vehicles had become common. The battalion's four companies, which operated out of Bagram and other bases in eastern Afghanistan, split up to conduct low-intensity searches in several towns along the road suspected of harboring weapons and ammunition. Staff Sergeant Charles Haskins of 1st Platoon, C Company described the searches as "low-intensity" because Soldiers paid great attention to the rights of homeowners and refrained from "busting down doors."[60] This sensitivity paid off when Afghans in the town of Surobi pointed out two different sites of unexploded ordnance. By the end of the mission, the 2-87 IN Soldiers recovered over 50 RPGs, dozens of mortar rounds and grenades, and improvised explosive device (IED) materials.[61]

On 22 April 2004 another small unit action took place in Khost province near the Pakistani frontier. In this incident, Corporal Pat Tillman, a former member of the National Football League's Arizona Cardinals, was killed when fire from his own unit mistakenly targeted his fire team, which included an Afghan militiaman. Tillman and his brother Kevin had joined the Army in 2002 in the wake of the attacks of 9/11. Both Tillman brothers were serving with the 2d Battalion, 75th Ranger Regiment when the incident occurred. Tillman's unit—2d Platoon, A Company—had been conducting security operations with Afghan forces near the village of Manah north of Khost. Because the platoon had a disabled vehicle that needed to be evacuated for repair, the company commander directed the platoon leader to split his unit into two serials. Serial 1 began moving toward the main road to the city of Khost while Serial 2 escorted the broken vehicle along a different route. The platoon planned to reunite at the same location on the Khost Road. Tillman was in Serial 1.

Along its route, the leader of Serial 2 determined that the path was too treacherous for the towed vehicle and switched routes, getting behind Serial 1. But the mountainous terrain prevented the two units from maintaining radio contact. The new route took both serials through a canyon. Tillman's serial passed through unharmed. When Serial 2 passed through, however, it came under RPG attack. Serial 1 saw the tracer and decided to provide covering fire for Serial 2 from high ground overlooking the exit from the canyon. To do this, the squad leader placed Tillman, another Ranger, and an Afghan militiaman on a ridge above the canyon exit. Tillman's group then began firing on enemy positions they could see on the opposite wall of the canyon. As they fired, Serial 2 came out of the canyon and identified Tillman's group as an enemy force. The presence of the Afghan militiaman and the lack of communications between the two serials contributed heavily to this mistake. Believing they had met a new threat, Serial 2 began directing heavy machinegun fire at the section on the ridge, mortally wounding Tillman and the Afghan.

The tragedy of this event was compounded when the incident was erroneously reported as the result of enemy rather than friendly fire.[62] Several investigations into the incident ensued, and in the summer of 2007, Mr. Pete Geren, Secretary of the Army, announced that he had issued a letter of censure to Retired Lieutenant General Phillip R. Kensinger Jr.[63] As commander of the Army's Special Operations Command (USASOC) in 2004, Kensinger had administrative authority over the 2d Ranger Battalion and was the senior officer involved directly in the investigation process. Mr. Geren asserted that Kensinger had not overseen the investigations correctly and had not informed Corporal Tillman's family in the immediate aftermath of the incident that the US Army was investigating the death as a possible fratricide. Seven other Soldiers received lesser forms of punishment for their roles in the flawed investigation process. Geren ultimately concluded the Army had "mishandled this matter from very early on" and apologized publicly to Tillman's family.[64]

In several cases, spikes in enemy violence or indications of enemy concentrations led CJTF-180 and TF *Warrior* to execute larger operations that featured the insertion of battalion-size formations into regions outside the sphere of Coalition bases. In late August 2003, for example, Coalition and Afghan forces launched Operation MOUNTAIN VIPER in the mountains north of Deh Chopan in Zabol province, an area believed to harbor a large number of Taliban fighters. Coalition SOF and Afghan security forces initiated the operation by conducting reconnaissance in the objective areas.[65] Once intelligence indicated where Taliban forces were located, TF *Warrior* inserted 2-22 IN into the region. Lieutenant Colonel Joseph Dichairo, the battalion commander, recalled that his Soldiers had only been in Afghanistan for several weeks before deploying into Zabol for MOUNTAIN VIPER.[66] This would be the first combat many of his infantrymen had seen.

Dichairo's battalion-size TF consisted of three rifle companies and a mix of CA, psychological operations (PSYOPs), and linguist support teams. On 30 August 2003 this force air assaulted into the Deh Chopan area and began conducting dismounted marches toward a set of objectives where they suspected Taliban forces were located. The TF *Warrior* staff expected 2-22 IN would meet enemy resistance, but they anticipated that the Taliban fighters would dissipate into the mountains or villages after initial contact. Instead, Taliban forces decided to stand and fight.[67] On the second day of operations, the battalion air assaulted into the area north of the target sites and came into contact with a small enemy element. Pushing deeper into the area, TF 2-22 continued the operation into the first week of September as ground and air assaults targeted an enemy cave complex and a suspected Taliban headquarters.[68] During MOUNTAIN VIPER, US Soldiers, Afghan security forces, and Coalition units killed between 150 and 200 Taliban fighters.[69]

Operation MOUNTAIN AVALANCHE in December, MOUNTAIN BLIZZARD in January 2004, and MOUNTAIN STORM in March 2004 also massed US, Coalition, and Afghan forces in specific provinces in reaction to Taliban and al-Qaeda activity. MOUNTAIN STORM, the last major operation conducted by TF *Warrior* before its return to the United States, and focused on setting the right security conditions for the presidential elections scheduled for late 2004. For the operation, CFC-A conducted simultaneous missions in all the southern and southeastern provinces, but concentrated on the border area of Pakistan in Oruzgan province.[70] Coalition intelligence had determined that the Taliban had created an important line of communication (LOC) between the city of Kandahar and the border crossing points in Oruzgan province along which people, money, and weapons moved. CJTF-180 sought to disrupt the LOC by launching a series of cordon and searches and other operations along this line. Two thousand Marines from the newly arrived 22d Marine Expeditionary Unit participated as did forces from two ANA battalions. The 2-22 IN completed five air assaults and over a dozen cordon and searches around Kandahar City in their portion of MOUNTAIN STORM.[71] During this operation and the others that preceded it, Coalition and Afghan forces succeeded in killing and capturing a relatively small number of Taliban fighters, but seized a significant number of weapons caches. Nevertheless, these successes were only temporary tactical victories in the larger campaign against an entrenched insurgent enemy.

In the midst of these large-scale security operations, the leaders of CFC-A and CJTF-180 were making a dramatic change in their approach to the campaign. Beginning in December and continuing through the early months of 2004, TF *Warrior*'s units began moving into and taking ownership of six new battalion-size AOs in the southern and southeastern provinces. The 2-22 IN, for example, took responsibility for an area that included Zabol province. In February 2004 they began that transition by establishing a new base near the town of Qalat, the capital of the province. That post, eventually called Firebase Lagman, began as nothing more than a mud hut surrounded by concertina wire. Likewise, 2-87 IN moved into Ghazni province by setting up a base outside the city of Ghazni. Other units assumed ownership of their areas by expanding their operations from bases that the Coalition had already established. The Soldiers of 1-501 PIR took control of their AO, called GERONIMO, from FOB Salerno near Khost.

Following Lieutenant General Barno's guidance, these tactical-level units began to interact with the Afghan population and to take responsibility for security and progress in that area. As noted earlier in this chapter, these battalions could not expect to secure their AOs in their entirety. AO GERONIMO, for example, was 10,000 square kilometers in area, roughly the size of the state of Vermont. But CFC-A did not expect 1-501 PIR to gain and maintain security across that AO. Instead, battalion commanders in TF *Warrior* began conducting full spectrum operations in conjunction with the PRTs and Afghan security forces to clear enemy elements from the area and then win the support of the population relying on reconstruction and other missions focused on creating stability and prosperity. That success would enlist the population in the larger effort to prevent the enemy from regaining strength in the AO.

The transition to area ownership and COIN operations was not easy for US commanders. Lieutenant General Barno recalled that he and the American officers on his staff had no COIN experience. Only a few British officers on the CFC-A staff had ever taken part in COIN operations.[72] Moreover, very few Soldiers in TF *Warrior* had any familiarity with COIN theory and had not trained to conduct COIN operations before deploying to Afghanistan. Thus, the shift directed by CFC-A caught many units off guard and unprepared. Most units adapted using initiative and common sense. For example, in spring 2004 Lieutenant Colonel Michael Howard, the commander of 1-87 IN, decided to assist his key leaders in this transition by ordering books about COIN theory and campaigns through the Internet.[73] After the books arrived, Howard directed his company commanders, first sergeants, platoon leaders, and platoon sergeants to read them and begin applying the lessons learned from those studies to their AOs.

Establishing the unit's new presence in an AO was the difficult first step in the new COIN campaign. Lieutenant Colonel Dichairo, the commander of 2-22 IN, recalled the progressive approach his battalion used in its initial operations in Zabol province. After moving into the Qalat Firebase, Dichairo's troops collected intelligence and then launched security operations to clear areas where enemy forces were detected. Dichairo attempted to ensure these regions remained free of Taliban by enlisting Afghan police units to conduct patrols and traffic control points with his Soldiers.

Barno had contended that a critical benefit to establishing AOs would be the increase in the quantity and quality of intelligence that US units would collect. Lieutenant Colonel David Paschal, commander of 2-87 IN, found that Barno's assumption was essentially accurate. Once his units assumed command of their AO, Soldiers were able to capitalize on the relationships built with local Afghans. A better situational awareness led to an improved understanding of the insurgent organization in the area.[74] But the information gathered in consultation meetings with local leaders also helped 2-87 IN plan and coordinate reconstruction projects to build the economic and political institutions that would sustain the population in the long run.

Reconstruction Operations in the New Approach

Throughout the course of 2003 and into 2004, reconstruction operations became increasingly important to the Coalition's campaign in Afghanistan. For this reason, the Coalition had put great effort into improving the delivery of humanitarian assistance and infrastructure improvement projects. By 2002 CJTF-180 had introduced the PRT concept that located all the resources for planning and conducting reconstruction projects within one organization. When TF *Warrior* arrived in July 2003, the PRTs were still in their infancy and existed in just four locations: Gardez, Bamian, Konduz, and Mazar-e Sharif. Thus, even before the adoption of CFC-A's new COIN approach, Coalition units operating out of their bases often took the initiative to improve conditions in the communities that they made contact. The emphasis on reconstruction only sharpened once Barno introduced the new approach, and the PRTs became the center of that effort.

For the senior Coalition leadership, the PRTs became symbolic of the means they hoped to use to foster stability and generate prosperity in Afghanistan. Lieutenant General Barno contended that the teams did more than just dig wells or refurbish schools. In his words, they also—

> Brought hope with them, they brought money with them, they brought the flag with them, and they brought recognition that this was not just the Americans. This was the [Afghan] government because there was always a Minister of Interior representative with the PRTs. . . . [T]hey were widely viewed as kind of outposts of hope in the future and optimism and a positive outlook for people who had not seen any sign of the government or the Coalition except for guys running around in HMMWVs with guns.[75]

Thus, in the thinking of the CFC-A commander, an increase in the number of PRTs helped sway the population to support the ATA and the Coalition. But the rapid increase of PRTs became necessary in 2003 also because increased insurgent violence against humanitarian organizations prompted many NGOs to pull out of Afghanistan. In May 2003 the UN suspended humanitarian demining activities in many areas after attacks against its workers. The organization then curtailed operations in several provinces in August 2003 after attacks on UN compounds. More violence against the UN, including the killing of a staffer for the High Commissioner for Refugees, plagued the reconstruction effort in fall 2003. The PRT concept promised to facilitate stability in insecure areas so that humanitarian and reconstruction work could continue.

Beginning in late 2003, Barno strived to elevate the status of the PRTs from what appeared to be a secondary matter limited to CA Soldiers to a concept that was critical to the main effort. To accelerate the timeline for standing up PRTs, Barno transferred CA personnel from the CJCMOTF headquarters as well as Soldiers from CJTF-180 to the staffs of new PRTs across the country.[76] By the summer of 2004, there were 12 PRTs operating throughout Afghanistan with a concentration in the southern regions. Nine US PRTs operated in Gardez, Jalalabad, Khost, Parwan, Herat, Qalat, Ghazni, Kandahar, and Asadabad. In addition, ISAF, which had come under NATO command in August 2003, coordinated three additional PRTs: Mazar-e Sharif, Bamian, and Konduz.[77] The decision to place these PRTs under ISAF command was part of the extension of the ISAF mission from Kabul to other parts of Afghanistan.

A typical US PRT contained a contingent of 60 to 80 Soldiers for force protection, a CA team, a US Army Corps of Engineers representative, a PSYOP element, and an SF Operational Detachment–Alpha (ODA). The PRT structure also had positions for representatives from other US agencies such as Department of State (DOS) and United States Agency for International Development (USAID), but these were not readily filled.[78] By design, each PRT also had an Afghan Ministry of Interior representative who facilitated communications with the provincial governors and local community. A CA lieutenant colonel commanded each PRT and reported to the commander of the CJCMOTF.

The force protection element of the PRT was not large enough to conduct combat operations. Instead, the force protection units provided general security and had other specific tasks including maintaining relationships with law enforcement and intelligence personnel and observing and assessing the capabilities of local military and police forces.[79] CA Soldiers coordinated reconstruction projects with NGO and ATA representatives and recommended reconstruction projects for funding. They established a Civil-Military Operations Center (CMOC)

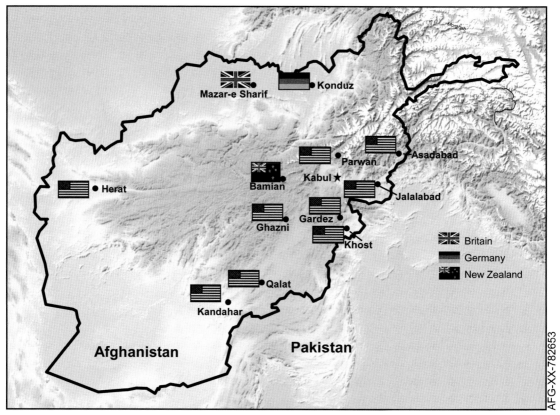

Figure 44. PRT locations.

and helped Afghan officials establish regional coordination offices. CA Soldiers also executed weekly assessments of IO and NGO activities, intraregional commerce, and Afghan acceptance of the rule of law and the Afghan central government.[80] Army Corps of Engineers representatives provided subject matter expertise, project identification assistance, quality control, and project inspections.[81]

The PRTs served as a way for the Kabul-centered ATA to extend its influence to remote and rural areas. In this capacity, Soldiers working in the PRTs were diplomats. As the Foreign Service Officer (FSO) stationed at the Parwan PRT explained when he addressed his military colleagues, "Every one of you is a diplomat. Every one of you is wearing that flag on your shoulder and is representing the United States of America and you need to conduct yourselves accordingly."[82] Included in this role was the necessity to extend the authority of the local governors. Soldiers coordinated with the governors and other local officials to plan projects according to local priorities. They also helped reinforce local security at a time when the Afghan police service was in its infancy.[83]

Although each PRT had the same mission to establish security, facilitate reconstruction, and promote the Afghan central government, CJTF-180 allowed individual teams to approach their mission in ways particularly suited to their unique environments throughout Afghanistan. The emphasis of the PRTs differed depending on the needs of the area. Some regions of Afghanistan required a greater emphasis on security while other areas required more reconstruction activities.

Colonel Darrel Branhagen, the director of the Civil Military Coordination Center in Kabul in 2003, explained: "Each PRT is tailored to the area [in] which it is located. If it is a particularly hazardous area, we expect to have more force protection teams. If it is an area where we need more reconstruction, we will probably have more civilians to help in the reconstruction."[84] Branhagen added that this unique character affected the shape and size of the PRTs that "vary from a low range of perhaps fifty person PRT teams to as many as two hundred to three hundred people as in Konduz." But he reiterated, "The mission is the same and the same mission parameters exist for all."[85]

Lieutenant Colonel John Lineweaver, the PRT commander in Herat in 2004, asserted that this flexibility was "the beauty" of the PRT concept.[86] Lineweaver used this flexibility to design a PRT uniquely suited to his region. The Herat PRT was based in the city of Herat but had responsibility for reconstruction in four western provinces. This area was huge but relatively secure. Thus, Lineweaver chose to take the 50 artillery Soldiers that he had as his security force, divide them into three teams, and pair them up with his CA Soldiers. The PRT commander then divided his AO into three smaller regions, each of which was assigned to a team. This strategy allowed for continual operations as one team worked in its community, one team provided base security in Herat, and one team refitted for future operations. Eventually, Lineweaver's goal was to establish safe houses throughout the four provinces in their AO. Together with the PRT base, the safe houses would provide a "hub and spoke organization" with which to conduct patrols and keep track of the security situation in the surrounding areas.[87]

Lineweaver's approach to reconstruction projects was representative of that taken by all of the PRTs. For his team in Herat, the point of the individual project was not just to build schools or repair roads. Instead, according to Lineweaver, the idea "was to develop the legitimacy of the local government and provide support for the central government and not make it look like the Americans were coming to save the day."[88] To do that, his three teams acted as facilitators who talked to local Afghan officials, assessed their needs, and planned and funded the project. Afghan communities would provide the labor. When the project, such as a new school, was complete, the PRT commander arranged for speakers from the provincial government and Ministry of Education to attend an opening ceremony. Lineweaver noted, "We tried to focus a lot on the local officials because that was the real purpose."[89]

The flexible approach in organizing PRT activities also applied to the Coalition partners who sponsored PRTs. The United Kingdom led the PRT in Mazar-e Sharif, New Zealand the PRT in Bamian, and Germany the Konduz PRT. Each of these countries took a slightly different approach to fostering progress and security in their areas. Germany's PRT had close to 400 personnel but most of this contingent was composed of civilians. The vision that drove the British effort in Mazar-e Sharif separated humanitarian work from PRT operations, preferring to focus PRT forces on government institution building and the DDR process while referring most of the reconstruction effort to NGOs.[90] This was possible because of the relative stability of Northern Afghanistan. But the British found that their emphasis on DDR could become a major security issue. In the fall of 2003, the militia forces of Generals Abdul Rashid Dostum and Atta Mohammed began clashing over dominance in Northern Afghanistan. The British PRT then found itself focusing a great deal of energy and resources on brokering an agreement between Dostum and Atta Mohammad simply to reestablish stability.

One of the objectives of the PRT concept was to better integrate civilian agencies such as the US DOS, USAID, and the Department of Agriculture into OEF. These agencies brought expertise and experience in specific fields that could not be matched by the Coalition's military forces. Historically, USAID has been the principal US agency involved in overseas assistance, and in Afghanistan USAID again assumed a primary role. In 2003 USAID provided $508 million for humanitarian, quick impact, and long-term projects while the DOD and the DOS spent $254 million and $64 million, respectively.[91] In September 2003 the United States attempted to reinforce the interagency effort in Afghanistan by introducing a new initiative called "Accelerating Success in Afghanistan." Congress appropriated $1 billion for that program in November 2003, but delays postponed the receipt of these fund that in turn postponed many long-term programs.[92]

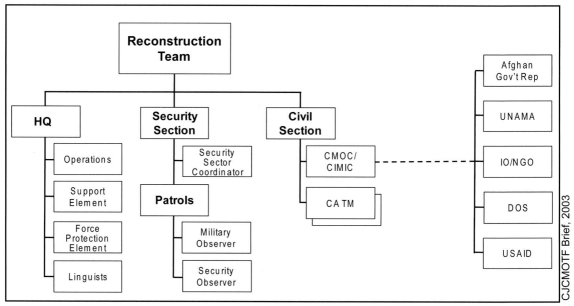

Figure 45. General structure for Provincial Reconstruction Teams, 2003.

Despite the emphasis on the interagency aspect of the PRT concept, most PRTs were not sufficiently manned with government civilians. An American PRT of 80 people typically included only 3 civilians with the remaining 77 positions manned by the military. A DOS official who served as Barno's political advisor expressed the general's disappointment at his inability to get US agencies to staff civilian positions. This frustration forced the CFC-A commander to turn to the US Army Reserve to man the PRTs. The DOS official described Barno as bewildered because "the Department of State didn't have one, two, three [foreign service officers] ready to roll to serve on each of these PRTs."[93] However, even Barno reluctantly admitted that the US military with its manpower and resources was the only entity capable of delivering results, stating, "It was clear with the capacity we had in the military, we actually had a chance of making that happen, whereas no one else had the remotest chance of getting close to that without the military playing an immense role."[94] Thus CFC-A adopted a "we own it all" philosophy rather than maintaining a narrow military mission.[95]

In areas where government civilians did serve on the PRTs, the military-civilian relationship was generally successful. Agencies such as USAID coordinated their reconstruction projects with the military projects to maximize their impact. For US units and PRT commanders, the primary reconstruction funding sources were the Overseas Humanitarian, Disaster, and Civic Aid (OHDACA) account and the Commander's Emergency Response Program (CERP), the latter an initiative that began earlier in 2003 in Iraq that allowed tactical-level units to contract for small reconstruction projects such as the refurbishing of schools. PRT commanders learned how to make use of all of these funding sources, often combining CERP, USAID's Quick-Impact Program (QIP), and the Economic Support Funds (ESF) to complete larger, phased programs. In Herat, for example, CERP funds and USAID funds were used sequentially to build a burn treatment hospital.[96] In Gardez, the military paid a contractor to grade and compact a road and USAID provided the asphalting and paving.[97] In Ghazni, USAID projects totaled $2,975,000 and included numerous road projects and building renovations.[98]

By the middle of 2003, the PRTs had launched 451 projects that required $20 million in funding from the DOD. These actions included road and bridge repair, rebuilding schools and hospitals, and providing educational and medical supplies to local facilities. Soldiers met with community officials to consult on these projects and to ensure that they implemented projects appropriately. Plans for water wells, for example, had to be confirmed to make certain that entire villages or towns had equal access to the water. Additionally, PRT staffs tended to view women as critical constituencies for their services, especially those that provided education and medical care. Facing some of the highest rates of illiteracy and the lowest standards of healthcare in the world, Afghan women were particularly grateful for the assistance they received from US military forces. The effective use of PRTs may be one reason for such favorable opinions of the United States and the Afghan Government in public polls in 2004.[99]

The overall Coalition reconstruction effort received a boost in fall 2003 when the US Government approved the Accelerated Success initiative that greatly expanded funding for Afghanistan. Beginning that fall, the fund that provided money for all manner of projects increased to $1.76 billion.[100] But this initiative also marked a conscious shift from an emphasis on smaller QIPs to larger infrastructure improvements. The accelerated funding also targeted improvements in the Afghan security forces and the mounting of elections, several of which were approaching in 2004 and 2005. Large-scale infrastructure projects such as road networks in the cities of Kabul and Kandahar received the largest portion of this aid. But the US Government, through USAID and DOD, sent $91 million to fund PRT projects so that the Coalition could continue to make an impact across the provinces of Afghanistan.[101]

Reconstruction Activities in the AOs

The PRTs were not the only Coalition organizations involved directly in the reconstruction pillar of the COIN campaign. The units of TF *Warrior* also played a role. Colonel William Garrett, the TF *Warrior* commander, believed that reconstruction was a key means of winning over local Afghan populations. He recalled thinking, "To win, we needed to separate the Taliban from the local population through hearts and minds, as well as combat operations. . . . Reconstruction could drive a wedge between the two groups by providing jobs and opportunities, while creating doubts that the Taliban offered a better life."[102] Previous Coalition maneuver units like TF *Devil* had reconstruction projects integrated into their operations. TF *Warrior*, however, had a new tool that made Garrett and his subordinate units more powerful agents of change in the Afghan countryside—the CERP. In November 2003 Congress expanded the program to Afghanistan and initially authorized $40 million in appropriations. CERP allowed both battalion commanders and PRT commanders to authorize small-scale projects up to $25,000 for quick impact. These projects demonstrated the Coalition's will to build a better future for Afghanistan, and built good will and trust between Coalition Soldiers and the population. Typical small-scale projects funded by CERP in Afghanistan included building wells, providing generators, and distributing school supplies.

Many units on their FOBs and firebases went further. Battalion and company commanders allowed local Afghans to access their medical facilities. For example, the 10th Forward Support Battalion Medical Company, augmented by 44th Medical Brigade and the 911th Forward Surgical Team, treated over 20,000 patients in their first 7 months at Kandahar. Local Afghans flocked to their gates and once inside the walls, no patient was turned away. After the Taliban detonated several IEDs in a local market, 25 children with horrific injuries arrived at the hospital and received treatment.[103] In the rural communities that surrounded the FOBs, veterinary care was also in high demand. The commander of 1-87 IN allowed local Afghans to bring their animals to the FOBs for treatment. The hired veterinarian distributed medicine to the animals and instructed their owners in proper care.[104]

Lieutenant Colonel Paschal, 2-87 IN commander, found that reconstruction projects often induced village leaders to help provide security. In 2003 one of his units was involved in drilling a well when an IED killed one of his Soldiers. Paschal stopped the project and told the village leadership, "You cannot secure your own area. You have affected me. Until you can secure your area, we are not going to have any other dealings."[105] Together, Paschal and the village leaders created a neighborhood watch program with each village elder responsible for security in an area. Paschal wrote a contract and translated the document into Pashto. Each elder stamped his thumbprint on the contract to seal the agreement. About 6 weeks later, villages alerted 2-87 IN to a roadside land mine. Paschal attributed this success to the local Afghan investment to the security process.[106]

Soldiers in 1-87 IN used CERP funds to launch a large agricultural project in Paktika province that they hoped would also foster security. Major Paul Wille, the battalion XO, knew that groves of fruit trees and a robust farming economy once prospered in the area, but years of war destroyed the infrastructure and the land. Wille wanted to regenerate the farming sector by helping the local Afghans plant crops other than poppies, the sale of which funded Taliban activities. Not knowing where to begin, he began to e-mail a number of agriculture professors located in US universities in the western states who knew how to sustain crops in arid, mountainous regions. He also researched irrigation systems that conserved water. To help the local economy, Wille purchased equipment, seed, and fertilizer from local vendors whenever possible. With the help of local labor, the unit built greenhouses to allow the community to continue the growing season through the winter and dug drip irrigation systems. To ensure the locals knew how to sustain the agricultural sector for the future, 1-87 IN hired Pashto speakers to teach classes on vocational agriculture, worked with local tribal leaders to ensure equitable distribution of resources, and to promote the local government's involvement in civic projects. In the first 3 months, the program distributed $1.5 million in resources throughout Paktika province.[107]

One of the goals of the reconstruction projects was to further the reach of the local and central governments. CJTF-180 was careful to credit Afghan leaders when projects were completed. Soldiers also conducted information operations to help teach locals about the new government. Lieutenant Colonel Bentley Nettles, the CJTF-180 information operations field support team chief, found that many Afghans did not have a strong national identity or feel a connection to the national government.[108] Most citizens had never seen President Karzai and were thrilled when Soldiers had pictures to share.[109] Nettles helped CA teams distribute Afghan flags to be displayed in the new schools or clinics.

CFC-A and CJTF-180 maintained that information operations was at the center of the strategy to defeat the Taliban and al-Qaeda. The enemy, however, had their own information operations campaigns intent on stimulating anti-Coalition sentiment. The Taliban broadcasted radio messages and blamed the Coalition for civilian deaths.[110] Propaganda efforts included leaflets showing US Soldiers violating the dignity of Afghan citizens and warning citizens not to cooperate with US reconstruction efforts.[111] Coalition information operations needed to overcome a widespread concern that the United States would abandon Afghanistan once combat ended.

CFC-A maintained a six-person information operations team that coordinated the various Coalition information efforts. Lieutenant Colonel Nettles, an information operations specialist and a team leader in 2003, used a variety of methods for strategic communications. His team coordinated radio shows hosted by local commanders and established a program that handed out radios powered by an attached hand crank to Afghans. Nettles' team also launched an initiative that built bulletin boards in villages that posted messages promoting the local and national governments.[112] Nettles even convinced the commercial airline carrier, Ariana Afghan Airlines, to distribute to passengers a newspaper highlighting the economic and social accomplishments of the new Afghanistan.[113] None of these measures, however, was as powerful as seeing the Afghan security forces, especially the soldiers of the ANA, working closely with Coalition troops.

Enabling the ANA

The CFC-A plan allotted an entire pillar to the enabling of the Afghan security forces. For Lieutenant General Barno, the reasoning behind this emphasis was sound. For most counterinsurgent forces throughout history, successful campaigns against insurgencies featured collaboration with host nation police, paramilitary, and military forces. Barno and the CFC-A staff knew this and also understood that the Coalition, relatively speaking, had very few forces inside Afghanistan. Thus, Coalition military units needed effective Afghan partners to be successful. Since 2002 the OMC-A had been working toward the establishment of the ANA and by mid-2003, was assisting the Afghan Government recruit, train, and equip a dozen battalions of light infantry. OMC-A reported that on 1 June 2003 it had trained over 7,000 Afghan soldiers of which approximately 4,000 were currently serving in units. Problems with pay, facilities, and other issues kept attrition rates high, but progress was steady and OMC-A officials believed that the ANA Central Corps, based in Kabul, would be completed by mid-2004.[114]

In December 2003 US Air Force Major General Craig Weston changed command with US Army Major General Karl Eikenberry as head of the OMC-A.[115] Under Eikenberry, the effort to train the soldiers of the ANA had transitioned from a US Army SF battalion to CJTF *Phoenix*, a unit that was focused solely on training and advising the ANA. US Army conventional forces formed the core of CJTF *Phoenix*, but individuals and units from other US services and the Coalition nations were also critical to the training and advising tasks. In the fall of 2003, the 2d Brigade, 10th Mountain Division, which had been serving as that core since mid-2003, was designated for deployment to Iraq as part of OIF. The Coalition then arranged for the 45th Infantry Brigade of the Oklahoma Army National Guard to provide the manning for CJTF

Phoenix beginning in November 2003. This move marked the first major commitment of a brigade-size Reserve Component force in OEF. Weston sought to continue the momentum built up by Eikenberry and hoped to solve some of the larger persistent issues, especially poor facilities and high attrition rates.

Recruiting, Retention, and Diversity

President Karzai's decree establishing the ANA had stipulated that the new army be a force of 70,000 soldiers composed of volunteers who represented all of Afghanistan's ethnic and social groups.[116] To meet these requirements, the ANA required a robust recruiting effort. A joint Afghan/OMC-A program to establish National Army Volunteer Centers in all 34 provinces began in July 2003. The initiative started slowly as the two recruiters from OMC-A faced challenges in securing ground and helicopter transportation to distant areas. Likewise, once new recruits enlisted, they often faced days of traveling to reach the ANA training centers in Kabul. But by winter 2004, Afghanistan's Recruiting Command was well established with 23 of the 34 centers open.[117]

Recruiters employed radio, television, posters, billboards, and flyers to encourage young Afghans to enlist using the recruiting motto, "One Nation, One Army"—a slogan that reflected the Coalition imperative of building a multiethnic national army. Many of the billboards featured that motto written under a picture of four Afghan Soldiers—a Pashtun, a Hazara, a Tajik, and an Uzbek. A large part of the recruiting effort was working with village leaders and elders who would nominate young men for the ANA.[118] While most Afghan families were familiar with weapons, the majority of the recruits had no military experience. Colonel David Francavilla, who served as OMC-A's first chief of recruiting, described the recruiting drive in 2003 as "absolutely starting from scratch. [The recruits] had no military training. They may have known how to pull a trigger, but no military discipline, no marksmanship, and no tactics other than hunting."[119] Because the Afghan MOD lacked a history of personnel records or census data, it was virtually impossible for the Afghan Government to check the records of young recruits for health problems, crimes, associations with criminal or terrorist organizations, and other things that might exclude them from military service. Village leaders had to serve in this capacity and often took responsibility for the young men they nominated. However, as the ANA developed, the intelligence section began to approve the accession of young soldiers.[120]

The Afghan MOD selected officers based on merit and ethnic representation. The minimal requirement for officer selection was the ability to read and write. When officers did not meet requirements or on recommendations from Coalition trainers, the MOD would remove or replace these officers. The ATA, recognizing the legacy of mujahideen leaders in the war against the Soviets, made every effort to encourage qualified mujahideen leaders to join the ANA.[121]

CJTF *Phoenix* and the ANA emphasized the many benefits offered to recruits by service in the ANA, including housing, steady meals, healthcare, literacy classes, and skills training. Recruiters advertised these benefits to potential soldiers. The most important reward of military service was a steady income. Basic pay began at $50 a month, but quickly increased to $70 when Afghan and Coalition officials realized that the initial amount was not enough to recruit and retain soldiers. Promotions added $15 a month, and soldiers earned an extra $1 a day when deployed. Officers earned considerably more. Despite attempts to ensure that pay was adequate and competitive in the labor market, enlisted pay often fell short, contributing to the larger problem of desertion. Mohammad Tahir, a platoon sergeant and sole income provider for a nine-member family explained to a journalist in December 2003: "If we can't pay rent, we have to find another job."[122] Other employment was available in Afghanistan and created competition for the ANA. Day laborers working for American contractors made more money than Afghan soldiers' earned.[123] Interpreters for ISAF earned $400 to $450 per month while Afghans serving in local Afghan militia forces sponsored by Coalition SOF earned up to $200 per month.[124]

Desertions continued to be a significant challenge as soldiers were tempted to use their newly gained marketable skills working for ISAF, IOs, or local militia forces.[125] Afghanistan's lack of a nationwide banking system also affected retention, because soldiers were forced to carry cash payments back to their families. After lengthy journeys of weeks or even months, many of these soldiers returned to the ANA but unit strength and efficiency suffered.[126] In January 2003 the OMC-A reported that the strength of the first and second battalions was 36 percent and 37 percent, respectively. The third, fourth, and fifth battalions, which had just completed basic training, maintained strengths of 59 percent, 58 percent, and 67 percent, respectively. The sixth battalion, which was still in basic training, sustained 99 percent strength.[127] Thus, battalions tended to lose soldiers through time, and maintaining their strength was a priority for recruiting and retention efforts. The average rate of attrition from December 2003 to July 2004 was 1.3 percent per month.[128]

President Karzai had directed that the ANA be ethnically balanced. Accordingly, both recruiters and trainers tried to ensure that the ANA represented all of Afghanistan's ethnic and sectarian groups. This principle was so important that on occasions when efforts fell short of providing recruits that represented ethnic demographics, the OMC-A delayed the start of basic training.[129] At each unit level—from squad to brigade—the ANA was ethnically integrated. Lieutenant Colonel Richard Gallant, commander of CJTF *Phoenix*'s 1st Brigade Training Team, recalled that the Pashtun, Uzbeks, and Tajiks each had command of one battalion in the brigade. Gallant emphasized that this step was a major achievement, stating, "These guys, who

	Afghanistan Ethnic Makeup	Ground Forces Ethnic Makeup	MoD/ General Staff Ethnic Makeup
Pashtun	44%	44%	39%
Tajiki	25%	34%	35%
Hazara	10%	8%	12%
Uzbek	8%	4%	8%
Other	13%	8%	6%

CFC-A Brief

Figure 46. ANA Ethnic balance, May 2004.

10 years ago were sworn enemies, would sit in brigade commander's calls together and they would work together like brothers. It was tremendous to see and it actually did work."[130] Despite these strides with ethnic diversity, women were not included in recruiting efforts because US and Afghan officials agreed that fighting had been traditionally viewed in Afghanistan as a job for males.

Basic Training

After recruitment, the Afghan soldier went through in-processing where his photo and fingerprints were taken and he was issued an identification card and uniform. Then the soldier began basic training, which was overseen by CJTF *Phoenix*. Basic training, officer school, and Noncommissioned Officer (NCO) Academy were conducted at Camp *Phoenix* and the Kabul Military Training Center (KMTC) located just east of Kabul. On arrival, enlisted soldiers would begin training with Afghan instructors and American mentors while the officers would enter officer training school led by the French Army.

Basic training consisted of weapons instruction, physical training, and small unit tactics. In building these skills, US trainers relied on basic US Army small unit tactical doctrine translated into Dari and given to the Afghan instructors. Brigadier General Joseph Prasek, the CJTF *Phoenix* commander in mid-2003, found teaching fundamentals was critical, and marksmanship, physical fitness, and fire and maneuver were the most important skills for ANA light infantry soldiers.[131] Originally, two battalions began the 10-week basic training program simultaneously, but when CFC-A directed CJTF *Phoenix* to train more units at a faster pace, basic training was shortened to 7 weeks and three battalions entered the KMTC at the same time.[132]

Soon after entering basic training, enlisted soldiers had the opportunity to volunteer for the British-led NCO school. This very competitive program had higher training standards for skills such as physical training and marksmanship. A soldier who successfully completed the program received a gold bar on his uniform and, depending on how well the soldier did in the NCO program, was then eligible for promotion. The NCO corps was a very new concept for most Afghans, because the Russian model with which they were familiar did not utilize NCOs. Senior Afghan officers, who emulated the Russian officers they had known, tended to micromanage their units and delegated mundane chores to the NCOs. Not surprisingly, they found it particularly difficult to accommodate the NCO corps.[133]

In the initial training, junior soldiers, NCOs, and officers progressed on separate but parallel tracks. Training was synchronized so that on graduation, soldiers of all ranks came together to form a battalion.[134] The 500 to 700 soldiers of the new battalion received their unit name and flag, and then moved into barracks at Darulaman Military Base near Kabul and other facilities where they would continue their training.

Mentoring the ANA: The Embedded Training Teams

Basic training was just the first step for the Afghan soldier. Once the soldier joined his battalion, he and his entire unit began training together under the tutelage of a Coalition embedded training team (ETT) from CJTF *Phoenix*. A fully staffed ETT at the battalion level consisted of 15 Soldiers led by a major. At the brigade level, ETTs numbered around 75 Soldiers. Embedded trainers developed training plans for their Afghan units, which included personal hygiene, physical fitness, tactical training, live fires, and night operations. Brigadier General

Prasek's training guidance stipulated that training should be "hands-on" with the primary focus on "shoot, move, and communicate."[135] In addition, Prasek directed the ETTs to conduct two 10-kilometer tactical foot marches per week, one monthly 20-kilometer foot march, squad and platoon live-fire exercises, a company-level 3-day field training exercise, and daily physical fitness events.[136]

In mid-2003, when the 45th Infantry Brigade from the Oklahoma Army National Guard received the mission to serve as the core of CJTF *Phoenix*, brigade leaders realized they had a major challenge in manning the ETTs. Brigadier General Thomas Mancino, who commanded the 45th Brigade and would in November 2003 become the commander of CJTF *Phoenix*, explained that the ETTs required Soldiers that were relatively high in rank.[137] For example, the lowest ranking Soldier on a battalion ETT was a sergeant (E5). As a large infantry formation, the 45th Infantry Brigade did not have enough senior NCOs and officers to fill the slots on the training teams. The US National Guard Bureau assisted the brigade by arranging for Soldiers from the Vermont Army National Guard and the South Carolina Army National Guard as well as the US Marine Corps to fill the ETTs.

This problem was exacerbated by the fact that CJTF *Phoenix* was also responsible for manning mobile training teams (MTTs), which augmented the ETTs by teaching specialty skills such as equipment repair, reconnaissance, heavy weapons, and even driver's training.[138] MTT courses were accelerated and designed to teach specialized skills in a very short amount of time. Both ETTs and MTTs would reinforce the basic skills developed in initial training, but for their battalions to sustain themselves independently, the ETTs had to shift the burden to Afghan commanders who gradually would assume responsibility to plan and supervise the training for their soldiers. ETTs mentored ANA commanders at the battalion, company, and platoon levels to teach commanders how to conduct effective meetings and how to plan training schedules.[139]

Captain Charles Di Leonardo served in 2003 as an embedded trainer for the Weapons Company of the ANA 1st Battalion, 1st Brigade. Di Leonardo quickly discovered that his most important task was to give the ANA company tools and processes that would make it more effective. After assessing the strengths and weaknesses of the company, Di Leonardo found that the leadership of the company had a great deal of military experience. Captain Sayeed Mohammad had served in the Soviet-trained Afghan Army of the 1980s, progressing to the rank of lieutenant colonel. His XO was also a veteran of the previous Afghan Army and his first sergeant had fought against that army on the side of the mujahideen. Weapons Company and the 1st Battalion had been together for a year and had conducted security missions in the Khost and Gardez areas.[140] When the company trained on the ranges, however, there was still a tendency for the officers to dominate the exercises while relegating NCOs to secondary positions.

After his initial assessment, Di Leonardo embarked on an aggressive training program to improve the company's operations. Di Leonardo began his program with 2 weeks of classes for the company's officers to teach operation orders, plan ranges, and live-fire exercises. Meanwhile, NCOs worked with the junior enlisted who trained separately under the watchful eyes of the corporals and sergeants. This training arrangement emphasized to the Afghans how the division of duties could give more time for unit administration to the officers while sharpening the leadership skills of the NCOs. Di Leonardo taught Sayeed Mohammad the US Army's after-action review (AAR) process so that the company could learn from their successes and mistakes. Both Di Leonardo and Sayeed Mohammad noted improvements as the company completed successive drills.

Captain Di Leonardo's mission extended beyond the training ranges. In August 2003, Di Leonardo accompanied his counterpart on a deployment to the town of Qalat in Zabol province. In that town, the ETT coordinated a linkup with an American ODA and both the Afghans and the Americans began coordinating with local government officials to plan a series of operations against insurgents in the province. Over the course of several weeks, Di Leanardo's ETT and the Afghan company conducted security patrols, traffic control points, and cordon and search operations.[141] One of the Coalition's objectives for this operation had been to increase the legitimacy of the ATA by demonstrating the competence of the ANA. Captain Di Leonardo believed that the missions in Zabol definitely had that effect. The American advisor was particularly struck by the positive reaction Afghans in Pashtun-dominated Zabol had when they saw how well they were treated by the soldiers in Weapons Company that were of multiple ethnicities.

Equipment and Facilities

Building competent and professional tactical-level units was just one part of the task that faced CJTF *Phoenix*. As noted in the previous chapter, the Coalition had committed to building an entire support structure that would educate, train, supply, equip, and pay those forces. Due to the urgency of imparting basic soldier skills, however, Coalition leaders had postponed the formation and training of combat service support units. Without even a rudimentary logistics system in place up through 2003, the ANA became dependent on Coalition support, including the basic coordinating and contracting for food and maintenance services.[142] In a 19 June 2003 memorandum, Brigadier General Prasek noted the problem:

> There is no reliable host-nation supply system in place for the ANA at any level . . . [battalions] themselves have no systemic mechanism for tracking requirements, resources, and unit hand receipts. Equipment accountability is nonexistent . . . the company and [battalion] logistics personnel have no system in place to request required equipment and supplies to support the units in garrison or on operational deployments.[143]

Still, by mid 2003 the first battalions were operational and new units were graduating from the KMTC at a steady pace. CJTF *Phoenix* could no longer ignore the need for a truly Afghan logistical infrastructure. Indeed, once Brigadier General Mancino took command of CJTF *Phoenix* in late 2003, he found that 80 percent of his time was focused on building the logistics system.[144]

Embedded trainers at battalion-level taught Afghan soldiers the proper way to request supplies, how to inventory their weapons and munitions, and how to track the supplies they had.[145] At the same time, ANA leaders worked with the Coalition to develop a quartermaster corps and logistical system complete with budgetary functions, acquisition systems, maintenance facilities, and distribution capability. Until the Afghan MOD could build that institutional capacity, the 210th Forward Support Battalion, 10th Mountain Division provided the acquisition and distribution of all incoming equipment and parts.

Managing the high volume of supply and equipment donations was a particular challenge for the ANA. In one instance, two large Condor transport aircraft unexpectedly arrived with full cargo loads of ammunition for the ANA, which CJTF *Phoenix* members scrambled to unload.[146] While the ANA and Coalition greatly appreciated all contributions, the variety of arms and equipment created difficulties for standardizing the ANA's organization and establishing its supply stores. The ANA's uniforms were a collection of donations from various nations, and thus varied appearance somewhat diminished the professionalism of the army. One embedded trainer found that his battalion was operating with three different types of mortars—Chinese, Czechoslovakian, and Hungarian—each with its own parts and ammunition requirements.[147] Countries that contributed weapons and equipment did not often send sustainment packages, spare parts, or training assistance. Therefore, it was difficult to ensure that the donations would be properly maintained and operated. Even US equipment, such as the over 500 2.5-ton trucks sent by CENTCOM, arrived without the proper supply of spare parts.[148]

Much of the existing Afghan weaponry was vintage Soviet equipment with which most Afghans were familiar because it was widely used by the former Afghan Army and Afghan militias. Several Coalition nations from Eastern Europe donated Soviet equipment from their arsenals.[149] Romanian and Bulgarian trainers provided extra instructional assistance. Still, Afghan units experienced severe equipment shortages, despite all the donations. A January 2003 assessment found that the Afghan Army needed 44 tanks, 108 armored personnel carriers, 496 RPK machineguns, over 7,000 AK-47 rifles, and over 66,000 rounds of RPG-7 ammunition.[150] The units also suffered from shortages in uniforms, boots, and communications gear.[151]

In 2003 and 2004 Afghan military facilities were also in a dismal state of affairs. Most egregious was that the KMTC lacked heat and sanitation. Almost all of Afghanistan's existing facilities required major renovation and many more facilities needed to be constructed. Given the increasing scope and complexity of ANA infrastructure development, Major General Eikenberry requested that the Army Corps of Engineers deploy increasing numbers of personnel from its Transatlantic Program Center, which provides engineering support to deployed Soldiers in the Middle East, Africa, and Russia. Their mission was to design master plans for the KMTC, Pol-e-Charki, and Darulaman.[152] In the OMC-A's estimation, providing basic facilities with roofing was the highest priority. The first barracks built by the Coalition resembled World War II American Army basic training buildings and were simple one-story concrete buildings with metal roofs and paved floors. Each battalion had a cluster of facilities including barracks, a headquarters building, an office for each company, a weapons storage area, and a mess hall. US engineers did not construct mosques, but assisted Afghan engineers in the MOD who designed mosques at the three bases.[153]

Engineers raced to keep up with the growing ANA and delivered new barracks and buildings as each new battalion graduated from basic training. Because Afghanistan lacked the ability to produce construction materials, all building supplies were imported. Steel, cement, electrical supplies, plumbing, and fixtures all came from Pakistan or from other overseas locations through the port of Dubai. Contractors provided most of the construction effort employing Turkish and Egyptian work crews and qualified Afghans for skilled labor and locals for unskilled labor.[154]

Although Afghanistan did not share US building codes, engineers and contractors were very careful to ensure that construction met high environmental and safety standards, including those that made a building earthquake resistant. Most buildings relied on wood stove heat or local generators, which were expensive to maintain so engineers tried to design heating systems that were not dependent on outside resources. Building and maintaining adequate sewage systems was also a paramount concern.[155]

Measuring Progress

By spring 2004 the OMC-A and CJTF *Phoenix* began to see significant, measurable signs of progress. May 2004 witnessed the grand opening of the 10th National Army Volunteer Center and the Recruiting Academy.[156] On 17 June 2004 the 20th ANA Battalion graduated from basic training and joined the Central Corps, which was on that date fully formed. By mid-2004 the OMC-A had helped Afghanistan train and equip the 10,000 soldiers that manned the Central Corps.[157] With this mission complete, the OMC-A began building the regional corps in Herat, Mazar-e Sharif, Gardez, and Kandahar.

Successful combat operations were another measure of progress. By early 2004 more ANA units were beginning to partner with CJTF-180 units in the field. Two ANA battalions, for example, were part of Operation MOUNTAIN STORM in March 2004. Moreover, the ANA began securing events and initiatives that directly enhanced the legitimacy of the ATA. In December 2003, for example, several ANA battalions provided security for the constitutional loya jirga in Kabul.[158] In March 2004, 1,500 ANA soldiers deployed to Herat to defuse tensions between regional leaders Ismail Khan and Abdul Zahir Navebzadeh. The two men had quarreled over a military garrison and the disagreement culminated with the assassination of Khan's son Mirwai Sadeq, the Minister of Civil Aviation and Tourism in President Karzai's cabinet. Just 1 month later, the ATA sent ANA units to Faryab province in northern Afghanistan where Dostum's forces were embroiled in a fight with units associated with General Hashim Habibi, the government-appointed commander in the region. The ANA battalions secured the main centers of the province and helped de-escalate the clash between a strong regional military leader and the central government.[159] President Karzai's employment of the ANA in these situations demonstrated how far Afghan security forces had progressed since 2002. More importantly, these cases reveal the degree to which the central government was willing to use its military forces to keep Afghanistan on the path toward greater political stability.

This success, however, led to a greater challenge for CFC-A and OMC-A. In 2003 officials in the US DOD began asking the Coalition command in Afghanistan to consider how it might accelerate the creation of Afghan security forces. By January 2004 the Bush administration had included this initiative in the aforementioned program known as "Accelerating Success in Afghanistan," which would also include an infusion of $2.2 billion for the funding of all types of projects.[160] In February 2004 Secretary of Defense Rumsfeld explained during a visit to Kabul that a key factor driving the acceleration of Afghan forces was his desire to begin decreasing the number of US troops in Afghanistan as soon as possible.[161] Thus, in 2004, OMC-A began making plans to increase the number of army battalions that would train simultaneously at KMTC and the rapidity with which these units would become operational.

Enabling Good Governance: The Constitutional Loya Jirga

As part of his new approach, Lieutenant General Barno had emphasized the partnership between CFC-A and the ATA. This effort fell within the campaign pillar labeled *Enable Reconstruction and Good Governance*. For Barno, the establishment of the PRTs and the ANA were the most direct ways of lending legitimacy to President Karzai and the ATA. But he and his staff also worked closely on a daily basis with the American Embassy, President Karzai, and the senior officials in the ATA. Like Lieutenant General McNeill, the CFC-A commander also spent a great deal of time dealing with regional leaders like Ismail Khan, Dostum, and others, to defuse tensions and armed conflicts.

Critical to the overall effort of strengthening the ATA's ability to govern was the political timetable established by the Bonn Agreement in 2002 that sought to move Afghanistan closer to democratic rule. In 2003 the most important political event was the constitutional loya jirga scheduled for December 2003. In preparation for the assembly, President Karzai created a Constitutional Commission, which created a draft document based on the 1964 Afghan Constitution. When the assembly met on 14 December 2003, it brought together delegates from the country's diverse tribes and ethnicities, including 89 women, who gathered to approve a new constitution.[162]

Tensions flared over the strength of the presidency in the new system to be established by the constitution. But the disconnect was ultimately ratified by consensus rather than by individual ballot. The charter established a two-chamber parliament and an elected president with two vice presidents. The constitution also included provisions that recognized women as equal citizens, protected the rights of Uzbeks and Turkmen to use their native languages in their regions, and designated former King Zahir Shah as the ceremonial Father of the Nation.[163] The new political process in Afghanistan had led to the peaceful creation of a new form of representative government. Neither regional leaders nor armed insurgents had been able to derail that forward momentum.

✦　✦　✦

The successful loya jirga was perhaps the most obvious sign of progress during the year that followed the XVIII Airborne Corps departure from Afghanistan. But the Coalition had also significantly altered the way it approached the campaign. This period saw numerous transitions in command: the arrival of 10th Mountain Division to take command of CJTF-180, the deployment of TF *Warrior* as the Coalition's main tactical force, and, most importantly, the creation of a new strategic-level headquarters in Afghanistan that introduced a new approach. CFC-A's counterinsurgency campaign focused on winning the support of the Afghan people to ensure that much of the progress made since 2001 was not undone by a growing enemy threat.

There were other signs of progress in this period. OMC-A continued to build the ANA and by spring 2004 had trained approximately 10,000 Afghan soldiers. Moreover, all units that composed the Afghan Central Corps, including combat support and combat service support, had completed basic training and were preparing for their mission to secure the national elections set for later in 2004. At the same time, the acceleration of the training program and the overall expansion of the ANA building effort placed great stress on OMC-A, CJTF *Phoenix*, and the Afghan MOD. CFC-A and CJTF-180 also saw the number of PRTs increase to 12 teams, many of which were now located in regions most threatened by the insurgency.

Despite these successes, Taliban and al-Qaeda forces continued to oppose the Coalition and the ATA as the spring of 2004 ended. As the summer began, the number of attacks continued to rise and as they did, CFC-A had to oversee another round of command transitions and troop deployments. CJTF-76, a task force composed primarily of units from the 25th Infantry Division, replaced CJTF-180 and the new Soldiers from the Indiana Army National Guard arrived to serve in CJTF *Phoenix*. Lieutenant General Barno and his staff faced the significant challenge of preserving the momentum they had created in their campaign to win the population's support for the Coalition and the ATA and thereby prevent the insurgent enemy from gaining further ground.

Notes

1. "Secretary Rumsfeld Joint Media Availability with President Karzai," *Department of Defense News Transcript*, 1 May 2003. http://www.defenselink.mil/transcripts/transcript.aspx?transcriptid=2562 (accessed 25 July 2007).

2. Lieutenant General (Retired) John R. Vines, interview by Contemporary Operations Study Team, Combat Studies Institute, Fort Leavenworth, KS, 27 June 2007, 19.

3. Vines, interview, 27 June 2007, 19.

4. Vines, interview, 27 June 2007, 19.

5. Lieutenant General (Retired) David W. Barno, interview by Contemporary Operations Study Team, Combat Studies Institute, Fort Leavenworth, KS, 29 January 2009, 2–3.

6. Colonel David W. Lamm, e-mail to Dr. Donald P. Wright, Combat Studies Institute, 28 September 2009. Colonel Lamm served as the CFC-A Chief of Staff between 2003 and 2005.

7. Robert Burns, "Mullen: Afghanistan Isn't Top Priority," *USA Today,* 11 December 2007. http://www.usatoday.com/news/washington/2007-12-11-3963072919_x.htm (accessed 6 November 2009).

8. Vines, interview, 27 June 2007, 19.

9. Seth G. Jones et al., *Establishing Law and Order After Conflict* (Santa Monica, CA: RAND Corporation, 2005), 91.

10. Jean-Marie Guehenno, "Briefings to the UN Security Council on the Situation in Afghanistan," *Open Meeting of the Security Council Afghanistan*, 17 June 2003. http://www.unama-afg.org/docs/_UN-Docs/_sc/_briefings/03jun17.htm (accessed 26 July 2007); Rory McCarthy, "22 Die as Taliban Attack Police Station," *The Guardian*, 18 August 2003, 11; Liz Sly, "Taliban Suspected in Attacks on Afghans Guarding Highway Work," *Knight Ridder Tribune News Service*, 1 September 2003, 1. http://www.libraryo.com/article.aspx?num=107133024 (accessed 24 September 2007).

11. "NGO Insecurity in Afghanistan," *Afghanistan NGO Safety Office (ANSO) and CARE,* May 2005. http://www.care.org/newsroom/specialreports/afghanistan/20050505_ansocare.pdf (accessed 16 August 2007).

12. Jones et al., *Establishing Law and Order,* 90.

13. Colonel Walter M. Herd, Combined Joint Special Operations Task Force, *Unconventional Warriors: Separate Insurgents from the Populace: Special Operations in Afghanistan from September 2003 to June 2004*, June 2004, slide 11.

14. Captain Bradley J. Armstrong, USAF, "Rebuilding Afghanistan: Counterinsurgency and Reconstruction in Operation ENDURING FREEDOM," Master's Thesis, Naval Postgraduate School, December 2003, 111.

15. Ahmed Rashid, *Descent into Chaos: The United States and the Failure of Nation Building in Pakistan, Afghanistan, and Central Asia* (New York, NY: Viking Press, 2008), 247.

16. Lieutenant Colonel (Retired) Lester W. Grau, "Something Old, Something New: Guerrillas, Terrorists, and Intelligence Analysis," *Military Review* (July–August 2004): 42.

17. Rashid, *Descent into Chaos*, 242.

18. Rashid, *Descent into Chaos*, 221.

19. Ahmed Rashid, "Taliban Mounted Militia Prepares for Border Strike," *The Daily Telegraph,* 8 August 2003. http://www.telegraph.co.uk/news/main.jhtml?xml=/news/2003/10/08/wafg08.xml (accessed 26 July 2007).

20. Rashid, *Descent into Chaos*, 223.

21. Rashid, *Descent into Chaos*, 247.

22. Ilana Ozernoy, "The Return of the Taliban," *U.S. News & World Report* (29 September 2003): 16.

23. Minister Ali Jalali, interview by Contemporary Operations Study Team, Combat Studies Institute, Washington, DC, 1 June 2007, 4.

24. George W. Bush, "The President's News Conference with President Pervez Musharraf of Pakistan at Camp David, Maryland," 24 June 2003. http://www.presidency.ucsb.edu/ws/index. php?pid=63119 (accessed 3 February 2009).

25. Rashid, "Taliban Mounted Militia Prepares for Border Strike."

26. Joint Publication (JP) 1-02, *DOD Dictionary of Military and Associated Terms* (Washington, DC, 2001), 265.

27. Lieutenant Colonel Michael F. Morris, USMC, "Al Qaeda as Insurgency," *Joint Force Quarterly* (October 2005): 39–42.

28. Bard O'Neill, *Insurgency & Terrorism: Inside Modern Revolutionary Warfare* (Dulles, VA: Brassey's Inc., 1990), 13.

29. Morris, "Al Qaeda as Insurgency," 39–42.

30. Morris, "Al Qaeda as Insurgency," 39–42.

31. Captain Bakhtiyorjon U. Hammidov, Uzbekistan Armed Forces, "The Fall of the Taliban Regime and Its Recovery as an Insurgent Movement in Afghanistan," Monograph, Fort Leavenworth, KS, 2004, 12.

32. Lieutenant General David W. Barno, interview by Center for Military History, 3 May 2006, 4.

33. Colonel Tucker B. Mansager, "Interagency Lessons Learned in Afghanistan," *Joint Force Quarterly*, First Quarter 2006, 82.

34. Mansager, "Interagency Lessons Learned in Afghanistan," 82.

35. Mansager, "Interagency Lessons Learned in Afghanistan," 82.

36. Afghanistan Experience Project Interview #5, interview by United States Institute for Peace, 13 April 2005.

37. Zalmay Khalilzad, "How to Nation-build: Ten Lessons from Afghanistan," *The National Interest* (Summer 2005): 26.

38. Barno, interview, 29 January 2009, 4.

39. Barno, interview, 29 January 2009, 4.

40. Lieutenant General David W. Barno, interview by Center for Military History, 21 November 2006, 10.

41. Barno, interview, 21 November 2006, 4.

42. Barno, interview, 29 January 2009, 8.

43. Colonel David Lamm, USA, "Success in Afghanistan means Fighting Several Wars at Once," *Armed Forces Journal,* November 2005. http://www.armedforcesjournal.com/2005/11/1174189 (accessed 11 September 2007).

44. Barno, interview, 29 January 2009, 4.

45. Barno, interview, 29 January 2009, 4.

46. Lieutenant General David W. Barno, interview by Center for Military History, 14 March 2007, 51.

47. Lieutenant General David W. Barno, "Fighting 'the Other War': Counterinsurgency Strategy in Afghanistan, 2003–2005," *Military Review* (September–October 2007): 35.

48. Barno, "Fighting 'the Other War,'" 41.

49. Barno, interview, 3 May 2006, 34.

50. Colonel Walter Herd, interview by Contemporary Operations Study Team, Combat Studies Institute, Fort Leavenworth, KS, 22 June 2007, 2.

51. Lieutenant Colonel Paul Wille, interview by Contemporary Operations Study Team, Combat Studies Institute, Fort Leavenworth, KS, 14 December 2006, 8.

52. Ann Scott Tyson, "Going in Small in Afghanistan," *Christian Science Monitor,* 14 January 2004, 1. http://www.csmonitor.com/2004/0114/p01s04-wosc.html (accessed 24 September 2007).

53. Wille, interview, 14 December 2006, 9–10.

54. Wille, interview, 14 December 2006, 9–10; Center for Army Lessons Learned (CALL), *Operation Enduring Freedom Initial Impressions Report,* December 2003, iii.

55. CALL, *OEF Initial Impressions Report*, December 2003, 4; Colonel Joseph Dichairo, interview by Contemporary Operations Study Team, Combat Studies Institute, Fort Leavenworth, KS, 27 August 2007, 4.

56. CALL, *OEF Initial Impressions Report*, December 2003, 18.

57. Wille, interview, 14 December 2006, 11.

58. Association of Graduates USMA, Ninger Award, http://www.aogusma.org/aog/awards/Nininger/06Gray_Matter_Article.htm (accessed 11 September 2007); Wille, interview, 14 December 2006.

59. Tim McGirk, "Battle in the Evilist Place," *Time Online*, 3 November 2003. http://www.time.com/time/magazine/article/0,9171,1006032-1,00.html (accessed 5 June 2007).

60. Sergeant Greg Heath, 4th Public Affairs Detachment, "2-87 Catamounts Keep Rolling in Afghanistan," *Fort Drum Blizzard Online*, 8 January 2004. http://www.drum.army.mil/sites/postnews/blizzard/blizzard_archives/hnews.asp?id=1&issuedate=1-8-2004 (accessed 11 September 2007).

61. Heath, "2-87 Catamounts Keep Rolling in Afghanistan."

62. Thomas Gimble, DOD Acting Inspector General, et al., "Special Defense Department Briefing—Inspector General Thomas Gimble Reports on the Death of Corporal Patrick Tillman in Afghanistan from the Pentagon Briefing Room, Arlington, Virginia," *News Transcript*, 26 March 2007. http://www.defenselink.mil/transcripts/transcript.aspx?transcriptid=3917 (accessed 11 September 2007).

63. Gerry J. Gilmore, "General Censured for Tillman Investigation Mistakes," *DefenseLink,* 31 July 2007. http://www.defenselink.mil/news/newsarticle.aspx?id=46888 (accessed 13 February 2009).

64. Gilmore, "General Censured for Tillman Investigation Mistakes."

65. 130th Military History Detachment Command Report, *Operation Enduring Freedom Rotation IV, July 2003–March 2004*, no date/place given, 4.

66. Dichairo, interview, 27 August 2007, 9.

67. 130th Military History Detachment, *Operation Enduring Freedom Rotation IV*, 4.

68. Colonel Rod Davis, USA, Director, Public Affairs, Coalition JTF 180, "Division Soldiers Help Kill Enemy Fighters in Operation Mountain Viper." http://www.drum.army.mil/sites/postnews/blizzard/blizzard_archives/hnews.asp?id=1&issuedate=9-11-2003 (accessed 8 August 2007).

69. The estimates of enemy casualties varied. In its report on TF *Warrior*'s operations, the US Army 130th Military History Detachment suggested that enemy radio intercepts during MOUNTAIN VIPER estimated between 150 and 200 killed. See 130th Military History Detachment, *Operation Enduring Freedom Rotation IV*, 4.

70. Terry Boyd, "Troops in Afghanistan Preparing Spring Offensive in Pursuit of Insurgents," *Stars and Stripes European Edition*, 10 March 2004. http://www.stripes.com/article.asp?section=104&article=20924 (accessed 17 February 2009).

71. Dichairo, interview, 27 August 2007, 11.

72. Barno, interview, 3 May 2006, 8.

73. Barno, interview, 29 January 2009, 8.

74. Colonel David Paschal, interview by Operational Leadership Experience, Combat Studies Institute, Fort Leavenworth, KS, 18 July 2006, 4.

75. Barno, interview, 21 November 2006, 42.

76. Barno, interview, 3 May 2006, 24.

77. Sima Alinejad, "Provisional Reconstruction Teams (PRT)," UNHCR, 1 April 2004. http://www.aims.org.af/services/sectoral/emergency_assistance/refugee/unhcr_return_issues/issue_54.pdf (accessed 10 September 2007).

78.   Lieutenant Colonel Steven Ford, interview by Contemporary Operations Study Team, Combat Studies Institute, Fort Leavenworth, KS, 14 September 2007, 7; Afghanistan Experience Project Interview #3, interview by United States Institute for Peace, 19 October 2004, 9.

79.   Lieutenant Colonel Steven Ford, Ghazni PRT VIP Briefing, *Provisional Reconstruction Team: Ghazni, Afghanistan,* 22 May 2004, slides 4–5; 18th Airborne Corps, CJCMOTF Brief, *101 Brief as of 31 March 2003,* slide 23.

80.   18th Airborne Corps, CJCMOTF Brief, slide 24.

81.   Colonel Richard Conte, *Working with the US Army Corps of Engineers in Afghanistan* Brief, 27 July 2004, slide 17.

82.   Afghanistan Experience Project Interview #2, interview by United States Institute for Peace, 10 December 2004, 7.

83.   Afghanistan Experience Project Interview #5, interview, 13 April 2005, 8.

84.   "Afghanistan: Interview with US-Led Coalition Civil Military Coordination Center," 8 January 2004. http:www.irinnews.org/report.asp?ReportID=22699 (accessed 1 August 2007).

85.   "Afghanistan: Interview with US-Led Coalition Civil Military Coordination Center."

86.   Lieutenant Colonel John Lineweaver, interview by Contemporary Operations Study Team, Combat Studies Institute, Fort Leavenworth, KS, 24 August 2007, 5.

87.   Lineweaver, interview, 24 August 2007, 5.

88.   Lineweaver, interview, 24 August 2007, 8.

89.   Lineweaver, interview, 24 August 2007, 8.

90.   "Afghanistan: Paper On UK PRT Experience," *Afghanistan Group, FCO, 20 January 2005.* http://www.fco.gov.uk/Files/kfile/UK%20paper%20on%20its%20PRT%20experience.pdf (accessed 9 August 2007); Michael J. McNerney, "Stabilization and Reconstruction in Afghanistan: Are PRTs a Model or a Muddle?" *Parameters* (Winter 2005–06): 38–39.

91.   US Government Accountability Office, GAO-04-403, *Afghanistan Reconstruction: Deteriorating Security and Limited Resources Have Impeded Progress; Improvements in U.S. Strategy Needed,* June 2004, 11.

92.   GAO-04-403, 51.

93.   Afghanistan Experience Project Interview #5, 13 April 2005, 19.

94.   Barno, interview, 21 November 2006, 48.

95.   Colonel David Lamm, interview by Contemporary Operations Study Team, Combat Studies Institute, Fort Leavenworth, KS, 20 September 2007, 4; Barno, interview, 21 November 2006, 48.

96.   Christopher Griffin, "A Working Plan: Hope Isn't the Only Strategy for Afghanistan," *Armed Forces Journal* (April 2007). http://www.armedforcesjournal.com/2007/04/2587549 (accessed 16 June 2007).

97.   Afghanistan Experience Project Interview #3, 19 October 2004, 16.

98.   Ford, *Ghazni* PRT VIP Briefing, *Provisional Reconstruction Team: Ghazni, Afghanistan,* 22 May 2004, slide 9.

99.   Cheryl Bernard et al., *Women and Nation-Building* (Santa Monica, CA: RAND Corporation, 2009), 29.

100. US Government Accountability Office, GAO-05-742, *Afghanistan Reconstruction: Despite Some Progress, Deteriorating Security and Other Obstacles Continue to Threaten Achievement of US Goals,* July 2005, 13.

101. GAO-05-742, 14.

102. Brigadier General William Garrett, written interview by Contemporary Operations Study Team, Combat Studies Institute, Fort Leavenworth, KS, 5 June 2007, 14.

103. Colonel Rodney Edge, interview by Contemporary Operations Study Team, Combat Studies Institute, Fort Leavenworth, KS, 5 June 2007, 13.

104. Wille, interview, 14 December 2006, 14.

105. Paschal, interview, 18 July 2006, 6.

106. Paschal, interview, 18 July 2006, 6.

107. Garrett, interview, 5 June 2007, 15.

108. Lieutenant Colonel Bentley Nettles, interview by Operational Leadership Experience, Combat Studies Institute, Fort Leavenworth, KS, 20 September 2006.

109. Paschal, interview, 7 March 2007, 17.

110. Wille, interview, 14 December 2006, 12.

111. Ann Scott Tyson, "Uphill Pursuit for Afghan Warlord," *Christian Science Monitor,* 22 December 2003. http://www.csmonitor.com/2003/1222/p06s01-wosc.html (accessed 10 September 2007).

112. Paschal, interview, 18 July 2006, 18.

113. Nettles, interview, 20 September 2006, 6.

114. OMC-A, *ANA Presentation to MG Ostenberg* Brief, 27 August 2003, slide 48.

115. Major General Craig Weston, *OMC-A Orientation*, 26 June 2004, slide 5.

116. UN Assistance Mission in Afghanistan, "Decree of the President of the Islamic Transitional State of Afghanistan on the Afghan National Army," 1 December 2002. http://www.unama-afg.org/docs/_nonUN%20Docs/_Internation-Conferences&Forums/Bonn-Talks/decree%20on%20army.pdf (accessed 18 August 2007).

117. Master Sergeant D. Keith Johnson, "Afghan National Army Volunteer Center Opens," 22 December 2004. http://www.defendamerica.mil/articles/Dec2004/a122204dw1.html (accessed on 20 August 2007).

118. Colonel David Francavilla, interview by Contemporary Operations Study Team, Combat Studies Institute, Fort Leavenworth, KS, 26 April 2007, 4.

119. Francavilla, interview, 26 April 2007, 5.

120. Lieutenant General Karl Eikenberry, interview by Contemporary Operations Study Team, Combat Studies Institute, Fort Leavenworth, KS, 27 November 2006, 16.

121. UN, "Decree of the President of the Islamic Transitional State of Afghanistan."

122. Ann Scott Tyson, "Desertions Deplete Afghan Army," *Christian Science Monitor Online*, 17 December 2003. http://www.csmonitor.com/2003/1217/p06s01-wosc.html (accessed 20 August 2007).

123. Colonel Richard Gallant, interview by Contemporary Operations Study Team, Combat Studies Institute, Fort Leavenworth, KS, 29 June 2007, 4.

124. Captain Michael Chagnon, Canadian Army, "Canadian Embedded Training Teams," *The Bulletin*, December 2004, 12. http://armyapp.dnd.ca/ALLC/Downloads/bulletin/Vol_10/Bulletin_Vol10No8Eng.pdf (accessed 10 August 2007); Brigadier General Joseph Prasek, interview by Contemporary Operations Study Team, Combat Studies Institute, Fort Leavenworth, KS, 7 September 2007, 16.

125. Chagnon, "Canadian Embedded Training Teams," 12.

126. Major General (Retired) Craig Weston, interview by Contemporary Operations Study Team, Combat Studies Institute, Fort Leavenworth, KS, 14 December 2006, 25.

127. Colonel Timothy Reese, *Afghan National Army—Karzai*, 6 January 2006, slide 55.

128. Major General Craig Weston, *Creating the Afghan Defense Sector*, July 2004, slide 25.

129. Eikenberry, interview, 27 November 2006, 5.

130. Gallant, interview, 29 June 2007, 8.

131. Prasek, interview, 7 September 2007, 11.

132. Prasek, interview, 7 September 2007, 8.

133. Chagnon, "Canadian Embedded Training Teams," 7.

134. Colonel Mark Milley, interview by Contemporary Operations Study Team, Combat Studies Institute, Fort Leavenworth, KS, 6 June 2007, 10.

135. Brigadier General Joseph Prasek, "CJTF *Phoenix* Training Guidance 4th Quarter, FY 03 (Draft)," Memorandum for Record, 19 June 2003.

136. Prasek, "CJTF *Phoenix* Training Guidance."

137. Brigadier General Thomas Mancino, interview by Contemporary Operations Study Team, Combat Studies Institute, Fort Leavenworth, KS, 15 September 2007, 8.

138. Colonel Timothy Reese, *Task Force Phoenix TRADOC Recon Overview* Brief, 8 April 2003, slide 16.

139. Prasek, "CJTF *Phoenix* Training Guidance."

140. Captain Charles Di Leonardo, USA, "Training the Afghan National Army," *Infantry* (March/April 2005): 31.

141. Di Leonardo, "Training the Afghan National Army," 38.

142. Gallant, interview, 29 June 2007, 6.

143. Prasek, "CJTF *Phoenix* Training Guidance."

144. Mancino, interview, 15 September 2007, 15.

145. Di Leonardo, "Training the Afghan National Army," 31–39.

146. Prasek, interview, 7 September 2007, 18.

147. Di Leonardo, "Training the Afghan National Army," 33.

148. Mancino, interview, 15 September 2007, 24.

149. US Government Accountability Office, GAO-05-575, *Afghanistan Security: Efforts to Establish Army and Police Have Made Progress, but Future Plans Need to be Better Defined*, June 2005, 16.

150. Reese, *Afghan National Army—Karzai*, slide 56.

151. GAO-05-575, 16.

152. Amy Clement, "TAC Helps Army Rebuild Afghan Forces, January 2003. http://www.hq.usace.army.mil/cepa/pubs/jan03/story17.htm (accessed 11 August 2007).

153. Colonel Richard Conte, interview by Contemporary Operations Study Team, Combat Studies Institute, Fort Leavenworth, KS, 6 July 2007, 6.

154. Conte, interview, 6 July 2007, 6.

155. Conte, interview, 6 July 2007, 12.

156. "Afghanistan Update," June 2004. http://www.defendamerica.mil/afghanistan/update/jun2004/ au062104.html (accessed 12 September 2007).

157. US Department of State, "New Afghan Initiatives Promote Growth, Education, Democracy," 15 June 2004. http://usinfo.state.gov/sa/Archive/2004/Jun/16-365926.html (accessed 12 September 2007).

158. Prasek, interview, 7 September 2007, 6.

159. UN High Commission for Refugees (UNHCR), *Chronology of Events in Afghanistan, April 2004*. www.unhcr.org/refworld/pdfid/415c64434.pdf (accessed 17 February 2009).

160. GAO-04-403, 4.

161. Major General Craig Weston, *Key to ANA Acceleration Briefings* memorandum, undated, 1.

162. Major Guy Turpin, "Preparing for the Constitutional Loya Jirga," 17 November 2006. http://www.nato.int/ISAF/Update/varia/getready.htm (accessed 11 September 2007).

163. Dr. Kenneth Katzman, "CRS Report for Congress," *CRS Web Afghanistan: Post-War Governance, Security, and U.S. Policy*, 28 December 2004, 17.

Chapter 10

The Path toward Stability: May 2004 to September 2005

In the spring of 2004, the future of Afghanistan appeared less than secure. A sense of guarded optimism did exist, reflecting the fact that President Hamid Karzai and the Afghan Transitional Authority (ATA) had made political progress with the constitutional loya jirga and in establishing the Central Corps of the Afghan National Army (ANA). However, the limited ability of Coalition forces to further the reach of the Afghan Government's authority tempered these successes. This problem was especially acute in the south and east where the insurgency mounted by Taliban and al-Qaeda forces showed no sign of dissipating. Not only were insurgent attacks continuing to increase, the enemy appeared better organized, better funded, and intent on disrupting the Afghan political process. Moreover, enemy attacks became more tactically sophisticated, involving improvised explosive devices (IEDs), suicide bombers, kidnappings, and targeted assaults on reconstruction projects.

This chapter describes how Coalition forces responded to the problems and opportunities in Afghanistan in the 16 months between the arrival of Combined Joint Task Force-76 (CJTF-76) in April 2004 and the parliamentary elections in September 2005. In this period, the Coalition military leadership in Afghanistan placed their confidence in the counterinsurgency (COIN) effort begun by Combined Forces Command–Afghanistan (CFC-A) in late 2003. In the initiation of that approach, Lieutenant General David W. Barno, the commanding general of CFC-A, had introduced a type of COIN campaign that focused on the population and sought to use popular support to neutralize the insurgent groups generating the violence.

With the presidential election scheduled for October 2004 and parliamentary elections set for the summer of 2005, Barno was acutely aware of the need to foster enough stability across the country to allow these critical political events to take place. Unlike the emergency loya jirga and the constitutional loya jirga, both of which had convened in Kabul in a tightly secured site, the elections of 2004 and 2005 would be held at polling stations nationwide and required months of voter registration and preparatory work. Thus, enemy forces intent on derailing the political process would have a much larger set of targets in easier reach of their sanctuaries in the south and east. Over the course of 2004, CFC-A made key changes in force size and command structure to place the COIN effort on a firmer foundation and generate a higher level of security.

Much of the burden for the COIN campaign fell to CJTF-76, the Coalition's new operational- and tactical-level military headquarters that replaced CJTF-180. The headquarters of the US Army's 25th Infantry Division (ID) served as the core headquarters of CJTF-76 until the spring of 2005 when the US Army Southern European Task Force (SETAF) would arrive to take command. In May 2004, CJTF-76's maneuver forces took over the areas of operations (AOs) established by CJTF-180 and began to work closely with the populations in those AOs by mounting a mix of security and stability operations.[*]

---

[*]The 1st Battalion, 501st Parachute Infantry Regiment (1-501 PIR), which had joined TF *Warrior* in November 2003, remained in its AO as part of CJTF-76 until August 2004 when it returned to its home station in Alaska.

While transitions in command are usually disruptive to ongoing military operations, the transfer of authority to CJTF-76 in spring 2004 provided opportunities to improve the Coalition's fledgling COIN campaign. When CFC-A introduced its new approach in fall 2003, its subordinate operational- and tactical-level commands—CJTF-180 and Task Force (TF) *Warrior,* respectively—had not trained or otherwise prepared for COIN operations. While the Soldiers in these units had adapted in the waning months of their deployments, they had only 5 months to move into their newly designated AOs and become familiar with the local population before they departed Afghanistan.

The Soldiers of CJTF-76, on the other hand, understood from the beginning of their deployment that their mission was to conduct COIN operations to win the support of the Afghan people. They trained for that mission and after arriving, moved directly into their AOs prepared to work closely with the Afghan communities. Further, CJTF-76 had deployed with more maneuver units than CJTF-180 had commanded in early 2004, and thus was able to commit more manpower to its AOs. By the summer of 2004, Barno further reinforced the CJTF-76 effort by giving regional commanders authority over the Provincial Reconstruction Teams (PRTs) in order to make the overall reconstruction effort more responsive to local Afghan needs. CJTF-76 also benefited from the unconventional warfare (UW) campaign launched by the Combined Joint Special Operations Task Force–Afghanistan (CJSOTF-A) in spring 2004. That effort, in which the CJTF-76 commander and staff were closely involved, focused on fostering security for the presidential elections and on interdicting enemy forces and materiel moving into Afghanistan from Pakistan.

Figure 47. Major General Karl W. Eikenberry who would take command of CFC-A in May 2005.

CFC-A complemented CJTF-76's actions by fostering the development of the Afghan Government. Barno and his staff worked closely with the US Embassy, Afghan officials in Kabul, and Afghanistan's powerful regional leaders to coordinate policies that would expand the control and legitimacy of the central government. The Office of Military Cooperation–Afghanistan (OMC-A) and CJTF *Phoenix* assisted in this effort through their programs to increase the size and capabilities of the ANA. In May 2005 Lieutenant General Karl W. Eikenberry, former commander of OMC-A, took command of CFC-A from Lieutenant General Barno. Eikenberry pledged to maintain the COIN approach in Afghanistan and in July 2005, reinforced the Coalition's overall role by directing OMC-A to assist German forces in the fielding of Afghan National Police (ANP) forces. This expansion in mission led CFC-A to change the name of OMC-A to the Office of Security Cooperation–Afghanistan (OSC-A). While this broadening of duties required more resources, the new CFC-A commander and staff viewed Afghan police forces as critical to the security of local communities across the country.

The Coalition Posture in Spring 2004

In May 2004 Coalition forces in Afghanistan numbered approximately 18,000 Soldiers under the command of CFC-A. On 15 April the headquarters of the US Army 25th ID arrived in Afghanistan and took command of CJTF-180 from the 10th Mountain Division. Lieutenant General Barno then decided to rename the CJTF because the "180" designation had traditionally been given to joint task forces (JTFs) led by the US Army XVIII Airborne Corps. Barno chose CJTF-76 as the new name to evoke America's history and the democratic spirit of 1776.[1] The CFC-A commander was hoping that this new designation would highlight the change in command at the operational level at a time when Afghanistan appeared to be moving closer to democracy.

Major General Eric T. Olson, the commanding general of the 25th ID, became the commander of CJTF-76. In the spring of 2004, nearly 13,000 US Army, Navy, Air Force, and Marine Corps personnel as well as forces from 18 Coalition nations made up this force. In the AOs of the southern and southeastern provinces, Olson deployed 11 battalion-size units, 6 of which were US Army light infantry battalions. By comparison, in early 2004 CJTF-180 had roughly half that number of units in the AOs. At the same time, the number of US Soldiers in Afghanistan increased by one-third between the early winter and mid-summer of 2004 to 15,000.[2] This was the high point in troop strength in Afghanistan since the beginning of OEF in 2001. US Army levels in Afghanistan would remain at this level, with minor fluctuations, for the remainder of 2004 and through 2005.

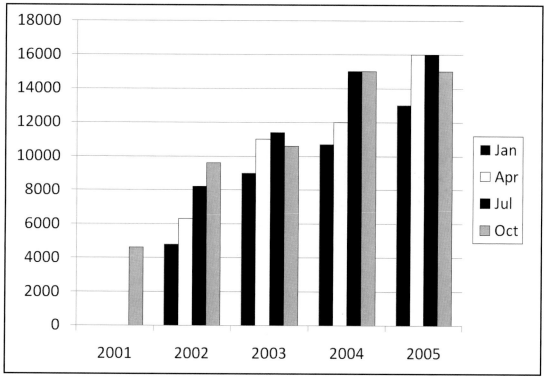

Figure 48. US Army troop levels in OEF, October 2001–September 2005.

Major General Olson organized CJTF-76 into six principal task forces. Combined Task Force (CTF) *Bronco*, commanded by Colonel Richard Pedersen and based on the 3d Brigade of the 25th ID, assumed responsibility for an AO that became known as Regional Command–South (RC-South). (See figure 54.) This large area included the provinces of Kandahar, Lashkar Gah, Zabol, Zaranj, and a part of Oruzgan. CTF *Bronco*'s

Figure 49. Major General Eric T. Olson, CJTF-76 Commander, talks with Afghan citizens during a patrol in the Cehar Cineh area of Afghanistan during Operation OUTLAW, 26 October 2004.

DOD Photo by SPC Jerry T. Combes

forces included four US Army light infantry battalions, one field artillery battalion, the French Task Group *Arés*, and a Romanian infantry regiment.[3] The 25th ID's Division Artillery reorganized as a maneuver force called CTF *Thunder* under the command of Colonel Gary H. Cheek. The new CTF included an Active Duty infantry battalion, an Army National Guard Infantry Battalion, a US Marine battalion, and Coalition and Afghan Army units. In July 2004 CTF *Thunder* took the reins of Regional Command–East (RC-East) made up of 16 provinces including the restive provinces of Paktika, Paktia, Khost, Ghazni, Nangarhar, and Laghman. In area, RC-East was roughly the size of the state of Iowa.

JTF *Wings*, led by Colonel B. Shannon Davis, provided aviation assets for all Coalition operations in Afghanistan. All of the US aviation assets in Afghanistan except those belonging to the US Air Force were controlled by JTF *Wings* and included US Army Blackhawk, Chinook, and Apache helicopters, plus Super Stallions and Cobras from the Marine Corps. JTF *Wings* was staffed by more than 2,500 pilots, crewmembers, and support personnel, and included Soldiers from the Alabama, Florida, Georgia, Hawaii, and Utah Army National Guard. The aviation JTF was the backbone of the Coalition supply chain and provided aeromedical evacuation and air traffic control services throughout the theater.

The 3d Squadron, 4th Cavalry Regiment (3-4 CAV) and Company B, 193d Aviation Regiment made up CTF *Saber* and operated in the vast provinces of western Afghanistan. In September 2004 CJTF-76 designated this area as Regional Command–West (RC-West) and created a new organization called CTF *Longhorn* based on 3-4 CAV. CTF *Coyote* oversaw engineering operations for CJTF-76 and was commanded by Colonel Nancy J. Wetherill, South Dakota Army National Guard. US Army Reserve and Army National Guard units from Alabama, Iowa, Louisiana, Minnesota, New York, and Wisconsin plus Coalition detachments from Australia, Korea, Poland, and Slovakia conducted a wide range of engineering missions as part of CTF *Coyote*. The 3d Special Forces Group (SFG) formed the core of CJSOTF-A. Four thousand soldiers from seven different countries made up the special operations TF, which was headquartered at Bagram Air Base.[4] Finally, on arriving in Afghanistan, the 25th

ID Support Command became the Joint Logistical Command and served all CJTFs from its headquarters at Bagram.

In addition to the six primary TFs organized under CJTF-76, several other US and Coalition units operated under Olson's authority during the spring of 2004. For example, the 22d Marine Expeditionary Unit, located at Bagram Air Base, was designated CTF *Stonewall* and conducted independent operations in northern Oruzgan province in RC-South. A Military Police TF (TF *Enforcer*) provided general support services to the regional commands and operated detainee holding facilities at Bagram and Kandahar.

The 45th Infantry Brigade of the Oklahoma Army National Guard, along with Army National Guard detachments from 20 additional states and contingents from 7 Coalition countries continued the CJTF *Phoenix* mission of training the ANA. In August, the 76th Infantry Brigade from the Indiana Army National Guard would take over from the Oklahoma Guard. The OMC-A, based in Kabul, was the parent organization for CJTF *Phoenix* and planned for six ANA battalions to be trained and ready by the summer of 2004 to assist in voter registration and presidential election security operations. Approximately 20,000 additional Afghans, graduates of Coalition-run Regional Law Enforcement Training Centers, were also expected to assist in election security as members of the ANP. The International Security Assistance Force (ISAF), under NATO authority since August 2003, provided security for the Kabul area and commanded the PRT in Konduz in northeast Afghanistan.

The US military was not the only US Government institution at work in Afghanistan. In the spring of 2004, Zalmay Khalilzad continued as the American ambassador in Kabul and additional representatives from the US Department of State (DOS) served with various PRTs. Other assistance came from the Afghan Reconstruction Group (ARG), an organization created in 2004 by the US National Security Council that featured professionals from the private sector, and the United Nations Assistance Mission in Afghanistan (UNAMA), which continued reconstruction activities and provided humanitarian assistance to the

Figure 50. Zalmay Khalilzad, US Ambassador to Afghanistan.

Afghan people.[5] The violent attacks against Western forces and interests continued, however, and led the nongovernment organization (NGO) *Medecins Sans Frontieres* (Doctors without Borders) to leave Afghanistan after five of its members were killed in Badghis province.[6]

The Maturing Threat

In the second half of 2004 and through 2005, the threat posed by the al-Qaeda organization, the Taliban, and the Hizb-i Islami Gulbuddin (HIG) appeared to be consolidating. In the second half of 2004 and much of 2005, enemy forces launched approximately 50 attacks per month against Coalition forces, Afghan security forces, and government infrastructure.[7] During this period, the Afghan insurgents began relying more heavily on IEDs. Enemy forces were also able and willing to mass combat power to attack the Coalition in a more direct manner. One of the most dramatic examples of this capacity occurred in the first week of June 2004 in the Deh Chopan district of Zabol province, when Afghan Army units, Coalition Special Operations Forces (SOF), and US Marines from CTF *Stonewall* conducted several battles against hundreds of well-organized Taliban fighters.[8]

A CTF *Bronco* assessment of the enemy in May 2004 described enemy activities as being a "Level One Insurgency." That term described an insurgent force that used small-scale assaults, raids, and ambushes on predominantly soft targets to harass security forces, weaken the government's resolve to fight, and erode popular support for the government.[9] While Taliban forces certainly mounted larger operations such as the actions in Deh Chopan in summer 2004, they generally avoided becoming embroiled in pitched battles with the Coalition forces that usually had an advantage in firepower and technology. Instead, the enemy relied primarily on smaller engagements to destabilize the security situation and create doubts within the population about the capacity and will of the Coalition and Afghan Government forces to create lasting improvements. For the accumulated effects of smaller attacks to be decisive, however, the Taliban and other enemy forces needed time.[10] Some Coalition military leaders believed that the Taliban's willingness to be patient was their greatest strength. Colonel Walter Herd, the commander of CJSOTF-A in 2003 and 2004, emphasized the asymmetry between the enemy in Afghanistan and the Coalition, quoting an oft-heard aphorism, "(the Taliban's) strength was their ability to endure and (the Coalition's) weakness was our willingness to endure. . . . The Americans have all the watches," Herd said, "but the Afghans have all the time."[11] In other words, Coalition forces were on a schedule in Afghanistan while the enemy was not.

Of course, the situation in each province was unique. HIG forces operated primarily in the northeast and mounted small-scale attacks. In the south and southeast, Coalition analyses offered a more complex picture. In the May 2004 assessment of the enemy, the staff of CTF *Bronco* described a mix of forces and capabilities in the provinces of RC-South. Al-Qaeda forces appeared to be lodged primarily in Paktia and Paktika provinces, but the Taliban was present as well. In Paktia province, for example, the CJTF-76 assessment described small Taliban forces that tended to use only indirect fire and IEDs against Coalition and Afghan forces.[12] Both Paktika and Zabol provinces, on the other hand, were the headquarters for key Taliban commanders and al-Qaeda leadership. Paktika was the AO for a Taliban commander, known to the Coalition as "Rocket Man," who had become infamous for his attacks against the forward operating bases (FOBs) at Shkin and Orgun-e using 107-mm rockets.[13] The Deh Chopan area in Zabol province had become both a training site and a staging area for Taliban operations elsewhere.

Most disconcerting was the situation in Helmand and Oruzgan provinces and the southern half of Kandahar province. The assessment stated that in 2004, the Taliban moved freely through the entire region, using vehicles to position troops and supplies.[14] Coalition intelligence indicated that the Taliban had established command centers north of Deh Rawod in Oruzgan and in the Baghran Valley in Helmand province. Mullah Omar and other senior enemy leaders were thought to use the Baghran Valley to make plans and issue orders. Enemy forces in this region became quite active in the summer, according to CJTF-76 reports, and normally moved south into friendly territory in Pakistan for the winter months.

CJTF-76 Adapts to COIN

In the 6 months before they deployed to Afghanistan, the Soldiers of CJTF-76 began to think about and train for the COIN effort in Afghanistan. This required a mental shift in the type of approach the command and staff of the TF intended to take. Brigadier General Bernard S. Champoux, the assistant division commander of the US Army 25th ID and the deputy commanding general of CJTF-76, recalled that this transition was not easy. In preparing for deployment, the senior staff viewed the mission as seeking battle with insurgent forces. Champoux stated, "I think we thought we were going to go kill/capture and defeat the Taliban and al-Qaeda and [Gulbuddin] Hikmetyar."[15] Gradually, the leadership of CJTF-76 began to see their role as separating the insurgents from the population. Champoux gave great credit to Lieutenant General Barno for assisting in this transition by explaining his vision for the campaign and the role of Coalition maneuver forces in winning over the population and preparing for the elections of 2004.[16]

This understanding flowed downward to the Soldiers in a number of ways. In March 2004 Colonel Pedersen, the commander of 3d Brigade, 25th ID, issued guidance in the form of a directive entitled *How to Think OEF*. The document contained 55 key points about the situation in Afghanistan and how 3d Brigade's Soldiers should operate once they were on the ground. Early in his guidance, Pedersen explained that military actions did not have primacy, emphasizing instead that "OEF is an environment characterized by the pursuit of national Obj[ectives] in a political dimension."[17] He went further by adding that even military operations were often characterized by "indirect rather than direct application of force/power."[18] Pedersen stressed the importance of the population, asserting that "the attitude of the Afghan people is the [center of gravity] for OEF; we must seek not just to defeat the enemy, but to defeat the enemy's strategy; we must seek not just to defeat the insurgents, but to defeat the insurgency."[19]

Colonel Cheek, the commander of CTF *Thunder* that had authority for the 16 provinces of RC-East, approached COIN in a manner similar to Pedersen. Cheek recognized the need to attack those enemy groups that espoused a radical form of Islam and required violence in support of that ideology. Cheek defined success as contingent on his command's ability to gain the support of local Afghans, asserting, "To be victorious we must win [the people's] trust and confidence."[20] By extension, Cheek saw the Afghan Government as the center of gravity for the Coalition. If the actions of his TF ultimately did not foster that government's capacity and its legitimacy within the eyes of the population, CTF *Thunder*'s campaign could not be considered successful.[21]

As these ideas took root within the units of CJTF-76, senior leaders grappled with the larger problem of finding the means of achieving abstract objectives such as winning popular support. One of the first steps in this process was to gain an understanding of the population's attitude toward the Coalition, the Afghan Government, and the Taliban. When CTF *Bronco* conducted an assessment in the spring of 2004, it found that levels of support in RC-South for the Coalition and Afghan Government varied across the provinces. In Khost, Paktia, and Paktika, the outlook was promising. According to the assessment, local Afghan leaders had a favorable response to the presence of Coalition soldiers and the sense that security was improving.[22]

Figure 51. Colonel Gary H. Cheek, Commander of CTF *Thunder,* and Captain Tage Rainsford, Commander of C Company, 2d Battalion, 27th Infantry, listen to village elders on 20 December 2004 in Waza Khwa, Afghanistan.

Still, Afghans in these areas were anxious about the willingness of Coalition forces to make a long-term commitment to Afghanistan, a theme emphasized in Taliban information operations. The situation in Zabol and Helmand provinces and the southern half of Kandahar province was far more troubling. In Zabol, CJTF-76 recognized that the Taliban presence prevented local populations from working closely with the Coalition and Afghan Government. The assessment considered the populace of Helmand a "closed society" controlled by Muslim clerics and strongmen involved in poppy cultivation.[23] This population cared little about Coalition projects or the plans of the Afghan Government.

For Pedersen and his subordinate commanders, the proper approach at the tactical-level was a combination of operations—tailored to conditions in each AO—that would concurrently weaken the influence of the enemy and win the support of the population. The CTF *Bronco* commander and staff used this concept as a basis for their operation order (OPORD) called *Bronco Strike.* This document established the overall mission and purpose for CTF *Bronco* operations during the course of an entire year and emphasized that the safe and successful conduct of the presidential elections in October 2004 was a key objective. In a sense, *Bronco Strike* established the parameters of a 12-month campaign more than a discrete tactical-level operation. Further, the order mandated that subordinate units conduct a mix of security, civil-military, and information operations aimed at achieving stability in RC-South. To give his Soldiers a more specific idea of how he defined success, Pedersen's end state in the order consisted of four key conditions: Afghan population generally rejects the enemy; population

Photo by SSG Bradley Rhen, PA NCOIC, CTF *Thunder*

trusts the Coalition's ability and will to create stability and security; RC-South prepared for expansion of Coalition and Afghan security force operations; and, insurgency in RC-South defeated.[24]

To begin this complex mission, the units of CTF *Bronco* began taking over AOs from TF *Warrior* in the late spring of 2004. Following the guidelines set by Lieutenant General Barno, the presence of Coalition units in the provinces was a key factor in the COIN campaign. For CJTF-76, the bases occupied by CTF *Bronco* and CTF *Thunder* in the spring and summer of 2004 were the starting points for an effort that would gradually dominate entire provinces. Brigadier General Champoux, the deputy commanding general of CJTF-76, described this process using the ink spot (or oil stain) metaphor often employed in COIN theory. Champoux explained, "The idea is, you have these ink spots, lily pads, that you're operating from, and that they expand; and eventually, over time, these ink spots would all connect."[25] No one within the Coalition command hoped to create security for the entire Afghan population. Instead, Major General Olson, the CJTF-76 commanding general, described his approach as establishing the right conditions with reconstruction and governance operations so that enemy forces would either lose their base of support within the population or lay down their arms to take advantage of the progress.[26] Colonel Pedersen became convinced that the ink spot concept was the correct concept given the resources and capabilities he had. Pedersen asserted, "In hindsight, the ink spot theory works for reconstruction where you plant permanent presence. If you want to sit here in these big bases and go out and whack bad guys and come back, the people don't trust you . . . if you go out and live with them, they start to trust you."[27]

Under the supervision of CJTF-76, bases spread across RC-East and RC-South. CTF *Thunder* would establish its headquarters at FOB Salerno in RC-East and push its forces out into previously established FOBs and newer bases. CTF *Bronco* did likewise. Headquartered at Kandahar Airfield, the TF began in spring 2004 with less than a dozen bases. The 1st Battalion, 501st Parachute Infantry Regiment (1-501 PIR) was headquartered at FOB Salerno; the 2d Battalion, 27th Infantry Regiment (2-27 IN) at FOB Shkin. Later in 2004, the provinces in which these bases were located, Khost and Paktika respectively, were transferred to RC-East. The French Task Group *Arés* operated out of the base at Spin Boldak. The 3d Battalion, 7th Field Artillery (3-7 FA) mounted both artillery and stability operations from Kandahar Airfield. Elements of these units were also located at FOB Qalat and FOB Spin Boldak.[28] The 2d Battalion, 5th Infantry Regiment (2-5 IN) deployed first to FOB Ghazni where it operated under the command of the US 6th Marine Regiment until the summer when it moved back into RC-South to a base at Tarin Kowt in Oruzgan province. By spring 2005 CTF *Bronco* operated from approximately 12 bases including PRT locations and the Kandahar headquarters.[29]

From these bases, the Soldiers of CJTF-76 conducted the aforementioned combination of security and stability operations. The security operations tended to be tied to the establishment of new bases or in reaction to specific intelligence about Taliban forces or individuals that played a significant role in the insurgency. Lieutenant Colonel Terry L. Sellers, commander of 2-5 IN in 2004, recalled that he conducted over 35 operations in restive Oruzgan province focused on fostering greater security.[30] Most of these missions involved company-size elements traveling into remote areas of the province by helicopter and conducting cordon and search operations. Contact with the enemy was relatively rare, although the Taliban did use IEDs—the type of ambushes perfected by the mujahideen in the 1980s.

Tactical-level commanders like Sellers, however, were under orders to integrate security operations into the larger effort. This was especially important in the summer and fall of 2004 when preparations for the presidential election required voter registration and the establishment of polling places. Sellers recalled that he launched Operation LANDGRAB in the summer of 2004 to set up a new base called FOB Cobra in the northwest district of the province.[31] That base would serve as the headquarters for the impending voter registration drive. At the same time, the Soldiers of 2-5 IN conducted a cordon and search operation near the new FOB where enemy forces had been located. During the operation and the voter drive, the Taliban lashed out in a series of attacks that killed several US Soldiers as well as UN election workers. Oruzgan would remain dangerous into the future despite the efforts of 2-5 IN.

As CJTF-76 placed greater emphasis on civil-military operations (CMO) and their role in the ink spot approach, the PRTs became more important than ever before. Tactical-level units worked closely with these teams, often coordinating closely on plans for development in the provinces. In most areas, the PRT efforts (discussed more completely below) focused on large-scale projects. Even so, battalion commanders still played a direct role in reconstruction by planning, funding, and supervising smaller projects with funds from the Commander's Emergency Response Program (CERP). These funds allowed for the drilling of water wells, simple refurbishing of schools, and other minor improvements to the physical infrastructure.

The presidential elections of October 2004 played a critical role in shaping Coalition operations. (This election, and the parliamentary elections of 2005, will be the subject of a section below.) In this discussion, it is important to emphasize the role that tactical-level units like 2-5 IN played in planning and conducting elections. Coordinating and staging an election in a well-developed stable democracy is difficult enough. To conduct an election in Afghanistan in 2004 was far more complex and required the resources and capabilities provided by Coalition military forces. In the registration campaign, commanders and staffs worked with the Afghan Government and the UN to give the population a chance to enroll as voters. On election day, many units provided quick reaction forces (QRFs) to secure polls and even transport ballots from regional sites to provincial centers. For example, 3-7 FA conducted an increasing number of patrols in the city of Kandahar in the weeks before the election and on election day moved most of its Soldiers from the Kandahar Airfield into the city to provide security.[32]

At the end of their deployment in spring 2005, the senior leaders in CJTF-76 believed they had made progress toward creating a more stable country with a government that had greater legitimacy and reach. The successful presidential election had been one indicator of that success. CTF *Bronco* had tracked other signs of progress. When they arrived, the TF staff assessed the security environment in RC-South and found they only had information on three of the five provinces, and in those three regions—Kandahar, Zabol, and southern Oruzgan provinces—the population feared the Coalition.[33] They knew almost nothing about the situation in Helmand and Nimruz provinces. One year later, CTF *Bronco* reported making inroads in gaining the support of the population in most of the districts of Kandahar, Zabol, and Oruzgan provinces and in a few districts of Helmand province.[34] This was not victory by any stretch of the imagination, but the Soldiers of CTF *Bronco* were convinced they had made significant gains.

The CJSOTF and Security Operations

In its COIN campaign, CJTF-76 had the support of the CJSOTF-A whose special operations teams were trained for and experienced in COIN operations. In addition to the Operational

Detachment–Alpha (ODA) teams provided by the 3d SFG in early 2004, the CJSOTF-A also included a US Naval Special Warfare Task Unit, Tactical Psychological Operations (PSYOP) Teams, a Civil Affairs (CA) Company, Joint Tactical Air Control Parties, and Irregular Afghan Security Forces. Headquartered at Bagram Airfield, CJSOTF-A operated out of a series of small bases, eventually locating its forces in 17 remote base camps and 6 border checkpoints in RC-South and RC-East.

In early 2004 the CJSOTF leadership began planning an unconventional warfare (UW) campaign focused on setting conditions for the presidential election in the fall. In Special Forces (SF) doctrine, the term "unconventional warfare" defined a type of approach that closely resembled COIN. The main difference between the two is the emphasis in UW on working with and through indigenous military forces. In the UW campaign in 2004, CJSOTF-A would attempt to partner with Afghan security forces, including the irregular militia found across the country.

CJTF-76 had operational control (OPCON) of the CJSOTF and in 2004 directed the CJSOTF commander, Colonel Herd, to operate along the Pakistani frontier that formed the southern border of RC-South and RC-East. In the spring, Herd began setting up what he called "A camps" along the frontier. In the Lawara district of Paktika province, for example, the SF-led contingent established a camp that included a US Army CA team, a company of soldiers from the ANA, and customs police officers. Their mission was to deny the enemy the use of an infiltration corridor and demonstrate the ability of the Coalition and the Afghan security forces to assert governmental control in a previously lawless region. Less than 24 hours after its establishment, al-Qaeda fighters attacked the camp and were not only stopped by the US and Afghan Soldiers, but pursued into the mountains by the ANA unit.[35] In the 4 months that followed this attack, the Soldiers at the A Camp invested approximately $50,000 into the local area in the form of reconstruction projects, such as water wells, that employed local labor. Colonel Herd recalled that the display of authority by the Coalition and ANA also led to a successful voter registration drive in the region with 40 percent of the registrants being female Afghans, an impressive figure given the traditional values of the area and the continued presence of both Taliban and al-Qaeda forces.[36]

At the same time that some elements of the CJSOTF were projecting military and civil power along the border, other teams were assisting CJTF-76 set conditions for the 2004 election by launching a series of operations aimed at breaking up enemy concentrations in the interior of the country. One of the first of these missions targeted Taliban transit corridors in the Baghran Valley in northern Helmand province. In Operation PRINCESS, two predawn simultaneous strikes resulted in the capture of Abdul Hafiz Mageed and Mohammed Dawood, both senior enemy commanders.[37]

Later in the summer, the CJSOTF launched two operations to build on the success of PRINCESS. During the first week of July 2004, two ODAs conducted Operation INDEPENDENCE, a follow-on sweep of the Baghran Valley. After finding that the Taliban had retreated from the valley, a local villager led the teams to a substantial weapons cache that included T-62 tanks, 105-mm howitzers, ZSU-23 antiaircraft guns, 107-mm rockets, and tens of thousands of rounds of assorted ammunition.[38] Operation TICONDEROGA, which followed, targeted the frontier area and the communication lines to Kabul and Kandahar from the border. The operations temporarily cut the enemy supply route through the Khyber Pass, which helped prevent Taliban groups from transiting southeastern Afghanistan and striking Kabul or

Kandahar. During the operation, a Navy SEAL team killed prominent Taliban leader Rozi Khan as he attempted to flee a cordoned village.

In early October the CJSOTF launched Operation TRENTON, a series of aggressive local operations to preempt pre-election attacks. Partly in response to the success of these missions, a force of more than 200 Taliban attacked an SF base camp at Deh Rawood in Oruzgan province on the day before the election. The SF team successfully fought off the attackers and killed 70 Taliban.[39] All told, enemy attacks in the month prior to the election were minimal. US Army General Bryan D. Brown, Commander, US Special Operations Command, asserted that in this pre-election period, "Special Operations Forces had killed or captured hundreds of terrorists and insurgents using precisely targeted offensive operations."[40]

Figure 52. General Bryan D. Brown (left), commander of US Special Operations Command, receives a base defense operations center briefing on 24 November at Camp Vance on Bagram Airfield, Afghanistan, from Captain Owen Ray of the 1st Special Forces Group (Airborne), Fort Lewis, Washington.

In December 2004 the 7th SFG took command of CJSOTF-A and began placing more emphasis on strengthening the Coalition and Afghan Government's presence in the provinces along the Pakistani frontier. With one eye on the parliamentary elections scheduled for the fall of 2005, the CJSOTF sought to decrease further enemy infiltration across the border while increasing the Afghan Government's legitimacy. This task relied heavily on the availability of trained Afghan security forces. In 2005 the number of these units working with Coalition SOF remained low, but did have some success with the few ANA battalions it advised.[41] In Operation NAM DONG, for example, 50 SOF advisors accompanied an ANA battalion into an enemy sanctuary in Oruzgan province and successfully cleared the district of organized enemy formations.[42] That operation was the largest ANA-led action since the fielding of the Afghan forces in 2002. Because of the success with NAM DONG and other actions, CJTF-76 directed the CJSOTF-A to focus its mission on assisting and advising Afghan security forces in preparation for the elections.[43]

The Continuing Militia Challenge

In 2004 and 2005 Coalition commanders at all levels continued to struggle with regional leaders and their armed militias. The individual leaders and their forces posed a direct obstacle to the expansion of the Afghan Government's sovereignty, and in some regions, served as potential adversaries. The Disarmament, Demobilization, and Reintegration (DDR) program, under the auspices of the UN, continued in 2004 and 2005 and enjoyed varying degrees of success. The Afghan Ministry of Defense (MOD) ran the program and received assistance from the Afghanistan New Beginnings Program (ANBP), the United Nations Development Program (UNDP), and the UNAMA. Japan was the lead country in Afghan DDR matters. However, problems had arisen early on regarding relationships between MOD officials and regional leaders, many of whom stubbornly refused to cooperate because of the alien nature of the concept of disarmament. At lower levels, Coalition leaders, like Colonel Pedersen, commander of CTF *Bronco,* found that his units were the only forces that had the will and the strength to put teeth into the DDR program. Pedersen recalled that they had some success in demobilizing and disarming the militia forces in RC-South. Nevertheless, he found there was little chance of reintegrating militiamen into society in a viable way, because opportunities for employment outside the militias and the Taliban were few.[44]

A few weeks prior to the 2004 presidential election, MOD announced a rededicated effort to get the DDR program back on track. Measuring progress was decidedly difficult. To begin with, various estimates of the number of eligible militiamen differed by as much as 600,000 troops.[45] Additionally, local militia commanders often inflated totals in an effort to seize the pay of "phantom" militiamen. Eventually, MOD settled on a baseline figure of 100,000 militia members eligible for the program.[46]

At the core of the DDR program was the idea of reintegration. Former militiamen and lower level officers each received a few hundred dollars as a reintegration stipend, while senior commanders—generals and some colonels—collected slightly more. Since many ex-combatants had been conscripts, they were genuinely appreciative of the DDR program, particularly now that they could spend more time with their families in a relatively stable environment. Many soldiers, though, were forced to wait for up to 6 months for their reintegration packages to arrive. This caused undue hardship for them and their families, since the food ration given them at the beginning of the program lasted only 2 months. Those former militiamen who were literate received vocational training such as carpentry, metal work, or teaching as a component of their packages, whereas illiterate soldiers were only offered payment in kind (grain or livestock). Unfortunately, many of those who successfully completed vocational training were forced to relocate to find appropriate work.

The DDR program had a measured amount of success in 2004 and 2005. UN figures indicated that slightly more than 60,000 ex-combatants had been disarmed and demobilized by the end of 2005. Further, 35,000 light/medium weapons and 11,000 heavy weapons had been collected by that date.[47] Even so, the failures of the program revealed the very real persistent political fractures in Afghanistan. In 2004 a commander of a militia force based in the Panjshir region refused to participate in the disarmament process.[48] Worse was the battle that broke out in the summer of 2004 in Herat province between the militia forces of Ismail Khan and Amanullah Khan. This crisis forced Major General Olson, the commander of CJTF-76, to intervene by sending CTF *Saber* (3-4 CAV), two SF ODAs, and an ANA company to the area.[49] This Coalition force quelled the battle, but Olson had to involve American Ambassador Zalmay Khalilzad and Hamid Karzai in the negotiations before the conflict was defused.

Expansion of the International Security Assistance Force (ISAF)

A key to the overall Western effort in Afghanistan was the successful expansion of ISAF's role in 2004. With forces strung out in the south and the east, CFC-A needed the ISAF to secure Kabul and expand security and reconstruction operations to the north. By mid-2004 ISAF was commanded by Lieutenant General Rick J. Hillier, a Canadian Army officer who reported to NATO's Allied Joint Forces Command in Brunssum, Netherlands. ISAF had assumed control of the German-led Konduz PRT in late 2003 and Hillier oversaw its takeover of the Mazar-e Sharif PRT from British forces in July 2004 and the German-led PRT at Feyzabab in October. During the summer of 2004, ISAF increased troop strength from 6,500 to 10,000 in anticipation of the upcoming presidential election and at that point controlled nine provinces (3,600 square kilometers) in northern Afghanistan.[50] French Lieutenant General Jean-Louis Py assumed command in August 2004, followed by Lieutenant General Etham Erdagi of the Turkish Army who took over in February 2005.

In 2005 ISAF expansion continued as the command took over PRTs at Herat and Farah along with the Herat Forward Support Base (FSB). The FSB was managed by 375 civilian and military personnel and included a QRF, a Spanish surgical hospital, and medical evacuation (MEDEVAC) units. With this increase in its mission scope, ISAF controlled nine PRTs and had security responsibility for 50 percent of Afghanistan's territory.[51] When Italian Lieutenant General Mauro Del Vecchio assumed command in August 2005, ISAF's troop strength dropped to 8,000 soldiers although its responsibilities in Afghanistan had never been greater.[52]

ISAF's expansion in Afghanistan faced critical problems. Low troop levels, insufficient transportation, incompatible communication systems, and underfunding by participating countries weakened the overall effort. Presenting more problems for tactical operations were the number of caveats or restrictions that governments placed on how troops could be used. Some caveats confined forces to certain geographical areas, and others limited the types of missions in which their troops could participate.[53] The German Government, for example, limited its forces in Afghanistan to operating in the northern provinces where the security environment was relatively benign. These limitations would have serious effects in 2006 and 2007 as the enemy threat worsened.

Transition at the Tactical Level: SETAF Takes Charge

In February 2005 Major General Jason Kamiya, commander of the Southern European Task Force (Airborne), known by the acronym SETAF, took command of CJTF-76 from Major General Olson. The SETAF deployment, primarily of airborne Soldiers from the 173d Airborne Brigade and the 1st Brigade, 82d Airborne Division, also included Army Active and Reserve units as well as Air Force, Navy, Marine Corps, and Coalition elements.[54]

Kamiya had taken command of SETAF in April 2004 and spent the following 9 months preparing the TF for deployment to Afghanistan. In that period, he recognized the Operation ENDURING FREEDOM (OEF) mission as a COIN campaign and emphasized balance between combat and stability operations in predeployment training.[55] Kamiya cautioned his troops that the CJTF-76 mission would be different from previous rotations and that the fight for Afghanistan was far from over. In his *Leader Preparation Monograph,* Kamiya described how the enemy forces in Afghanistan were mounting a classic insurgency intent on deposing President Karzai's government. He went on to describe the complexity of counterinsurgencies, noting that they are primarily political in nature and that patience, perseverance, initiative, and discipline on the part of all SETAF forces would be required to defeat the insurgency. Kamiya further explained SETAF's unique opportunity to positively impact Afghanistan's future on all levels of national power: diplomatic, informational, military, and economic. "We must be astute to recognize these opportunities and transform them to our advantage," he wrote, adding, "When opportunities are seized, they multiply. When they are not, they die."[56]

DOD Photo by SPC Jerry T. Combes

Figure 53. Major General Jason Kamiya (left), commander of CJTF-76, and Oruzgan province Governor Hajji Jan Mohammed discuss concerns and solutions to recent flooding that occurred in the village of Cekzai, Afghanistan, 20 March 2005.

Ultimately, Kamiya synthesized his COIN guidance into 15 key points, which he titled his *Warfighting Focus* and published in wallet-size card format for distribution to all members of the CJTF. These points emphasized the importance of CMO and the overall goal of supporting the political process in Afghanistan and the legitimacy of the democratically elected government. The points stressed flexibility, creativity, the need to carefully gather intelligence, and to understand how local populations perceive US Soldiers.[57]

Armed with this guidance, SETAF's units flowed into Afghanistan and moved into their AOs. The 173d Airborne Brigade, the main element within SETAF, took the designation CTF *Bayonet*, deployed to RC-South at Kandahar Airfield, and then into most of the bases previously established by CTF *Bronco*. US Army Colonel Kevin Owens, who commanded the 173d Airborne Brigade, became the commander of RC-South. CTF *Bayonet* was comprised of 2d Battalion, 503d Parachute Infantry Regiment (2-503 PIR); 74th Infantry Detachment (Long-Range Surveillance); 173d Support Battalion (Airborne); elements of 3d Battalion, 319th Field Artillery Regiment (3-319 FA); along with additional Coalition elements from Romania and Canada. In all, nearly 3,500 men and women served in CTF *Bayonet*.[58]

The other main maneuver force in the new CJTF-76 was CTF *Devil*, a brigade-size force built around the 1st Brigade of the US Army 82d Airborne Division. This force consisted of four US Army light infantry battalions: 1st Battalion, 325th Airborne Infantry Regiment (1-325 AIR); 2d Battalion, 504th Parachute Infantry Regiment (2-504 PIR); 1st Battalion, 508th Parachute Infantry Regiment (1-508 PIR); and 3d Battalion, 141st Infantry Regiment from the Texas Army National Guard. A series of US Marine battalions also rotated through the area including 2d Battalion, 3d Marine Regiment. Field artillery and support units brought the TF manpower up to 5,000 Soldiers, Sailors, Marines, and Airmen. Colonel Patrick Donahue, the CTF *Devil* commander, took over RC-East, which quickly became the main effort for CJTF-76, because Coalition intelligence indicated enemy forces used the eastern and northeastern provinces adjacent to the Pakistani border as sanctuaries.[59] Donahue became especially concerned about the Korengal River Valley in Kunar province that served as a stronghold for Wahhabist radicals.[60] In July 2005 an MH-47 Chinook was shot down while supporting operations in that valley, demonstrating the tenacity and capacity of enemy forces in the area. All 16 US crewmembers and passengers onboard were killed.

While preparing for the deployment, Major General Kamiya was aware that his units would not be able to replace the units of the 25th ID on a one-for-one basis. Thus, he had to accept some risk by using the teams of the CJSOTF to create a Coalition presence in some areas. For example, with no forces left to replace the 2-5 IN in Oruzgan province, Kamiya chose to support the PRT at Tarin Kowt with an ODA. Because RC-East had become the main effort, Kamiya actually looked to increase the Coalition presence in Nangarhar province around the city of Jalalabad. While there was an ODA there, SETAF started constructing a FOB and by early 2006, the base had grown to include a PRT and an airstrip that could accommodate C-130 transport aircraft.

Like CTF *Bronco* and CTF *Thunder* before them, Donahue and Owens pursued a combination of security, governance, information, and reconstruction operations from the bases established in battalion and company AOs. As the PRTs increased and came more firmly under the authority of the regional commands, the effects of reconstruction became more pronounced. As in 2004, tactical-level commanders supported their own reconstruction projects using CERP funds and other means. In RC-East, the CTF *Devil* commander directed his battalion commanders to coordinate closely with the PRTs to create a larger effect, especially in the improvement of the road network and other highly visible infrastructure.[61] Serving as a guidepost for all of these actions was the parliamentary elections scheduled for September 2005. CJTF-76 focused on setting conditions in which the Afghan Government and the UN could launch the voter registration process and set up polls to move Afghanistan further on the path toward stability.

The Interagency Reconstruction Effort in 2004–2005

In March 2004 the US DOS issued a progress report on the Afghan reconstruction effort, which noted that US expenditures for Afghan reconstruction between 2001 and 2004 totaled $4.2 billion with an additional $1.2 billion slated for fiscal year (FY) 2006. The primary objective in Afghanistan—the avoidance of a major humanitarian crisis—had been achieved. The report highlighted major improvements to the infrastructure: re-opening Kabul-Kandahar highway and Salang Tunnel; rebuilding 203 schools, 140 clinics, and 700 miles of secondary roads; repairing several electrical power plants, the Kandahar-Kajaki Dam, and the Pyanj Bridge to Tajikistan; completing 7,000 irrigation projects; vaccinating 4.2 million Afghan children against measles and polio; and providing 25 million school books.[62]

In contrast to the DOS report, a 2005 US Government Accountability Office (GAO) report recognized the efforts of United States Agency for International Development (USAID), but concluded that the United States had still neglected to meet its long-term reconstruction targets or project objectives over the course of OEF.[63] Since 2002, the report contended, the United States had provided $1.5 billion to head off the production of opiates in the region;

however, by 2005 there was little progress to show for that major effort.[64] Along with this strategy, the DOS and USAID portions of the reconstruction campaign re-emphasized the 2004 shift to larger-scale reconstruction and infrastructure-oriented projects to assist Afghanistan's local communities and national programs. To facilitate the reconstruction plan, USAID now accounted for the majority of reconstruction expenditures, while the DOS concentrated on refugee assistance funding.

DOD's reconstruction focus, nevertheless, did not change and continued contributing to the campaign by financing small projects using the Overseas Humanitarian, Disaster, and Civic Aid (OHDACA) Program and the CERP funds with the PRTs.[65] The main responsibilities of OHDACA were improving DOD visibility, building security, and generating DOD goodwill. CERP, on the other hand, was meant solely for quick-response projects that would have an immediate impact on local populations. Unlike USAID projects, the DOD did not require PRT commanders to conduct technical assessments and involve Afghan Government officials in their plans before receiving CERP funding. DOD regulations allowed funds to be turned over more quickly, which resulted in what appeared to be more rapid implementation of small-scale projects.[66]

Another key component of the United States' broad reconstruction plan in Afghanistan was the US Army Corps of Engineers, which also helped to meet the common goal among the agencies: securing and stabilizing the war-torn region. From the Afghanistan Engineer District (AED) in Kabul, more than 200 Corps personnel managed projects for ISAF, the OSC-A, CJTF-76, and USAID.[67] By 2005 the AED work force of 14,000 workers was made up of primarily Afghans. In FY 2004, US engineers awarded $600 million in contracts for work in Afghanistan, and a significant portion of the funds were allocated to companies who trained and employed local workers.[68] Afghan plumbers, electricians, masons, and carpenters significantly contributed to a myriad of construction projects in progress—including buildings, bridges, runways, and public-works projects.[69]

Colonel John B. O'Dowd, commander of AED and Director of the Engineer Division for CFC-A from 2004 to 2005, described the strategy he saw for interagency cooperation and how progress could be made in Afghanistan:

> In this environment, you need the skill sets each agency brings to the table. When you combine the social programs that USAID can do—institution building and capacity building—with the engineering and technical skills of the Corps of Engineers, it's a really powerful developmental tool and it is a particularly useful tool for a country like Afghanistan that has seen a man-made disaster.[70]

Because the situation in Afghanistan required a broad-based reconstruction response, the US military and the development community continued to strive for a better understanding of one another's procedures and policies to collaborate with comparative advantages in mind.[71]

Expansion of the PRT Program

To further empower the PRTs and the overall military portion of the reconstruction campaign, USAID began expanding the scope of its reconstruction assistance to include programs for agriculture, education, health, road construction, and power generation. In all, USAID identified 12 distinct Afghanistan reconstruction program categories, including continued humanitarian needs such as food and assistance for internally displaced persons, from which specific projects would be identified and implemented by PRTs.[72] Between mid-2004 through the fall of 2005, the PRT effort grew in size and was refined in concept. By July 2005, 22 PRTs were functioning in Afghanistan—9 controlled by the NATO-led ISAF and 13 directed by the United States. The mix shifted by 1 in September to 10 NATO and 12 United States.[73] Lieutenant Colonel Jennifer Caruso, who deployed with the 25th ID in March 2004 and was initially stationed at CJTF-76 headquarters in Bagram, witnessed this PRT expansion. Caruso remembered working with two PRTs, one in Asadabad and another in Kandahar when she first arrived in theater. Caruso remembered, "After a while, they started popping up all over the place and really populating the idea of PRTs versus just the military unit on the ground . . . doing those same functions."[74]

During the 2004–2005 period, PRTs across Afghanistan supported the Coalition's larger reconstruction objectives. Lieutenant Colonel Steven Ford, commander of the Ghazni PRT from January through October 2004, oversaw his team's expansion from a "PRT with just dirt and an old madrassa, to being a whole forward operating base (FOB) with approximately 30 buildings."[75] While in theater, Ford ensured his team conducted CMO that improved security, facilitated reconstruction, and strengthened "the reach of the central government to the

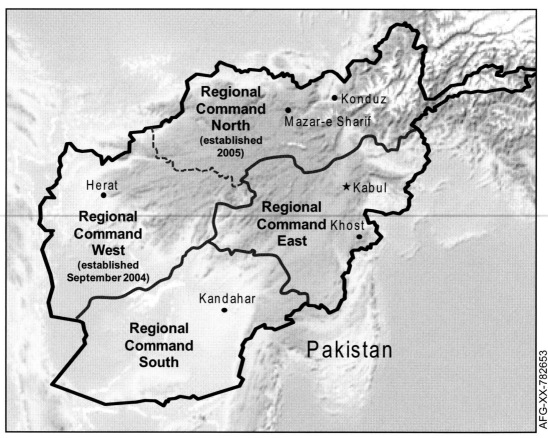

Figure 54. Regional command structure as of September 2005.
RC-South and RC-East established in May 2004.

provinces."[76] Two of the critical ways Ford accomplished this mission was through assisting USAID in its many projects, such as building the Ghazni City Library and refurbishing the Ghazni Hospital Road. As of 1 June 2004, Ford's PRT was juggling a half-million dollars worth of projects focused on sanitation, clean-up, education, and public safety and communication."[77]

The PRT commander who replaced Ford described his mission as that of winning over the people of the province and isolating them from Taliban influence. His team visited every district and met regularly with local council elders. Afghans lined the streets and waved enthusiastically when his PRT convoys came through their villages. "We were looking to make their lives better," he explained, but cautioned against expecting too much too quickly, noting "we can't make it happen overnight—this is a long term investment."[78]

Soldiers from the 25th ID also involved themselves in the everyday reconstruction activities of engaging with the local population. As CJTF-76 development projects were established, the Afghan people began to see the PRTs make a difference. Lieutenant Colonel Caruso emphasized the capacity of the PRTs to provide the lives of Afghan women by "showing up, doing benevolent things, building schools" with women's interests specifically in mind.[79] Caruso understood that her presence in Afghanistan as a female leader could generate cultural obstacles, especially among Afghan men. Despite these issues, Caruso pursued connections with the Afghans while, at the same time, maintaining her identity as an authority and representative of democratic ideals. During these trips, many Afghan women mentioned their interest in better schools and healthcare as well as their appreciation of their new freedom to vote.[80] Sergeant Flora Estrada recalled enjoying the humanitarian missions she participated in by delivering blankets and food to the people. According to Estrada, "Whenever we went out there and we saw those kids smiling and people waiting for us to get there, that was when we felt like we were actually doing something for them."[81]

Perhaps the biggest change to the reconstruction campaign during this time was the subordination of the PRTs to the commanders of the regional commands. Caruso recalled participating in a staff meeting at CJTF-76 headquarters when the regional commanders began to realize that their forces now included the PRTs. Caruso noted that their immediate reaction was positive, characterizing it as, "[The PRT] is a part of my team."[82] These leaders immediately saw the ways in which the PRTs could magnify the presence of their maneuver forces and help spread Coalition and Afghan governmental authority across the AOs.

Colonel Cheek, commander of CTF *Thunder* and RC-East in 2004, had nine PRTs under his authority. Six of the nine PRTs were led by US Army Reserve CA officers. Two others were commanded by a US Navy commander and a US Marine Corps lieutenant colonel. The ninth PRT, in Bamian province, was staffed primarily by New Zealanders, along with DOS and the United States Department of Agriculture (USDA) representatives. Cheek emphasized a multidimensional approach to PRT management and the sharing of information among the various teams. His message to the Afghan people was clear: "We're here to restore order, we're here to assist with the reconstruction of your country by building schools and establishing institutions."[83] Cheek described the enemy's message as violent and destructive, noting that Taliban and al-Qaeda forces intended to "burn down the schools and kill people."[84] In RC-South, Colonel Pedersen had four PRTs in Kandahar, Qalat, Lashkar Gah, and Tarin Kowt. Colonel Phil Bookert who took command of CTF *Longhorn* in September 2004 gained authority over the PRT already in Herat and later established a new PRT in Farah.[85]

Task Force *Victory*: Supporting the PRTs

In spring 2004, the Soldiers of the 1st Battalion, 168th Infantry deployed to Afghanistan to assist the Coalition's reconstruction effort. The battalion, originally 750 strong, swelled to over 1,000 Soldiers as other units including detachments of engineers, medics, and civil affairs specialists joined its ranks. The task force mission was to provide security, communications, and logistical support to the provincial reconstruction teams (PRTs) across Afghanistan. This mission grew as the number of PRTs increased from 7 in spring 2004 to over a 12 by the time of the unit's departure in June 2005.

Most of the task force's Soldiers were assigned to specific PRTs as security elements. They manned the towers and gates at the team compounds and provided convoy security when PRT members moved around the countryside. The task force also created "Log cells" that provided all classes of supply to the PRTs as well as maintenance and medical support and items to be distributed to the Afghan population in the provinces. Task force Soldiers also helped build the PRT compounds, relying on their civilian plumbing, carpentry, and electrician skills to make the sites functional. Lieutenant Colonel Scott Visser, the commander of Task Force *Victory*, stated, "My guidance to our Soldiers was that they were to do everything so that civil affairs could do their mission."

That mission often became dangerous. In September 2004, after Afghan president Hamid Karzai removed Ismail Khan as governor of Herat province, task force elements at the Herat PRT became heavily involved in protecting civilian aid workers after riots erupted. In November, a PRT convoy in Paktika province that was under escort by Soldiers from Task Force *Victory* was ambushed by insurgents. Several members of the security element were hit by enemy fire and one ultimately died from his wounds. But quick action by other task force Soldiers to pull the wounded away from the ambush site and call for a MEDEVAC aircraft and close air support saved lives. The PRT security elements also played a critical role in the 2004 presidential election by providing patrols around polling sites and escorts for ballot boxes.

Lieutenant Colonel Visser commented that his guardsmen gained the confidence of both the civilians and the Active Duty Soldiers with whom they served in Afghanistan. Visser recalled one senior officer in the 25th Infantry Division telling him, "I'd take your Soldiers with me anytime, anywhere."

Task Force 168 Unit History, 2006.

Interview with Lieutenant Colonel Scott Visser, 2006.

Effectiveness of the PRT

After completing his deployment to Afghanistan in June 2005, Colonel Cheek, commander of CTF *Thunder* and RC-East in 2004, recognized the key assets and capabilities the PRTs offered the Coalition COIN campaign: "The PRT is a huge plus. It is exactly what we need to really fight the insurgency at the population level—it's a brilliant idea and one that should be expanded."[86] However, he also recommended a number of potential improvements to the PRT program. For example, he believed that more attention should be paid to the centers of intellectual and cultural influences in Afghanistan, such as religious leaders, teachers, businessmen, women, and elders. Getting the Coalition message out to these types of leaders and, in turn, having them share it with the general population promised to enhance the Coalition's stature. Additionally, Cheek observed an absence of civilian experts on the PRTs and noted that each team should be organized in accordance with the needs of its respective location. Nangarhar province and the city of Jalalabad, for example, were manufacturing centers and needed more business expertise, while Paktika province was an agricultural area in an arid zone and thus required agricultural assistance. Cheek recognized that PRT commanders had to be rotated, but better predeployment training and relief-in-place measures could improve effectiveness.

Colonel Pedersen, commander of RC-South in 2004, largely agreed with his counterpart from RC-East. Pedersen emphasized that the four PRTs in RC-South were successful in extending the presence of the Coalition and the legitimacy of the Afghan Government for two reasons. First, they were under his command and thus fully integrated into the COIN plan as well as CTF *Bronco's* logistical plan. Second, the PRTs were collocated with maneuver units that could provide direct support, especially in unstable areas. According to Pedersen, these two factors were critical to the success the PRTs enjoyed.[87]

Dr. Kenneth Katzman, a specialist in Middle Eastern Affairs for the US Congress, also generally agreed with the optimistic assessment of the overall PRT performance. Having visited the US-run Gardez PRT during this time, he praised the program's flexibility and increasing effectiveness. PRTs in contested areas resolved disputes between local governments and supported combat operations and intelligence gathering, while those in more secure regions of the north and west concentrated on reconstruction. Because of the presence of the PRTs, electrical substations and new roads were even built in some rural villages in more unstable regions of southern Afghanistan.[88]

As CFC-A began transferring responsibility for the PRTs to ISAF in 2004 and 2005, reconstruction priorities changed to reflect those of the donor nation. In turn, the reorganization created a sense of overall lack of direction, because centralized control was now diminished. Also, the continued presence of PRTs remained a contentious issue for many NGOs and others in the civilian humanitarian relief community. These groups felt that affiliation with PRTs would bring about enemy retaliation, that the line between military and civilian operations was obscured, and that their appearance of impartiality would be lost.[89] For example, *Doctors without Borders* pulled its teams from Afghanistan after five volunteers were killed by enemy groups on 2 June 2005 in Badghis province.[90] Civilian workers contended they needed more "humanitarian space" to perform their mission.[91] These notions appeared to have at least some merit as attacks on aid workers increased during the year; yet, the former PRT military commander in Ghazni provided a differing opinion on the humanitarian space issue, noting, "The fact that you wear a camouflage uniform and you've got an M-16, and you're building schools and giving school supplies to kids, that bothers [NGO representatives]. They don't like to see that."[92] In contrast to what was said by NGO representatives, PRT leadership perceived aid workers as feeling "threatened" by uniformed officers also assisting the Afghan people.

The United States Institute for Peace (USIP) compiled insights and experiences from more than 50 interviews conducted with US and foreign officials, military officers, and representatives of NGOs that worked directly with PRTs in Afghanistan in 2004 and 2005. Dr. Robert Perito, who led the USIP project, pinpointed recurring problems that prevented the PRTs from being more successful. Among the problems he identified was, first, the reliance on improvisation, which originated in the lack of interagency agreement regarding roles, missions, and concept of operations; and, second, the need for the nonmilitary agencies of the US Government to become more serious about staffing the PRTs with qualified people.[93] After 3 years in existence, the PRTs still needed to be improved. The concept, however, was original and revolutionary, and, despite a myriad of obstacles, the teams had made significant contributions to the Afghanistan campaign.

Enabling the Afghan National Army and Police

In 2004 the OMC-A continued to exert its control of the programs fostering the ANA. The OMC-A mission remained essentially the same in 2004 as it had been earlier: reconstruct the Afghan security and defense sectors and train the ANA. United States Air Force (USAF) Major General Craig P. Weston, the chief of OMC-A, stated, "For our mission, we really took the Phase IV OPORD to heart and said that our mission was to create the entire Afghan defense sector, from the Ministry of Defense to the sustaining institutions, like the logistics command and a recruiting command and a training center, all the way down to training combat troops."[94] Throughout his tenure, Weston described his plan as working with the Afghan people to "sustain and establish" defense policies that would last under Afghan leadership long after the support of the US Army was available. Under Weston's leadership, OMC-A functioned, in part, as an acquisition program while also providing oversight of CJTF *Phoenix*, the organization primarily responsible for training and mentoring the ANA.

During the summer of 2004, the 76th Infantry Brigade, Indiana Army National Guard, commanded by Brigadier General Richard Moorhead, relieved the 45th Infantry Brigade, Oklahoma Army National Guard as the core of CJTF *Phoenix*. Assisting the 1,000 Soldiers

DOD Photo by SGT Dennis Schultz

Figure 55. The Tropic Lightning Division's Major General Eric Olson, commanding general of CJTF-76, poses with soldiers of the ANA's Thunder Corps at the activation ceremony for the Gardez regional command, 22 September.

from the 76th Brigade were approximately 500 additional Army Guardsmen from 15 other states along with detachments of US Marines and USAF officers and airmen. France, Germany, Romania, Canada, New Zealand, the United Kingdom, and Mongolia also provided military trainers for CJTF *Phoenix*.[95] By September 2004 the expanded CJTF *Phoenix* had successfully trained nearly 15,000 ANA soldiers and the Afghan MOD had activated regional commands in Kandahar (205th ANA Corps) and Gardez (203d). In addition to maintaining ANA Central Corps (201st ANA Corps) headquarters in Kabul, by year end the Afghan MOD activated two more regional commands at Mazar-e Sharif (209th) and Herat (207th).[96]

OMC-A and the MOD planned for each ANA corps to have three brigades, each consisting of three light infantry battalions, one combat support (CS) battalion, and one combat service support (CSS) battalion. Third Brigade, 201st Corps in Kabul eventually became the ANA QRF and, as such, had one commando battalion, one mechanized infantry battalion, and one armor battalion. By 2004 all of the ANA recruits that manned these units received 7 weeks of basic training at the Kabul Military Training Center (KMTC), after which

Figure 56. Brigadier General Richard Moorhead (left), commanding general of CJTF *Phoenix,* and ANA Brigadier General Ibrahim Ahmad Zai, the Recruiting Command Chief of Staff, are greeted by local residents of Khost on arrival at the NAVC.

a few were chosen to attend the British-run noncommissioned officer (NCO) school, while those remaining went on to complete 6 additional weeks of advanced individual training (AIT). Also by this date, Afghan instructors taught nearly all classes at these basic levels. After basic and advanced training, recruits were sworn in as ANA soldiers and joined NCOs and ANA officers for 2 more weeks of small unit field exercises conducted by the Canadian military detachment to facilitate cohesion and esprit. Newly trained soldiers earned the equivalent of $70 a month while NCOs received a monthly salary of $180.[97]

As 2004 progressed, the capacities of the ANA increased. ANA units conducted operations with Coalition units in RC-South, RC-East, and with the CJSOTF. President Karzai also dispatched an ANA battalion to Herat in the summer of 2004 to quell the conflict between Ismail Khan and Amanullah Khan.[98] The success of the Herat operation led one Afghan officer to assert, "The Afghan National Army is the spine of this country and of our president—the central government can defend itself now."[99] Still, concerns regarding the effectiveness of the ANA persisted. "A few months of training are not going to make an illiterate young Afghan boy a soldier. It takes time to build an army," noted Ahmad Fahim Noori, a weapons instructor at the KMTC. "The US military is the backbone of the ANA—without them the ANA could not stand alone."[100] Despite advances, Coalition forces still faced a difficult mission in training the ANA.

Several of the problems that had hindered the development of the ANA in 2003 and early 2004 persisted. Low pay caused attrition rates to climb and recruitment became more difficult. The inability to create a formal banking system created a monthly absent without leave (AWOL) crisis, because many ANA soldiers were forced to hand carry money home to their families. Soldiers also disappeared during the month of Ramadan and the celebratory week that followed. Additionally, the general hardships of winter and the lucrative poppy-growing season caused season-long desertions. Moreover, the Taliban issued a directive declaring ANA soldiers as infidels for their association with Coalition forces, creating a certain level of ambivalence in the ranks. Budgetary constraints delayed the proper arming of ANA soldiers, leaving many with the feeling that enemy forces often outgunned them. In mid-2005 average battalion manning levels, which were based on the number of soldiers actually available for duty, hovered around 50 percent for many units.[101]

Although remaining optimistic about the steady progress being made, leaders at OMC-A and in CJTF *Phoenix* understood by 2005 that developing a fully functioning Afghan fighting force would require considerable time. In the summer of that year, when the 53d Separate Infantry Brigade, Florida Army National Guard, commanded by Brigadier General John Perryman, arrived in Afghanistan to assume the CJTF *Phoenix* mission, the Coalition had trained and equipped more than 20,000 ANA soldiers since 2002 and 6,000 more were currently in training.[102] Yet, much still needed to be done if the ANA expected to hit its mark of 70,000 soldiers in the near future.

The National Military Academy of Afghanistan

As important as the overall manpower was the development of an efficient professional corps for the ANA. In the fall of 2003, Colonel George Forsythe, Vice Dean for Education at the United States Military Academy (USMA), began developing a concept plan for a new military academy in Afghanistan. As chief of the newly established Military Academy Study Team (MAST), Forsythe, along with Army Lieutenant Colonel Casey Neff, and Turkish Defense Attache Colonel Sener Tekbas, prepared a comprehensive plan for what was to be called the National Military Academy of Afghanistan (NMAA). The operational premise for the academy drew on examples from several countries without duplicating any one in particular. MAST then focused on the explicit needs of Afghanistan in developing the following core concepts: a 4-year university level education for all Afghan officers; training consistent with the overall ANA vision based on Western standards but sustainable by the Afghan Government and in harmony with Afghan culture; emphasis on leadership skills and the role of military officers in an Islamic democracy; the value of loyalty to one's country; and the notion of a career dedicated to national service.[103] The academy that resulted featured a 4-year curriculum that would produce 350 professional officers per year who were competent and loyal to the democratically-elected government of Afghanistan.[104]

Lieutenant General Barno approved the concept plan in November 2003. In the conclusion, Forsythe recommended initiating work on the implementation plan as soon as possible to ensure the academy's opening by February 2005. He further urged the superintendent at West Point to continue sending military academy faculty to Afghanistan at regular intervals to facilitate progress and continuity. In early 2004 Lieutenant Colonel Donna Brazil and Major William Caruso, both from the Behavioral Science and Leadership Department, and Colonel Barry Shoop, Director of the USMA Electrical Engineering Program, deployed to Afghanistan to oversee the project—"to put meat on the bones," as Forsythe described it.[105] US Army Reserve Colonel James Wilhite, a college education professor, then arrived in June 2004 to finalize work on the implementation plan that addressed a number of facets including faculty, staff, and cadet selection; facilities; supplies; and equipment.

The MOD chose the former site of the Afghan Air Corps Training Center at Kabul International Airport as the academy's home. Plans for the future included a new facility west of Kabul in Qarghah that could house 1,600 cadets, both men and women.[106] By December 2004, 350 cadet applicants had completed the NMAA entrance exam. Subsequently, 120 were offered admission to the class that began studies in 2005, NMAA's first official class.[107] In January 2005 Lieutenant Colonel Ray Nelson assumed responsibility for Cadet Basic Training (CBT) and CJTF *Phoenix* assigned six of its members to assist Nelson with the task of training the Afghan trainers. By the end of January, 16 ANA NCOs and 8 Afghan officers completed the crash course in US Army basic training. Official NMAA CBT began on 3 February and ended with a formal graduation ceremony on 17 March at which each cadet swore his oath of allegiance to the Afghan Government.[108] With this event, the new Afghan Army began forming its professional officer corps.

The Afghan National Police Mission

At the 2002 Geneva Conference on Afghanistan's future, Germany had accepted responsibility for the second pillar of security sector reforms: reorganizing and rebuilding the ANP. Between 2002 and 2005, several sections of the US Embassy staff in Kabul and the DOS's Bureau for International Narcotics and Law Enforcement Affairs (INL) also provided extensive support to the ANP reform effort. Germany focused primarily on refurbishing the National Police Academy in Kabul and on reestablishing the 3-year professional commissioned police officer training program. INL concentrated on training noncommissioned police officers and patrolmen/women at several facilities throughout Afghanistan and at the Kabul Central Training Center. Under an INL contract, DynCorp International built, equipped, and staffed the various ANP training centers, and also provided embedded advisors to the Afghan Ministry of Interior (MOI). Eventually, MOI established five ANP Regional Command Centers at Kabul, Gardez, Herat, Kandahar, and Mazar-e Sharif. By the Afghan presidential election in October 2004, nearly 20,000 ANP had completed training and were operational. Through 2005, the United States had invested more than $800 million in reforming the ANP.[109]

In light of OMC-A's success in training the ANA, CFC-A requested that OMC-A develop a comprehensive plan for conducting comparable ANP training. Although German forces had developed and were now running the ANP Academy, they were seriously limited by inadequate funding and a shortage of personnel. Therefore, Major General Weston and members of his OMC-A staff prepared a detailed plan for restructuring the ANP training program. Then, with a series of briefings in late 2004 and early 2005, Weston gained the necessary approvals from Lieutenant General Barno at CFC-A and from US Central Command (CENTCOM) to become substantially more involved.[110] By this time, nearly 35,000 ANP officers and patrolmen/women had been trained and were on duty throughout the country.[111]

General Weston's plan recommended that Germany retain its role as lead nation in reforming the Afghan police sector and that the United States (OMC-A) assume a strong supportive role. The fully integrated plan was based on Western police policies, systems, and processes, and emphasized quality over quantity, local recruiting, and adequate pay to attract literate officers. Weston further proposed a complete overhaul of the entire police sector, including certain aspects of the Afghan MOI. Issues of restructuring, rehiring, retraining, re-equipping, and reinforcing with mentors were all critical aspects addressed by General Weston, as was expanding the ANP training program from 8 to 12 weeks. Implementing the plan would require nearly $1 million in incremental funding and more than 1,500 additional Coalition personnel.[112]

Figure 57. Major General John T. Brennan.

DOD Photo

In February 2005 Air Force Major General John T. Brennan succeeded General Weston as Chief, OMC-A. As Brennan's office officially assumed responsibility for the ANP reform mission in July 2005, it was redesignated as the OSC-A. In 2006 the name would change once again to the Combined Security Transition Command–Afghanistan (CSTC-A) and would command CJTF *Phoenix* and the newly-formed CJTF *Police*.[113] During Major General Brennan's first 4 months in Afghanistan, he was consumed with the process of taking responsibility for ANP training, securing the necessary congressional funding, and convincing the Germans to accept the takeover.[114] In a short week in the middle of June, Brennan briefed Coalition, NATO, UN, and Afghan leadership, culminating in a meeting with President Karzai.[115] In all of his presentations, Brennan emphasized the need for political support from the international community for the ANP program to be successful. He reminded his audiences that law and order was crucial to establishing stability and creating economic growth for the citizens of Afghanistan.[116]

At the OSC-A reorganization ceremony in Kabul on 12 July, Major General Brennan's Chief of Staff, British Army Colonel Mark van der Lande, described how institutional reform experience gained in rebuilding the ANA would influence restructuring of the ANP. Likewise, Maureen Quinn, US Charge d'Affairs, acknowledged the significance of OSC-A's heightened responsibilities, noting that "this command is crucial to the future success of Afghanistan . . . our ability to further develop the ANA and to train an effective police force will have a direct impact on democracy and reconstruction in Afghanistan."[117] OSC-A headquarters added nearly 100 new positions, filled mostly by US Army Reserve officers, as it assumed the ANP training role. "We restructured some of the [battalions] to improve the quality of training these folks were getting," Brennan explained. "We changed our focus with the ANA from quantity to quality."[118]

State Building and Democracy in Afghanistan: The October 2004 Election

In political terms, the Afghans had made remarkable progress since the Taliban defeat in 2001. The Afghan Government was up and running in Kabul under a new constitution and was in mid-2004 planning for upcoming presidential and parliamentary elections. The elections had been stipulated by the constitution that had been approved by the loya jirga in early 2004. The constitution called for a presidential form of government with elections for the office of president to be held in June 2004. That government would also feature a bicameral legislature consisting of a lower house, *Wolesi Jirga*, to be chosen by direct elections, and an upper house, *Meshrano Jirga*, selected by the president and provisional/district councils. The parliamentary elections would follow the presidential elections by about 12 months. Security concerns and delayed voter registration, however, caused Hamid Karzai to postpone the presidential election until September 2004. A few weeks later, the Joint Electoral Management Body (JEMB), a combined Afghan and UN organization responsible for ensuring transparent and credible elections, designated 9 October the official election date.[119] A new election law issued in May 2004 certified one-man, one-vote for every Afghan man and woman 18 years or older, and specified that a simple majority would determine the presidential winner.

Early projections indicated that 10.5 million Afghan citizens would be eligible to vote. Because no voter registry and no census data existed in Afghanistan, registration estimates were difficult at best. In particular, registering Afghan women posed unique problems in the traditional male-oriented culture. As a result, separate teams of men and women were established to register male and female voters. Issuing voter registration cards with photo identification to fully veiled women was one difficulty encountered, nevertheless, the JEMB decided to do so in the interest of expediency.[120] In addition to registration concerns, female candidates were at serious risk. Despite significant improvements in the lives of Afghan women since 2001, women interested in running for office did so in an atmosphere of fear. One female candidate for the parliament from Kandahar province said, "Security is different for men and women. Men candidates have put their pictures everywhere in the bazaar. Women candidates can't do that, because they are afraid. Somebody might come during the night and kill them. Anything can happen."[121] Restrictive societal norms, threats from local warlords, and the increasing activity of the Taliban deterred both women candidates and voters from participating in the election.[122] Still, by September 2004, 10 million potential voters had registered.[123] Allegations arose questioning the validity of the registration process, because many voters appeared to have registered more than once.[124] Nevertheless, on election day, more than 8 million Afghans from all 34 provinces voted at 24,000 polling stations located in 4,800 polling centers, each of which had separate facilities for men and women. Afghan refugees were also able to cast their votes at 2,800 polling stations established in Iran and Pakistan.[125] Unfortunately, with only 200 election officials available for monitoring, most polling areas lacked oversight. Such a small number of observers violated European Union election standards, thus requiring observer teams to be renamed "democracy support teams" at the last minute.[126]

In July 2004 the JEMB had announced the Afghan presidential ticket—a list of official candidates who had registered to run in the upcoming presidential election. The 18 approved candidates included 14 independents and 4 with various party affiliations. President Karzai, an ethnic Pashtun, ran as an independent as did his former Minister of Planning, Hazara leader Mohammad Mohaqeq. Former Uzbek Northern Alliance General Abdul Rashid Dostum also registered as an independent along with Masooda Jalal, a physician and the only female candidate in the race. Finally, Karzai's previous Minister of Education, Mohammad Yunus Qanuni, represented the Tajik Nuhzat-e-Mili political party in the presidential race.

Security concerns prior to the presidential election persisted during the summer of 2004. Continued enemy threats to disrupt or prevent the election worried leaders of the Afghan Government, ISAF, and Coalition forces. By August, 12 election registration staff members had been killed and 33 more wounded. Six IEDs were found near voter registration locations or JEMB officials' homes, and four direct attacks on personnel or sites had occurred.[127] In mid-September unknown forces launched an unsuccessful rocket attack on Afghan President Karzai's helicopter near Gardez; 3 weeks later vice-presidential candidate Zia Massoud was the victim of an assassination attempt in Badakhshan province. Even though enemy attacks were up slightly, CJTF-76 commander Major General Olson optimistically pointed out at the time that "the bottom line is . . . we're getting done the business we need to get done."[128]

Afghan authorities, primarily the MOI, assumed overall responsibility for developing and implementing election security procedures. A concentric circle approach called for the ANP, estimated at 46,000 strong, to secure the polling centers and immediate surroundings. Police commanders were authorized to deputize local citizens as necessary to serve as temporary police officers. Soldiers from the ANA formed the second ring and provided more widespread polling center security, manned checkpoints, conducted patrols, and served as backup support for the ANP. All existing ANA battalions—approximately 16,000 soldiers and officers—were committed to the election security mission. ISAF and Coalition forces, representing the outer ring, functioned as a QRF, could only be called on in cases of emergency, and would be located out of sight of polling facilities. Global positioning system (GPS) coordinates were established in advance for each polling center, facilitating a rapid Coalition response if required.[129] Subordinate plans outlined additional security measures involving roads used to transport ballots; roads to polling places; JEMB regional offices; and ballot collection, transfer, and counting locations.[130]

Despite ongoing intimidation, allegations of fraud, and a perceived unfair advantage held by President Karzai, the 9 October election turned out to be nearly free of violence. Security operations were deemed a major success because of the close cooperation between the JEMB, APA, ANA, ISAF, and Coalition forces. MOI officials cited extensive pre-election training, interdiction of planned enemy attacks by Coalition and ANA forces, highly-effective offensive operations carried out along the Afghanistan-Pakistan border, and election-day Coalition air patrols as being instrumental in creating a reasonably safe environment for the Afghan people.[131]

More than 8 million Afghans voted, 40 percent of whom were women. The overall turnout rate of 70 percent was much higher than anticipated.[132] Controversies were minimal given the conditions. At a few voting locations, however, the indelible ink used to mark voters' thumbs could apparently be washed off. Subsequent accusations of multiple voting prompted several presidential candidates to threaten a boycott. In light of the exceptionally high voter turnout and the overwhelming enthusiasm of the Afghan people, boycott proceedings never materialized.[133] "This is one of the happiest days of my life," an elderly woman said. "I don't even care who wins. I just want peace and security and to live long enough to come and vote again."[134] Regarding the election, Lieutenant Colonel Caruso, Deputy Commander of CTF *Longhorn* in Herat, emphasized the monumental nature of the event, asserting, "Just the whole idea of getting an election to happen in Afghanistan, even if there were a billion things that weren't perfect about it, was cool and you could really see that the local Afghans were proud—especially the women."[135] Overall, 82 percent of Afghan citizens considered the election to have been free and fair as determined by a post-election nationwide survey of 17,000 voters.[136]

Transporting the completed ballots from the polling centers to the counting centers was a laborious task. Seven counting centers had been established in Kabul, Mazar-e Sharif, Herat, Konduz, Jalalabad, Gardez, and Bamian. Ballots from polling centers in Pakistan and Iran were brought to the Kabul counting center. Vehicles of all shapes and descriptions, plus horses, donkeys, and Afghans on foot participated in the process. Official counting did not begin until 20 October when national and international members of the JEMB staff completed the process. Various agents and observers were present during all stages of the counting process to ensure transparency. Results from each counting center were then reported to the national tally room in Kabul.[137]

On 3 November JEMB announced the official, certified results of Afghanistan's first democratic presidential election. As anticipated, Karzai won with a majority of 4.4 million votes (55.4 percent), thus precluding a run-off election. Yonous Qanuni, Mohammad Mohaqeq, and Abdul Rashid Dostum ran second, third, and fourth with 16.3 percent, 11.7 percent, and 10.0 percent of the votes, respectively. Dr. Masooda Jalal finished in sixth place with 91,415 (1.1 percent) votes.[138] Following his decisive win, Karzai's inauguration took place on 7 December in the former royal palace. During his acceptance speech, he elaborated on campaign speeches when he said, "We have now left a hard and dark past behind us, and today we are opening a new chapter in our history. On this day of a new, peaceful, prosperous era for our country, I would like to wish the best for Afghanistan." The crowd in attendance, which included Vice President Richard Cheney and more than 150 international representatives, stood to applaud the historic occasion.[139]

President Karzai's New Cabinet

On 23 December 2004 Karzai announced his new cabinet, which would eventually be approved by the National Assembly. The 27-member cabinet included numerous Afghan intellectuals and only one regional leader—Minister of Energy Ismail Khan. Former Deputy Defense Minister Abdul Rahim Wardak replaced Fahim Khan as Defense Minister. Ali Ahmad Jalali retained his post as Interior Minister, and Karzai's presidential election opponent, Masooda Jalal, received a special appointment as Minister of Women's Affairs.[140] Eight Tajiks and several Hazaras and Uzbeks were appointed to ministerial seats. President Karzai's running mates, Ahmad Zia Massoud and Mohamad Karim Khalili, became first and second vice presidents.

By the spring of 2005, the announcement of a US–Afghan agreement recognized Afghanistan's political progress toward full sovereignty. The new partnership emphasized a renewed dedication to the rule of law; protection of human rights; support for democratic governance; defeat of international terrorism; and ensuring Afghanistan's security, sovereignty, independence, and territorial integrity. "We are confident that the US–Afghan strategic partnership will play a central role in helping Afghanistan achieve these goals," declared President George W. Bush and Afghan President Karzai as they jointly announced the new partnership.[141]

In an effort to spread democracy to the provincial and district levels, the Afghan Government initiated a National Solidarity Program that encouraged rural governing councils to better manage local reconstruction projects. Nearly 40 percent of the governing council members were women. To further assist the Afghan Government, the US DOS established an Afghan Reconstruction Group at the Embassy in Kabul and an Office of Afghanistan Affairs in Washington, DC. As an additional measure of support for the Afghan Government, Secretary of Defense Donald

Rumsfeld visited every 3 months, Secretary of State Condoleezza Rice met with Karzai twice in 2005, and First Lady Laura Bush traveled to Afghanistan in March 2005.[142]

Afghanistan Parliamentary and Provincial Council Elections 2005

Parliamentary and provincial elections in Afghanistan represented the last milestone in implementing the requirements of the 2001 Bonn Agreement. The 2004 Afghanistan Constitution and the 2005 Afghan Electoral Law had described the form that the legislature and local government would take. A National Assembly with a Lower House with 249 seats and an Upper House with 102 seats would serve at the national level. At lower levels, provincial councils, district councils, and municipal councils and mayors would ensure that the country was governed in a representative fashion. In Afghanistan's new National Assembly, Lower House representatives would be elected directly by the people and each province's share of seats was proportional to its population.[†] Women were guaranteed 68 seats. In the Upper House, members would be either selected by Provincial Councils (34 members) and District Councils (34 members) or appointed by the president (34 members).[143]

At a March 2005 meeting in Kabul, US Secretary of State Rice and Afghan President Karzai decided to postpone the parliamentary and provincial council elections from April 2005 until 18 September and to put off district council elections until 2006. Recognizing that this election plan would leave a 34-seat shortfall in the Upper House, Afghan officials adopted a temporary measure that reduced President Karzai's appointments from 34 to 17, thereby retaining the 2 to 1 relationship between selected and appointed members. Secretary Rice and President Karzai indicated that the reasons for postponing the elections involved the perception of deteriorating security in Afghanistan and complicated election logistical issues. For example, 34 separate ballots would be required, one for each province. Hundreds of candidates were listed on each ballot, and all the ballots—many of which had not yet been completely designed—needed to be printed and distributed to the 6,000 polling stations.[144] More time would be needed to design, print, and distribute all the ballots.

To take the initiative against enemy forces and preempt any offensives aimed at disrupting the elections, Coalition forces expanded offensive operations over the summer. To bolster CFC-A's combat power before the elections, CENTCOM deployed the 1st Battalion, 325th Airborne Infantry Regiment (1-325 AIR) to Afghanistan during the summer of 2005. As elections approached, the new CFC-A commander, Lieutenant General Eikenberry, stressed the need to "keep on taking the fight to the enemy. . . . It is a battle of wills out there—we are up against a determined enemy."[145] Indeed, the Taliban planned an information campaign and attacks to deter the elections. Mofti Latifollah Hakimi, a Taliban spokesman, issued anti-parliamentary election propaganda in the summer of 2005, calling the elections deceptive, fraudulent, and illegal, and threatening to attack electoral offices, staff, and legislative candidates.[146] Taliban leader Mullah Mohammad Omar threatened to disrupt the Afghan parliamentary elections at any cost, describing them as merely a "toll to legitimize the US occupation of Afghanistan."[147]

Enemy forces did step up attacks in 2005. By September more than 1,000 Afghans and 77 American servicemen and women had been killed since the year began.[148] Most notable was

---

[†]Kabul province, with its large population, has 33 seats. The smaller province of Panjshir, for example, has two seats.

the downing of the MH-47 Chinook helicopter in Kunar province mentioned earlier in this chapter.[149] In southern Kabul province, Taliban insurgents threw hand grenades into a police vehicle, killing five officers and the police chief of Musehi District. Seven parliamentary candidates and four election officials were also killed, and official reports surfaced of kidnappings, beheadings, and suicide bombing attacks.[150] In August, 1 police officer was killed and 14 were wounded by a remote control bomb in Kandahar, where a district judge had been fatally shot a month earlier.[151] Although these attacks and others were serious, they were sporadic and did little to interfere with voter registration, candidate registration, or campaigning.[152]

Election day security measures were similar to those followed for the presidential election a year earlier. ANP officers and patrolmen were on duty inside each polling station, while ANA and additional ANP forces encircled the outside. Coalition and ISAF troops would remain nearby, but out of sight, to serve as backup. CJTF-76's weekly intelligence meetings with both UNAMA and the JEMB proved invaluable in developing a common understanding of the threat environment and in the subsequent preparation of an appropriate election security plan.[153] Scattered but minimal violence did occur on 18 September 2005—19 polling stations were attacked and rockets hit a UN compound, the ISAF headquarters in Kabul, and the airport at Jalalabad. However, it was hardly the cataclysm promised by the Taliban. The most serious incident involved an IED attack that killed a French officer near the Spin Boldak border crossing in Kandahar province. In all, there were 12 deaths attributed to enemy attacks during the elections.[154]

By that day, 2 million more Afghan citizens had registered to vote since the October 2004 presidential election, bringing the total number of registered voters to 12.5 million. More than 1,000 Afghan and international observers, including teams from the European Union and the UNAMA, were present to monitor the election process.[155] The JEMB, which then consisted of nine Afghan members of the Independent Electoral Commission (IEC) and four international experts, retained responsibility for developing election rules, regulations, and procedures. Each Afghan voter would be allowed to cast one vote for one candidate from his or her province for the Lower House, in accordance with Afghanistan's Single Non-Transferable Vote (SNTV) policy.[156]

In July, during a televised lottery held at the Kabul Intercontinental Hotel, Afghan children had hand-picked pieces of paper with the names of all 6,000 parliamentary and provincial council candidates (of whom over 500 were women) from cardboard boxes to determine the order in which the names would be listed on the ballot. This selection process could have been accomplished more quickly using computers; however, Peter Erben, head of the UN–Afghan election secretariat, thought transparency was important. "We wanted to demonstrate what it means to have free and open elections," Erben explained.[157]

Despite the massive voter registration effort and the relatively low rate of violence, the turnout rate was 53 percent, lower than anticipated and lower than that of the 2004 presidential election. Various explanations for the low turnout emerged, including security issues, inclusion of some regional leaders as candidates, failure to accommodate Afghan refugees in the voting process, and voter apathy stemming from dissatisfaction with government performance since the presidential election. Nevertheless, this second successful Afghan election in less than a year, which had cost donor countries nearly $150 million, was a giant step forward and represented genuine progress for a newly democratic nation.[158] President Bush, CFC-A Commander

Lieutenant General Eikenberry, and CJTF-76 Commanding General Major General Kamiya all pledged continued US support for Afghanistan and congratulated President Karzai and the Afghan people for their significant achievement and for surmounting the many obstacles that had stood in their way.[159] The JEMB would go on to certify the final parliamentary results on 12 November and the National Assembly would eventually be seated on 19 December 2005. Afghans would now wait patiently to see how their new parliament would govern.

✦   ✦   ✦

From mid-2004 to the election of September 2005, Afghanistan not only took critical steps toward forming a truly representative government but also consolidated military power within the hands of that government. By the fall of 2005, more than 26,000 ANA troops had been trained, equipped, and readied to fight. Also by that date, the Coalition and the international community had poured billions of dollars into Afghanistan in the form of reconstruction aid and used the 22 PRTs in operation to help the Afghans efficiently employ those funds. These milestones led many Coalition leaders to express optimism about Afghanistan's future.

Despite the generally positive outlook, there was anxiety about the security situation in the country. Clearly, Taliban and al-Qaeda forces were better organized than they were in 2002 and were launching attacks that had greater lethality. The Coalition and ISAF had responded partly by increasing the number of their troops inside Afghanistan and employing those forces in a COIN campaign designed to gain and retain the support of the population as the means of denying the insurgent forces support. Why then was the insurgency enduring? What part of the Coalition military approach needed to be retooled?

These questions remained unanswered as the end of 2005 approached. The Coalition and the US Army had been operating in Afghanistan for exactly 4 years and had accomplished a great deal. Most importantly, it had freed the Afghan people from the grips of a tyrannical regime that harbored and enabled a deadly international terrorist group. These were victories that American Soldiers made possible and of which they could be proud. However, it was clear that the struggle to secure a stable and prosperous future for Afghanistan was not yet won.

Notes

1. Lieutenant General David W. Barno, interview by Center for Military History, 21 November 2006, 31–32.

2. Department of the Army G3, *US Army Troop Levels in OEF Spreadsheet*, 2008.

3. Colonel Richard Pedersen, "BRONCO 6 Guidance: How to Think about OEF," 16 March 2004, 6.

4. US Department of Defense, "Into Afghanistan: Rooting Out Terrorists," *DefenseLink*, 1–2. http://www.defenselink.mil/home/features/1082004d.html (accessed 24 May 2007); 25th Infantry Division Association, "Global War on Terrorism," 9–10. http://www.25thida.com/division.html, (accessed 16 May 2007).

5. Pedersen, "BRONCO 6 Guidance," 7–9.

6. Dr. Robert Perito, interview by Contemporary Operations Study Team, Combat Studies Institute, Fort Leavenworth, KS, 26 June 2007, 6–8.

7. Major General Michael Flynn, *State of the Insurgency: Trends, Intentions and Objectives* Briefing, 22 December 2009, slide 8.

8. Ahmed Rashid, *Descent into Chaos: The United States and the Failure of Nation Building in Pakistan, Afghanistan, and Central Asia* (New York, NY: Viking Press, 2008), 253.

9. Pedersen, "BRONCO 6 Guidance," 1–2.

10. Colonel Walter M. Herd, Combined Joint Special Operations Task Force Briefing, *Unconventional Warriors: Separate Insurgents from the Populace: Special Operations in Afghanistan September 2003–June 2004*, slide 9.

11. Colonel Walter M. Herd, interview by Contemporary Operations Study Team, Combat Studies Institute, Fort Leavenworth, KS, 22 June 2007, 8.

12. CJTF-76, "OPORD 04-01, Bronco Strike (OEF-5 Combat Operations), 3d Brigade, 25th Infantry Division," 22 May 2004, 2.

13. CJTF-76, "OPORD 04-01, Bronco Strike," 2.

14. CJTF-76, "OPORD 04-01, Bronco Strike," 3.

15. Christopher N. Koontz, ed., *Enduring Voices: Oral Histories of the US Army Experience in Afghanistan, 2003–2005* (Washington, DC: US Army Center of Military History, 2008), 273.

16. Koontz, ed., *Enduring Voices,* 273.

17. Pedersen, "BRONCO 6 Guidance," 1.

18. Pedersen, "BRONCO 6 Guidance," 1.

19. Pedersen, "BRONCO 6 Guidance," 1.

20. Colonel Gary H. Cheek, "So You Want to Be a Maneuver Brigade Commander? CTF Thunder in Afghanistan," *Field Artillery,* March–April 2005, 5.

21. Cheek, "So You Want to Be a Maneuver Brigade Commander?" 6.

22. CJTF-76, "OPORD 04-01, Bronco Strike," 10.

23. CJTF-76, "OPORD 04-01, Bronco Strike," 10.

24. CJTF-76, "OPORD 04-01, Bronco Strike," 11–12.

25. Koontz, ed., *Enduring Voices,* 295.

26. Koontz, ed., *Enduring Voices,* 260.

27. Colonel Richard N. Pedersen, interview by Contemporary Operations Study Team, Combat Studies Institute, Fort Leavenworth, KS, 8 November 2006, 16.

28. CJTF-76, "OPORD 04-01, Bronco Strike," 23–24.

29. CTF *Bronco, OEF V Historical Command Brief*, 22 April 2005, slide 43.

30. Koontz, ed., *Enduring Voices,* 388–391.

31. Koontz, ed., *Enduring Voices,* 390.

32. Koontz, ed., *Enduring Voices,* 359–360.

33.   CTF *Bronco*, *OEF V Historical Command Brief*, 22 April 2005, slide 26.

34.   CTF *Bronco*, *OEF V Historical Command Brief*, 22 April 2005, slide 27.

35.   Herd, interview, 22 June 2007, 6–7.

36.   Herd, interview, 22 June 2007, 7.

37.   Adrian T. Bogart III, *One Valley at a Time* (Hurlburt Field, FL: Joint Special Operations University Press, 2006), 59–60.

38.   Bogart, *One Valley at a Time,* 61.

39.   Bogart, *One Valley at a Time,* 66.

40.   US Congress, Senate, Senate Armed Services Committee, *Statement of General Bryan D. Brown, US Army,* 109th Cong., 1st Sess., 22 April 2005, 7.

41.   US Special Operations Command History Office, *United States Special Operations Command HISTORY, 1987–2007, 20th Anniversary Edition* (MacDill Air Force Base, FL: USSOCOM, 2007), 110.

42.   *USSOCOM History*, 110.

43.   *USSOCOM History*, 110.

44.   Pedersen, interview, 8 November 2006, 11.

45.   Antonio Giustozzi, *Working Paper No. 33: Respectable Warlords? The Politics of State-Building in Post-Taleban Afghanistan*, Crisis States Programme Development Research Centre (London: DESTIN, 2003). http://www.crisisstates.com/download/wp/WP33.pdf (accessed 29 July 2007).

46.   "Afghanistan." United Nations Disarmament, Demobilization, and Reintegration Resource Centre. http://www.unddr.org/countryprogrammes.php?c=121 (accessed 17 May 2007).

47.   "Afghanistan," UN DDR Resource Center, 4; IRIN Humanitarian News and Analysis, "Afghanistan: Year in Review 2005–Fragile Process, Insecurity Remains," 11 January 2006, 2. http://www.irinnews.org/report.aspx?reportid=33637 (accessed 24 July 2007).

48.   International Crisis Group Update Briefing, *Afghanistan: Getting Disarmament Back on Track*, Asia Briefing No. 35, 23 February 2005, 5–6. http://www.crisisgroup.org/home/index.cfm?l=1&id=3290 (accessed 28 July 2007).

49.   Koontz, ed., *Enduring Voices,* 317; Major Edward Croot, interview by Contemporary Operations Study Team, Combat Studies Institute, Fort Leavenworth, KS, 2 February 2007, 14–15.

50.   Donna Miles, "NATO Makes Key Decisions on Iraq, Afghanistan," *American Forces Press Service*, 28 June 2004, 1–2. http://www.defenselink.mil/news/newsarticle.aspx?id=26186 (accessed 4 June 2007); Allied Joint Forces Command Headquarters (PIO), "Expansion of NATO Presence in Afghanistan." http://www.nato.int/isaf/topics/expansion/index.html (accessed 4 June 2007).

51.   Allied Joint Forces Command Headquarters (PIO), "ISAF Takes Command of Western PRTs in Herat and Farah" (31 May 2005), Press Release #2005-036, 1–2. http://www.nato.int/isaf/docu/pressrelease/2005/Release_31May05.htm (accessed 8 July 2007).

52.   Allied Joint Forces Command Headquarters (PIO), "ISAF Holds Change of Command Ceremony in Kabul" (4 August 2005), Press Release #2005-47, 1. http://www.nato.int/isaf/docu/pressrelease/2005/ Release_04Aug_47.htm (accessed 8 July 2007).

53.   Helle Dale, "NATO in Afghanistan: A Test Case for Future Missions," *The Heritage Foundation Backgrounder* #1985, 27 November 2006, 3–5. http://www.heritage.org/Research/Europe/upload/bg_1985.pdf (accessed 21 May 2007).

54.   Scott Schonauer, "SETAF Takes Command of Afghan Mission," *Stars and Stripes European Edition* (16 March 2005): 1–3. http://www.military.com/NewContent/0,13190,SS_031605_Setaf,00.html (accessed 21 May 2007).

55.   Major General Jason Kamiya, interview by Contemporary Operations Study Team, Combat Studies Institute, Fort Leavenworth, KS, 11 September 2007, 4.

56.   Major General Jason Kamiya, *Leadership Preparation Monograph #1*: *Insurgency/ Counterinsurgency Historical Perspectives* (Vincenza, Italy: USASETAF, 2004), 3–4.

57.   Kamiya, *Leadership Preparation Monograph #1*, 47–49.

58.   Colonel Kevin Owens, "News Briefing with Colonel Kevin Owens" (23 September 2005), Office of the Assistant Secretary of Defense for Public Affairs, 1–2. http://www.defenselink.mil/transcripts/transcript.aspx?transcriptid=2580 (accessed 21 May 2007).

59.   Kamiya, interview, 11 September 2007, 4.

60.   Colonel (P) Patrick Donahue, "Combating a Modern Insurgency: Combined Task Force Devil in Afghanistan," *Military Review* (March–April 2008): 30.

61.   Donahue, "Combating a Modern Insurgency," 32.

62.   US Department of State, "Fact Sheet: Progress in Afghanistan's Reconstruction," 26 March 2004, 1–2. http://www.state.gov/r/pa/prs/ps/2004/30803.htm (accessed 19 June 2007).

63.   US Government Accountability Office, GAO-05-742, *Afghanistan Reconstruction: Despite Some Progress, Deteriorating Security and Other Obstacles Continue to Threaten Achievement of US Goals*, July 2005, 3–4. www.gao.gov/new.items/d05742.pdf (accessed 21 May 2007).

64.   US Government Accountability Office, GAO-07-801SP, *Securing, Stabilizing, and Reconstructing Afghanistan*, May 2007, 23. www.gao.gov/new.items/d07801sp.pdf (accessed 21 July 2007).

65.   GAO-05-742, 10–18.

66.   GAO-05-742, 18–19.

67.   Eric Aubrey, Afghanistan Engineer District, "The Corps Needs You," 1 July 2005. http://www.aed.usace.army.mil/news/releases/exitinterview.html (accessed 23 February 2009); US Army Corps of Engineers, "Afghanistan Engineer Fact Sheet." http://usace.army.mil/CEPA/FactSheets/Pages/AED.aspx (accessed 23 February 2009).

68.   US Department of Defense, "Afghan Engineer District Chief Updates Projects," *American Forces Press Service*, 11 April 2005. http://www.defenselink.mil/news/newsarticle.aspx?id=31457 (access 23 February 2009).

69.   Corps of Engineers, "Afghanistan Engineer Fact Sheet."

70.   Afghanistan Engineer District, "Colonel O'Dowd Reflects on Afghan Mission," 10 July 2005. http://www.aed.usace.army.mil/news/releases/exitinterview.html (accessed 23 February 2009).

71.   Andrew S. Natsios, "The Nine Principles of Reconstruction and Development," 16. www.carlisle.army.mil/usawc/parameters/05autumn/natsios.pdf (accessed 18 February 2009).

72.   GAO-07-801SP, 28–29.

73.   Dr. Robert M. Perito, *United States Institute of Peace Special Report: The US Experience with Provincial Reconstruction Teams in Afghanistan*, Special Report 152, October 2005, 1–15; Lieutenant General David W. Barno, interview by Center for Military History, 21 November 2006, 46, 50.

74.   Lieutenant Colonel Jennifer Caruso, interview by Contemporary Operations Study Team, Combat Studies Institute, Fort Leavenworth, KS, 25 July 2007, 7.

75.   Lieutenant Colonel Steven Ford, interview by Contemporary Operations Study Team, Combat Studies Institute, Fort Leavenworth, KS, 14 September, 2007, 3.

76.   Lieutenant Colonel Steven Ford, Ghazni PRT VIP Briefing, *Provisional Reconstruction Team: Ghazni, Afghanistan*, 22 May 2004, slide 2.

77.   Ford, Ghazni PRT VIP Briefing, slides 6, 9, 11.

78.   Anonymous US military PRT commander, interview by United States Institute of Peace, Afghanistan Experience Project, Washington, DC, interview #45, 20 September 2005, 2–14.

79.   Caruso, interview, 25 July 2007, 8.

80.   Caruso, interview, 25 July 2007, 8–9.

81.   Sergeant Flora Estrada, interview by Contemporary Operations Study Team, Combat Studies Institute, Schofield Barracks, Hawaii, 24 July 2007, 3–4.

82.   Caruso, interview, 25 July 2007, 14.

83.   Colonel Gary Cheek, interview by United States Institute of Peace, Afghanistan Experience Project, Washington, DC, interview #51, 24 August 2005, 5.

84.   Cheek, interview, 24 August 2005, 5.

85. Caruso, interview, 25 July 2007, 11–13.

86. Cheek, interview, 24 August 2005, 18.

87. Pedersen, interview, 8 November 2006, 5–6.

88. Dr. Kenneth Katzman, interview by Contemporary Operations Study Team, Combat Studies Institute, Fort Leavenworth, KS, 25 June 2007, 5.

89. Perito, *US Experience with PRTs in Afghanistan*, Special Report 152, 9.

90. MSF Press Release, "MSF Pulls Out of Afghanistan," 28 July 2004, 1–2. http://www.msf.org/msfinternational/invoke.cfm?component=pressrelease&objectid=8851DF09-F62D-47D4-A8D3EB1E876A1E0D& method=full_html (accessed 20 September 2007).

91. Michael Dziedzic and Colonel Michael Seidl, Special Report #147, "United States Institute of Peace Special Report: Provincial Reconstruction Teams," September 2005, 5.

92. Anonymous US military PRT commander, interview #45, 20 September 2005, 13.

93. Perito, *US Experience with PRTs in Afghanistan*, Special Report 152, 11–12.

94. Major General (Retired) Craig P. Weston, interview by Contemporary Operations Study Team, Combat Studies Institute, Fort Leavenworth, KS, 18 July 2007, 7.

95. "GIs to Help Train Afghan National Army," 14 July 2004, 1–3. http://www.military.com/NewsContent/0,13319,FL_train_071404,00.html (accessed 12 June 2007); Mitch Perryman, "Letter from Afghanistan," undated, 1–2. http://www.halllakeland.com/troops/letter.htm (accessed 1 August 2007).

96. Halima Kazem, "New Afghan Army Asserts Itself," *Christian Science Monitor,* 23 August 2004, 6; "Afghan National Army Activates Second Regional Command," *American Forces Press Service,* 23 September 2004, 1–3. http://www.defenselink.mil/news/newsarticle.aspx?id=25226 (accessed 1 August 2007); Ron Synovitz, "Afghanistan: New National Army Bases Planned in Four Provinces," 17 March 2004, 1–2. http://www.rferl.org/featuresarticle/2004/3/360A06F8-2DE5-4B3D-8DCF-55F0CE3A648E.html (accessed 18 June 2007).

97. Samuel Chan, "Sentinels of Afghan Democracy: The Afghan National Army," S. Rajaratnam School of International Studies, 1 June 2007, unpublished paper, 4–8.

98. 3d Squadron, 4th Cavalry, 3d BCT, 25th Infantry Division (Light) was also sent at this time to Herat. Caruso, interview, 25 July 2007, 10.

99. Kazem, "New Afghan Army Asserts Itself," 2.

100. Kazem, "New Afghan Army Asserts Itself," 2.

101. Samuel Chan, "Sentinels of Afghan Democracy," 14; Aryn Baker, "Can the Afghans Defend Themselves?" *Time in Partnership with CNN,* 3 January 2007, 1–3. http://www.time.com/time/world/article/0,8599,1573742,00.html (accessed 24 June 2007).

102. Frederick Rice, "Afghanistan Unit Takes on New Mission and Name," *American Forces Press Service,* 13 July 2005, 1–3. http://www.defenselink.mil/news/newsarticle.aspx?id=16650 (accessed 22 May 2007); Combined Security Transition Command–Afghanistan Fact Sheet, 12 April 2006, 1. http://oneteam.centcom.mil/fact_sheets/CSTC-A%20Fact%20sheet%20-%2012%20April%202006.pdf (accessed 22 June 2007).

103. Colonel George B. Forsythe, "Final Report of the Military Academy Study Team," official correspondence to OMC-A, 11 November 2003, 1–2.

104. Colonel George B. Forsythe, "National Military Academy of Afghanistan: Concept Plan," unpublished, 11 November 2003, 2.

105. Brigadier General (Retired) George B. Forsythe, interview by Contemporary Operations Study Team, Combat Studies Institute, Fort Leavenworth, KS, 18 April 2007, 16. (Note: Forsythe was promoted to brigadier general in 2004.)

106. CSTC-A Info Paper, "National Military Academy of Afghanistan," April 2007, 1.

107. Rick Peat and Frederick Rice, "Afghan Military Academy Opens Gates to Future Leaders," Special to *American Forces Press Service,* 28 March 2005, 1–2. http://www.defenselink.mil/news/newsarticle.aspx?id=31081 (accessed 9 April 2007).

108. Ray Nelson, "The National Military Academy of Afghanistan: A First-Hand Account," *First Call*, 27 March 2005, 1–12. http://www.west-point.org/users/usma1983/40505/First_Call_Article/article.doc (accessed 12 April 2007).

109. US Government Accountability Office, GAO-05-575, "Afghanistan Security: Efforts to Establish Army and Police Have Made Progress, but Future Plans Need to Be Better Defined," June 2005, 1–27; US Department of State and US Department of Defense, "Interagency Assessment of Afghanistan Police Training and Readiness," DOS Report No. ISP-IQO-07-07, DOD Report No. IE-2007-001, 14 November 2006, 5–32.

110. Major General Craig P. Weston, "Key to Afghan National Police Mission Assumption," unpublished, undated notes.

111. GAO-05-575, 3.

112. Major General Craig P. Weston and the OMC-A Staff, *OMC-A's Estimate, COAs, and Recommendation for Police Sector Reform: Brief to LTG Barno as of 3 January 2005*, unpublished, slides 1–44.

113. Rice, "Afghanistan Unit Takes on New Mission and Name," 1–3.

114. Major General John Brennan, interview by Contemporary Operations Study Team, Combat Studies Institute, Fort Leavenworth, KS, 12 September 2007, 4.

115. Major General John Brennan, "Proposed Briefing Flow for ANP Plan," unpublished, undated, 1.

116. Major General John Brennan, *Afghan National Police Program* Brief, unpublished, undated, slides 3–4.

117. Rice, "Afghanistan Unit Takes on New Mission and Name," 1–3.

118. Brennan, interview, 12 September 2007, 8.

119. Larry P. Goodson, "Afghanistan in 2004: Electoral Progress and an Opium Boom," *Caliber Asian Survey* (January/February 2005): 93.

120. US Department of State, "Fact Sheet: Afghanistan Elections 2004: Women's Participation," 1–2. http://www.state.gov/g/wi/rls/24792.htm (accessed 1 May 2007).

121. Human Rights Watch, "Afghanistan: Protect Women Candidates," 16 August 2005. http://www.hrw.org/en/news/2005/08/16/afghanistan-protect-women-candidates (accessed 23 February 2009).

122. Human Rights Watch, "Afghanistan: Protect Women Candidates."

123. Tim McGirk, "Inside Karzai's Campaign," *Time* (11 October 2004): 44.

124. "Special Report: Voting in Warlord Country–Afghanistan," *The Economist* (9 October 2004): 21–24.

125. Joint Electoral Management Body, "Afghanistan Presidential Election Results 2004: On Voting." http://www.elections-afghanistan.org.af/Election%20Results%20Website/english/english.htm (accessed 24 July 2007); Goodson, "Afghanistan in 2004: Electoral Progress and an Opium Boom," 94.

126. "Special Report: Voting in Warlord Country–Afghanistan," 21–24.

127. Andrew Reynolds and Andrew Wilder, "Free, Fair or Flawed: Challenges for Legitimate Elections in Afghanistan," Afghanistan Research and Evaluation Unit (AREU), 6–7. http://www.areu.org.af/?option=com_docman&Itemid=&task=doc_download&gid=225 (accessed 21 May 2007).

128. Eric Schmitt and David Rohde, "Taliban Fighters Increase Attacks, with Troubling Toll Among G.I.'s and Afghans," *New York Times,* 1 August 2004, 1.11.

129. Sergeant Douglas DeMaio, interview by Contemporary Operations Study Team, Combat Studies Institute, Fort Leavenworth, KS, 12 February 2007, 23.

130. Joint Electoral Management Body, "Afghanistan Presidential Election Results 2004: On Security." http://www.elections-afghanistan.org.af/Election%20Results%20Website/english/english.htm (accessed 20 July 2007).

131. Jawad Sharifzada, "Election Security a Success," *Institute for War & Peace Reporting*, 26 October 2004, ARR No. 143. http://www.iwpr.net/?p=arr&s=f&o=152833&apc_state=heniarr2004 (accessed 21 May 2007).

132. Joint Electoral Management Body, "Afghanistan Presidential Election Results 2004: Turnout by Province." http://www.elections-afghanistan.org.af/Election%20Results%20Website/english/english.htm (accessed 24 July 2007).

133. Hafizullah Gardesh, "Elections Close Not with a Bang, But a Whimper," *Institute for War & Peace Reporting*, 11 October 2004, ARR No. 140. http://www.iwpr.net/?p=arr&s=f&o=152833&apc_state=heniarr2004 (accessed 21 May 2007).

134. US Department of State, "Road to Democracy: Afghan Elections" (posted November 2004), 1. http://usinfo.state.gov/products/pubs/afgelect/afghanistan.htm (accessed 25 July 2007).

135. Caruso, interview, 25 July 2007, 20.

136. US Department of State, "The First Democratic Elections in Afghanistan: A Report by the Bipartisan Observer Team," 15 October 2004, 1–7. http://fpc.state.gov/fpc/37133.htm (accessed 21 May 2007).

137. Joint Electoral Management Body, "Afghanistan Presidential Election Results 2004: On Counting." http://www.elections-afghanistan.org.af/Election%20Results%20Website/english/english.htm (accessed 12 June 2007).

138. Joint Electoral Management Body, "Afghanistan Presidential Election Results 2004: Decision of the Joint Electoral Management Body—Certification of Results." http://www.elections-afghanistan.org.af/Election%20Results%20Website/english/english.htm (accessed 12 June 2007).

139. Lisa Stein, "The Week," *US News and World Report*, 12 December 2004. http://www.usnews.com/usnews/news/articles/041220/20week.lede.htm (accessed 18 February 2009).

140. Goodson, "Afghanistan in 2004: Electoral Progress and an Opium Boom," 96.

141. "Joint Declaration of the United States–Afghanistan Strategic Partnership." http://www.whitehouse.gov/news/releases/2005/05/20050523-2.html (accessed 20 June 2007).

142. Dr. Kenneth Katzman, "Afghanistan: Post-War Governance, Security, and US Policy," Congressional Research Service Report RL 30588, 11 January 2006, 12–13. www.fas.org/sgp/crs/row/RL30588.pdf (accessed 20 June 2007).

143. Andrew Reynolds, Lucy Jones, and Andrew Wilder, "A Guide to Parliamentary Elections in Afghanistan," Afghan Research and Evaluation Unit, August 2005, 3–6. http://unplan1.un.org/intradoc/groups/public/documents/APCITY/UNPLAN021668.pdf (accessed 12 June 2007).

144. Declan Walsh, "Afghan Elections Put Back to the Autumn: Rice Renews US Commitment as 5 Bomb Deaths Mar Her Visit," *The Guardian*, 18 March 2005, 18; N.C. Aizenman, "Long-Delayed Afghan Vote Is Set for September; One House of Parliament Will Remain Incomplete," *Washington Post*, 21 March 2005, A.11.

145. Thom Shanker, "Coalition Steps Up Raids as Afghan Elections Approach," *New York Times*, 20 August 2005, A.5.

146. "Taliban Denounce Afghan Elections, Vow to Resist Future Parliament," *BBC Monitoring Newsfile*, 21 September 2005, 1; "Taliban Pledge to Disrupt Afghan Elections, Rule out Polling Day Attacks," *BBC Monitoring South Asia,* 21 August 2005, 1.

147. "NATO to Boost Troops to 12,000 Ahead of Afghan Elections," *Xinhua News Agency–CEIS*, 27 July 2005, 1.

148. "Leaders: Putting Steel into Karzai; Afghanistan's Parliamentary Elections," *The Economist*, 24 September 2005, 17.

149. John Hendren, "Lucky Shot Brought Down Helicopter in Afghanistan," *Houston Chronicle*, 1 July 2005, 23.

150. Kim Barker, "Targeted Attacks Intended to Disrupt Afghan Elections," *Knight Ridder Tribune News Service*, 17 September 2005, 1; Jonathan Landay, "Afghan Election Prompts Fighting," *Knight Ridder Newspapers*, 21 August 2005, A.8.

151. Carlotta Gall, "Fatal Bombing Mars Start of Afghan Election Campaign," *International Herald Tribune*, 19 August 2005, 3; "3 Afghan Election Workers Abducted; Judge Shot," *Washington Post*, 24 July 2005, A.18.

152. Barker, "Targeted Attacks Intended to Disrupt Afghan Elections," 1.

153. Kamiya, interview, 11 September 2007, 12–13.

154. "Asia: Democracy, Sort of; Afghanistan's Elections," *The Economist,* 24 September 2005, 84; "Afghan Elections Begin Amidst Taliban Attacks," *Hindustan Times*, 18 September 2005, 1.

155. Esther Pan, "Afghan Parliamentary Elections," Council on Foreign Relations Backgrounder, 16 September 2005, 1–4. http://www.cfr.org/publication/8867/afghan_parliamentary_elections.html (accessed 21 May 2007).

156. Reynolds, Jones, and Wilder, "A Guide to Parliamentary Elections in Afghanistan," 7, 12.

157. "Asia: Getting the Vote Out; Afghanistan," *The Economist*, 2 July 2005, 60.

158. "Afghanistan Votes," *Washington Post*, 16 September 2005, A.30; Aizenman, "Long-Delayed Afghan Vote Is Set for Sept.," A.11.

159. "President Congratulates Afghan People and Government on Successful Parliamentary Elections," The White House, Office of the Press Secretary, 18 September 2005, 1.

Chapter 11

Implications

All wars are improvisations. Given the influence on military engagements of a myriad of factors—some of which are within human control and many that are not—how could warfare be characterized otherwise? The 19th-century German military theorist Carl von Clausewitz acknowledged this fact capturing the importance of the improvisational nature of war in the word *friction,* a term that describes the unpredictable factors in war that alter conditions, plans, and objectives. Clausewitz emphasized the unique and unpredictable character of military campaigns by contending, "Each is an uncharted sea, full of reefs."* It is imperative, according to Clausewitz, for the commander and staff to make allowances for friction in their planning and decisions, although they can never completely overcome random and unforeseen events that have often undone the most experienced military leader.

From its inception in the chaotic weeks after the attacks of 9/11, the course of Operation ENDURING FREEDOM (OEF) was heavily shaped by improvisation. Without a contingency plan for a campaign to overthrow the Taliban regime in Afghanistan, the US Department of Defense (DOD) and US Central Command (CENTCOM) rapidly created a response that took advantage of the technological strengths of the United States and the political weaknesses of the Taliban. This campaign, which featured Coalition aircraft launching precision weapons that were guided onto targets by Special Operations teams working with the Taliban's domestic enemies, was a resounding success in achieving the initial objectives of the United States. Within the 3-month period that began in October 2001, the US-led Coalition and its Northern Alliance allies overthrew the Taliban regime, pushed most of al-Qaeda's operatives out of Afghanistan, and installed a new Afghan Government. This successful coordination of air power and Special Operations Forces (SOF) in support of a proxy force—essentially an unprecedented combination—led to President George W. Bush's characterization of OEF as a "different kind of war." This statement simultaneously suggested that the Afghanistan campaign would feature new techniques and avoid the deployment of large numbers of US forces and materiel normally used to gain control of an entire country.

The 4-year Coalition effort that followed the victory over the Taliban was also heavily improvised, but it enjoyed less success in achieving the Coalition's ultimate objective—the creation of a stable Afghanistan that no longer served as a haven for international terrorist groups such as al-Qaeda. To be sure, as OEF matured the US Army and its joint, interagency, and Coalition partners became far more adept at working within the Afghan environment. Significant innovations such as the creation of the Provincial Reconstruction Teams (PRTs) demonstrated flexibility in thought and action. Changes in the direction of the overall effort, most importantly Lieutenant General David W. Barno's introduction of a formal counterinsurgency (COIN) campaign in 2003, displayed a very real commitment to making critical corrections. As parliamentary elections were held in September 2005, however, Afghanistan was experiencing its highest rate of violence since the fall of the Taliban, suggesting that the country was not moving inexorably toward stability. Moreover, that year saw the highest US casualties since the beginning of OEF.

---

*Carl von Clausewitz, *On War*, eds. Peter Paret and Michael Howard (Princeton, NJ: Princeton University Press, 1976), 120.

To understand why the Coalition campaign did not foster a more stable environment after 2001, one must look beyond the *friction* that, as Clausewitz noted, is universal to the practice of warfare. This chapter highlights the key decisions and processes that shaped OEF from October 2001 to September 2005 to present the implications that the campaign during this period offers the US Army today.

Envisioning the Campaign: "Nation Building" and Planning for OEF

The departure point for this discussion must be the initial vision for OEF and how key senior military and political officials saw the campaign developing over time. With the emphasis on projecting a viable military force into Afghanistan in a matter of weeks, the CENTCOM commander, General Tommy Franks, and his staff quickly facilitated the marriage of Coalition forces with Northern Alliance militia. Franks had few options. The Afghan theater of war was remotely located in central Asia, a great distance from the sea and in a region that was unwilling to support a large US presence.

The traditional American approach that featured the nation's ability to project large amounts of combat forces and materiel to crush an enemy was essentially nullified. There would be no forced entry, such as the invasion of France in 1944 or building up massive forces as in Saudi Arabia during DESERT SHIELD and DESERT STORM in 1990. Even if this type of massing of forces had been politically feasible, the poor and mountainous neighboring nations possessed no infrastructure or road network to support it. Conditions in poverty-stricken and war-ravaged Afghanistan were even worse. Diplomatic persuasion initially yielded only a ramshackle former Soviet airbase in Uzbekistan, thereby forcing a reliance on air rather than sea and ground lines of communications (LOCs). These factors necessitated a small and highly capable force that barely called on the services of the US Army's conventional maneuver units, but rather relied on two unified commands (CENTCOM and Special Operations Command [SOCOM]). The speed with which these teams were able to depose the Taliban and chase al-Qaeda terrorist groups into their mountain redoubts surprised observers and participants alike and revealed the severe weakness in the Taliban's hold over Afghanistan.

The fall of the Taliban regime in December 2001, nevertheless, did not mark the end of the Coalition campaign. When it came time to turn this victory into a lasting success that would achieve the Coalition's strategic goals, planners at CENTCOM, SOCOM, and the US DOD became less certain of the proper course. The single greatest obstacle to conceptualizing OEF in a holistic sense was the ambivalence among senior American political officials about what was often derogatorily referred to as "nation building," the large-scale, time-consuming reconstruction and governance-building efforts such as those that had characterized American involvement in Bosnia and Kosovo. When the Bush administration took power in 2001, Secretary of Defense Donald Rumsfeld and other officials thought missions like those in the Balkans were essentially quagmires in which the combat power of the US military had become trapped. The lack of clear objectives and vague timetables made nation-building efforts anathema to proponents of a foreign policy that would rely on a military instrument that was highly responsive. The Rumsfeld DOD instead pushed hard to transform the military into a smaller, more agile force that would react quickly to contingencies and avoid nation building.

That attitude survived the attacks of 9/11 essentially intact. When planning for OEF began at the CENTCOM level, Franks and his staff did follow joint doctrine and created a campaign for Afghanistan that consisted of four phases terminating with Phase IV, Transition.

That final phase, according to doctrine, included economic reconstruction, the establishment of law and order, and actions taken to address any lingering humanitarian concerns. Phase IV normally terminated once US forces turned responsibility for operations over to a multinational peacekeeping force or to a new domestic government. In its OEF plan, the CENTCOM staff titled this phase, "Establish Capability of Coalition Partners to Prevent the Re-Emergence of Terrorism and Provide Support for Humanitarian Assistance Efforts." Some planning for this phase did occur, especially for operations that sought to mitigate the expected humanitarian crises. In fact, the OEF plan directed Coalition forces to begin humanitarian assistance operations, traditionally a component of Phase IV, during earlier phases. But in the fall of 2001 and winter of 2002, neither Franks nor his staff offered any detailed concept of how the Coalition would move Afghanistan from Taliban rule to a stable state that no longer harbored terrorist organizations.

At DOD and CENTCOM levels, the need for a plan that not only offered a clear vision for this transition should have been obvious. For most observers of Afghanistan, it was clear that general conditions in the country in 2001 were extremely unstable. Behind the façade constructed by the Taliban, Afghanistan remained a failed state. Two decades of war had left the country with a shattered society and an economy that was smaller than that of Albania. When Coalition forces arrived in October 2001, Afghanistan was still in the midst of civil war with the Northern Alliance controlling significant portions of the country's northeast. To a certain degree, CENTCOM planners became aware of the conditions inside Afghanistan and that cognizance led to the inclusion of humanitarian assistance operations in the early phases of the campaign.

Yet in the months following the beginning of OEF, the US Government struggled to initiate a concerted effort to create a coordinated and comprehensive approach to transitioning Afghanistan to stability. Certainly, at the DOD and CENTCOM levels, the monumental tasks of projecting Coalition power into central Asia and using that power to overthrow the Taliban and destroy al-Qaeda dominated the planners' thinking and energy. But, even after the capture of Kabul and Kandahar, the installation of a new interim Afghan Government, and Operation ANACONDA, there was no major planning initiated to create long-term political, social, and economic stability in Afghanistan.

In fact, the message from senior DOD officials in Washington was for the US military to avoid such efforts. Lieutenant General Dan K. McNeill, the commander of Combined Joint Task Force-180 (CJTF-180) recalled that in the spring of 2002 senior officials in the Pentagon told him to plan for US forces to be in Afghanistan for a very limited period and to ensure that American Soldiers did not become involved in nation building.[†] This stance about avoiding nation building was passed along to those directly involved in the early reconstruction effort in Afghanistan. Brigadier General David Kratzer, the first commander of the Combined Joint Civil Military Operations Task Force (CJCMOTF), remembered that as he left for Afghanistan in late 2001, General Franks pointedly directed him to avoid becoming enmeshed in nation building. The strong antipathy toward large-scale reconstruction and governance efforts at high levels in the US Government persisted through 2002 and into 2003, shaping the development of OEF as well as the nascent plans to overthrow the Saddam regime in Iraq.

[†]See chapter 7 of this study for details.

Senior Coalition military officers in Afghanistan, like Kratzer and McNeill, then faced a conundrum. Given the conditions of Afghanistan in 2002, achieving the overall Coalition objective meant the launching of major state-building initiatives, such as the creation of an army and the reconstruction of the physical infrastructure. On the other hand, the establishment of those programs ran contrary to general guidance from senior military officials. Not surprisingly, McNeill and his headquarters arrived in Afghanistan with only a basic concept for progress and very limited resources to focus on these missions. To be sure, the United Nations (UN) and the Coalition partners had taken the lead to create a political roadmap for a new Afghan state. The Bonn Agreement in 2001 established that roadmap. The Coalition's formation of the International Security Assistance Force (ISAF) also provided assurance that the US would not be alone in fostering security inside Afghanistan. However, the Bonn Agreement and the ISAF were just the first steps in the much larger project to create a stable state in Afghanistan. It would take another 12 months for the Coalition to gradually assess the conditions inside the country and construct the organizations needed to begin the process of stabilizing the country. During that period, most of Afghanistan remained untouched by Coalition forces and the fledgling Afghan Government. Taliban and al-Qaeda forces, although pressured in some regions by rapid Coalition strikes, were free to reconstitute and conduct operations.

The weaknesses in the US planning effort for OEF and Operation IRAQI FREEDOM (OIF) have already helped change US joint doctrine. The new version of Joint Publication (JP) 5-0, *Joint Operation Planning*, published in 2006, emphasized the need for planners to ensure that concepts of campaigns are complete and place equal emphasis on both the decisive offensive operations that lead to military victory and the myriad stability operations that transform that victory into strategic success. JP 5-0 reinforced that point by introducing a new phasing template for campaigns consisting of six phases, including a transition phase (Phase IV) in which stability operations became the focus of US forces and a final phase called "Enable Civil Authority," which prescribed actions taken to strengthen a newly-established government. This new doctrine should help military leaders plan for entire campaigns and help senior commanders understand the perils of focusing too heavily on decisive combat operations. The new joint campaign framework is not a panacea. New theories on the use of military power and guidance from political officials will always exert an influence on operations. It is hoped that the new planning doctrine, combined with the experience of OEF and OIF, will induce future planners to conceive campaigns in their entirety.

The Evolution of Command Structures

Because of the difficulties with envisioning the campaign, US officials and planners experienced challenges with shaping command structures for OEF. From October 2001 through 2004, Coalition forces saw a variety of headquarters established, altered, and disestablished. At the beginning of the campaign, the ad hoc arrangement of 10th Mountain Division's headquarters serving as both Combined Forces Land Component Command (CFLCC) (Forward) and then CJTF *Mountain* soon gave way to a new CJTF based on the headquarters of the US Army's XVIII Airborne Corps. CJTF-180's structure allowed the senior commander, Lieutenant General McNeill, to focus on theater strategic- and operational-level concerns that included relations with Afghan military and political officials. McNeill placed the burden for tactical-level operations on Combined Task Force (CTF) 82, which had been constructed from the US Army's 82d Airborne Division headquarters and was commanded by Major General

John Vines. But even this command structure had been weakened by the insistence that half of the XVIII Airborne Corps headquarters staff remain in the United States to keep force levels in Afghanistan low and to prepare for other contingencies, specifically the campaign in Iraq. Thus, CJTF-180 deployed with a less than robust ability to command and control just as the campaign in Afghanistan was becoming more complex. Further, the decision to limit the size of the CJTF staff reflected the initial de facto classification of Afghanistan as an economy of force theater.

As OEF progressed, the campaign's status as an economy of force continued to shape command structure. The Coalition chose not to sustain the size and capacity of the CJTF-180 staff, even in its reduced state. In spring 2003 McNeill and the staff from XVIII Airborne Corps redeployed to Fort Bragg. They were replaced by the headquarters of the 10th Mountain Division, a much smaller organization. By fall 2003 the 10th Mountain commanding general, Major General Lloyd Austin, had taken the reins of CJTF-180, which left him and his staff to oversee high-level political matters as well as tactical operations. If the threat level had remained minimal and the Coalition operations decreasing in scope and complexity, this transition might have been suitable. The fact that attacks were increasing and the efforts to train the Afghan National Army (ANA) and rebuild the physical infrastructure of Afghanistan were growing should have recommended a command structure with more capacity for planning and oversight, not less.

The creation of Combined Forces Command–Afghanistan (CFC-A) was an attempt to rectify that situation. The Coalition installed this new three-star level command to oversee affairs at the theater-strategic and high-operational level. CFC-A would work closely with the Afghan Government and with regional Afghan leaders who continued to play an important role in the development of the country. Lieutenant General David Barno, the initial CFC-A commander, eventually generated an unprecedented level of unity of effort in the Coalition campaign by partnering with US Ambassador Zalmay Khalilzad, Embassy staff, and other US agencies in Afghanistan. However, all of these improvements took time. When Barno arrived in Afghanistan in fall 2003, his staff numbered in the dozens and only grew to the proper size over the course of the next 12 months. Barno has acknowledged that in attempting to build a larger staff, he was competing for manpower with the Baghdad-based CJTF-7 and the overall needs for the campaign in Iraq. Still, the problems and delays encountered by CFC-A in forming a full staff that could coordinate the high-level political-military effort and direct the new COIN approach that Barno introduced are difficult to understand.

The evolution of command structures in OEF between 2001 and 2005 was a result of both shortcomings in fully envisioning the scope of and requirements for the campaign and the limitations of resources available to the Afghan theater of operations. This uncertain succession of commands strongly suggests that in the future planners must carefully think through the size and capacity of the headquarters required to successfully end the campaign. In an economy of force theater, arguably, the planning for command structure is both more difficult and more critical. Further, in their planning documents, planners should clearly identify the specific headquarters designated for command. Equally important is the paramount objective of creating and retaining unity of effort. In both OEF and OIF, unity of effort greatly improved when the Coalition formed commands at the theater-strategic level. These decisions allowed senior commanders to focus on political affairs that were often far more important than military operations.

Troop Levels and Troop Dispositions

Debates about the US troop commitment to Afghanistan grew in volume and importance after 2005 when levels of violence in the country began to rise precipitously. Any serious discussion about current and future troop deployments should consider the three key factors shaping troop levels in the first 4 years of OEF. First was the prevailing attitude about nation building and the related assumption that US forces would be in the country for a limited time. Dovetailing with that incomplete vision of the campaign was the second factor, the belief in the first 24 months of the campaign that a large "footprint" of Western forces inside Afghanistan would alienate the population and lead to disaffection and violence. Finally, the status of Afghanistan as an economy of force theater placed real limitations on troop levels, even as OEF matured after 2003 and senior commanders became less concerned about expanding the Coalition military presence across Afghanistan.

Among senior US political and military officials, the initial emphasis on maintaining a small footprint came from an understanding of the Soviet experience in Afghanistan that was at best incomplete. This interpretation of that decade-long conflict explained the Soviet failure as stemming from the deployment of large mechanized formations that appeared and acted as an army of occupation. The presence of this large alien force, so the interpretation suggested, bred the insurgency that ultimately forced the Soviets to leave in disgrace a decade after they arrived.

Often overlooked in this version of the Soviet-Afghan War was the ways in which the Soviet military used its power in Afghanistan. Early in the conflict, for example, the Soviet Air Force directly attacked civilian populations to deny insurgents safe havens. Large-scale casualties and refugee populations resulted, generating a high level of support for the mujahideen. Moreover, when the Soviet Union sent its military forces across the Afghan border in 1979 to support the Afghan Communist government, Afghanistan was already in the midst of a civil war. Thus, much of the resistance the Soviets encountered was not generated by the size of their footprint, but by the fact that they had intervened in support of one side in the preexisting conflict.

For many senior-level policymakers and military commanders, maintaining a small footprint appeared to be the best way of avoiding failure in Afghanistan. This policy led to CENTCOM's close management of troop levels in 2001 and 2002. In May 2002 force-level limitations contributed to the decision to deploy only half of the XVIII Airborne Corps staff in the establishment of CJTF-180. Further, troop limits severely restricted the amount of combat power available to senior Coalition commanders in Afghanistan. Excluding ISAF, which was limited to Kabul and its immediate environs, between late 2001 and the beginning of 2003 there was an average of six maneuver battalions—mostly light infantry—available to conduct operations. These battalions did enjoy the support of aviation units that provided both mobility and close air support. Still, these six units, with approximately 800 Soldiers each, provided the entire Coalition presence in a country the size of Texas.

Between 2003 and the end of 2005, the Coalition's combat power and overall troop strength in Afghanistan grew steadily if not dramatically. Romanian and French units reinforced CJTF-180 and CJTF-76, as did US Marine Corps forces that deployed for relatively short periods. Additional US and Coalition partners staffed CJTF *Phoenix,* taking the burden of training the ANA off of the Combined Joint Special Operations Task Force–Afghanistan

(CJSOTF-A). Further, as OEF progressed, US Army manpower doubled from 8,000 in fall 2002 to 16,000 in fall 2005.

In the first 18 months of the campaign, the small force footprint did not constrain the Coalition. Given the intent to maintain a low profile, most of the infantry battalions remained on the large bases at Bagram and Kandahar Airfields. CJTF-180 sought to use its combat forces only in those instances where Coalition intelligence indicated significant enemy activity, primarily in the provinces along the Pakistani frontier. In the series of rapid security operations that became emblematic of CJTF-180's approach in 2002 and 2003, elements of these battalions air assaulted into regions where Taliban or al-Qaeda formations were suspected to be operating. After a week of successive operations, which included raids, cordon and searches, and humanitarian assistance missions, these units would return to their bases located hundreds of miles away. Only in fall 2003 did CJTF-180 begin to extend its presence in Afghanistan by establishing a handful of small bases in the provinces of the south and southeast. This general disposition of forces made the Coalition heavily dependent on aviation support, which required a great deal of logistical management. It also meant that in 2002 and 2003, few Afghans outside of Kabul, Kandahar, and a small number of other cities ever saw Coalition soldiers or directly felt their presence. Even in 2004, almost 3 years after OEF began, there were areas of Afghanistan about which the Coalition knew almost nothing.

Once Lieutenant General Barno introduced the formal COIN campaign in late 2003, the small footprint became far more problematic. Barno's new effort hinged on Coalition forces taking ownership of specific areas of operation (AOs) and conducting a mix of reconstruction, security, and information operations to win the support of the population. Barno asserted that by taking this population-centric approach to COIN, he could magnify the presence of the Coalition. This was a reasonable response, given that OEF was an economy of force theater. Simply put, from 2003 on, the United States was directing the lion's share of its military manpower to its main effort: the campaign in Iraq. In fact, from the fall of 2003 through 2005, US troop levels in Afghanistan remained only 15 to 20 percent of the troop levels in Iraq. The CFC-A commander recognized that there were severe constraints on units available for deployment to Afghanistan and used what resources and units he had to mount his COIN effort.

Still, as Barno admitted, many battalion commanders "owned" AOs that were the size of small American states. How well could these relatively small units achieve the desired effects across such large territories? It is true that in 2004 and 2005 there was an increased number of battalions operating in AOs in the south and southeast, but Coalition forces remained thinly spread across Afghanistan. That meant that much of the country remained vulnerable to enemy forces increasingly willing to reassert their power.

The problems associated with the commitment of forces to campaigns are complex. Senior political and military officials have to make difficult decisions about where to focus manpower and other assets when ongoing campaigns make simultaneous demands for resources. They must also consider factors outside the military realm, such as domestic support for campaigns that might involve placing large numbers of troops in harm's way. Military planners in the future will have to consider the number of troops required for nation building in general and COIN specifically. These types of campaigns are troop and time intensive. Field Manual (FM) 3-24, *Counterinsurgency*, published in 2006 by the US Army and US Marine Corps, established new COIN doctrine for the US military and underlines the protracted nature of these campaigns and the problems that this can create for the counterinsurgent force. Moreover, the manual emphasizes the paramount importance of securing the population from the insurgents and that the counterinsurgent force should have 20 to 25 soldiers, police, and other security personnel per 1,000 inhabitants to provide that security. That guidance suggests that the Coalition and the Afghan Government should have had a force level of approximately 500,000. Between 2001 and 2005, the number of troops never approached that goal.

Full Spectrum Operations and Counterinsurgency

When the first US Army units arrived in Afghanistan in October 2001, few if any had trained or otherwise prepared for what the Army called full spectrum operations. Although FM 3-0, *Operations*, published in 2001, had introduced the concept, the new doctrine had not yet taken root within the Army. At its core, full spectrum operations established that during campaigns the US Army would have to be capable of conducting a mix of offensive, defensive, and stability operations simultaneously. This mandate was as relevant to the tactical-level commander as it was to the operational-level leader in overall command of the campaign. Between 2002 and 2005, the conventional units that deployed in OEF essentially validated the doctrine of full spectrum operations by demonstrating that with some preparation and coordination they could conduct concurrent cordon and searches, defensive operations to secure bases, information operations, and reconstruction. In 2002 the rough beginnings of this capacity could be seen in CJTF *Mountain's* and CTF 82's inclusion of civil affairs (CA) teams on their security operations that took infantry battalions into the far-flung districts of Afghanistan. As OEF matured and the PRTs were established to focus on reconstruction, maneuver elements continued to conduct a mix of offensive missions and civil-military operations using the Commander's Emergency Response Program (CERP). As tactical-level commanders became more comfortable with the concept, they became far more adept at preparing their own organic forces to do these myriad operations concurrently. The progress the Army has made in both OEF and OIF toward creating a force that is truly capable of full spectrum operations should be reinforced in the Army's training base, its combat training centers, and its educational institutions.

Closely related to the transition to full spectrum operations was the similarly difficult adoption of COIN as the Coalition's formal approach in 2003. By directing that US Army units launch a COIN campaign, Lieutenant General Barno was saddling Soldiers with an imposing task. The Army's COIN doctrine had languished over the previous two decades. With the exception of the Army's Special Forces (SF), no units had trained to conduct COIN. While commanders in late 2003 and 2004 made the transition to COIN with enthusiasm and flexibility, there was still a gap in knowledge and experience that had to be overcome. The previously discussed issue concerning the number of troops available to commanders in the COIN campaign was yet another obstacle.

Since 2003 the US Army has gained an immeasurable amount of experience in COIN. Soldiers who operated in Afghanistan, Iraq, the Philippines, the Horn of Africa, and other locations have honed their understanding of COIN principles and practices. Equally important was the introduction of new COIN doctrine in 2006. FM 3-24 offered a critical updating of US Army thinking about COIN. That doctrine places the US practice of COIN onto the larger doctrinal foundation of full spectrum operations. By so doing, the Army has prevented COIN from becoming a unique form of warfare, practiced only by SF Soldiers and thus vulnerable to marginalization by those more focused on and comfortable with conventional combat operations. Soldiers who were given the difficult responsibility of conducting COIN early in the OEF and OIF campaigns should not allow the Army as an institution to overlook this doctrine in the coming decades. Of critical importance for consideration in future COIN campaigns is the lingering issue of troop levels. How will commanders in those conflicts, armed though they might be with thoughtful doctrine and a trained force, deal with an insurgent enemy if their force is too small to conduct all the necessary operations including the securing of a large population? This is a critical question for policymakers and planners—both civilian and military—to grapple with in an objective and straightforward manner.

Intelligence and Detainee Operations

Accurate and timely intelligence was critical to successful COIN operations in Afghanistan. However, US Army units that found themselves conducting full spectrum and COIN operations in 2002 faced a major obstacle in understanding their enemy. The intelligence system that had enabled US Army operations since 1945 began losing relevance as soon as the planes struck the towers in New York on 9/11. Based on a hierarchical structure that pushed information from the top down and was heavily dependent on signals intelligence (SIGINT) and imagery intelligence (IMINT), this system struggled to adapt in the opening phases of OEF. Detainee and interrogation policy at the national level and within the theater also evolved haltingly as US forces found themselves confronting a new type of enemy in Afghanistan.

What emerged by mid-2002 was a system in which human intelligence (HUMINT) was the dominant discipline and information primarily flowed from the bottom up. These changes were innovations made by Soldiers at the tactical level seeking ways of improving their understanding of the enemy. At times there were failures, most dramatically in the arena of detainee operations in which guidance and leadership was sometimes lacking. However, the first 4 years of OEF also saw remarkable examples of joint and interagency cooperation as with the creation of Task Force (TF) *Bowie* as early as October 2001 and intelligence fusion cells in other commands. This period also witnessed the widespread practice of intelligence collection, analysis, and dissemination by widely separated teams that greatly leveraged their technology to create a detailed picture of the enemy.

Since 2005 the US Government and US Army have tried to come to grips with the new realities of intelligence and detainee operations, codifying some of these changes in law, doctrine, and organizational structure. To better deal with the type of detainee operations that the Global War on Terrorism (GWOT) requires, the US Congress passed the 2005 Detainee Treatment Act that sets clear standards for detainee treatment. New Army HUMINT doctrine, especially FM 2-22.3, *Human Intelligence Collector Operations* (2006), goes further in providing specific guidance about the techniques allowed for use by interrogators. This new doctrine is an excellent foundation, but future individual and collective training should continue to reinforce the lessons learned in places like Kandahar and Bagram by placing Soldiers in realistic settings and giving them serious problems to solve. The Army schools supporting both the Military Intelligence (MI) and Military Police (MP) branches should likewise find ways to impart to current and future Soldiers the fundamentals of doctrine and law governing detainee operations so that they are prepared to operate in a dangerous and alien environment in which guidance and resources might be limited or nonexistent.

The Interagency Effort

One important bright spot in OEF was the significant amount of interagency coordination and cooperation that had an ultimately salutary effect on the campaign. Beginning with the remarkable successes of the SOF teams in 2001, there was a steady growth of operations that involved more than a few agencies and resulted in improvements in intelligence gathering, planning at the theater-strategic level, and other areas. Most revolutionary were the steps taken to improve the delivery of humanitarian assistance and reconstruction support to the Afghan population. The Coalition's creation of a separate command called the CJCMOTF and then its formation of the PRTs in late 2002 best represented the new ways of thinking about coordinating difficult tasks that were spread across a variety of units and organizations. The PRTs especially were the result of frustrations encountered earlier in OEF in the coordination of the many stakeholders and resource providers involved in the reconstruction program. The obstacles involved in trying to bring Coalition civil-military operations together with those of other Coalition governmental agencies, nongovernment organizations, and international organizations were significant. Nevertheless, by the end of 2005, 22 PRTs had integrated these disparate components together to make the nation-building project in Afghanistan more feasible. Moving the PRTs under the authority of the regional commanders in 2004 was yet another step that more firmly integrated the reconstruction effort into the larger campaign. Still, the Coalition experienced difficulties in staffing PRTs with enough members from the Department of State (DOS), United States Agency for International Development (USAID), and other nonmilitary agencies. Thus, this concept must be developed further and given permanence in doctrine and practice at the combatant command level, DOD, and other agencies of the US Government.

Training Indigenous Forces

The American experience in OEF, as well as in OIF, included major efforts to train indigenous security forces. However, in neither campaign did US military planners allocate resources to these critical training missions until Coalition forces were in the midst of operations. Clearly, with the US Government emphasis on avoiding nation building in Afghanistan, commanders and planners did not expect to become involved in building a new Afghan Army. But in spring 2002, both ISAF and Coalition forces had to adopt that additional task when it became clear that any viable and stable Afghan state had to have its own security forces, if only to foster stability and legitimacy within its own borders.

The gradual realization of the scope of the mission meant that the overall effort was tentative and suffered from a lack of resources. The initial agency designated to oversee the building of the new ANA—the Office of Military Cooperation–Afghanistan (OMC-A)—was "calved" from the CJCMOTF and had to rely primarily on Coalition SF to conduct the training of that new force. As 2002 progressed, Coalition commanders began to realize that the OMC-A had to become involved not only in training ANA battalions, but in constructing an entire military edifice from the Ministry of Defense (MOD) down to the bases in which the Afghan soldiers would live and train. The staff and resources grew accordingly. Most importantly, in 2003 the Coalition established CJTF *Phoenix* to train and advise the new ANA units. These improvements allowed the ANA to complete its establishment of the Central Corps in 2005. By that date, the Coalition had also begun training the Afghan National Police (ANP).

The substantial programs in Afghanistan and Iraq to train, build, and advise indigenous armies are not unprecedented. A brief survey of the US Army's campaigns in the 20th century will reveal that these types of programs were common. In the Philippines, South Korea, Vietnam, El Salvador, and other countries, America Soldiers served as trainers and advisors to foreign forces. Despite the primary role of conventional units and officers in these programs, in the aftermath of Vietnam, few units outside of Army SF prepared for this type of mission. SF battalions and teams certainly played a key role in establishing new national forces in both Iraq and Afghanistan. Even so, these units are few in number and are neither trained nor resourced to build the administrative, logistical, and training institutions that modern armies require.

The US Army's history in the GWOT suggests that Soldiers will become involved in the training of indigenous forces in future campaigns. Planners at the DOD and combatant command levels will need to identify the headquarters and other resources necessary to initiate these efforts as smoothly as possible. Commanders at the tactical level will also need to consider how this mission fits into their training for full spectrum operations. At the very least, Soldiers at this level should expect to work closely with and perhaps advise indigenous military and police units. Policymakers at the DOD level should also give serious thought to forming commands and units focused on this mission, perhaps transforming formations in the US Army Reserve or National Guard into foreign army assistance units.

The Integration of SOF and Conventional Forces

SOF played a larger role in OEF than in all other recent US campaigns. Not only were the Operational Detachment–Alpha (ODA) teams instrumental in the initial military victory over the Taliban, but the missions pursued by the CJSOTF-A after December 2001 were multifaceted and critical to the overall Coalition effort. American and Coalition SOF conducted raids on Taliban and al-Qaeda targets, worked with Afghan militia forces along the Pakistani border to interdict enemy troops and materiel, and served as trainers and advisors for the ANA. At times, the Coalition's senior commands appear to have given the CJSOTF too many tasks, thus diluting the strengths brought to the battlefield by these forces. Indeed, some in the SOF community seemed to chafe under the constraints that prevented them from practicing a more developed form of unconventional warfare (UW) with a larger contingent of ANA units. The inability or unwillingness of the Coalition senior command to commit more ANA to the UW campaign in 2004 and 2005 hindered the ability of the ODAs to have a broader affect, especially along the border.

Despite these apparent shortcomings, the level of integration and coordination between SOF and conventional forces during the 4-year period in this study was an improvement from previous campaigns. The CJSOTF-A was under operational control of the senior Coalition headquarters from 2002 forward and SOF were integrated into the larger campaign plans. Moreover, from Operation ANACONDA through the operations preparing for parliamentary elections in 2005, SOF and conventional forces worked closely at the tactical level. In many cases, the ODAs integrated indigenous Afghan forces into conventional operations, enhancing the Coalition's ability to foster relationships and build legitimacy for the new Afghan Government.

Given the success of SOF in OEF, the Army should be ready to place these forces together with conventional forces on most if not all battlefields of the future. To achieve the benefits seen in Afghanistan, however, the Army will need to prepare and train for this type of operational integration. Certainly, SOF will continue to hone their ability to work with air power and indigenous forces. Accordingly, the US Army's combat training centers, Battle Command

Training Program (BCTP), and Officer and Noncommissioned Officer Education Systems must also reinforce the steps taken in Afghanistan to enhance the operational integration between SOF and conventional forces.

Operating in Foreign Cultures

The campaigns of the GWOT have deployed American Soldiers to countries where the cultures are quite different from American life. Mounting basic military operations in these distant lands has been difficult, and success has often hinged on the ability to navigate competently within these strange cultures. This task not only requires linguistic skills, but also a fairly sophisticated understanding of religious, political, and social structures that differ from those familiar to most Soldiers. Moreover, officers and noncommissioned officers have often had to wade into these cultures and employ local Afghan or Iraqi norms to be successful.

In the first year of OEF, many units struggled within the alien cultural environment. Not all Soldiers were aware, for example, of important religious and social norms that prohibited close contact between unrelated men and women. Poor understanding of tribal and ethnic relationships hindered negotiations and even some operations. However, US units became more knowledgeable about Afghan history and society as OEF progressed. By late 2002 battalions from the 82d Airborne Division were regularly using female Soldiers to search Afghan women during routine operations. Since 2002 commanders at all levels became heavily involved in sophisticated and successful negotiations with local Afghan leaders. The Afghan experience reinforces the critical point that regardless of the nature of the Army's future campaigns, US Soldiers will almost inevitably interact with foreign cultures. If these campaigns are focused on nation building, cultural awareness will become not just a necessity but perhaps a critical skill like marksmanship or land navigation. The Army's training courses and schools must impress this point on Soldiers at all levels by making cultural classes and even language instruction mandatory. The combat training centers should sustain the training scenarios that place Soldiers of all ranks in situations where they must act and react with at least some sensitivity to local norms. Commanders must follow through with this aspect of deployment training by preparing their Soldiers to navigate through and even thrive in cultures that are a world apart from the United States.

✦   ✦   ✦

The Coalition effort in Afghanistan between 2001 and 2005 was an extraordinary and complex campaign, one that was replete with the use of high-technology weaponry, such as the Joint Direct Attack Munition (JDAM), and small SOF teams moving around the battlefield with their tribal allies on horseback. In this sense, this study of OEF should remind the reader that many aspects of warfare—especially the importance of small, well-trained, and adaptive teams—remain constant, regardless of the tools that they employ. This is not to underestimate the importance of the technology brought to bear on the Afghan battlefield. After all, the small teams at Tora Bora in 2001 were equipped with very sophisticated devices that helped direct the air attack and thus greatly magnified the power of Coalition air forces. However, even the high-precision bombing of the al-Qaeda redoubt did not conclude with the killing or capture of Osama bin Laden. In the same way, none of the Coalition's technological advantages were able to prevent the reemergence of the Taliban in the south and east of Afghanistan between 2003 and 2005.

Also striking is the manner and rapidity with which the campaign evolved between 2001 and 2005. In the relatively brief span of 4 years, the Coalition found itself drawn from a small scale operation that featured focused counterterrorist operations into a counterinsurgency that required units and commands to become involved in training Afghan security forces and assisting the Afghan Government consolidate its authority. Essentially, the US military and its allies in the Coalition were helping the new Afghan Government build a new nation. From the perspective of the young Soldier who arrived in Afghanistan in 2002 and 2003, the campaign must have looked like "a different kind of war," unlike any of the well-known conflicts recently fought by the US Army. Yet by the end of 2003, the Army and the other branches of the US military found themselves in a campaign in Iraq that, in its objectives and the characteristics of its operations, closely resembled the one in Afghanistan. This fact leads to the conclusion that at least for the duration of the GWOT, the Army will be involved in campaigns that are heavily focused on nation building and bear more of a resemblance to OEF and OIF than to World War II. It is hoped that this study will equip the Soldiers facing those future challenges with insights that can illuminate their way forward on an often dark and precarious path.

Appendix A

US Army Units in Operation ENDURING FREEDOM–Afghanistan
Order of Battle: October 2001–September 2005

The following depicts the US Army units that participated in Operation ENDURING FREEDOM (OEF) between 19 October 2001 and September 2005. This 4-year period included multiple rotations of forces, not all of the same length. Accordingly, this order of battle generally follows a chronological course to document the evolving Coalition command structure and the US Army units that served under those headquarters.

The units listed below were often not operating with their full complement of Soldiers or subordinate commands. This order of battle attempts to capture the major operational- and tactical-level headquarters in OEF in this period as well as larger tactical-level formations. As such, this document does not capture smaller US Army elements like the security forces and civil-military operations staff on the Provincial Reconstructions Teams.

US Central Command

Joint Psychological Operations Task Force
    HQ/4th Psychological Operations Group
    8th Psychological Operations Battalion

Joint Special Operations Task Force–*North* (October 2001–March 2002)
    HQ/5th Special Forces Group (October 2001–May 2002)
        1st Battalion, 5th Special Forces Group
        2d Battalion, 5th Special Forces Group
        3d Battalion, 5th Special Forces Group
    19th Special Forces Group

    2d Battalion, 160th Special Operations Aviation Regiment

Combined Forces Land Component Command (CFLCC) (Forward)
    HQ/10th Mountain Division
    Task Force *Rakkasan*
        HQ/3d Brigade, 101st Airborne Division (January 2002–July 2002)
            1st Battalion, 187th Infantry
            2d Battalion, 187th Infantry
            1st Battalion, 87th Infantry
            7th Battalion, 101st Aviation
            B/1st Battalion, 159th Aviation
            3d Battalion, 101st Aviation
            626th Support Battalion

    Task Force *Commando*
        HQ/2d Brigade, 10th Mountain Division (November 2001–July 2002)
            4th Battalion, 31st Infantry
            B/7th Battalion, 101st Aviation

> > B/1st Battalion, 159th Aviation
> > 7-101st Aviation
> HQ/507th Corps Support Group
> HQ/561st Corps Support Group
> > 530th Corps Support Battalion

202d Military Intelligence Battalion
92d Engineer Battalion
A/112th Signal Battalion
96th Civil Affairs Battalion

Joint Special Operations Task Force–*South* (November 2001–March 2002)
HQ/3d Special Forces Group
> HQ/3d Battalion, 3d Special Forces Group
> C/112th Signal Battalion
3d Battalion, 160th Special Operations Aviation Regiment

Combined Joint Civil Military Operations Task Force (CJCMOTF)
96th Civil Affairs Battalion
489th Civil Affairs Battalion (2002–June 2003)
403d Civil Affairs Battalion (June 2003–May 2004)
407th Civil Affairs Battalion (August 2003–May 2004)

Combined Joint Special Operations Task Force–Afghanistan (March 2002–present)
> 3d US Army Special Forces Group
> 7th US Army Special Forces Group
> 19th US Army Special Forces Group
> 20th US Army Special Forces Group
> 160th Special Operations Aviation Regiment
> 75th Ranger Regiment

Office of Military Cooperation–Afghanistan (September 2002–July 2005) (After July 2005, Office of Security Cooperation–Afghanistan)
> 1st Battalion, 3d Special Forces Group (May 2002–June 2003)

Task Force *Phoenix* (June 2003–September 2005)
> HQ/2d Brigade, 10th Mountain Division (August 2003–November 2003)
> 2d Battalion, 87th Infantry (August 2003–November 2003)
> 210th Forward Support Battalion (August 2003–March 2004)

> HQ/45th Infantry Brigade (Separate) (November 2003–August 2004)
> 1st Battalion, 179th Infantry (November 2003–August 2004)
> 1st Battalion, 180th Infantry (November 2003–August 2004)
> 1st Battalion, 279th Infantry (November 2003–August 2004)
> 1st Battalion, 160th Field Artillery (November 2003–August 2004)
> 700th Support Battalion (November 2003–August 2004)

> HQ/76th Infantry Brigade (Separate) (August 2004–August 2005)
> 1st Battalion, 151st Infantry (August 2004–August 2005)
> 113th Support Battalion (August 2004–August 2005)

Combined Joint Task Force-180 (June 2002–April 2004)
    HQ/XVIII Airborne Corps (June 2002–May 2003)
    HQ/10th Mountain Division (May 2003–April 2004)

Combined Task Force 82 (August 2002–May 2003)
    HQ, 82d Airborne Division

        Task Force *Panther* (August 2002–January 2003)
            HQ/3d Brigade, 82d Airborne Division
            1st Battalion, 505th Parachute Infantry
            1st Battalion, 504th Parachute Infantry
            3d Battalion, 505th Parachute Infantry
            1-319th Field Artillery
            C/3d Battalion, 4th Air Defense Artillery
            C/307th Engineer Battalion
            C/769th Engineer Battalion
            313th Military Intelligence Battalion
            A/9th Psychological Operations Battalion
            3/82d Military Police Company
            118th Military Police Company
            C/450th Civil Affairs Battalion
            C/82d Signal Battalion
            82d Forward Support Battalion

        Task Force *Devil* (December 2002–May 2003)
            HQ/1st Brigade, 82d Airborne Division
            2d Battalion, 504th Parachute Infantry
            3d Battalion, 504th Parachute Infantry
            2d Battalion, 505th Parachute Infantry
            3d Battalion, 319th Field Artillery
            307th Forward Support Battalion
            307th Engineer Battalion
            50th Signal Battalion
            126th Finance Battalion

        Task Force *Pegasus* (September 2002–May 2003)
            HQ/Aviation Brigade, 82d Airborne Division

            Task Force *Corsair*
            HQ, 2-82d Aviation Brigade
            B/7-101st Aviation
            B/1-58 Aviation
            C/3-229th Aviation
            I/4-159th Aviation
            D/3-229th Aviation

        Task Force *Angel*
            HQ/3-229th Aviation (December 2002–May 2003)
            A/2-82d Aviation

A/3-229th Aviation (December 2002–May 2003)
B/3-229th Aviation (December 2002–May 2003)
C/159th Aviation (December 2002–May 2003)

63d Ordnance Battalion (EOD)

Task Force *Warrior* (August 2003–May 2004)
HQ/1st Brigade, 10th Mountain Division (August 2003–May 2004)
1st Battalion, 87th Infantry (August 2003–May 2004)
2d Battalion, 87th Infantry (August 2003–May 2004)
2d Battalion, 22d Infantry (August 2003–May 2004)
1st Battalion, 501st Infantry (October 2003–April 2004)
3d Squadron, 17th Cavalry (August 2003–April 2004)
3d Battalion, 6th Field Artillery (August 2003–April 2004)
10th Forward Support Battalion (August 2003–April 2004)
C/159th Aviation (August 2003–April 2004)
3d Battalion, 229th Aviation (August 2003–April 2004)
A/41st Engineer Battalion (August 2003–April 2004)
A/3d Battalion, 62d Air Defense Artillery (August 2003–May 2004)

519th Military Intelligence Battalion

Combined Forces Command–Afghanistan (October 2003–September 2005)

Combined/Joint Task Force-76 (April 2004–April 2005)
HQ, 25th Infantry Division (Light) (February 2004–April 2005)
HQ, Southern European Task Force (April 2005–March 2006)

Combined Task Force *Bronco* (February 2004–April 2005)
HQ, 3d Brigade, 25th Infantry Division (Light) (February 2004–April 2005)
2d Battalion, 5th Infantry (February 2004–April 2005)
2d Battalion, 35th Infantry (February 2004–April 2005)
3d Battalion, 7th Field Artillery (February 2004–April 2005)
325th Forward Support Battalion (February 2004–April 2005)

Combined Task Force *Thunder* (February 2004–April 2005)
Division Artillery, 25th Infantry Division (February 2004–April 2005)
2d Battalion, 27th Infantry (February 2004–April 2005)
3d Battalion, 116th Infantry (July 2004–August 2005)
1st Battalion, 505th Infantry (September 2004–October 2004)

Combined Task Force *Saber*
3d Squadron, 4th Cavalry

Task Force *Victory*
1st Battalion, 168th Infantry

Combined Task Force *Coyote*
65th Engineer Battalion (February 2004–April 2005)
367th Engineer Battalion (May 2004–June 2005)
528th Engineer Battalion (March 2004–March 2005)

Joint Task Force *Wings* (May 2004–April 2005)
    HHC/Aviation Brigade, 25th Infantry Division (February 2004–April 2005)
    2d Battalion, 25th Aviation (February 2004–April 2005)
    1st Battalion, 111th Aviation (February 2004–April 2005)
    1st Battalion, 211th Aviation (February 2004–April 2005)
    68th Aviation Company (February 2004–April 2005)

HHC/Division Support Command (February 2004–April 2005)
    725th Support Battalion (February 2004–April 2005)
    556th Personnel Services Battalion (February 2004–April 2005)
    125th Military Intelligence Battalion (February 2004–April 2005)
    125th Signal Battalion (February 2004–April 2005)

Combined Task Force *Bayonet* (April 2005–March 2006)
    HQ, 173d Airborne Brigade (April 2005–March 2006)
    2d Battalion, 503d Parachute Infantry (April 2005–March 2006)
    3d Battalion, 319th Field Artillery (April 2005–March 2006)
    74th Infantry Detachment (Long Range Surveillance)
    173d Support Battalion (April 2005–March 2006)

Combined Task Force *Devil* (April 2005–March 2006)
    HQ, 1st Brigade, 82d Airborne Division
    1st Battalion, 325th Airborne Infantry
    2d Battalion, 504th Parachute Infantry
    1st Battalion, 508th Parachute Infantry

Appendix B

Chronology

Operation ENDURING FREEDOM
Major Events, September 2001 to September 2005

2001

11 September 2001 Nineteen al-Qaeda terrorists hijack four passenger airliners and crash them into targets in New York City, Washington, DC, and rural western Pennsylvania. Two of the planes hit the Twin Towers in New York City; another hit the Pentagon in Washington, DC; and the last one crashed near Shanksville, Pennsylvania, apparently when passengers attempted to regain control of the aircraft. The death toll for all four planes was over 3,000.

12 September 2001 Secretary of Defense Donald Rumsfeld requests options for military strikes against the planners of the 9/11 attacks.

5 October 2001 United States (US) receives permission from the Uzbekistan Government to fly planes and base troops at Karshi-Khanabad (K2). Television crews had spotted US transport planes at Khanabad prior to this date.

7 October 2001 Forces from the United States and United Kingdom bomb Taliban positions for first time.

12 October 2001 United States and Uzbekistan Governments sign agreement allowing US forces to use Uzbek soil as a staging area for operations in Afghanistan.

19 October 2001 Insertion of Operational Detachments–Alpha (ODAs) 555 and 595.

19–20 October (night) 2001 Four MC-130 planes drop 199 Rangers of the 3d Battalion, 75th Ranger Regiment at Objective RHINO.

24 October 2001 Insertion of ODA 585.

31 October 2001 Insertion of ODA 553.

2 November 2001 ODA 553 lands near Bamian to support General Karim Khalili (Hazara General).

4 November 2001 Insertion of ODA 534.

8 November 2001 Insertion of ODAs 586 and 594.

10 November 2001 Mazar-e Sharif falls to General Dostum's militia and US Special Operations Forces (SOF).

13 November 2001 Taliban abandons Kabul.

14 November 2001	Special Forces (SF) ODA 574 inserted and links up with Hamid Karzai.
17 November 2001	SF ODA 574 directs United States Air Force (USAF) bombing of a Taliban convoy of troops near Tarin Kowt—30 trucks destroyed.
18 November 2001	160th Special Operations Aviation Regiment (SOAR) inserts SF ODA 583 to link up with Gul Agha Sherzai.
25 November 2001	Major General Franklin Hagenbeck, commanding general of the 10th Mountain Division, is directed to deploy his division headquarters staff to Uzbekistan to establish the Combined Forces Land Component Command (CFLCC)–Forward headquarters.
26 November 2001	Konduz falls to Generals Dostum and Daoud Khan and US SOF.
23 November 2001	Battle of Tahk-te-pol between ODA 583, forces of Gul Agha Sherzai, and the Taliban.
24 November 2001	The town of Tahk-te-pol falls to ODA 583 and the forces under Gul Sherzai.
25 November 2001	Taliban prisoners in the 18th century fortress of Qala-i-Jangi revolt.
1 December 2001	The revolt inside Qala-i-Jangi prison is finally crushed.
3 December 2001	Sherzai's 2,000-man force probes defenses of Kandahar Airport, south of the city, and is thrown back and bailed out by US air power.
	Elements of ODA 583, Sherzai's men, and US air power thwart a Taliban attack on Sherzai's southern outpost near Thak-te-pol.
	Fighting starts at Tora Bora between Eastern Alliance and al-Qaeda forces.
4 December 2001	Karzai's soldiers and ODA 574 turn back another Taliban attack 40 miles north of Kandahar.
	ODA 572 joins the fighting at Tora Bora.
5 December 2001	A 2,000-pound Joint Direct Attack Munition (JDAM) bomb is mistakenly dropped on ODA 574 killing three and wounding nine of the team members. It also killed 23 Pashtun soldiers and injured Hamid Karzai.
	In Bonn, Germany, an agreement establishing the Afghan Interim Authority (AIA) is approved.
7 December 2001	Mullah Omar abandons Kandahar.
	Sherzai reoccupies the Governor's Palace, and ODA 583 enters shortly thereafter.

12 December 2001	Taliban and al-Qaeda rear guard fights to give remainder of their force time to escape into the mountains and complexes within Tora Bora.
	US Army 10th Mountain Division HQ arrives at K2 to serve as CFLCC (Forward).
14 December 2001	US Marines at Camp Rhino relocate to Kandahar Airport.
	Osama bin Laden identified talking on radio at Tora Bora.
17 December 2001	Last elements of al-Qaeda in Tora Bora are overrun. Bin Laden is not among those captured or killed.
20 December 2001	UN adopts Resolution 1386 authorizing an International Security Force to be used in Afghanistan.
	ODA 561 joins ODA 572 in searching the caves of Tora Bora.
28 December 2001	First Taliban and al-Qaeda prisoners arrive at Guantanamo Bay (GTMO).

2002

2 January 2002	US B-52 and B-1 bombers, F-18 fighters, and AC-130 gunships strike a suspected al-Qaeda regrouping point, the Zawar Kili compound, southwest of Khost.
24 January 2002	US forces use an AC-130 gunship strike to destroy a "very large cache" of arms and ammunition in a raid on two Taliban compounds at Hazar Qadam north of Kandahar. The raid netted 27 Taliban detainees. Later reports suggested that the gunships may have killed some Karzai allies.
4 February 2002	A strike by a Predator unmanned aerial vehicle reportedly killed several al-Qaeda leaders at a site near Zawar Kili, Afghanistan.
15 February 2002	Combined Joint Task Force (CJTF) *Mountain* forms around CFLCC–Forward headquarters to plan and command Operation ANACONDA.
	CJTF *Mountain* moves to Bagram Airfield.
2 March 2002	Operation ANACONDA begins.
4 March 2002	Action on Takur Ghar—nine US military personnel killed in operation.
19 March 2002	Operation ANACONDA ends.
25 March 2002	Secretary of Defense announces plans for US and Coalition forces to help create and train the Afghan National Army (ANA).
15 April 2002	Operation MOUNTAIN LION begins.

17 April 2002	An American F-16 fighter jet drops a bomb on Canadian forces conducting training. Four Canadian soldiers are killed and eight wounded as a result of the accident.
6 May 2002	Operation SNIPE, a part of MOUNTAIN LION, begins.
14 May 2002	The ANA's first 250 soldiers begin training. US SOF kill five suspected Taliban and al-Qaeda fighters and capture 32 others during a raid on a compound 50 miles north of Kandahar.
17 May 2002	British forces launch Operation CONDOR to support an Australian Special Air Service patrol engaged in combat with al-Qaeda and Taliban forces in the mountains of southeastern Afghanistan.
31 May 2002	American and allied Afghan military forces conducting a raid mistakenly fire on other friendly Afghan troops.
31 May 2002	CJTF-180, commanded by Lieutenant General Dan K. McNeill, assumes control of Coalition operations in Afghanistan.
11 June 2002	The emergency loya jirga (grand council) convenes and ultimately selects Hamid Karzai as interim president with 80 percent of the votes. Karzai had been chairman of the AIA.
1 July 2002	Coalition forces mistakenly fire on a wedding party in Oruzgan province after pilots allegedly mistook celebratory fire for hostile fire.
20 July 2002	TF *Panther* takes over from TF *Rakkasan*.
23 July 2002	The first battalion of the ANA graduates from the Afghan Military Academy.
24 July 2002	Afghanistan–American Reconstruction Summit.
19 August 2002	Operation MOUNTAIN SWEEP begins in southeastern Afghanistan.
5 September 2002	Afghan President Hamid Karzai survives an apparent assassination attempt in the city of Kandahar.
29 September 2002	Operation ALAMO SWEEP begins.
14 October 2002	Major General Karl W. Eikenberry arrives to be the OMC-A commander.

2003

10 January 2003	TF *Panther* transfers authority to TF *Devil*, manned by the 1st Brigade Combat Team, 82d Airborne Division.

27 January 2003	Operation MONGOOSE begins near Spin Boldak with troops of the 82d Airborne Division and Afghan militia against Afghan fighters loyal to Gulbuddin Hekmatyar in the caves of the Adi Ghar Mountains.
19 February 2003	Operation VIPER begins.
19 March 2003	Coalition forces in Afghanistan launch Operation VALIANT STRIKE at villages and cave complexes east of Kandahar in the Sami Ghar Mountains.
May 2003	TF *Warrior,* manned with forces from the 10th Mountain Division, replaces TF *Devil.*
27 May 2003	Lieutenant General McNeill transfers command of CJTF-180 to Major General John R. Vines.
4 June 2003	CJTF *Phoenix,* under Brigadier General Joseph Prasek and elements of 2d Brigade, 10th Mountain Division, is activated.
7 June 2003	Suicide car bombing in Kabul injures more than 20 German peacekeepers and kills 4 German soldiers, part of the International Security Assistance Force (ISAF) conducting security and peacekeeping operations in Afghanistan.
11 August 2003	NATO assumes strategic command, control, and coordination of the ISAF in Afghanistan. The force had been under the leadership of Germany and the Netherlands.
August 2003	Operation MOUNTAIN VIPER launched.
October 2003	Combined Forces Command–Afghanistan (CFC-A) is established under Lieutenant General David W. Barno.
November 2003	Operation MOUNTAIN RESOLVE begins. 45th Separate Infantry Brigade from Oklahoma Army National Guard takes command of CJTF *Phoenix.*
14 December 2003	Constitutional loya jirga begins.

2004

5 January 2004	Delegates to Afghanistan's loya jirga agree on a new constitution.
13 March 2004	Operation MOUNTAIN STORM begins.
15 April 2004	CJTF-76, commanded by Major General Eric T. Olson, replaces CJTF-180.

22 April 2004	Friendly fire during a firefight in southeastern Afghanistan kills Specialist Pat Tillman, 27, deployed with the 75th Ranger Regiment from Fort Benning, Georgia.
28 July 2004	Improvised explosive device (IED) goes off inside a mosque in Ghazni province killing two UN employees registering voters.
August 2004	76th Infantry Brigade from Indiana Army National Guard takes command of CJTF *Phoenix*.
3 October 2004	Coalition forces capture 16 enemy insurgents during a day-long battle near the city of Spin Boldak.
9 October 2004	Afghan presidential elections held.
3 November 2004	Election officials announce that Hamid Karzai elected president.

2005

February 2005	Major General Jason K. Kamiya, commanding general of Southern European Task Force (SETAF), takes command of CJTF-76.
3 February 2005	National Military Academy of Afghanistan opens doors.
3 March 2005	President Hamid Karzai appoints the country's first woman governor.
17 March 2005	A bombing in Kandahar kills 5 and injures up to 40 people.
18 March 2005	US helicopter crews rescue more than 200 villagers after flooding from 3 days of intense rain strands them along the Helmand River near Deh Rawod in Oruzgan province.
6 April 2005	CH-47 Chinook helicopter crashes killing 19 Americans.
3 May 2005	Lieutenant General Karl W. Eikenberry assumes command of CFC-A from Lieutenant General Barno.
28 June 2005	While on a rescue mission to recover SOF personnel, Chinook helicopter downed by insurgents, killing 16 American troops.
12 July 2005	The Office of Military Cooperation–Afghanistan (OMC-A) changes its name to the Office of Security Cooperation–Afghanistan (OSC-A) and officially assumes responsibility for the US role in reforming the Afghan National Police (ANP) force.
19 September 2005	Afghans vote in elections for parliament.

Glossary

1st BANG	1st Battalion, Afghan National Guard
AA	antiaircraft
AACA	Afghan Assistance Coordination Authority
AAR	after-action review
ACM	Anti-Coalition Militia
AED	Afghanistan Engineer District
AFB	Air Force Base
AFSOC	Air Force Special Operations Command
AIA	Afghan Interim Authority
AIT	advanced individual training
AMF	Afghan Militia Forces
ANA	Afghan National Army
ANBP	Afghanistan New Beginnings Program
ANP	Afghan National Police
AO	area of operation
AOR	area of responsibility
APOD	aerial port of debarkation
AQ	al-Qaeda
AREU	Afghanistan Research and Evaluation Unit
ARG	Afghan Reconstruction Group
ARSOF	Army Special Operations Forces
ASOC	Air Support Operations Center
ASOS	Air Support Operations Squadron
ATA	Afghan Transitional Authority
AWACS	Airborne Warning and Control System
AWOL	absent without leave
BCTP	Battle Command Training Program
BN	battalion
BP	blocking position
BPT	be prepared to
C2	command and control
CA	civil affairs
CAC	Combined Arms Center
CALCM	Conventional Air Launched Cruise Missile
CAOC	Combined Air Operations Center
CAOCL	Center for Advanced Operational Cultural Learning
CAS	close air support
CAT	Crisis Action Team
CAT-A	Civil Affairs Team–Alpha
CAV	cavalry
CBT	Cadet Basic Training
CENTCOM	US Central Command
CENTRASBAT	Central Asian Battalion
CERP	Commander's Emergency Response Program
CFACC	Combined Forces Air Component Commander
CFC-A	Combined Forces Command–Afghanistan
CFLCC	Combined Forces Land Component Command

CG	commanding general
CHLC	Coalition Humanitarian Liaison Cell
CIS	Commonwealth of Independent States
CJ2	Intelligence Section at Combined Joint Staff
CJCMOTF	Combined Joint Civil Military Operations Task Force
CJSOTF	Combined Joint Special Operations Task Force
CJSOTF-A	Combined Joint Special Operations Task Force–Afghanistan
CJSOTF-S	Combined Joint Special Operations Task Force–South
CJTF	combined joint task force
CMIC	Civil-Military Cooperation
CMO	civil-military operations
CMOC	Civil-Military Operations Center
COG	center of gravity
COIN	counterinsurgency
CONUS	continental United States
COST	Contemporary Operations Study Team
CP	command post
CS	combat support
CSAR	Combat Search and Rescue
CSI	Combat Studies Institute
CSIS	Center for Strategic and International Studies
CSS	combat service support
CSTC-A	Combined Security Transition Command–Afghanistan
CTC	Counterterrorism Center
CTF	Combined Task Force
DART	(Canadian) Disaster Assistance Response Team
DC	District of Columbia
DDR	Disarmament, Demobilization, and Reintegration
DEFCON	Defense Condition
DFID	(United Kingdom) Department for International Development
DOD	Department of Defense
DOS	Department of State
DRA	Democratic Republic of Afghanistan
DS	direct support
EA	Eastern Alliance
EOD	explosive ordnance disposal
EPW	enemy prisoner of war
ESF	Economic Support Fund
ETAC	enlisted terminal attack controller
ETT	embedded training team
EU	European Union
FA	field artillery
FARP	forward arming and refueling point
FBI	Federal Bureau of Investigation
FID	foreign internal defense
FM	field manual; frequency modulation
FOB	forward operating base
FORSCOM	Forces Command
FSB	forward support base

FSO	Foreign Service Officer
fwd	forward
FY	fiscal year
G2	Intelligence Section at Corps and Division Staff
G3	Operations Section at Corps and Division Staff
GAO	Government Accountability Office
GDI	ground-directed interdiction
GPS	Global Positioning System
GS	general support
GTMO	Guantanamo Bay, Cuba
GWOT	Global War on Terrorism
HAST	Humanitarian Assistance Survey Team
HDR	humanitarian daily rations
HHC	headquarters and headquarters company
HIG	Hizb-i Islami Gulbuddin
HLZ	helicopter landing zone
HMMWV	high-mobility multipurpose wheeled vehicle
HQ	headquarters
HSC	headquarters and service company
HUMINT	human intelligence
HVT	high-value target
ID	Infantry Division
IED	improvised explosive device
IMINT	imagery intelligence
IMU	Islamic Movement of Uzbekistan
IN	Infantry
INL	International Narcotics and Law Enforcement Affairs
IO	international organization
IRR	individual ready reserve
ISAF	International Security Assistance Force
ISI	Inter Services Intelligence
ISIM	Institute for the Study of Islam
ISOFAC	isolation facilities
ISR	intelligence, surveillance, and reconnaissance
ITGA	Islamic Transitional Government of Afghanistan
JAG	Judge Advocate General
JCS	Joint Chiefs of Staff
JDAM	Joint Direct Attack Munition
JEMB	Joint Electoral Management Body
JFACC	Joint Forces Air Component Command
JFSOCC	Joint Force Special Operations Component Command
JIF	Joint Interrogation Facility
JMD	Joint Manning Document
JP	joint publication
JPOTF	Joint Psychological Operations Task Force
JRT	joint regional team
JRTC	Joint Readiness Training Center
JSOTF	Joint Special Operations Task Force
JSOTF-N	Joint Special Operations Task Force–North

JTF	joint task force
JUI	Jamiat Ulema-e Islam
K2	Karshi-Khanabad (air base)
KGB	(Russian abbreviation of Committee for State Security)
KHAD	(Afghan security force similar to the Soviet KGB)
KIA	killed in action
KMTC	Kabul Military Training Center
LAV	light armored vehicle
LOC	line(s) of communications
LOO	line of operation
LTF	Logistics Task Force
LZ	landing zone
MAST	Military Academy Study Team
MEDCAP	Medical Civic Action Program
MEDEVAC	medical evacuation
MI	Military Intelligence
MIT	mobile interrogation team
mm	millimeter
MMC	Materiel Management Center
MOD	Ministry of Defense
MOI	Ministry of Interior
MP	Military Police
MRE	meal, ready to eat
MSDF	Maritime Self-Defense Force
MT	Mountain
MTT	mobile training team
NA	Northern Alliance
NATO	North Atlantic Treaty Organization
NAVC	National Army Volunteer Center
NCO	noncommissioned officer
NGO	nongovernment organization
NLF	National Liberation Front
NMAA	National Military Academy of Afghanistan
NORAD	North American Air Defense Command
NTC	National Training Center
NVG	night vision goggles
obj	objective
ODA	Operational Detachment–Alpha
ODC	Operational Detachment–Charlie
OEF	Operation ENDURING FREEDOM
OEMA	Office of Economic and Manpower Analysis
OGA	other governmental agency
OHDACA	Overseas Humanitarian, Disaster, and Civic Aid
OIF	Operation IRAQI FREEDOM
OMC-A	Office of Military Cooperation–Afghanistan
ONE	Operation NOBLE EAGLE
OP	observation point; operation
OPCON	operational control
OPORD	operation order

OSC-A	Office of Security Cooperation–Afghanistan
OUSD(P)	Office of the Under Secretary of Defense for Policy
PDPA	People's Democratic Party of Afghanistan
PIR	Parachute Infantry Regiment
PKSOI	US Army Peacekeeping and Stability Operations Institute
PL	phase line
PM-CPP	Political–Military Bureau for Contingency Planning and Peacekeeping
POG	Psychological Operations Group
POL-MIL	Political–Military
PPCLI	Princess Patricia's Canadian Light Infantry
PRT	Provincial Reconstruction Team
PSAB	Prince Sultan Air Base
PSYOP	psychological operations
PUC	persons under control
PZ	pickup zone
QIP	Quick-Impact Program
QRF	quick reaction force
RAOC	Rear Area Operations Center
RC-East	Regional Command–East
RC-South	Regional Command–South
RC-West	Regional Command–West
ROC	Rear Operations Center
ROE	rules of engagement
RPG	rocket-propelled grenade
RTO	radio-telephone operator
SAR	search and rescue
SAS	Special Air Service
SATCOM	satellite communications
SAW	Squad Automatic Weapon
SEAL	Sea, Air, Land
SETAF	Southern European Task Force
SF	Special Forces
SFG	Special Forces Group
SIGINT	signals intelligence
SNTV	Single Non-Transferable Vote
SO	Special Operations
SOAR	Special Operations Aviation Regiment
SOCCE	Special Operations Command and Control Element
SOCCENT	Special Operations Command Central
SOCOM	Special Operations Command
SOF	Special Operations Forces
SOFLAM	Special Operations Forces Laser Acquisition Markers
SOP	standing operating procedure
SOSB	Special Operations Support Battalion
SOSCOM	Special Operations Support Command
SR	Special Reconnaissance
SSD	Strategic Studies Detachment
SSE	sensitive site exploitation
SSR	Security Sector Reform

STANAVFORMED	Standing Naval Forces Mediterranean
SUV	sport utility vehicle
TAC	tactical command post
TACON	tactical control
TACP	Tactical Air Control Party
TALC	Theater Airlift Control Element
TF	task force
THREATCON	Threat Condition
TLAM	Tomahawk land attack missile
TOC	tactical operations center
TOE	table of organization and equipment
TRADOC	Training and Doctrine Command
TRANSCOM	US Transportation Command
TSC	Theater Support Command
TSgt	technical sergeant
UAV	unmanned aerial vehicle
UK	United Kingdom
UN	United Nations
UNAMA	United Nations Assistance Mission in Afghanistan
UNHCR	United Nations High Commission for Refugees
US	United States
USAF	United States Air Force
USAID	United States Agency for International Development
USASOC	United States Army Special Operations Command
USDA	United States Department of Agriculture
USIP	United States Institute for Peace
USMA	United States Military Academy
USMC	United States Marine Corps
USSOCOM	United States Special Operations Command
UW	unconventional warfare
VMI	Virginia Military Institute
VTC	video teleconference
WIA	wounded in action
XO	executive officer

Bibliography

Interviews, Discussions, Notes, and e-mail Correspondence

General John Abizaid
General Bryan Brown
General Abdul Rashid Dostum, Chief of Staff of the Afghanistan Army
General Dan K. McNeill
General Victor Eugene Renuart

Lieutenant General David W. Barno
Lieutenant General (Retired) Michael DeLong
Lieutenant General Karl Eikenberry
Lieutenant General Franklin L. Hagenbeck
Lieutenant General (Retired) Paul T. Mikolashek

Major General John Brennan
Major General (Retired) Dennis Jackson
Major General Jason Kamiya
Major General David E. Kratzer
Major General Benjamin Mixon
Major General (Retired) Eric Olson
Major General (Retired) John R. Vines
Major General (Retired) Craig Weston

Brigadier General (Retired) George B. Forsythe
Brigadier General William Garrett
Brigadier General John Kern
Brigadier General Thomas Mancino
Brigadier General John Mulholland
Brigadier General Jeffery Marshall
Brigadier General Stanley A. McCrystal
Brigadier General Joseph Prasek

Colonel (Retired) Bruce Boevers
Colonel Gary Cheek
Colonel Richard Conte
Colonel B. Shannon Davis
Colonel Joseph Dichairo
Colonel Edward Dorman III
Colonel Kevin Doxey
Colonel Rodney Edge
Colonel David G. Fox
Colonel (Retired) Michael Fitzgerald
Colonel David Francavilla
Colonel Richard Gallant
Colonel Bruce Haselden
Colonel Michael Hawrylak
Colonel (Retired) Michael Hayes
Colonel Walter Herd
Colonel Terry Lambert
Colonel David Lamm

Bibliography

Colonel Robert Landry
Colonel Orlando Lopez
Colonel (Promotable) Phillip McGhee
Colonel George P. Maughan
Colonel Mark Milley
Colonel David Paschal
Colonel Richard N. Pedersen
Colonel Charles A. Preysler
Colonel Timothy Reese
Colonel Robert Sharp, British Army
Colonel Thomas Snukis
Colonel John Spiszer
Colonel Michael Stout
Colonel Michael Toner
Colonel Stephen J. Townsend
Colonel (Retired) James Treadwell
Colonel (Retired) Mike Weimer
Colonel Mark Wentlent
Colonel Francis J. Wiercinski

Lieutenant Colonel Donald Bolduc
Lieutenant Colonel David Carstens
Lieutenant Colonel Jennifer Caruso
Lieutenant Colonel (Retired) Ronald Corkran
Lieutenant Colonel Roland de Marcellus
Lieutenant Colonel Carl E. Fischer
Lieutenant Colonel David Fitzgerald
Lieutenant Colonel Steven Ford
Lieutenant Colonel Brian Hilferty
Lieutenant Colonel John Lineweaver
Lieutenant Colonel David Miller
Lieutenant Colonel Bentley Nettles
Lieutenant Colonel Mary Ann O'Connor
Lieutenant Colonel William Owen
Lieutenant Colonel Tom Reilley
Lieutenant Colonel (Retired) Bruce Stanley
Lieutenant Colonel Patrick Stogran
Lieutenant Colonel Dennis Sullivan
Lieutenant Colonel Stephen C. Walker
Lieutenant Colonel Mike Warmack
Lieutenant Colonel Paul Wille

Major David Baker
Major Franklin Baltazar
Major William Bialozor
Major Mark Campbell
Major Roger Crombie
Major Edward Croot
Major Peter Dawe
Major Mike DeJarnette

Major Michael L. Gibler
Major James Hall
Major Nelson Kraft
Major Christine Locke
Major Kevin Lovell
Major Tim Miller
Major Troy O'Donnell
Major Luther Webster
Major Fred Wolanski

Captain Curtis Anderson
Captain Charles Fowler
Captain Benjamin Houston
Captain Patrick O'Hara
Captain Smith (First Name Withheld)

Lieutenant Matt Stafford

Command Sergeant Major Thomas Capel

Master Sergeant Armand J. Bolduc
Master Sergeant Michael Threatt

Staff Sergeant Tyler Ekwell

Technical Sergeant John McCabe

Sergeant Douglas DeMaio
Sergeant Flora Estrada

Afghan Experience Project Interview, #2, 3, 5, 23, 29
Deborah Alexander, USAID Field Program Manager for Afghanistan
Dr. David Champagne
Dr. Ehsan Entezar
Dr. Kenneth Katzman, CRS
Dr. Robert Perito, USIP
Minister Ali Jalali

US Military

Briefings

2d Brigade, 10th Mountain Division. *"Commandoes," Afghanistan: December 2001–April 2002, After Action Review* Briefing.
3d Brigade, 101st Airborne Division. *After Action Report*, undated brief.
10th Mountain Division. *10th Mountain Afghanistan and Opn Anaconda Brief*, undated, slide 33.
10th Mountain Division (Light Infantry). *Operation Enduring Freedom—V IBOS AAR*, date unknown, slide 16.
18th Airborne Corps CJCMOTF Brief. *101 Brief as of 31 March 2003*, slides 18, 23, 24.
130th Military History Detachment Command Report. *Operation Enduring Freedom Rotation IV, July 2003–March 2004*, date unknown.
Beradini, Vince. *Office of Military Cooperation–Afghanistan: ANA Development Brief*, Fall 2004, unpublished.

Bolduc, Donald (Lieutenant Colonel). *Operations in Southern Afghanistan* Briefing, slide 9.

Brennan, Major General John. *Afghan National Police Program* Brief, unpublished, undated.

C8 Resource Management. *Commander's Emergency Response Program (CERP)* Brief, slide 3.

Center for Strategic and International Studies. *The Afghanistan–Pakistan War: The Rising Threat: 2002–2008* Briefing, 27 January 2009.

Chambers, Major Christopher M., Deputy Director, OEMA (ANA Reconstruction Team, CJTF-180). *Recruiting for the Afghan National Army* Brief, 3 October 2002.

CJTF-76. "OPORD 04-01, Bronco Strike (OEF-5 Combat Operations), 3d Brigade, 25th Infantry Division." 22 May 2004.

CJTF *Mountain. Operation Anaconda: Combat Operations Brief*, 26 February 2002, slides 2 and 6.

CJTF *Mountain*, Headquarters, 10th Mountain Division. *Afghanistan and Operation ANACONDA* Brief, undated, slide 19.

Clinton, President William. Presidential Decision Directive 39, 21 June 1995. http://www.fas.org/irp/offdocs/pdd39.htm (accessed 11 April 2007).

CTF *Bronco. OEF V Historical Command Brief*, 22 April 2005.

Coalition Joint Civil-Military Operations Task Force. *Coalition Joint Civil-Military Operations (CJCMOTF)* Brief, January 2002. MacDill AFB, FL.

CJTF–180 Afghanistan. *10th Mountain Division's Mountain Story—OEF IV*, Spring 2004.

Conte, Colonel Richard. *Working with the US Army Corps of Engineers in Afghanistan* Brief, 27 July 2004, slide 17.

Franks, General Tommy. Presentation to the Army War College, April 2002, slide 9.

Ford, Lieutenant Colonel Steven. Ghazni PRT VIP Briefing. *Provisional Reconstruction Team: Ghazni, Afghanistan,* 22 May 2004.

Forte, Major Robert. Combined Task Force *Mountain* Briefing. *Operation Mountain Lion Assessment Briefing,* 13 July 2002, slides 1–5.

Garrett, Brigadier General William Burke. *10th Mountain Postmortem: Insights and Implications from Operation Enduring Freedom IV*, date unknown, slides 5 and 12.

Hagenbeck, General Franklin L. 10th Mountain Division (LI) Briefing. *10th Mountain Division AAR, Anaconda, 2001–2002*, 29 March 2007, slide 33.

Herd, Colonel Walter M. Combined Joint Special Operations Task Force Briefing. *Unconventional Warriors: Separate Insurgents from the Populace: Special Operations in Afghanistan from September 2003 to June 2004,* June 2004, slide 11.

Hollifield, Major Tim. Office of Military Cooperation–Afghanistan (OMC-A) Briefing. *Building the Afghan Army: Some Keys to Cultural Understanding,* no date/place given, 33 slides.

———. Office of Military Cooperation–Afghanistan (OMC-A) Briefing. *Ethnic Overview of Afghanistan*, no date/place given.

International Crisis Group Update Briefing. *Afghanistan: Getting Disarmament Back on Track.* Asia Briefing, No. 35, 23 February 2005, 5–6. http://www.crisisgroup.org/home/index.cfm?1=1&id=3290 (accessed 28 July 2007).

Kraft, Major Nelson. *Lessons Learned from a Light Infantry Company During Operation Anaconda* Brief, undated, slide 3.

Mancino, Brigadier General Thomas. *TF Phoenix II Brief, 76th Update to Command Briefing*, date unknown, slide 4.

Marshall, Colonel Jeffery. OMC-A Brief. *Force Development Concept Brief*, 15 October 2002, slide 8.

McCullagh, 1st Lieutenant Kevin J. *Coalition Joint Task Force Phoenix* Brief, date unknown, slide 4.

OMC-A. *ANA Presentation to MG Ostenberg* Brief, 27 August 2003, slide 48.

OMC-A. *Building the Afghan National Army* Brief, January 2003, slide 54.

OMC-A. CSA Brief, *Afghan National Army*, 28 November 2002, slide 3.

Reese, Colonel Timothy. *Office of Military Cooperation—Afghanistan Command Information* Brief, slide 7.

———. OMC-A Brief. *Afghan National Army—Karzai*, 6 January 2006, slides 55 and 56.

———. OMC-A Brief. *Task Force Phoenix TRADOC Recon Overview* Brief, 8 April 2003.

———. *Successful Fielding of the Afghan National Army, Central Corps*, 3 April 2003, slide 6.

Shah Mahmood. *MOD National Military Strategy*, 21 October 2004.

Snukis, Colonel Thomas. AEI Briefing, *Afghanistan Military Update*, date unknown, slides 3 and 14.

Stout, Colonel Michael. *Afghanistan: Effects Based Operations as a "Roadmap to Transition."* US Army War College Briefing.

Sumners (no first name given). 10th Mountain Division (LI) Briefing, *2d Brigade, 10th Mountain Division (LI) "Commandos": Afghanistan, December 2001–April 2002*, 25 July 2002.

US Central Command. *Operation ENDURING FREEDOM, Humanitarian Assistance (HA) Strategic Concept* Briefing, 12 November 2001. USCENTCOM, MacDill AFB, FL.

Weston, Major General Craig. OMC-A Brief. *Creating the Afghan Defense Sector*, July 2004.

———. OMC-A Brief. *G8 ANA Presentation*, 27 March 2004, slide 11.

———. OMC-A Brief. *OMC-A Orientation*, 26 June 2004, slide 5.

Weston, Major General Craig P., and the OMC-A Staff. *OMC-A's Estimate, COAs, and Recommendation for Police Sector Reform: Brief to LTG Barno as of 3 January 2005*, unpublished, slides 1–44.

Documents

1st Battalion, 505th PIR, *1-505 AAR MTN SWEEP*, 27 August 2002.

25th Infantry Division Association. "Global War on Terrorism." http://www.25thida.com/division.html (accessed 16 May 2007).

"173rd Airborne Brigade: History." http://www.173abnbde.setaf.army.mil/history.htm (accessed 13 August 2007).

Air Force Special Operations Command. "Fact Sheets." http://www.af.mil/factsheets (accessed 14 February 2007).

Allied Joint Forces Command Headquarters (PIO). "Expansion of NATO Presence in Afghanistan." http://www.nato.int/isaf/topics/expansion/index.html (accessed 4 June 2007).

———. "ISAF Fact Sheet." http://www.nato.int/isaf/docu/epub/pdf/isaf_leaflet.pdf (accessed 11 July 2007).

———. "ISAF Holds Change of Command Ceremony in Kabul," 4 August 2005. Press Release #2005-47. http://www.nato.int/isaf/docu/pressrelease/2005/Release_04Aug_47.htm (accessed 8 July 2007).

———. "ISAF Takes Command of Western PRTs in Herat and Farah," 31 May 2005. Press Release #2005-036. http://www.nato.int/isaf/docu/pressrelease/2005/Release_31May05.htm (accessed 8 July 2007).

Brennan, Major General John. "Proposed Briefing Flow for ANP Plan," unpublished, undated.

Center for Army Lessons Learned (CALL). *82d Airborne Division Initial Impressions Report*. Fort Leavenworth, KS, January 2003.

———. *Operation Enduring Freedom Initial Impressions Report*. Fort Leavenworth, KS, December 2003.

CJTF-180. Memorandum for the Commander (ATTN: CJCMOTF LNO to CJTF180), OHDACA Status Report as of 1 January 2003, 5 January 2003.

"Coalition Forces in Afghanistan." http://www.cfc-a.centcom.mil/Information/Coalition%20forces%20in%20Afghanistan.htm (accessed 22 May 2007).

Cubbison, Douglas R., Command Historian, 10th Mountain Division. *Summary History of Operation Enduring Freedom*.

Davis, Colonel Rod, USA. Director, Public Affairs, CJTF-180. "Division Soldiers Help Kill Enemy Fighters in Operation Mountain Viper." http://www.drum.army.mil/sites/postnews/blizzard/ blizzard_archives/ hnews.asp?id=1&issuedate=9-11-2003 (accessed 8 August 2007).

Department of the Army G3. *US Army Troop Levels in OEF Spreadsheet*, 2008.

Doxey, Lieutenant Colonel Kevin. "CCCA Progress Update: Information Paper," 16 June 2003.

Forsythe, Colonel George B. "Final Report of the Military Academy Study Team," unpublished official correspondence to OMC-A, 11 November 2003.

———. "National Military Academy of Afghanistan: Concept Plan," 11 November 2003, unpublished.

Hancock, Colonel Mackey K. Memorandum for Commander, CJTF-180, Bagram Airfield Afghanistan. Subject: CJCMOTF Lessons Learned, 3 May 03–19 Jan 04, 20 January 2004.

Headquarters, 1st Battalion, 187th Infantry. Memorandum: Subject: Task Force 1-187 IN After Action Report: Operation ANACONDA, 21 March 2001.

Heath, Sergeant Greg, 4th Public Affairs Detachment. "10th Mountain Division Shows its Mettle in Operation Mountain Resolve."

Helmy, Lieutenant General James, USA. Defense Subcommittee Hearing Statement, 7 May 2003.

O'Hara, Patrick. "ODA 586 (Texas 11) Historical Vignette of Afghanistan," unpublished, undated.

Operation Mountain Sweep AAR from ODAs 986 and 314, 25 August 2002.

Olson, Major General Eric. "CJTF-76 Commander's Guidance," 15 May 2004.

Pedersen, Colonel Richard. "BRONCO 6 Guidance: How to Think about OEF," 16 March 2004.

Prasek, Brigadier General Joseph. "CJTF *Phoenix* Training Guidance 4th Quarter, FY 03 (Draft)." Memorandum for Record, 19 June 2003.

Press Release. Combined Joint Task Force Headquarters, MacDill AFB, FL. Release Number 02-05-01, 14 May 2002. www.centcom.mil/sites/uscentcom1 (accessed 28 February 2007).

Smith, Lieutenant Colonel Hopper, Commander, 1/179 Infantry, 45th Infantry Brigade. "After Action Review submitted to Brigadier General Thomas Mancino," 28 September 2003.

TF *Devil*. Desert Devil Dispatch. 17 January 2003; 28 February 2003.

"TF Devil Operation Mongoose After Action Review," 18 March 2003.

TF *Devil. Significant Actions Daily Staff Journal*, March 2003.

TF 3-505th PIR. *AAR Comments for Operation MOUNTAIN SWEEP*, 26 August 2002.

"TF 3-505th PIR Operation Enduring Freedom (OEF) After Action Review," 5 December 2002.

"TF Panther, 3d Brigade, Battle Captain After Action Review," 27 August 2002.

"Task Force *Rakkasan* Warning Order #2," 21 June 2002.

US Army Accessions Support Brigade. "Colonel Walter M. Herd Biography." http://www.usarec.army. mil/asb/pages/CDR2.htm (accessed 5 June 2007).

US Army Corps of Engineers. "Afghanistan Engineer Fact Sheet." http://usace.army.mil/CEPAFact Sheets/Pages/AED.aspx (accessed 23 February 2009).

US Army Operation ENDURING FREEDOM Web site. http://www.army.mil/operations/oef/images42. html (accessed 15 August 2007).

US Central Command. "Afghanistan: Excerpts from Statement of General John P. Abizaid, United States Army Commander, United States Central Command, before the Senate Armed Services Committee on the 2006 Posture of the United States Central Command," 14 March 2006. http:// www.centcom.mil/sites/uscentcom2/Misc/Afghanistan.aspx (accessed 14 August 2007).

US Marine Corps Center for Advanced Operational Cultural Learning (CAOCL). http://www.tecom. usmc.mil/caocl/Caucasus_and_Central_Asia/Central_Asia_Former_Sov (accessed 11 January 2007).

US Special Operations Command History Office. *United States Special Operations Command HISTORY, 1987–2007, 20th Anniversary Edition*. MacDill Air Force Base, FL: USSOCOM, 2007.

United States Transportation Command Annual Command Report. USTRANSCOM, 2001.

Weston, Major General Craig P. "Key to Afghan National Police Mission Assumption," unpublished, undated notes.

———. *Key to ANA Acceleration Briefings* memorandum, undated.

Joint Publications, Field Manuals, and Army Regulations

Joint Chiefs of Staff. Joint Publication (JP) 1-02, *DOD Dictionary of Military and Associated Terms*. Washington, DC, 2001.

———. JP 3-05, *Doctrine for Special Operations*. Washington, DC, 17 April 1998.

———. JP 3-57, *Joint Doctrine for Civil-Military Operations*. Washington, DC, 8 February 2001.

———. JP 5-0, *Doctrine for Planning Joint Operations*. Washington, DC, 1995.

———. JP 30-8, *Interagency Cooperation During Joint Operations, Volume 1*. Washington, DC, 1996.

Headquarters, Department of the Army. Field Manual (FM) 3-0, *Operations*. Washington, DC, 2001.

———. FM 3.05-201, *Special Forces Unconventional Warfare Operations*. Washington, DC, 2003.

———. FM 5-0, *Army Planning and Orders Production*. Washington, DC, 2005.

———. FM 27-100, *Legal Support to Operations*. Washington, DC, 2000.

———. FM 41-10, *Civil Affairs Operations*. Washington, DC, 2000.

———. FM 90-8, *Counterguerrilla Operations*. Washington, DC, 1986.

———. FM 100-20, *Military Operations in Low Intensity Conflict*. Washington, DC, 1990.

———. FM 100-25, *Doctrine for Army Special Operations Forces*. Washington, DC, 1999.

Headquarters, Department of the Army. Army Regulation (AR) 310-25, *Dictionary of United States Army Terms*. Washington, DC, 1983.

Books, Articles, and Reports

"3 Afghan Election Workers Abducted; Judge Shot." *Washington Post,* 24 July 2005.

9/11 Report Staff Statement. "Remarks by the Vice President to the Heritage Foundation," 10 October 2003. http://www.whitehouse.gov/news/releases/2003/10/text/20031010-1.html (accessed 6 April 2007).

"1997 Annual Defense Report." http://www.dod.gov/execsec/adr97/chap18.html (accessed 27 April 2007).

Abney, Steve. "DLA Activities in Europe in Support of Operation Enduring Freedom." *Dimensions* (Winter 2003): 6–9.

"AC-130H/U Gunship." Air Force Fact Sheet. http://www.af.mil/factsheets/factsheet.asp?fsID=71 (accessed 24 April 2007).

Ackerman, Robert K. "Infowarriors Ensure Local Citizenry Gets the Message." *Signal Magazine* (March 2002): 20–21.

"Address by President General Pervez Musharraf to the Pakistani Nation," 19 September 2001. http://www.un.int/pakistan/14010919.html (accessed 17 January 2007).

"Afghan Elections Begin Amidst Taliban Attacks." *Hindustan Times,* 18 September 2005.

"Afghan National Army Activates Second Regional Command." *American Forces Press Service,* 23 September 2004. http://www.defenselink.mil/news/newsarticle.aspx?id=25226 (accessed 1 August 2007).

Afghanistan Engineer District. "Colonel O'Dowd Reflects on Afghan Mission," 10 July 2005. http://www.aed.usace.army.mil/news/releases/exitinterview.html (accessed 23 February 2009).

"Afghanistan Fact Sheet Jan 2003." United Kingdom Department for International Development, 29 January 2003. http://www.reliefweb.int/rw/rwb.nsf/AllDocsByUNID/9d624e84e3da4d40c1256cbd004ceafc (accessed 28 August 2007).

"Afghanistan: Interview with US-led Coalition Civil Military Coordination Center," 8 January 2004. http://www.irinnews.org/report.asp?ReportID=22699 (accessed 1 August 2007).

"Afghanistan: Paper On UK PRT Experience." *Afghanistan Group, FCO, 20 January 2005.* http://www.fco.gov.uk/Files/kfile/UK%20paper%20on%20its%20PRT%20experience.pdf (accessed 9 August 2007).

"Afghanistan." United Nations Disarmament, Demobilization, and Reintegration Resource Centre. http://www.unddr.org/countryprogrammes.php?c=121 (accessed 17 May 2007).

"Afghanistan Update," June 2004. http://www.defendamerica.mil/afghanistan/update/jun2004/au062104.html (accessed 12 September 2007).

"Afghanistan Votes." *Washington Post,* 16 September 2005.

Ahari, M.E., and James Beal. *The New Great Game in Muslim Central Asia.* McNair Paper 47, National Defense University, Institute for National Strategic Studies. Washington, DC: National Defense University Press, 2001.

Aizenman, N.C. "Long-Delayed Afghan Vote Is Set for Sept.; One House of Parliament Will Remain Incomplete." *Washington Post,* 21 March 2005.

Albright, Secretary of State Madeleine K. "Statement for the Record before the Senate Committee on Appropriations Hearing on Terrorism." US Department of State, Washington, DC, 13 May 1997. http://www.milnet.com/state/1997/albright.htm (accessed 20 April 2007).

Alinejad, Sima. "Provisional Reconstruction Teams (PRT)." UNHCR, 1 April 2004. http://www.aims.org.af/services/sectoral/emergency_assistance/refugee/unhcr_return_issues/issue_54.pdf (accessed 10 September 2007).

"Al Qaeda's Fatwa." *PBS Online News Hour,* 23 February 1998. http://www.pbs.org/newshour/terrorism/international/fatwa_1998.html (accessed 5 April 2007).

"America and the War on Terror." *Soldier Magazine* 58, No. 9, September 2003.

Amin, Hussein Abdulwaheed. "The Origins of the Sunni/Shia Split in Islam." *Islam for Today.* http://www.islamfortoday.com/shia.htm (accessed 11 January 2007).

"Analysis: Masood's Regional Allies." *BBC News Online,* 11 September 2001. http://news.bbc.uk (accessed 7 February 2007).

Anderson, Benedict. *Imagined Communities: Reflections on the Origin and Spread of Nationalism.* Rev. ed. New York, NY: Verso, 2006.

Anderson, Jon Lee. "The Surrender." *New Yorker* 77, no. 39 (10 December 2001): 70.

Andrade, Dale. *The Battle of Mazar-e Sharif, October–November 2001.* Washington, DC: US Army Center of Military History Information Paper, 2002.

Annan, Kofi A. "The Situation in Afghanistan and its Implications for International Peace and Security." *Report of the Secretary-General.* General Assembly, Fifty-sixth session, United Nations, NY, 18 March 2002.

Archick, Kristin. "European Approaches to Homeland Security and Counterterrorism." *CRS Report to Congress,* 24 July 2006.

Arguello, Jon. "Task Force Rock Paratroopers Repel Ambush." *Defend America—U.S. Department of Defense News about the War on Terrorism,* 18 May 2005. www.defendamerica.mil/articles/may2005/a051805la2.html (accessed 13 August 2007).

———. "Task Force Rock Takes Control in Zabol." *The Outlook* (3 May 2005): 1–4.

Arkin, William. "Response to Terror; Military Memo; Old-Timers Prove Invaluable in Afghanistan Air Campaign." *Los Angeles Times,* 10 February 2002.

Armitage, US Deputy Secretary of State Richard, and Lord Robertson, Secretary General of NATO. "Press Availability: U.S. Deputy Secretary of State Armitage and NATO Secretary General Lord Robertson," 20 September 2001. http://www.nato.int/docu/speech/2001/s010920a.htm (accessed 15 April 2009).

Armstrong, Captain Bradley J., USAF. "Rebuilding Afghanistan: Counterinsurgency and Reconstruction in Operation Enduring Freedom." Master's Thesis, Naval Postgraduate School, December 2003.

Arnold, Anthony. *Afghanistan: The Soviet Intervention in Perspective*. Stanford, CA: Hoover Institution Press, 1986.

"Asia: Democracy, Sort of; Afghanistan's Elections." *The Economist* (24 September 2005): 84.

"Asia: Getting the Vote Out; Afghanistan." *The Economist* (2 July 2005): 60.

"Asia Overview: Patterns of Global Terrorism." Office of the Coordinator for Counterterrorism, 30 April 2001. http://www.state.gov/s/ct/rls/crt/2000/2432.htm (accessed 6 April 2007).

"Assembly Concludes Debate on Report of Secretary-General with Reiterated Calls for Action to Combat Terrorism." Press Release/9918, Fifty-Sixth General Assembly, 11th Meeting (AM), 26 September 2001.

Associated Press. "Afghan Chief Touts Reconciliation Plan." *Kansas City Times*, 22 July 1987.

———. "Afghan Leader Tells of Helping Osama Get Away." *Beaumont (Texas) Enterprise,* 12 January 2007.

Association of Graduates USMA, Nininger Award. http://www.aogusma.org/aog/awards/Nininger/06Gray_Matter_Article.htm (accessed 11 September 2007).

Aubrey, Eric. Afghanistan Engineer District. "The Corps Needs You," 1 July 2005. http://www.aed.usace.army.mil/news/releases/exitinterview.html (accessed 23 February 2009).

Aziz, Christine, and Smruti Patel. "Defiance and Oppression: The Situation of Women." In *Afghanistan,* 2d edition, edited by Edward Girardet and Jonathan Walter, co-editors Charles Norchi and Mirwais Masood. Geneva, Switzerland: Crosslines Publications, 2004.

Badstibner, Ellen. "Supporting Operation Enduring Freedom." *Dimensions* (Winter 2002): 30–31.

Baker, Aryn. "Can the Afghans Defend Themselves?" *Time in Partnership with CNN,* 3 January 2007. http://www.time.com/time/world/article/0,8599,1573742,00.html (accessed 24 June 2007).

Baker, Stephen, and Emily Clark. "Forces in Play." *Center for Defense Information Bulletin*, 26 October 2001.

Balance, Edward O. *Afghan Wars: Battles in a Hostile Land, 1839–Present*. London: Brassey's, 2002.

Bansahel, Nora. *The Counterterror Coalitions: Cooperation with Europe, NATO, and the European Union.* Santa Monica, CA: RAND Corporation, 2003.

Barakat, Sultan. "Setting the Scene for Afghanistan's Reconstruction: The Challenges and Critical Dilemmas." *Third World Quarterly* 23, no. 5 (2002): 802.

Barker, Kim. "Targeted Attacks Intended to Disrupt Afghan Elections." *Knight Ridder Tribune News Service,* 17 September 2005.

Barno, Lieutenant General David. "Central Command Briefing," 17 June 2004. http://www.defenselink.mil/transcripts/transcript.aspx?transcriptid=3345 (accessed 16 July 2007).

Barno, Lieutenant General (Retired) David W., USA. "Fighting 'The Other War': Counterinsurgency Strategy in Afghanistan, 2003–2005." *Military Review* (September–October 2007): 32–44.

Barton, Frederick, Bathsheba Crocker, and Morgan L. Courtney. *In the Balance: Measuring Progress in Afghanistan*. Washington, DC: The CSIS Press, 2005.

Baumann, Dr. Robert F. *Russian-Soviet Unconventional Wars in the Caucasus, Central Asia, and Afghanistan.* Leavenworth Papers No. 20. Fort Leavenworth, KS: Combat Studies Institute, Command and General Staff College Press, 1993.

Bay, Austin. "A Full Report on Operation Anaconda—America's First Battle of the 21st Century, A Complete After Action Interview with COL Wiercinski." *StrategyPage*. http://www.strategypage.com/on_point/20020627. aspx (accessed 30 May 2007).

Bedford, Ian. "Nationalism and Belonging in India, Pakistan, and South Central Asia: Some Comparative Observations." *Australian Journal of Anthropology* 7, no. 2, August 1996. http://findarticles. com/p/articles/mim2472/is_n2_v7/ai_18912022/print (accessed 16 November 2006).

Ben-Aryeah, David. "British Troops Face the Reality that is Afghanistan." *Asia Times Online,* 16 November 2001. http://www.atimes.com (accessed 16 February 2007).

Berke, Richard L., and Janet Elder. "NY Times/CBS Poll." *New York Times,* 25 September 2001.

Bernard, Cheryl, Seth G. Jones, Olga Oliker, Cathryn Quantic Thurston, Brooke Stearns Lawson, Kristen Cordell. *Women and Nation-Building.* Santa Monica, CA: RAND Corporation, 2009.

Biddle, Stephen. *Afghanistan and the Future of Warfare: Implications for Army and Defense Policy.* Carlisle, PA: US Army War College Strategic Studies Institute, 2002.

Bindra, Satinder. "Northern Alliance Takes Khanabad." Interview by Catherine Callaway. *CNN.com Transcripts,* 25 November 2001. http://transcripts.cnn.com (accessed 19 January 2007).

Birtle, Andrew. *Afghan War Chronology.* Washington, DC: US Army Center of Military History Information Paper, 2002.

Blanchard, Christopher M. "Al Qaeda: Statements and Evolving Ideology." *CRS Report to Congress,* 16 November 2004.

Blood, Peter R., Foreign Affairs, Defense, and Trade Division. "Pakistan–U.S. Relations." *CRS Issue Brief for Congress,* 10 March 2002.

Blood, Peter R., ed. *Afghanistan: A Country Study.* Washington, DC: Library of Congress, 1998.

Blum, Bill, trans. "Interview with Dr. Zbigniew Brzezinski, Paris, France, January 15–21, 1998, *Le Nouvel Observateur*." http://www.globalresearch.ca/articles/BRZ110A.html (accessed 1 February 2007).

Blum, Lieutenant General H. Steven, USA. "A Vision for the National Guard." *Joint Force Quarterly* 36, no. 24.

Bocharov, Gennadi. *Byl I videl . . . Afganistan 1986/87 go.* Moscow: Politizdat, 1987.

Bogart, Adrian T. III. *One Valley at a Time.* Hurlburt Field, FL: Joint Special Operations University Press, 2006.

Bogdanos, Matthew F. "Joint Interagency Cooperation: The First Step." *Joint Forces Quarterly* 35 (April 2005): 10–18.

Bonin, John A., and Mark H. Gerner. "Continuous Concentric Pressure." *The Land Warfare Papers,* September 2003.

Boot, Max. "Special Forces and Horses." *Armed Forces Journal* (November 2006): 18–25. http://www. armedforcesjournal.com/2006/11/2146103 (accessed 1 April 2007).

Bowie, Christopher J., Robert P. Haffa Jr., and Robert E. Mullins. *Future War: What Trends in America's Post-Cold War Military Conflicts Tell Us About Early 21st Century Warfare.* Arlington, VA: Northrop Grumman Analysis Center, 2003.

Boyd, Terry. "Troops in Afghanistan Preparing Spring Offensive in Pursuit of Insurgents." *Stars and Stripes European Edition*, Wednesday, 10 March 2004. http://stripes.com/article.asp?section= 104&article=20153&archive=true (accessed 24 September 2007).

Briscoe, Charles H., Richard L. Kiper, James A. Schroder, and Kalev I. Sepp. *Weapon of Choice: US Army Special Operations Forces in Afghanistan.* Fort Leavenworth, KS: Combat Studies Institute Press, 2003.

Bureau of South and Central Asian Affairs. "Afghanistan." *US Department of State.* http://www.state. gov/p/sca/ci/af/ (accessed 19 December 2006).

Burgess, Mark. "CDI Fact Sheet: International Security Assistance Force (December 2002)." *Center for Defense Information Terrorism Project*, 17 December 2002. http://www.cdi.org/terrorism/ isaf_dec02-pr.cfm (accessed 30 May 2007).

"Bush Calls on US to Defend Freedom: Authorizes Guard and Reserve Call-ups." *TALON* 7, no. 38 (22 September 2001): 4.

Bush, George W. "Address to a Joint Session of Congress and the American People," 20 September 2001. http://www.whitehouse.gov/news/releases/2001/09/20010920-8.html (accessed 19 September 2008).

———. "Blocking Property and Prohibiting Transactions with Persons Who Commit, Threaten to Commit, or Support Terrorism." Executive Order 13224, 23 September 2001.

———. "Presidential Address to the Nation," 8 October 2001. http://www.whitehouse.gov/news/releases/2001/10/20011007-8.html (accessed 10 July 2007).

———. "Radio Address of the President to the Nation," 29 September 2001. http://www.whitehouse.gov/news/releases/2001/09/20010929.html (accessed 8 October 2008).

———. "Radio Address of the President to the Nation," 6 October 2001. http://www.whitehouse.gov/news/releases/2001/10/20011006.html (accessed 14 March 2001).

———. "Statement by the President in His Address to the Nation," 11 September 2001. http://www.whitehouse.gov/news/releases/2001/09/20010911-16.html (accessed 15 September 2008).

———. "The National Security Strategy of the United States of America," 17 September 2002.

———. "The President's News Conference with President Pervez Musharraf of Pakistan at Camp David, Maryland," 24 June 2003. http://www.presidency.ucsb.edu/ws/index.php?pid=63119 (accessed 3 February 2009).

Butt, John. "The Taliban Phenomenon." In *Afghanistan,* 2d edition, edited by Edward Girardet and Jonathan Walter, co-editors Charles Norchi and Mirwais Masood. Geneva, Switzerland: Crosslines Publications, 2004.

Caffrey, Matthew. "Afghanistan: Current Operational Lessons from the Soviet Experience." *Air Command and Staff College Quick Look* 05-01 (January 2005). http://research.airuniv.edu (accessed 5 January 2007).

Caldwell, Jacob. "Operation Diablo Reach Back Targets Militia." *Defend America—U.S. Department of Defense News about the War on Terrorism,* 28 June 2005. http://www.defendamerica.mil/articles/june2005/a0628051a4.html (accessed 13 August 2007).

"Campaign Against Terror, Behind the Scenes at Bonn: Colin Powell, U.S. Secretary of State." *PBS FRONTLINE.* http://www.pbs.org/wgbh/pages/frontline/shows/campaign/withus/cbonntheme.html (accessed 29 March 2007).

"Campaign Against Terror, Behind the Scenes at Bonn: Condoleezza Rice, U.S. National Security Adviser." *PBS FRONTLINE.* http://www.pbs.org/wgbh/pages/frontline/shows/campaign/withus/cbonntheme.html (accessed 29 March 2007).

"Campaign Against Terror, Behind the Scenes at Bonn: James Dobbins, U.S. Special Envoy to Afghanistan." *PBS FRONTLINE.* http://www.pbs.org/wgbh/pages/frontline/shows/campaign/withus/cbonntheme.html (accessed 29 March 2007).

"Campaign Against Terror, Interview: Colonel John Mulholland." *PBS FRONTLINE* (undated). http://www.pbs.org/wgbh/pages/frontline/shows/campaign/interviews/mulholland.html (accessed 1 April 2007).

"Campaign Against Terror, Interview: Condoleezza Rice." *PBS FRONTLINE,* 12 July 2002. http://www.pbs.org/wgbh/pages/frontline/shows/campaign/interviews/rice.html (accessed 6 December 2006).

"Campaign Against Terror, Interview: General Tommy Franks." *PBS FRONTLINE,* 12 June 2002. http://www.pbs.org/wgbh/pages/frontline/shows/campaign/interviews/franks.html (accessed 6 December 2006).

"Campaign Against Terror, Interview: Lt. Col. David Fox." *PBS FRONTLINE* (undated). http://www.pbs.org/wgbh/pages/frontline/shows/campaign/interviews/fox.html (accessed 1 April 2007).

"Campaign Against Terror, Interview: Paul Wolfowitz." *PBS FRONTLINE* (undated). http://www.pbs.org/wgbh/pages/frontline/shows/campaign/interviews/wolfowitz.html (accessed 23 January 2007).

"Campaign Against Terror, Interview: President Hamid Karzai." *PBS FRONTLINE,* 7 May 2002. http://www.pbs.org/wgbh/pages/frontline/shows/campaign/interviews/karzai.html (accessed 29 March 2007).

"Campaign Against Terror, Interview: U.S. Army Captain Jason Amerine." *PBS FRONTLINE,* 12 July 2002. http://www.pbs.org/wgbh/pages/frontline/shows/campaign/interviews/amerine.html (accessed 29 March 2007).

"Campaign Against Terror, Interview: U.S. Army General Tommy Franks." *PBS FRONTLINE*, 8 September 2002. http://www.pbs.org/wgbh/pages/frontline/shows/campaign/interviews/franks.html (accessed 27 August 2007).

"Campaign Against Terror, Interview: U.S. Special Forces ODA 555, Frank [No last name available] (SFC)." *PBS FRONTLINE* (undated). http://www.pbs.org/wgbh/pages/frontline/shows/campaign/interviews/555.html (accessed 4 September 2007).

"Campaign Against Terror, Interview: U.S. Special Forces ODA 572, Bill [No last name available] (SSG)." *PBS FRONTLINE* (undated). http://www.pbs.org/wgbh/pages/frontline/shows/campaign/interviews/572.html (accessed 8 April 2007).

"Campaign Against Terror, Interview: U.S. Special Forces ODA 572, Jeff [No last name available] (SSG)." *PBS FRONTLINE* (undated). http://www.pbs.org/wgbh/pages/frontline/shows/campaign/interviews/572.html (accessed 8 April 2007).

"Campaign Against Terror, Interview: U.S. Special Forces ODA 572, Shane [No last name available] (MSG)." *PBS FRONTLINE* (undated). http://www.pbs.org/wgbh/pages/frontline/shows/campaign/interviews/572.html (accessed 8 April 2007).

"Campaign Against Terror, Interview: U.S. Special Forces ODA 595, Mark [No last name available] (CAPT)." *PBS FRONTLINE,* 8 September 2002. http://www.pbs.org/wgbh/pages/frontline/shows/campaign/interviews/595.html (accessed 4 December 2008).

"Campaign Against Terror, The Battle of Tarin Kowt, Capt. Jason Amerine, U.S. Special Forces A-Team Captain." *PBS FRONTLINE,* 12 July 2002. http://www.pbs.org/wgbh/pages/frontline/shows/campaign/ground/tarinkowt.html (accessed 31 March 2007).

"Campaign Against Terror, Working with the Warlords: Reuel Gerecht, Former CIA Agent." *PBS FRONTLINE,* 19 June 2002. http://www.pbs.org/wgbh/pages/frontline/shows/campaign/ground/warlord.html (accessed 1 April 2007).

"Canadian Forces' Contribution to the International Campaign Against Terrorism." *Canadian Forces Backgrounder*. Canadian Department of National Defence, BG-02.001p, 7 January 2004. http://www.forces.gc.ca/site/Newsroom/view_news_e.asp?id+490 (accessed 17 August 2007).

"CENTCOM Commander Franks Press Conference in Uzbekistan," 27 September 2000. Transcript archived at the Department of State, Press Relations.

Chagnon, Captain Michael, Canadian Army. "Canadian Embedded Training Teams." *The Bulletin,* December 2004. http://armyapp.dnd.ca/ALLC/Downloads/bulletin/Vol_10/Bulletin_Vol10No8 Eng.pdf (accessed 10 August 2007).

Chan, Samuel. "Sentinels of Afghan Democracy: The Afghan National Army." S. Rajaratnam School of International Studies, 1 June 2007, 4–8. Unpublished paper.

Chayes, Sarah. *The Punishment of Virtue: Inside Afghanistan after the Taliban.* New York, NY: The Penguin Press, 2006.

Cheek, Colonel Gary H. "So You Want to Be a Maneuver Brigade Commander? CTF Thunder in Afghanistan." *Field Artillery Journal* (March–April 2005).

Church, Vice Admiral Albert T. III. *Review of Department of Defense Detention Operations and Detainee Interrogation Techiques (The Church Report)*, 7 March 2005.

"CinC CENTCOM and the Chief of the Defence Staff: Press Conference—26 April 2002." *Operation Veritas*. UK Ministry of Defence, 26 April 2002. http://www.operations.mod.uk/veritas/press_brief_26apr.htm (accessed 6 July 2007).

Clark, Emily, and Mark Burgess. "Action Update (Complete Archive)." *Center for Defense Information Terrorism Project*, 8 October 2001–1 September 2002. http://www.cdi.org/terrorism/actionupdate-archive-pr.cfm (accessed 28 February 2007).

Clement, Amy. "TAC Helps Army Rebuild Afghan Forces," January 2003. http://www.hq.usace.army.mil/cepa/pubs/jan03/story17.htm (accessed 11 August 2007).

CNN Cold War Series. "Episode 17: Good Guys, Bad Guys: Interview with Dr. Zbigniew Brzezinski." http://www.gwu.edu/~nsarchiv/coldwar/interviews/episode-17/brzezinski1.html (accessed 10 January 2007).

CNN Perspective Series. "Episode 14: Red Spring." http://www.cnn.com/SPECIALS/cold.war/episodes/14/documents/doctrine (accessed 18 December 2006).

"CNN Presents House of War: Uprising at Mazar-e Sharif," 3 August 2002. http://www.cnn.com/CNN/Programs/presents/shows/house.of.war/interactive/interactive/house.of.swf (accessed 3 March 2007).

"Coalition in Afghanistan Wraps Up Mountain Blizzard." *American Forces Press Service News Articles*, 13 March 2004. http://www.defenselink.mil/news/newsarticle.aspx?id=27073 (accessed 10 July 2007).

Coll, Steve. *Ghost Wars: The Secret History of the CIA: Afghanistan, and bin Laden, from the Soviet Invasion to September 11, 2001.* New York, NY: Penguin Press, 2004.

Combined Security Transition Command–Afghanistan Fact Sheet, 12 April 2006. http://oneteam.centcom.mil/fact_sheets/CSTC-A%20Fact%20sheet%20-%2012%20April%2006.pdf (accessed 22 June 2007).

"Conspiracy to Attack Defense Utilities of the United States." United States District Court Southern District of New York, 6 November 1998. http://www.fas.org/irp/news/1998/11/indict1.pdf (accessed 17 April 2007).

Cordesman, Anthony H. *The Ongoing Lessons of Afghanistan: Warfighting, Intelligence, Force Transformation, and Nation Building.* Washington, DC: Center for Strategic and International Studies, 2004.

Crane, Conrad. *Final Report: The U.S. Army's Initial Impressions of Operation Enduring Freedom and Noble Eagle.* Carlisle, PA: US Army War College, 2002.

Crumpton, Henry A. "Intelligence and War: Afghanistan, 2001–2002." In *Transforming U.S. Intelligence,* edited by Jennifer E. Sims and Burton Gerber, 162–179. Washington, DC: Georgetown University Press, 2005.

CSTC-A. Information Paper. "National Military Academy of Afghanistan," April 2007.

Curtis, Glenn E., ed. *Kazakstan, Kyrgyzstan, Tajikistan, Turkmenistan and Uzbekistan: Country Studies.* Washington, DC: Library of Congress Federal Research Division, 1997.

Dagger, Jacob. "The Mind of Bin Laden: Interview with Professor Bruce Lawrence." *Duke Magazine* 91, Issue 6, November–December 2005. http://www.dukemagazine.duke.edu/dukemag/issues/111205/depqa.html (accessed 10 May 2007).

"Daily Press Briefing by the Office of the Spokesman for the Secretary-General." *United Nations Press Briefing*, 6 September 2001. http://www.un.org/News/briefings/docs/2001/db090601.doc.htm (accessed 25 January 2007).

Dale, Helle. "NATO in Afghanistan: A Test Case for Future Missions." *The Heritage Foundation Backgrounder* #1985, 27 November 2006. http://www.heritage.org/Research/Europe/upload/bg_1985.pdf (accessed 21 May 2007).

Davis, Anthony. "Basic Training." *Time*, 3 June 2002. http://www.time.com/time/printout/0,8816,257159,00.html (accessed 5 July 2007).

Davis, Jacquelyn K. "Radical Islamist Ideologies and the Long War: Implications for US Strategic Planning and US Central Command Operations." Washington, DC: Defense Threat Reduction Agency, Institute for Foreign Policy Analysis, Inc., January 2007.

Davis, Major Mark G. "Operation ANACONDA: Command and Confusion in Joint Warfare." Masters Thesis. Maxwell AFB, AL: School of Advanced Air and Space Studies, Air University, June 2004.

"Debating Report of the Secretary-General on Work of Organization." Press Release/9915, Fifty-Sixth General Assembly, Plenary, 8th Meeting (PM), 24 September 2001.

Dehghanpisheh, Babak. "The Death Convoy of Afghanistan." *Newsweek* 140, no. 9 (26 August 2002): 20.

DeLong, Lieutenant General Michael, and Noah Lukeman. *Inside CentCom: The Unvarnished Truth about the Wars in Afghanistan and Iraq.* Washington, DC: Regnery Publishing, Inc., 2004.

"Department of Defense's Role in Combating Terrorism and Force Protection Lesson, Before the Special Oversight Panel on Terrorism, House Committee of Armed Services," 14 June 2001. http://commdocs.house.gov/committees/security/has165240.000/has165240_0f.htm (accessed 12 April 2001).

"Deputy Secretary Wolfowitz Press Briefing with Afghan Foreign Minister." *US Department of Defense News Transcript,* 15 July 2002. http://www.defenselink.mil/transcripts/transcript. aspx?transcriptid=3601 (accessed 26 January 2009).

"Detainee Helped Bin Laden Flee, Document Says." *Washington Post,* 23 March 2005.

"DIAG: History and Background." DIAG home page. http://www.diag.gov.af/ (accessed 20 June 2007).

Di Leonardo, Captain Charles, USA. "Training the Afghan National Army." *Infantry* (March/April 2005): 28–39.

DOD Commission on Beirut International Airport Terrorist Act. *Report of the DOD Commission on Beirut International Airport Terrorist Act, October 23, 1983* [aka The Long Commission]. Washington, DC: US Department of Defense, 20 December 1983. http://www.ibiblio.org/hyperwar/AMH/XX/MidEast/Lebanon-1982-1984/DOD-Report/index.html (accessed 12 December 2006).

Donahue, Colonel (P) Patrick. "Combating a Modern Insurgency: Combined Task Force Devil in Afghanistan." *Military Review* (March–April 2008): 30.

Dowell, William. "Blowing Hot and Cold: 20 Years of US Policy." In *Afghanistan,* 2d edition, edited by Edward Girardet and Jonathan Walter, co-editors Charles Norchi and Mirwais Masood. Geneva, Switzerland: Crosslines Publications, 2004.

Downing Assessment Task Force. *Report of the Assessment of the Khobar Towers Bombing.* Washington, DC: The Pentagon, 30 August 1996.

Drumsta, Staff Sergeant Raymond, USA. "Rainbow Soldiers at Ground Zero." *Guard Times* 9, Issue 5, September–October 2001.

Dupree, Louis. *Afghanistan.* Princeton, NJ: Princeton University Press, 1973.

———. "Afghanistan in 1982: Still No Solution." *Asian Survey* 23, no. 2 (1983).

Dziedzic, Michael, and Colonel Michael Seidl. Special Report #147, "United States Institute of Peace Special Report: Provincial Reconstruction Teams," September 2005.

Emadi, Hafizullah. *Culture and Customs of Afghanistan.* Westport, CT: Greenwood Press, 2005.

Erwin, Sandra I. "Air Warfare Tactics Refined in Afghanistan: Planners, Air Crews Fine-Tuning Target Techniques and Rules of Engagement." *National Defense Magazine* (April 2002). http://www.nationaldefensemagazine.org/issues/2002/Apr/Air_Warfare.htm (accessed 7 February 2007).

Eyre, Lieutenant Vincent. *The Military Operations at Cabul: The Retreat and Destruction of the British Army, 1842.* Gloucestershire, Great Britain: Nonsuch Publishing, LTD, 2005 (first published 1843).

Fang, Bay. "They Were All Fighting to Die." *U.S. News & World Report* 131, no. 24 (10 December 2001): 18–21.

Fanning, Lieutenant Colonel Paul, USA. "Responding to Terror: The New York National Guard at Ground Zero." *Guard Times* 9, Issue 5, September–October 2001.

Fathi, Nazila. "Iran Won't Join US Campaign, Leader Says." *New York Times,* 27 September 2001.

Federal Bureau of Investigation Web site. http://www.fbi.gov/ (accessed 11 April 2007).

Feickert, Andrew. "U.S. Military Operations in the Global War on Terrorism: Afghanistan." Congressional Research Service Report RL 32758, 20 June 2006. www.italy.usembassy.gov/pdf/other/RL32758.pdf (accessed 8 June 2007).

Feith, Douglas J., Under Secretary of Defense for Policy. Foreign Press Center Briefing. "Operation Enduring Freedom: 1 Year Later." Washington, DC: US Department of State, 8 October 2002. http://fpc.state.gov/fpc/14209.htm (accessed 22 January 2007).

———. *War and Decision: Inside the Pentagon at the Dawn of the War on Terrorism.* New York, NY: HarperCollins, 2008.

Filkins, Dexter, and Thom Shanker. "Afghan Rebels Report Capture of Major City from the Taliban." *New York Times,* 10 November 2001. http://query.nytimes.com/gst/fullpage.html?res=9A03EEDF1538F933A25752C1A9679C8B63 (accessed 2 January 2009).

Findley, Mike, Robert Green, and Eric Braganca. "SOF on the Contemporary Battlefield." *Military Review* (May–June 2003): 11.

Finlayson, Kenneth. "Not Just Doing Logistics: LTF 530 in Support of TF Dagger." *Veritas* 3, no. 2, 2007. Fort Bragg, NC: United States Special Operations Command.

Flavin, William. *Civil Military Operations: Afghanistan.* Carlisle, PA: US Army Peacekeeping and Stability Operations Institute, 2004.

———. *Observations on Civil Military Operations during the First Year of Operation Enduring Freedom.* US Army Peacekeeping and Stability Operations Institute, 23 March 2004.

Franks, General Tommy. *American Soldier.* New York, NY: HarperCollins, 2004.

Franks, Tommy (GEN). "War of Words." *New York Times,* 19 October 2004. http://www.nytimes.com/2004/10/19/opinion/19franks.html?ex=1255924800&en=dfe849b12233309f&ei=5090&partner=rssuserland (accessed 9 April 2007).

Friedman, Herbert A. "Psychological Operations in Afghanistan." *Perspectives, the Journal of the Psychological Operations Association* 14, no. 4 (2002): 1–4.

Fulghum, David A., and Robert Wall. "Heavy Bomber Attacks Dominate Afghan War; New Real-Time Targeting, Plus Long Endurance, has Recast the Bomber Fleet as a Full-time Battlefield Menace." *Aviation Week & Space Technology* 155, no. 23 (3 December 2001): 22.

Fusco, Vincent. "Eikenberry Takes Command of Coalition Forces in Afghanistan." *American Forces Press Service,* 4 May 2005. http://www.defenselink.mil?news/newsarticle.aspx?id=31741 (accessed 5 May 2007).

"Future of War, Interviews: General Erik K. Shinseki." *PBS FRONTLINE*, 2000. http://www.pbs.org/wgbh/pages/frontline/shows/future/interviews/shinseki.html (accessed 8 December 2008).

Gadbois, Karen. *Improving the Financial Resourcing Process for Civil/Military Operations.* Strategy Research Project, 19 March 2004. Carlisle Barracks, PA: US Army War College. http://www.strategicstudiesinstitute.army.mil/ksil/files/000110.doc (accessed 22 August 2007).

Galeotti, Mark. *Afghanistan: The Soviet Union's Last War.* London: Frank Cass, 1995.

Gall, Carlotta. "A Deadly Siege At Last Won Mazar-e Sharif." *New York Times,* 19 November 2001. http://query.nytimes.com/gst/fullpage.html?res=9C0DE0D7103BF93AA25752C1A9679C8B63&n=Top/Reference/Times%20Topics/Organizations/T/Taliban (accessed 2 January 2009).

———. "Fatal Bombing Mars Start of Afghan Election Campaign." *International Herald Tribune,* 19 August 2005.

———. "In Tunnels Full of Bodies, One of Them Kept Firing." *New York Times,* 30 November 2001. http://query.nytimes.com/gst/fullpage.html?res=9904E6D8153DF933A05752C1A9679C8B63 (accessed 2 January 2009).

———. "U.S. Bomb Wounds G.I.'s as Battle Rages at Fort." *New York Times,* 27 November 2001. http://query.nytimes.com/gst/fullpage.html?res=9900EED71E3AF934A15752C1A9679C8B63 (accessed 2 January 2009).

Galula, David. *Counterinsurgency Warfare: Theory and Practice.* Praeger Security International Paperback, 1964.

Garamone, Jim. "Humanitarian Success Story in Afghanistan." *Armed Forces Press Service News Articles*, 18 January 2002. http://www.defenselink.mil/news/newsarticle.aspx?id=43839 (accessed 18 January 2007).

———. "India-Pakistan Situation is Bush Administration's 'Highest Priority.'" *American Forces Press Service News Articles,* 31 May 2002. http://www.defenselink.mil/news/newsarticle. aspx?id=43992 (accessed 9 December 2008).

———. "Joint Force Concept Comes of Age in Afghanistan." *DefenseLink,* 15 November 2001. http://www.defenselink.mil/news/Nov2001/n11152001_200111151.html (accessed 9 February 2007).

———. "Operation Snipe Ends, Efforts in Afghanistan Continue." *American Forces Press Service News Articles*, 13 May 2002. http://www.defenselink.mil/news (accessed 9 December 2008).

Gardesh, Hafizullah. "Elections Close Not with a Bang, But a Whimper." *Institute for War & Peace Reporting,* 11 October 2004. ARR No. 140. http://www.iwpr.net/?p=arr&s=f&o=152833&apc_state=heniarr2004 (accessed 21 May 2007).

———. "Veteran General Goes for Presidency." *Institute for War & Peace Reporting,* 13 August 2004. ARR No. 129. http://www.iwpr.net/?p=arr&s=f&o=153408&apc_state=heniarrebff8caa76e1d 6640626a56452ba35b1 (accessed 21 May 2007).

"George Tenet interview by Scott Pelley." *CBS News 60 Minutes,* 25 April 2007. Washington, DC. Aired 29 April 2007. http://www.cbsnews.com/stories/2007/04/25/60minutes/main2728375.shtml (accessed 30 April 2007).

Gerelman, David J., Jennifer E. Stevens, and Steven A. Hildreth. "Operation Enduring Freedom: Foreign Pledges of Military & Intelligence Support." *CRS Report for Congress,* 17 October 2001.

German, Michael. "Squaring the Error." *Competing Approaches to Fighting Terrorism Conference Report.* Carlisle, PA: Strategic Studies Institute, July 2005.

Gerth, Jeff. "U.S. Detainee is Questioned, But His Fate is Still Unclear." *New York Times,* 10 December 2001.

Gilmore, Gerry J. "Air Force Fliers Continue Afghan Food Drop Operations." *American Forces Press Service*, 12 October 2001. http://www.defenselink.mil (accessed 17 January 2007).

———. "Bush Authorizes Guard and Reserve Call-Ups." *DefenseLink*, 14 September 2001. http://www. defenselink.mil/news/Sep2001/n09142001_200109148.html (accessed 29 January 2007).

———. "General Censured for Tillman Investigation Mistakes." *DefenseLink,* 31 July 2007. http://www. defenselink.mil/news/newsarticle.aspx?id=46888 (accessed 13 February 2009).

———. "'Millennium Challenge' Experiment to Test Joint Capabilities." *American Forces Press Service News Articles*, 22 May 2002. http://www.defenselink.mil/utility/printitem.aspx? (accessed 9 December 2008).

———. "U.S Military Will Help Train Afghan Army, Rumsfeld Says." http://www.defenselink.mil/ news/newsarticle.aspx?id=44220 (accessed 29 August 2007).

Gimble, General Thomas, DOD Acting Inspector; Brigadier General Rodney Johnson, Commander, US Army Criminal Investigations Command; Pete Geren, Acting Secretary of the Army; General Richard Cody, Army Vice Chief of Staff. "Special Defense Department Briefing—Inspector General Thomas Gimble Reports on the Death of Corporal Patrick Tillman in Afghanistan from the Pentagon Briefing Room, Arlington, Virginia." *News Transcript*, 26 March 2007. http://www. defenselink.mil/transcripts/transcript. aspx?transcriptid=3917 (accessed 11 September 2007).

Girardet, Edward, and Jonathan Walter, editors, Charles Norchi and Mirwais Masood, co-editors. *Afghanistan.* 2d edition. Geneva, Switzerland: Crosslines Publications, 2004.

"GIs to Help Train Afghan National Army," 14 July 2004. http://www.military.com/NewsContent/ 0,13319,FL_train_071404,00.html (accessed 12 June 2007).

Giustozzi, Antonio. *Working Paper No. 33: Respectable Warlords? The Politics of State-Building in Post-Taleban Afghanistan.* Crisis States Programme Development Research Centre. London: DESTIN, 2003. http://www.crisisstates.com/download/wp/WP33.pdf (accessed 29 July 2007).

Gohari, M.J. *The Taliban: Ascent to Power.* Oxford, UK: Oxford University Press, 2000.

Goodson, Larry P. "Afghanistan in 2004: Electoral Progress and an Opium Boom." *Caliber Asian Survey* (January/February 2005): 93.

———. *Afghanistan's Endless War: State Failure, Regional Politics, and the Rise of the Taliban.* Seattle, WA: University of Washington Press, 2001.

Grant, Rebecca. *An Air Force Association Special Report: The Afghan Air War.* Arlington, VA: The Air Force Association, 2002.

———. "The War Nobody Expected." *Air Force Magazine* 85, no. 4, April 2002. http://www.afa.org/ magazine/april2002/0402airwar.asp (accessed 10 February 2007).

Grau, Lester W. "The Takedown of Kabul: An Effective Coup de Main." In *Block by Block: The Challenges of Urban Operations*, edited by William G. Robertson and Lawrence A. Yates. Fort Leavenworth, KS: US Army Command and General Staff College Press, 2003.

Grau, Lester W., ed. *The Bear Went Over the Mountain: Soviet Combat Tactics in Afghanistan.* Washington, DC: National Defense University Press, 1996.

Grau, Lester W., and Michael A. Gress, eds. *The Soviet-Afghan War: How a Superpower Fought and Lost.* Lawrence, KS: University of Kansas Press, 2002.

Grau, Lieutenant Colonel (Retired) Lester W., USA. "Something Old, Something New: Guerrillas, Terrorists, and Intelligence Analysis." *Military Review* (July–August 2004): 42–49.

Gresham, John D. "Forces Fighting for Enduring Freedom." *United States Naval Institute Proceedings* 127, no. 11 (November 2001): 45–48.

Griffin, Christopher. "A Working Plan: Hope Isn't the Only Strategy for Afghanistan." *Armed Forces Journal* (April 2007). http://www.armedforcesjournal.com/2007/04/2587549 (accessed 16 June 2007).

Guehenno, Jean-Marie. "Briefings to the UN Security Council on the Situation in Afghanistan." *Open Meeting of the Security Council Afghanistan*, 17 June 2003. http://www.unama-afg.org/docs/_ UN-Docs/_sc/_briefings/03jun17.htm (accessed 26 July 2007).

Haass, Richard M. *Intervention: The Use of American Military Force in the Post-Cold War World.* Washington, DC: Carnegie Endowment, 1984.

Hamblet, William P., and Jerry G. Kline. "Interagency Cooperation: PDD 56 and Complex Contingency Operations." *Joint Force Quarterly* (Spring 2000): 92–97.

Hammidov, Captain Bakhtiyorjon U., Uzbekistan Armed Forces. "The Fall of the Taliban Regime and its Recovery as an Insurgent Movement in Afghanistan." Monograph, Fort Leavenworth, KS, 2004.

Haskell, Master Sergeant Bob, USA. "Guard Responds." *National Guard Bureau,* 14 September 2001.

Haulman, Daniel L. *Intertheater Airlift Challenges of Operation Enduring Freedom.* Maxwell Air Force Base, AL: Air Force Historical Research Agency, 2002.

Heath, Sergeant Greg, 4th Public Affairs Detachment. "2-87 Catamounts Keep Rolling in Afghanistan." *Fort Drum Blizzard Online,* 8 January 2004. http://www.drum.army.mil/sites/postnews/blizzard/ blizzard_archives/hnews.asp?id=1&issuedate=1-8-2004 (accessed 11 September 2007).

Hendren, John. "Lucky Shot Brought Down Helicopter in Afghanistan." *Houston Chronicle,* 1 July 2005.

Herd, Colonel Walter M., Colonel Patrick M. Higgins, Lieutenant Colonel Adrian T. Bogart III, Major Mark A. Davey, and Captain Daudshah S. Andish. "One Valley at a Time: Victory in Afghanistan." Unpublished monograph.

Hines, Jay E. "From Desert One to Southern Watch: The Evolution of U.S. Central Command." *Joint Forces Quarterly* (Spring 2000): 42–48.

Hirsh, Michael, and John Barry. "The Hunt Heats Up." *Newsweek* (15 March 2004): 46–48.

Hoffman, Bruce. *Inside Terrorism.* New York, NY: Columbia University Press, 1998.

———. "Terrorism, Trends, and Prospects." In *Countering the New Terrorism,* edited by Ian O. Lesser, Bruce Hoffman, John Arquilla, David Ronfeldt, Michele Zanini, and Brian Michael Jenkins. Santa Monica, CA: RAND Corporation, 1999.

Holzworth, Major C.E., USMC. "Operation Eagle Claw: A Catalyst for Change in the American Military." Command and Staff College (CSC), 1997. http://www.globalsecurity.org/military/library/report/1997/Holzworth.htm (accessed 12 December 2006).

Hoon, Mr. Geoffrey. "Operations in Afghanistan." *House of Commons Hansard Debates, Part 5*, 20 June 2002. http://www.publications.parliament.uk/pa/cm200102/cmhansrd/vo020620 (accessed 16 August 2007).

Hopkirk, Peter. *The Great Game: The Struggle for Empire in Central Asia.* New York, NY: Kodansha, 1992.

House National Security Committee. *The Khobar Towers Bombing Incident: Staff Report*, 14 August 1996. http://www.fas.org/irp/threat/saudi.pdf (accessed 21 November 2006).

Howell, Llewellyn D. "Terrorism: The 21st-Century War." *USA Today,* March 2001.

Huffman, Captain James W. III, USA. "B/3-6 FA: 120-mm Mortar Battery in Afghanistan." *Field Artillery Journal* (January–February 2005): 42–44.

Human Rights Watch. "Afghanistan: Protect Women Candidates," 16 August 2005. http://www.hrw.org/en/news/2005/08/16/afghanistan-protect-women-candidates (accessed 23 February 2009).

"Humanitarian Leaders Ask White House to Review Policy Allowing American Soldiers to Conduct Humanitarian Relief Programs in Civilian Clothes." Letter to National Security Advisor Dr. Condoleezza Rice from InterAction, 2 April 2002. http://interaction.org/library/bushletter1.html (accessed 7 December 2006).

Hussain, Hamid. "The Bear and the Eagle: Operations in Afghanistan by Two Superpowers." http://www.defencejournal.com/2003/apr/bear-eagle.htm (accessed 26 January 2007).

Hussain, Rifaat. "Pakistan Walks a Tightrope." *Jane's Defense Weekly* (24 October 2001): 23.

Illinois Institute of Technology, Paul V. Galvin Library. "Afghanistan Country Study" (14 January 2002): 1–4. http://www.gl.iit.edu/govdocs/afghanistan (accessed 29 January 2007).

"In Afghanistan, A Population in Crisis." United Nations Press Release AFG/145, ORG1336, 24 September 2001.

"India, Pakistan Put Their Missiles on Alert." *PBS Online Newshour Update*, 26 December 2001. http://www.pbs.org/newshour/updates/december01/india_pakistan_12-26.html (accessed 18 January 2007).

Ingle, Saul. "First Strike: Launching of Tomahawk Missiles from USS John Paul Jones As Part of War on Terrorism." *All Hands* (December 2001).

Interagency OPSEC Support Staff, Global History—January to June. http://www.ioss.gov/docs/jantojune.html (accessed 23 April 2007).

"International Security Assistance Force (Operation Fingal)." UK Ministry of Defence, 20 June 2002. http://www.operations.mod.uk/fingal (accessed 11 December 2008).

"Into Afghanistan, Rooting Out Terrorists, Operation Enduring Freedom Marks 3 Years: Fact Sheet—Provincial Reconstruction Teams Sept. 27, 2004." US Department of Defense. http://www.defenselink.mil/home/articles/2004-10/a100107b.html (accessed 8 December 2008).

IRIN Humanitarian News and Analysis. "Afghanistan: Year in Review 2005—Fragile Process, Insecurity Remains," 11 January 2006. http://www.irinnews.org/report.aspx?reportid=33637 (accessed 24 July 2007).

Islamic Republic of Afghanistan. "A Brief Biography of President Hamid Karzai." http://www.president. gov.af/english/president_biography.mspx (accessed 14 March 2007).

Jackson, Major Scott A. *Tactical Integration of Special Operations and Conventional Forces Command and Control Functions.* School of Advanced Military Studies Monograph, US Army Command and General Staff College, Fort Leavenworth, KS, 2003.

Jalali, Ali A. "Afghanistan in 2002: The Struggle to Win the Peace." *Asian Survey* 43, no. 1. A Survey of Asia in 2002 (January–February 2003). Berkeley, CA: University of California Press, 2002. http://links.jstor.org/sici?sici=00044687%28200301%2F02%2943%3A1%3C174%3AAI2TS T%3E2.0.CP%3B2-L (accessed 26 July 2007).

———. "Afghanistan: The Anatomy of an Ongoing Conflict." *Parameters* (Spring 2001): 92–93.

———. "Rebuilding Afghanistan's National Army." *Parameters* (Autumn 2002).

———. "The Future of Afghanistan." *Parameters* (Spring 2006): 4–19.

Jalali, Ali Ahmad, and Lester W. Grau. *The Other Side of the Mountain: Mujahideen Tactics in the Soviet-Afghan War.* Fort Leavenworth, KS: Foreign Military Studies Office, 1995.

Jaquish, Douglas W. "Uninhabited Air Vehicles for Psychological Operations—Leveraging Technology for PSYOPs Beyond 2010." *Air & Space Power Journal—Chronicles Online* (6 April 2004): 2. http://www.airpower.maxwell.af.mil/airchronicles (accessed 14 March 2007).

Jenkins, Brian M. "Defense Against Terrorism." *Political Science Quarterly* 101, no. 5 (1986): 773–786.

Joffe, Lawrence. "Abdul Haq: Veteran Afghan Leader Seeking post-Taliban Consensus Rule." *The Guardian,* 29 October 2001. http://www.guardian.co.uk/waronterror/story/0,,582692,00.html (accessed 3 April 2007).

Johnson, Christine. "Aid and Recovery." In *Afghanistan,* 2d edition, edited by Edward Girardet and Jonathan Walter, co-editors Charles Norchi and Mirwais Masood. Geneva, Switzerland: Crosslines Publications, 2004.

Johnson, Master Sergeant D. Keith, USA. "Afghan National Army Volunteer Center Opens," 22 December 2004. http://www.defendamerica.mil/articles/Dec2004/a122204dw1.html (accessed 20 August 2007).

Johnson, Thomas H. "Ismail Khan, Herat, and Iranian Influence." *Strategic Insights,* quoting the *New Yorker.* http://www.ccc.nps.navy.mil/si/2004/jul/johnsonJul04.asp (accessed 10 September 2007).

"Joint Declaration of the United States–Afghanistan Strategic Partnership." http://www.whitehouse.gov/ news/releases/2005/05/20050523-2.html (accessed 20 June 2007).

Joint Electoral Management Body. "Afghanistan Presidential Election Results 2004: Decision of the Joint Electoral Management Body—Certification of Results." http://www.elections-afghanistan.org. af/Election%20Results%20Website/english/english.htm (accessed 12 June 2007).

———. "Afghanistan Presidential Election Results 2004: On Counting." http://www.elections-afghanistan.org.af/Election%20Results%20Website/english/english.htm (accessed 12 June 2007).

———. "Afghanistan Presidential Election Results 2004: On Security." http://www.elections-afghanistan. org.af/Election%20Results%20Website/english/english.htm (accessed 20 July 2007).

———. "Afghanistan Presidential Election Results 2004: On Voting." http://www.elections-afghanistan. org.af/Election%20Results%20Website/english/english.htm (accessed 24 July 2007).

———. "Afghanistan Presidential Election Results 2004: Turnout by Province." http://www.elections-afghanistan.org.af/Election%20Results%20Website/english/english.htm (accessed 24 July 2007).

"Joint Statement of Ms. Pamela B. Berkowsky, Assistant to the Secretary of Defense for Civil Support, and Mr. Charles Cragin, Principle Deputy Assistant Secretary of Defense for Reserve Affairs, before the United States Senate Committee on Armed Services," 24 March 2000. http://armed-services.senate.gov/statemnt/2000/000324pb.pdf (accessed 12 April 2007).

Jones, Seth G., Jeremy M. Wilson, Andrew Rathmell, and K. Jack Riley. *Establishing Law and Order After Conflict.* Santa Monica, CA: RAND Corporation, 2005.

Kahaner, Larry. "Weapon of Mass Destruction." *Washington Post*, 26 November 2006.

Kalic, Sean. *Combating a Modern Hydra: Al Qaeda and the Global War on Terrorism.* Fort Leavenworth, KS: Combat Studies Institute Press, 2005.

Kamiya, Major General Jason. *Leadership Preparation Monograph #1: Insurgency/Counterinsurgency Historical Perspectives.* Vincenza, Italy: USASETAF, 2004.

Kaplan, Robert D. *Soldiers of God: With the Mujahidin in Afghanistan.* Boston, MA: Houghton-Mifflin Company, 1990.

———. "The Coming Anarchy." *The Atlantic Monthly* 273.2 (February 1994), 44–76.

Katzman, Dr. Kenneth. "Afghanistan: Post-War Governance, Security, and U.S. Policy." Congressional Research Service Report RL 30588, 11 January 2006. www.fas.org/sgp/crs/row/RL30588.pdf (accessed 20 June 2007).

———. "CRS Report for Congress.*" CRS Web Afghanistan: Post-War Governance, Security, and U.S. Policy*, 28 December 2004.

Kazem, Halima. "New Afghan Army Asserts Itself." *Christian Science Monitor*, 23 August 2004.

Kennedy, Harold. "More Life Needed, Avers US Transportation Chief." *National Defense Magazine*, July 2002. http://www.nationaldefensemagazine.org/issues/2002/Jul/More_Lift.htm (accessed 1 February 2007).

Khalilzad, Zalmay. "How to Nation-build: Ten Lessons from Afghanistan." *The National Interest* (Summer 2005): 19–27.

Khan, Rais Ahmad. "Pakistan in 1992: Waiting for Change." *Asian Survey* 43, no. 2 Part II (February 1993).

Khoshal Khan Khattak. *Dastarnama. A Classic Treatise on Norms and Practice of Leadership (in Pashto).* Kabul, 1967.

Kiper, Richard L. "Of Vital Importance: The 4th PSYOP Group." *Special Warfare* (September 2002).

———. "We Support to the Utmost: The 528th Special Operations Support Battalion." *Special Warfare* 15, no. 3 (September 2002): 13–15.

Klaidman, Daniel, and Michael Isikoff. "Walker's Brush with bin Laden." *Newsweek* 139, no. 1 (7 January 2002): 20–21.

Knarr, William, and John Frost. *Operation Enduring Freedom Battle Reconstruction.* Alexandria, VA: Institute for Defense Analyses, 2004.

Koontz, Christopher N., ed. *Enduring Voices: Oral Histories of the US Army Experience in Afghanistan, 2003–2005.* Washington, DC: US Army Center of Military History, 2008.

Kosnik, Captain Mark E., US Navy. "The Military Response to Terrorism." *Naval War College Review* LIII, no. 2, Spring 2000. http://www.nwc.navy/PRESS/Review/2000/spring/art1-sp).htm (accessed 4 December 2006).

Kozaryn, Linda D. "British-led Coalition Battle Al Qaeda, Taliban Fighters." *American Forces Press Service News Articles*, 17 May 2007. http://www.defenselink.mil/news/newsarticle.aspx?id-44048 (accessed 4 December 2008).

———. "Families, Friends Honor Desert Storm Fallen." *Armed Forces Press Service*, 27 February 2001. http://www.defenselink.mil/news/Feb2001/n02272001_200102271.html (accessed 24 April 2007).

———. "New Weapons Cache Found: Oruzgan Deaths Investigated." *Defend America*, 8 July 2002. http://www.defendamerica.mil/archive/2002-07/20020708.html (accessed 5 February 2009).

———. "Pakistan-India Conflict Concerns U.S. Military." *American Forces Press Service News Articles*, 28 May 2002. http://www.defenselink.mil/news (accessed 8 December 2008).

———. "U.S. Focus Turns to Afghanistan's Reconstruction." *American Forces Press Service,* 16 January 2003. http://www.defenselink.mil/news/newsarticle.aspx?id=29568 (accessed 16 July 2007).

Krulak, General Charles C., USMC. "The Strategic Corporal: Leadership in the Three Block War." *Marines Magazine,* January 1999. http://www.au.af.mil/au/awc/awcgate/usmc/strategic_corporal.htm (accessed 11 September 2007).

Lamb, Christopher J., and Paris Genalis. *Review of Psychological Operations Lessons Learned from Recent Operational Experience.* Washington, DC: National Defense University Press, 2005.

Lambert, William C. "US-Central Asian Security Cooperation: Misunderstandings, Miscommunications & Missed Opportunities." In *Security Assistance, U.S. and Historical Perspectives: Proceedings from the Combat Studies Institute 2006 Military History Symposium,* edited by Kendall Gott and Michael Brooks, 123–159. Fort Leavenworth, KS: Combat Studies Institute Press, 2006.

Lambeth, Benjamin S. *Air Power Against Terror: American's Conduct of Operation Enduring Freedom.* Santa Monica, CA: RAND Corporation, 2005.

Lamm, Colonel David, USA. "Success in Afghanistan means Fighting Several Wars at Once." *Armed Forces Journal* (November 2005). http://www.armedforcesjournal.com/2005/11/1174189 (accessed 11 September 2007).

Landay, Jonathan. "Afghan Election Prompts Fighting." *Knight Ridder Newspapers,* 21 August 2005.

Lansford, Tom. *All for One: Terrorism, NATO and the United States.* Aldershot, UK: Ashgate Publishing Limited, 2002.

"Largest Afghan Campaign since Anaconda Ends." *CNN,* 25 August 2002. http://archives.cnn.com/2002/WORLD/asiapcf/central/08/25/afghan.operation/index.html (accessed 10 February 2009).

Laqueur, Walter. "Terror's New Face." *Harvard International Review* 20 (Fall 1998): 48–51.

Lavrov, Sergey V. "Building a Collective Response to Terrorism." *UN Chronicle,* June–August 2004. http://www.un.org/Pubs/chronicle/2004/issue2/0204p35.asp (accessed 10 May 2007).

Lawrence, Bruce, ed. *Messages to the World: The Statements of Osama Bin Laden.* New York, NY: Verso, 2005.

"Leaders: Putting Steel into Karzai; Afghanistan's Parliamentary Elections." *The Economist* (24 September 2005): 17.

"Legal Lessons Learned from Afghanistan and Iraq, Volume I." Center for Law and Military Operations, The Judge Advocate General's Legal Center and School, 1 August 2004.

Levy, Gaea. "Objectives Rhino and Gecko: SOF's Opening Salvo in Operation Enduring Freedom." *Tip of the Spear,* November 2006.

Library of Congress Country Studies. "Afghanistan: The Peshawar Accord, April 25, 1992." http://www.photius.com/countries/afghanistan/government/afghanistan_government_the_peshawar_accord~72.html (accessed 6 February 2007).

———. "Afghanistan: The Soviet Decision to Withdraw." http://lcweb2.loc.gov/cgi-bin/query/r?/frd/cstdy:@field(DOCID+af0094 (accessed 5 February 2007).

Library of Congress—Federal Research Division. *Country Profile Afghanistan,* May 2006. http://www.lcweb2.loc.gov (accessed 6 February 2007).

"Lion of Panjshir Ahmed Shaw Massoud." http://www.massoudhero.com/English/biography.html (accessed 10 February 2007).

Mack, Raneta Lawson, and Michael J. Kelly. *Equal Justice in the Balance: America's Legal Response to the Emerging Terrorist Threat.* Ann Arbor, MI: University of Michigan Press, 2004. http://www.press.umich.edu/pdf/0472113941-ch2.pdf (accessed 14 December 2006).

Magni, Sergeant Frank, USA. "Vermont Guardsmen Train, Mentor Afghan Soldiers," August 2004. http://defendamerica.gov/articles/aug2004/a081304b.html (accessed 10 August 2007).

Magnus, Ralph H., and Eden Naby. *Afghanistan: Mullah, Marx, and Mujahid.* Boulder, CO: Westview Press, 1998.

"Major Afghan Offensive Launched." *CNN Online,* 8 December 2003. http://www.cnn.com/2003/WORLD/asiapcf/central/12/08/afghan.offensive/index.html (accessed 10 September 2007).

Malik, Nadeem. "US Military Seeks Deeper Roots in Pakistan." *Asia Times Online,* 30 January 2002. http://www.atimes.com/c-asia/DA30Ag01.html (accessed 14 February 2007).

Mansager, Colonel Tucker B., USA. "Interagency Lessons Learned in Afghanistan." *Joint Force Quarterly* (First Quarter 2006): 80–84.

Manwaring, Max G. "Peace and Stability Lessons from Bosnia." *Parameters,* Winter 1998. http://www.carlisle.army.mil/usawc/Parameters/98winter/manwarin/htm (accessed 10 May 2007).

"Marines Launch Operation Buzzard in Afghanistan." *ABC News Online*, 30 May 2002. http://www.abc.net.au/news/newsitems/200205 (accessed 16 August 2007).

Marion, Forrest L. "Building USAF 'Expeditionary Bases' for Operation ENDURING FREEDOM—AFGHANISTAN, 2001–2002." *Air & Space Power Journal.* http://www.airpower.maxwell.af.mil/airchronicles/cc/marion.html (accessed 31 July 2007).

Marquis, Christopher. "Before He Died, C.I.A. Man Interrogated U.S. Captive." *New York Times,* 7 December 2001.

Marsden, Peter. "Exile for a Cause: The Plight of Refugees." In *Afghanistan,* 2d edition, edited by Edward Girardet and Jonathan Walter, co-editors Charles Norchi and Mirwais Masood. Geneva, Switzerland: Crosslines Publications, 2004.

Martin, Susan Taylor. "The Man Who Would Have Led Afghanistan." *St. Petersburg Times,* 9 September 2002. http://www.sptimes.com/2002/09/09/news_pf/911/The_man_who_would_hav.shtml (accessed 19 January 2007).

Mazach, John. "The 21st Century Triad." *Sea Power* 45, no. 3 (March 2002): 51–55.

Mazzetti, Mark. "A Matter of Death and Life." *U.S. News & World Report*, 18 June 2004. http://www.usnews.com/usnews/news/articles/040426/26afghan.htm (accessed 21 September 2007).

McCarthy, Rory. "22 Die as Taliban Attack Police Station." *The Guardian*, 18 August 2003. http://www.guardian.co.uk/afghanistan/story/0,,1020828,00.html (accessed 24 September 2007).

———. "Warlords Bury their Differences in Readiness for Long and Bloody Battles." *The Guardian,* 7 November 2001. http://www.guardian.co.uk (accessed 9 February 2007).

McElroy, Robert H. "Interview with Franklin L. Hagenbeck—Afghanistan Fire Support for Operation Anaconda." *Field Artillery Journal* (September–October 2002).

McFall, Major Joseph D. "From Rogue to Vogue: Why Did Libya Give up its Weapons of Mass Destruction?" Master's Thesis, Naval Postgraduate School, September 2005.

McGeary, Johanna, Massimo Calabresi, and Mark Thompson. "Shell Game." *Time* 158, no. 24 (3 December 2001): 26.

McGirk, Tim. "Battle in the Evilist Place." *Time Online*, 3 November 2003. http://www.time.com/time/magazine/article/0,9171,1006032-1,00.html (accessed 5 June 2007).

———. "Inside Karzai's Campaign." *Time* (11 October 2004): 44.

McGrath, John J. *Boots on the Ground: Troop Density in Contingency Operations.* Fort Leavenworth, KS: Combat Studies Institute Press, 2006.

McIntyre, Jamie. "U.S. Vows Terrorist Bomb Won't Affect Saudi Relationship." *CNN.com*, 13 November 1995. http://www.cnn.com/WORLD/9511/saudi_blast/pm/ (accessed 28 December 2006).

McKenzie, Kenneth, Robert Shea, and Christopher Phelps. "Marines Deliver in Mountain Storm." *United States Naval Institute Proceedings* (November 2004): 48–51.

McNerney, Michael J. "Stabilization and Reconstruction in Afghanistan: Are PRTs a Model or a Muddle?" *Parameters* (Winter 2005–06): 38–39.

Meyer, Karl E., and Shareen Blair Brysac. *Tournament of Shadows: The Great Game and the Race for Empire in Central Asia.* Washington, DC: Counterpoint, 1999.

Mientka, Matt. *US Medics Reach Out In Afghanistan,* December 2002. http://www.usmedicine.com/article.cfm?articleID=550&issueID=45 (accessed 23 August 2007).

Miles, Donna. "NATO Makes Key Decisions on Iraq, Afghanistan." *American Forces Press Service*, 28 June 2004. http://www.defenselink.mil/news/newsarticle.aspx?id=26186 (accessed 4 June 2007).

"Military Technical Agreement Between the International Security Assistance Force (ISAF) and the Interim Administration of Afghanistan ('Interim Administration')," 4 January 2002.

MIPT Terrorism Knowledge Base. http://www.tkb.org/Home.jsp (accessed 9 April 2007).

Mirza, Mateen. "Taming the 'Wild West': Integrating the Federally Administered Tribal Areas of Pakistan." Master's Thesis, Naval Postgraduate School, December 2005.

"Mobilization Reform: A Compilation of Significant Issues, Lessons Learned and Studies Developed Since September 11, 2001." Office of the Secretary of Defense, Reserve Forces Policy Board, October 2003.

Monaco, Annalisa. "Beyond Kabul: Testing ISAF Potential and Limits." *ISIS Europe* 5, no. 7, October 2003. http://isis-europe.org/Beyond%20Kabul-NN%20v5n7.PDF (accessed 11 September 2007).

Moore, Robin. *The Hunt for Bin Laden: Task Force Dagger.* New York, NY: Random House, 2003.

Morgan, Matthew J. "The Origins of New Terrorism." *Parameters* (Spring 2004): 29–43.

Morgan Shane P., Robert H. Levis, and Harry C. Glenn III. "B/377 PFAR: Platoon-Based Fires in Afghanistan." *Field Artillery Journal* (March–April 2005): 29–33.

Morris, Lieutenant Colonel Michael F., USMC. "Al-Qaeda as Insurgency." *Joint Force Quarterly* (October 2005). http://www.ndu.edu/inss/Press/jfq_pages/i39.htm (accessed 4 December 2004).

MSF Press Release. "MSF Pulls Out of Afghanistan," 28 July 2004. http://www.msf.org/msfinternational/invoke.cfm?component=pressrelease&objectid=8851DF09-F62D-47D4-A8D3EB1E876A1E0D&method= full_html (accessed 20 September 2007).

Murrey, Thomas W. Jr. "Khobar Towers' Aftermath: The Development of Force Protection." *Air & Space Power Journal,* 25 October 2000. http://www.airpower.maxwell.af.mil/airchronicles/cc/Murrey.html (accessed 8 January 2007).

Musharraf, Pervez. *In the Line of Fire.* New York, NY: Free Press, 2006.

Mylroie, Laurie. "The World Trade Center Bomb: Who is Ramzi Yousef? And Why It Matters." *The National Interest,* Winter 1995/96. http://www.fas.org/irp/world/iraq/956-tni.htm (accessed 27 December 2006).

Naftali, Timothy. *Blind Spot: The Secret History of American Counterterrorism.* New York, NY: Basic Books, 2005.

National Commission on Terrorism. *Countering the Changing Threat of International Terrorism: Report of the National Commission on Terrorism.* Washington, DC, 2000.

"National Guard and Reserve Mobilized as of Dec. 5." *DefenseLink*, 5 December 2001. http://www.defenselink.mil/releases/release.aspx?releaseid=3176 (accessed 17 December 2008).

"National Guard Homeland Defense White Paper: September 11, 2001, Hurricane Katrina, and Beyond." *Army National Guard,* 11 October 2005.

"NATO in Afghanistan Factsheet." North Atlantic Treaty Organization, 21 February 2005. http://www.nato.int./issues/afghanistan/040628-factsheet.htm (accessed 22 May 2002).

"NATO to Boost Troops to 12,000 Ahead of Afghan Elections." *Xinhua News Agency-CEIS,* 27 July 2005.

Natsios, Andrew S. "The Nine Principles of Reconstruction and Development." www.carlisle.army.mil/usawc/parameters/05autumn/natsios.pdf (accessed 18 February 2009).

Naylor, Sean. *Not A Good Day to Die: The Untold Story of Operation Anaconda.* New York, NY: Berkley Caliber Books, Paperback ed., 2006.

Nelson, Ray. "The National Military Academy of Afghanistan: A First-Hand Account." *First Call,* 27 March 2005. http://www.west-point.org/users/usma1983/40505/First_Call_Article/article.doc (accessed 12 April 2007).

Newell, Nancy Peabody, and Richard S. Newell. *The Struggle for Afghanistan.* Ithaca, NY: Cornell University Press, 1981.

"NGO Insecurity in Afghanistan." *Afghanistan NGO Safety Office (ANSO) and CARE,* May 2005. http://www.care.org/newsroom/specialreports/afghanistan/20050505_ansocare.pdf (accessed 16 August 2007).

Nichol, Jim. "Central Asia's Security Issues and Implication for US Interests." *CRS Report for Congress.* Updated 7 February 2006.

Nichols, Robert, ed. *Colonial Reports on Pakistan's Frontier Tribal Areas.* Oxford, NY: Oxford University Press, 2005.

Noonan, Michael, and Mark Lewis. "Conquering the Elements: Thoughts on Joint Force (Re)Organization." *Parameters* (Autumn 2003): 38.

Nyrop, Richard F., and Donald M. Seekins. *Afghanistan: A Country Study.* Washington, DC: American University, 1986.

O'Balance, Edgar O. *Afghan Wars: Battles in a Hostile Land, 1839 to the Present.* Revised Paperback Edition. London: Brassey's, 2002.

O'Connor, Phillip. "Two Men Who Fought Terror." *St. Louis Post-Dispatch,* 22 February 2004.

Office for the Coordinator of Counterterrorism Web site. http://www.state.gov/s/ct/ (accessed 11 April 2007).

Office of Counterintelligence, Spy and Terrorist Briefing Center, Terrorist Attacks. http://www.hanford.gov/oci/ci_terrorist.cfm?dossier=46 (accessed 11 April 2007).

Office of the Assistant Secretary of Defense (Public Affairs). "Opening Statement by Secretary of Defense William J. Perry before the House National Security Committee on the Downing Assessment Task Force." Press Release No. 544-96, 19 September 1996. http://www.defenselink.mil/releases/release.aspx?releaseid=1043 (accessed 20 April 2007).

Office of National Drug Control Policy. "Estimated Poppy Cultivation in Afghanistan." Press Release, 28 November 2003. http://www.whitehousedrugpolicy.gov/NEWS/press03/112803.html (accessed 29 August 2007).

Oliker, Olga, Richard Kauzlarich, James Dobbins, Kurt W. Basseuner, Donald L. Sampler, John G. McGinn, Michael J. Dziedzic, Adam Grissom, Bruce Pirnie, Nora Bensahel, and A. Istar Guven. *Aid During Conflict: Interaction Between Military and Civilian Assistance Providers in Afghanistan, September 2001– June 2002.* Santa Monica, CA: RAND Corporation, 2004.

"One House of Parliament Will Remain Incomplete." *Washington Post,* 21 March 2005.

O'Neill, Bard. *Insurgency & Terrorism: Inside Modern Revolutionary Warfare.* Dulles: VA: Brassey's Inc: 1990.

"Opening of the Fifty-Sixth Session, General Assembly Condemns Heinous Acts of Terrorism Perpetrated in Host City and Washington." Fifty-Sixth General Assembly Plenary, 1st Meeting, 12 October 2001.

"Opening Statement of Admiral Harold W. Gehman Jr., US Navy Commander in Chief, United States Joint Forces Command, Before the Subcommittee on Emerging Threats and Capabilities of the Committee on Armed Services of the United States Senate," 24 March 2000. http://armed-services.senate.gov/statemnt/2000/000324hg.pdf (accessed 12 April 2007).

"Operation Apollo." *Backgrounder: Land Force Western Area*, n.d. Department of National Defence/Canadian Forces. www.army.forces.ca/lfwa (accessed 17 August 2007).

"Operation Condor." *Operation Veritas*. UK Ministry of Defence, 22 May 2002. http://www.operations.mod.uk/veritas/condor.htm (accessed 4 December 2008).

"Operation Enduring Freedom: Coalition Military Fatalities by Year." http://www.icasualties.org/oef/ (accessed 9 July 2007).

"Operation Enduring Freedom Overview." White House Fact Sheet, 1 October 2001. http://www.state.gov/s/ct/index.cfm?docid=5194 (accessed 1 January 2007).

"Operation Snipe." *Operation Veritas*. UK Ministry of Defence, 13 May 2002. http://www.operations.mod.uk/veritas/snipe.htm (accessed 6 July 2007).

"Operation Valiant Strike." *Army*, 1 May 2003.

"Osama bin Laden: A Chronology of His Political Life." *PBS FRONTLINE.* http://www.pbs.org/wgbh/pages/frontline/shows/binladen/etc/cron.html (accessed 10 January 2007).

"Osama bin Laden interview by Peter Arnett." Transcript. *CNN*, March 1997. http://www.anusha.com/osamaint.htm (accessed 21 November 2006).

Owens, Colonel Kevin. "News Briefing with Colonel Kevin Owens." Office of the Assistant Secretary of Defense for Public Affairs, 23 September 2005. http://www.defenselink.mil/transcripts/transcript.aspx?transcriptid=2580 (accessed 21 May 2007).

Ozernoy, Ilana. "The Return of the Taliban." *U.S. News and World Report* (29 September 2003): 16–17.

Pakistan Mission to the United Nations, New York, 7 March 1993. "Afghan Peace Accord or the Islamabad Accord of March 1993." *Important Documents.* http://www.un.int/pakistan/15islbad.htm (accessed 6 February 2007).

"Pakistan Vows to Help US 'Punish' Attackers." *CNN.com World,* 13 September 2001. http://archives.cnn.com/2001/WORLD/asiapcf/central/09/13/Pakistan.support/index.html (accessed 28 March 2007).

Pan, Esther. "Afghan Parliamentary Elections." Council on Foreign Relations Backgrounder (16 September 2005). http://www.cfr.org/publication/8867/afghan_parliamentary_elections.html (accessed 21 May 2007).

Patterns of Global Terrorism: 1992. "Appendix A: Chronology of Significant Terrorist Incidents." http://www.fas.org/irp/threat/terror_92/chron.html (accessed 21 February 2007).

"Patterns of Global Terrorism." US Department of State, 30 April 2001. http://www.state.gov/s/ct/rls/crt/2000/2419.htm (accessed 15 April 2007).

Paul, James, and Martin Spirit. "Operation Fingal, International Security Assistance Force." *Afghanistan: The War on Terror*, 2003. http://www.britains-smallwars.com/Terror/Fingal.html (accessed 11 December 2008).

Peat, Rick, and Frederick Rice. "Afghan Military Academy Opens Gates to Future Leaders." *Special to American Forces Press Service*, 28 March 2005. http://www.defenselink.mil/news/newsarticle.aspx?id=31081 (accessed 9 April 2007).

Perito, Dr. Robert M. *United States Institute of Peace Special Report: The U.S. Experience with Provincial Reconstruction Teams in Afghanistan.* Special Report 152, October 2005.

Perry, Alex. "Inside the Battle at Qala-i Jangi." *Time* 158, no. 25 (10 December 2001): 52.

Perryman, Mitch. "Letter from Afghanistan" (undated). http://www.halllakeland.com/troops/letter.htm (accessed 1 August 2007).

Peters, Rudolph. *Islam and Colonialism: The Doctrine of Jihad in Modern History.* The Hague, Netherlands: Moulton Publishers, 1979.

Phillips, Kyra. "Where and What is Mazar-e Sharif?" *CNN.com Transcripts,* 9 November 2001. http://www.transcripts.cnn.com (accessed 24 February 2007).

Pike, John. "Reserve & National Guard Mobilized Since 9/11." *GlobalSecurity.org.* http://www.globalsecurity.org/military/ops/res-ng-callup.htm (accessed 6 July 2007).

Portman, Gunnery Sergeant Charles. "Green Berets Standing Up Afghan Army." *Special Forces*, 31 May 2002. http://www.groups.sfahq.com/3rd/mc_donnell_afgan_31_05_03.htm (accessed 11 December 2008).

Powell, Bill. "The Strange Case of Haji Basha Noorzai." *Time* 169, no. 8 (19 February 2007), 29–37. http://www.time.com/time/printout/0,8816,1587252,00.html (accessed 9 February 2007).

Prados, Alfred B. "Saudi Arabia: Current Issues and U.S. Relations." *CRS Issue Brief to Congress,* 17 June 2005. http://fpc.state.gov/documents/organization/50262.pdf (accessed 19 April 2007).

"President Congratulates Afghan People and Government on Successful Parliamentary Elections." The White House, Office of the Press Secretary, 18 September 2005.

"President Orders Ready Reserves of Armed Forces to Active Duty: Executive Order Ordering the Ready Reserve of the Armed Forces to Active Duty and Delegating Certain Authorities to the Secretary of Defense and the Secretary of Transportation," 14 September 2001. http://www. whitehouse.gov/news/releases/2001/09/20010914-5.html (accessed 3 December 2008).

"President Outlines War Effort: Remarks by the President to the George C. Marshall ROTC Award Seminar on National Security." Office of the Press Secretary, The White House, 17 April 2002. http://www.whitehouse.gov/news/releases/2002/04 (accessed 3 July 2007).

"President Urges Readiness and Patience: Remarks by the President, Secretary of State Colin Powell and Attorney General John Ashcroft, Camp David, Thurmont, MD, 15 September 2001." http:// www.whitehouse.gov/news/releases/2001/09/20010915-4.html (accessed 18 September 2008).

"Press Statement by Security Council President on Terrorist Attacks in United States." Press Release SC/7141, 11 September 2001.

Price, Johann. "Operation Enduring Freedom Chain of Command." *Center for Defense Information Terrorism Project*. Washington, DC: Center for Defense Information, 26 June 2002. http:// www.cdi.org/terrorism/OEFcommand-pr.cfm (accessed 11 December 2008).

Prokhanov, A. "Russian Journalist Sorts Among the Ruins of Nine-Year Afghan War." *Kansas City Times,* 5 May 1998, in *Russian-Soviet Unconventional Wars in the Caucasus, Central Asia, and Afghanistan,* edited by Robert F. Baumann. Leavenworth Papers No. 20. Fort Leavenworth, KS: Combat Studies Institute, Command and General Staff College Press, 1993.

"Provisional Irish Republican Army." *Council on Foreign Relations Backgrounder*, November 2005. http://www.cfr.org/publication/9240/ (accessed 2 April 2007).

Quddus, Syed Abdul. *The Parthans*. Lahore, Pakistan: Ferozsons, 1987.

Rafeedie, Fadia. "Review of Benedict Anderson's *Imagined Communities: Reflections on the Origin and Spread of Nationalism.*" http://socrates.berkeley.edu/~mescha/bookrev/Anderson,Benedict. html (accessed 5 January 2007).

Rashid, Ahmed. *Descent into Chaos: The United States and the Failure of Nation Building in Pakistan, Afghanistan, and Central Asia.* New York, NY: Viking Press, 2008.

———. "Pakistan, the Taliban and the US." *The Nation,* 8 October 2001. http://www.thenation.com/ doc/20011008/rashid (accessed 21 January 2007).

———. *Taliban: Militant Islam, Oil, and Fundamentalism in Central Asia.* New Haven, CT: Yale University Press, 2001.

———. "Taliban Mounted Militia Prepares for Border Strike." *The Daily Telegraph,* 8 August 2003. http://www.telegraph.co.uk/news/main.jhtml?xml=/news/2003/10/08/wafg08.xml (accessed 26 July 2007).

———. "War without Borders." In *Afghanistan,* 2d edition, edited by Edward Girardet and Jonathan Walter, co-editors Charles Norchi and Mirwais Masood. Geneva, Switzerland: Crosslines Publications, 2004.

Reagan, President Ronald. National Security Decision Directive 207, 20 January 1986.

———. *Remarks at the Annual Convention of the American Bar Association*, 8 July 1985. http://www. reagan.utexas.edu/archives/speeches/1985/70885a.htm (accessed 10 April 2007).

Reddy, B. Muralidhar. "The Northern Players." *PBS FRONTLINE* 18, no. 24 (24 November–7 December 2001). http://www.hinduonnet.com (accessed 8 February 2007).

Report of the Accountability Review Boards Bombings of the US Embassies in Nairobi, Kenya and Dar es Salaam, Tanzania on August 7, 1998. US Department of State, January 1999. http://www. state.gov/www/regions/africa/accountability_report.html (accessed 28 December 2006).

"Resolution to Eliminate International Terrorism." A/RES/49/60, UN General Assembly, 9 December 1994. http://www.un.org/documents/ga/res/49/a49r060.htm (accessed 10 April 2007).

Reynolds, Andrew, and Andrew Wilder. "Free, Fair or Flawed: Challenges for Legitimate Elections in Afghanistan." Afghanistan Research and Evaluation Unit (AREU).

Reynolds, Andrew, Lucy Jones, and Andrew Wilder. "A Guide to Parliamentary Elections in Afghanistan." Afghan Research and Evaluation Unit, August 2005. http://unplan1.un.org/intradoc/groups/public/documents/APCITY/UNPLAN021668.pdf (accessed 12 June 2007).

Rhem, Kathleen T. "Officials Laud Rebuilding of Afghan Girls School." *Armed Forces Press Service,* 31 October 2002. http://www.defenselink.mil (accessed 18 January 2007).

Rhem, Sergeant First Class Kathleen T. "Bush Sending Rumsfeld to Meet Leaders in India, Pakistan." *American Forces Press Service News Articles*, 30 May 2002. http://www.defenselink.mil/news/newsarticle.aspx?id=43995 (accessed 11 December 2008).

Rice, Frederick. "Afghanistan Unit Takes on New Mission and Name." *American Forces Press Service,* 13 July 2005. http://www.defenselink.mil/news/newsarticle.aspx?id=16650 (accessed 22 May 2007).

Richard, Alain. "The European Union, A Rising Feature on the International Stage." Remarks by the Minister of Defence of France, 12 Forum, *Bundeswehr & GesellschaftWelt am Sonntag,* Berlin, 2 October 2001. http://www.defense.gouv.fr/sites/defense/english_contents/the_ministry_of_defence/archive/the_minister_of_defence_1998-2002/discours/051001.htm (accessed 6 December 2006).

Ricks, Thomas E., and Alan Sipress. "Attacks Restrained by Political Goals." *Washington Post,* 23 October 2001.

Risen, James, and David Johnston. "Bush Has Widened Authority of C.I.A. to Kill Terrorists." *New York Times,* 15 December 2002.

Robertson, Lord, NATO Secretary General. "Statement by the Secretary General of NATO." PR/CP(2001)121, 11 September 2001. http://www.nato.int/docu/pr/2001/p01-121e.htm (accessed 16 April 2009).

———. "Statement to the Press on the North Atlantic Council Decision on Implementation of Article 5 of the Washington Treaty following the 11 September Attacks against the United States," 4 October 2001. http://www.nato.int/docu/speech/2001/s011004b.htm (accessed 16 April 2009).

Rodriquez, Jorge E. "What's Missing in ARSOF Logistics?" *Army Logistician* 36, no. 1 (January/February 2004): 7–9.

Roy, Olivier. "Ethnic Identity and Political Expression in Northern Afghanistan." In *Muslims in Central Asia: Expressions of Identity and Change*, edited by Jo Ann Gross. Durham, NC: Duke University Press, 1992.

———. *Afghanistan, From Holy War to Civil War*. Princeton, NJ: Princeton University Press, 1995.

———. *Islam and Resistance in Afghanistan*. Cambridge, MA: Cambridge University Press, 1986.

Rumsfeld, Secretary of Defense Donald. "Kansas State University Landon Lecture." Speech, US Department of Defense (Public Affairs), Manhattan, KS, 9 November 2006. http://www.defenselink.mil/Speeches/Speech.aspx?SpeechID=1060 (accessed 5 January 2007).

Rumsfeld, Donald. "Statement of the Secretary of Defense." United States Department of Defense, No. 560-01, 1 November 2001. http://www.defenselink.mil/releases/2001/b11012001_bt560-01.html (accessed 6 December 2006).

"Russia and Central Asia." Berlin Information Center for Transatlantic Security (BITS). http://www.bits.de/NRANEU/CentralAsia.html#II (accessed 10 January 2007).

Said, Edward. *Orientalism.* New York, NY: Pantheon Books, 1978.

Saikal, Amin. *Modern Afghanistan: A History of Struggle and Survival.* London: I.B. Taurus, 2004.

Sanger, David, and Eric Schmitt. "New US Effort Steps Up Hunt for bin Laden." *New York Times,* 29 February 2004.

Savranskaya, Svetlana. "The Soviet Experience in Afghanistan: Russian Documents and Memoirs." *Volume II: Afghanistan: Lessons from the Last War.* Document 21, 9 October 2001. CC CPSU Letter on Afghanistan, 10 May 1988 [Source: Alexander Lyakhovsky, *Tragedy and Valor of*

Afghan, Iskon, Moscow 1995, Appendix 8, Translated by Svetlana Savranskaya]. http://www. gwu.edu/~nsarchiv/NSAEBB/NSAEBB57/soviet.html (accessed 20 January 2007).

Scales, General Robert H., USA. *Certain Victory: The US Army in the Gulf War.* Fort Leavenworth, KS: US Army Command and General Staff College Press, 1994.

Scarborough, Rowan. "US Search for bin Laden Intensifies; Unit that Tracked Saddam Moves to Afghanistan." *Washington Times,* 23 February 2004.

Schmitt, Eric, and David Rohde. "Taliban Fighters Increase Attacks, with Troubling Toll Among G.I.'s and Afghans." *New York Times,* 1 August 2004.

Schmitt, Eric, and James Dao. "Use of Pinpoint Airpower Comes of Age in New War." *New York Times,* 24 December 2001.

Schonauer, Scott. "SETAF Takes Command of Afghan Mission." *Stars and Stripes European Edition,* 16 March 2005. http://www.military.com/NewContent/0,13190,SS_031605_Setaf,00.html (accessed 21 May 2007).

Schrader, Esther. "Response to Terror; War, on Advice of Counsel." *Los Angeles Times,* 15 February 2002.

Schroder, James A. "Observations: ARSOF in Afghanistan." *Special Warfare* (September 2002): 50–52.

"Secretary-General Urges Assembly to Respond to 11 September Attacks by Reaffirming Rule of Law." Press Release SG/SM/7865, 24 September 2001.

"Secretary of State Colin L. Powell Written Remarks Submitted to The National Commission on Terrorist Attacks Upon the United States." *9/11 Commission Report,* 23 March 2004. http:// www.9-11commission.gov/hearings/hearing8/powell_statement.pdf (accessed 12 February 2007).

"Secretary of State for Defence's Statement in the Commons—18 March 2002." *Operation Veritas.* UK Ministry of Defense, Statement, 18 March 2002. http://www.operations.mod.uk/veritas/ statements (accessed 30 May 2007).

"Secretary Rumsfeld Joint Media Availability with President Karzai." *Department of Defense News Transcript,* 1 May 2003. http://www.defenselink.mil/transcripts/transcript.aspx?transcript id=2562 (accessed 25 July 2007).

"Security Council Resolution 1386 (2001) on the Situation in Afghanistan." *Security Council Resolutions-2001,* 20 December 2001. http://www.un.org/Docs/scres/2001/sc2001.htm (accessed 2 May 2007).

Sepp, Kalev. "Uprising at Qala-i Jangi: The Staff of the 3/5th SF Group." *Special Warfare* 15, no. 3 (September 2002): 17.

Shahrani, M. Nazif. "The Taliban Enigma: Person-Centered Politics and Extremism in Afghanistan." *International Institute for the Study of Islam (ISIM) Newsletter*, June 2000. http://isim. leidenuniv.nl (accessed 5 February 2007).

Shahzad, Syed Saleem. "Afghanistan: Dogs of War in Full Cry." *Asia Times Online,* 16 March 2004. http://www.atimes.com/atimes/South_Asia/FC16Df04.html (accessed 16 July 2007).

Shanker, Thom. "Coalition Steps Up Raids as Afghan Elections Approach." *New York Times,* 20 August 2005.

Shanker, Thom, and Steven Lee Myers. "U.S. Special Forces Step up Campaign in Afghan Areas." *New York Times,* 19 October 2001. http://query.nytimes.com/gst/fullpage.html?res= 9E00E2DB133 EF93AA25753C1A9679C8B63 (accessed 2 January 2008).

Sharifzada, Jawad. "Election Security a Success." *Institute for War & Peace Reporting,* 26 October, ARR No. 143. http://www.iwpr.net/?p=arr&s=f&o=152833&apc_state=heniarr2004 (accessed 21 May 2007).

Siddiqi, A.R. "Pakistan-Afghan Ties: A Critical Appraisal." *Dawn,* 7 April 2006. http://www.dawn. com/2006/04/07/fea.htm (accessed 6 February 2007).

Significant Terrorist Incidents, 1961–2003: A Brief Chronology. US Department of State. http://www. state.gov/r/pa/ho/pubs/fs/5902.htm (accessed 23 April 2007).

Sipress, Alan, and Vernon Loeb. "U.S. Uncouples Military, Political Efforts; Officials Decide to Step Up Bombing Without a Postwar Government Arranged." *Washington Post,* 1 November 2001.

Skinner, Elizabeth. "Strategic Insight: Russia and Eurasia: Enduring Freedom for Central Asia?" *Center for Contemporary Conflict, Naval Postgraduate School,* 2 April 2002. http://www.ccc.nps. navy.mil/si/apr02/russia.pdf (accessed 14 May 2007).

Sloan, Stanley R. "The United States and the Use of Force in the Post-Cold War World: Toward Self-Deterrence?" *Congressional Research Service: Report for Congress*, 20 July 1994.

Slosser, Specialist John. "82d's 'White Devils' make Valiant Return." *Defend America,* April 2003. http://www.defendamerica.mil/articles/apr2003/a040103a.html (accessed 9 November 2008).

Sly, Liz. "Taliban Suspected in Attacks on Afghans Guarding Highway Work." *Knight Ridder Tribune News Service*, 1 September 2003. http://www.libraryo.com/article.aspx?num=107133024 (accessed 24 September 2007).

Smith, Brigadier General James. "Special Briefing on Millennium Challenge 2002." *US Department of Defense News Transcript*, 22 May 2002. http://www.defenselink.mil (accessed 9 December 2008).

Smith, Michael. *The Killer Elite: The Inside Story of America's Most Secret Special Operations Team.* New York, NY: St. Martin's Press, 2006.

Smucker, Philip. "How bin Laden Got Away: A Day-by-Day Account of How Osama bin Laden Eluded the World's Most Powerful Military Machine." *Christian Science Monitor,* 4 March 2002. http://www.csmonitor.com/2002/0304/p01s03-wosc.html (accessed 4 May 2007).

Soloway, Colin. "I Yelled at Them to Stop." *Newsweek*, 7 October 2002. http://www.newsweek.com/ id/65868/page/1 (accessed 10 February 2009).

Soskis, Benjamin. "Why All Pashtuns Aren't Alike." *The New Republic*, 3 December 2001. http:// wwwca-politicaltransitions.com/Classes/PoliticalIdeas/Nationalism/Afghan%2Onati (accessed 13 February 2007).

"Special Report: Voting in Warlord Country-Afghanistan." *The Economist* (9 October 2004): 21–24.

Stack, Megan K. "U.S. Strikes Back: The Bombing Campaign; Afghan Mission Offers Navy Pilots Endurance Lessons; Military: The Round-Trip Bombing Runs from the Carl Vinson Can Last as Long as Seven Hours." *Los Angeles Times,* 14 October 2001.

"Staff Statement 6: The Military." *The 9/11 Commission Report: Final Report of the National Commission on Terrorist Attacks Upon the United States.* Washington, DC: Government Printing Office, 2004.

Stallings, Major Ron, and Specialist First Class Michael Foley. "CI and HUMINT Operations in Support of Operation Enduring Freedom." *Military Intelligence Professional Bulletin,* October–December 2003.

Stapleton, Barbara J. *A British Agencies Afghanistan Group Briefing Paper on the Development of Joint Regional Teams in Afghanistan*, January 2003. http://www.baag.org.uk/downloads/reports/ Barbara_JRT_report.pdf (accessed 22 July 2007).

"State Sponsors of Terrorism Overview: Patterns of Global Terrorism." Office of the Coordinator for Counterterrorism, 30 April 2001. http://www.state.gov/s/ct/rls/crt/2000/2441.htm (accessed 6 April 2007).

"Statement by the President of the Security Council." United Nations, 7 April 2000. http://www.un.int/ usa/spst0012.htm (accessed 10 April 2007).

Steele, Dennis. "U.S. Army Line Battalion in the War on Terrorism: The Mountains." *Army*, June 2002. http://findarticles.com/p/articles/mi_qa3723/is_200206/ai_n9124771 (accessed 9 May 2007).

———. "Unconventional Logistics." *Army* 52, no. 11 (November 2002): 58.

Stein, Lisa. "The Week." *US News and World Report*, 12 December 2004. http://www.usnews.com/ usnews/news/articles/041220/20week.lede.htm (accessed 18 February 2009).

Stewart, Richard W. *The United States Army in Afghanistan, Operation Enduring Freedom, October 2001–March 2002*. CMH Publication 70-83-1. Washington, DC: Center of Military History, 2006.

Stockton, Nicholas. *Strategic Coordination in Afghanistan*. Afghanistan Research and Evaluation Unit, August 2002.

Stogran, Colonel Patrick. "Fledgling Swans Take Flight: The Third Battalion, Princess Patricia's Canadian Light Infantry in Afghanistan." *Canadian Army Journal*, Fall/Winter 2004/2005. http://64.233.167.104/search?q=cache:BayRyeT7CsJ:www.army.forces.gc.ca/caj/documents/ vol_7/iss_3 (accessed 15 August 2007).

Symon, Fiona. "Afghanistan's Northern Alliance." *BBC News Online,* 19 September 2001. http://news. bbc.uk (accessed 31 January 2007).

Synovitz, Ron. "Afghanistan: New National Army Bases Planned in Four Provinces," 17 March 2004. http://www.rferl.org/featuresarticle/2004/3/360A06F8-2DE5-4B3D-8DCF-55F0CE3A648E. html (accessed 18 June 2007).

"Taliban Denounce Afghan Elections, Vow to Resist Future Parliament." *BBC Monitoring Newsfile,* 21 September 2005.

"Taliban Pledge to Disrupt Afghan Elections, Rule out Polling Day Attacks." *BBC Monitoring South Asia,* 21 August 2005.

"Target America: Terrorist Attacks on Americans, 1979–1988: Bombing of La Belle Discoteque." *PBS FRONTLINE.* http://www.pbs.org/wgbh/pages/frontline/shows/target/etc/cron.html (accessed 4 April 2007).

"Target America: Terrorist Attacks on Americans, 1979–1988: Bombing of Rome, Vienna Airports." *PBS FRONTLINE.* http://www.pbs.org/wgbh/pages/frontline/shows/target/etc/cron.html (accessed 4 April 2007).

"Target America: Terrorist Attacks on Americans, 1979–1988: Hijacking of Cruise Ship Achille Lauro." *PBS FRONTLINE.* http://www.pbs.org/wgbh/pages/frontline/shows/target/etc/cron.html (accessed 4 April 2007).

"Target America: Terrorist Attacks on Americans, 1979–1988: Threats from Libya." *PBS FRONTLINE.* http://www.pbs.org/wgbh/pages/frontline/shows/target/etc/cron.html (accessed 4 April 2007).

Tarzi, Shah M. "Politics of the Afghan Resistance Movement: Cleavages, Disunity, and Fragmentation." *Asian Survey* 31, no. 6 (June 1991): 479–495.

Tehranian, Majid. "Communication Global Terrorism: Searching for Appropriate Responses." *Pacifica Review* 14, no. 1 (February 2002): 57–65.

"Terrorism 2000/2001." FBI Publication 0308, US Department of Justice, 2001.

"Terrorism in the United States 1996: Counterterrorism Threat Assessment and Warning Unit." National Security Division, Federal Bureau of Investigation, 1996.

"Terrorist Network Fact Sheet." White House Press Release, 7 November 2001. http://www.whitehouse. gov/news/releases/2001/11/20011107-6.html (accessed 6 April 2007).

"Text of Bush's Act of War Statement." *BBC News,* 12 September 2001. http://news.bbc.co.uk/1/hi/ world/americas/1540544.stm (accessed 23 April 2007).

The 9/11 Commission Report: Final Report of the National Commission on Terrorist Attacks Upon the United States. Washington, DC, 2004.

The 9/11 Commission Report. New York, NY: W.W. Norton & Company, 2004.

"The Campaign for Mazar-e Sharif." CD of re-enactment of Mazar-e campaign prepared by the Institute for Defense Analyses.

"The Gulf War, Oral History: Richard Cheney." *PBS FRONTLINE.* http://www.pbs.org/wgbh/pages/frontline/gulf/oral/cheney/2.html (accessed 24 April 2007).

"The Heartbreak of Mazar-e Sharif." *CBC News Online,* 27 January 2004. http://www.cbc.ca/news/background/Afghanistan/mazaresharif.html (accessed 23 February 2007).

"The Liberation of Mazar-e Sharif: 5th SF Group Conducts UW in Afghanistan." *Special Warfare* 15, no. 2 (June 2002): 37–39.

The North Atlantic Treaty, Article V, 4 April 1949.

Todd, Sandler. "Collective Action and Transnational Terrorism." *World Economy* (June 2003): 779–802.

"Transcript of Usama Bin Laden Video Tape," 13 December 2001. http://www.defenselink.mil/news/Dec2001/d20011213ubl.pdf (accessed 25 May 2007).

"Transforming While Mobilizing: Part I of a Two-Part Interview with LTG James R. Helmly." *Army Reserve Magazine* 49, no. 1 (Summer 2003): 8–11.

Tucker, David. "Combating International Terrorism." In *The Terrorism Threat and U.S. Government Response: Operational and Organizational Factors,* edited by James M. Smith and William C. Thomas. US Air Force Academy, CO: USAF Institute for National Security Studies, 2001.

Turpin, Guy Major, KMNB PIO. "Preparing for the Constitutional Loya Jirga," 17 November 2006. http://www.nato.int/ISAF/Update/varia/getready.htm (accessed 11 September 2007).

Tyler, Patrick. "U.S. and Britain Strike Afghanistan, Aiming at Bases and Terrorist Camps; Bush Warns 'Taliban Will Pay a Price.'" *New York Times,* 8 October 2001.

Tyrangiel, Josh, Hannah Bloch, Matt Forney, and Mark Thompson. "Inside Tora Bora." *Time* 158, no. 27 (24 December 2001).

Tyson, Ann Scott. "Desertions Deplete Afghan Army." *Christian Science Monitor Online,* 17 December 2003. http://www.csmonitor.com/2003/1217/p06s01-wosc.html (accessed 20 August 2007).

———. "Going in Small in Afghanistan." *Christian Science Monitor,* 14 January 2004. http://www.csmonitor.com/2004/0114/p01s04-wosc.html (accessed 24 September 2007).

———. "Uphill Pursuit for Afghan Warlord." *Christian Science Monitor,* 22 December 2003. http://www.csmonitor.com/2003/1222/p06s01-wosc.html (accessed 10 September 2007).

"UK Marines in New Afghan Mission." *BBC News,* 29 May 2002. http://news.bbc.co.uk/1/hi/world/south_asia/2014774.stm (accessed 16 August 2007).

UN. *Agreement on Provisional Arrangements in Afghanistan Pending the Re-Establishment of Permanent Government Institutions.* http://www.un.org/News/dh/latest/afghan/afghan-agree.htm (accessed 19 January 2009).

UN Assistance Mission in Afghanistan. "Decree of the President of the Islamic Transitional State of Afghanistan on the Afghan National Army," 1 December 2002. http://www.unama-afg.org/docs/_nonUN%20Docs/_Internation-Conferences&Forums/Bonn-Talks/decree%20on%20army.pdf (accessed 18 August 2007).

UN Department of Peacekeeping Operations. "Disarmament, Demobilization and Reintegration of Ex-Combatants in a Peacekeeping Environment: Principles and Guidelines," 2000.

UN Development Program—Afghanistan. "Disbandment of Illegal Armed Groups," 2004. http://www.undp.org.af/about_us/overview_undp_afg/psl/prj_anbp.htm (accessed 20 June 2007).

UN General Assembly Security Council. "The Situation in Afghanistan and its Implications for International Peace and Security," 7 March 2007.

UN High Commission for Refugees (UNHCR). *Chronology of Events in Afghanistan, April 2004.* www.unhcr.org/refworld/pdfid/415c64434.pdf (accessed 17 February 2009).

UN. "Plight of Civilian Afghan Population Desperate, Says Secretary-General: Those Deliberately Withholding Food and Attacking Relief Workers will be Held Responsible." Press Release SG/SM/7968,AFG/146, 25 September 2001.

UN Preamble. Charter of the United Nations, 26 June 1945.

UN Press Release, SC/7311. "Afghanistan Political Progress Faster than Expected; Security Threats Remain, Under-Secretary-General for Political Affairs Tells Security Council." http://www.un.org/News/Press/docs/2002/sc7311.doc.htm (accessed 4 December 2008).

UN Resolution 1269, 19 October 1999. http://daccessdds.un.org/doc/UNDOC/GEN/N99/303/92/PDF/N9930392.pdf?OpenElement (accessed 10 April 2007).

UN Security Council Resolution 1401, 4501st Meeting, 28 March 2002, Report of the Secretary General. "The Situation in Afghanistan and its Implications for International Peace and Security," 18 March 2002.

UN. "Security Council Unanimously Adopts Wide-Ranging Anti-Terrorism Resolution." Press Release SC/7158, Security Council, 4385th Meeting (Night), 28 September 2001.

UN. "Senior Inter-Agency Network on Internal Displacement Mission to Afghanistan." *Findings and Recommendations from the UN Special Coordinator on Internal Displacement from Mission*, 18–25 April 2001.

UN. "United Nation's Role Essential in 'Moral Imperative' of Preventing Conflict General Assembly Told, As Debate Continues on Secretary-General's Report." Press Release/9916, Fifty-sixth General Meeting, 9th Meeting (AM), 25 September 2001.

US Agency for International Development. "USAID Fact Sheet on Humanitarian Aid for Afghanistan," 26 April 2002. http://geneva.usmission.gov/press2002 (accessed 23 January 2007).

US Congress. Goldwater-Nichols Act of 1986. http://www.au.af.mil/au/awc/awcgate/congress/title_10.htm (accessed 29 January 2007).

US Congress. House. House Armed Services Committee. *Statement of General Tommy R. Franks.* 107th Cong., 27 February 2002.

———. *Statement of Lieutenant General Karl W. Eikenberry, U.S. Army.* 110th Cong., 1st Sess., 13 February 2007, 3.

US Congress. Joint Resolution. *Authorization for Use of Military Force.* 107th Cong., S.J. Res. 23, *Congressional Record*, Vol. 147 (18 September 2001). http://www.usconstitution.net/newsarch_01.html (accessed 20 February 2007).

US Congress. Senate. Senate Armed Services Committee. *Prepared Testimony of U.S. Secretary of Defense Donald H. Rumsfeld before the Senate Armed Services Committee on Progress in Afghanistan.* As Delivered by Secretary of Defense Donald H. Rumsfeld, Dirksen Senate Office Building, Washington, DC, 31 July 2002. http://www.defenselink.mil/speeches/2002/s20020731-secdef.html (accessed 20 January 2007).

———. *Statement of General Bryan D. Brown, U.S. Army.* 109th Cong., 1st Sess., 22 April 2005.

———. *Statement of General Henry H. Shelton, Chairman of the Joint Chiefs of Staff.* 107th Congress, 3 May 2001. http://armed-services.senate.gov/statemnt/2001/010503shelton.pdf (accessed 12 April 2007).

———. *Statement of General John P. Abizaid, U.S. Army-CENTCOM Posture Statement,* 109th Cong., 1st Sess., 1 March 2005.

———. *Statement of General John P. Abizaid, U.S. Army-CENTCOM Posture Statement.* 109th Cong., 1st Sess., 16 March 2006.

———. *Statement of General Joseph W. Ralston, Vice Chairman of the Joint Chiefs of Staff.* 106th Congress, 9 March 1999. http://armed-services.senate.gov/statemnt/1999/990309jr.pdf (accessed 12 April 2007).

———. *Statement of General Tommy R. Franks, Commander in Chief of US Central Command.* Transcript, 22 March 2001.

———. *Statement of General Tommy R. Franks, Commander, US Central Command,* 31 July 2002.

US Congress. Senate. Senate Foreign Relations Committee, Subcommittee on Central Asia and the Caucasus. *Statement of Elizabeth A. Jones, Assistant Secretary for European and Eurasian Affairs.* Washington, DC, 13 December 2001.

US Department of Defense. "Afghan Engineer District Chief Updates Projects." *American Forces Press Service,* 11 April 2005. http://www.defenselink.mil/news/newsarticle.aspx?id=31457 (accessed 23 February 2009).

———. "DOD News Briefing—Gen Myers." *DefenseLink News Transcript* (20 October 2001). http://www.defenselink.mil/transcripts/transcript/aspx?transcriptid=2145 (accessed 1 April 2007).

———. "DOD News Briefing—Secretary Rumsfeld and Gen Myers." *DefenseLink News Transcript,* 18 October 2001. http://www.defenselink.mil (accessed 21 February 2007).

———. "DOD News Briefing—Secretary Rumsfeld and Gen Myers." *DefenseLink News Transcript,* 26 November 2001. http://www.defenselink.mil (accessed 2 March 2007).

———. "Executive Summary of the Battle of Takur Ghar," 24 May 2002.

———. "Into Afghanistan: Rooting Out Terrorists." *DefenseLink.* http://www.defenselink.mil/home/features/1082004d.html (accessed 24 May 2007).

———. "Rumsfeld Visits, Thanks U.S. Troops at Camp X-Ray in Cuba." *DefenseLink News Transcripts,* 27 January 2002. http://www.defenselink.mil/news/Jan2002/n01272002_200201271.html (accessed 3 March 2007).

US Department of Justice/OIG Special Report. "The FBI Laboratory: An Investigation into Laboratory Practices and Alleged Misconduct in Explosives-Related and Other Cases, Section D: The Bush Assassination Attempt," April 1997. http://www.usdoj.gov/oig/special/9704a/ (accessed 17 April 2007).

US Department of State. "Fact Sheet: Afghanistan Elections 2004: Women's Participation." http://www.state.gov/g/wi/rls/24792.htm (accessed 1 May 2007).

———. "Fact Sheet: Progress in Afghanistan's Reconstruction," 26 March 2004. http://www.state.gov/r/pa/prs/ps/2004/30803.htm (accessed 19 June 2007).

———. "Road to Democracy: Afghan Elections" (posted November 2004). http://usinfo.state.gov/products/pubs/afgelect/afghanistan.htm (accessed 25 July 2007).

———. "Road to Democracy: Afghan Elections, President Karzai's Inauguration" (posted December 2004). http://usinfo.state.gov/products/pubs/afgelect/karzi.htm (accessed 25 July 2007).

———. "The First Democratic Elections in Afghanistan: A Report by the Bipartisan Observer Team," 15 October 2004. http://fpc.state.gov/fpc/37133.htm (accessed 21 May 2007).

———. "New Afghan Initiatives Promote Growth, Education, Democracy," 15 June 2004. http://usinfo.state.gov/sa/Archive/2004/Jun/16-365926.html (accessed 12 September 2007).

US Department of State and US Department of Defense. "Interagency Assessment of Afghanistan Police Training and Readiness." DOS Report No. ISP-IQO-07-07, DOD Report No. IE-2007-001, 14 November 2006.

US Government Accountability Office. GAO-04-403, *Afghanistan Reconstruction: Deteriorating Security and Limited Resources Have Impeded Progress; Improvements in U.S. Strategy Needed,* June 2004.

———. GAO-05-575, *Afghanistan Security: Efforts to Establish Army and Police Have Made Progress, but Future Plans Need to Be Better Defined,* June 2005.

———. GAO-05-742, *Afghanistan Reconstruction: Despite Some Progress, Deteriorating Security and Other Obstacles Continue to Threaten Achievement of U.S. Goals,* July 2005. www.gao.gov/new.items/d05742.pdf (accessed 21 May 2007).

———. GAO-07-801SP, *Securing, Stabilizing, and Reconstructing Afghanistan,* May 2007. www.gao.gov/new.items/d07801sp.pdf (accessed 21 July 2007).

———. GAO Report, *Combating Terrorism: Federal Agencies' Efforts to Implement National Policy and Strategy*, 26 September 1997.

———. GAO Report, *Combating Terrorism: Issues to be Resolved to Improve Counterterrorism Operations,* 13 May 1999.

US Institute of Peace. "Afghanistan: Prospects for Peace and Reconstruction." http://www.usip.org/events/2002/es20020117.html (accessed 16 March 2007).

———. "Agreement on Provisional Arrangements in Afghanistan Pending the Re-Establishment of Permanent Government Institutions. http://www.usip.org/library/pa/Afghanistan/pa_afghan_12052001.html (accessed 16 March 2007).

"U.S. Largest Single Donor of Aid to Afghans." US State Department Archives, 2 October 2000. http://usinfo.state.gov/is/Archive_Index/U.S._Largest_Single_Donor_of_Aid_to_Afghans.html (accessed 25 January 2007).

"U.S. Missiles Pound Targets in Afghanistan, Sudan." *CNN.com,* 21 August 1998. http://www.cnn.com/US/9808/20/us.strikes.02/ (accessed 16 April 2007).

"US Nets 'Al Qaeda' Financier." *BBC News Online*, 12 September 2002. http://news/bbc.co.uk/2/hi/south_asia/ 2253299.stm (accessed 16 August 2007).

"US Rejects Taliban Offer to Try Bin Laden." *CNN.com,* 7 October 2001. http://archives.cnn.com/2001/us/10/07.ret.us.taliban/ (accessed 19 September 2008).

US Special Operations Command Mission. http://www.socom.mil/Docs/Command_Mission-060214.pdf (accessed 7 February 2007).

"US Troops Finish 'Operation Mountain Lion.'" *CNN.com/TRANSCRIPTS*, 7 April 2002. http://transcripts.cnn.com/TRANSCRIPTS?0204/07/SM.04.html (accessed 25 January 2009).

Vigar, Said Habib, and Ghulam Sayeed Najami. "Massouda Jalal: Physician Talks Up Her Neutrality." *Institute for War & Peace Reporting* (7 October 2004). ARR No. 139. http://www.iwpr.net/?p=arr&s=f&o=152957&apc_state=heniarrfa49b7fa178d15b16701ac2f9f263bbe (accessed 24 July 2007).

von Clausewitz, Carl. *On War.* Edited and translated by Michael Howard and Peter Paret. Princeton, NJ: Princeton University Press, 1976.

Waldman, Amy. "Masters of Suicide Bombing: Tamil Guerrillas of Sri Lanka." *New York Times* (Late Edition), 14 January 2003.

Waller, Douglas. "Using Psywar against the Taliban." *Time Online,* 10 December 2001. http://www.time.com/time/columnist/waller/article/0,9565,187810,00.html (accessed 31 January 2007).

Walsh, Declan. "Afghan Elections Put Back to the Autumn: Rice Renews US Commitment as 5 Bomb Deaths Mar Her Visit." *The Guardian,* 18 March 2005.

Walters, Tome H. Jr. "The Office of Humanitarian Assistance and Demining: Supporting Humanitarian Needs Around the Globe—Brief Article." *DISAM Journal*, Winter 2000. http://findarticles.com/p/articles/mi_m0IAJ/is_2_23/ai_71837319 (accessed 22 August 2007).

Wardak, Ali. "The Ethnic and Tribal Composition of Afghan Society." In *Afghanistan,* 2d edition, edited by Edward Girardet and Johnathan Walter, co-editors Charles Norchi and Mirwais Masood. Geneva, Switzerland: Crosslines Publications, 2004.

Weaver, Mary Anne. "Lost At Tora Bora." *New York Times Magazine* (11 September 2005): 55.

Weinberger, Caspar W. "The Uses of Military Power." Speech delivered to the National Press Club, Washington, DC, 28 November 1984. http://www.pbs.org/wgbh/pages/frontline/shows/military/force/weinberger.html (accessed 4 April 2007).

"What the World Thinks in 2002." *The Pew Global Attitudes Project.* Washington, DC: Pew Center for People and the Press, 4 December 2002.

White House. "Operation Enduring Freedom: One Year of Accomplishments," 7 October 2002. http://www.whitehouse.gov (accessed 14 February 2007).

———. "Remarks by the President Upon Arrival at Barksdale Air Force Base," 11 September 2001. http://www.whitehouse.gov (accessed 26 February 2007).

Whittle, Jennifer, and Steve Alvarez. "Special Forces Officer Honored for Heroism in Mazar-e Sharif Prison Battle." *Defend America News,* 14 November 2003. http://www.defendamerica.mil (accessed 23 January 2007).

Wilber, Donald M. *Afghanistan*. New Haven: HRAF Press, 1962.

Windows on Asia. *Geography of Afghanistan*. http://www.asia.msu.edu/centralasia/Afghanistan/geography.html (accessed 5 February 2007).

Wirsing, Robert. "Precarious Partnership: Pakistan's Response to U.S. Security Policies." *Asia-Pacific Center for Security Studies, Special Assessment* (2003). http://www.apcss.org/Publications/SAS/SASAPResponse030320/PrecariousPartnershipPakistansResponsetoUSSecurityPolicies.pdf (accessed 14 May 2007).

Wishnick, Elizabeth. *Growing US Security Interests in Central Asia*. Carlisle, PA: Strategic Studies Institute, 2002.

Woodrow Wilson International Center for Scholars. *Proceedings of the Conference: The U.S. Role in the World: Enhancing the Capacity to Respond to Complex Contingency Operations*. Washington, DC, 19 September 2001.

"Words Alone Inadequate as Response to Terrorist Attacks, Secretary General Tells Opening of Fifty-Sixth General Assembly." Press Release SG/SM7851, GA 9906, 12 September 2001.

"Working to Bring Peace and Stability to Afghanistan." NATO Briefing, 1 August 2003. http://www.nato.int/issues/afghanistan/briefing_afghanistan_01.pdf (accessed 2 August 2007).

World Bank. "Afghanistan Reconstruction Trust Fund," 21 July 2007. http://go.worldbank.org/GO3S1MDO60 (accessed 1 August 2007).

"Younis Qanuni: Panjshiri With National Ambitions." *Institute for War & Peace Reporting*. ARR No. 139, 6 October 2004. http://www.iwpr.net/?p=arr&s=f&o=152949&apc_state=heniarrfa49b7fa178d15b16701ac 2f9f263bbe (accessed 24 July 2007).

Zubok, Vladislav, and Constantine Pleshakov. "Stalin's Road to the Cold War." In *The Origins of the Cold War*, 4th ed., edited by Robert J. McMahon and Thomas G. Patterson. New York, NY: Houghton Mifflin Co., 1999.

Zucchino, David. "The Changing Face of Battle." *Los Angeles Times*, 14 October 2002. http://www.dailytimes.com.pk/default.asp?page=story_14-10-2002_pg7_11 (accessed 16 August 2007).

Zulfiqar, Shahzada. "Altered States." *Newsline* (January 2002). http://www.newsline.com.pk/NewsJan2002/newsreport1.htm (accessed 15 March 2007).

Index

V

W

X

Y

Z

About the Contributors

Donald P. Wright is the chief of the Contemporary Operations Study Team at the Combat Studies Institute (CSI) and a lieutenant colonel in the US Army Reserve. He holds a Ph.D. in History from Tulane University and has served as an Army historian for 6 years. Wright was the co-author of *On Point II: Transition to the New Campaign, The US Army in Operation IRAQI FREEDOM, May 2003–January 2005* (Fort Leavenworth, KS: CSI Press, 2008). He also authored several publications on the Russian Imperial Army including "That Vital Spark: Japanese Patriotism in Russian Military Perspective" in John Steinberg et al., *The Russo-Japanese War in Global Perspective* (Brill, 2005).

James R. Bird, Lieutenant Colonel, US Army, Retired, joined the Contemporary Operations Study Team in January 2006 and was a contributor to *On Point II.* Bird holds a M.A. in History and is a Ph.D. candidate in History at the University of Arkansas.

Steven E. Clay, Lieutenant Colonel, US Army, Retired, is the senior writer for the Contemporary Operations Study Team. Clay retired after 27 years of Active Duty service and holds a M.A. from Texas State University. He is the author or co-author of several publications, to include *Blood and Sacrifice: The History of the 16th Infantry Regiment from the Civil War to the Gulf War*; *Iroquois Warriors in Iraq;* and *Staff Ride Handbook for the Overland Campaign, A Study in Operational-Level Command.*

Peter W. Connors was a charter member of the Contemporary Operations Study Team and contributed to *On Point II.* He holds a Ph.D. in Economics. Connors served as a US Marine Corps aviator in Vietnam and later served with and retired as a major from the Kansas Army National Guard.

Lieutenant Colonel Scott C. Farquhar is a historian at the Combat Studies Institute. He holds a M.A. in History from Kansas State University. Farquhar has served in a variety of command and staff positions, most recently in Iraq in 2007 and 2008 where he served as senior advisor to an Iraqi infantry brigade.

Lynne Chandler Garcia has served on the Contemporary Operations Study Team since 2005 and was a contributor to *On Point II*. She holds a M.A. in Political Science from the University of Maryland and is a Ph.D. candidate in Government and Political Science at that university.

Dennis Van Wey was a member of the Contemporary Operations Study Team from 2005 to 2007 and contributed to *On Point II.* Van Wey is a Civil Affairs officer who served with the 4th Infantry Division in Iraq in 2003 and 2004.